Cliff Charpentier's
1998 FANTASY FOOTBALL DIGEST

by

Cliff Charpentier

Lerner Publications Company • Minneapolis

The author and publisher believe all information regarding NFL player transactions to be accurate up to May 1, 1998, when this book was set to go to press. For subsequent information, please consult the Fantasy Football Newsletter. An order form is provided on the color insert in this book.

Cover photo: © Mickey Pfleger/Sports California 1998

Composed in Times Ten and Helvetica
by Interface Graphics, Inc., Minneapolis, Minnesota

International Standard Book Number: 0-8225-9947-3
1 2 3 4 5 6 —   — 03 02 01 00 99 98

DEDICATIONS AND ACKNOWLEDGMENTS

When you have been writing text for 15 years, it may seem redundant to be giving thanks to many of the same people every year. However, for me, going through this process year after year, the task seems almost more difficult each time out, trying to get bigger, better, faster so the thanks when all is done is given in genuine spirit to each and everyone who contributes.

Many thanks,

To my wife Lori, who although not much of a sports fan, tolerates my passion for sports, which adds to her burden of maintaining our family responsibilities. For this I am deeply appreciative and I truly admire her patience.

To my children, Kelly, Cliff Jr. and Matthew, you are very special indeed. Fantasy football may be a distraction for me at certain times of the year but your understanding and patience makes our time together just that much more to cherish.

To my business partner and long time friend, Tom Kane Jr. Our relationship and friendship goes well beyond our fantasy connection. It's been a triumph of ups and downs through the last 15 years, hasn't it?

To my sister Denise, no company is deserving of such a dedicated person let alone a brother deserving of such a sister. Thanks again and again, Den.

To my editor Julie Jensen. As we continue to work on this project together, Julie you continue to make the completion of the project very workable.

To my friend Fred Livermore. Fred, you continue to take us into the age of software and hardware advances, making our job easier each and every year.

To my nephew, Ben Fleischhacker. Ben, you have become a big asset to our team. I appreciate all your dedication and help.

To my friend Tom Nemo. First as a friend and now a member of our fantasy team. Tom, thanks very much for all your time, effort and support.

To Julie Pedersen, our typist. Thank you for your timely manner in handling things.

And now thank you to all the others that help throughout the year:

Jim Rubbelke	Tom Fleischhacker
Terri Elizondo	Teri Schierenbeck
Mike Evans	Cathy Evans
Bernie Fleischhacker	Vicky Thibedeau
Rex Estby	Brenda Geisselman
Michelle Stein	Jodi Thibedeau

Now last, but certainly not least, thanks to all of our readers. Your countless ideas and suggestions continue to be a source for our improvement. I hope you enjoy this year's digest, and I wish you luck in your 1998 fantasy season. Hope to see you in the Fantasy Bowl.

CONTENTS

FANTASY FOOTBALL BASICS 301

THE AUTHOR'S 1997 SEASON

COULD HAVE BEEN A "BOOMER" SEASON

The toughest thing about fantasy football that there is nothing you can do to stop your opponent from scoring. In going head to head weekly in our league, you could score a ton of points but if you happen to play the top-scoring team of the week and you score the second most points, you still lose. This could leave you with a bad taste, especially if the other teams in your division score significantly fewer points and win. Such was the season I was about to embark on in 1997.

Going into the 1997 Fantasy Draft, I believed that, beyond Brett Favre, there were very few players who stood out as exceptional picks. Perhaps Emmitt Smith, who had scored 62 touchdowns the previous three seasons, was one. But even his consistency had shown signs of sliding when he scored 15 times in 1996 compared to 25 times a year earlier.

THE DRAFT

Unlike most seasons, I was not as concerned about getting a top-five pick at our draft, believing there were many players available who were capable of scoring in the 12-plus touchdown range. And I felt that there were very few quarterbacks worthy of top draft pick consideration like Brett Favre. Favre was the only quarterback I believed was certain to throw 35-plus touchdowns.

As the draft cards were shuffled and dealt, I got some pretty good news. I had the No.3 overall pick. In the short recess before the start of the draft, however, I decided to do some wheeling and dealing. Following my theory that there were many good players out there but few "great" players, I opted to trade my No.3 overall pick, which would have given me the 14th pick in the second round. In other words, I traded my first- and second-round picks. In return, I received the No.12 overall pick, which gave me the fifth pick in the second round. I truly believed I could still get a legitimate 12-plus touchdown scorer at No.12.

As the draft began, Brett Favre, Emmitt Smith, Curtis Martin, Barry Sanders, Terrell Davis, Ricky Watters, Jerry Rice, Jerome Bettis, Terry Allen, Steve Young and Natrone Means went before I was able to select at No.12. Looking over my draft list, I chose Karim Abdul-Jabbar as my favorite to score 12-plus. So, despite trading down, I believed I had done well. Besides, now I'd have an earlier second-round pick. In the second round, I made Jeff Blake my quarterback, believing he would throw for 25-30 scores because he had the previous two seasons. (Wrong!) The rest of my draft went like this:

Round	Player	Position	Team
3rd	Isaac Bruce	WR	St. Louis
4th	Tim Biakabatuka	RB	Carolina
5th	Keyshawn Johnson	WR	N. Y. Jets
6th	Gary Anderson	K	San Francisco
7th	Darnay Scott	WR	Cincinnati
8th	Bam Morris	RB	Baltimore
9th	Kerry Collins	QB	Carolina
10th	Tony Gonzalez	TE	Kansas City
11th	Brett Conway	K	Green Bay
12th	Jeff Graham	WR	N. Y. Jets

Looking at my team, I'd have Blake to start at quarterback with Kerry Collins as a backup. At running back, Abdul-Jabbar would start alongside Biakabatuka, if he was ready, and I could hang onto Bam Morris for an ace in the hole when he returned from his suspension. At wideout, Isaac Bruce, Keyshawn Johnson and Darnay Scott could start, depending on team matchups. At tight end rookie, Tony Gonzalez looked good in the preseason so I took a chance on him. At kicker; I have always liked having the 49ers' kicker so I grabbed Gary Anderson. Later I took a chance on injured Packer rookie Brett Conway.

REGULAR SEASON

For the regular-season opener, my lineup looked like this:

QB	Jeff Blake	QB	Cincinnati
RB	Karim Abdul-Jabbar	RB	Miami
RB	Tim Biakabatuka	RB	Carolina
WR	Jeff Graham	WR	N. Y. Jets
WR	Darnay Scott	WR	Cincinnati
TE	Tony Gonzalez	TE	Kansas City
K	Gary Anderson	K	San Francisco

WEEK No.1

On the Sunday of Labor Day weekend, I watch the games with relatives. My nephew, who is my opponent, and I watch as Abdul-Jabbar scores early and I jump out to a 6-0 lead. This, however, is the last enjoyable moment of the day for me. His running back, Lawrence Phillips, scores once, then twice, then a third time. Despite Abdul-Jabbar's score and two touchdowns from Jeff Graham, I get thrashed, 63-28, as my nephew Ben also gets a three-touchdown performance out of Tim Brown and two scores from Terry Allen.

WEEK No.2

With Biakabatuka now playing behind Anthony Johnson in Carolina, I pick up Stephen Davis. He is to get the call for the Redskins since Terry Allen is banged up. Neither Davis nor any of my six-point players, score as I lose 27-9 to go 0-2.

WEEK No.3

Time to get it going. I now decide to replace Stephen Davis with Atlanta rookie Byron Hanspard. Still I get no help as my players score four total points—one touchdown pass out of Jeff Blake and an extra point. I lose 16-4 in a defensive, ugly contest.

WEEK No.4

Never having been 0-3 before, I was hoping things could not get any worse. I do get a score out of Abdul-Jabbar and 10 points out of kicker Gary Anderson, but my opponent scores 26. I drop my fourth in a row, losing 26-19. Worst of all, my opponent was F-Troop, my long-time nemesis. F-Troop is the only team close to me on the all-time win-loss list. I hate losing to them.

WEEK No.5

At 0-4, I decide to make a couple of pickups and grab running back Corey Dillon, who is stepping in for Ki-Jana Carter in Cincinnati, and Tennessee tight end Frank Wycheck, who is getting the majority of the receptions for the Oilers. Wycheck pays immediate dividends with a touchdown and a two-point conversion. I also get another touchdown out of Abdul-Jabbar, my most consistent scorer, and a nine-point play out of Jeff Blake and Darnay Scott. Blake adds another and Anderson boots for 10 as I finally get my first win, 36-12.

WEEK No.6

Bam Morris is back and I start him. Morris scores, as does Abdul-Jabbar. Blake throws for two and Anderson kicks for another 10 as I win my second straight, 28-23.

WEEK No.7

Morris and Abdul-Jabbar both score for the second straight week. A new pickup, wide receiver Rae Carruth, also scores. Wycheck puts up six, Blake throws for two scores and Anderson gets 12 at I continue my scoring roll with 36. My opponent, however, gets five scores out of James Stewart, who steps in for an injured Natrone Means. He also gets three TDs out of Barry Sanders as I get thrashed, 66-36. It was just my bad luck to match up against this guy on this week because I would have beaten all of the other 14 teams in the league. Despite the loss, I'm excited about the points I'm scoring.

WEEK No.8

Abdul-Jabbar continues to fare well, scoring three times, but I only get one touchdown pass out of Kerry Collins and three points out of Gary Anderson. My opponent scores 31 points as I lose 31-24 and fall to 2-6. Despite my record, I remain only one game out of a possible playoff berth.

WEEK No.9

Abdul-Jabbar does it again with a touchdown. Bam Morris and Isaac Bruce also score to help me to a 32-20 win. Despite my 3-6 record, I'm starting to believe that if I can make the playoffs I may do well considering that my team's consistency has improved immensely. Abdul-Jabbar, Bam Morris and Corey Dillon are all doing well. Gary Anderson and his potent 49ers continue to play well. *Watch out!*

WEEK No.10

I'm back within my division for the last three games. I'm battling for the final playoff spot in our division. My nephew, who blew me out 63-28 on week No.1, has struggled since then. Neither of my consistent running backs, Abdul-Jabbar and Bam Morris, score but I get two scores out of Isaac Bruce, six points out of quarterback Kerry Collins and five out of kicker Gary Anderson. I need all of them as I sneak by with a crucial 23-22 win. I have now won four out of my last six games. Had I won the week when I was the second-highest scoring team, I would have won five out of six.

WEEK No.11

Matching up against my brother-in-law Rex, with whom I am battling for the last playoff spot, makes this a huge game. He sits at 3-7 and I am 4-6. His lineup, which includes Jerome Bettis and the Drew Bledsoe—Terry Glenn combo, scares me.

Bledsoe does throw for one score but not to Glenn. Bettis scores but kicker Eddie Murray's three points are his only other points for a total of 12. Abdul-Jabbar equals that number by himself with two scores. Blake throws for one, Anderson kicks for 6 points and I win 21-12. That moves me up to 5-6 and virtually locks up a playoff spot.

WEEK No.12

Matching up the final week against the league's leading scorer looks tough. He had both Terrell Davis and Jamal Anderson. Anderson scores twice but it is tight end Harvey Williams who inflicts the worst damage with four touchdowns. Yes, that's right! Harvey Williams for four. I get scores from Karim "Mr. Consistent" Abdul-Jabbar and Frank Wycheck but lose, 45-21. I end the regular season 5-7 but I remember that I started out 0-4. I did lead the league handily in points against, which means I had to face the league's toughest schedule. Regardless, I have battled back to make the playoffs and I am ready to make a run for it.

PLAYOFFS

Preparing for the playoffs, I make my one Playoff Player Addition. I grab Boomer Esiason, who is replacing a struggling Jeff Blake.

ROUND 1

Matching up against my nephew, with whom I had split during the year, I feel I have a great chance to win, especially considering how well I have been doing lately. My "Mr. Consistent" continues his productive ways, as Karim Abdul-Jabbar explodes for three scores. I had elected to go with Kerry Collins at quarterback since Jeff Blake had not been playing well and Boomer Esiason just recently stepped in for the Bengals. Collins throws for one and Gary Anderson adds five as I cruise 26-12. My nephew gets scoring from only his kicker. His Jeff George-to-Tim Brown combo shuts down and Terry Allen also fails to score.

I am now among the "final eight" in our league. I have a good chance to make the "final four" despite getting off to a horrendous 0-4 start.

ROUND 2

This wasn't going to be easy. I was to face our division champ, the league's leading scorer, G & H Empire, who had beaten me twice during the year. They had been successful on the strength of their running game of Terrell Davis and Jamal Anderson.

While preparing for this game, I took a close look at game matchups. At quarterback, I had to decide between Kerry Collins (Carolina was playing at home against a pretty poor New Orleans Saints team) or Boomer Esiason, who had done well recently after taking over for Jeff Blake. The Bengals were at Philadelphia. I elected to go with Collins because I figured playing three Bengals was too risky. I already had running back Corey Dillon and wide receiver Darney Scott in the lineup. The games started on Thanksgiving Day. My opponent has Troy Aikman of Dallas going and I have tight end Frank Wycheck of Tennessee playing. G & H jumps out 6-0 as Aikman throws for two scores and Wycheck fails to score.

On Sunday, my sons were in a hockey tournament. I was in and out of the arena to the car as often as I could be to catch the scores on ESPN radio. In the early games, Cincinnati starts by scoring readily on Philadelphia. Esiason has already thrown for two and one is to Darnay Scott when I get the first update. Corey Dillon, however, has failed to score. Throughout the afternoon, Boomer continues to roll and throws for four on the day. Scott only scores once and Dillon fails to score. (The next week Dillon scores four times!) I hope Esiason's four TD passes don't haunt me but after hearing about the low-scoring affair between Carolina and New Orleans, I fear they will. Collins fails to throw for any scores. More bad news. Isaac Bruce fails to score. My kicker, Gary Anderson, does get 9 points so I'm actually ahead 15-6 going into the late games.

Once the 3 o'clock games start, I get a score out of Abdul-Jabbar but that's the end of my run. G & H Empire gets two touchdowns out of Jamal Anderson, one score out of Terrell Davis and five out of kicker Todd Peterson to win 29-21. Let's see, 21 plus 12 (Boomer's four TD passes) equals 33. Yep, had I started Boomer I would have beaten G & H 33-29. A blunder! A bad move! Still, I liked the matchup of Kerry Collins against the Saints. Well, I had liked it. Not to worry, not starting Boomer will only eat at me until . . . next season.

And, just to continue the what if's, I would have stomped on the next week's opponent, led by Corey Dillon's four touchdowns, to get to the Fantasy Bowl. And I would have outscored my opponent in the Fantasy Bowl. So one bad move cost me a Fantasy Bowl. I hate when that happens! I hate thinking about it! *Wow*, I just hate it.

MEASURING UP MY 1997 SEASON

How do I assess my season? The toughest thing to swallow was the fact that I had faced our league's toughest schedule. I had the misfortune to play teams when they were "hot" and twice had more than 60 points scored against me. There is nothing that you or I can do about that. Had I faced a bit easier schedule, I may have finished with three or four more wins.

Despite a horrible 0-4 start, I rebounded to win 5 of the next 7 games to reach the playoffs. Moves such as trading down to draft Karim Abdul-Jabbar (16 TDs) and drafting Bam Morris despite his early-season suspension eventually paid off. Picking up Jeff Blake's backup, Boomer Esiason, turned out to be an excellent move to start the playoffs although not starting him in the second week of the playoffs was a blunder.

When all was said and done, I maintained my most precious league bragging right, holding the top all-time win-loss percentage (.593) with a 124-85 mark. But my closest challenger, long-time rival F-Troop, moved three games closer with an 8-4 season, despite scoring nine fewer points than I did. *Where's the justice?* They sit at 118-91 (.564).

On to next year when I hope I can regain some much-needed luck, especially in the schedule I face. A 10-2 season, a division title and a Fantasy Bowl win is all I expect. But then, doesn't everybody?

I
INITIAL CONSIDERATIONS
Every Year is a New Year

A frequent mistake made by many Fantasy Football participants is to draft a Fantasy team based purely on the previous year's statistics and events. Don't get caught in this mindset. Remember: "That was then and this is now." Every year takes on its own characteristics. Because a player fares well or poorly one year, doesn't mean he'll do the same in the next. Injuries, contract holdouts, and poor play are all factors that contribute to a player doing well or poorly. These same factors may also affect another player's performance.

The 1997 season, like numerous seasons before it, was a year of much player movement. Were you able to predict which players who joined new teams would do well? Did you have the foresight to grab Jeff George, who signed on to become the Raiders signal-caller and finished with an AFC-high 29 touchdown passes? How about Kordell Stewart, who took over the permanent quarterback job in Pittsburgh to produce 21 passing touchdowns and 11 more on the ground? Or did you grab one of our "sleeper" picks like wide receiver Rod Smith of Denver, who exploded for 12 touchdowns?

What about the rookies? How about second-round pick Corey Dillon of Cincinnati? Were you fortunate enough to draft him or pick him up early as he unseated Ki-Jana Carter as the starter? Dillon finished with 10 scores. Or how about Antowain Smith, who pushed veteran Thurman Thomas for playing time and production and finished with eight scores and just over 1,000 rushing-receiving yards? Warrick Dunn started out strong and tailed off but finished with 1,440 rushing-receiving yards and seven touchdowns. The rookies at the wide receiver position were a pretty big disappointment. Miami first-rounder Yatil Green injured a knee in the preseason and never played a down. Fellow first-rounders Ike Hilliard (Giants), Reidel Anthony (Buccaneers) and Rae Carruth (Panthers) all had less than spectacular seasons.

Why is it that many of our preseason picks or predictions don't work out as well as we believed they would? Because, of course, each season is unique. Injuries, holdouts, suspensions, trades and playing time all play very big roles in a player's success or failure. The previously mentioned knee injury to rookie first-round pick Yatil Green cost him his entire NFL season. How will he fare in 1998? A broken leg suffered by Rashaan Salaam cost him his last 13 games. His injury opened the door for Raymont Harris, who scored 10 times. What happens when Salaam returns healthy in 1998 or now that the Bears have brought aboard Edgar Bennett and made Curtis Enis their No. 1 draft pick? A knee injury to Jerry Rice helped boost the stats of Terrell Owens and J.J. Stokes. Rice's healthy return will surely affect their numbers in 1998. There were also many short-term injuries that cost a player one to four or five weeks of action and certainly adversely affected their year-end results. Players like Isaac Bruce, Carl Pickens and Garrison Hearst all missed short stints because of injuries. How will the return of these players in 1998 affect their statistics and those of the players who filled in for them?

Another thing to consider when planning your 1998 fantasy draft is the direction the teams are headed. Which teams are on the upswing, and which teams may be on their way down? Pittsburgh, behind the running of Jerome Bettis and the talent of young signal-caller Kordell Stewart, looks to be good for years to come. Tony Dungy sure seems to have the Tampa Bay Buccaneers on the right track. On the flip side, the Dallas Cowboys have quickly fallen from prominence, as have the Buffalo Bills with the departure of quarterback Jim Kelly. Meanwhile, Green Bay, San Francisco and Denver continue to find ways to stay among the league's elite.

Many teams are changing coaches. In Oakland, Joe Bugel is out and Philadelphia offensive coordinator Jon Gruden is in. In Dallas, Jerry Jones has finally given Barry Switzer his walking papers following a 6-10 finish. Jones brought in Chan Gailey to replace Switzer. Gailey, the Philadelphia Eagles' offensive coordinator in 1997, was chosen over George Seifert and other notables.

Also, while preparing for your 1998 fantasy season, be sure to keep a close eye on off-season happenings, such as progress of significant injuries and, of course, player moves. Free agency continues to have a startling effect on the makeup of teams and the league. Big-money players changed teams last year and will again this year. In 1997, Garrison Hearst went to San Francisco, Elvis Grbac went to Kansas City and free agents Jeff George and Gary Brown signed with Oakland and San Diego, respectively. These are just a few of the many players who changed teams in 1997, either via trade or free agency. Many more key transactions will have a big impact on the 1998 season. Such changes deserve your attention because they will affect the performance of the team the player is leaving as well as the one he's joining.

Which trends will carry over from 1997 to 1998? Which teams and, more specifically, which players will come to the forefront in 1998? The performance of a player or a team can change quickly and unexpectedly from year to year, especially with so many key players moving to new squads. To demonstrate just how wildly and significantly the statistical leaders can fluctuate from year to year, we're going to compare 1996's top-10 lists with those of 1997. We'll be comparing the leaders from each fantasy position in both the Basic and the Combined Basic-Performance Scoring Methods. By doing this, you will gain a sense of the changes that have occurred among scoring and yardage leaders from year to year. (NOTE: A kicker's fantasy points are the same in both scoring methods so they're shown just once.)

BASIC SCORING METHOD—RUNNING BACKS

	1996					1997		
NAME	TEAM	TDs	FANTASY POINTS		NAME	TEAM	TDs	FANTASY POINTS
1. T. Allen	WASH	21	126		1. Abdul-Jabbar	MIA	15	96
2. Martin	NE	17	104		2. Davis	DEN	15	96
3. Smith	DALL	15	90		3. Sanders	DET	14	84
4. Davis	DEN	15	90		4. Levens	GB	12	74

5.	Watters	PHIL	13	78
6.	Sanders	DET	11	66
7.	Abdul-Jabbar	MIA	11	66
8.	Bettis	PITT	11	66
9.	Levens	GB	10	60
10.	Stewart	JAC	10	60

5.	M. Allen	KC	11	72
6.	Anderson	ATL	10	63
7.	Harris	CHI	10	60
8.	Dillon	CIN	10	60
9.	Alstott	TB	10	60
10.	Means	JAC	9	54
	Stewart	JAC	9	54
	Bettis	PITT	9	54

Of the top 10 (expanded to 12 in 1997 by ties), six returned to that production level in 1997. They were Terrell Davis, Barry Sanders, Karim Abdul-Jabbar, Jerome Bettis, Dorsey Levens and James Stewart. Injuries to Terry Allen, Curtis Martin and Emmitt Smith were big reasons they fell out of the group, while Ricky Watters just saw his consistent touchdown production take a big hit.

Aging Marcus Allen continued his scoring prowess, while rookie Corey Dillon joined youngsters Mike Alstott, Raymont Harris and Jamal Anderson as solid touchdown performers for their respective teams.

BASIC SCORING METHOD—WIDE RECEIVERS

1996				1997			
NAME	TEAM	TDs	FANTASY POINTS	NAME	TEAM	TDs	FANTASY POINTS
1. Jackson	BALT	14	88	1. Carter	MINN	13	84
2. Martin	SD	14	84	2. Smith	DEN	12	72
3. Pickens	CIN	12	74	3. Freeman	GB	12	72
4. Fryar	PHIL	11	66	4. Jett	OAK	12	72
5. Kennison	STL	11	66	5. Galloway	SEAT	12	54
6. C. Carter	MINN	10	60	6. Emanuel	ATL	9	54
7. Alexander	BALT	9	56	7. Irvin	DALL	9	54
8. Moore	DET	9	56	8. D. Alexander	BALT	9	54
9. Freeman	GB	9	54	9. R.Moore	ARIZ	8	50
10. Brown	OAK	9	54	10. H.Moore	DET	8	50
Rice	SF	9	54	Calloway	NYG	8	48
				Owens	SF	8	48
				McCaffrey	DEN	8	48
				J. Lewis	BALT	8	48

This group got nearly an entire facelift. Of the 11 top-10 performers in 1996, only four returned to that distinction in 1997. That group included only Chris Carter, Antonio Freeman, Derrick Alexander and Herman Moore. There were huge touchdown falloffs for Michael Jackson, Tony Martin, Carl Pickens and Jerry Rice, with injuries to Pickens and Rice taking a heavy production toll.

In Denver, with Anthony Miller off to Dallas, Rod Smith became John Elway's go-to guy, producing 12 scores. James Jett became a frequent touchdown target for strong-armed Jeff George, while Joey Galloway reaped the benefits of a resurgent Warren Moon in Seattle. Terrell Owens benefited statistically from the injury to Jerry Rice.

BASIC SCORING METHOD—TIGHT ENDS

	1996				1997			
NAME	TEAM	TDs	FANTASY POINTS		NAME	TEAM	TDs	FANTASY POINTS
1. Walls	CAR	10	60	1.	Coates	NE	8	48
2. Sharpe	DEN	10	60	2.	Dudley	OAK	7	42
3. Jackson	GB	10	60	3.	McGee	CIN	6	38
4. Coates	NE	9	56	4.	Walls	CAR	6	36
5. Wycheck	HOUS	6	36	5.	Chmura	GB	6	36
6. Popson	SF	6	36	6.	Bruener	PITT	6	36
7. McGee	CIN	4	24	7.	Williams	OAK	5	32
8. Dilger	IND	4	24	8.	Green	BALT	5	30
9. Dudley	OAK	4	24	9.	Wycheck	TENN	4	26
10. Asher	WASH	4	24	10.	Drayton	MIA	4	24
					Gedney	ARIZ	4	24
					Mitchell	JAC	4	24
					Conwell	STL	4	24
					C. Lewis	PHIL	4	24
					Moore	TB	4	24

Half of the top-10 finishers in 1996 returned to that group in 1997. Ben Coates, Ricky Dudley, Tony McGee, Wesley Walls and Frank Wycheck made up that group. Shannon Sharpe, although having a productive year, saw his touchdown level drop as Rod Smith became more of Denver's go-to guy. Keith Jackson retired, opening a top-10 slot for fellow Packer, Mark Chmura.

Converted running back Harvey Williams became a tight end scoring force for the Raiders, while Mark Bruener began seeing more action near the goal line for Pittsburgh. Eric Green returned a bit to the production of his younger days, scoring five times for Baltimore.

BASIC SCORING METHOD—QUARTERBACKS

	1996					1997			
NAME	TEAM	PS TDs	RSH TDs	FANTASY POINTS	NAME	TEAM	PS TDs	RSH TDs	FANTASY POINTS
1. Favre	GB	2	39	131	1. Stewart	PITT	11	21	130
2. Testaverde	BALT	2	33	116	2. Favre	GB	1	35	112
3. Elway	DEN	4	26	102	3. McNair	TENN	8	14	91
4. Blake	CIN	2	24	85	4. George	OAK	0	29	89
5. Bledsoe	NE	0	27	85	5. Elway	DEN	1	27	88
6. Brunell	JAC	3	19	82	6. Bledsoe	NE	0	28	84
7. Mitchell	DET	4	17	75	7. Moon	SEAT	1	25	81
8. Hostetler	OAK	1	23	75	8. Young	SF	3	19	75
9. Hebert	ATL	1	23	75	9. Dilfer	TB	1	21	69
10. Young	SF	4	14	68	10. Brunell	JAC	2	18	67

Here's another group where exactly half the group returned in 1997 to the top-10 list. Brett Favre, John Elway, Drew Bledsoe, Mark Brunell and Steve Young made up that group, which comes as no surprise. Scott Mitchell's significant drop was a surprise, while Jeff Blake's poor play lost him his starting job and Vinny Testaverde's performance was affected by a late-season knee injury.

The newcomers to the list included a few surprises in Trent Dilfer and aging Warren Moon. Youngsters Kordell Stewart and Steve McNair began demonstrating their skills, including their running ability, which propelled them into the elite group. Jeff George's appearance in the group with 29 TD passes after coming to the Raiders was really not a very big surprise.

BASIC SCORING METHOD—KICKERS

	1996				1997		
NAME	**TEAM**	**FANTASY POINTS**		**NAME**	**TEAM**	**FANTASY POINTS**	
1. Kasay	CAR	145		1. Hollis	JAC	134	
2. Blanchard	IND	135		2. Cunningham	DALL	126	
3. Del Greco	HOUS	131		3. Anderson	SF	125	
4. Wilkins	SF	130		4. Elam	DEN	124	
5. Boniol	DALL	120		5. Longwell	GB	120	
6. Vinatieri	NE	120		6. Hall	NYJ	120	
7. Carney	SD	118		7. Hanson	DET	117	
8. Blanton	WASH	118		8. Blanchard	IND	117	
9. Hollis	JAC	117		9. Mare	MIA	117	
10. Anderson	PHIL	115		10. Vinatieri	NE	115	

Like most years, very few kickers return to the top-10 group. In this case, there were only three: Cary Blanchard, Adam Vinatieri and Mike Hollis. However, with the 49ers and the Cowboys changing kickers (to Gary Anderson and Rickie Cunningham, respectively) their kickers again made it to the group.

COMBINED BASIC/PERFORMANCE POINT METHOD
RUNNING BACKS

	1996					1997			
NAME	**TEAM**	**YARDS**	**TD's**	**FANTASY POINTS**	**NAME**	**TEAM**	**YARDS**	**TD's**	**FANTASY POINTS**
1. Allen	WASH	1,547	21	268	1. Sanders	DET	2,358	14	305
2. Davis	DEN	1,848	15	263	2. Davis	DEN	2,037	15	286
3. Watters	PHIL	1,855	13	248	3. Levens	GB	1,805	12	245
4. Martin	NE	1,485	17	242	4. Bettis	PITT	1,775	9	222
5. Smith	DALL	1,453	15	225	5. Kaufman	OAK	1,697	8	207
6. Sanders	DET	1,700	11	223	6. Abdul-Jabbar	MIA	1,153	16	198
7. Bettis	PITT	1,553	11	211	7. Faulk	IND	1,525	8	188
8. George	HOUS	1,550	8	193	8. Dillon	CIN	1,388	10	185
9. Abdul-Jabbar	MIA	1,255	11	178	9. Watters	PHIL	1,550	7	183
10. Anderson	ATL	1,528	6	175	10. Anderson	ATL	1,286	10	179
					George	TENN	1,443	7	179

Here is one of the strongest returning groups. Of the top-10 finishers in this method in 1996, seven of them returned in 1997. Only Terry Allen, Curtis Martin and Emmitt Smith, all of whom were slowed by injury in 1997, did not return to their top-10 rank in 1997.

Newcomer Dorsey Levens' playing time and statistics grew with Edgar Bennett out. Marshall Faulk stayed away from injuries well enough to have a rebound season. Napoleon Kaufman continued to improve and so did his numbers. Rookie Corey Dillon just kept getting better as the season wore on.

COMBINED BASIC/PERFORMANCE POINT METHOD
WIDE RECEIVERS

	1996					1997			
NAME	TEAM	YARDS	TD's	FANTASY POINTS	NAME	TEAM	YARDS	TD's	FANTASY POINTS
1. Jackson	BALT	1,204	14	203	1. R. Moore	ARIZ	1,584	8	200
2. Martin	SD	1,171	14	193	2. Freeman	GB	1,257	12	192
3. Pickens	CIN	1,182	12	185	3. Smith	DEN	1,196	12	187
4. Fryar	PHIL	1,191	11	180	4. Carter	MINN	1,069	13	182
5. Moore	DET	1,296	9	177	5. Thigpen	PITT	1,401	7	178
6. Rice	SF	1,331	9	174	6. Galloway	SEAT	1,121	12	176
7. Carter	MINN	1,163	10	169	7. H. Moore	DET	1,293	8	172
8. Bruce	STL	1,342	7	168	8. Brown	OAK	1,427	5	166
9. Reed	MINN	1,320	7	166	9. Irvin	DALL	1,180	9	164
10. Smith	JAC	1,244	7	161	10. Fryar	PHIL	1,316	6	161

This wide receiver group returned only three players to the top 10 in 1997. Those members are Irving Fryar, Herman Moore and Cris Carter. Significant injuries to Jerry Rice, Carl Pickens, and Isaac Bruce greatly affected their seasons.

On the upswing, Rob Moore and Antonio Freeman rebounded well from injuries in 1996 and Rod Smith became the go-to guy for John Elway in Denver.

COMBINED BASIC/PERFORMANCE POINT METHOD
TIGHT ENDS

	1996					1997			
NAME	TEAM	YARDS	TD's	FANTASY POINTS	NAME	TEAM	YARDS	TD's	FANTASY POINTS
1. Sharpe	DEN	1,062	10	162	1. Sharpe	DEN	1,107	3	124
2. Walls	CAR	713	10	126	2. Coates	NE	737	8	114
3. Coates	NE	682	9	117	3. Dudley	OAK	787	7	113
4. Jackson	GB	505	10	105	4. Walls	CAR	746	6	104
5. Wycheck	HOUS	514	6	79	5. Wycheck	TENN	748	4	93
6. Dilger	IND	503	4	68	6. Green	BALT	601	5	84
7. Asher	WASH	481	4	65	7. McGee	CIN	414	6	73
8. Popson	SF	301	6	62	8. Drayton	MIA	558	4	73
9. McGee	CIN	446	4	61	9. Chmura	GB	417	6	71
10. Dudley	OAK	386	4	58	10. Conwell	STL	404	4	57

Of 1996's top-10 finishers, six returned to that group in 1997. Shannon Sharpe, Wesley Walls, Ben Coates, Frank Wycheck, Tony McGee and Ricky Dudley all returned. Keith Jackson retired, and Ken Dilger and Ted Popson were slowed by injuries in 1997.

Newcomer Mark Chmura gained statistically from Keith Jackson's retirement. Eric Green rebounded in Baltimore, Troy Drayton became a bigger factor for Miami in his second season there, as did young Ernie Conwell for the Rams.

COMBINED BASIC/PERFORMANCE POINT METHOD
QUARTERBACKS
1996

	NAME	TEAM	RSH YDs	PS YDs	RSH TDs	PS TDs	FANTASY PTS
1.	Testaverde	BALT	188	4,177	2	33	330
2.	Favre	GB	136	3,899	2	39	328
3.	Brunell	JAC	400	4,367	3	19	325
4.	Blake	CIN	313	3,624	2	24	273
5.	Elway	DEN	249	3,328	4	26	283
6.	Bledsoe	NE	27	4,086	0	27	283
7.	Hebert	ATL	59	3,162	1	22	228
8.	Mitchell	DET	83	2,917	4	17	219
9.	Hostetler	OAK	179	2,548	1	23	209
10.	Young	SF	310	2,410	4	14	207

1997

	NAME	TEAM	RSH YDs	PS YDs	RSH TDs	PS TDs	FANTASY PTS
1.	Stewart	PITT	476	3,020	11	21	314
2.	Favre	GB	187	3,867	1	35	311
3.	Elway	DEN	218	3,635	1	27	281
4.	McNair	TENN	674	2,665	8	14	280
5.	George	OAK	45	3,917	0	29	279
6.	Bledsoe	NE	55	3,706	0	28	265
7.	Moon	SEAT	40	3,678	1	25	261
8.	Brunell	JAC	257	3,281	2	18	243
9.	Mitchell	DET	83	3,484	1	19	236
10.	Young	SF	199	3,029	3	19	235

Sixty percent of the quarterbacks who were in the top 10 in 1996 regained that status in 1997. Brett Favre, Mark Brunell, John Elway, Drew Bledsoe, Scott Mitchell and Steve Young all returned. Vinny Testaverde, the No.1 finisher in 1996, missed the last three games of 1997 with a knee injury, which hurt his performance. Jeff Blake lost his starting job, while Bobby Hebert and Jeff Hostetler left their 1996 teams and those starting jobs.

Newcomers include two youngsters, Kordell Stewart and Steve McNair, who can get it done on the ground as well as in the air. Veterans Jeff George and Warren Moon both had resurgent seasons after joining new teams.

Can this two-year comparison help you? It shows how radically top performers can change from year to year. This widespread change occurs for a variety of reasons: injuries, holdouts, trades, and personnel movement. We can see that roughly 50 percent of the players from any one position who make the top-10 list one year make it back the next year. That's quite a change from one year to the next, and that's just the top-10 players.

Comparing these lists demonstrates how poorly we would have drafted in 1997 if we had based our decisions purely on statistics from the previous year. A review like this reminds us how many circumstances influence the success of a season. Again, overall in 1997, about half the players at fantasy positions who were top-10 finishers in 1996 returned to that list. This rate holds fairly true, year to year. Successful fantasy players realize that one great season (or a horrible one) does not necessarily indicate a trend. Injuries, holdouts, trades, suspensions and free-agent moves can all determine how a player does. To win consistently, a successful franchise owner will make forecasts for the upcoming season by examining helpful facts from the previous year, by keeping track of off-season player movement, by considering the general upward or downward movement of a player's team, and by combining these considerations with a general feel for the game.

Such successful fantasy owners probably had the foresight to gamble on Jeff George, Kordell Stewart or Corey Dillon in 1997. George came to Oakland in 1997 to open up the Raiders' offense and did just that, throwing for 29 touchdowns. The very athletic Kordell Stewart took over the quarterback job in Pittsburgh and rushed for 11 scores, while throwing for 21 more. And rookie second-round pick Corey Dillon just kept pushing Ki-Jana Carter until he took over the starting job and finished with 10 touchdowns.

We have already found that free-agent signings, injuries, retirements, contract holdouts and suspensions can affect players' careers. Merely studying the 1997 statistics, although helpful, will not be enough to make you successful in 1998. That is why, in the following sections, we'll study many variables, such as the injuries, trades, contract holdouts, and other factors that may have influenced a player's statistics last year. We will also look at the effects these variables may have on the upcoming 1998 season. We'll look at off-season roster moves, such as free-agent moves, trades, acquisitions, and retirements. We'll take a close look at injury updates to see what effect they may have on the upcoming season. Then I hope you can combine all this information with your feel for both NFL football and fantasy football to make your 1998 season a huge success.

II
HELPFUL FACTS FROM THE 1997 SEASON
(Key injuries, trades, holdouts, and other events that affected
1997 performances and how the 1997 rookies fared)

Many fantasy franchise owners preparing for the draft make a big mistake by considering only the previous year's statistics. Many factors contribute to a player's success or failure, and all of them should be carefully examined.

In this section, we will review the 1997 season to learn some of the reasons for the statistical success or failure of certain players. We'll look at injuries, trades, contract holdouts, suspensions, and other events to see how each may have helped one player but hurt another. We'll also review the 1997 rookies' performances to see how they were affected by injuries and by other players' performances. (A rookie isn't always able to prove himself in his first year in the NFL.) We do this to evaluate players' potential for 1998. We may be able to forecast a "sleeper" or predict which veterans may have comebacks.

Injuries, suspensions and holdouts to key players always play a significant role in statistics. A knee injury to Jerry Rice led to greatly expanded roles for Terrell Owens and J.J. Stokes, which inflated their year-end numbers. Injuries to prominent standout Terry Allen (thumb, knee and ankle) limited him to only 724 rushing yards and five touchdowns as he missed six games. Isaac Bruce missed the first five games of 1997 with a hamstring injury and finished with only 815 receiving yards and five touchdowns. Others, like Rashaam Salaam (broken ankle), Jim Harbaugh (hand) and Brad Johnson (neck), all missed significant playing time, which damaged their year-end numbers. There are a number of other players who missed significant time and whose 1997 numbers are deceiving.

These are circumstances from the previous year we should consider. Without acknowledging all the missed time due to injuries, holdouts, etc., we're likely to overlook a significant player this year. What follows is a team-by-team discussion of events that may have played a part in a certain player's success or failure in 1997 and what lingering effects they may have going into 1998.

HERE'S THE KEY TO THIS BREAKDOWN:

IR — Injured and on injured reserve
PUPL — Physically unable to perform list
I — Injured but never on injured reserve
S — Suspended
TR — Traded
RT — Retired
RS — Re-signed
RL — Released
AC — Acquired
HO — Contract holdout
L — Leave of absence
AO — Absent for other reason

ARIZONA CARDINALS

I—Le Shon Johnson (Running Back)
Johnson struggled through a hamstring injury late in the year but was mainly just inconsistent and ineffective. None of the Cardinal backs did much consistently including Leeland McElroy, which is why the Cardinals will be looking for help at running back in 1998. Johnson has moved on as a free agent to join the New York Giants in 1998.

ATLANTA FALCONS

I—Chris Chandler (Quarterback)
Chandler threw for 20 touchdowns and 2,692 yards in his first year as the Falcons starter in 1997. Those numbers would have been better had he not missed two games with chest and head injuries.

I—O.J. Santiago (Tight End)
The rookie's first-year production was marred by a leg injury late in the year. Santiago finished with only 17 receptions and two touchdowns.

BALTIMORE RAVENS

I—Vinny Testaverde (Quarterback)
After putting up whopping numbers in 1996—throwing for 4,177 yards and 33 touchdowns—Testaverde finished with 2,971 passing yards and only 18 touchdowns in 1997. A major factor was a knee injury that was

part of the reason he missed the last three games of 1997. In 1998, he'll likely be forced to a backup role behind newly acquired Jim Harbaugh.

I—Jermaine Lewis (Wide Receiver)
Despite missing three games with knee and arm injuries, Lewis produced 35 receptions and eight touchdowns in 1997. Over the full 16-game schedule, it's likely Lewis would have hit the double-digit touchdown plateau and could again in 1998 especially with Derrick Alexander moving on to Kansas City.

I—Eric Green (Tight End)
An impressive 65 receptions and five touchdowns for Green in 1997, despite missing two games with hamstring and knee injuries.

S,I—Bam Morris (Running Back)
Morris missed the first four games of 1997 serving a suspension for breaking the league's policy on drugs. Later a toe injury kept him out of a game. Ultimately, despite the fact that he led the team with 774 yards rushing in 1997, the Ravens chose not to bring him back for 1998.

BUFFALO BILLS

No significant or lengthy injuries.

CAROLINA PANTHERS

I—Kerry Collins (Quarterback)
A broken jaw suffered in the preseason kept Collins out of the first two games of 1997. He never seemed to get on track, throwing for only 2,124 yards and 11 touchdowns.

I—Anthony Johnson (Running Back)
Johnson won the starting job over Tim Biakabatuka to begin the 1997 season but a toe injury forced him out of action. He was replaced by Biakabatuka and, eventually, undrafted rookie Fred Lane. Late in the year, Lane stole the show and, apparently, the starting job for 1998.

I—Tim Biakabatuka (Running Back)
Biakabatuka, a former first-round draft pick, began the 1997 season as a backup to Anthony Johnson. He got his chance when Johnson was hurt but could not hold off the challenge of rookie Fred Lane.

I—Muhsin Muhammed (Wide Receiver)
The Panthers were hoping for their former second-round pick to step up in a big way in 1997. Muhammed, however, missed over half the season with a fractured wrist and finished with only 27 receptions and no touchdowns.

I—Rocket Ismail (Wide Receiver)
Ismail missed the last three games of 1997 with a shoulder injury. To that point, he had amassed 36 receptions for 419 yards and scored twice.

CHICAGO BEARS

I—Rashaam Salaam (Running Back)
After missing a good portion of 1996, Rashaam Salaam was hoping to stay injury-free in 1997. Such was not the case, however. Salaam played in only three games before suffering a season-ending broken ankle. Looking to 1998, Salaam is likely to be traded since the Bears added free-agent Edgar Bennett and rookie first-round pick Curtis Enis.

I—Raymont Harris (Running Back)
A rib injury kept Harris out of one game, and a broken leg kept him out of two games at the end of the 1997 season. Despite missing three games, Harris rushed for 1,063 yards and scored 10 times. Looking to 1998 however, the Bears have brought aboard Edgar Bennett and made Curtis Enis their No. 1 draft pick, which could make Harris trade bait.

I—Curtis Conway (Wide Receiver)
Conway had become one of the league's more feared receivers, grabbing 81 receptions for more than 1,000 yards in 1996. 1997 was a much different situation. Conway finished with only 30 receptions for 476 yards and one touchdown after playing in only seven games because of a broken collarbone.

I—Bobby Engram (Wide Receiver)
With the Bears' premier receiver, Curtis Conway, hurt, the Bears were hoping for Bobby Engram to step up. Engram also fell to injury. Engram missed five weeks with an ankle injury and finished with 45 receptions for 399 yards and two touchdowns. The injuries to Conway and Engram boosted the playing time and year-end numbers of Ricky Proehl.

CINCINNATI BENGALS

I—Carl Pickens (Wide Receiver)
Pickens, one of the league's best receivers, missed the last four weeks of 1997 with a groin injury. On the season, Pickens recorded only 52 receptions for 695 yards and five touchdowns, compared to 100 receptions for 1,180 yards and 12 scores a year earlier.

DALLAS COWBOYS

I—Eric Bjornson (Tight End)
With Jay Novacek retiring, the Cowboys were looking for someone to step in. Eric Bjornson battled first-round pick David LaFleur for the job. Bjornson got the job for the most part, recording 47 receptions before being forced to miss the last three games of the season with a leg injury.

DENVER BRONCOS

I—Terrell Davis (Running Back)
Davis's 1,750 rushing yards, 2,037 overall yards and 15 touchdowns are quite impressive. However, Davis would easily have boosted those numbers had he not missed the regular-season finale with an injured shoulder.

DETROIT LIONS

No significant injuries or events.

GREEN BAY PACKERS

I—Edgar Bennett (Running Back)
Bennett's preseason, season-ending knee injury boosted Dorsey Levens into a more prominent role. Looking to 1998, Bennett, saw Levens becoming the primary ball-carrier and has moved on by signing a free-agent deal with Chicago.

INDIANAPOLIS COLTS

I—Jim Harbaugh (Quarterback)
Harbaugh missed four weeks of action with a hand injury. He finished the season with only 2,060 passing yards and 11 touchdown passes. He has since signed with Baltimore to play the 1998 season.

I—Sean Dawkins (Wide Receiver)
Despite missing two games in 1997, Dawkins boosted his reception total to 68 (57 in 1996) for 800 yards. Certainly 80 catches for 1,000 yards is possible if he stays healthy in 1998. He has signed with New Orleans.

I—Ken Dilger (Tight End)
After grabbing 42 receptions for four touchdowns both in 1995 and 1996, Dilger dropped to 27 catches and three touchdowns in 1997. Dilger missed five games in 1997, three because of a hamstring injury.

JACKSONVILLE JAGUARS

I—Mark Brunell (Quarterback)
Brunell missed the first two games of 1997 with a knee injury. Had he been healthy all year, he may have topped the 20-touchdown mark, finishing with 18. His yardage numbers also took a big hit, dropping from 4,367 in 1996 to 3,281 in 1997.

I—Natrone Means (Running Back)
Missing two games in 1997 with an ankle injury likely kept Means from rushing for more than 1,000 yards and scoring more than 10 times. He finished the year with 823 rushing yards and nine touchdowns. Looking to 1998, Means has signed a free-agent contract to play for the San Diego Chargers.

MIAMI DOLPHINS

IR—Yatil Green (Wide Receiver)
Green, the Dolphins' No.1 draft pick of 1997, did not play a regular-season down after he suffered a season-ending knee injury during the preseason. The Dolphins are looking forward to a healthy return of Green in 1998.

RL—Fred Barnett (Wide Receiver)
The veteran Barnett was released mid-season after his production slumped.

AC—Lawrence Phillips (Running Back)
Phillips was acquired late in the year after his release from St. Louis. Although he didn't do much for Miami in the 1997 season, he could become a factor in 1998, challenging for playing time.

AC—Brett Perriman (Wide Receiver)
Perriman was signed in the seventh week by Miami in 1997 following his release by Kansas City. He had also been resigned by Miami for the 1998 season but has since been released.

MINNESOTA VIKINGS

I—Brad Johnson (Quarterback)
Johnson threw for 3,000 yards (3,036) and 20 touchdowns despite missing the last three games of 1997 with a neck injury. He was well on his way to increasing those numbers.

I—Robert Smith (Running Back)
Almost a full season for Smith. Smith, who has a history of missing action because of injury, missed only two games in 1997 due to an ankle injury. His 1,493 rushing-receiving yards and seven touchdowns begin to give us an idea of what he could do over a full season if he's injury-free.

NEW ENGLAND PATRIOTS

I—Curtis Martin (Running Back)
Despite missing the last three games of 1997 with a shoulder injury, Martin still finished with 1,456 rushing-receiving yards but only five touchdowns. Look for both numbers to grow in 1998 if he is healthy all season. And this time out in 1998 Martin will take his services to the New York Jets who signed him in the offseason

I—Terry Glenn (Wide Receiver)
After a brilliant 90-reception rookie year in 1996, Glenn's reception level dropped to 27 in 1997, in part because he missed nine games with ankle and hamstring injuries. Here is a player you should make sure not to overlook in 1998 just because of his injury-riddled 1997 campaign.

NEW ORLEANS SAINTS

I—Irv Smith (Tight End)
Missing nearly half the season with a knee injury in 1997, Smith recorded only 17 receptions and one touchdown. Numbers he'll easily rebound from in 1998 if healthy. He'll have to do it in San Francisco, though, since he signed an offseason free-agent deal with the 49ers.

NEW YORK GIANTS

I—Rodney Hampton (Running Back)
The veteran Hampton missed the first 14 games of 1997 with a knee injury and finished the year with only 81 rushing yards He has since been released.

I—Ike Hilliard (Wide Receiver)
The Giants were looking for a big-play receiver when they made Hilliard their No.1 draft pick in 1997. They were sorely disappointed when a neck injury forced Hilliard to miss the last 14 games. His status for the upcoming season is unknown. We will keep an eye on this injury.

I—Tiki Barber (Running Back)
Barber was used in numerous roles as a rookie in 1997. He missed four games with a knee injury midseason and finished with 810 rushing-receiving yards and four touchdowns.

I—Dave Brown (Quarterback)
A chest injury sidelined Brown just before midseason. That cost him statistically, and he also lost his job to Danny Kanell.

I—Tyrone Wheatley (Running Back)
Wheatley, a former No.1 draft pick, continued his injury-prone ways in 1997, missing a couple of games late in the year with an ankle injury. Wheatley did finish the year with 583 rushing yards and four touchdowns but he does not seem durable enough to be an every-down back.

I—Thomas Lewis (Wide Receiver)
Lewis, another former first-round pick of the Giants, also continued being prone to injury in 1997. He missed the last 13 weeks of the year with a toe injury. Lewis finished the year with only five receptions. In 1998 Lewis will take his services to the Chicago Bears, who signed him in the offseason.

NEW YORK JETS

No significant injuries or events.

OAKLAND RAIDERS

No significant injuries or events.

PHILADELPHIA EAGLES

I—Chris T. Jones (Wide Receiver)
Starting wideout Chris T. Jones missed 12 games of 1997 with a knee problem, finishing with only five receptions. A year earlier, Jones had latched onto 70 receptions. Jones's absence also pushed the numbers of Michael Timpson, who stepped in to grab 42 receptions in 1997 and will challenge him and newly acquired Jeff Graham for the No. 2 job alongside Irving Fryar in 1998.

I—Jason Dunn (Tight End)
Dunn, the Eagles' No.2 draft pick of 1996, battled injury, including a prolonged stint with a hamstring injury. On the season, Dunn recorded only seven receptions, playing in seven games.

PITTSBURGH STEELERS

I—Charles Johnson (Wide Receiver)
Johnson, who recorded 60 receptions a year earlier in 1996, fell to 46 receptions for 568 yards in 1997. He missed four games with a knee injury and in 1998 with Yancy Thigpen off to Tennessee chould be the Steelers #1 receiver and boost his numbers in a big way.

I—Jerome Bettis (Running Back)
Another very productive season for Bettis in 1997. He recorded 1,775 combined rushing-receiving yards and nine touchdowns. Those numbers would have been even better had he not missed the season finale with a knee injury.

ST. LOUIS RAMS

I—Isaac Bruce (Wide Receiver)
Certainly one of the league's premier receivers, Bruce's numbers were down in 1997 as he missed the first give games of the season with a hamstring injury. After recording 84 receptions for 1,338 yards and seven touchdowns in 1996, Bruce dropped to 56 catches for 815 yards and five scores in 1997. If he's healthy in 1998, look for a big rebound.

I—Eddie Kennison (Wide Receiver)
A groin injury sidelined Kennison for three weeks in 1997. Kennison finished the year with only 25 receptions and no touchdowns after recording 54 catches and 11 scores as a rookie in 1996. In 1998 the Rams have signed Ricky Proehl to come in and challenge for the job.

RL—Lawrence Phillips (Running Back)
Phillips, the Rams' No.1 draft pick of 1996, continued to struggle on and off the field in 1997. He was released midseason and was eventually signed by the Miami Dolphins.

SAN DIEGO CHARGERS

I—Stan Humphries (Quarterback)
Humphries took his hits in 1997, including one that led to a concussion and sidelined him for the final seven weeks of the season. He has since opted to retire.

I—Gary Brown (Running Back)
Brown returned in 1997 after a year off to become the Chargers' main ball carrier. Rushing for 945 yards, Brown would likely have topped the 1,000-yard mark had he not been bothered by a knee injury late in the year that sidelined him for a game. Looking to 1998, Brown was signed by the New York Giants. The Chargers signed Natrone Means to a free-agent deal in the offseason.

I—Fred Jones (Tight End)
Rookie Fred Jones recorded an impressive 41 receptions and two touchdowns in 1997. He would have had even better numbers but he missed two games late in the year with a leg injury.

SAN FRANCISCO 49ERS

IR—Jerry Rice (Wide Receiver)
The game's best receiver saw action in only one game in 1997 because of a knee injury. His absence ballooned the stats of Terrell Owens and J.J. Stokes, which will obviously take a dip in 1998 when a healthy Rice returns.

I—Garrison Hearst (Running Back)
Hearst produced 1,213 rushing-receiving yards and six touchdowns in 1997. Those numbers could have been much larger had he not missed the last three games of the season with an injured collarbone.

I—Brent Jones (Tight End)
Jones suffered a leg injury midseason that sidelined him for three games. Jones, however, had already decided that 1997 was his final year in the NFL and has retired.

I—Steve Young (Quarterback)
Young missed one entire game and a good portion of three others early in the year, which certainly contributed to his year-end results. Young threw for 3,029 yards but only 19 touchdowns.

SEATTLE SEAHAWKS

I—John Friesz (Quarterback)
Friesz fractured the thumb on his throwing hand in the regular-season opener and spent the rest of the season watching veteran Warren Moon have an astounding season and steal his starting job.

I—Joey Galloway (Wide Receiver)
Galloway missed one game in 1997 with an ankle injury but still had an incredible season with 72 receptions, for 1,049 yards and 12 touchdowns.

I—Brian Blades (Wide Receiver)
Blades missed the last five games of 1997 with a hand injury. In Blades' absence, Mike Pritchard and James McKnight expanded their playing time and year-end stats.

I—James McKnight (Wide Receiver)
McKnight missed the first four weeks of 1997 with a knee injury but came on to produce 34 catches and six touchdowns after that, showing some promising potential.

I—LaMar Smith (Running Back)
Smith missed four games with a leg injury midseason, finishing with only 575 rushing-receiving yards and two touchdowns while sharing time with Chris Warren and Steve Broussard. Looking to 1998, Smith has signed a free-agent deal to play in New Orleans.

TAMPA BAY

I—Jackie Harris (Tight End)
A prolonged groin injury hampered Harris for virtually the entire second half of 1997, limiting him to 20 receptions and one touchdown. Looking to 1998, a healthier Harris is taking his services to Tennessee, joining the Oilers in the offseason.

I—Horace Copeland (Wide Receiver)
Copeland was limited to 32 receptions in 1997, missing action in three of the last four games.

TENNESSEE OILERS

I—Chris Sanders (Wide Receiver)
Sanders missed a number of games midseason with a hamstring injury in 1997. He finished with only 31 receptions after leading the team with 48 catches in 1996.

WASHINGTON REDSKINS

I—Terry Allen (Running Back)
In 1996, Allen led the NFL with 21 touchdowns and amassed 1,547 rushing-receiving yards. In 1997, Allen missed six games with a broken thumb and knee and ankle injuries. Allen finished the year with only 896 total rushing-receiving yards and five touchdowns.

I—Gus Frerotte (Quarterback)
Frerotte missed the last three games of 1997 with a hip injury, limiting him to 2,682 passing yards and 17 touchdowns.

I,S—Michael Westbrook (Wide Receiver)
Westbrook was suspended for the first game of the season for taking a swipe at a teammate. He later missed time with a knee injury. In all, Westbrook saw action in 10 games, and caught 34 passes and three touchdowns.

I—Leslie Shepard (Wide Receiver)
Shepard was the Redskins' most consistent receiver until he missed the last six games of the year with a dislocated wrist. Before the injury, Shepard recorded 29 catches for 562 yards and scored five times.

HOW THE 1997 ROOKIES FARED

A rookie doesn't always have an opportunity to prove himself in his first year of NFL action, so it's a good idea to look back and see what events—such as injuries or contract holdouts—may have affected his season. Keep in mind that many prize rookie prospects, especially contract holdouts, may have missed some action not because of injury but because they had trouble learning their team's strategies and systems. Still, these are prime, blue-chip players who somehow impressed the scouts while they were in college. Chances are that they still have potential, even if it wasn't fully realized in their first season.

Here's a look at how the rookies of 1997 performed. First, we'll take a look at the players from the first two rounds—the NFL scouts' blue-chippers—and then we'll look at potential standouts who were picked in later rounds of the draft.

ROUND 1

POSITION IN DRAFT	NAME	POS	TEAM DRAFTED BY
7	Ike Hilliard	WR	N.Y. Giants

The Giants were hoping to have a big-play receiver in Hilliard but a neck injury forced him out of action just two weeks into the season. Hilliard finished the year with only two catches, but that could be deceiving when looking to his sophomore campaign in 1998.

12	Warrick Dunn	RB	Tampa Bay

The Buccaneers have to be happy with their first-round pick. Dunn showed real explosiveness and finished the year with 1,440 rushing-receiving yards and seven touchdowns. 1998 should bring even better numbers.

13	Tony Gonzalez	TE	Kansas City

Gonzalez had a very good preseason but finished the regular season with only 33 receptions and two touchdowns. Those are numbers he can easily expand on in 1998.

15	Yatil Green	WR	Miami

The Dolphins' hope for a "deep-threat" receiver fell apart when Green suffered a season-ending knee injury in the preseason. Keep an eye on Green's progress in 1998.

16	Reidell Anthony	WR	Tampa Bay

Anthony showed some signs of becoming the Bucs' "deep-threat" receiver, catching four touchdowns as a rookie, but his total of 35 receptions was a disappointment.

22	David LaFleur	TE	Dallas

LeFleur played second-fiddle to Eric Bjornson for most of 1997 but with Bjornson injured late in the year, LaFleur recorded 11 catches, two for touchdowns over the last four games. Perhaps signs of what's to come.

23 Antowain Smith RB Buffalo

Smith shared the rushing load with veteran Thurman Thomas in 1997, rushing for 840 yards and scoring eight times. Look for those numbers to expand in 1998 as the young Smith continues to expand his duties.

26 Jim Druckenmiller QB San Francisco 49ers

As the heir apparent to Steve Young, the 49ers were hoping to bring Druckenmiller along slowly. However, when Young was hurt early in the 1997 season Druckenmiller did see some action, hitting 21 of 52 passes for 239 yards and one touchdown in four games. With Young still around, Druckenmiller's potential is unlikely to be seen for quite awhile.

27 Rae Carruth WR Carolina Panthers

A productive rookie year for Carruth, with 44 receptions and four touchdowns in 1997. He'll work to improve those numbers in 1998.

ROUND 2

36 Tiki Barber RB New York Giants

Barber began the year as the Giants' primary back and ended the year that way. In between he missed four games with a knee injury. On the season, Barber produced 810 rushing-receiving yards and four touchdowns. His role for 1998 is uncertain though he's likely to see plenty of work.

41 Byron Hanspard RB Atlanta Falcons

Hanspard did see some backfield work alongside Jamal Anderson in 1997 but also returned kicks. On the year, Hanspard rushed for only 335 yards and scored three times, twice on kickoff returns. An expanded role in 1998 is very possible.

42 Jake Plummer QB Arizona Cardinals

Plummer began the year as the backup to Kent Graham but took over midseason and never looked back. Over the season's last 10 weeks, Plummer threw for 2,203 yards and 15 touchdowns. He sparked the Cardinals to wins over Philadelphia, Baltimore and Atlanta and has given Cardinal fans hope for the future.

43 Corey Dillon RB Cincinnati Bengals

Dillon did not rush the ball until the Bengals' third game of the season. In the season's last 14 games, Dillon ousted Ki-Jana Carter as the starter, rushed for 1,129 yards, added 259 more on 27 receptions and scored 10 times. He should be a huge fantasy force in 1998.

45 Freddie Jones TE San Diego Chargers

A pleasant surprise for San Diego. Jones grabbed 41 receptions for 505 yards but only two touchdowns as a rookie.

ROUND 3

62 Troy Davis RB New Orleans Saints

During the preseason, Davis was thought to have a chance to win the starting running back job. Instead he saw limited action, with Mario Bates and Ray Zellars seeing much of the work. He finished his rookie season with only 271 rushing yards and no touchdowns.

64   Jay Graham   RB   Baltimore Ravens

Graham got a shot early in his rookie year when Bam Morris was suspended but he never played well enough to keep the job. He may get another chance in 1998 since the Ravens declined to resign Morris, though they have been signed ex-Tampa Bay Buccaneer, Errict Rhett.

70   O.J. Santiago   TE   Atlanta Falcons

Santiago caught 17 passes, two for touchdowns, before a leg injury sidelined him late in the 1997 season. In 1998, the Falcons will try to get him more involved in the offense.

90   Brett Conway   K   Green Bay Packers

Conway lost his confidence during the preseason and then hurt his leg. Ryan Longwell stepped in and Conway became history.

ROUND 4

99   Danny Wuerffel   QB   New Orleans

Wuerffel got his chance in the quarterback merry-go-round orchestrated by Mike Ditka in 1997. Playing in six games, Wuerffel threw for 518 yards and four touchdowns.

105   Darnell Autry   RB   Chicago Bears

With Rashaam Salaam and Raymont Harris out injured, Autry saw more playing time as the season wore on. He finished the year with 319 rushing yards and two touchdowns.

III
FREE AGENTS
(AND OTHER PLAYER MOVES)
FREE AGENCY AGAIN
SHAKES UP TEAM ROSTERS

As the 1998 offseason gets into gear, free-agent signings have begun again. Teams are trying to balance signing competitive talent and meeting the salary cap requirements. In 1995, each team had to meet a $36.5 million salary cap. In 1996, the cap rose to $40.7 million; in 1997, the cap went to $41.45 million, and, in 1998, the salary cap jumped to $51.5 million, in part because of the NFL's new TV contract. Teams like Green Bay and San Francisco, which already have high payrolls, continue to meet this limit with great ingenuity and maintain their winning ways. Now Denver is on top. Will the Broncos be able to keep their key players happy and in Bronco uniforms? These questions certainly provide for an interesting offseason.

Will teams aggressively chase players in the 1998 offseason the way they did in 1997? Last year, one of the key moves was Garrison Hearst (Bengals) to the 49ers. And if this year's early signings of Edgar Bennett (Bears), Ricky Watters (Seattle) and Jim Harbaugh (Ravens) are any indication, we're off and running with lots of player movement again this offseason.

Keep as up-to-date as you can. Let's start this section with a review of some of the terms and dates associated with free agency in the NFL.

- **Unrestricted Free Agents**
  Unrestricted free agents are players who have completed four or more seasons in the NFL and whose contracts have expired. On July 16, 1998, their exclusive rights revert to their original NFL clubs, assuming that the clubs have made a June 1 tender to them. NFL teams have until Nov. 3 to sign these unrestricted free agents. If the players are not signed by this date, they must sit out the rest of the season. Players with fewer than four years of experience also become unrestricted free agents if they have not received a qualifying offer or a minimum tender offer from their current teams.

- **Restricted Free Agents**
  Restricted free agents are defined as players who have completed at least three, but fewer than four, seasons in the NFL and whose contracts have expired. These players were given qualifying offers from their original NFL teams and were free to negotiate with any club until April 13. At that time, if a restricted free agent had not accepted an offer from another team, his original team had the right to match the offer and retain him. If the original team chooses not to match the offer, it may receive draft-pick compensation. The value of the compensation depends on the amount of the qualifying offer made to the restricted free agent.

- **Franchise Players**
  An NFL team may designate one player as its "Franchise" player. There are two types of franchise players.

  First option, Exclusive: A team commits to an "exclusive" franchise player by committing to a minimum offer of the average salary of the top five players at the player's position.

  Second option: If a new team submits an offer sheet to a franchise player, it must offer compensation of two No.1 draft choices to that player's team. Offer sheets to these players must be submitted by 4 p.m. (EST) on July 15. Once a franchise player is so designated, his team must offer him either 120 percent of his previous year's salary or the average salary of the top five players in the league at his position, whichever is greater.

- **Transition Players**
  An NFL team may also designate a player as a "transition" player. This gives the team the right of first refusal and the right to match any offer given to the player by another team, but not the right to draft-pick compensation. The minimum offer to a transition player must be either 120 percent of his previous year's salary or the average salary of the top 10 players in the league at his position, whichever is greater.

1998 DATES TO KEEP IN MIND

February 1:　　Contracts of veteran players expire.

February 12:　Teams must designate franchise and/or transition players by this date.

Clubs must submit qualifying offers to their restricted free-agents (those for whom they wish to retain the right of first refusal). Clubs must submit minimum salary offers to players with less than three years of experience (those for whom they wish to retain exclusive negotiating rights).

February 13:　Veteran free-agent signings begin.

NFL trading begins.

April 13:　　　Offer sheets must be submitted to restricted free agents by this date.

April 17:　　　Original teams must exercise their right of first refusal on restricted free agents by this date.

April 18–19:　NFL college draft.

June 1:　　　Teams must make offers to their own unrestricted free agents by this date, if they wish to retain rights to those players. This gives teams exclusive negotiating rights to these players for the rest of the season if the players are not signed by another team by July 15.

Teams must send tender to unsigned restricted free agents or extend qualifying offer to retain exclusive negotiating rights.

July 15:   Exclusive rights to unrestricted veteran free agents revert to original clubs on this date, provided that those clubs have tendered an offer by June 1.

September 6:   NFL regular season begins.

Once again this year, teams will try to find ways to avoid losing their highly coveted players who have become free agents. However, many of these good players will again jump ship in 1998. Many of these players will have an immediate impact on their new teams while others may become free-agent busts. In 1997, Jeff George, released by Atlanta a year earlier, signed a five-year, $27.5 million deal to play in Oakland for the Raiders. George exploded for 3,917 passing yards and 29 touchdown passes. Garrison Hearst, who left Cincinnati and signed as a free agent with San Francisco, managed 1,213 rushing-receiving yards and six touchdowns before being sidelined the last three weeks with a collarbone injury. Warren Moon signed on as a free agent with Seattle to back up John Friesz. Friesz's early-season injury led to Moon's 3,678 passing yards and 25 touchdowns. Andre Rison, let go by Green Bay, was signed by Kansas City and went on to lead the Chiefs with 72 receptions for 1,092 yards and scored seven times.

On the flip side, Rick Mirer signed by Chicago to take over the starting job; was out-performed by Erik Kramer and became a huge free-agent bust for the Bears. Heath Shuler, the former first-round pick of the Redskins, was dealt to New Orleans, presumably to take over the starting job. Just as he did in Washington, Shuler played his way out of a job.

Another group to keep in mind is this year's crop of rookie draft picks. Each of these first-year players must sign a contract before appearing in training camp. Missed time in training camp sets any player back physically and mentally, but it is especially harmful to a rookie because it delays his number one job—learning his new team's system so he can play as soon as possible. Long holdouts by rookies have decreased, however, since the NFL is forcing them to sign early in August or sit out the season.

In summary, it's important to keep an eye on both veteran free agents and on early-round draft choices. As the veterans are signed, we need to evaluate their effects both on the teams they are leaving and the teams they are joining. What vacancies are these teams filling? How must they manipulate their salary structure to sign the new player and stay under the salary cap? The biggest concern with rookies is to sign them early and get them into training camp. It is a great advantage to keep up with possible holdouts or free agents who may have signed with a new team in 1998. As the season approaches and these players begin missing preseason conditioning and games, tracking their progress becomes even more important. Following are lists of the various free agents whose contracts have expired, along with their 1998 signing status. Also, a list of key players who are not free agents but who have either been released or have switched teams via another means, follows.

NOTE: This list of free-agent signings, along with incoming rookies signings, will be updated in our first Fantasy Sports, Inc. preseason newsletter, available in early August—a must if you want to prepare properly for your fantasy draft.

1998 FREE AGENTS

Free-Agent Types	Status Key	
U—Unrestricted	S w/=Signed with	TR=Traded
R—Restricted	RS=Re-signed with Current Team	NCO=No Contract Offer
T—Transitional	RT=Retired	EXP S w/=Expansion Draft Signed with
F—Franchise	RL=Released	Blank=No Status Update Yet

RUNNING BACKS

NAME	TEAM	TYPE	STATUS	NAME	TEAM	TYPE	STATUS
LeShon Johnson	ARI	U	S w/NYG	Robert Smith	MINN	U	RS
Derrick Moore	ARI	U		Robert Green	MINN	U	
Cedric Smith	ARI	U		Keith Byars	NE	U	S w/NYJ
Gary Downs	ATL	U	RS	Sam Gash	NE	U	S w/BUF
Harold Green	ATL	U	RS	Curtis Martin	NE	R	S w/NYJ
Bam Morris	BALT	U		Mario Bates	NO	U	S w/ARIZ
Darick Holmes	BUF	R		Derek Brown	NO	U	
Tim Tindale	BUF	R	S w/CHI	Erric Pegram	NYG	U	
Tony Carter	CHI	U	S w/NE	Derrick Fenner	OAK	U	
Raymont Harris	CHI	T		Charlie Garner	PHIL	U	RS
Herschel Walker	DALL	U		Mel Gray	PHIL	U	
Derek Loville	DEN	U		Ricky Watters	PHIL	U	S w/SEAT
Ron Rivers	DET	R		Amp Lee	STL	U	RS
Dorsey Levens	GB	F		Gary Brown	SD	U	S w/NYG
Edgar Bennett	GB	U	S w/CHI	Aaron Craver	SD	U	S w/NO
Aaron Hayden	GB	R		Terrell Fletcher	SD	R	
William Henderson	GB	R		William Floyd	SF	U	S w/CAR
Travis Jervey	GB	R		Steve Broussard	SEAT	U	RS
Zack Crockett	IND	R		Lamar Smith	SEAT	U	S w/NO
Ty Hallock	JAC	U	S w/CHI	Jerry Ellison	TB	R	
Randy Jordan	JAC	U		Errict Rhett	TB	R	S w/BALT
Natrone Means	JAC	U	S w/SD	Rodney Thomas	TENN	R	
Greg Hill	KC	U		Marc Logan	WASH	U	
Bernie Parmalee	MIA	U	RS	Brian Mitchell	WASH	U	RS
Roosevelt Potts	MIA	U	S w/BALT				

OTHER KEY RUNNING BACK MOVES
(Not Involving Free Agents)

NAME	TEAM	STATUS
Adrian Murrell	NYJ	TR to ARIZ
Terry Kirby	SF	Released
Chris Warren	SEAT	Released then signed by DALL
Marcus Allen	KC	Retired
Rodney Hampton	NYG	Released
Glyn Milburn	DEN	Traded to GB
Irving Spikes	MIA	Released

WIDE RECEIVERS

NAME	TEAM	TYPE	STATUS	NAME	TEAM	TYPE	STATUS
Frank Sanders	ARI	R	RS	Sean Dawkins	IND	U	S w/NO
Anthony Edwards	ARI	U	RS	Brian Stablein	IND	U	S w/NE
Kevin Williams	ARI	U	S w/BUF	Lake Dawson	KC	U	
Bert Emanuel	ATL	T	S w/TB	Danan Hughes	KC	U	RS
Derrick Alexander	BALT	U	S w/KC	Qadry Ismail	MIA	U	
Nate Singleton	BALT	U		Brett Perriman	MIA	U	RS then RL
Steve Tasker	BUF	U		Chris Walsh	MINN	U	RS
Michael Bates	CAR	U		Randal Hill	NO	U	
Mark Carrier	CAR	U	RS	Omar Douglas	NYG	U	
Raghib Ismail	CAR	U		Thomas Lewis	NYG	U	S w/ CHI
Ernie Mills	CAR	U	S w/DALL	Chris T. Jones	PHIL	R	
Dwight Stone	CAR	U	RS	Michael Timpson	PHIL	U	
Ricky Proehl	CHI	U	S w/STL	Yancey Thigpen	PITT	U	S w/TENN
David Dunn	CIN	R	RS	Jimmy Oliver	SD	U	S w/DALL
Anthony Miller	DALL	U		Johnny Thomas	STL	R	
Billy Davis	DALL	R	RS	Keith Crawford	STL	U	S w/ATL
Kez McCorvey	DET	R	RS	Malcolm Floyd	STL	U	
Robert Brooks	GB	U	RS	Torrance Small	STL	U	S w/IND
Terry Mickens	GB	U		James McKnight	SEAT	U	RS
Antonio Freeman	GB	R		Henry Ellard	WASH	U	

OTHER KEY WIDE RECEIVER MOVES
(Not Involving Free Agents)

NAME	TEAM	STATUS
Andre Hastings	NO	Released then Resigned
Eric Metcalf	SD	Traded to Arizona
Jeff Graham	NYJ	Traded to Philadelphia
Kevin Alexander	NYG	Traded to Miami

TIGHT ENDS

NAME	TEAM	TYPE	STATUS	NAME	TEAM	TYPE	STATUS
Pat Carter	ARI	U		Greg DeLong	MINN	U	
Chris Gedney	ARI	U	RS	Andrew Glover	MINN	U	RS
Brian Kozlowski	ATL	U	RS	Mike Bartrum	NE	U	RS
Eric Green	BALT	U		Irv Smith	NO	U	S w/SF
Rob Coons	BUF	U		John Burke	NYJ	U	S w/SD
Lonnie Johnson	BUF	U	RS	Kirk Botkin	PITT	R	
Tony Cline	BUF	R		Aaron Laing	STL	R	
Walter Rasby	CAR	U		David Binn	SD	U	
Harper LeBel	CHI	U		Frank Hartley	SD	U	
Ryan Wetnight	CHI	U	RS	Shannon Mitchell	SD	U	
Scott Galbraith	DALL	U		Chad Fann	SF	U	
Eric Bjornson	DALL	R		Carlester Crumpler	SEAT	U	
David Sloan	DET	R		Christian Fauria	SEAT	R	
Pete Metzelaars	DET	U		Jackie Harris	TB	U	S w/TENN
Jeff Thomason	GB	U	RS	Roderick Lewis	TENN	U	
Marcus Pollard	IND	R	S w/PHIL	Jamie Asher	WASH	R	
Pete Mitchell	JAC	R		David Frisch	WASH	U	
Derek Brown	JAC	U		Rick Griffith	JAC	U	RS

OTHER KEY TIGHT END MOVES
(Not Involving Free Agents)

NAME	TEAM	STATUS
Alfred Pupunu	Free-Agent	Signed w/NYG
Aaron Pierce	NYG	Released
Brent Jones	SF	Retired
Derrick Walker	KC	Released

QUARTERBACKS

NAME	TEAM	TYPE	STATUS	NAME	TEAM	TYPE	STATUS
Stoney Case	ARI	R		Craig Erickson	MIA	U	RS
Kent Graham	ARI	U	S w/NYG	Randall Cunningham	MINN	U	RS
Jim Miller	ATL	U	S w/DET	Jay Walker	MINN	R	
Eric Zeier	BALT	R		Doug Nussmeier	NO	U	S w/DEN
Kerry Collins	CAR	R		Ty Detmer	PHIL	U	S w/SF
Shane Matthews	CAR	U	RS	Will Furrer	STL	U	
Erik Kramer	CHI	U	RS	Mark Rypien	STL	U	S w/ATL
Steve Stenstrom	CHI	R		Jim Everett	SD	U	
Matt Blundin	DET	U		Todd Philcox	SD	U	
Paul Justin	IND	R	S w/CIN	Casey Weldon	SD	U	RS

OTHER KEY QUARTERBACK MOVES
(Not Involving Free Agents)

NAME	TEAM	STATUS
Doug Flutie	Free Agent/CFL	Signed w/BUF
Steve Bono	GB	Tr to STL
Rob Johnson	JAC	Tr to BUF
Jim Harbaugh	IND	Tr to BALT
Stan Humphries	SD	Retired
Boomer Esiason	CIN	Retired
Wade Wilson	DALL	Released
Dave Brown	NYG	Released then signed w/ARIZ
Bill Musgrave	Free Agent	Signed w/IND

KICKERS

NAME	TEAM	TYPE	STATUS	NAME	TEAM	TYPE	STATUS
Eddie Murray	MINN	U		Gary Anderson	SF	U	S w/MINN
Brad Daluiso	NYG	U	RS	Todd Peterson	SEAT	R	
Cole Ford	OAK	R		Scott Blanton	WASH	R	RS
Greg Davis	SD	U					

OTHER KEY KICKER MOVES
(Not Involving Free Agents)

NAME	TEAM	STATUS
Jon Baker	Free Agent	Signed w/MIA
Jay Kirchoff	Free Agent	Signed w/CIN
Mike Vanderjagt	Free Agent	Signed w/IND
John Becksvoort	Free Agent	Signed w/SF
Danny Kight	Free Agent	Signed w/WASH

IV
OFFSEASON NOTES
Key Player Movements and Their Effects/
Significant Injury Updates/New NFL Head Coaches

Marcus Allen (Running Back)
RETIRED from: Kansas City Chiefs
Year after year it seemed everyone believed would be the last season for aging Marcus Allen. Allen however, kept returning and proved critics wrong by being productive, especially as a touchdown scorer. But now the time has come for Allen to finally hang up his running shoes. Allen leaves the game as the all-time holder of touchdown scored with 123, all-time receptions leader among running backs with 587 and sixth all-time in rushing yards with 12,243. His retirement leaves and opens a hole at running back for the Chiefs, where at least for now Donnell Bennett and Kimble Anders are penciled in at running back.

Gary Anderson (Kicker)
Unrestricted free agent with: San Francisco 49ers
Signed with: Minnesota Vikings
Anderson, one of the league's more consistent kickers takes his services to Minnesota in 1998. His departure leaves a very promising spot for a replacement to do well with the 49ers. In 1997, while with San Francisco, Anderson was good on 29 of 36 (.806) field goals and all 38 extra point tries.

Jon Baker
Free agent signed with: Miami Dolphins
Baker, a free agent, comes in to push Olindo Mare for the Dolphins' 1998 kicking duties. In 1997, Mare was 28 of 36 (.778) on field goal attempts and hit all 33 extra point tries.

Mario Bates (Running Back)
Unrestricted free agent with: New Orleans Saints
Signed with: Arizona Cardinals
An off-and-on starter for the New Orleans Saints the last couple of years, Mario Bates moves to join the Arizona Cardinals. Bates rushed for 440 yards, caught five passes for 42 yards and scored four times for New Orleans in 1997. In 1998, he joins a team that is desperate to improve its running attack, which has struggled in a big way the last few seasons. However, Adrian Murrell is also joining the Cardinals, coming in a trade from the New York Jets. Murrell's appearance will make it tough for Bates to push for playing time.

John Becksvoort (Kicker)
Free agent signed with: San Francisco 49ers
With veteran Gary Anderson going to Minnesota, the 49ers are looking to fill a need. Thus far, they have brought in free agent John Becksvoort out of Tennessee.

Edgar Bennett (Running Back)
Unrestricted free agent with: Green Bay Packers
Signed with: Chicago Bears
Bennett, who missed the entire 1997 season with a knee injury, comes to
the Bears. Bennett once split time with Dorsey Levens in the Packer backfield but when Bennett saw that he was no longer in the Packers' plans,
he opted to take his services to Chicago. With the Bears, Bennett is the
presumed starter, which means Rashaan Salaam and Raymont Harris may
be taking a backseat or looking for work elsewhere. In 1996, when he was
healthy, Bennett rushed for 899 yards, caught 31 passes for 176 yards and
scored three times.

Dave Brown (Quarterback)
RELEASED by: New York Giants
Signed by: Arizona Cardinals
Inconsistency led to Dave Brown's losing his starting job to Danny Kanell
and, ultimately, to Brown's release. Brown was later signed by the Ari-
zona Cardinals to battle for backup duty behind Jake Plummer.

Gary Brown (Running Back)
Unrestricted free agent with: San Diego Chargers
Signed with: New York Giants
With the signing of Natrone Means by San Diego in the offseason, Gary
Brown took his services to the New York Giants, signing as a free agent.
Brown, who rushed for 945 yards in 1997 with the Chargers, will try to
help the Giants resolve their running back woes. He'll battle Tiki Barber,
Tyrone Wheatley and Charles Way for playing time.

Keith Byars (Tight End/Running Back)
Unrestricted free agent with: New England Patriots
Signed with: New York Jets
Byars, once one of the league's better receiving backs, moves his services
to New York. Not as effective as he once was, Byars tallied only 20 receptions for 189 yards while rushing for only 24 yards and scoring three
times in 1997.

Tony Carter (Running Back)
Unrestricted free agent with: Chicago Bears
Signed with: New England Patriots
Carter, who produced 56 rushing yards and 24 receptions for 152 yards
but no touchdowns in 1997, comes to New England to likely do more
blocking than anything. He's not likely to have much fantasy impact.

Sean Dawkins (Wide Receiver)
Unrestricted Free Agent with: Indianapolis Colts
Signed with: New Orleans Saints
Dawkins, who caught 68 passes for 804 yards and scored twice in 1997 for
Indianapolis, was signed as a free agent by New Orleans in the offseason.
With the Saints, Dawkins will bring immediate help to a team in need of
a consistent passing game. Dawkins, however, can't be expected to fare
exceptionally well statistically while playing for the Saints because they
will likely run much more often than force the pass in 1998. Dawkins' departure from the Colts leaves a vacancy to fill opposite Marvin Harrison.

Ty Detmer (Quarterback)
Unrestricted free agent with: Philadelphia Eagles
Signed with: San Francisco 49ers
Having lost his starting job, not to Rodney Peete but to Bobby Hoying, Detmer decided it was time to exit. Detmer takes his experience to the 49ers where he'll battle for backup duty.

Bert Emanuel (Wide Receiver)
Transitional free agent with: Atlanta Falcons
Signed with: Tampa Bay Buccaneers
The Falcons leading receiver of the last couple seasons was offered $16 million over four years by the Tampa Bay Buccaneers and the Falcons having the chance to match the offer because of tagging Emanuel as a 'transitional' free agent chose not to. Emanuel goes to Tampa Bay where his experience will be a huge asset for a young receiving crew, however don't expect huge numbers because the Bucs and Trent Dilfer just won't pass as often as Atlanta would have. Departing the Falcons, Emanuel leaves a huge void where Terrence Mathis will have to step up and where the Falcons will need to quickly fill the #2 role. In 1997 Emanuel caught 65 passes for 991 yards and scored nine times for the Falcons.

Boomer Esiason (Quarterback)
RETIRED from: Cincinatti Bengals
Despite having a huge rebound season in 1997, Esiason elected to retire to the TV booth, joining the Monday Night Football broadcast team. Esiason's departure likely gives Jeff Blake his starting job back.

Doug Flutie (Quarterback)
Free Agent
The ineffectiveness of both Todd Collins and Alex Van Pett has led to the continuing search for a replacement for the retired Jim Kelly. Doug Flutie, who failed early in his career to impress in NFL but went to Canada and realized tremendous success, returns to the NFL's Bills. Flutie comes aboard to battle Rob Johnson, who looked virtually spectacular when subbing for an injured Mark Brunell in Jacksonville in 1997 and Todd Collins to compete for the starting job. This is a battle we'll have to monitor as the regular season nears.

William Floyd (Running Back)
Unrestricted free agent with: San Francisco 49ers
Signed with: Carolina Panthers
Perhaps seeing the writing on the wall when the 49ers made Marc Edwards their second-round pick in 1997, William Floyd moves on to join the Carolina Panthers. Floyd had come back from a severe knee injury and in 1997 produced 231 rushing yards, 37 receptions for 321 yards and scored four times.

Jeff Graham (Wide Receiver)
Traded from: New York Jets
Acquired by: Philadelphia Eagles
Graham who caught only 42 passes in 1997 and would have cost the New York Jets over $2 million toward the salary cap, was dealt to the Philadelphia Eagles on draft day. Graham arrives in Philadelphia to provide in-

surance toward the serious concern over Chris T. Jones knee which has been scoped three times since last fall. Graham will battle Michael Timpson and Jones if he's healthy for the #2 spot opposite Irving Fryar. Graham's departure from the Jets should push much more playing time for the likes of Wayne Chrebet, Dedric Ward and Alex Van Dyke.

Kent Graham (Quarterback)
Unrestricted free agent with: Arizona Cardinals
Signed with: New York Giants
Graham began 1997 as the starter for the Arizona Cardinals, but eventually lost his job to young Jake Plummer. With the writing on the wall that Arizona was likely to stick with Plummer in 1998, Graham returns to the Giants to back up Danny Kanell.

Rodney Hampton (Running Back)
Released by: New York Giants
Hampton, the Giants' all-time leading rusher with 6,897, was released by the Giants. Just a year ago the Giants had matched an offer of $16.4 million over six years by the San Francisco 49ers to retain Hampton. Last season Hampton rushed for only 81 yards on 23 carries.

Jim Harbaugh (Quarterback)
Traded from: Indianapolis Colts
Acquired by: Baltimore Ravens
With Vinny Testaverde's performance slipping in a big way in 1997, the Ravens are looking for an alternative. In the offseason, the Ravens acquired Jim Harbaugh from Indianapolis for their third- and fourth-round draft picks. As a fantasy player, Harbaugh has never excited me. In 1997, Harbaugh threw for 2,060 yards and 10 touchdowns while playing in 12 games with the Colts.

Jackie Harris (Tight End)
Unrestricted free agent with: Tampa Bay Buccaneers
Signed with: Tennessee Oilers
Once recognized as one of the league's better tight ends, Harris has struggled through injuries in recent years. In 1997, a groin injury limited Harris to action in only nine games, for 20 receptions and one touchdown. Joining the Oilers in 1998, Harris will take some of the pressure off Frank Wycheck. Don't be surprised to see Harris record decent numbers himself if he stays healthy.

Stan Humphries (Quarterback)
RETIRED from: San Diego Chargers
After suffering yet another concussion, the sixth of his career, Humphries opted to retire, despite being given clearance to play. His retirement obviously creates an opportunity for Craig Whelihan, who played all right in his absence in 1997, or newly drafted Ryan Leaf, the Charger's #1 draft choice, who will be the Chargers future and possibly in short order their present.

LeShon Johnson (Running Back)
Unrestricted free agent with: Arizona Cardinals
Signed with: New York Giants
The off-and-on starter for the Cardinals goes to the Giants, who have a strange backfield situation. Johnson joins Tiki Barber, Tyrone Wheatley,

Rodney Hampton and Charles Way in the battle for playing time. I can't see much improvement from his erratic performance in Arizona. In 1997, Johnson produced only 81 rushing yards and no touchdowns while struggling with a hamstring injury and poor performance.

Rob Johnson (Quarterback)
Traded from: Jacksonville Jaguars
Acquired by: Buffalo Bills
The Bills traded for the services of Johnson, to add to the equation trying to find a replacement for Jim Kelly. Johnson had looked spectacular when subbing for the injured Marc Brunell in Jacksonville in 1997. Johnson will battle Doug Flutie another Buffalo offseason acquisition and Todd Collins for the Bills quarterback duties in 1998.

Brent Jones (Tight End)
RETIRED from: San Francisco 49ers
Jones, a big contributor to the 49ers' offense throughout most of the 1990s, opted to retire. Jones's retirement opens up a huge opportunity. In line for the job are Greg Clark, who caught eight passes in 1997 with San Francisco and who the 49ers really like, and Irv Smith, who was signed away from New Orleans as a free agent. Smith missed about six weeks of the 1997 season with a knee injury, finishing with 17 receptions and one touchdown.

Paul Justin (Quarterback)
Unrestricted free agent with: Indianapolis Colts
Signed with: Cincinnati Bengals
Likely knowing the Colts were going to go with youth in 1998, Justin, like Jim Harbaugh (Ravens), left the scene, signing with the Bengals. In Cincinnati, Justin will likely battle for the backup job behind Jeff Blake. If Blake falters early, Justin may get a chance to start.

Danny Kight (Kicker)
Free agent signed with: Washington Redskins
Danny Kight, who battled for the Dallas Cowboys' kicking job in 1997 only to lose out to Richie Cunningham, has been signed by the Redskins. In Washington, Kight will battle Scott Blanton, who hit only 16 of 24 (.667) field goal tries in 1997.

Jay Kirchoff (Kicker)
Free agent signed with: Cincinnati Bengals
The Bengals signed free agent Jay Kirchoff to battle veteran Doug Pelfrey in 1998. Pelfrey in 1997 hit 12 of 16 field goals and 41 of 43 extra points.

Terry Kirby (Running Back)
Released by: San Francisco 49ers
After acquiring Garrison Hearst in 1997 and seeing him produce as they had hoped he would, the 49ers elected to give Terry Kirby his release. Kirby had produced 418 rushing yards, 23 receptions for 279 yards and eight touchdowns in 1997.

Thomas Lewis
Unrestricted free agent with: New York Giants
Signed with: Chicago Bears
Lewis, a former first-round pick of the Giants has signed with Chicago.

Lewis had struggled through injuries since being drafted by New York including last season when he missed 13 weeks with a toe toe injury. In Chicago he'll likely compete for playing time behind Curtis Conway, Chris Penn and Bobby Engram.

Curtis Martin (Running Back)
Restricted free agent with: New England Patriots
Signed with: New York Jets
In one of the biggest offseason transactions, Curtis Martin was offered $36 million over six years by the Jets, an offer that the Patriots elected not to match. Martin's arrival made Adrian Murrell expendable and he was dealt to Arizona. Martin's departure means the Patriots will have to rebuild their running game perhaps behind Derrick Cullors, Sedrick Shaw or more likelynewly drafted Robert Edwards out of Georgia. Martin, missing three games with a shoulder injury in 1997, fell to only five touchdowns but did still produce 1,456 total rushing-receiving yards. He'll be a huge factor for the Jets in 1998.

Natrone Means (Running Back)
Unrestricted free agent with: Jacksonville Jaguars
Signed with: San Diego Padres
Means, who spent two productive years in Jacksonville, returns to San Diego, a place he had been dismissed from just three years ago. Means signed a six-year, $19.1-million deal to again be their featured back. As the Chargers' main back and with the Chargers' uncertain quarterback situation, look for Means to get plenty of work.

Eric Metcalf (Wide Receiver)
Traded from: San Diego Chargers
Acquired by: Arizona Cardinals
Metcalf, who caught 40 passes for 576 yards in 1997, goes to Arizona to most likely to return kicks. Metcalf scored five touchdowns in 1997, three of which came on punt returns.

Glyn Milburn (Running Back)
Traded from: Detroit Lions
Acquired by: Green Bay Packers
Milburn, who caught only five passes for 77 yards in 1997 for the Lions and accumulated no rushing yards was dealt to the Green Bay Packers. In Green Bay he will likely spend most of his time returning kicks much like he did for the Lions.

Ernie Mills (Wide Receiver)
Unrestricted free agent with: Carolina Panthers
Signed with: Dallas Cowboys
Following a disappointing season from Anthony Miller, the Cowboys are still looking for someone to team with Michael Irvin. Ernie Mills joins Stepfret Williams and Billy Davis in battling for playing time in 1998. In 1997, Mills recorded only 11 receptions for 127 yards and one touchdown with Carolina.

Adrian Murrell (Running Back)
Traded by: New York Jets
Acquired by: Arizona Cardinals
The Jets made a huge move in the offseason, luring Curtis Martin to New York for a reported $36 million over six years. Martin's arrival made Adrian Murrell's services expendable despite his back-to-back 1,000-yard seasons. Murrell was dealt to Arizona for the Cardinals' first- and third-round picks. In Arizona, Murrell likely becomes the every-down back the Cardinals have desperate needed.

Brett Perriman (Wide Receiver)
Released by: Miami Dolphins
Perriman, who came to the Dolphins following his release by Kansas City in 1997, had been resigned by the Dolphins in the offseason and then given his release. Perriman recorded 25 receptions, playing eight games with Miami and three with Kansas City in 1997. The previous two years Perriman had recorded 96 and 108 receptions with Detroit.

Roosevelt Potts (Running Back)
Unrestricted free agent with: Miami Dolphins
Signed with: Baltimore Ravens
Potts brings his blocking services to Baltimore and will likely team with Errict Rhett in the Ravens' backfield. Don't look for any significant fantasy numbers from him in 1998.

Ricky Proehl (Wide Receiver)
Unrestricted free agent with: Chicago Bears
Signed with: St. Louis Rams
Proehl, who stepped in for an injury-riddled Chicago Bears' team in 1997 to record 58 receptions for 753 yards and seven touchdowns, takes his services to the Rams. In St. Louis, Proehl will push Eddie Kennison for the No.2 wide receiver spot opposite Isaac Bruce. Kennison struggled miserably in 1997 with only 25 receptions and no touchdowns following an impressive rookie campaign in 1996.

Alfred Pupunu (Tight End)
Free agent
Signed with: New York Giants
Pupunu, who spent some time as a starter in San Diego before being let go, signed on with the Giants for 1998. The signing of Pupunu is probably what led to the release of Aaron Pierce. Pupunu will challenge veteran Howard Cross.

Errict Rhett (Running Back)
Unrestricted free agent with: Tampa Bay Buccaneers
Signed with: Baltimore Ravens
Rhett, a former two-time 1,000-yard rusher, had taken a backseat to Warrick Dunn in Tampa Bay and was looking for a trade to a team where he'd get more work. The Bucs obliged by dealing Rhett to Baltimore for a third-round pick. Rhett will get his chance to again be a team's featured back and perhaps get paid what he thinks he's worth. He always felt short-changed in Tampa Bay.

Torrence Small (Wide Receiver)
Unrestricted free agent with: St. Louis Rams
Signed with: Indianapolis Colts
With Sean Dawkins not espected back the Colts were looking for help for newly drafted quarterback Peyton Manning. The Colts signed Torrence Small away from St. Louis where he caught 32 passes in 1997. Small will battle for playing time alongside the Colts #1 receiver Marvin Harrison.

Irv Smith (Tight End)
Unrestricted free agent with: New Orleans Saints
Signed with: San Francisco 49ers
Following the retirement of Brent Jones, the 49ers are in search of a replacement. Smith comes in to likely battle Greg Clark for playing time. Smith, normally a consistent performer, struggled through a knee injury in 1997 to record only 17 receptions and one touchdown, seeing action in only nine games.

Lamar Smith (Running Back)
Unrestricted free agent with: Seattle Seahawks
Signed with: New Orleans Saints
The Saints, obviously unhappy with their running game, have signed Lamar Smith to a four-year, $7.1-million deal. Smith, mainly a backup to Chris Warren in Seattle, has had his share of starts. He comes to New Orleans, however, pushing for the starting job. In 1997, Smith rushed for 392 yards, had 23 receptions for 183 yards and scored twice for Seattle.

Irving Spikes (Running Back)
Released by: Miami Dolphins
Spikes, who had pushed for the No. 1 running back spot with the Dolphins but never could quite get there was released. In 1997, Spikes rushed for 180 yards, caught seven passes for 70 yards and scored two touchdowns.

Brian Stablein (Wide Receiver)
Unrestricted free agent with: Indianapolis Colts
Signed with: New England Patriots
Stablien, who caught 25 passes and one touchdown in 1997, goes to New England to battle for playing time. The Patriots' receiving crew really struggled a year ago.

Yancey Thigpen (Wide Receiver)
Unrestricted free agent with: Pittsburgh Steelers
Signed with: Tennessee Oilers
Thigpen, the Steelers' best receiver, leaves Pittsburgh to join the Oilers and help bolster their receiving crew. I don't see, however, the same amount of passes for him there. Pittsburgh is hunting for a new go-to receiver, likely Charles Johnson. In 1997, Thigpen recorded 79 catches for 1,398 yards and seven touchdowns.

Mike Vanderyagt (Kicker)
Free agent with: Indianapolis Colts
After hitting a sterling 36 of 40 (.900) field goals in 1996, Cary Blanchard dropped to hitting only 32 of 41 (.780) in 1997. The Colts are perhaps a bit concerned about that because they've signed free agent Mike Vanderyagt to compete for the job.

Chris Warren (Running Back)
Released by: Seattle Seahawks
Signed with: Dallas Cowboys
Once one of the league's premier backs, and the Seahawk's all-time leading rusher, Chris Warren was given his release by the Seahawks. Warren became expendable when the Seahawks signed Ricky Watters in the offseason. Shortly thereafter however, Warren was signed by the Dallas Cowboys. The Cowboys were looking for better insurance behind Emmitt Smith, who has struggled with injury recently.

Ricky Watters (Running Back)
Unrestricted free agent with: Philadelphia Eagles
Signed with: Seattle Seahawks
In another of the big offseason moves, Ricky Watters signed a four-year, $13-million deal and takes his services to Seattle. Watters actually had an off year in 1997 with 1,550 rushing-receiving yards and only seven touchdowns. Those are very low numbers by his standards. His arrival in Seattle has also triggered the release of Chris Warren and was possibly a factor in the departure of Lamar Smith, who has gone to New Orleans. But, his departure opens up an opportunity for Charlie Garner and Duce Staley.

SIGNIFICANT INJURY UPDATES

What follows is a list of significant fantasy players who are recovering from injuries. When possible, I have also included statements on their status by their teams. These status reports were from April and May. Be sure to track further progress in our preseason Fantasy Football Newsletters, which begin in August.

Terry Allen (Running Back, Washington Redskins)
Allen missed the last three games of 1997 with an ankle injury but is expected to be 100% and ready for the '98 season.

John Carney (Kicker, San Diego Chargers)
Carney, who suffered a knee injury in 1997, passed his physical, was practicing and was expected to compete for his job again in 1998.

Mark Carrier (Wide Receiver, Carolina Panthers)
Carrier, who missed the last four games of the 1997 season with a wrist injured, has been re-signed for 1998, his wrist is healed according to the Panthers and was ready to play in Carolina's mini-camp.

Gus Frerotte (Quarterback, Washington Redskins)
Frerotte ended the 1997 on injured reserve, missing the last three games with a broken hip. Frerotte's recovery is going well and the Redskins say he's doing fine and is expected ready for the 1998 season.

Yatil Green (Wide Receiver, Miami Dolphins)
The Dolphins' No.1 draft pick of 1997 missed his entire rookie season with a knee injury. In the spring, the Dolphins commented that Green was not completely healed yet and he remained in rehab. Their hope was that he'd be in mini-camp and would eventually be ready for training camp. This is another injury we'll keep an eye on.

Jackie Harris (Tight End, Tennessee Oilers)
Harris missed the last game of 1997 with a hernia. In the offseason, Harris signed a free-agent contract with the Tennessee Oilers and is expected to be 100 percent and ready to go in 1998.

Raymont Harris (Running Back, Chicago Bears)
Harris broke his leg late in 1997, which forced him to miss the last two games. The Bears said that Harris had the pins removed, was in rehab, was walking and was expected to be ready for training camp. However, looking to 1998, Harris will have a tough time getting significant playing time because the Bears signed Edgar Bennett away from the Packers in the offseason.

Ike Hilliard (Wide Receiver, New York Giants)
Hilliard, who suffered a neck injury as a rookie in 1997, was cleared by doctors to play and the Giants said he was ready when they were contacted in early April.

Brad Johnson (Quarterback, Minnesota Vikings)
Johnson, who took over as the Vikings' full-time starter in 1997, missed the last three games of the season with a neck injury. In April, the Vikings reported that Johnson underwent successful surgery in the obviously delicate area and they were, at that time, still waiting for him to heal. The true test will be if, and when, he can take a hit. This is an injury we'll keep a close eye on during the preseason and report in our newsletter.

Daryl Johnston (Running Back, Dallas Cowboys)
Johnston had surgery to remove a bulging disk in his neck. After surgery, Johnson was given permission to practice but the Cowboys had a wait-and-see attitude in the spring.

Chris T. Jones (Wide Receiver, Philadelphia Eagles)
Jones underwent arthroscopic surgery three times since late last season. The Eagles remain very concerned about the condition of the knee. This is an injury that we'll keep an eye on as the '98 season nears and we'll update in our Preseason Newsletters.

Jeff Lewis (Quarterback, Denver Broncos)
The backup to John Elway, Lewis tore the anterior cruciate ligament in his left knee during the offseason. The Broncos report surgery went well, he's improving daily and they anticipate he'll be ready for camp in July.

Curtis Martin (Running Back, New York Jets)
Martin suffered a shoulder injury at the tail end of the 1997 season, forcing him to miss the last three games. Martin is healed and ready for training camp. However, during the offseason he signed with the Jets so he'll be in a new uniform come the 1998 season.

Carl Pickens (Wide Receiver, Cincinnati Bengals)
Pickens missed the last four games of 1997 with a groin injury. The Bengals say he is at full speed and ready for the 1998 season.

Jerry Rice (Wide Receiver, San Francisco 49ers)
Rice missed most of the 1997 season with a knee injury only to return late in the year to, again, fall victim to a second knee injury. The 49ers com-

mented that Rice said he was believed to be 80% recovered in May and is excited about playing in the upcoming '98 season.

Rashaan Salaam (Running Back, Chicago Bears)
Salaam had suffered a broken ankle on week #3 against Detroit and was lost for the season. When the Bears tried to trade him in the offseason to Miami in late April he had not recovered well enough to pass the physical and the trade was ruled void. It is believed the ankle will continue to improve and the Bears are likely to try and deal Salaam because of their offseason additions of free agent Edgar Bennett and first-round draft pick Curtis Enis.

O.J. Santiago (Tight End, Atlanta Falcons)
Santiago suffered a leg injury late in 1997, forcing him to miss the season's last five games. The Falcons commented that he is fully healed and working out daily.

Leslie Shepherd (Wide Receiver, Washington Redskins)
Shepard, who missed the last six games of 1997 with a dislocated wrist, is said to be doing well and expected ready for the upcoming season.

Tyrone Wheatley (Running Back, New York Giants)
The Giants' former first-round pick continued to be hampered by injury, as he missed the last two games of 1997 with an ankle injury. Wheatley had been given the doctors' clearance to practice, was in good shape and was expected to be ready for 1998.

Alex Van Pelt (Quarterback, Buffalo Bills)
Van Pelt is recovering from surgery on his throwing shoulder and is expected out until about training camp. This will put him far behind his competition of Rob Johnson, Doug Flutie and Todd Colllins.

NEW NFL HEAD COACHES

Buffalo Bills
In: Wade Phillips
Out: Marv Levy
After Marv Levy's retirement, the Bills were forced to look for a new head coach. They didn't have to look far as they promoted their own defensive coordinator, Wade Phillips. Phillips is well liked by the players, which is a big plus for him. The Bills think he has done an excellent job with the defense, and they hope he can expand that success to the entire team in this post-Jim Kelly era. The quarterback situation is still a big key and a big question. The Bills have brought in CFLer Doug Flutie and traded for Jacksonville backup Rob Johnson. Phillips has an uphill battle and will need some time to see if he can accomplish it.

Indianapolis Colts
In: Jim Mora
Out: Lindy Infante
The Colts' new president, Bill Polian, elected to hire former New Orleans Saint head coach Jim Mora. Mora resigned from the Saints' job after compiling a 93-74 record in just more than 10 seasons. The rip on Mora was his lack of playoff success. The Colts and Polian were looking for an experienced coach to get them back on track following a 3-13 campaign in

1997. With Jim Harbaugh gone, Mora's job will be very tough. He'll have to try to turn around a team behind a new and perhaps inexperienced signal-caller. Mora and the Colts will have to look down the road for long-term success because I don't see much for them in the near future.

Dallas Cowboys
In: Chan Gailey
Out: Barry Switzer
Cowboys owner, Jerry Jones, spoke to Terry Donohue, (UCLA), George Seifert (ex SF), and Sherman Lewis (GB offensive coordinator), before deciding on Chan Gailey. Gailey, the Pittsburgh Steelers' offensive coordinator from a year ago, takes over a team that was 6-10 last season. This isn't just any team. This used to be "America's Team." The Cowboys, despite still having Emmitt Smith, Troy Aikman and Michael Irvin, have fallen quickly and far. Gailey's work is cut out for him. Known to be well organized, disciplined and extremely hard-working, Gailey will need all those traits to turn this team back around and satisfy his boss, Jerry Jones.

Oakland Raiders
In: Jon Gruden
Out: Joe Bugel
After committing to more than $25 million to bring in quarterback Jeff George in 1997, Al Davis was expecting something better than the Raiders' 4-12 finish. Davis has settled on young (34) Jon Gruden, who last year was the offensive coordinator for the Philadelphia Eagles. Gruden, a product of some Mike Holmgren tutoring, should bring some great presence to the talented Raider offense. Jeff George, along with receivers Tim Brown, James Jett, Ricky Dudley and running back Napoleum McCallum, should all benefit from Gruden's arrival and presence. Davis and the Raiders are intrigued by what the young coach might bring to them for years to come.

V
1998 ROOKIE CLASS
Manning and Leaf Capture Pre-Draft Attention

Certainly the center of this year's pre-draft attention was quarterbacks Peyton Manning and Ryan Leaf. The belief was that they would go 1-2 in the draft. Both were talented with plenty of potential but each brought unique qualities with him. Manning, out of Tennessee, was said to be more mature and more likely to show immediate results. Leaf, out of Washington State, was more rebellious and headstrong, but also probably more gifted as an athlete. The hype and comparisons went on forever in every publication you could get your hands on, making pre-draft speculation much more exciting. Then, as expected, Manning and Leaf did go 1-2. Manning went to Indianapolis and Leaf to San Diego. Most years not too much is expected out of rookie quarterbacks. However, this is likely to change in 1998 with Manning and Leaf. Both are expected to be both the future and the present for their teams. Immediate success, however, may be another issue. Remember just a few short years ago when Heath Shuler and Trent Dilfer were highly touted and were drafted numbers 3 and 6 overall? Obviously, neither has burned up the NFL as yet, and I really don't look for them to in the future. So don't get too excited.

Other than Manning and Leaf, the first round saw four running backs drafted: Curtis Enis (Chicago), Frey Taylor (Jacksonville), Robert Edwards (New England), and John Avery (Miami). Enis, with the Bears, and Avery, with the Dolphins, may have a tough time making an immediate impact in situations where teams already looked fairly strong at running back. Enis joins a cast in Chicago that includes newly acquired Edgar Bennett, who came over from Green Bay in the offseason and is the likely starter. Besides Bennett, the Bears also have Raymont Harris and Rashaan Salaam. Either or both could be moved now that Enis is aboard. In Miami, John Avery is small but very quick. He joins Karim Abdul-Jabbar and Lawrence Phillips but is likely to find himself in a third-down or kick-returning role. For Fred Taylor and Robert Edwards, the scenario is different. Both players come to teams in need of running backs. Edwards goes to the Patriots, who lost all-pro Curtis Martin to the Jets in the off-season. There's certainly an opportunity there. Taylor joins the Jaguars, who lost Natrone Means to San Diego in the offseason. Both players are in a position to make an impact as rookies.

Three wide receivers were taken in this year's first round: Kevin Dyson (Oilers), Randy Moss (Vikings) and Marcus Nash (Broncos). Although all three are big talents, I don't look for overwhelming success for them in their first year. Dyson joins the Oilers, who added Yancey Thigpen in the offseason. The Oilers seem to want to run more than throw, which would hinder Dyson's immediate success. Moss comes to the Vikings with a few underlying factors. First, with his talent Moss could have been rated as high as a top-five overall pick but his off-the-field problems slid him down a long way. Even if he gets beyond his off-field distractions, he joins an offense that already has a talented cast of receivers, including Cris Carter and Jake Reed. Immediate success as a rookie is unlikely for Moss. Nash goes to Denver where he'll likely have time to develop under veterans Rod Smith and Ed McCaffrey.

Who will actually stand out and make an impact from this year's draft? Keep in mind that one of today's best running backs is Terrell Davis of Denver. Davis was a sixth-round pick of the Broncos in 1995 and the 196th overall selection. Success doesn't always come from the first couple of rounds. Even the pro scouts who watch these players all year long very often misjudge a player's potential for a number of reasons. So who will really stand out from this draft? It's not an easy prediction. In this section, I will evaluate the 1998 rookies to try to determine who will make waves and who will be groomed for future stardom. The rookies who will make a difference right away in 1998 are those going to teams with immediate needs. The players whose success will come later are those headed for teams that are planning for the future.

When evaluating this year's rookies, we'll first take a look at last year's draftees from the first couple of rounds-the "Blue Chippers." Analyzing both successful and unsuccessful seasons by these players helps us see how this year's rookies may fare. After a quick look at last year's draft choices, I will list this year's draft choices from fantasy positions only-quarterbacks, running backs, wide receivers, tight ends and kicker-and, finally, I will give a key player-by-player evaluation of this year's rookie crop. (For a more extensive look or review of the 1997 rookies, see Section II, How the 1997 Rookies Fared.

1997 BLUE-CHIPPERS
ROUND #1

OVERALL PICK	NAME	POS	COLLEGE	NFL TEAM
7	Ike Hilliard	WR	Florida	NY Giants
12	Warrick Dunn	RB	Florida State	Tampa Bay
13	Tony Gonzalez	TE	California	Kansas City
15	Yatil Green	WR	Miami	Miami
16	Reidel Anthony	WR	Florida	Tampa Bay
22	David LaFleur	TE	LSU	Dallas
23	Antowain Smith	RB	Houston	Buffalo
26	Jim Druckenmiller	QB	Colorado	Carolina

ROUND #2

OVERALL PICK	NAME	POS	COLLEGE	NFL TEAM
36	Tiki Barber	RB	Virginia	NY Giants
38	John Allred	TE	USC	Chicago
41	Byron Hanspard	RB	Texas Tech	Atlanta
42	Jake Plummer	QB	Arizona State	Arizona
43	Corey Dillon	RB	Washington	Cincinnati
45	Freddie Jones	TE	North Carolina	San Diego
46	Joey Kent	WR	Tennessee	Tennessee
47	Kevin Lockett	WR	Kansas State	Kansas City
53	Will Blackwell	WR	San Diego State	Pittsburgh
55	Marc Edwards	RB	Notre Dame	San Francisco

Of last year's first-rounders, Warrick Dunn and Antowain Smith were really the only two that made significant impacts as rookies. Injuries to Ike Hilliard curtailed any possibilities for hIm to make an impact in his inaugural season. Tony Gonzalez, Reidel Anthony, David LaFluer and Rae Carruth were heard from but not in a big way, while the only quarterback of the bunch, Jim Druckenmiller was rarely seen.

From the second round, running backs Tiki Barber, Byron Hanspard and Corey Dillon all made significant contributions to their respective teams, with Dillon's being the most notable. Fullback Marc Edwards of the 49ers did very little as a rookie but may change for him as a second-year player now that William Floyd has gone to Carolina. Of the wide receivers, Joey Kent, Kevin Lockett and Will Blackwell, none did much as fantasy players. At tight end, John Allred was a bust, while Freddie Jones did well and shows plenty of future promise. The lone quarterback of the second-rounders, Jake Plummer, took a while but became a very big hit in the second half of 1997.

Surely we could not have predicted injuries such as the season-ending knee injury to Yatil Green of the Dolphins, which was obviously a huge setback for his rookie season. So even if a player is deemed to be a blue-chipper and is drafted by a team in need at his position, he is not always successful as a rookie. This, however, is not to say he won't be as a second-year player. Although the performances by Tony Gonzalez, Reidel Anthony and Rae Carruth did not set the world on fire as rookies in 1997, they developed and gained knowledge, which may lead to much better accomplishments this year.

1998 ROOKIE CLASS BY ROUND

ROUND #1

OVERALL PICK	NAME	POS	COLLEGE	NFL TEAM
1	Peyton Manning	QB	Tennessee	Indianapolis
2	Ryan Leaf	QB	Washington State	San Diego
5	Curtis Enis	RB	Penn State	Chicago
9	Fred Taylor	RB	Florida	Jacksonville
16	Kevin Dyson	WR	Utah	Tennessee
18	Robert Edwards	RB	Georgia	New England
21	Randy Moss	WR	Marshall	Minnesota
29	John Avery	RB	Mississippi	Miami
30	Marcus Nash	WR	Tennessee	Denver

ROUND #2

32	Jerome Pathon	WR	Washington	Indianapolis
34	Jacquez Greene	WR	Florida	Tampa Bay
37	Robert Holcombe	RB	Illinois	St. Louis
40	Cameron Cleeland	TE	Washington	New Orleans
42	Pat Johnson	WR	Oregon	Baltimore
48	Stephen Alexander	TE	Oklahoma	Washington
50	Germane Crowell	WR	Virginia	Detroit
52	Tony Simmons	WR	Wisconsin	New England
54	Rod Rutledge	TE	Alabama	New England
55	Joe Jurevicius	WR	Penn State	NY Giants
59	Mikhael Ricks	WR	Stephen F. Austin	San Diego
60	Charlie Batch	QB	Eastern Michigan	Detroit

ROUND #3

63	Jon Ritchie	RB	Stanford	Oakland
69	Skip Hicks	RB	UCLA	Washington
70	Brian Alford	WR	Purdue	NY Giants
71	E.G. Green	WR	Florida State	Indianapolis
74	Jammi German	WR	Miami	Atlanta
76	Ahman Green	RB	Nebraska	Seattle
81	Chris Floyd	RB	Michigan	New England
82	Larry Shannon	WR	East Carolina	Miami
86	John Quinn	QB	Middle Tennessee State	Jacksonville
88	Rashaan Shehee	RB	Washington	Kansas City
91	Brian Griese	QB	Michigan	Denver
92	Hines Ward	WR	Georgia	Pittsburgh

ROUND #4

94	Alonzo Mayes	TE	Oklahoma State	Chicago
95	Michael Pittman	RB	Fresno State	Arizona
96	Az-Zahir Hakim	WR	San Diego State	St. Louis
98	Roland Williams	TE	Syracuse	St. Louis
101	Tavian Banks	RB	Iowa	Jacksonville
106	Donald Hayes	WR	Wisconsin	Carolina
114	Tim Dwight	WR	Iowa	Atlanta
122	Curtis Alexander	RB	Alabama	Denver
123	Carlos King	RB	North Carolina State	Pittsburgh

ROUND #5

125	Terry Hardy	TE	Southern Mississippi	Indianapolis
127	Jeremy Brigham	TE	Washington	Oakland
129	Raymond Priester	RB	Clemson	St. Louis
131	Jonathan Linton	RB	North Carolina	Buffalo
132	Wilmont Perry	RB	Livingstone (N.C.)	New Orleans
146	Blake Spence	TE	Oregon	NY Jets
150	Corey Bradford	WR	Jackson State	Green Bay
153	Chris Howard	RB	Michigan	Denver

ROUND #6

160	Fred Coleman	WR	Washington	Buffalo
167	Jason Tucker	WR	Texas Christian	Cincinnati
169	Bobby Shaw	WR	California	Seattle
170	Pat Palmer	WR	NW Louisiana	Washington
172	John Dutton	QB	Nevada	Miami
174	Chris Brazzell	WR	Angelo State	NY Jets
176	Harold Shaw	RB	Southern Mississippi	New England
177	Todd Pollack	TE	Boston College	NY Giants
178	Chris Fuamatu-Ma'afala	RB	Utah	Pittsburgh
180	Fred Beasley	RB	Auburn	San Francisco
182	Kevin McLeod	RB	Auburn	Jacksonville
183	Dustin Johnson	RB	Brigham Young	NY Jets
187	Matt Hasselbeck	QB	Boston College	Green Bay

ROUND #7

192	Alvin Whitted	WR	North Carolina State	Jacksonville
193	Phil Savoy	WR	Colorado	Arizona
195	Lawrence Hart	TE	Southern University	NY Jets
201	Ken Oxendine	RB	Virginia Tech	Atlanta
202	Marcus Parker	RB	Virginia Tech	Cincinnati
204	Andy McCullough	WR	Tennessee	New Orleans
215	Ryan Thelwell	WR	Minnesota	San Francisco
218	Ed Watson	RB	Purdue	Green Bay
222	Damien Vaughn	TE	Miami (Ohio)	Cincinnati
223	Tarik Smith	RB	California	Dallas
224	Ernest Blackwell	RB	Missouri	Kansas City
228	Jim Turner	WR	Syracuse	Carolina
232	Moses Moreno	QB	Colorado State	Chicago
233	Ron James	RB	Missouri	Arizona
234	Kio Sanford	WR	Kentucky	San Diego
237	Rodrick Monroe	TE	Cincinnati	Dallas
238	Kamil Loud	WR	Cal Poly-San Luis Obispo	Buffalo
241	Cam Quayle	TE	Weber State	Baltimore

GOOD ROOKIE PROSPECTS
FROM THE 1998 DRAFT

How many good fantasy players will come from this year's draft? Or, more accurately and perhaps importantly, which players have a shot at making an immediate impact, and which ones are being groomed for the future? Let's take a look at some of these prospects.

RUNNING BACKS

Curtis Enis *(1st Round: Chicago Bears/College: Penn State)*
The Bears' selection of Enis in the first round was a bit of a surprise. The Bears' backfield is already very crowded. In the offseason, the Bears signed free agent Edgar Bennett to likely be their every-down back. And Raymont Harris, along with Rashaan Salaam, are still in the picture, although likely as expendable trade bait. Enis himself, at just over 6 feet and 240 pounds, is tough, quick and can catch the ball out of the backfield. During his last two college seasons, he scored 32 times and rushed for 2,573 yards. He is a workhorse back who may have difficulty finding a workhorse's load in the Bears' backfield, at least initially.

Fred Taylor *(1st Round: Jacksonville Jaguars/College: Florida)*
With Natrone Means off to San Diego, the Jaguars are looking for help for James Stewart. Taylor, who rushed for just under 1,300 yards and scored 13 times in 1997 at Florida, should be able to provide that support. The situation is certainly right for Taylor to be a significant and immediate fantasy prospect as a rookie in 1998.

Robert Edwards *(1st Round: New England Patriots/College: Georgia)*
With Curtis Martin off to the New York Jets in the offseason, Edwards steps into a pretty good situation with New England in 1998. The Patriots need someone to step in and Edwards should have his chance to battle Sedric Shaw and Derrick Cullors for playing time. At just over 6 feet 2 and 208 pounds, Edwards has the build and running ability to make his mark. He, however, has a couple of drawbacks, including inconsistency and a tendency to fumble. He's certainly one to watch as training camp rolls around.

John Avery *(1st Round: Miami Dolphins/College: Mississippi)*
With Karim Abdul-Jabbar and Lawrence Phillips already aboard, Jimmy Johnson was not looking for an every-down back. Instead, the Dolphins selected Avery perhaps for a third-down option and/or to return kicks. Avery is just over 5 feet 9 and weighs only 184 pounds but he is quick and would make an excellent target out of the backfield.

Robert Holcombe *(2nd Round: St. Louis Rams/College: Illinois)*
With the Rams abandoning hopes for their former first-round pick Lawrence Phillips and releasing him in 1997, the search is on for a replacement. Jerald Moore stepped in and played admirably in 1997 but the Rams were looking for depth and some insurance when they drafted Hol-

comb. Holcomb is a workmanlike back, that is, he's not a great breakaway threat. He did, however, rush for more than 1,000 yards in three straight college seasons.

Jon Ritchie *(3rd Round: Oakland Raiders/College: Stanford)*
Ritchie, at just over 6 feet 1 and weighing 248 pounds, is a true fullback. He was drafted to open holes for Napoleon Kaufman. I see little fantasy impact from him.

Skip Hicks *(3rd Round: Washington Redskins/College: UCLA)*
With Terry Allen banged up for much of 1997, the Redskins have to be a bit worried. In Hicks, they get a gifted runner who doesn't play with a true sense of urgency at times. He did, however, rush for 1,142 yards and 25 scores.

Rashaan Shehee *(3rd Round: Kansas City Chiefs/College: Washington)*
With Marcus Allen retiring and Greg Hill unlikely to be back, the Chiefs are looking for help at running back. Shehee, however, is not likely to be their answer as an every-down player. He may fit more into a third-down role because he has good hands and would be an excellent receiver out of the backfield.

WIDE RECEIVERS

Kevin Dyson *(1st Round: Tennessee Oilers/College: Utah)*
The Oilers, looking to improve their passing game, already had acquired Yancey Thigpen (Steelers) in the offseason. Now adding Kevin Dyson will give them an added boost and a target for quarterback Steve McNair. Dyson is an excellent deep threat with great speed but he can also be used as a kick returner. He'll need to work on his concentration and route running in the pros but he has plenty of potential. He's a player to keep a close eye on in training camp to see just how the Oilers will use him.

Randy Moss *(1st Round: Minnesota Vikings/College: Marshall)*
Loaded with talent, Moss's draft value slipped due to his off-the-field problems. He was projected by many as a top-five overall pick but he wasn't drafted until the 21st pick by the Vikings. His off-the-field problems include jail time but his skill, talent and potential are just too hard to ignore. Moss, at just under 6 feet 5, is a great size for a target, and he possesses great speed, jumping ability and soft hands. He has all the tools, if he can just concentrate on football. He has two excellent veterans to learn from in Cris Carter and Jake Reed but they also likely stand in the way of his immediate success.

Marcus Nash *(1st Round: Denver Broncos/College: Tennessee)*
Nash is an improving receiver who produced 1,170 receiving yards on 76 catches while scoring 13 times as the favorite target of Peyton Manning at Tennessee in 1997. He's a nice sized target at just under 6 feet 3 who isn't afraid to catch the ball in a crowd. Nash will benefit from playing behind Rod Smith and Ed McCaffrey in Denver.

Jerome Pathon *(2nd Round: Indianapolis Colts/College: Washington)*
Now that the Colts have secured their quarterback of the future by drafting Peyton Manning, they must provide help around him. Pathon brings with him big-play ability that should complement Marvin Harrison well. With Sean Dawkins unlikely to return, Pathon will get his chance to play.

Jacquez Greene *(2nd Round: Tampa Bay Buccaneers/College: Florida)*
With the Buccaneers adding Bert Emanuel (Falcons) to their receiving crew just before the draft, it's most likely Greene was brought in to return kicks. At just under 5 feet 9, Greene is not a good size for an NFL target but he has great quickness and speed and is an excellent receiver. Don't be surprised to see Greene work both as a receiver and kick returner in 1998.

Pat Johnson *(2nd Round: Baltimore Ravens/College: Oregon)*
With Derrick Alexander off to Kansas City, the Ravens may be looking for a little more depth behind Michael Jackson and Jermaine Lewis. Johnson has excellent quickness and speed but is not yet believed to be an accomplished or refined receiver. Johnson could see time as both a receiver and as a return man.

Germane Crowell *(2nd Round: Detroit Lions/College: Virginia)*
The Lions, looking to build depth at wide receiver behind Herman Moore and Johnnie Morton, have an excellent prospect. Crowell possesses good size at just over 6 feet 3, good hands and the ability to catch the ball in traffic. I don't see Crowell with any immediate fantasy impact but he could blossom in the future.

Tony Simmons *(2nd Round: New England Patriots/College: Wisconsin)*
Simmons comes to a team whose receiving crew struggled through injuries in 1997. Simmons will come in to battle for playing time but, because he was an inconsistent college player, I believe it's very unlikely he'll make a significant impact as a rookie. He has the potential, if he works at it, to be a solid NFL receiver.

Joe Jurevicius *(2nd Round: New York Giants/College: Penn State)*
The Giants have drafted so many receivers in the early rounds in recent years, it's hard for me to get too excited about this one. In Jurevicius, the Giants have a big target who's just under 6 feet 5 inches tall, with good hands and deceptive speed. Again, I have a hard time getting too excited about Giant receivers, let alone a rookie draft pick.

Michael Ricks *(2nd Round: San Diego Charges/College: Stephen F. Austin)*
At 6 feet 5, Ricks has excellent size but he brings with him a history of knee trouble. If he can overcome his knee problem, he'll make an excellent target for Ryan Leaf for years to come.

Brian Alford *(3rd Round: New York Giants/College: Purdue)*
At just over 6 feet 1, Alford is a decent-sized target, with good but not great speed. Continuing to improve his skills, Alford joins a crowded Giants receiving corps.

E. G. Green *(3rd Round: Indianapolis Colts/College: Florida State)*
Green comes to a team in need of a wide receiver. He doesn't possess great speed or size (just under 6 feet) but he is very skilled and accelerates well. He can make the big-play.

TIGHT ENDS

Cameron Cleeland *(2nd Round: New Orleans Saints/College: Washington)*
Cleeland joins the Saints, who lost veteran Irv Smith to San Francisco in the offseason, via free agency. This creates an opportunity for the rookie. Cleeland, 6 feet 4, 272 pounds, has good size and hands but is not yet a refined player. The skills to develop are there.

Stephen Alexander *(2nd Round: Washington Redskins/College: Oklahoma)*
Alexander is a solid athlete with good jumping ability and decent hands. He has been known to drop passes but is working hard to improve. With the Redskins, he'll likely develop behind Jamie Asher.

Rod Rutledge *(2nd Round: New England Patriots/College: Alabama)*
Rutledge may be used more as a blocker than a receiver. Playing on the same team as Ben Coates, it's unlikely Rutledge would see much fantasy production as a rookie.

Alonzo Mayes *(4th Round: Chicago Bears/College: Oklahoma State)*
At just over 6 feet 4 and 250 pounds, Mayes has the size and the potential to be a solid NFL tight end. He also has the rare ability to get down field. I don't see him unseating Ryan Wetnight for Chicago in 1998, so look for Mayes's potential to be more long-term than short.

QUARTERBACKS

Peyton Manning *(1st Round: Indianapolis Colts/College: Tennessee)*
Polished and poised as both a quarterback and a person, Manning was the Colts' choice over another very talented signal-caller in Ryan Leaf. Manning, the son of former NFL quarterback Archie Manning, has the size (6 feet 5), great work ethic, good but not great arm, and the intangibles of desire and poise that all great quarterbacks need. Keep in mind he joins a team that went 3-13 in 1997, so success, though likely to come, may not present itself immediately.

Ryan Leaf *(1st Round: San Diego Chargers/College: Washington State)*
At just over 6 feet 5 and fluctuating between 250 and 265 pounds, Leaf is a solid athlete. He has great arm strength and is very tough both physically and mentally. He is a great leader on the field. The Chargers, who lost Stan Humphries to retirement, love Leaf's tools. They believe he's their future and they're hoping he's their present as well.

Charlie Batch *(2nd Round: Detroit Lions/College: Eastern Michigan)*
Looking to their future, the Lions made Batch their No. 2 draft pick. At Eastern Michigan, Batch played in a wide-open, run-and-shoot offense

where he was able to show off his passing skills. He's certainly more of a long-term project than immediate boon.

John Quinn *(3rd Round: Jacksonville Jaguars/College: Middle Tennessee State)*
Quinn has played both tight end and quarterback. At 6 feet 5 inches-plus, he has nice size for both positions. As a quarterback, he has a strong arm, and as a tight end, he has good speed and can jump. He isn't likely to have any immediate impact at either position with the Jaguars, playing behind Mark Brunell at quarterback and Pete Mitchell at tight end.

Brian Griese *(3rd Round: Denver Broncos/College: Michigan)*
The son of former NFL quarterback Bob Griese, Griese joins the Broncos hoping to be groomed under John Elway. Griese does not possess a great arm but he is a very smart, effective passer.

KICKERS

There were no placekickers selected in this year's draft. Look for comments on the free agent kickers picked up by various teams in the team-by-team sections.

VI
RATING THE 1998 NFL TEAM SCHEDULES

Which players from which teams should you pick in your fantasy draft? Who's going to fare well in 1998? One thing to consider when selecting your fantasy team for 1998 is the strength or weakness of the teams your players will face during the 1998 NFL season. Obviously, a player playing an easy schedule has a good chance of having a statistically successful year.

First, we'll look at last year's standings and see how each team did. Then we'll look at each team's 1998 schedule and rate that schedule according to how the current year's opposition performed in 1997.

This is not a foolproof method of selecting players, but it is an important factor to consider when choosing between two players whom you have rated almost equal.

The following pages show the final 1997 NFL standings, followed by rankings for each team's 1998 schedule.

1997 AMERICAN CONFERENCE STANDINGS

Eastern Division

TEAM	W	L	T	PCT.	PTS.	OPP.
New England	10	6	0	.625	369	289
Miami	9	7	0	.563	339	327
N.Y. Jets	9	7	0	.563	348	287
Buffalo	6	10	0	.375	255	367
Indianapolis	3	13	0	.188	313	401

Central Division

TEAM	W	L	T	PCT.	PTS.	OPP.
Jacksonville	11	5	0	.688	394	318
Pittsburgh	11	5	0	.688	372	307
Tennessee	8	8	0	.500	333	310
Cincinnati	7	9	0	.438	355	405
Baltimore	6	9	1	.406	326	345

Western Division

TEAM	W	L	T	PCT.	PTS.	OPP.
Kansas City	13	3	0	.813	375	232
Denver	12	4	0	.750	472	287
Seattle	8	8	0	.500	365	362
Oakland	4	12	0	.250	324	419
San Diego	4	12	0	.250	266	425

1997 NATIONAL CONFERENCE STANDINGS

Eastern Division

TEAM	W	L	T	PCT.	PTS.	OPP.
N. Y. Giants	10	5	1	.657	307	265
Washington	8	7	1	.531	327	289
Philadelphia	6	9	1	.406	317	372
Dallas	6	10	0	.375	304	314
Arizona	4	12	0	.250	283	379

Central Division

TEAM	W	L	T	PCT.	PTS.	OPP.
Green Bay	13	3	0	.813	422	282
Tampa Bay	10	6	0	.625	299	263
Detroit	9	7	0	.563	379	306
Minnesota	9	7	0	.563	354	359
Chicago	4	12	0	.250	263	421

Western Division

TEAM	W	L	T	PCT.	PTS.	OPP.
San Francisco	13	3	0	.813	375	265
Atlanta	7	9	0	.438	320	361
Carolina	7	9	0	.438	265	314
New Orleans	6	10	0	.375	237	327
St. Louis	5	11	0	.313	299	359

How can this ranking of schedules help you? I recommend that when deciding on a fantasy draft pick you lean toward players on teams that face the easier overall schedules. The flip side is, obviously, that you should shy away from players on teams that face tough schedules because you recognize that they will have a harder time coming up with productive seasons. The exceptions to this are great players from good teams. Players like Brett Favre and Terrell Davis will produce for you no matter what kind of schedules they face. For the most part, however, it is a good idea to grab players from teams facing weaker foes.

What are some of the tentative conclusions we can draw from this year's schedule-difficulty rankings? Arizona faces the league's easiest schedule. Arizona plays Chicago, Oakland and San Diego, all of which were 4-12 in 1997, at home in 1998. Perhaps young Jake Plummer and receivers Rob Moore and Frank Sanders can put together good numbers under those conditions in 1998. Other prospects include the Miami Dolphins and the San Francisco 49ers, both of whom face rather easy schedules. This could mean another solid season out of Karim Abdul-Jabbar and the 49ers offense led by Steve Young. The 49ers and Dolphins are tied with Baltimore and Buffalo for the league's second-easiest schedule in 1998. Their 1998 opponents all had a .465 winning percentage in 1997.

From whom should we shy away? Stay away from Kordell Stewart and Jerome Bettis because the Steelers face the league's toughest schedule, facing teams with a combined 140-114-2 (.551) record in 1997? Not necessarily. Sure the Steelers face a very tough schedule but this is one of those instances where players like Jerome Bettis and Kordell Stewart are just too good to pass up. The Steelers' schedule includes Jacksonville (11-5) twice within the division and Green Bay (13-3), Kansas City (13-3), New England (10-6) and Tampa Bay (10-6) outside their division. Other teams with tough schedules include Chicago, which faces teams with a combined 140-115-1 (.549) record, and Tampa Bay and Cincinnati, which both face teams with a 1997 record of 138-116-2 (.543) in 1998. This will make things tough for Pittsburgh, Cincinnati, Tampa Bay and especially Chicago, which is struggling anyway.

This schedule is not a precise way to pick players, especially considering the amount of player movement that has taken place during the off-season in recent years, but the ranking should give you a sense of what kind of opposition your fantasy players will face in 1998.

Here, then, are the 1998 schedule rankings. They are based on the win-loss records of opponents during the 1997 season. Rankings go from the easiest schedule, at the top, to the most difficult schedule at the bottom.

1998 DIFFICULTY RANKINGS OF TEAM SCHEDULES
1998 Opponents' Combined 1997 Records

	TEAM	WON	LOST	TIE	PCT.
1.	Arizona	113	137	6	.453
2.	Baltimore	119	137	0	.465
3.	Buffalo	119	137	0	.465
4.	Miami	119	137	0	.465
5.	San Francisco	118	136	2	.465
6.	Washington	119	133	4	.473
7.	New Orleans	121	135	0	.473
8.	Dallas	119	131	6	.477
9.	Seattle	121	133	2	.477
10.	Atlanta	122	132	2	.480
11.	St. Louis	123	132	1	.482
12.	N. Y. Jets	123	132	1	.482
13.	Kansas City	123	131	2	.484
14.	N. Y. Giants	124	128	4	.492
15.	Carolina	126	129	1	.494
16.	Indianapolis	126	129	1	.494
17.	Denver	125	128	3	.494
18.	San Diego	125	127	4	.496
19.	Philadelphia	127	125	4	.504
20.	New England	129	127	0	.504
21.	Minnesota	129	125	2	.508
22.	Oakland	130	123	3	.510
23.	Green Bay	132	121	3	.521
24.	Jacksonville	136	118	2	.535
25.	Tennessee	137	117	2	.539
26.	Detroit	137	117	2	.539
27.	Cincinnati	138	116	2	.543
28.	Tampa Bay	138	116	2	.543
29.	Chicago	140	115	1	.549
30.	Pittsburgh	140	114	2	.551

VII
A TEAM-BY-TEAM
1997 REVIEW / 1998 PREVIEW

Here is a team-by-team review/preview, with teams listed alphabetically. I first evaluate each team by fantasy position, then give an overall estimation of the team's offensive potential, and, finally, list all the players the team has either gained or lost as of May 1, 1998.

RB = Running Back, **WR** = Wide Receiver, **TE** = Tight End, **QB** = Quarterback, **K** = Kicker, and **KR** = Kick Returner

ARIZONA CARDINALS

Home Stadium: Sun Devil Stadium
Playing Surface: Grass
Head Coach: Vince Tobin
1997 Record: 4-12

Cardinals Call On a "Plummer" to Unclog Offense
Running Game Still "Centers" Around Fullback

RB: The Cardinals were hoping to finally establish a ground attack in 1997. LeShon Johnson and Leeland McElroy were both returning after inconsistent and sporadic performances in 1996. The Cardinals also brought in veteran Derrick Moore for a boost, but a knee injury quickly ended any hope of a contribution from him. As the season progressed, the performances of both McElroy and Johnson became all too familiar and neither stepped forward to grab the main back's duties. As the season wound down, the Cardinals brought aboard Ron Moore, who had been with the Rams. Moore closed the year as the team's main rusher. The only good sign for Arizona was, again, fullback Larry Centers. Centers, however, also saw his production drop. Centers rushed for 276 yards but more importantly caught only 54 passes after averaging more than 100 receptions the previous two seasons. McElroy led the Cardinals with 424 rushing yards in 1997, so it's certainly no secret that they need a back who can give them every-down production. In the offseason, they first did sign free agent Mario Bates, from New Orleans. Then, they made a much bigger move by acquiring Adrian Murrell and a seventh-round pick for the Jets third-round draft pick. Murrell became expendable for the Jets when they signed Curtis Martin away from New England. Murrell, who rushed for over 1,000 yards in each of his last two seasons with New York, looks to be the answer for the Cardinals search for an every down back. The Cardinals are a young, improving team where Bates and especially Murrell emencly help their running game. Meanwhile LeShon Johnson has moved on to New York, signing a free agent deal with the Giants.

WR: Veteran Rob Moore had a tremendous season in 1997 and improved as the year went on. Moore fared well with Kent Graham at the helm and exploded when rookie Jake Plummer took over about mid-season. Moore finished the year with a whopping 97 receptions for 1,584 yards and eight touchdowns. Moore had eight 100-yard games and three more in the 90-yard range. Seven of his eight touchdowns came in the last nine games when Plummer was inserted into the lineup. Moore was not the only receiver who did well. Frank Sanders also topped the 1,000-yard mark with 1,017 on 75 receptions while scoring four times. Anthony Edwards and Kevin Williams both chipped in 20 catches. Williams has gone, via free agency, to Buffalo. Looking to 1998, the passing game looks good if young Plummer continues to improve. This is especially true for Rob Moore, who has quickly developed a chemistry with Plummer. Certainly Frank Sanders will again be a big factor. The Cardinals wanting to ensure he would stay, signed Sanders to a 5 year, $16 million deal in the offseason. The Cardinals have also added Eric Metcalf to the mix. Metcalf was acquired in a trade with San Diego in the offseason. Metcalf will return kicks but could be very useful as a receiver as well. Metcalf grabbed 40 receptions for the Chargers in 1997.

TE: Although they already had a pretty good receiving tight end in Pat Carter and despite having taken Johnny McWilliams with their third-round pick in 1996, the Cardinals opted to bring in Chris Gedney from the Bears in 1997. Gedney, often injured with Chicago, stayed healthy and put together decent numbers. He recorded 23 receptions for 261 yards and scored four times. Three of his four touchdowns came in the season's last four games, which could be a sign that the Cardinals will use him more in future scoring situations.

QB: Kent Graham took the starting job away from Boomer Esiason at the close of the 1996 season and maintained that status in 1997. Graham remained the starter until he suffered an ankle and knee injury and played poorly against the Giants in week seven, going 4 of 14 for 40 yards. Stoney Case replaced Graham. Two games later, head coach Vince Tobin turned to rookie Jake Plummer. Plummer played with enthusiasm and when Graham returned, he saw little action. Plummer kept the starting job for the last six weeks of the season. In the 10 games in which Plummer played, he threw for 2,203 yards and 15 touchdowns. That performance has the Cardinals excited about their future.

K: A year earlier, Kevin Butler replaced Greg Davis about halfway through the season. In 1997, Butler was replaced after six games. He had hit on only 8 of 12 (.667) field goals. Butler's replacement was Joe Nedney, who had been released by Miami. Nedney hit only 11 of 17 (.647) field goals attempts. That should mean that the Cardinals will again be looking for a kicker in 1998.

Overall: The Cardinals need a running game to complement the passing of young signal-caller Jake Plummer. LeShon Johnson and Leeland McElroy confirmed in 1997 that they are not the answer. Ron Moore, who was used at the tail end of the season, isn't likely either. The Cardinals hope to turn to Adrian Murrell (Jets) and Mario Bates (Saints), two offseason acquisitions. Murrell is a two-time 1,000 yard man that should help in a big way. Through the air, head coach Vince Tobin seems to have found his future in Jake Plummer. Plummer has injected enthusiasm and hope into the team, and has elevated the play of veterans Rob Moore and Frank Sanders. I wouldn't be surprised to see Arizona push the .500 mark in 1998 if they can get their running attack going, especially since it faces the league's easiest schedule.

Offseason Fantasy-Position Moves

	Arriving	From:		Departing	To:
QB	Dave Brown	NYG	RB	LeShon Johnson	NYG
RB	Adrian Murrell	NYJ	WR	Kevin Williams	BUF
RB	Mario Bates	NO	QB	Kent Graham	NYG
WR	Eric Metcalf	SD			

ATLANTA FALCONS
Home Stadium: Georgia Dome
Playing Surface: Astro Turf
Head Coach: Dan Reeves
1997 Record: 7-9

Winning Last 5 Out of 6 has Falcons' Hopes Soaring for 1998

RB: Jamal Anderson rushed for more than 1,000 yards for the second straight season in 1997. Anderson's 1,002 yards were gained, however, with the help of just two 100-yard games. Anderson also grabbed 29 receptions for 284 yards and scored 10 times. The Falcons, looking to enhance their running game, also added Byron Hanspard to the fold. Hanspard, their No.2 draft pick in 1997, rushed for only 335 yards but was very effective as a kick returner, scoring twice on kickoff returns. Harold Green chipped in 438 total rushing-receiving yards, 360 of which came on 29 receptions. Looking to 1998, Green, a free agent, has been re-signed, however, Jamal Anderson can again be expected to carry the bulk of the rushing load but look for the Falcons to give Hanspard, and his ability to run well in the open field, more involvement in the offense.

WR: 1997 marked the second straight season the Falcons went without a 1,000-yard receiver. Bert Emanuel again led the team in receiving with 65 catches for 991 yards while scoring nine times. Terrance Mathis followed with 62 catches for 802 yards and six scores. This is a far cry from the run-and-shoot years in Atlanta when a 1,000-yard season from a Falcon receiver, or two, or three was the norm. Besides Emanuel and Mathis, the Falcons got contributions of 16 receptions from Todd Kinchen and 12 catches from Michael Haynes, who returned to Atlanta after a short stint in New Orleans. The key to the Falcon passing game again in 1998 is a healthy Chris Chandler. When he's on the field, the receivers will likely produce. In 1998, however, the Falcons will be without the services of Bert Emanuel, who departed to Tampa Bay via free agency. The Buccaneers offered Emanuel $16 million over four years, and the Falcons chose not to match it. This is a big loss for the Falcon passing game. The result should see bigger numbers from Terence Mathis who'll likely be forced to step into a bigger role. The Falcons will need help in looking for a solid

#2 receiver. They'll likely have their eyes and options open, looking to fill Emanuel's shoes. They did make Jimmi German out of Miami their third-round draft pick, helping them to fill the vacancy.

TE: The Falcons were hoping to get their tight end more involved in the offense. In 1997, the Falcons added veteran Ed West and, knowing he was a better blocker than receiver, and made O.J. Santiago their third-round draft pick. West did as expected, blocking well but recording only seven receptions. Santiago began to establish himself with 17 receptions and two touchdowns in the first 11 games. However, a leg injury then sidelined Santiago for the remainder of the year. Looking to 1998, West may retire while Santiago is expected to continue to exploit what seems to be a ton of potential.

QB: It was an impressive season for Chris Chandler, who was brought aboard to take over for Jeff George. Chandler missed two entire games with chest and concussion injuries and was sidelined in four other games. Despite all that, he threw for 2,692 yards and 20 touchdowns. The team was 0-6 when Chandler did not play the full game and 7-3 when he did. Chandler was a big factor as the Falcons won six of their last eight games, which is why, if Chandler stays healthy in 1998, I expect very productive fantasy numbers from him.

K: Morten Anderson had a mediocre 1996 season, hitting 22 of 29 (.759) on field goal attempts, but rebounded to hit 23 of 27 (.852) attempts in 1997. All of Anderson's four misses were from farther than 40 yards, and one was from more than 50 yards. The Falcons were smart to re-sign Anderson, who had become a free-agent in the offseason.

Overall: The Falcons have much to look forward to in 1998. In winning their last five out of six games in 1997 and last six out of eight, they established that they can win. On the ground, Jamal Anderson provided solid work and Byron Hanspard should provide more help in his sophomore season. Chris Chandler, however, is the key. With Chandler at the helm, the Falcons' offense plays well. Receivers Bert Emanuel, Terrance Mathis and up-and-coming tight end O.J. Santiago will benefit. Look for an interesting season from Dan Reeves and Co.

Offseason Fantasy-Position Moves

	Arriving	From:		Departing	To:
QB	Mark Rypien	STL	QB	Jim Miller	DET
QB	Brian Brennan	Free Agent	WR	Bert Emanuel	TB
RB	Darren Fisk	Free Agent			
WR	Keith Crawford	STL			
WR	Corey Allen	Free Agent			
WR	Octavus Barnes	Free Agent			

Derrick Alexander/Baltimore Ravens; with Chiefs in 1998

BALTIMORE RAVENS

Home Stadium: Memorial Stadium
Playing Surface: Grass
Head Coach: Ted Marchibroda
1997 Record: 6-9-1

'Bam' Morris is Gone, Baltimore now 'Raven' about Harbaugh, Rhett
who Hope to Spark Offense

RB: Bam Morris was serving another suspension (for four weeks) at the start of the 1997 season, so the Ravens first used veteran Earnest Byner and then rookie Jay Graham to handle the rushing load. They did an adequate job but when Morris's suspension ended, he returned to the starting lineup. Morris rushed for 774 yards and added 176 more on 29 receptions while scoring four times. Byner, seeing sporadic duty the rest of the year, rushed for 313 yards. Graham finished with 299 yards on the ground, 154 of which came on a brilliant performance with 35 carries against Philadelphia when Morris sat out with an injured toe. Looking to 1998, however, things are changing in a huge way. Earnest Byner has been released. Morris won't be re-signed after he served four months in jail for violating his probation. The Ravens, not certain that young Jay Graham was the answer after he suffered an ankle injury late in the year, have acquired Errict Rhett from Tampa Bay for a third-round pick in 1999. Rhett, a former 1,000-yard rusher for the Buccaneers, had taken a backup role in Tampa Bay behind Warrick Dunn and Mike Alstott. In Baltimore, Rhett will again be able to try to establish himself as one of the league's better backs. The Ravens have also added Roosevelt Potts, likely to play alongside Rhett. The Ravens are gambling on Potts, who's had a troubled past that includes missing the 1996 season because of he violated the league's substance abuse policy. However, the Ravens thought he was the best fullback available in the free-agent pool. Only time will tell what Rhett, and perhaps Potts, will do, though I do believe Rhett has something to prove and will put up respectable numbers.

WR: 1997 was a disappointing season for Michael Jackson. Benefiting from a career season by Vinny Testaverde in 1996, Jackson had produced 1,201 receiving yards on 76 receptions and 14 touchdowns. In 1997, with Testaverde no longer in pro bowl form, Jackson's numbers fell to 69 catches for 918 yards and only four touchdowns. Receiving mate Derrick Alexander, however, did not see his numbers drop as far in 1997. He went from 62 catches for 1,099 yards and nine touchdowns in 1996 to 65 catches for 1,009 yards and another nine touchdowns in 1997. Besides Jackson and Alexander, the Ravens got big help from Jermaine Lewis, who grabbed 42 receptions for 648 yards and six touchdowns. Ryan Yarborough added 16 catches. Looking to 1998, I don't see big receiving numbers from Michael Jackson and Jermaine Lewis. Quarterback, Vinny Testaverde is likely to take a back seat to newly acquired Jim Harbaugh. I look for the Ravens to become more run-oriented with Harbaugh. Regardless, Derrick Alexander is gone, leaving via free-agency to Kansas City in the off-season, which will hurt Baltimore's passing game and obviously the receiving numbers for Michael Jackson and Jermaine Lewis who is likely to slide in as the #2 receiver with Alexander gone. The Ravens also added speedy Pat Johnson out of Oregon to the mix. Johnson was the Ravens #2 draft pick and could see time as a receiver and/or a return man.

TE: What a turnaround season for veteran Eric Green in 1997. Green struggled with knee problems in 1996 but, in 1997, exploded with 65 receptions for 601 yards and five touchdowns. Brian Kinchen chipped in 11 catches after producing 54 a year earlier when he filled in for the injured Green. In 1998, Green, re-signed in the offseason, should produce good numbers again.

QB: Coming off a 4,177-yard, 33-touchdown season in 1996, Vinny Testaverde was expected to do big things in 1997. Testaverde, however, was never able to duplicate the level of his 1996 performance. He finished the year nursing a knee injury and watching Eric Zeier run the team. On the season, Testaverde threw for 2,971 yards and 18 touchdowns, a far cry from a year earlier. In the offseason, the Ravens chose to go yet another direction by signing Jim Harbaugh. Harbaugh comes in as the starter. Don't expect the huge passing numbers for the Ravens that were evident when Testaverde was the starter. Harbaugh is not that kind of player. Meanwhile, Testaverde could be released, with Eric Zeier remaining the team's backup.

K: Matt Stover was having a pretty good season in 1997, hitting 26 of his first 29 (.897) field goal attempts. However, Stover ended the season by missing his last five tries. This has to have the Ravens very concerned as they look at possibilities for the upcoming 1998 season, thus for signing free agent Nelson Garner to battle for the job.

Overall: The 1998 Ravens will look very different. With Bam Morris not returning, Errict Rhett should be the mainstay of the Ravens' ground attack. This is not a bad thing since Rhett is a former 1,000-yard back with something to prove. I expect Rhett will get plenty of work, especially with the Ravens bringing in Jim Harbaugh at quarterback. Harbaugh, historically, is not a big numbers man, which also means the receiving group of Michael Jackson, Jermaine Lewis and tight end Eric Green will likely suffer statistically. Losing Derrick Alexander to free agency (Kansas City) will hurt.

Offseason Fantasy-Position Moves

	Arriving	From:		Departing	To:
QB	Jim Harbaugh	IND	WR	Derrick Alexander	KC
QB	Bill Ward Jr.	Free Agent			
RB	Errict Rhett	TB			
RB	Roosevelt Potts	MIA			
RB	Roddrick Newhouse	Free Agent			
RB	Ben Snell	Free Agent			
RB	Rob Robertson	Free Agent			
WR	Bryan Kish	Free Agent			
WR	Duane Gregory	Free Agent			
WR	MacArthur Johnson	Free Agent			
K	Nelson Garner	Free Agent			

BUFFALO BILLS

Home Stadium: Rich Stadium
Playing Surface: Astro Turf
Head Coach: Wade Phillips
1997 Record: 6-10

Levy Retires, Wade Phillips Steps in to Rebuild Bills

RB: With Thurman Thomas's career winding down, the Bills knew they had to make a move at running back for their future. They did just that in 1997 by making Antowain Smith, out of Houston, their No. 1 draft pick. The two backs pretty much split the duties with Smith getting just a little more work. On the season, Thomas finished with 643 rushing yards on 154 carries and added 208 more on 30 receptions while scoring only once. Smith, in his inaugural season, rushed for 840 yards, added 177 more on 28 receptions and scored eight times. Darick Holmes was almost a non-factor, chipping in only 106 rushing yards. Looking to 1998, I expect young Smith to expand his role under new head coach Wade Phillips. If Thomas stays on, he'll be in more of a supporting role. I wouldn't be surprised to see Smith top both the 1,000-yard mark and the 10-touchdown mark in 1998, especially with the Bills landing free agent Sam Gash in the offseason. Gash comes over from New England to open holes for Smith and Thomas.

WR: It seems that the Bills continue to believe that Andre Reed's next season is his last, but he continues to prove them wrong. Reed did this again in 1997. Despite hurting a shoulder late in the year and missing the season finale, Reed tied for the team lead with 60 receptions for 880 yards and scored five times. Reed's receiving mate, Quinn Early, rebounded to 60 receptions for 853 yards and five scores after a disappointing first year with Buffalo in 1996 when he grabbed only 49 receptions. Besides Reed and Early, second-year player Eric Moulds was the only other significant contributor, with 29 receptions but no touchdowns. Looking to 1998, I wonder if the Bills still think Andre Reed's career is over. If he's around, I expect another productive campaign. Quinn Early should also put up decent numbers but, with the quarterback situation still a question mark, don't look for either to put up numbers like those in the days of Jim Kelly. The Bills have added Kevin Williams via free agency from Arizona. Williams, who caught 20 passes for the Cardinals in 1997, may see action both as a receiver and kick returner. This is a team rebuilding its passing game and in need of a solid quarterback.

TE: Not a flashy, but a consistent, position for the Bills as they got contributions from both Lonnie Johnson and Jay Riemersma in 1997. Johnson finished with 41 catches for 340 yards and two touchdowns, while Riemersma finished with 26 catches for 208 yards and also two touchdowns. The Bills, under a new quarterback, will try to keep the tight ends involved again in 1998.

QB: A huge undertaking is continuing in Buffalo as the Bills try to fill the huge hole left by the retirement of Jim Kelly. In 1997, Kelly's first year of retirement, the Bills went with Todd Collins. Collins, their No.2 draft pick in 1995, was under incredible pressure to step in after the very successful Jim Kelly. Collins got the bulk of work in the Bills' 6-10 season. However, Billy Joe Hobert and Alex Van Pelt also saw action. Collins's 2,367 passing yards and 13 touchdown passes were not very satisfying to the Bills management, and Hobert and Van Pelt didn't show much either. After evaluating their 1997 campaign, the Bills are looking in a new direction in 1998. In the offseason, the Bills first signed CFL standout Doug Flutie. Flutie has already had a stint in the NFL that was less than impressive but, after his success in Canada, the Bills thought he was worth the chance. The Bills didn't stand pat there. They also traded for Rob Johnson from Jacksonville. Johnson showed great promise when he stepped in for injured Mark Brunell in 1997. Johnson cost the Bills their first- (ninth overall) and fourth-round picks in 1998. The battle is on for the starting spot. My money is on Rob Johnson, though Doug Flutie and Collins may have something to say about that. Alex Van Pelt is likely out of the picture following surgery on his throwing shoulder in the offseason. He is expected out until about training camp which would put him well behind his competition.

K: Veteran Steve Christie's 24 of 30 (.800) completions on field goal attempts in 1997 is likely to keep him around in 1998. However, the Bills must be concerned that three of his six misses came from inside 40 yards.

Overall: Looking to 1998, the Bills continue to evolve in the post-Jim Kelly era. Marv Levy's retirement now turns the team over to Wade Phillips. Phillips is faced with bettering a 6-10 team that is basically young and has to retool. The quarterback spot is the key, where Rob Johnson and Doug Flutie, both newcomers, battle for the top job. The pressure could put more emphasis on the running game, which should push young Antowain Smith's numbers as Thurman Thomas continues to be phased out. It could be another long winter in Buffalo.

Offseason Fantasy-Position Moves

	Arriving	From:		Departing	To:
QB	Doug Flutie	Free Agent/CFL	RB	Tim Tindale	CHI
QB	Rob Johnson	JAC			
RB	Sam Gash	NE			
WR	Kevin Williams	ARIZ			

Antowain Smith/Buffalo Bills

Fred Lane/Carolina Panthers

CAROLINA PANTHERS

Home Stadium: Ericsson Stadium
Playing Surface: Grass
Head Coach: Dom Capers
1997 Record: 7-9

Panthers Looking for the (Fred) Lane to Success

RB: After producing 1,120 rushing yards and six touchdowns in 1996 with Tim Biakabatuka out hurt, Anthony Johnson earned a shot at the starting role for 1997. Johnson did hold the starting job to open the 1997 season despite the return of a healthy Tim Biakabatuka. Johnson started out hot, rushing for 134 yards in the season opener against Washington. Slowly, however, a toe injury slowed his play. The Panthers opted to give their former first-round pick, Biakabatuka, another shot, along with undrafted and unheralded rookie Fred Lane. Biakabatuka seemed to be faring well, rushing for more than 100 yards once (a 104-yard performance against Atlanta in week nine) but it was Lane that turned some heads. Biakabatuka suffered a rib injury that gave Lane more opportunity and he took off. Over the season's last eight weeks, Lane rushed for 719 yards and scored five touchdowns. During that stint, he produced four 100-yard games. On the year, Lane finished with 809 rushing yards, Anthony Johnson with 358 and Biakabatuka with 299. The Panthers also got help from Scott Greene who rushed for 157 yards and added 277 more on 40 receptions. Looking to 1998, Lane has clearly stolen the show and the No.1 running back spot. He could post some big numbers, considering how strongly he finished 1997. The Panthers have also added fullback William Floyd via free agency from San Francisco. Floyd signed a four-year deal worth $6.2 million and should be a big help to the Panther running game, likely opening holes for Fred Lane.

WR: The Panthers, looking to the future, were hoping for productive years out of their young receivers in 1997. The hope was that 1996 second-round pick Muhsin Muhammad would step up. Also, the Panthers made Rae Carruth out of Colorado their No.1 draft pick. The Panthers elected not to re-sign veteran Mark Carrier, but instead added Ernie Mills via free agency from Pittsburgh. The hope was never realized. Muhammad, often injured, finished with only 27 receptions for 317 yards and no touchdowns. Carruth did demonstrate some speed and ability and led the club with 44 receptions for 545 yards and four touchdowns. Rocket Ismail chipped in 36 receptions and two scores. And Mark Carrier was eventually re-signed about three weeks into the season and tallied 33 receptions for 436 yards and two touchdowns in just nine games before a wrist injury forced him to miss the last four games. Looking to 1998, perhaps the Panthers have grown wiser. Carrier was re-signed quickly, to a two-year, $1.3 million deal. Now the Panthers can mix experience with their talented youth. With Ernie Mills gone via free agency to Dallas in the offseason, look for Muhammad to see action opposite Rae Carruth, with Carrier, Ismail and fourth-round pick Donald Hages out of Wisconsin chipping in playing time and production.

TE: In his second season as a Panther, Wesley Walls continued to prove what a valuable acquisition he was. In 1997, Walls recorded 58 receptions for 746 yards and six touchdowns. In his first year with Carolina in 1996, Walls produced 61 catches for 713 yards and 10 scores. Expect big numbers again in 1998.

QB: Perhaps, following a 12-4 season in 1996, the expectations were too high in 1997. Kerry Collins never got on track. Collins missed the first two games of the season with a battered jaw, suffered in the preseason. After returning, he just never got going, looked unpoised and wound up with a league-high 21 interceptions. His 2,124 passing yards and 11 touchdowns were less than impressive. Veteran Steve Beuerlein stepped in on a few occasions but he couldn't get Carolina on track either. Looking to 1998, the Panthers opted not to exercise the $6 million re-signing bonus for Collins, a free agent, which raises plenty of questions for the upcoming campaign.

K: Certainly one of the league's best, John Kasay proved his worth again in 1997. Kasay was good on 22 of 26 (.846) field goal attempts, with three of his four misses coming from beyond 50 yards. The problem for Kasay is the number of chances he got in 1997. The Panthers gave him only 26 field goal attempts in 1997, compared to 45 a year earlier. That's something they'll work to improve in 1998.

Overall: The Panthers' 7-9 finish in 1997 was a huge disappointment following their 12-4 1996 season. To rebound in 1998, they may be looking for new leadership under center. Kerry Collins struggled most of the year and was not awarded his scheduled re-signing bonus, so his days in Carolina may be numbered. The bright spot when looking to 1998, is undrafted and unheralded Fred Lane. In 1997, Lane came on to beat out Anthony Johnson and Tim Biakabatuka at running back, finishing with 809 rushing yards. His topping the 1,000-yard mark looks likely in 1998, especially with new fullback William Floyd leading the way.

Offseason Fantasy-Position Moves

	Arriving	From:		Departing	To:
QB	Dameyune Craig	Free Agent	WR	Ernie Mills	DALL
RB	William Floyd	SF			
WR	Thabiti Davis	Free Agent			
TE	Seth Thomas	Free Agent			

CHICAGO BEARS

Home Stadium: Soldier Field
Playing Surface: Grass
Head Coach: Dave Wannstedt
1997 Record: 4-12

Edgar Bennett Hopes to Keep 1998 Season 'Bear'able

RB: Raymont Harris and Rashaan Salaam are both pretty good running backs when they are healthy. The problem in 1997 was that the Bears could not keep either on the field all season. Salaam was lost for the season early on when he suffered a broken ankle in week three. Raymont Harris didn't break his leg until much later, and he missed just the last two games. Harris still managed to rush for 1,033 yards, catch 28 passes for 115 yards and score 10 times. Salaam finished with only 112 rushing yards. The Bears also got 319 rushing yards out of fourth-round pick Darnell Autry, who saw sporadic action as the year went on. With the uncertainty about both Harris and Salaam because of their injuries and their inconsistent performances, the Bears took action in the offseason. They signed Packer free agent Edgar Bennett to a four-year, $6.2-million deal. Bennett, too, was injured in 1997. He missed the entire year because of a knee injury. He is, however, said to be healthy now, and the Bears will likely use him as their main back. The Bears did also add Curtis Enis to the mix, making him their #1 draft pick. Picking Enis out of Penn State was a big surprise for the Bears who seemed to already be stockpiled at running back. Enis should push Bennett and either will run behind Ty Hallock, another offseason free-agent acquisition, from Jacksonville. This meant that the Bears would likely deal Salaam, and perhaps Harris also, now that they have their new-look backfield. Salaam was dealt to Miami, however after failing a physical, he was still considered likely to regain 100% status and return to the trading block for the Bears.

WR: Curtis Conway had just started to establish himself as one of the league's better receivers by grabbing 62 receptions and 12 touchdowns in 1995 and 81 receptions and 7 touchdowns in 1996. The 1997 season, however, was a huge setback. Conway missed the first six games of the year with a broken collarbone and later missed four more games with a shoulder injury. Playing in just seven games, Conway recorded only 30 receptions for 476 yards and one touchdown. With Conway ailing, the Bears hoped Bobby Engram would step up. Engram, however, caught the injury bug, too, missing five games with an ankle injury. Engram did record 45 receptions for 399 yards and two touchdowns in 11 games, but was a disappointment. The Bears did get good production out of veterans Ricky Proehl and Chris Penn. Proehl stepped in to lead the team with 58 catches for 753 yards and seven touchdowns. Penn recorded 47 receptions for 576 yards and three scores. Looking to 1998, the Bears hope to have Conway healthy all year. Proehl won't be back, however. He went to St. Louis, via free agency, in the off-season. That leaves the No.2 position for Engram, Penn and newly signed free agent Thomas Lewis. Lewis, a former first-round pick of the New York Giants missed most of 1997 with a toe injury. Don't be surprised to see Penn push hard to win the job.

TE: With Chris Gedney off to Arizona in 1997, Ryan Wetnight had the opportunity to step up his production. Wetnight did just that, more than doubling his production from a year earlier. Wetnight recorded 46 receptions (after 21 receptions in 1996) for 464 yards but only one touchdown. Keith Jennings chipped in 14 catches, and rookie second-round pick John Allred was a big disappointment with only eight catches. I look for Wetnight to again carry the bulk of the tight end duties for Chicago in 1998. The Bears did make Alonzo Mayes out of Oklahoma State their fourth-round draft pick. Mayes has a good down-field ability and long term potential but I don't think he'll make much of an impact as a rookie.

QB: I don't know what the Bears were thinking, but going into 1997, they acquired Rick Mirer from Seattle to improve their quarterback situation. Mirer is a former first-round pick who has struggled since his rookie season and, in most estimations, was turning into a bust. In defense of the Bears, there was uncertainty over Erik Kramer because of a herniated disc in his lower back. Kramer got the OK to return, and he beat out Mirer as the team's starter to begin the year. Mirer saw some action during the course of the year when Kramer was struggling but Kramer got the bulk of the work. On the year, Kramer threw for 3,011 yards and 14 touchdowns. Mirer threw for 420 yards and six scores. Looking to 1998, Kramer, who was an unrestricted free agent, has already been re-signed. There's little doubt he'll be the Bears' No.1 signal-caller.

K: Jeff Jaeger hit his first 13 field goal attempts last year but then struggled down the stretch, hitting only eight of his last 13 tries. That performance could worry the Bears as they face the upcoming season. Three of Jaeger's five misses were from inside 40 yards.

Overall: The Bears are retooled in the backfield for 1998 with Edgar Bennett and rookie Curtis Enis running behind Ty Hallock. Dave Wannstedt is hoping Bennett can perform the way he did when he was healthy in Green Bay. By re-signing quarterback Erik Kramer in the offseason, the Bears have apparently committed to him. Kramer should experience reasonable success if Curtis Conway can stay healthy all year. One big obstacle for Chicago, however, is facing the league's second-toughest schedule in 1998.

Offseason Fantasy-Position Moves

	Arriving	From:		Departing	To:
RB	Ty Hallock	JAC	RB	Tony Carter	NE
RB	Edgar Bennett	GB	WR	Ricky Proehl	STL
RB	Tim Tindale	BUF			
WR	Thomas Lewis	NYG			

CINCINNATI BENGALS

Home Stadium: Cinergy Field
Playing Surface: Astro Turf
Head Coach: Bruce Coslet
1997 Record: 7-9

'Boom'er Esiason Retires, Bengals Hope Blake
Can Again be 'Picken' Apart Defenses in '98

RB: With Garrison Hearst off to San Francisco in 1997, the Bengals needed insurance for the suspect knees of Ki-Jana Carter. The Bengals got that insurance by making Corey Dillon, out of Washington, their No.2 draft pick. Carter was the starter to begin the season in 1997 but as the season progressed, Dillon saw more and more playing time. By the halfway point of the season, Dillon had earned his shot as the starter and he never looked back. Over the season's last eight games, Dillon rushed for 933 yards and scored eight times. He was certainly one of the league's best runner during that stint. Overall Dillon recorded 1,129 rushing yards, 27 catches for another 259 yards and scored 10 times. Carter finished with 464 yards on the ground, 157 through the air on 21 catches, and seven touchdowns. The Bengals also got contributions from Eric Bienemy (97 rushing yards, 31 catches for 249 yards and two scores) and Brian Milne, who recorded only 32 rushing yards but had 23 catches for 138 yards and two touchdowns. The story, however, was Dillon and I believe that will again be the case in 1998. Phenomenal yardage and scoring numbers are possible for him.

WR: After his 100-reception, 1,180-yard, 12-touchdown performance in 1996, Carl Pickens faced huge expectations in 1997. Pickens did not start out having a great season, with only 52 receptions and five touchdowns in the first 12 games. He was not entirely to blame, however, as quarterback Jeff Blake was struggling. Pickens never got a chance to rebound late in the year because a groin injury knocked him out of the last four games. That was unfortunate timing for Pickens because that's about the time the Bengals turned their offense over to Boomer Esiason. Darnay Scott was perhaps the biggest beneficiary, producing 22 receptions for 423 yards and three touchdowns in the last three games. On the year, Scott produced only 54 receptions for 797 yards and five touchdowns. His work late in the year, however, convinced the Bengals to ante up a 3-year, $9-million deal following the season. Besides Pickens and Scott, the Bengals got 27 receptions and two touchdowns out of David Dunn and 16 catches and two scores out of James Hundon, most of which came when Esiason was hot. Looking to 1998, there's disappointment that Boomer Esiason has decided to retire to the TV booth. This leaves questions on how productive Pickens and Scott will be with Jeff Blake returning as the starter. At the #3 receiver look for newly acquired free agent Chris Doering (IND) to push David Dunn for playing time.

TE: Tony McGee's receptions production continues to drop. In 1995, he recorded 55 catches, 38 in 1996 and only 34 in 1997. That's the bad news. The good news is that McGee's touchdowns production jumped to six in

'97. Second-year player Marco Battaglia, a former second-round pick, continued to be less than impressive with only 12 catches. In 1998, McGee is hoping to increase his reception total and continue his scoring ways.

QB: In 1996, Jeff Blake threw for 24 touchdowns, 19 of which came over the season's last 10 games. That had many observers excited going into 1997. Blake, however, never recaptured that success and, after struggling much of the season, gave way to veteran Boomer Esiason. Blake finished with 2,145 passing yards and only eight touchdowns while playing in 11 games. Esiason, on the other hand, was very impressive. He threw for 1,478 yards and 13 touchdowns while playing in just seven games. The fun and success won't carry over to 1998, however, as Esiason has opted to give up on-the-field action for the TV booth. He signed with ABC to do Monday Night Football. This likely leaves the Bengals' starting job back in the hands of Jeff Blake. The Bengals hope that Blake can repeat the success he showed late in 1996, but if he can't, the Bengals have brought in free agent Paul Justin from Indianapolis to push the matter.

K: After a rocky start in 1997, Doug Pelfrey finished strong. Pelfrey missed five of his first nine kicks but rebounded to hit his last eight in a row. In his defense, two of his five misses were from beyond 50 yards. However, his 12 of 16 (.750) overall performance drew some attention. The Bengals have already signed free agent Jay Kirchoff to battle for the 1998 kicking chores.

Overall: After Boomer Esiason's remarkable 1997 finish, when he threw for 1,327 yards and 11 touchdowns in the last five games, it's disappointing that he has chosen the Monday Night TV booth for 1998. This throws the signal-calling back into the hands of Jeff Blake. For the Bengals' passing game to work, Blake has to regain his confidence and play the way he did late in 1996. Blake will get help from the return of a healthy Carl Pickens, along with Darnay Scott and good ground support from young Corey Dillon, who tore up the league the second half of 1997. One huge drawback will be the Bengals' schedule, which is the league's third toughest.

Offseason Fantasy-Position Moves

	Arriving	From:		Departing	To:
QB	Paul Justin	IND	RB	Scottie Graham	Free Agent
QB	Chad May	Free Agent			
RB	Brandon Bennett	Free Agent			
RB	Buddy Rogers	Free Agent			
WR	Chris Doering	IND			
WR	Damon Gibson	Free Agent			
WR	Alonzo Clayton	Free Agent			
K	Jay Kirchoff	Free Agent			

Corey Dillon/Cincinnati Bengals

Emmitt Smith/Dallas Cowboys

DALLAS COWBOYS

Home Stadium: Texas Stadium
Playing Surface: Texas Turf
Head Coach: Chan Gainey
1996 Record: 6-10

Cowboys give Switzer the Boot
Gainey has Tough Task of Turning Around 'America's' Team

RB: As the Cowboys continue to decline, so does Emmitt Smith. Or perhaps it's vice versa. As Smith's performance and numbers have dropped, so have the once-mighty Cowboys. Just two years earlier, in 1995, Smith had recorded 1,773 rushing yards and 25 touchdowns. In 1997, Smith's numbers continued their descent to 1,080 rushing yards, 234 receiving yards on 40 receptions and a meager four touchdowns. What a huge drop. Losing Daryl Johnston to a neck problem didn't help. Johnston missed the last 11 games of the season. Johnston had surgery in the offseason to remove a bulging disc in his neck and his return is uncertain. Smith and the Cowboys did get some help from Sherman Williams, who rushed for 468 yards and caught 21 passes for another 159 yards, scoring twice. Herschel Walker chipped in only 20 rushing yards but did catch 14 passes for 149 yards and also scored twice. Is Emmitt Smith done? Can he rebound to his days of glory? He can't do it alone. The offensive line has to improve and once again open holes consistently. The return of a healthy Daryl Johnston would help. Smith has to stay healthy. In the event Smith does not rebound or stay healthy the Cowboys added some insurance in the offseason by signing former Seattle Seahawk, Chris Warren. Warren had been released by Seattle following their signing of Ricky Watters. Coming to Dallas, Warren adds immediate depth to the running game. Warren was the Seahawks all-time leading rusher and once was considered among the league's elite backs. So look for Smith to get the call but I'm sure Warren will see action dependent on Smith's health and performance. Also the Cowboys face the league's eighth-easiest schedule which should help the Cowboys turn things around.

WR: With the Cowboys' running game struggling, the passing game obviously came under more pressure. For Michael Irvin, this meant he'd have to try to carry more of the offensive load. Although the Cowboys brought in Anthony Miller to help open up the offense, Irvin was the key. Irvin put together decent numbers: 75 receptions for 1,180 yards and nine touchdowns. Miller did not live up to the Cowboys' hopes. Despite grabbing four touchdowns in the first five weeks, he finished the year with only 46 catches for 645 yards and those four touchdowns. He did not score after week five. Strepfret Williams chipped in 30 catches for 308 yards and one touchdown. The passing game really couldn't hold up the offense as the Cowboys struggled all year. Looking to 1998, the Cowboys will again expect big things from Michael Irvin. The big question will be, who will help him. The Cowboys already have brought in Ernie Mills to compete for work. Mills did not do much in Carolina in 1997, recording only 11 receptions, but he has potential. Otherwise, Williams or little known Billy

Davis will be expected to step up.

TE: The retirement of Jay Novacek opened up the starting job. The battle was between Eric Bjornson and young David LaFleur, the 6-foot-7 first-round draft choice of the Cowboys. Bjornson had the starting job until he injured his leg, forcing him to miss the last three games of the year. On the year, Bjornson recorded 47 receptions for 442 yards but failed to score in the 13 games in which he saw action. La Fleur finished with 18 catches and 11 of those came in the last four games, along with his two touchdowns. Look for the Cowboys to utilize both Bjornson and La Fleur and to use them at the same time occasionally in 1998.

QB: Troy Aikman threw for 3,283 yards and 19 touchdowns in 1997. He began the year by throwing for four touchdowns against Pittsburgh. As the season wore on, however, he was asked to do too much when the running game stalled. Actually his yardage and touchdown numbers weren't bad for him. He's normally been able to rely on the ground game. Looking to 1998, the key for the Cowboys is to get their running game back on track and not rely so heavily on Aikman's arm. About 3,000 yards and 15 to 20 touchdowns is what I expect from him in 1998.

K: Richie Cunningham, who beat out a number of no-name free agents to win the Dallas kicking job, didn't disappoint the Cowboys. Cunningham hit a remarkable 34 of 37 (.919) field goal attempts in 1997. There's good reason to believe the Cowboys will want him around for years to come.

Overall: The Cowboys' slide continued in 1997 as they went 6-10. Jerry Jones finally ousted head coach Barry Switzer after the season. For a replacement, Jones hired Pittsburgh Steelers offensive coordinator Chan Gailey. Gailey's task won't be easy. He has to revitalize "America's Team." The components are still there. They're just older. The big three—Emmitt Smith, Troy Aikman and Michael Irvin—have to regain the desire and determination they had just a short time ago. They can't do it alone. Their supporting cast has been whittled away some. I don't look for a huge turnaround but facing the league's eighth-easiest schedule may help them improve.

Offseason Fantasy-Position Moves

	Arriving	From:		Departing	To:
RB	Chris Warren	SEAT	QB	Wade Wilson	Released
WR	Ernie Mills	CAR			
WR	Jimmy Oliver	SD			

DENVER BRONCOS

Home Stadium: Mile High Stadium
Playing Surface: Grass
Head Coach: Mike Shanahan
1997 Record: 12-4

Broncos Bucking for Another Super Win!

RB: Terrell Davis just got better in 1997. Despite missing the season finale with a shoulder injury, Davis rushed for a whopping 1,750 yards, added 287 yards on 42 catches and scored 15 times. Davis's performance included starting the year with four consecutive 100-yard games. He had ten 100-yard games in all and two 200-yard performances. Davis and the Broncos got great help from the blocking and 11 receptions of Howard Griffith. Vaughn Hebron chipped in 222 rushing yards and Derek Loville had 124. But the main show was Davis. Those who jumped on Davis at your fantasy draft had to be happy, regardless of the scoring method you use. Though he tailed off toward the end of the season with the troublesome shoulder, Davis returned for the playoffs and was a key factor in the Broncos' terrific Super Bowl run. Looking to 1998, I look for plenty more highlight films of the hardworking Davis, who will continue to push for very high numbers.

WR: With Anthony Miller off to Dallas in 1997, the Broncos were looking for a new go-to receiver. The Broncos brought in Willie Green from Carolina via free agency, but many felt Rod Smith would finally get the chance to show his stuff. Smith had been with the Broncos but hadn't done much. In 1996, Smith recorded 16 receptions for 237 yards and scored twice, seeing action in eight games. He got his chance in 1997 and he took advantage. Smith opened the year with two 100-yard games in the first three weeks and scored four times in the first four weeks. He continued to develop as the season wore on, finishing with 70 receptions for 1,180 yards and 12 touchdowns. Opposite Smith most of the year was big Ed McCaffrey. McCaffrey was bothered by a hamstring injury late in the year but finished with 45 catches for 590 yards and eight touchdowns. Green, the free-agent acquisition, finished with only 19 receptions and two touchdowns. Looking to 1998, we now know who the Broncos' go-to guy is. Smith should have another big year but much depends on whether John Elway returns, now that he's finally won a Super Bowl. McCaffrey remains an excellent target, especially because of his height, which means 7-10 touchdowns is again a possibility for him. And the Broncos have added another option in first-round draft pick Marcus Nash out of Tennessee. Nash grabbed 76 receptions in 1997 for 1,170 yards while scoring 13 times. He is a receiver that isn't afraid to go over the middle and will in time be a nice contributor to the Bronco offense.

TE: It was another solid season for Shannon Sharpe in 1997. Although his touchdown level dropped from 10 in 1996 to three last year, Sharpe still recorded 72 catches for 1,107 yards. Those are remarkable numbers for a tight end, and numbers that I believe he'll be near again in 1998 if John Elway is still around.

QB: To have such a great career as John Elway has but not win a Super Bowl was obviously disappointing. But in 1997, Elway's fourth try became the charm as the Broncos beat Green Bay. During the regular season, Elway put up excellent numbers, throwing for 3,635 yards and 27 touchdowns. It seems in recent years that Elway's numbers have grown. In his younger years, he rarely threw for 20-some touchdown passes. The question is, with a Super Bowl win finally under his belt, does he have any reason to return? And if he returns, will he have the fire that pushed him for all those years? Time will tell but I, for one, was happy to see him finally complete his "Super" quest in 1997. Who's waiting in the wings? It was Jeff Lewis but he suffered a torn anterior cruciate ligament in a pickup basketball game in the offseason and was presumed to be out four to six months. That makes him questionable for training camp. His is an injury we'll keep an eye on. Meanwhile, the Broncos signed free agent Doug Nussmeier from New Orleans. Nussmeier threw for 182 yards and no touchdowns with the Saints in 1997. Bubby Brister will likely open camp as the No.2 quarterback, unless Lewis is ready to go.

K: When a team wins a Super Bowl, you assume that everything went pretty well for it. In 1997, things did go well for Denver, but kicker Jason Elam had his struggles. Elam finished the year hitting 26 of 36 (.722) field goal chances. Of his 10 misses, only two were from farther than 50 yards and that may concern the Broncos as they look to 1998.

Overall: John Elway looked more relieved than happy following the Broncos' Super Bowl win over Green Bay in January. After four tries for Elway, five for Denver, the Broncos finally got the Super Bowl win. Things surely don't look bad for a return visit for Denver. Terrell Davis has become one of the league's elite backs. Receivers Rod Smith, Ed McCaffrey and tight end Shannon Sharpe are a talented cast. But how about John Elway? With a ring on his hand, does he have the drive to try to do it again? The parts for another big productive season are there. Only time will tell if the desire returns with them.

Offseason Fantasy-Position Moves

	Arriving	From:	Departing	To:
QB	Doug Nussmeier	NO		

Terrell Davis/Denver Broncos

DETROIT LIONS

Home Stadium: Pontiac Silverdome
Playing Surface: Astro Turf
Head Coach: Bobby Ross
1997 Record: 9-7

Ross Put Roar Back into Lions' Barry Sanders

RB: How would new head coach Bobby Ross use Barry Sanders? Every fantasy football buff wanted and needed to know that going into 1997. I hope you didn't panic when Sanders only produced 53 rushing yards in the first two weeks of 1997. From that point on, Sanders rolled off an incredible 14-game streak of 100 rushing yards or more. On the season, Sanders rushed for a whopping 2,053 yards, added 305 more on 33 receptions and scored 14 times. Wow! So what had Wayne Fontes been thinking? Sanders ran, rumbled, juked and entertained all year. He was a joy to watch. Fourteen 100-yard games, two of more than 200 yards. He could easily have scored more than 14 touchdowns, too, since Tommy Vardell plowed over with six 1-yard touchdown runs. Vardell rushed for only 122 yards and caught 16 passes for another 218. The story, however, was Barry Sanders. He certainly proved that he is not only getting older but, when given the chance, he's getting better, too. I can't wait to see what 1998 brings. Perhaps he won't have the numbers of 1997, but they'll be pretty hefty, I'm sure.

WR: With Barry Sanders running wild on the ground, you would think that something had to drop and that it would likely be the passing game. Surprisingly, however, the Lions' top receivers fared pretty well statistically. Herman Moore again topped the 100-reception mark with 104 catches for 1,293 yards and eight touchdowns. Moore finished with six 100-yard games. On the other side, with Brett Perriman off to Kansas City and then Miami, Johnnie Morton got more playing time and boosted his numbers. He went from 55 receptions in 1996 to 80 receptions for 1,057 yards and six touchdowns. The Lions rewarded Morton in the offseason by re-signing him to a 5-year, $15-million deal. Despite the huge success of Barry Sanders, the Lion receivers fared well in 1997 and should again in 1998 as long as Scott Mitchell continues to get them the football. I look for Moore to again reach or at least approach the 100-reception plateau while Morton closes the gap as he matures. The Lions have also added to their receiving arsenal by making Germaine Crowell out of Virginia their #2 draft selection. Crowell, at just over 6' 3", has good hands and will be a nice addition to the Lion receiving cast.

TE: David Sloan returned to the Lions in 1997 after he missed most of 1996 with a knee injury. There had been much talk that he would be a big part of their offense. That didn't happen. He finished with only 29 catches for 264 yards and no touchdowns. Veteran Pete Metzelaars chipped in 17 catches for 144 yards. Pete Chryplewicz recorded only three catches but caught the only touchdown scored by a Lion tight end. The Lions still just don't use their tight ends often. It would not surprise me, however, to see David Sloan's numbers expand in 1998.

Barry Sanders/Detroit Lions

QB: Since Scott Mitchell peaked in 1995 with his 4,338-yard, 32-touchdown performance, he's had back-to-back disappointing seasons. In 1996, slowed by a rib injury, Mitchell produced 2,917 passing yards and 17 touchdowns. Last year, despite being healthy most of the year, Mitchell produced 3,484 passing yards and only 19 touchdowns. Yes, this is partly due to the phenomenal year Barry Sanders had on the ground. However, Mitchell has not played with any consistency. He may find himself battling to hang onto his job if he doesn't improve quickly. The Lions added young Jim Miller in the offseason, possibly hoping to groom him for the future and later made Charlie Batch out of Eastern Michigan their #2 draft pick.

K: The Lions got a very solid season from kicker Jason Hanson in 1997. Hanson hit 26 of 30 (.867) field goal attempts, with two of his four misses coming from farther than 50 yards. It was a nice rebound season for him, following his very disappointing 1996 campaign when he hit only 12 of 17 (.706) tries. I look for his continued success in 1998, now that he's back on track.

Overall: Looking to 1998, the Lions again will display the league's best back in Barry Sanders. Sanders's incredible 1997 numbers will be hard to match or even come close to, especially since Detroit faces the league's fifth-toughest schedule. Sanders will need more support from Scott Mitchell and his aerial attack, led by Herman Moore and Johnnie Moore. The keys for the Lions will be Sanders staying healthy and Mitchell regaining some consistency. Head coach Bobby Ross is doing a good job of getting the Lions back on track.

Offseason Fantasy-Position Moves

	Arriving	From:		Departing	To:
QB	Jim Miller	ATL	RB	Glyn Milburn	GB
WR	Tutu Atwell	Free Agent			

GREEN BAY PACKERS
Home Stadium: Lambeau Field
Playing Surface: Grass
Head Coach: Mike Holmgren
1997 Record: 13-3

The 'Pack Was Back' in the Super Bowl but 'Favre' from Winners

RB: Losing your leading rusher of two straight seasons might send most teams into a huge tailspin but not the Green Bay Packers. The Packers lost Edgar Bennett for the season with a knee injury before the 1997 season began. After thinking about using Aaron Hayden, signed in the offseason; Travis Jervey or Chris Darkins, the Packers elected to expand Dorsey Levens's role. Levens became the Packers' main back in 1997, with William Henderson at fullback most of the time. Levens was superb, giving the Packers every bit of the running game they needed. On the year, Levens exceeded expectations. He rushed for 1,435 yards, added 370 more on 53 receptions and scored 12 times, seven on the ground and five through the air. Aaron Hayden chipped in 148 rushing yards. William Henderson added 113 yards rushing, but was much more effective receiving with 41 receptions for 367 yards. Both players scored once. Looking to 1998, there will certainly be plenty more of Dorsey Levens. Edgar Bennett, although healthy, saw the writing on the wall and signed a free-agent deal with Chicago in the offseason, leaving Levens to again be the Packers main ground weapon.

WR: After both of their primary receivers missed significant playing time in 1996, the Packers were hoping to keep both Robert Brooks (knee) and Antonio Freeman (arm) healthy for all of 1997. For the most part, they did. There was some concern over Brooks's return from the knee injury, but 60 receptions, 1,010 yards and seven touchdowns later, that concern disappeared. Freeman was even better than that. He recorded 81 receptions for 1,243 yards and 12 touchdowns. In addition to this talented duo, the Packers got a little help from Derrick Mayes, who chipped in 18 catches but no touchdowns. They also got five total receptions, two for touchdowns, out of the trio of Don Beebe, Terry Mickens and Bill Schroeder. Looking to 1998, I expect more of the same, with both Freeman and Brooks putting up significant numbers and likely topping both the 1,000-yard mark and the 10-touchdown plateau, as Brett Favre's favorite targets.

TE: Following the Packers' Super Bowl victory in January of 1997, tight end Keith Jackson retired. Jackson had caught 40 passes for 505 yards and 10 touchdowns during that season. Jackson's retirement left an obvious vacancy. In 1997, Mark Chmura stepped back into that role, a role he had held in 1995 when he produced ProBowl numbers. Chmura put up decent numbers in 1997, recording 38 receptions for 417 yards and six touchdowns. Jeff Thomason chipped in nine receptions for 115 yards while scoring once. Looking to 1998, Chmura will retain the bulk of the tight end duties and, as a target of Brett Favre's, he could easily expand his numbers.

QB: What a run it's been for Brett Favre statistically. He may have lost the 1997 Super Bowl but he again produced great numbers for fantasy football participants. The 1997 season was the fourth straight of 30-plus touchdowns for him. On the year, Favre threw for 3,867 yards and 35 touchdowns. What's in store for 1998? With both Robert Brooks and Antonio Freeman back healthy, the 4,000-yard, 40-touchdown marks are well within his reach.

K: The Packers made Penn State standout Brett Conway their No.3 draft pick in 1997. Conway was the only kicker chosen in the draft. Once training camp started, however, he struggled with an injured thigh muscle and began losing his confidence. The Packers eventually chose to go with undrafted Ryan Longwell. Longwell first came on as a temporary fix but won the job and went on to hit a solid 24 of 30 (.800) field goal tries. His performance will keep him in a Packer uniform in 1998 and longer, signing a 3 year deal in the offseason.

Overall: Losing the Super Bowl to Denver was, perhaps, something of a wakeup call for the Packers. I think many people, including the Packers, believed they were invincible. They weren't, obviously, and now maybe they are hungry again. They certainly have the weapons. Dorsey Levens became an every-down back in 1997 and just exploded statistically. Brett Favre's 30-plus touchdowns and near 4,000 yards have become norms. Receivers Antonio Freeman and Robert Brooks are both healthy and ready to produce. Look for another big season from the Green and Gold in 1998 as the Packers have something to prove.

Offseason Fantasy-Position Moves

	Arriving	From:		Departing	To:
RB	Glyn Milburn	DET	RB	Edgar Bennett	CHI
WR	Mike Bowman	Free Agent	QB	Steve Bono	STL
WR	Delonte Perkins	Free Agent			
TE	Tyrone Davis	Free Agent			

Dorsey Levens/Green Bay Packers

INDIANAPOLIS COLTS
Home Stadium: RCA Dome
Playing Surface: Astro Turf
Head Coach: Jim Mora
1997 Record: 3-13

Colts Looking for a Turnaround 'Mora' Less

RB: After the 1996 season, when a foot injury slowed him, Marshall Faulk returned to the 1,000-yard club in 1997. Faulk's 1,054 rushing yards marked the third time in four years he has surpassed 1,000 yards. In addition to his 1,054 rushing yards, Faulk recorded 47 receptions for another 471 yards and scored eight times. Faulk got better as the season wore on. He didn't rush for more than 100 yards in any of the first nine games, but then he hit the 100-yard mark four times in the last seven weeks. He also scored four times in the season's last three weeks. Supporting Faulk were Zack Crockett, who rushed for 300 yards and added 112 more on 15 receptions while scoring once, and Lamont Warren, who rushed for only 80 yards but caught 20 passes for 192 yards and scored once on the ground. Cliff Groce chipped in 66 rushing yards. Looking to 1998, the Colts have to be pleased with how Faulk finished the 1997 season when he was getting better play from his offensive line. If he stays healthy, I look for him to gain another 1,000-1,200 rushing yards and, possibly, top double-digits in touchdowns.

WR: For the second straight season, Marvin Harrison led the Colts in receptions. Harrison recorded 73 catches for 866 yards and scored six times. Not far behind was Sean Dawkins. Dawkins, in fact, might have topped Harrison's reception mark had he not missed two games early in the year with stomach trouble. On the season, Dawkins recorded 68 catches for 804 yards and scored twice. Besides the Colts' big two, they got 26 receptions for 329 yards and three touchdowns out of Aaron Bailey and 25 receptions for 253 yards and one score out of Brian Stablein. Looking to 1998, the Colts have a potential 1,000-yard receiver in Marvin Harrison. Sean Dawkins signed with New Orleans in the offseason. With Jim Harbaugh off to Baltimore, perhaps his replacement—rookie first-round pick Peyton Manning—will provide more passing consistency to help Harrison reach that plateau. However, until the picture for the Colts' 1998 offense comes clearer, I expect somewhere between 800 and 1,000 yards rushing from Marvin Harrison and six to eight scores. And with Brian Stablein already off to New England via free agency and Sean Dawkins not returning, look for newly acquired Torrance Small to step in and push Aaron Bailey and rookie draft picks Jerome Pathon out of Washington and E.G. Green out of Florida State. Pathon was the Colts second-round and Green their third-round draft choice.

TE: After two straight seasons of exactly 42 receptions and four touchdowns, Ken Dilger's numbers took a slight dip in 1997. Dilger finished with 27 receptions for 380 yards and three touchdowns. The Colts also got 10 receptions out of Marcus Pollard and three from Scott Slutzker. Dilger, however, is the Colts' primary tight end. In 1998, he will hope to improve his reception and touchdown totals. Pollard, meanwhile, left for Philadelphia in the offseason as a free agent.

QB: Bothered by hand and ankle injuries, Jim Harbaugh was forced to miss a number of games in 1997. However, even when he was healthy, his performance was not very impressive. He had just one 300-yard game all year and only three 200-yard performances. Because of Harbaugh's injuries and ineffectiveness, the Colts turned to Paul Justin and Kelly Holcomb. On the year, Harbaugh finished with only 2,060 passing yards and 10 touchdowns in 12 games. Following the season, the Colts dealt Harbaugh to Baltimore for the Ravens' third- and fourth-round picks. This leaves the Colts' quarterback vacancy for highly-touted rookie first-round draft pick Peyton Manning out of Tennessee. The Colts made Manning the #1 overall pick of draft and have invested heavily into their present and future. With Harbaugh already gone and Justin also departed via free-agency to Cincinatti, Manning has the opportunity to step right in and make an impact.

K: After missing three out of his first four field goal attempts in the season opener in 1997, Cary Blanchard straightened himself out. On the season, Blanchard hit 32 of 41 (.780) field goals. Even so, Blanchard is going to have competition going into 1998. The Colts have signed CFL standout Mike Vanderjagt. Vanderjagt kicked last year for the CFL champion Toronto Argonauts.

Overall: After finishing 3-13 in 1997, the Colts certainly need to go in a new direction. They've already made a couple of moves. The Colts parted ways with head coach Lindy Infante and brought in former New Orleans Saint head coach Jim Mora. Mora was a winner in New Orleans but always struggled at playoff time. The Colts, at this point, just want to get back to the playoffs. The Colts also dealt quarterback Jim Harbaugh to Baltimore. This means the Colts will have new leadership on the field as well with rookie, #1 draft pick Peyton Manning stepping in. After going 3-13, any move is a good move. The Colts are just looking to shake things up, they hope in the right direction. One highlight in 1997 was the play of running back Marshall Faulk, which the Colts hope will carry over to 1998.

Offseason Fantasy-Position Moves

	Arriving	From:		Departing	To:
QB	Bill Musgrave	Free Agent	WR	Brian Stablein	NE
RB	Charles Kirty	Free Agent	WR	Chris Doering	CIN
WR	Torrance Small	STL	WR	Marcus Pollard	PHIL
WR	Marlon Evans	Free Agent	WR	Sean Dawkins	NO
WR	Peter McFadden	Free Agent	QB	Jim Harbaugh	BALT
TE	Melvin Dearsall	Free Agent	QB	Paul Justin	CIN
K	Mike Vanderjagt	Free Agent			

Keenan McCardell/Jacksonville Jaguars

JACKSONVILLE JAGUARS
Home Stadium: Jacksonville Municipal Stadium
Playing Surface: Grass
Head Coach: Tom Coughlin
1997 Record: 11-5

No Longer a 'Means' to an End, Natrone Returns to San Diego
Stewart and Rookie Taylor Likely to Get Their Shots

RB: Although he led the team in rushing, I don't think Natrone Means was the most impressive back for Jacksonville in 1997. Means finished the year with a respectable 823 rushing yards on 244 carries and scored nine touchdowns, missing two games with an ankle injury. James Stewart, who carried the ball only 136 times, recorded 555 rushing yards, added 336 more on 41 receptions and also scored nine times, with five touchdowns in one game. Means never had a 100-yard game; Stewart had one. What does this mean going into 1998? Well, Means has departed, via free agency, for his former team, the San Diego Chargers and a six-year, $19.1-million deal. This leaves the main tailback spot open for Stewart, but there's always been talk that he's not big enough to carry an every-down load. Because of the uncertainty of Stewart's durability the Jaguars made Fred Taylor out of Florida their #1 draft pick. Taylor, who rushed for just under 1,300 yards and scored 13 times for Florida in 1997, will push Stewart for playing time and statistical production in 1998.

WR: Last season was another solid one for the Jaguars' dynamic duo of receivers—Keenan McCardell and Jimmy Smith. Once again, neither receiver had great touchdown numbers (McCardell scored five times and Smith four) but their reception and yardage numbers were fabulous. Much like the previous year, McCardell recorded 85 catches for 1,164 yards and his five touchdowns. He had four 100-yard games and two more in the 90-yard range. A year earlier, in 1996, his numbers were 85 catches for 1,129 yards and three touchdowns. Smith recorded 82 receptions for 1,324 yards and four touchdowns, including six 100-yard games and two more in the 90s. A year earlier, he produced 83 receptions for 1,244 yards and seven scores. Jacksonville got great consistency from both. Willie Jackson also chipped in 17 catches for 206 yards and two touchdowns. Looking to 1998, you can't ignore the consistency of both McCardell and Smith. Smith, will with certainty remain with the Jaguars for quite some time. He had his contract extended in the offseason. He receives $19 million over the next six years. If you're in a yardage fantasy league, both Smith and McCardell are good candidates. For scoring leagues, the Jaguars prefer to score on the ground. I'm looking for another 1,000 to 1,200 yards out of both in 1998 and I expect at least one of them to top the six-touchdown plateau.

TE: Pete Mitchell's receptions took a dip in 1997 but his touchdowns jumped up. After producing 41 and 53 receptions in 1995 and 1996, respectively, Mitchell dropped to 35 catches for 380 yards in 1997. Mitchell had recorded two and one touchdowns in 1995 and 1996, respectively, but jumped to four scores in 1997. The added scoring is welcome to the

Jaguars. In addition to Mitchell, the Jaguars also got 18 catches out of Ty Hallock, one touchdown and eight catches out of Derek Brown, and one score and five catches out of Damon Jones. Looking to 1998, Hallock went to Chicago as a free agent and it seems unlikely the Jaguars will bring back Derek Brown. This leaves Pete Mitchell to expand both his reception and scoring numbers as the team's main force at tight end.

QB: Despite missing the first two games of the year with a knee injury, Mark Brunell returned to put up respectable numbers. On the year, Brunell threw for 3,281 yards and 18 touchdowns. He also ran for 257 yards and scored twice on the ground. Perhaps the biggest thing the Jaguars discovered while Brunell was out with his knee injury was that backup Rob Johnson was a player. Johnson played extremely well in the preseason and was 20 of 24 for 294 yards and two touchdowns in the regular-season opener against Baltimore. The bad news, however, is that in displaying his talent and potential, Johnson became a sought-after commodity. In the offseason, the Jaguars took advantage of his appeal and dealt him to Buffalo for the Bills' first- (ninth overall) and fourth-round picks. Looking to 1998, as long as Mark Brunell is healthy, the Jaguars are fine. If he gets hurt, there's now some uncertainty at backup.

K: Mike Hollis gave another solid performance in 1997. After hitting 30 of 36 (.833) field goal tries in 1996, Hollis followed that up with a 31 of 36 (.861) effort in 1997. Those performances should keep him around in 1998.

Overall: The Jaguars, under Tom Coughlin, continue to play well, improving their record from 9-7 in 1996 to 11-5 last year. Despite losing Natrone Means in the offseason to San Diego, James Stewart is still around. Stewart has shown some real explosiveness though there remains some uncertainty about his durability which is why the Jaguars made Fred Taylor their #1 draft pick. Taylor will push Stewart for work. Through the air, lefty Mark Brunell continues to be impressive especially because he has very consistent and underrated receivers in Keenan McCardell, Jimmy Smith and tight end Pete Mitchell. This is a young, well-coached team that continues to improve.

Offseason Fantasy-Position Moves

Arriving	From:		Departing	To:
		RB	Natrone Means	SD
		RB/TE	Ty Hallock	CHI
		QB	Rob Johnson	BUF

KANSAS CITY CHIEFS

Home Stadium: Arrowhead Stadium
Playing Surface: Grass
Head Coach: Marty Schottenheimer
1997 Record: 13-3

Allen will no Longer be 'Chief' Scorer
Adding Alexander Will Help

RB: Every year, it seems, we deem the last for ageless Marcus Allen. But 1997 certainly wasn't it. Allen no longer gets large yardage numbers but he continues to amaze us with his nose for the goal line. In 1997, Allen was close to leading the Chiefs in rushing yards with 505, and he led the Chiefs, by far, with 11 touchdowns. Greg Hill led the Chiefs' rushing-by-committee backfield with a meager 550 yards on the ground while adding 12 catches for 126 yards but he failed to score. Next was Kimble Anders with 397 rushing yards, but he was actually more effective through the air with 59 catches for 453 yards while scoring twice. Donnell Bennett chipped in 369 rushing yards and one touchdown. In 1998, Greg Hill, who is an unrestricted free-agent, might be gone, while the veteran Marcus Allen will be with certainty. Allen opted to retire to the TV booth in the offseason, believing his body should no longer take the punishment. If Hill now leaves and the Chiefs don't bring in a prominent back, look for more rushing by committee. Donnell Bennett is the most likely bet to begin the year as the team's main back and with Marcus Allen now retired, the Chiefs will need a new go to guy around the goal line. As the preseason approaches we'll get a better feel for just how the Chiefs will handle the upcoming season on the ground though it looks like Bennett will likely team with Kimble Anders in the backfield. The Chiefs also gave themselves another option by making Rashann Shehee out of Washington their third-round draft choice. Shehee will likely be a third-down option, possessing good hands and not having the build to be an every-down back.

WR: When your leading receiver has only 49 receptions in a season, perhaps it's time to look for help. Chris Penn led Kansas City in 1996 with 49 catches, so the Chiefs went looking for help. They brought in both Andre Rison and Brett Perriman. Rison, who has jumped from team to team in recent years after making a big name for himself in Atlanta, surprised many with his performance. On the year, Rison recorded 72 receptions for 1,092 yards and scored seven times. Perriman, who averaged more than 100 receptions in 1995 and 1996 while he was with Detroit, struggled in Kansas City. He recorded only six receptions, playing in just three games before he was released. He was later signed by Miami. With Perriman unproductive, the Chiefs turned to Lake Dawson, but he managed only 21 catches and two touchdowns. Danan Hughes and Tamarick Vanover were also less than impressive, both recording only seven catches. Looking to 1998, the Chiefs are happy to have Rison back. In fact, they went looking for help so that teams couldn't double-team him. They got that help by signing Derrick Alexander away from the Baltimore Ravens for $17 million over five years. The addition of Alexander, who recorded 65 catches for 1,009 yards and nine touchdowns for Baltimore in 1997, gives the Chiefs their best receiving tandem in years. With Alexander and Rison in place, the Chiefs can now be assured of a solid passing game to back up their running attack.

TE: Despite making Tony Gonzalez their No.1 draft pick in 1997, the Chiefs also lured Ted Popson away from the San Francisco 49ers. The two put on a good fight for recognition and playing time. By season's end, their numbers were almost identical. Popson recorded 35 receptions for 320 yards and two touchdowns; Gonzalez recorded 33 receptions for 368 yards and two scores also. Having two talented tight ends is certainly a big plus for the Chiefs, though I believe they'll try to develop young Gonzalez more in 1998.

QB: The Chiefs, looking to their future, lured Elvis Grbac away from the San Francisco 49ers in 1997. Grbac won the starting role, as expected. He was not setting the world on fire but he was gaining experience and confidence until he injured his shoulder, which knocked him out of five games. In stepped Rick Gannon, who played so well that many questioned whether, when Grbac returned, Gannon shouldn't have kept the starting job. The Chiefs and head coach Marty Schottenheimer went back to Grbac, believing he is their future. On the year, Grbac threw for 1,943 yards and 11 touchdowns, playing in 10 games. He'll easily improve those numbers in 1998 as he matures, stays healthy and uses his new receiving corps, which now includes Derrick Alexander alongside Andre Rison.

K: It's hard to find a flaw in a kicker who hits a phenomenal 26 of 27 (.963) field goal attempts. That's exactly what veteran Pete Stoyanovich did for Kansas City in 1997. His only miss came from 48 yards.

Overall: Looking to 1998, perhaps there's some question about Kansas City's running game. Greg Hill, long thought to be the Chiefs' main back of the future, is no longer held in that regard. The Chiefs may continue to spread the wealth in the running game especially with ageless Marcus Allen opting to retire in the offseason. The bright spot may be the Chiefs' passing game. In adding free agent Derrick Alexander to Andre Rison and tight ends Ted Popson and Tony Gonzalez, the Chiefs may have something, especially as Elvis Grbac matures.

Offseason Fantasy-Position Moves

	Arriving	From:		Departing	To:
RB	James Bostic	Free Agent	RB	Marcus Allen	Retired
WR	Derrick Alexander	BALT	TE	Derrick Walker	Released
WR	Shawn Washington	Free Agent			
WR	Kevin Huntley	Free Agent			
WR	Toussant Waterman	Free Agent			
TE	Brian Gaine	Free Agent			
TE	Jim Moore	Free Agent			
TE	Chad Flick	Free Agent			
TE	Damien Johnson	Free Agent			

Andre Rison/Kansas City Chiefs

Karim Abdul-Jabbar/Miami Dolphins

MIAMI DOLPHINS

Home Stadium: Pro Player Stadium
Playing Surface: Grass
Head Coach: Jimmy Johnson
1997 Record: 9-7

Dolphins Show Subtle Improvement
Starting to Swim under Johnson

RB: After rushing for 1,116 yards as a rookie in 1996, Karim Abdul-Jabbar and the Dolphins were looking to improve his numbers in 1997. The yardage numbers, however, suffered. Abdul-Jabbar produced only two 100-yard games and finished the year with only 892 rushing yards. He did add 261 more yards on 29 receptions. The one category he did improve in was in touchdowns. Abdul-Jabbar finished the year with 16 touchdowns, after scoring 11 as a rookie in 1996. Fifteen of the 16 touchdowns came on the ground and all were from 10 yards or less. In addition to Abdul-Jabbar, the Dolphins got 180 rushing yards and seven receptions for 70 yards and a couple of scores out of Irving Spikes. Jerris McPhail chipped in 146 rushing yards and became a force out of the backfield with 34 receptions for 262 yards and two touchdowns. Bernie Parmalee rushed for only 59 yards but added 301 more on 28 receptions and scored once. Late in the year, the Dolphins gambled by signing Lawrence Phillips after his release from the Rams. Phillips, a former No.1 pick of the Rams who has struggled with off-the-field problems, rushed for only 44 yards after joining the Dolphins. His presence, however, sets up an interesting scenario for 1998. How will the Dolphins effectively use both Abdul-Jabbar and Phillips? It's a situation we'll be keeping a close eye on. The Dolphins will also have the services of 5' 9", first-round draft pick John Avery out of Mississippi. Avery looks to help the Dolphins as both a third-down option and possibly as a kick returner. The Dolphins also tried to continue stockpiling running back talent by acquiring Rasheen Salaam from the Bears in the offseason. The trade was quickly ruled void after Salaam failed his physical. Meanwhile Irving Spikes was given his release.

WR: When looking to 1997, the Dolphins must have thought they had a handle on their receiving situation, with O.J. McDuffie, rookie first-round pick Yatil Green, and Fred Barnett. McDuffie did mostly as expected, finishing the year with 76 receptions for 943 yards and just one touchdown. Green, however, was lost for the season when he suffered a knee injury in the preseason. Barnett was also not so fortunate. He recorded 17 receptions and one touchdown in the first five games, was phased out of the offense and, ultimately, released. The Dolphins turned to Lamar Thomas, who recorded 28 receptions for 402 yards and two touchdowns; Charles Jordan, who grabbed 27 receptions for 471 yards and three touchdowns, and, eventually, Brett Perriman. Perriman, signed after his release from Kansas City, recorded 19 receptions for 309 and one touchdown over the last nine weeks. He played well enough for the Dolphins to originally re-sign him for 1998 but was later released. This makes the Dolphins a more solid team, going into the upcoming season. McDuffie's return as the primary wideout is a certainty. A healthy Yatil Green should be the No.2 receiver. Lamar Thomas, Charles Jordan and

Brian Manning, who had a good preseason in 1997, and new free agent acquisition Kevin Alexander (Giants) will compete for playing time behind them in 1998. The Dolphins and head coach Jimmy Johnson are also experimenting with bringing speedster Jerris McPhail into the receiving mix and made Larry Shannon out of East Carolina their #3 draft choice, who might surprise many and push for a good amount of playing time.

TE: Coming to the Dolphins during the middle of the 1996 season, Troy Drayton took a while to work his way into the offense. In 1997, Drayton expanded his role and produced 39 receptions for 558 yards and four touchdowns. The Dolphins also got 11 receptions for 45 yards and one touchdown from Ed Perry. In 1998, I look for Drayton to continue to build on his contributions to the Miami offense, which will help his numbers grow.

QB: Much like John Elway, Dan Marino continues to hang on for one more shot at a Super Bowl. Elway got his chance last year. Marino obviously did not, and it's more than likely the Dolphins aren't going to get there this year. In 1997, Marino threw for 3,780 yards but only 16 touchdowns. As a fantasy football participant, I'm not too concerned about Marino getting another shot at a Super Bowl. As a football fan, I'd like to see it, just like I enjoyed seeing John Elway's run last year. I'm concerned, though, that Marino, both because of his age and Jimmy Johnson's system, is not likely to reach any prized offensive numbers any longer. For Marino, sadly, the best days are long past.

K: The Dolphins went hunting for a new kicker in 1997, after a dismal 18 of 29 (.621) kicking performance from Joe Nedney a year earlier. They settled on free-agent Olindo Mare. Mare hit a respectable 28 of 36 (.778) field goal tries but missed two of his last four kicks. Both the misses, however, were from 50 yards out. On the year, Mare hit only 4 of 9 (.444) kicks from beyond 40 yards, which might concern the Dolphins for 1998. They have already signed free agent Jon Baker for a look.

Overall: Head coach Jimmy Johnson saw his team improve by one game, to 9-7, in his second season in 1997. Johnson has some tough decisions to make for the Dolphins' future. How long does he go with veteran Dan Marino? Marino's skills are slowly diminishing, and he doesn't really fit the style Johnson would like to employ. Is it time to give Craig Erickson a shot? The Dolphins re-signed Erickson in the offseason. How about at running back? The Dolphins brought in Lawrence Phillips late in the 1997 season. How will they use Phillips and/or Karim Abdul-Jabbar? Johnson and the Dolphins will be an interesting team to watch as the preseason begins.

Offseason Fantasy-Position Moves

	Arriving	From:		Departing	To:
QB	Stan White	Free Agent	RB	Roosevelt Potts	BALT
RB	Landon Smith	Free Agent	RB	Irving Spikes	Released
WR	Kevin Alexander	NYG	WR	Qadry Ismail	NO
WR	Derrick Steagall	Free Agent	WR	Brett Perriman	Released
WR	Geoff Turner	Free Agent			
TE	Chris Fontenot	Free Agent			
K	Jon Baker	Free Agent			

MINNESOTA VIKINGS

Home Stadium: Hubert H. Humphrey Metrodome
Playing Surface: Astro Turf
Head Coach: Denny Green
1997 Record: 9-7

Vikings Still Looking for 'Green'er Pastures

RB: Having a back as explosive and talented as Robert Smith but seeing him injured on a regular basis had to be frustrating for the Vikings. Smith had missed a good portion of both the 1995 (ankle) and 1996 (knee) seasons. What would 1997 bring? As usual, Smith got off to a strong start, rushing for 775 yards and scoring five times in the first eight games, but almost like clockwork he suffered yet another injury. This ankle injury, however, only sidelined him for two weeks. Smith returned and played better as the season progressed. Despite missing those two games, Smith still finished with 1,266 rushing yards, recorded another 197 yards on 37 receptions and seven touchdowns. The Vikings always knew that if he could stay healthy, big numbers would surface. In addition to Smith, the Vikings got 235 rushing yards and 84 more on 11 receptions out of Leroy Hoard, along with four touchdowns. Charles Evans chipped in 157 yards on the ground along with 21 receptions for 152 yards and two scores. David Palmer produced 36 rushing yards, 26 receptions for 193 yards and two touchdowns. The story, however, was Robert Smith. Smith stayed healthy for most of the year and finally performed as he had been expected to. The story in the offseason was also Smith. The Vikings elected to make Smith their "franchise" player. Smith didn't like that restriction. Eventually, an arbitrator changed him to a "transition" player. Shortly thereafter, Smith re-signed with the Vikings for $25 million over five years, including a $5 million signing bonus. As long as he stays healthy in 1998, everyone will be happy. Smith is the key to the Vikings' offense when he's healthy, and if he stays that way, even bigger numbers could be in store.

WR: Since the departure of Warren Moon, Cris Carter's reception numbers continue to drop. However, the 89 receptions for 1,069 yards and 13 touchdowns that he recorded in 1997 are certainly career-year numbers for most players. They are, however, far from the 122 receptions he recorded in both 1995 and 1996. The other side of the talented Viking receiving duo is Jake Reed. Reed's numbers have also declined slightly. Like Carter, Reed's 68 receptions for 1,138 yards and six touchdowns are very good yearly numbers for most receivers. Besides Carter and Reed, the Vikings got 11 receptions out of Chris Walsh and three out of rookie seventh-round pick Matthew Hatchette. Walsh was re-signed in the offseason but in 1998, it'll again be the talented Carter and Reed putting up big numbers for us fantasy buffs. The numbers for Carter should again top the 1,000-yard, 10 to 12 touchdown range. Reed should be in the 1,000-yard, 6 to 10 touchdown range. That's perhaps not quite what they did three or four years ago but it's still significant enough to make them excellent fantasy choices in 1998. There is another player to throw into the mix, that is the Vikings first-round draft pick Randy Moss out of Marshall.

Moss was at one time a projected top-five overall selection whose value slipped because of off the field problems which included jail time. Moss was finally selected by the Vikings at #21 overall. He brings huge talent and potential to a team that is already very loaded on offense.

TE: The Vikings, looking for some production from their tight end position, picked up Andrew Glover, the former Oakland Raider. The Vikings' tight end production had been dismal in recent years. Glover provided some spark. On the year, he produced 32 receptions for 378 yards and three touchdowns. The Vikings also got eight and seven receptions, respectively, out of Greg DeLong and Hunter Goodwin. It was Glover, however, who revived the tight end position for the Vikings.

QB: After winning the starting job, Brad Johnson had the Vikings and their fans excited about their future. He had thrown for 2,258 yards and 17 touchdowns, playing in just 12 games in 1996. In 1997, Johnson was gaining confidence and experience until he suffered a herniated disc in his neck that forced him to miss the last three games of the year. His 3,036 passing yards and 20 touchdowns in just 13 games was impressive. In his absence, veteran Randall Cunningham stepped in. Cunningham did a good job, throwing for six touchdowns in four games. However, the Vikings' future rests on the arm of the much younger Brad Johnson, which is why we'll be very interested in his return in 1998.

K: The Vikings had their problems with kickers in 1997. Greg Davis lasted only four games before being released after he hit only 7 of 10 (.700) field goal tries, with all three misses from inside 45 yards. The Vikings then signed veteran Eddie Murray. Murray hit 12 of 17 (.706) field goals to complete the season. The Vikings, hoping to ensure not having the same problem in 1998, signed free agent Gary Anderson in the offseason. Anderson, who signed a three-year, $2.4-million deal, hit 29 of 36 (.806) field goal tries for San Francisco in 1997.

Overall: By re-signing Robert Smith in the offseason, the Vikings ensured a sound running attack as long as Smith stays healthy. In signing Gary Anderson from the 49ers, the Vikings solidified their kicking game. The question may come in the passing game. Yes, standout receivers Cris Carter and Jake Reed return and they have added talented first-round pick Randy Moss, but how will Brad Johnson fare when he returns from his neck injury? That could be the key to the Vikings' 1998 success.

Offseason Fantasy-Position Moves

	Arriving	From:	Departing	To:
K	Gary Anderson	SF		

Cris Carter/Minnesota Vikings

Drew Bledsoe/New England Patriots

NEW ENGLAND PATRIOTS
Home Stadium: Foxboro Stadium
Playing Surface: Grass
Head Coach: Pete Carroll
1997 Record: 10-6

Bledsoe Just Hitting Stride But Receiving Crew Leaves Questions

RB: In his first two NFL seasons, Curtis Martin drew plenty of attention to himself with solid performances. Coming into 1997, everyone was expecting more of the same. Martin again was putting together a solid season until a groin injury sidelined him for the last three games. Actually, some believe the groin injury had bothered Martin for most of the year. In the 13 games in which Martin played, he tallied 1,160 rushing yards, 296 receiving yards on 41 receptions but only five touchdowns. That's not bad for a player who was bothered by an injury for most of the year. With Martin ailing, Derrick Cullors and Mario Grier stepped in. Cullors finished with 101 rushing yards and one touchdown; Grier rushed for 75 yards and a score. Also during the season, the Patriots got 60 rushing yards and 203 receiving yards on 19 receptions and two touchdowns from Dave Meggett. Sam Gash, besides providing solid blocking, produced only 10 rushing yards but did catch 22 passes for 154 yards and also scored three times. Looking to 1998, the Patriots would have liked Martin back healthy but he'll no longer be a Patriot, as the Jets lured the restricted free agent to signing a six-year, $36 million deal that the Patriots chose not to match. In addition to losing Martin, the Patriots also lost Sam Gash to free agency. Gash departs to Buffalo. Gash's fullback responsibilities will likely be taken up by Tony Carter, who comes to the Patriots via free agency from Chicago. Martin's role and contributions won't be as easy to replace. The Patriots did make Robert Edwards out of Georgia their #1 draft pick. Edwards will come aboard to push and likely beat out Sedrick Shaw and Derrick Cullors for the #1 running back spot. Certainly a position that will provide ample opportunity for big statistical production in 1998.

WR: Big expectations usually follow a player who has a good rookie season. Terry Green had such a season in 1996, with 90 receptions for 1,132 yards and six touchdowns. In 1997, Glenn wasn't as fortunate. He missed nine games, first with an ankle injury and later with a hamstring problem. Limited to action in just seven games Glenn recorded only 27 receptions for 431 yards and two touchdowns. With Glenn out quite a bit, the Patriots' other receivers were called on to step up their game. Shawn Jefferson responded with 54 receptions for 841 yards but only two touchdowns. A nice surprise was Troy Brown, who recorded 41 receptions for 607 yards and six touchdowns. Vincent Brisby, who had missed all of 1996 with a hamstring injury, was a continuing disappointment with only 23 catches for 276 yards and two touchdowns. Looking to 1998, the Patriots are concerned. Shawn Jefferson has had his good games, but he's not a consistent go-to guy. Terry Glenn, who had shown so much potential as a rookie in 1996, now has question marks regarding injuries. Vincent Brisby just hasn't done much to create hope. Troy Brown can help but he is not a dominant figure. Add Brian Stablein to the fold. Stablein comes over from Indianapolis. He caught 25 passes and one touchdown for the Colts in 1997. The Patriots will also bring into the mix their #2 draft choice, Tony Simmons out of Wisconsin. The Patriots hope to sort out these questions and problems as the regular season draws near. A situation to keep a close eye on.

TE: Last year was another solid performance by one of, if not the, best tight ends in the league, Ben Coates. In 1997, Coates grabbed 66 receptions for 737 yards and eight touchdowns. Lovett Purnell chipped in five catches, three for touchdowns, while Keith Byars recorded 20 receptions for 189 yards and also three touchdowns. Looking to 1998, another big year can be expected from Ben Coates. Keith Byars, however, is gone. Byars has left, as a free agent, to join the New York Jets. The Patriots did make a move here, in drafting Rod Rutledge out of Alabama. Rutledge is unlikely however, to see much fantasy success playing behind Ben Coates.

QB: Thus far in his young career, quarterback Drew Bledsoe had not put together consecutive productive seasons. In 1993, as a rookie, Bledsoe threw for only 2,494 yards and 15 touchdowns. In 1994, he jumped to 4,555 yards and 25 touchdown passes. So, after struggling to 3,507 passing yards and 13 touchdowns in 1995, and then rebounding to 4,086 yards and 27 touchdowns in 1996, it looked like 1997 should be a down year. Bledsoe, however, broke with that trend. In 1997, Bledsoe recorded 3,706 passing yards and 28 touchdown passes despite injured and struggling receivers. With the trend broken, Bledsoe has now asserted himself among the consistent, proven signal-callers in the league. This is why he'll get plenty of attention at fantasy drafts, come August.

K: Despite hitting a very impressive 25 of 29 (.862) field goal tries in 1997, there is some concern over Adam Vinatieri for 1998. Vinatieri, despite good year-end numbers, missed four times in the last seven games, hitting only 9 of 13 attempts. All four of his misses came inside 45 yards, two were inside 35 yards. The Patriots tried to sign Gary Anderson away from the 49ers but the Vikings beat them to it. Now they're looking to try out others for the job.

Overall: On the ground, the Patriots have become a huge question mark following the departures of Curtis Martin and Sam Gash. Tony Carter, an offseason free agent signee is likely to step in for Gash but who steps in for Martin? It won't be easy to replace a back of Martin's all-pro dimension, though first-round pick Robert Edwards will be a big help in that direction. Through the air, Drew Bledsoe is getting better and more consistent. His receiving crew has a few question marks, however, except for, of course, tight end Ben Coates. The Patriots may be forced to throw more in 1998 because of the departure of Curtis Martin which could boost Drew Bledsoe's numbers if his receivers come through.

Offseason Fantasy-Position Moves

	Arriving	From:		Departing	To:
RB	Tony Carter	CHI	RB	Curtis Martin	NYJ
WR	Brian Stablein	IND	RB	Keith Byars	NYJ
			RB	Sam Gash	BUF

NEW ORLEANS SAINTS

Home Stadium: Louisiana Superdome
Playing Surface: Astro Turf
Head Coach: Mike Ditka
1997 Record: 6-10

Ditka hasn't Reached 'Saint'hood Quite Yet

RB: There's one thing about Mike Ditka: if he doesn't like the way a player is performing, he'll make a switch without hesitating. In his first year with the Saints in 1997, Ditka demonstrated that style. During the preseason, the word was that Iron Mike really liked third-round pick Troy Davis. By the season opener, however, Davis was carrying the ball less than Mario Bates or Ray Zellars. The load shifted between the players for about half of the season until Ray Zellars got locked into a more permanent job. On the year, Zellars led the team with 552 rushing yards, added 263 more on 31 receptions and scored four times. Bates was next with 440 rushing yards, only 42 receiving yards on five catches and four touchdowns also. Davis, the rookie, finished with 271 rushing yards, 13 catches for 85 yards and no touchdowns. Looking to 1998, things will be changed again. In the offseason, Mario Bates realized he wasn't in the Saints' plans and signed a free-agent contract with Arizona. In turn, the Saints signed Seahawk free agent Lamar Smith to a four-year, $7.1-million deal. Smith had missed four games with a leg injury in 1997. He finished with 392 rushing yards, 23 receptions for another 182 yards and two scores for the Seahawks. Presumably he is going to be the main force for the Saints' running game, though Zellars will push to see time and the Saints have added Aaron Craver to supply blocking for both. Craver comes over via free agency from San Diego.

WR: The Saints' passing game, both at quarterback and at wide receiver, took on a completely new look under Mike Ditka in 1997. Ditka cleaned house by releasing Haywood Jeffires, Torrance Small and Michael Haynes. The Saints brought in such household names as Randall Hill, Andre Hastings, Daryl Hobbs and Eric Guliford. How did they fare? Actually not as bad as I believed they would. Hill, a former first-round pick who never panned out in Miami, led the team with 55 receptions for 761 yards and two touchdowns. Hastings was next with 48 catches for 722 yards and five touchdowns. Guliford finished with 27 receptions for 362 yards and one touchdown, and Hobbs had only two catches for 41 yards. Those were certainly not great numbers, but then again, what do you expect when their quarterback was changed regularly. Looking to 1998, the Saints have made a huge move to address their wide receiver needs by signing unrestricted free agent Sean Dawkins from Indianapolis. Dawkins missed two games in 1997 because of injuries but still caught 68 passes for the colts. They brought in Qadry Ismail from the Dolphins but, perhaps, more for kick-returning. They released Andre Hastings but re-signed him a short time later. Before I'd make one of the Saints' receivers a viable fantasy consideration, including Sean Dawkins, I'd want to believe they've settled on a quarterback to build their future on. That's a decision I don't believe Mike Ditka and the Saints have made yet.

TE: For the second straight season, a knee injury forced Irv Smith to miss a good portion of the season. Playing in just nine games, Smith recorded only 17 receptions for 180 yards and one touchdown. The Saints got some help from John Farquhar, who produced 17 receptions for 253 yards and scored once. Looking to 1998, the Saints no longer have to worry about Smith's knees. Smith has moved on, via free agency, to join the San Francisco 49ers. This leaves a big hole for the Saints to fill before the upcoming season. The Saints did make Cameron Cleeland out of Washington their #2 draft pick. Cleeland will likely battle John Farquhar for playing time and statistical success in 1998.

QB: Well, we've heard about the Saints' musical running backs, now we'll talk about their musical quarterbacks in 1997. The Saints, under new head coach Mike Ditka, were looking for a young quarterback to lead them into the future. In the 1997 offseason, they acquired Heath Shuler, who had lost his starting job with the Redskins. Shuler began the year as the starter but his dismal performances quickly led to appearances by rookie Danny Wuerffel, Doug Nussmeier and, eventually, Billy Joe Hobert. Hobert finished the year strong, throwing for six touchdowns in the last three games. Looking to 1998, unless the Saints make a change, Hobert is likely to begin the year as the starter. Nussmeier is gone, signing as a free agent with Denver. Shuler's future is looking dimmer all the time, and young Danny Wuerffel may still be groomed for the future.

K: Doug Brien did his job in 1997 in trying to help the Saints improve. On the year, Brien hit 23 of 27 (.852) field goal tries. One of his four misses was from 50 yards and the other three were from beyond 40 yards. That's one performance you'd think even Iron Mike would be happy with.

Overall: A 6-10 mark isn't usually considered very good, but that's three games better than the Saints finished a year earlier. Mike Ditka knew he had his work cut out for him when he took the job and he must still realize it when looking ahead. Decisions at running back and quarterback may be key. Signing Lamar Smith to a four-year deal should certainly help the running back situation. The quarterback problem seems like a "worst of all evils" situation, although Billy Joe Hobert showed some promise at the tail-end of 1997. Facing the league's seventh-easiest schedule should give Mike Ditka and the Saints a chance to improve in 1998.

Offseason Fantasy-Position Moves

	Arriving	From:		Departing	To:
RB	Lamar Smith	SEAT	QB	Doug Nussmeier	DEN
RB	Aaron Craver	SD	RB	Mario Bates	ARIZ
WR	Qadry Ismail	MIA	TE	Irv Smith	SF
WR	Sean Dawkins	IND			

NEW YORK GIANTS

Home Stadium: Giants Stadium
Playing Surface: Astro Turf
Head Coach: Jim Fassel
1997 Record: 10-5-1

Fassell Generates 'Giant' Turnaround

RB: Going into 1997, the San Francisco 49ers sought the services of Rodney Hampton. They offered Hampton $16.4 million over four years. The Giants put a stop to the move by matching the offer and keeping Hampton in New York. Too bad for the Giants. After they spent all that money, a knee injury prevented Hampton from playing until week 16. That was just the start of New York's backfield woes. Former first-round pick Tyrone Wheatley continued his history of injuries and battled ankle problems in 1997. Second-round draft pick Tiki Barber, once thought to be a third-down contributor, was at times thrown into a more extensive role but he missed four games midseason with a knee injury. On the season, Hampton finished with only 81 rushing yards and one touchdown, playing in just two games. Wheatley, seeing action in 13 games, rushed for 583 yards, caught 16 passes for 140 more yards and scored four times. Barber contributed 511 rushing yards, 34 receptions for another 299 yards and four touchdowns playing in 12 games. Erric Pegram, coming to the Giants midstream from San Diego, contributed 72 rushing yards and 19 receptions while scoring once. None of these players, however, was the Giants' most productive runner. That distinction went to Charles Way. Way finished with 698 rushing yards and added 304 more on 37 receptions while scoring five times. There are certainly plenty of questions for 1998. Hampton, too expensive at this stage of his career for the Giants to retain, was released. Wheatley has yet to stay injury-free long enough to show much. Barber looks too small and not durable enough to be an every-down back. Way did a nice job in 1997, but will the Giants commit to him? The Giants did add, via free agency, LeShon Johnson from Arizona. Johnson, however, never showed any consistency while with the Cardinals so this move is a bit confusing. The Giants also added free agent Gary Brown. Brown rushed for 945 yards and scored four times for San Diego in 1997, but was given his release when the Chargers acquired Natrone Means in the offseason. Brown can certainly be considered a remedy for the Giants running back woes. For now, this is a situation to monitor as the season draws near.

WR: Looking for a big-play receiver to strengthen their receiving crew, the Giants made Ike Hilliard out of Florida their No.1 pick in 1997. Hilliard, however, never was able to develop. He suffered a season-ending neck injury after playing in just two games and catching only two passes. One bright spot for the Giants was Chris Calloway. For the second straight season, Calloway led the Giants in receiving. On the year, Calloway produced 58 receptions for 849 yards and eight touchdowns. Calloway got very little support. Thomas Lewis, a former first-round pick, reverted to his injury-prone ways, missing 13 games with an injured toe. Lewis produced only five receptions. Kevin Alexander chipped in 18 receptions and one touchdown. Amani Toomer, the Giants' second-round pick of 1996, recorded only 16 catches while being used mostly as a kick returner. And David Patten added 13 catches, two for touchdowns. Looking to 1998, Chris Calloway looks to be the only certainty. Kevin Alexander has gone to Miami, via free agency. The Giants hope to have Ike Hilliard back healthy from his neck injury which is looking more likely. If Hilliard returns healthy he and Calloway will likely start. Thomas Lewis and his injury problems won't return, as he signed as free agent with the Chicago Bears leaving some questions that will only be answered during training camp and as the season draws near. The Giants are also hoping for a turnaround from Amani Toomer, which would bolster their receiving corps. The Giants added wide receivers to their receiving mix via the early rounds of the draft. Joe Jurevicius out of Penn State was the Giants #2 draft choice and Brian Alford out of Purdue was the Giants third-round choice. For me however, at this point, it's hard for me to get excited about any Giant early-round wide receiver pick.

TE: The Giants didn't get anything extraordinary out of this position, just 21 receptions for 150 yards and two touchdowns by veteran Howard Cross, while Aaron Pierce contributed 10 receptions for 147 yards and no scores. The Giants, hoping to strengthen their tight end position, have added former San Diego Charger Alfred Pupunu. With Pupunu's arrival, it's unlikely Aaron Pierce will return but Cross should remain a consistent but low performer.

QB: When he took over a 6-10 team in 1997, new head coach Jim Fassel knew his work was cut out for him. At quarterback, Fassel had returning starter Dave Brown, who had yet to establish himself as a consistent NFL signal-caller. Fassel opened the year with Brown as his starter. Brown remained there until a chest injury against Dallas sidelined him in week six. In stepped second-year man Danny Kanell. The Giants rolled off three straight wins with Kanell as the starter and Kanell retained the starting job. Playing in 12 games, Kanell threw for 1,740 yards and 11 touchdowns. He has a virtual lock on the starting job for 1998. Dave Brown was released in the offseason, later signed by Arizona, and the Giants signed former Giant Kent Graham (Arizona) to be Kanell's backup. The Giants and Jim Fassel have found a new young quarterback to lead them into the future.

K: The 1997 season was not very impressive for kicker Brad Daluiso, who hit only 22 of 32 (.688) field goal attempts. Of his 10 misses, only three were from farther than 50 yards. Four were from beyond 40 yards and three were from inside 40 yards, all of which should raise some concern. The Giants may have been looking back to a year earlier when Daluso was good on 24 of 27 (.889) field goal attempts when they re-signed him in the offseason.

Overall: Under Jim Fassel, the Giants improved from 6-10 in 1996 to 10-5-1 in 1997. Fassel did this without a consistent ground game and with a new young quarterback in Danny Kanell. Defense played a big part in the Giants' success; how will the offense look in 1998? Through the air, young Kanell will continue to mature and improve. He has only one consistent target, Chris Calloway. The rest of the receiving crew is questionable, especially last year's first-round pick, the recovering Ike Hilliard. The ground game has more questions with all the injuries that took place in 1997. Tiki Barber will be used often but he probably can't handle every-down duty. Rodney Hampton was too expensive to retain and was released. Gary Brown, who rushed for just under 1,000 yards in San Diego in 1997 could be an answer. Tyrone Wheatley has lost his allure. Adding LeShon Johnson, who showed little consistency while in Arizona, doesn't do much for me either.

Offseason Fantasy-Position Moves

	Arriving	From:		Departing	To:
QB	Kent Graham	ARIZ	QB	Dave Brown	ARIZ
RB	Gary Brown	SD	RB	Rodney Hampton	Released
RB	LeShon Johnson	ARIZ	WR	Kevin Alexander	MIA
WR	Eddie Goines	Free Agent	WR	Thomas Lewis	CHI
TE	Alfred Pupunu	Free Agent			

Keyshawn Johnson/New York Jets

NEW YORK JETS

Home Stadium: Giants Stadium
Playing Surface: Astro Turf
Head Coach: Bill Parcells
1997 Record: 9-7

Parcells has Jets Beginning to Soar Again

RB: Under new head coach Bill Parcells, Adrian Murrell put together his second straight 1,000-yard season. However, because Parcells is known to like his teams to run the ball, Murrell's 1,086 rushing yards are actually surprisingly low. Murrell began the year with three 100-yard games in the first five weeks but he never again topped that mark. His performance just seemed to slide as the year went on. In his defense, he got more than 20 carries in a game only three times in the last 10 weeks. In addition to his 1,086 rushing yards, Murrell tallied 27 receptions for 106 yards and scored seven times. The Jets also got 158 rushing yards and 142 receiving yards on 16 receptions, along with four touchdowns, out of rookie fourth-round pick Leon Johnson. Richie Anderson chipped in 70 rushing yards and, more importantly, 26 receptions for 150 yards while scoring once. Free-agent acquisition Lorenzo Neal, coming over from New Orleans, was a bust with only 28 rushing yards and eight receptions. Looking to 1998, the Jets running game will have a much different look. First, they have lured restricted free agent Curtis Martin to New York for a reported $36 million over 6 years. Martin's arrival will bring him back to work for Bill Parcell's who drafted him as a rookie in 1995 when he was the head coach of the Patriots. This is a huge move to bring in one of the league's top backs though Martin struggled through injury in 1997. With Martin aboard the Jets turned their attention to dealing Murrell. Murrell and a seventh-round pick were soon there after traded to Arizona for the Cardinals third-round draft pick. If Martin can stay healthy look for him to likely team with Leon Johnson in the Jet backfield and put up significant numbers in 1998.

WR: Second-year receiver and former first-round pick Keyshawn Johnson continued to improve in 1997. On the year, Johnson recorded 70 receptions for 963 yards but a disappointingly low five touchdowns. Next to Johnson in receiving was Wayne Chrebet. Each season, Chrebet is labeled as the odd man out but each year, he responds. Jeff Graham was actually the No.2 receiver going into the year but Chrebet just kept producing and eventually won that role. Chrebet finished the year with 58 receptions for 799 yards and three touchdowns. Graham finished with a disappointing 42 catches for 542 yards and two scores. In addition, the Jets got 18 catches and a touchdown out of Dedric Ward but only three receptions out of former second-round pick Alex Van Dyke. Looking to 1998, Keyshawn Johnson will again be the Jets' go-to guy. Jeff Graham, who would have cost the Jets more than $2 million, will not be back. Graham was dealt to the Philadelphia Eagles on draft day. This should expand the roles of Chrebet, Ward and Van Dyke. Their roles will be more defined as the season approaches.

TE: Would 1997 be the year former first-round pick Kyle Brady would step up and become more of a part of the New York Jets' offense? It was, but not to the degree the Jets had hoped. After producing only 15 receptions for 144 yards and one touchdown in 1996, Brady finished 1997 with 22 catches for 238 yards and two touchdowns. Brady was actually bested by Fred Baxter, who tallied 27 catches for 276 yards and three scores. Looking to 1998, the Jets are still disappointed that Brady hasn't blossomed into the first-round pro they had originally sought. They have taken an extended step to better their tight end position for 1998, signing free agent Keith Byars away from New England. The veteran Byars numbers have slid in recent years but he remains a solid blocker and receiver.

QB: The Jets' $25 million quarterback, Neil O'Donnell, started the 1997 season as if he was worth every dime of it. In the season opener against Seattle, O'Donnell threw for 270 yards and five touchdowns in a 41-3 romp. It was pretty much downhill from there. O'Donnell was so inconsistent that head coach Bill Parcells elected to give Glenn Foley a chance to revitalize the offense. Foley provided some spark until he injured a knee, giving O'Donnell a chance to take the job back. On the year, O'Donnell finished with 2,796 passing yards and 17 touchdowns playing in 15 games. Foley, playing in four games, threw for 705 yards and three scores. In 1998, Bill Parcells is not tipping his hand as to who'll be his starter. Maybe he doesn't know. He may lack confidence in both the high-priced O'Donnell and unproven Foley. Perhaps only training camp can answer these questions and, even then, Parcells could like change his mind as he did in 1997.

K: Following an unimpressive kicking performance by Nick Lowery in 1996, the Jets went looking for a kicker in 1997. They settled on John Hall. Hall's woeful 28 of 41 (.683) performance on field goals, however, will probably send the Jets out shopping again in 1998.

Overall: New head coach Bill Parcells was deemed a savior in 1997, lifting the Jets from their 1-15 record of 1996 to a 9-7 mark last year. However, for the Jets to continue to improve, Parcells has some questions to answer. Who'll get the call at quarterback, expensive Neil O'Donnell or young Glenn Foley? How will the Jets look at wide receivers other than Keyshawn Johnson? With Jeff Graham gone will Wayne Chrebet, Dedric Ward or Alex Van Dyke step up? One answer Parcells may have is on the ground where he now has Curtis Martin. The Jets bring aboard the talented running back by offering him a huge $36 million, 6 year deal that the Patriots chose not to meet.

Offseason Fantasy-Position Moves

	Arriving	From:		Departing	To:
RB	Curtis Martin	NE	RB	Adrien Murrell	ARIZ
RB	Keith Byars	NE	RB	Lorenzo Neal	TB
RB	Keith Lozowski	Free Agent	WR	Jeff Graham	PHIL
WR	Brian Musso	Free Agent	TE	Sean Burke	SD
WR	Nakia Jenkins	Free Agent			

OAKLAND RAIDERS

Home Stadium: Oakland Coliseum
Playing Surface: Grass
Head Coach: Jon Gruden
1997 Record: 4-12

Raiders Blow Off Bugel
Eagles' Gruden Gets Chance to Help Turnaround

RB: Napoleon Kaufman, in his first season as a season-long starter, put together some very impressive numbers. Showing an explosive, quick-hitting style, Kaufman was fun to watch, especially early in the year. On the season, Kaufman finished with 1,294 rushing yards, 403 receiving yards on 40 receptions and eight touchdowns. He did this despite really tailing off in the second half. After producing five 100-yard games and seven touchdowns over the first eight games of 1997, Kaufman managed only one 100-yard game and one touchdown over the second half of the season. Besides Kaufman, the Raiders got very little other production. Tim Hall produced 120 rushing yards, and Derrick Fenner had 24 rushing yards along with 14 receptions for 92 yards. From all other contributors, the Raiders got 12 rushing yards. No running back other than Kaufman scored a touchdown. Looking to 1998, I look for more of the same for Napoleon Kaufman. The Raiders finally have the every-down back they've been seeking, despite his dramatic dropoff in the second half in 1997. The 1,500–1,800 range in yards and the double-digit scoring plateau are certainly well within reach for the explosive Kaufman in 1998, especially if he's running behind big, third-round draft pick, Jon Ritchie out of Stanford, who should provide solid blocking.

WR: With Jeff George coming in as quarterback in 1997, wide receiver Tim Brown had to be licking his chops when thinking of the numbers he could produce. Brown, without George in 1996, had a 90-reception, 1,104-yard, nine-touchdown campaign. How much higher could he drive those numbers? Brown began the 1997 season as if the sky was the limit, producing three touchdowns on eight receptions and 158 yards against Tennessee in the season opener. In all, Brown finished the season with seven 100-yard games. On the year, Brown recorded 104 receptions for 1,408 yards but only five touchdowns. So George's arrival did help Brown's numbers, except for his touchdown total. George's arrival also benefited another receiver, James Jett. Jett's reception level went from 43 in 1996 to 46 in 1997 but his yardage numbers jumped to 804 (from 601) and his touchdown numbers leapt to 12 scores after only four the year before. Jett became one of the league's most feared deep threats, catching two 50-plus yard touchdowns. In addition to Brown and Jett, Kenny Shedd chipped in 10 receptions and one touchdown, Olando Truitt recorded seven catches and a score, and Desmond Howard, who had hoped to get more of a receiving role in Oakland, managed only four receptions and no touchdowns. In 1998, fantasy football owners have to once again be high on the potential of both Tim Brown and James Jett. I'm especially convinced that even though Brown caught only five touchdowns in 1997, he will surpass the 10-touchdown level in 1998.

TE: Did Jeff George's arrival also affect the year-end numbers of tight ends Ricky Dudley and Harvey Williams in 1997? Of course it did. As a rookie in 1996, Dudley had 34 catches for 386 yards and four touchdowns. In 1997, Dudley's numbers climbed to 48 catches for 787 yards and seven scores. Harvey Williams, who saw action at both tight end and running back, grabbed 16 receptions for 147 yards, along with rushing for 70 yards and scoring five times. Looking to 1998, Ricky Dudley is another player whose fantasy stock has climbed since strong-armed Jeff George arrived in Oakland.

QB: The Raiders and general manager Al Davis never seem to shy away from a guy who has been less than a boy scout elsewhere. They were a perfect fit for Jeff George, whose relationship with the Falcons had deteriorated in Atlanta. The Raiders, ready to gamble, signed George to a five-year, $27.5-million deal. Although the Raiders stumbled to a 4-12 record, George's season was impressive. On the year, George threw for 3,917 yards and 29 touchdowns, and he didn't throw for a touchdown in just two games. Five times George threw for three touchdowns or more in a game. George seems to have found a home in Oakland, where his strong arm fits the Raiders' downfield philosophy and should reap rewards for both team and player for years to come.

K: Cole Ford's dismal 13 of 22 (.591) field goal performance in 1997 certainly has the Raiders concerned. It's surprising they kept Ford around all year in1997, since he hit only 1 of 5 field goal attempts in a game early in the year. The Raiders are likely looking for challengers to Ford for their 1998 kicking chores, thus far bringing in Scott Bentley, Chris Jacke, Greg Davis and Steve McGlaughlin, all with NFL experience, for tryouts.

Overall: Despite nice offensive performances by Napoleon Kaufman on the ground and Jeff George with receivers Tim Brown, James Jett and Ricky Dudley through the air in 1997, the Raiders finished 4-12. Following the season, the Raiders quickly dismissed head coach Joe Bugel. In his place, they hired 34-year-old Jon Gruden. Gruden was the Philadelphia Eagles' offensive coordinator in 1997. With all the offensive talent the Raiders possess, Gruden's focus may quickly shift to defense. However, because he is a former offensive coordinator, he has to be happy with the offensive talent already in place.

Offseason Fantasy-Position Moves

Arriving	From:	Departing	To:

Napoleon Kaufman/Oakland Raiders

PHILADELPHIA EAGLES

Home Stadium: Veterans Stadium
Playing Surface: Astro Turf
Head Coach: Ray Rhodes
1997 Record: 6-9-1

Hoying Could Be Eagles Future 'Rhodes' to Success

RB: In 1997, Ricky Watters produced 1,110 rushing yards and 440 more on 48 receptions while scoring seven times. That's a pretty good season for most running backs, but it was a down year for Watters. A year earlier, Watters had recorded 1,411 rushing yards, added 444 more on 51 receptions while scoring 13 times. In addition to Watters' production, the Eagles got 547 rushing yards and 24 receptions for 225 yards and three touchdowns out of Charlie Garner. Kevin Turner continued in his role as a featured receiver out of the backfield, grabbing 48 receptions for 443 yards and three scores while rushing for 96 yards. Rookie Duce Staley didn't show much during the regular season with 29 rushing yards and two receptions. Looking to 1998, the Eagles' ground attack will take on a new complexion. First, the Eagles ensured that Charlie Garner would be back, re-signing him to a four-year, $6.4-million deal. Watters, however, won't be back. Watters is taking his services to Seattle where he signed a four-year, $13-million deal. This leaves Garner to carry the bulk of the rushing load in 1998. The Eagles, however, realize that Garner is unlikely to be able to carry the full load all season. It's a question of durability. I wouldn't be surprised to see Duce Staley's role greatly enlarged to support Garner, while Kevin Turner continues coming out of the backfield.

WR: The 1997 season was another solid one for Irving Fryar, who produced 86 receptions for 1,316 yards and six touchdowns in his second season with the Eagles. Chris T. Jones, who had a breakout year in 1996 with 70 receptions, wasn't so fortunate in 1997. Bothered by a knee problem for most of the season, Jones finished with only five catches for 73 yards, seeing action in just four games. With Jones hobbling because of his knee, Michael Timpson received more playing time and that resulted in 42 receptions for 484 yards and two touchdowns. In addition, Freddie Solomon chipped in 29 receptions and three touchdowns, and Mark Seay added 13 catches and one score. Looking to 1998, the Eagles have the luxury of having Irving Fryar who, year in and year out, produces consistently good numbers. The question will be at the second wideout spot where Chris T. Jones is still struggling to overcome his knee injury, having it scoped three times since last fall. If Jones should be back healthy, will he get the call over Michael Timpson, who did well in his absence in 1997 or newly acquired Jeff Graham? Graham was a draft day acquisition and adds to the Eagles insurance. Graham comes over from the New York Jets where he was a bit of a disappointment in 1997. Last season Graham began the year as the Jets #2 wide out but lost his job to Wayne Chrebet. He finished the season with only 42 receptions and two touchdowns. However, a year earlier Graham recorded 50 receptions and six touchdowns despite missing four games with a knee injury, giving us a better idea of what he is capable of.

TE: The Eagles were hoping that 1996 second-round pick Jason Dunn would step up in 1997. As a rookie, Dunn was a bit of a disappointment. He recorded only 15 receptions for 332 yards and two touchdowns. Dunn's 1997 performance did not even match those results. Hampered by a hamstring injury for part of the year, Dunn finished with only seven receptions for 93 yards and two touchdowns. The Eagles got 14 receptions for 177 yards and one touchdown and 12 catches for 94 yards and four touchdowns out of Chad Lewis. This means the Eagles' tight ends scored seven touchdowns on just 33 receptions. Look for the Eagles to continue that trend in 1998 with a healthy Jason Dunn reaping most of the statistical rewards.

QB: Coming off a 10-6 season in 1996, the Eagles looked to continue their winning ways in 1997 behind Ty Detmer, who had played so well, especially down the stretch, in 1996. Detmer, however, did not find the same success and the Eagles were back to shuffling him in and out of the lineup with Rodney Peete. Peete was also less than impressive so head coach Ray Rhodes and the Eagles turned to young Bobby Hoying. Hoying threw for 1,573 yards and 11 touchdowns in just seven games. Hoying's second-half performance has the Eagles looking more enthusiastically to their future. Hoying should be the starter in 1997 with Rodney Peete serving as his backup. Detmer moved on, signing a free-agent deal with San Francisco.

K: The Eagles lured division rival Dallas's kicker Chris Boniol to Philadelphia in 1997. Boniol was coming off a season in which he hit a remarkable 32 of 36 (.889) field goal tries for the Cowboys. Boniol, however, did not put up the same type of numbers in 1997 for Philadelphia. Boniol hit 22 of 31 (.710) field goal tries. It was, obviously, not the performance that the Eagles were looking for, but one Boniol will work to improve on in 1998.

Overall: The Eagles took a step backward in 1997, going from a 10-6 mark in 1996 to their 6-9-1 finish last year. For 1998, changes are being made. Running back Ricky Watters has gone to Seattle via free agency. This leaves the ground game to be handled by Charlie Garner, Duce Staley and Kevin Turner. The Eagles also got a good look at young Bobby Hoying at quarterback last year. Hoying showed potential to grow, mature and evolve into a solid NFL quarterback. His second-half finish has the Eagles more excited about their future, though success may be a while off, especially with the departure of Watters.

Offseason Fantasy-Position Moves

	Arriving	From:		Departing	To:
QB	Mike McCoy	Free Agent	QB	Ty Detmer	SF
RB	Jeff Cothran	Free Agent	RB	Ricky Watters	SEAT
RB	Mike Reed	Free Agent			
RB	Brian McKensie	Free Agent			
WR	Jeff Graham	NYJ			
WR	Karl Hankton	Free Agent			
WR	Jake Hoffart	Free Agent			
WR	Harvey Middleton	Free Agent			
WR	Jason Dulick	Free Agent			
WR	Josh Dolbin	Free Agent			
TE	Kevin Hickman	Free Agent			
TE	Marcus Pollard	IND			
K	Jaret Holmes	Free Agent			

Kordell Stewart/Pittsburgh Steelers

PITTSBURGH STEELERS

Home Stadium: Three Rivers Stadium
Playing Surface: Astro Turf
Head Coach: Bill Cowher
1997 Record: 11-5

Bettis and Stewart 'Steel'ing the Show

RB: New scenery seemed to serve Jerome Bettis well when he went to Pittsburgh in 1996 after a couple of down years with the Rams. Bettis recorded 1,431 rushing yards, had ten 100-yard games and scored 11 times. Would he be able to maintain that success in 1997? Bettis answered that question loud and clear. Despite missing the season finale with knee and back injuries, Bettis recorded a whopping 1,665 rushing yards, added 110 more on 15 receptions and scored nine times. Bettis again recorded another ten 100-yard games. He's certainly found a suitable home in Pittsburgh. Bettis and the Steelers also got help from fifth-round pick George Jones. Jones recorded 235 rushing yards and 16 receptions for another 96 yards while scoring twice. Ultimately, however, it was the Jerome Bettis show—a demonstration of consistently hard running that should produce big numbers again in 1998. Surely 1,500-plus rushing yards and the 10-touchdown mark are well within reach for Bettis again.

WR: With Yancey Thigpen and Ernie Mills hurt much of the 1996 season, Andre Hastings and Charles Johnson were forced to step up. They recorded 72 and 60 receptions, respectively. Going into 1997, the Steelers were without the services of Mills and Hastings. Mills was off to Carolina and Hastings to New Orleans. This left Yancey Thigpen, Charles Johnson, Courtney Hawkins and rookie second-round pick Will Blackwell. Thigpen returned to form, leading the team with 79 receptions for 1,398 yards and seven touchdowns. Johnson was next with 46 receptions for 568 yards and two touchdowns. Johnson missed four games midseason with a knee injury. Hawkins chipped in 45 catches for 555 yards and three touchdowns. Looking to 1998, the Steelers are going to need stepped-up performances from a number of players. Leading receiver Yancey Thigpen was a free agent and went to the Tennessee Oilers. Thigpen's departure likely leaves Charles Johnson and young Will Blackwell likely as starters and Courtney Hawkins as the No.3 receiver. This is, of course, if the Steelers don't make a move for another proven receiver. They did make Hines Ward out of Georgia their third-round pick. However, it's Charles Johnson who I believe if he stays healthy could put up significant numbers in 1998.

TE: The Steelers' No.1 draft pick of 1995, Mark Bruener, had yet to show much, being hindered by injuries. Going into 1996, Bruener was healthy and began the year well, producing four touchdowns in the first five games. By season's end, however, Bruener finished with only five touchdowns on 18 receptions. In addition to Bruener, the Steelers got six total receptions and no touchdowns from Mitch Lyons, Kirk Botkin and Troy Sadowski. Looking to 1998, Mark Bruener will again be the main focus at tight end. As history has shown, however, the Steelers certainly don't overuse the tight end position on pass routes, although that can change in scoring situations. Don't rule out another four to six touchdown receptions for Bruener again in 1998.

QB: Because of his multiple talents, young Kordell Stewart had been used in a variety of ways before the 1997 season. The Steelers and head coach Bill Cowher had to make a decision coming into 1997. Would they give Stewart his shot at full-time quarterbacking duties? They did, and the results were very welcome. Stewart started rather slowly but quickly matured and made his statements on the ground, through the air and as a leader. On the season, Stewart produced 3,020 passing yards and 21 touchdown passes along with 476 rushing yards and a whopping 11 rushing touchdowns. Those are staggering numbers for a young quarterback who was playing his first full season as the team's No.1 quarterback. Where does Stewart go from here? Can his numbers grow? That may be difficult in 1998 because the Steelers face the league's most difficult schedule. Stewart also will face the year without his best wide receiver of a year ago, Yancey Thigpen, who has departed for Tennessee.

K: Veteran Norm Johnson just keeps getting it done. In 1997, Johnson hit 22 of 25 (.880) field goals with all three misses coming from farther than 40 yards (one of the three was from beyond 50 yards). Consistency like that keeps the veteran Johnson around year after year.

Overall: The Steelers went one better in 1997, going 11-5 following a 10-6 season in 1996. The stability that Jerome Bettis has provided at running back for the last two years has been a great asset. At quarterback, the Steelers made young Kordell Stewart their starter. Both in the air and on the ground, Stewart was everything they hoped for and more. Looking to 1998, Bettis and Stewart are again the obvious keys. Both, however, along with the entire Pittsburgh team, will have an uphill battle as they face the league's toughest schedule.

Offseason Fantasy-Position Moves

	Arriving	From:		Departing	To:
QB	Pete Gonzalez	Free Agent	WR	Yancey Thigpen	TENN

ST. LOUIS RAMS

Home Stadium: Trans World Dome
Playing Surface: Astro Turf
Head Coach: Dick Vermeil
1997 Record: 5-11

The Future 'Banks' on more from 'Moore' and from Bruce

RB: After a disappointing rookie season for first-round pick Lawrence Phillips in 1996, the Rams were hoping to get their money's worth in 1997. Phillips began the season strong, rushing for 125 yards and three touchdowns in the season opener against New Orleans. That game, however, was the season highlight as Phillips, playing in nine more games with the Rams, never again hit the 100-yard mark. With his numbers going down and his struggles off the field and with team management, Phillips was released. He was shortly thereafter picked up and signed by the Dolphins. With Phillips gone, the Rams turned to Jerald Moore. Moore improved in the second half of the season and finished the year with his lone 100-yard performance against the Panthers in the season finale. In the eight games in which Moore played, he produced 379 rushing yards and caught eight passes for 69 yards while scoring three times. Another big contributor was Amp Lee. Lee rushed for only 104 yards but tallied 61 receptions for 825 yards and scored three times. Craig Heyward's contribution was minor—84 rushing yards and eight receptions for 77 yards and one touchdown. Looking to 1998, the Rams will likely feature Jerald Moore as their main back though rookie second-round pick Robert Holcombe out of Illinois will push for playing time and the running back spot. Look for Amp Lee to provide some speed for the Rams, especially on pass routes out of the backfield.

WR: After averaging more than 100 receptions in each of his two previous seasons, Isaac Bruce had joined the league's elite. In 1997, however, a hamstring injury forced Bruce to miss the first five games of the season. The result was a huge drop to only 56 receptions for 815 yards and five touchdowns, playing in 11 games. Bruce's highlight was a 10-reception, 233-yard, two-touchdown performance against Atlanta in week 10. Another player who did not reach expectations in 1997 was Eddie Kennison. In his rookie season of 1996, Kennison had produced 54 receptions, for 924 yards and 11 touchdowns. In 1997, with Bruce out, Kennison drew more coverage. Kennison slipped to only 25 catches for 404 yards and no touchdowns. The Rams did get 32 receptions for 488 yards and one touchdown out of Torrance Small who, was signed after his release from New Orleans. Looking to 1998, the Rams would like to get more than just the six touchdowns out of their wide receivers that they did in 1997. A year earlier, Isaac Bruce and Eddie Kennison had 24 touchdowns between them. The Rams obviously need to keep Bruce healthy. He is one of the league's best and having him will open things up for the other receivers. Eddie Kennison will have a challenge to retain the No.2 receiver spot. The Rams signed Ricky Proehl away from Chicago, via free agency, in the off-season to a four-year, $6-million deal. Proehl, who led the Bears with 58 receptions in 1997, will push Kennison hard for the No.2 spot. Meanwhile,

Torrance Small has departed the Rams equation for 1998 by signing a free agent deal with Indianapolis in the offseason.

TE: When Troy Drayton left for Miami in mid-1996, the Rams turned their attention to their No.2 draft pick of 1996, Ernie Conwell. In 1997, Conwell began to assert himself, recording 38 receptions for 404 yards and four touchdowns. Besides Conwell, the Rams got five catches and a touchdown out of Mitch Jacoby. In 1998, Ernie Conwell will continue to improve and so should his year-end numbers. Totals of 500 yards and five-plus touchdowns are well within his reach.

QB: Young Tony Banks had won the starting job in short order as a rookie in 1996. The Rams' second-round draft choice finished his rookie season with 2,544 yards and 15 touchdown passes. His performance pleased the Rams and new head coach Dick Vermeil. In 1997, however, Banks did not seem to progress as well as expected. On the year, Banks threw for 3,254 yards and only 14 touchdowns. Certainly his low touchdown pass levels were hurt by the injury to Isaac Bruce and the inconsistent play of all the wideouts. Looking to 1998, the Rams hope to get young Banks back on track because they believe he's still their future.

K: With a history of poor consistency from their kickers in recent years, the Rams opted to lure free agent Jeff Wilkins away from the 49ers in 1997. Wilkins had hit 30 of 34 (.882) field goal attempts with San Francisco in 1996. Wilkins, however, wasn't as successful in 1997, hitting only 25 of 37 (.676) field goal tries. Of his 11 misses, five were from inside 40 yards. That's something that concerns the Rams, going into 1998.

Overall: The Rams, under new head coach Dick Vermeil, actually took a step backward in 1997. Their 5-11 finish was one game worse than their 6-10 record of 1996. Looking to 1998, the Rams hope to improve. Running back Lawrence Phillips was let go in 1997, which likely means Jerald Moore steps in as the team's main back. Moore should get help from Amp Lee out of the backfield and possibly from some addition who will provide more speed. Young Tony Banks should get back on track, especially if he has standout Isaac Bruce healthy all year. Bruce may have Ricky Proehl aboard to challenge speedster Eddie Kennison for the No.2 wide receiver spot. Head coach Dick Vermeil would like to see significant signs of improvement, keeping his "burnout" from a quick relapse.

Offseason Fantasy-Position Moves

	Arriving	From:		Departing	To:
WR	Ricky Proehl	CHI	QB	Mark Rypien	ATL
QB	Steve Bono	GB	WR	Torrance Small	IND
			WR	Keith Crawford	ATL

SAN DIEGO CHARGERS

Home Stadium: Jack Murphy Stadium
Playing Surface: Grass
Head Coach: Kevin Gilbride
1997 Record: 4-12

Chargers may again have 'Means' to an End

RB: The Chargers, looking for a back who could handle every-down responsibilities, took a new direction in 1997. Aaron Hayden had come on late in 1996 to produce 475 rushing yards and three touchdowns in the last three weeks and looked like the likely starter for 1997. The Chargers, however, had not been pleased with their running game as a whole and opted to sign Gary Brown in the offseason. Brown, a former 1,000-yard rusher, had sat out all of 1996. Hayden was let go and eventually signed with Green Bay. Brown became the Chargers' main back. On the year, Brown came close to topping the 1,000-yard mark and might have if he hadn't missed a game late in the year with a knee injury. Brown finished with 945 rushing yards, added 137 more yards on 21 receptions and scored four times. In addition to Brown, the Chargers got 161 rushing yards and, more importantly, 39 receptions for 292 yards but no touchdowns out of Terrell Fletcher. Aaron Craver chipped in 97 total rushing-receiving yards. Looking to 1998, despite Brown's 1997 performance, the Chargers elected not to bring him back as he eventually signed with the New York Giants. Instead, the Chargers elected to sign Natrone Means from Jacksonville. Means, who had been released by the Chargers just two years earlier, signed a six-year, $19-million deal. In 1997, Means produced 927 rushing-receiving yards and nine touchdowns for the Jaguars but had topped the 1,300 yard rushing mark four years earlier when with San Diego. He will obviously carry the bulk of the Chargers' rushing load while Terrell Fletcher will likely remain a big weapon out of the backfield. The Chargers also may be looking for some blocking help, losing Aaron Craver to New Orleans via free agency in the offseason.

WR: The 1995 and 1996 seasons were two straight remarkable seasons for Tony Martin. Following an 85-reception, 1,171-yard, 14-touchdown performance in 1996, Martin was not so remarkable or productive in 1997. Martin's year-end numbers tallied up to only 63 receptions for 904 yards and six touchdowns. There were a number of reasons for the dropoff, including the loss of veteran quarterback Stan Humphries about midway through the season because of a concussion. Regardless, Martin was not pleased with his performance nor his team's by the season's end and voiced his opinion. Besides Martin, the Chargers got 40 receptions for 576 yards and two touchdowns out of Eric Metcalf, 32 receptions for 423 yards and only one touchdown out of second-year man and 1996 fourth-round pick Charlie Jones, and 24 catches for 324 yards and no touchdowns out of 1996 second-round pick Bryan Still. Looking to 1998, the Chargers first need to get their quarterback position in order, following the retirement of Stan Humphries. Young Craig Whelihan stepped in when Humphries was injured in 1997 and did an adequate job but now, following the NFL draft the Chargers can likely bank on the arm of first-round draft Ryan Leaf. They got Leaf by dealing Eric Metcalf to Arizona, to move up to the No.2 overall spot in the draft. With Leaf aboard the future looks bright though the present may suffer for a bit while Leaf gains experience. Regardless, look for the Chargers to utilize Leaf's strong arm which should bode well for Tony Martin, Charlie Jones, Bryan Still and rookie second-round draft pick Mikhael Ricks out of Stephen F. Austin.

TE: In looking to develop a tight end for their future, the Chargers made Freddie Jones out of North Carolina their second-round draft pick in 1997. Jones quickly responded by recording an impressive 41 receptions for 505 yards and two touchdowns as a rookie, despite missing two games late in the year with a leg injury. The Chargers also got 19 receptions, for 246 yards and one touchdown, out of Frank Hartley, along with only one catch each by Shannon Mitchell and Alfred Pupunu. Looking to 1998, Alfred Pupunu was let go and eventually signed with the Giants. The Chargers plan on continuing to develop second-year man Freddie Jones, who should see his numbers continue to climb.

QB: Quarterback Stan Humphries has a history of injuries. The 1997 season was no different as he missed the last seven weeks of the season following another severe blow to the head. That was his sixth concussion in 10 years. In his absence, the Chargers turned to young Craig Whelihan, despite having veteran Jim Everett on hand. Whelihan showed some promise, throwing for 1,357 yards and six touchdowns, playing in nine games. Following the season, Humphries got the OK to return but opted to retire. Where does that leave the Chargers? Jim Everett is not likely to be asked back, which leaves Craig Whelihan and rookie Ryan Leaf. Leaf, the Chargers #1 draft pick and the #2 overall, has a ton of potential and is expected to be San Diego's future, however he'll be trying to turn around a team that was 4–12 in 1997. So don't expect huge immediate success.

K: John Carney had a decent season in 1996 when he hit 29 of 36 (.806) field goal attempts. He looked to be on his way to another successful campaign in 1997. However, a knee injury sidelined Carney for the season, after he had hit all seven field goal tries. With Carney out, veteran Greg Davis came aboard and finished the season hitting 19 of 22 (.864) field tries. Looking to 1998, if Carney's knee is ready, it's likely the Chargers will bring him back.

Overall: Dropping to 4-12 in 1997, the Chargers know they have to make some changes. They've already brought back running back Natrone Means. Means spent two years in Jacksonville but has returned to the tune of a six-year, $19-million deal. He'll be the main focus on the ground. Through the air, the Chargers have lost quarterback Stan Humphries to retirement. Humphries called it quits after suffering his sixth concussion during the 1997 season. The question is, who'll replace him? Craig Whelihan, or rookie Ryan Leaf? Or perhaps how quickly will Leaf be given the starting job. It could be immediate. Whichever takes over, it will take him a while to realize success, which means the Chargers aren't going very far, very fast, after a 4–12 finish in 1997.

Offseason Fantasy-Position Moves

	Arriving	From:		Departing	To:
QB	Jeff Baker	Free Agent	QB	Stan Humphries	Retired
RB	Natrone Means	JAC	RB	Gary Brown	NYG
RB	Tremayne Stephens	Free Agent	RB	Aaron Craver	NO
RB	Justin Watson	Free Agent	WR	Eric Metcalf	ARIZ
WR	Jeremy Earp	Free Agent	WR	Jimmy Oliver	DALL
WR	Dan Gmelin	Free Agent			
WR	Tyrone Taylor	Free Agent			
TE	Wendell Davis	Free Agent			
TE	Eric Smith	Free Agent			
TE	Champ Taylor	Free Agent			
TE	Sean Burke	NYJ			

Garrison Hearst/San Francisco 49ers

SAN FRANCISCO 49ERS

Home Stadium: 3Com Park
Playing Surface: Grass
Head Coach: Steve Mariucci
1997 Record: 13-3

13–3 Mark Gets Thumbs Up for 'Young' Coach Mariucci

RB: Looking to find that every-down back they've been looking for since the departure of Ricky Watters, the 49ers first tried to lure Rodney Hampton away from the Giants in 1997. The 49ers offered Hampton $16.4 million over six years, but the Giants matched the offer and Hampton stayed put in New York. The 49ers then turned their attention to Garrison Hearst of Cincinnati. Hearst was signed and brought aboard. Hearst then beat out Terry Kirby for the main back duties, which resulted in 1,019 rushing yards, 21 receptions for 194 yards and six touchdowns, playing in 13 games. Hearst missed the last three games of the season with a shoulder injury. Kirby was next in production with 418 rushing yards, 23 receptions for 279 yards and eight touchdowns. William Floyd chipped in 231 rushing yards, 37 receptions for 321 yards and four touchdowns. Looking to 1998, it's apparent that the 49ers were pleased with Hearst's performance since they re-signed him for $15.1 million over five years. Hearst will again carry the major load for the 49ers, which should mean even bigger numbers for him if he can stay healthy. Terry Kirby and William Floyd won't be back. Kirby was released because of salary cap concerns and Floyd left as a free agent to join the Carolina Panthers. This could create an opportunity for Marc Edwards, the 49ers' second-round pick of a year ago. Edwards rushed for only 17 yards and caught six passes for 48 yards as a rookie in 1997.

WR: If he's not the best receiver of all-time, he's certainly among the very top. Jerry Rice has had a phenomenal career. Because of that, you just expect him to have fabulous numbers each year, which makes him always a top fantasy pick. Those who took him as their top fantasy pick in 1997 were sadly disappointed when he suffered a terrible knee injury in the season opener. Rice worked hard to return and did, only to get hurt in the very game in which he returned. His seven receptions and one touchdown playing in just two games was devastating. With Rice hurt, the door opened for youngsters Terrell Owens and J.J. Stokes. Neither had really stepped up previously. They did, however, in 1997. Owens led the club with 60 receptions for 936 yards and eight touchdowns, while Stokes compiled 58 catches for 733 yards and scored four times. Iheanyi Uwaezuoke chipped in 14 catches but no touchdowns. Owens and Stokes were the real story, producing 118 receptions and 12 touchdowns between them. Those are numbers you might expect Jerry Rice to produce on his own. That's not to belittle what Owens and Stokes did, but just to point out what may be termed the norm for the incredible Jerry Rice. With Rice back healthy in 1998, the 49ers and fantasy fans hope things return to normal with Rice again putting up big numbers. Meanwhile, Owens and Stokes have earned respect but they'll be battling for playing time as the team's No.2 and No.3 receivers.

TE: For years, Brent Jones had been considered one of the league's premier tight ends. In recent years, injuries have begun to take their toll. In 1997, a leg injury sidelined Jones for three weeks, resulting in only 29 receptions for 383 yards and two touchdowns. That performance was not up to his normal standards. As the injuries increased, Jones was starting to believe his career was nearing its end. Following the 1997 season, Jones finally retired. Looking to 1998 and for a replacement for Brent Jones, the 49ers have lured Irv Smith from the Saints with a two-year, $1.75-million deal to come to San Francisco. Smith is a very respected tight end talent. Smith, too, was injured in 1997, missing six games with a knee injury. He's back healthy but don't give him the starting job quite yet. The 49ers are also very high on Greg Clark. Clark produced only eight receptions for 96 yards and one touchdown in 1997 but has impressed the 49ers. This is a situation to monitor as the 1998 season draws near. Either could produce good numbers as the starter.

QB: It was commonly believed that if you kept Steve Young healthy for most of the year, big statistical numbers would follow. In 1997, Young saw action in 15 games but finished with 3,029 passing yards and only 19 passing touchdowns and three on the ground—far short of what you'd expect. Remember, though, his favorite and perhaps the best receiver of all time, Jerry Rice, missed virtually the entire season. Young, looks to be back in 1998. The 49ers made Jim Druckenmiller their No.1 draft pick in 1997 but as long as Young wants to go, he will. Young will be back and so should a healthy Rice, which should help Young's numbers rebound in a healthy way in 1998.

K: Following a stellar 30 of 34 (.882) field goal performance in 1996, Gary Anderson slipped a few notches to 29 of 36 (.806) attempts in 1997. Certainly, that was still a very solid performance. In 1998, however, the 49ers won't be using Anderson's services. He was a free agent and has gone to Minnesota. This leaves the 49ers' kicking job wide open. The 49ers have begun their candidate considerations which includes John Becksvoort out of Tennessee.

Overall: How would the 49ers do under new head coach Steve Mariucci, fresh out of the college ranks? Their 13-3 record should have answered that. They did this without the services of all-world receiver Jerry Rice for virtually the entire season. The 49ers just keep rolling along. Quarterback Steve Young got older and more banged-up but he keeps coming back. In 1998, Young should have Rice back healthy along with Terrell Owens and J.J. Stokes, who picked up valuable experience with Rice out in 1997. On the ground, Garrison Hearst will be back. Hearst finally gives the 49ers the every-down capability they've long awaited. Looks like 1998 will be another successful season for the 49ers, especially since they face the league's fifth-easiest schedule.

Offseason Fantasy-Position Moves

	Arriving	From:		Departing	To:
TE	Irv Smith	NO	RB	Terry Kirby	Released
QB	Ty Detmer	PHIL	RB	William Floyd	CAR
K	John Becksvoort	Free Agent	TE	Brent Jones	Retired
			K	Gary Anderson	MINN

SEATTLE SEAHAWKS

Home Stadium: Kingdome
Playing Surface: Astro Turf
Head Coach: Dennis Erickson
1997 Record: 8-8

Seahawks Hope to Run like Watters

RB: After struggling with injuries in recent years, Chris Warren stayed healthy for most of 1997, missing only one entire game with a hamstring injury. For the season, Warren finished with 847 rushing yards, 45 receptions for 257 yards and four touchdowns. Those are decent numbers, but far from the numbers of the Warren of old. Lamar Smith, who missed four games with a leg injury, produced 392 rushing yards, 183 more on 23 receptions while scoring only twice. Steve Broussard was something of a surprise. He hadn't done much in recent years, but he tallied 418 yards on the ground, 24 receptions for another 183 yards and scored six times. The Seahawks, however, were not very pleased with the overall performance of their running game and made major changes for 1998. Lamar Smith took off as a free agent, for New Orleans. Steve Broussard was re-signed but Chris Warren's days in Seattle became numbered when the Seahawks signed Ricky Watters away from Philadelphia for a four-year deal worth a reported $13 million. Warren was soon there after released, though shortly after that signed on with the Dallas Cowboys to serve as a backup to Emmitt Smith. No more shuffling backs in and out of lineup. Watters, as long as he's healthy, will get the bulk of the rushing load and perhaps much of the receiving load out of the backfield for the Seahawks in 1998.

WR: Third-year receiver Joey Galloway rebounded to the 1,000-yard mark in 1997 after his numbers dipped in 1996. Galloway missed one game with an ankle injury but still finished with 72 receptions for 1,049 yards and 12 touchdowns. Veteran Brian Blades wasn't so fortunate as knee and hand injuries limited his action to just 10 games, resulting in only 30 receptions for 319 yards and two touchdowns. Blades missed the last five games of the year on injured-reserve with his injured hand. Mike Pritchard, in his second year with the Seahawks, stepped up his play when Blades was injured, finishing with 64 receptions for 843 yards and two touchdowns. Another significant contributor was James McKnight. McKnight missed the first four games of the year with a knee injury but then returned to record 34 receptions for 637 yards and a surprising six scores. Looking to 1998, there's concern Blades won't be back because of his injury. Regardless, speedster Joey Galloway should again put up big numbers. However, keep in mind that much of his success in 1997 can be attributed to the play of Warren Moon. Moon's return and health could be a big factor for the Seahawks' passing game. Look for Mike Pritchard to be the starter opposite Galloway, and James McKnight, who signed a three-year deal in the offseason, continuing to make big-plays as he did in 1997 with his six touchdowns.

TE: Carlester Crumpler continued to push former second-round pick Jeff Fauria for playing time in 1997. Crumpler and Fauria both saw action but

Crumpler got the better of it, by far. Crumpler finished the season with 31 catches for 361 yards and one touchdown. Fauria continued to be unimpressive, producing only 10 receptions for 110 yards and no touchdowns. Look for Crumpler to continue to get the bulk of the work in 1998 but not enough to draw very much fantasy interest.

QB: Life after 40 years of age is supposed to get easier and less hectic. Perhaps that's what Warren Moon thought when he signed a contract that virtually guaranteed he'd be the backup for John Friesz in 1997. So much for the life of leisure. Friesz broke his thumb in the season opener and Moon was thrust right back into a starting role. Did he do an adequate job for an aging quarterback? No, he did a terrific job for any age. Moon lit it up, throwing for 3,678 yards and 25 touchdowns, playing in 15 games. Moon had one game with four touchdown passes and one game with five. He was fun to watch, even though he wasn't on my fantasy team. How do the Seahawks handle this for 1998? Does Moon get another shot based on his performance or does Friesz get his job back? We'll monitor those questions closely as the season draws near.

K: Todd Peterson's 1997 performance was solid, 22 of 28 (.786), on field goal tries. However, four of his six misses came in his last 10 attempts at the end of the season, which may have raised some concern with the Seahawks.

Overall: Led by aging Warren Moon's resurgence in 1997, the Seahawks finished at 8-8. Looking to 1998, questions surround the quarterback situation because of Moon's 1997 performance. Do the Seahawks try to win now or do they look to the future with John Friesz and push Moon back into a backup role? On the ground, the Seahawks, after using Chris Warren, Lamar Smith and Steve Broussard in 1997, have set a new path for 1998. The Seahawks brought aboard Ricky Watters from Philadelphia. For the $13 million over four years they'll be paying him, it's a certainty that Watters will get plenty of work. With Watters aboard, Chris Warren's future in Seattle is pretty much over. Lamar Smith has already moved on to New Orleans. The Seahawks look to 1998 with hopes of climbing past the .500 mark since they face the league's ninth-easiest schedule.

Offseason Fantasy-Position Moves

	Arriving	From:		Departing	To:
RB	Michael Black	Free Agent	RB	Lamar Smith	NO
RB	Vershan Jackson	Free Agent	RB	Chris Warren	DALL
RB	Ricky Watters	PHIL			
WR	Michael Finneran	Free Agent			
TE	Furnell Hankton	Free Agent			

TAMPA BAY BUCCANEERS
Home Stadium: Houlihan's Stadium
Playing Surface: Grass
Head Coach: Tony Dungy
1997 Record: 10-6

Dungy has Bucs Getting it 'Dunn'

RB: It seems like each season Errict Rhett pleads his case for more money and threatens a holdout ,or actually holds out. It was hard to blame him in 1996, when he was scheduled to make around $400,000 after a 1,207-yard, 11-touchdown season. For whatever reason, the Bucs wouldn't give in and, instead, in 1997 made Warrick Dunn their No.1 draft pick, apparently sending a message to Rhett. Rhett assumed he would continue as the team's main back at the season's outset. That was not the case. By the season opener, Dunn and Mike Alstott were lining up in the backfield as Rhett watched from the sidelines. On the year, Rhett rushed for only 96 yards and three touchdowns. Meanwhile, Dunn fell just short of 1,000 yards, rushing for 978 while adding 462 more on 39 receptions and scoring seven times. Dunn recorded five 100-yard games. Alstott, the team's fullback, recorded 665 rushing yards and saw his receiving levels drop to only 23 receptions for 178 yards but he did score 10 times. A year earlier, Alstott had recorded 65 receptions. Looking to 1998, Rhett saw the writing on the wall and requested a trade. His wish was granted, and was dealt to Baltimore for a third-round pick. This leaves Warren Dunn and Mike Alstott, two young talented backs, to carry the Bucs to success in the future. I look for Dunn to easily surpass the 1,000-yard rushing mark and push the 1,500 to 1,800 range in total rushing-receiving yards in 1998.

WR: As the young Buccaneers continue to evolve under head coach Tony Dungy, new young talent is being brought in. The Buccaneers, who had two first-round picks in 1997, not only made running back Warrick Dunn a first-round pick, they also made wide receiver Reidel Anthony out of Florida a first-round selection. The Bucs were hoping that Anthony could be the big-play receiver they desperately needed. Anthony showed some signs of potential, but although his 35 receptions, totaling 448 yards, led Buccaneer wide receivers, they were a disappointment. Anthony also scored only four times. Besides Anthony, the Buccaneers got 33 receptions for 486 yards and five touchdowns out of Karl Williams, who also spent time returning kicks. And Horace Copeland, returning from a knee injury in 1996, recorded 32 receptions for 421 yards and one touchdown. He missed almost four entire games late in the year with an ankle injury. The Buccaneers had hoped Copeland could become their go-to receiver following a strong preseason but that never happened. Looking to 1998, the addition of Bert Emanuel should help immensely. Emanuel comes over from Atlanta where he caught 65 passes for 991 yards and 9 touchdowns a year ago. Emanuel was offered $16 million over 4 years by the Bucs, an offer the Falcons chose not to match. Emanuel will start, with Reidel Anthony, Karl Williams and rookie second-round pick Jacquez Greene out of Florida likely battling for the #2 and #3 spots, with Horace Copeland pushing for playing time. Because the

Buccaneers will again run the ball often under Tony Dungy, none of their receivers could be considered too much of a prime fantasy candidate. Perhaps a No.2 fantasy receiver for Emanuel or, better yet, someone you could stick on your roster or bench until you can get a feel for his development.

TE: Bothered by a groin and hernia type injury in 1997, Jackie Harris's performance continued to fall. On the season, Harris recorded only 20 receptions for 216 yards and one touchdown. That was a big disappointment for someone who was once considered one of the league's more respected tight ends. With Harris bothered by injury, Dave Moore saw enough playing time to produce 19 catches for 217 yards and four touchdowns. Patrick Hape and John Davis also chipped in four and three receptions, respectively, with Hape scoring once. Looking to 1998, Harris won't be back, having signed a free-agent deal with Tennessee in the offseason. This leaves Moore, Hape and Davis to battle for playing time. Moore is the most likely beneficiary and should easily boost his previous year's numbers.

QB: Under head coach Tony Dungy, Trent Dilfer seems to continue to develop. Dungy has stuck with Dilfer, who had struggled, to put it mildly, before Dungy. In 1997, it was not so much the 2,555 passing yards but the 21 touchdown passes that were a pleasant surprise to Buccaneers and fantasy fans. Dilfer's performance was a big factor in the Bucs' sudden turnaround. Can he improve on those numbers? He has a young set of receivers and a very difficult schedule to face, which may make that tough, at least in 1998.

K: Michael Husted didn't have many chances to show his stuff in 1997 but he made good on 13 of 17 (.765) field goal attempts. A year earlier, Husted was 25 of 33 (.758), which in a way demonstrates how much more effective the Bucs were in the red zone in 1997. Looking to 1998, with the Bucs up against a tough schedule, I look for Husted to get many more field goal tries and that will obviously lift his numbers.

Overall: In just two short seasons, head coach Tony Dungy has turned the Bucs into winners who finished 10-6 in 1997. He's done it with youth and by believing in the talent he has. The Buccaneers, obviously happy with his work, signed Dungy to a five-year, $6.5-million deal in the offseason. Choosing running back Warrick Dunn and wide receiver Reidel Anthony, both in the first round in 1997, has set the stage for the future. Dungy has also let Trent Dilfer continue to develop into a much more confident player and the addition of Bert Emanuel should help Dilfer's game. The Bucs' future looks brighter all the time. However, in 1998, they'll have to prove themselves in a big way because they face the league's third-toughest schedule.

Offseason Fantasy-Position Moves

	Arriving	From:		Departing	To:
RB	Rabih Abdullah	Free Agent	RB	Errict Rhett	BALT
RB	Lorenzo Neal	NYJ	TE	Jackie Harris	TENN
WR	Nigea Carter	Free Agent			
WR	Kendrick Lee	Free Agent			
WR	Bert Emanuel	ATL			
TE	Lamont Hall	Free Agent			

Warrick Dunn/Tampa Bay Buccaneers

Eddie George/Tennessee Oilers

TENNESSEE OILERS

Home Stadium: Vanderbilt
Playing Surface: Astro Turf
Head Coach: Jeff Fisher
1997 Record: 8-8

McN'air' Will be Helped by Addition of Thigpen,
but Ground Attack Still the Key 'By George'

RB: Young Eddie George had a second straight very productive yardage year in 1997. After producing 1,368 rushing yards as a rookie in 1996, George went on to top that with 1,399 rushing yards in 1997. George also added just seven catches for 44 yards while scoring seven times. On the year, George topped the 100-yard mark eight times and actually began the year with a 216-yard performance against Oakland in the season opener. In addition to George, the Oilers got 310 rushing yards and 14 catches for 111 yards, along with three touchdowns, out of Rodney Thomas. Thomas, who rushed for nearly 1,000 yards (947) in 1995 before George's arrival, has been pushed to the backseat since George joined the club. With Thomas supplying an occasional breather, there looks to be little to slow George down. Topping the 1,500-yard mark in rushing is surely well within George's reach. The only other category fantasy fans would like to see is for George to top the 10-touchdown mark, which is another very reachable goal for George in 1998.

WR: With Eddie George handling the bulk of the offensive load on the ground and with the Oilers having a young quarterback in Steve McNair, the Oilers' passing game has taken a bit of a backseat. In 1997, Willie Davis led the Oilers' receivers with just 43 receptions that went for 564 yards while he scored four times. Chris Sanders, who led the Oilers with 48 receptions in 1996, slipped to 31 receptions for 498 yards and scored three times but he did miss three games with a hamstring injury. Besides Davis and Sanders, the Oilers got 14 catches for 141 yards and no touchdowns out of Derrick Mason, 12 receptions for 141 yards and one touchdown out of Derek Russell, and only six catches and one touchdown out of second-round pick Joey Kent out of Tennessee. Looking to 1998, the Oilers tried to improve their passing game by signing free agent Yancey Thigpen from Pittsburgh in the offseason. Thigpen, who signed a five-year, $21-million deal, will be the featured receiver with Chris Sanders and/or rookie first-round draft pick Kevin Dyson out of Utah in a more minor role. Dyson will add speed to the Oiler passing game giving them a nice 'deep threat' potential. Willie Davis and Derek Russell are presumed unlikely to be back. This leaves Thigpen and Sanders to be the main receiving statistical beneficiaries. For them to put up decent numbers, the Oilers and Steve McNair must take to the air more often in 1998.

TE: Frank Wycheck's numbers just continue to climb for the Tennessee Oilers. In the last three seasons, Wycheck has recorded 40, 53 and 63 receptions, respectively. Wycheck's 63 receptions went for 748 yards, while he scored four times. Of Wycheck's four touchdowns, two of them were for more than 30 yards, proving he's a nice downfield asset. In addition to

Wycheck, Michael Roan chipped in 12 receptions for 159 yards. Looking to 1998, it's become evident how important Frank Wycheck has become to the Oiler passing game, which is why his success will continue. The Oilers, however, have also added Jackie Harris to the fold. Harris comes, via free agency, from Tampa Bay. Harris, once one of the league's more respected tight ends, has been slowed by injury the couple of seasons. In 1997, he produced only 20 receptions and one touchdown with Tampa Bay. His presence, however, should make Frank Wycheck even more effective in 1998.

QB: The Oilers, now looking to their future, gave the starting reins to Steve McNair on a full-time basis in 1997. McNair had split time with Chris Chandler in 1996 but Chandler, knowing the Oilers' plans, departed for Atlanta. McNair did not set the world on fire, finishing with 2,665 passing yards and only 14 touchdown passes. He was, however, very effective on the ground, rushing for 674 yards and scoring eight rushing touchdowns. Moving on to 1998, McNair is only going to get better. Adding wide receiver Yancey Thigpen should also help his passing numbers, which could easily approach the 3,000-yard, 20-touchdown pass range. And also, remember how effective he is on the ground. In 1997, he rushed for 674 yards and eight touchdowns.

K: It wasn't an overly impressive season, but a solid one for veteran Al Del Greco in 1997. Del Greco hit 27 of 35 (.771) field goal attempts, including both of his attempts from beyond 50 yards. His performance will likely keep the veteran around again in 1998.

Overall: After back-to-back 8-8 seasons, the Oilers are looking to take a bigger step toward a brighter and more successful future, now located in Tennessee. They have a solid ground game as Eddie George has played extremely well in his first two seasons in the NFL. It's time, however, for young Steve McNair to continue to mature and improve, getting the passing attack on board. Adding Steeler free agent Yancey Thigpen will help as will rookie first-round pick Kevin Dyson. Thigpen caught 79 passes for 1,398 yards in Pittsburgh in 1997. Frank Wycheck, quickly becoming one of the league's better tight ends, also provides great help and he will get help from free-agent acquisition Jackie Harris. Facing the league's fifth-toughest schedule won't help, however.

Offseason Fantasy-Position Moves

	Arriving	From:	Departing	To:
QB	Ron Powlus	Free Agent		
RB	Ricky Whittle	Free Agent		
WR	Yancey Thigpen	PITT		
WR	Maurice Bryant	Free Agent		
TE	Jackie Harris	TB		
TE	Josh Brady	Free Agent		

WASHINGTON REDSKINS
Home Stadium: Robert F. Kennedy Stadium
Playing Surface: Grass
Head Coach: Norv Turner
1997 Record: 8-7-1

Redskins Need Healthy Allen, Frerotte to Get Back on Track

RB: How do you follow up a season in which you produced 1,325 rushing yards, 32 receptions for another 194 yards and scored a whopping 21 touchdowns, winning Fantasy Player of the Year Honors? Terry Allen, after that 1996 performance, had his sights set on another big year in 1997. So did many fantasy football owners, who made Allen a prime fantasy pick going into the season. Both Allen and his fantasy fans were very disappointed. Allen began the year as if he was about to repeat or better his 1996 performance, rushing for 141 yards and scoring twice in the season opener against Carolina. However, he suffered a broken thumb, which forced him to miss the next game. He returned, but knee and ankle injuries sidelined him for five more games. For the season, Allen finished with only 724 rushing yards, 20 receptions for 172 yards and five touchdowns. With Allen hurt, second-year man Stephen Davis saw more action and finished with 567 rushing yards, 18 catches for 134 yards and three touchdowns. Brian Mitchell was again effective out of the backfield with 36 receptions for 438 yards, while rushing for 107 more and scoring four times. Larry Bowie was also helpful out of the backfield with 34 catches for 388 yards, while rushing for 100 yards and scoring four times. Looking to 1998, the Redskins would love to keep Terry Allen healthy because he is a key to their offense, but Stephen Davis should continue to see action and third-round pick Skip Hicks out of UCLA, who rushed for over 1,100 yards in 1997 is another added option. Both Larry Bowie and Brian Mitchell will remain assets out of the backfield.

WR: The Redskins kept hoping in 1997 that Michael Westbrook, their former No.1 draft pick, would step up to be their go-to guy. Westbrook, who caught only 34 passes in 1996, was again a disappointment in 1997. First, he was suspended for the season opener for punching teammate Stephen Davis. Later in the year, a knee injury kept him out of three games. On the season, Westbrook did lead the Redskins receivers but with only 34 catches for 559 yards while scoring three times. Veteran Henry Ellard, whom the Redskins phased out of the offense, finished with 32 catches for 485 yards and four touchdowns. Leslie Shepherd, was actually playing well until he dislocated his wrist, which sidelined him for the last six weeks of the season. To that point, Shepard had produced 29 catches for 562 yards and five touchdowns, playing in just 10 games. Chris Thomas chipped in 11 catches for 93 yards. Looking to 1998, the Redskins are likely to seek help at wide receiver. Michael Westbrook continues to be a disappointment, and aging Henry Ellard is being phased out. Leslie Shepherd has been their most consistent receiver but he can't do it alone.

TE: Jamie Asher continued to improve in 1997 and finished the year as the leading overall receiver for the Redskins with 49 catches for 474 yards but he scored only once. In addition to Asher, the Redskins got only four receptions out of James Jenkins but three of the four went for touchdowns. Looking to 1998, Asher will again be a main fixture in the Redskins' offense. He'll be hoping, however, to improve his touchdown production to more like that of 1996 when he scored four times on 42 receptions. The Redskins have also made Stephon Alexander out of Oklahoma their #2 draft pick. Alexander will be a nice addition to the offense. He's a big, fast tight end who'll push Asher as the season goes on.

QB: In his second season as the team's lone starter (he used to share playing time with former first-round pick Heath Shuler), Gus Frerotte did not set the world on fire with his passing numbers. It was not all his fault, however, as the Redskins' receiving group battled injuries and inconsistency. Frerotte's yardage numbers dropped from 3,453 yards in 1996 to 2,682 in 1997, but he did miss three games at the season's end with a broken hip. Frerotte's touchdown pass numbers actually went up from 12 in 1996 to 17 in 1997. With Frerotte out, veteran Jeff Hostetler stepped in to throw for 674 yards and six touchdowns in leading the Redskins to two wins in those last three games. Looking to 1998, however, it is believed that if Frerotte recovers fully from his broken hip, he'll reassume the starting role over Hostetler. Then, if he and his receivers can stay healthy, 3,000 passing yards and 20 touchdown passes are well within reach.

K: Kicker Scott Blanton struggled in 1997, hitting only 16 of his 24 (.667) field goal attempts. To his credit, three of his eight misses came from farther than 50 yards and five of the eight were from beyond 45 yards. This, after hitting 26 of 32 (.813) field goal tries a year earlier in 1996. He'll have to fare much better or the restricted free agent may be looking for work elsewhere. The Redskins have already brought in Danny Kight to battle for the job. Kight, a free agent also was a candidate for the Dallas Cowboy kicking chores a year ago, eventually losing out to Ritchie Cunningham.

Overall: Losing a player like Terry Allen for a major part of a season because of injury is very costly. That was 1997. Stephen Davis, Brian Mitchell and Larry Bowie tried to pick up the slack and did well, but not nearly as well as Allen had done a year earlier. Keeping Allen healthy is the key to the Redskins' ground attack. The Redskins' wide receiver group also took its injuries in 1997, as did quarterback Gus Frerotte, who ended the year with a broken hip. Frerotte's recovery is very important for the Redskins' future. The Redskins are still looking for a go-to receiver because former No.1 pick Michael Westbrook just can't seem to step up. One positive for the Redskins in 1998 is the fact that they face the league's sixth-easiest schedule.

Offseason Fantasy-Position Moves

	Arriving	From:	Departing	To:
K	Danny Kight	Free Agent		
WR	Junior Lord	Free Agent		
WR	Ousmane Tounkara	Free Agent		
RB	Norman Miller	Free Agent		
RB	Kevin Pesak	Free Agent		
RB	Chris Shelton	Free Agent		

Terry Allen/Washington Redskins

VIII
RATING THE PLAYERS:
BASIC SCORING METHOD

In the Basic Scoring Method, points are awarded to the players who actually score or throw touchdowns (or kick field goals or extra points, in the case of kickers), with no consideration for the yardage a player may accumulate or the distance covered by a touchdown play.

The Basic Scoring Method is the simplest scoring method, but it may be the hardest to draft for. This method probably involves more luck than skill in predicting who will score touchdowns. When most sports enthusiasts sit down at their first fantasy football draft, they feel they are pretty much up on the game. Their tendency is to draft well-known, established names; but during the season, they may get a rude awakening. Their highly paid scatback rushes up and down the field week after week, but when it's time for the two-yard touchdown plunge, the ball is given to the big fullback. Such had been the case in Detroit in recent years, as Barry Sanders ran and received up and down the field but gave the ball up to Derrick Moore when the team got near the goal line. This limited Sanders to seven and three touchdowns, respectively, in 1993 and 1994. But with Moore gone in 1995, Sanders's touchdown total climbed to 11, and in 1997 hit the 14 mark. In 1995 Edgar Bennett rushed and received for 1,715 yards but scored only seven times. Bam Morris rushed for only 559 yards but scored nine times. In 1996, Garrison Hearst led the Bengals with 847 rushing yards but never scored a rushing touchdown. Ki-Jana Carter became the designated scorer, rushing for only 264 yards but scoring eight rushing touchdowns. In 1997 Karim Abdul-Jabbar running for Miami, rushed for only 892 yards but scored 16 times. Marcus Allen rushed for only 505 yards but scored 11 times. In recent years, more teams have left their scatback players in near the goal line to reap some scoring rewards after laboring to pick up all that yardage. Nevertheless, don't think that a roster of million-dollar players guarantees a successful fantasy football team.

In the following pages, I'm going to help you plan your basic drafting strategy. I'll follow that with some things to keep in mind when choosing players from each position. Next, I'll offer a look at the players' 1997 statistical results. And, finally, I'll rate the players for 1998. No rookies are included in my player ratings. It's too early to size up how rookies will fit into each team's scheme, so I rate them separately, in Section V of this chapter.

DRAFTING STRATEGY BY ROUNDS
(A Guide for the Beginner)

1 The draft consists of 12 rounds.

2. Of the 12 players, seven are starters and five are reserves.

3. The starting seven comprise:

1 Quarterback		1 Quarterback
2 Running Backs	OR	2 Running Backs
2 Wide Receivers	FLEX OPTION	3 Receivers
1 Tight End		1 Kicker
1 Kicker		

4. The five reserves can be from any position.

5. Any player from any starting position can be drafted in any round.

What are the keys to drafting a successful fantasy football team? Why are some franchises consistent winners, year after year? In studying the successful franchises of the leagues I participate in, I have found a number of factors. One of these is preparation: successful franchise owners are always ready for the unexpected. If a player they were hoping to get is grabbed just before their turn, they have an alternate choice. These owners also make sure they review the previous season to learn about significant injuries that might have drastically reduced the year-end stats of prime players. They won't overlook these players as candidates for their drafts. (In Section II: "Helpful Facts from the 1997 Season," I note which players sustained significant injuries last season. Take a look at it before you head into your 1997 draft.) Following is a system that will give you the best chances for a successful draft.

ROUND 1: For the first round, I recommend grabbing the best six-point player available. In the past, this would almost automatically have been a running back, but in recent years, wide receivers such as Jerry Rice, Herman Moore, Carl Pickens, and Cris Carter have also turned into consistent scorers. Quarterbacks may throw a lot of touchdown passes, but they are awarded only three points for each, as opposed to the six awarded to the player who actually scores the touchdown. However, a quarterback like Steve Young may throw for 25 touchdowns and run for five more (when he's healthy), so he merits first-round consideration, as does Brett Favre, who may throw 30 to 40 touchdowns. Young Kordell Stewart, who rushed for an incredible 11 touchdowns in 1997, may now get first-round consideration. Kickers, especially in recent years, are scoring a lot of points; but I still recommend taking a six-point player first. Though a kicker may occasionally top 140 points, you can still get a good 100-point kicker in later rounds, whereas the six-point players will be picked up early.

ROUND 2: In this round, choose the best player available, perhaps with six-point players—running backs, wide receivers, and tight ends. There is another possibility: If you have an inkling that a particular quarterback may be on his way to an outstanding year (30-plus touchdowns), you may elect to grab him in this round if none of the six-point players really excites you. (Some owners get panicky in the early rounds if they think they might get stuck with a mediocre player at a key position. If you pick a quarterback in this round, you might just set off a chain reaction of quarterback picking by other owners. This works to your advantage if it happens, because it leaves you more six-point players to choose from in the third round.

ROUND 3: Now it's time to consider a three-point player, either a quarterback or a kicker if you haven't already chosen one. I find that a trend usually develops in the third round. If the first two or three choices are quarterbacks, the rest of the franchises will panic and choose a quarterback. If the first few picks are kickers, the rest will follow that lead. Kickers and quarterbacks play important roles on your fantasy football team. I've seen kickers carry a fantasy team for two or three weeks. A quarterback who throws 30 touchdowns in a year gives you (on the average) six points weekly from that position. (If you have already selected your quarterback by this round, it's a good idea to again pick the best six-point player available.)

ROUNDS 4 and 5: It's time to pick up at least one of your wide receivers. By now the best ones are gone, but how about taking a stab at somebody? In 1997 those who grabbed less heralded Rod Smith, James Jett and Joey Galloway in the middle rounds were all rewarded with 12 touchdowns.

ROUNDS 6, 7, and 8: By the end of the eighth round, you should have your seven starting positions filled.

ROUNDS 9 through 12: This is the time to pick your reserves and take some long shots on rookies. Those who picked rookies Corey Dillon or Antowain Smith in 1997 are certainly glad they did. Make sure that you have at least one backup at quarterback, running back, and wide receiver, since these seem to be the most injury-prone positions.

NOTE: If you draft a receiver who is a favorite target of your quarterback, you get a nine-point play every time there is a touchdown completion between the two (three points for the pass and six points for the touchdown). This can make a difference, especially if you have tandems like Jeff Blake and Carl Pickens, or Brett Favre and Antonio Freeman. Now let's take a look at what to consider in choosing players at the various positions

A LOOK AT THE RUNNING BACKS
(A Guide for the Beginner)

Considerations in Choosing a RUNNING BACK

Choosing a good running back is usually crucial to putting together a competitive team. Here, listed in order of usefulness, are some considerations for choosing your running backs. After this review are the 1997 statistics, followed by my 1998 player ratings.

1. First, review players' previous performances, especially from last season. Injuries, player movement, holdouts and the like should be noted. Players like Curtis Martin, Terry Allen, and Garrison Hearst had significant injuries.

2. Look for running backs that both play for good teams and who are the primary back for their team. And most importantly, make sure this back is used in goal-line situations. You don't want a back who is removed when his team gets inside the ten-yard line.

3. Next, review backs that are used as designated scorers, such as Marcus Allen, who in 1993 rushed for only 764 yards but scored 15 times. In 1995 Bam Morris rushed for only 559 yards but scored nine times. In 1996 Ki-Jana Carter of Cincinnati rushed for only 264 yards but scored eight times. In 1997 Marcus Allen again rushed for only 505 yards but scored 11 times.

4. Finally, consider the trend of a number of teams now trying to protect their "franchise" backs in goal-line situations. In Detroit, for example, the Lions began to use Derrick Moore for many goal-line situations in 1994. Moore has since departed, however, and Barry Sanders is once again a scoring force.

In looking at the 1997 statistics, you'll find the players ranked by their fantasy-point totals. Remember that in the Basic Scoring Method, fantasy points are calculated by scoring six points for every touchdown rushed or caught and three points for every touchdown pass thrown.

NAME	TEAM	GP	RSH	YARDS	REC	YARDS	TOTAL YARDS	RSH TDs	REC TDs	TOTAL TDs	CONV PTS	FAN-TASY PTS
1. Te. Davis	DEN	15	369	1,750	42	287	2,037	15	0	15	6	96
1996		16	345	1,538	36	310	1,848	13	2	15	0	90
1995		14	237	1,117	49	367	1,484	7	1	8	0	48
3 Yr - TOTALS		45	951	4,405	127	964	5,369	35	3	38	6	234
2. Abdul-Jabbar	MIA	16	283	892	29	261	1,153	15	1	16	0	96
1996		16	307	1,116	23	139	1,255	11	0	11	0	66
1995		–	–	–	–	–	–	–	–	–	–	–
3 Yr - TOTALS		32	590	2,008	52	400	2,408	26	1	27	0	162
3. Sanders	DET	16	335	2,053	33	305	2,358	11	3	14	0	84
1996		16	307	1,553	24	147	1,700	11	0	11	0	66
1995		16	314	1,500	48	398	1,898	11	1	12	0	72
3 Yr - TOTALS		48	956	5,106	105	850	5,956	33	4	37	0	222
4. Levens	GB	16	329	1,435	53	370	1,805	7	5	12	2	74
1996		16	121	566	31	226	792	5	5	10	0	60
1995		15	36	120	48	434	554	3	4	7	0	42
3 Yr - TOTALS		47	486	2,121	132	1,030	3,151	15	14	29	2	176
5. M. Allen	KC	16	124	505	11	86	591	11	0	11	0	72
1996		16	206	830	27	270	1,100	9	0	9	0	54
1995		16	207	890	27	210	1,100	5	0	5	0	30
3 Yr - TOTALS		48	537	2,225	65	566	2,791	25	0	25	0	156
6. J. Anderson	ATL	16	290	1,002	29	284	1,286	7	3	10	0	63
1996		16	232	1,055	49	473	1,528	5	1	6	0	36
1995		7	39	161	4	42	203	1	0	1	0	6
3 Yr - TOTALS		39	561	2,218	82	799	3,017	13	4	17	0	105
7. R. Harris	CHI	13	275	1,033	28	115	1,148	10	0	10	0	60
1996		12	194	748	32	296	1,044	4	1	5	0	30
1995		1	0	0	1	4	4	0	0	0	0	0
3 Yr - TOTALS		26	469	1,781	61	415	2,196	14	1	15	0	90
8. Dillon +	CIN	14	233	1,129	27	259	1,388	10	0	10	0	60
1996		–	–	–	–	–	–	–	–	–	–	–
1995		–	–	–	–	–	–	–	–	–	–	–
3 Yr - TOTALS		14	233	1,129	27	259	1,388	10	0	10	0	60
9. Alstott	TB	15	176	665	23	178	843	7	3	10	0	60
1996		16	96	377	65	557	934	3	3	6	0	36
1995		–	–	–	–	–	–	–	–	–	–	–
3 Yr - TOTALS		31	272	1,042	88	735	1,777	10	6	16	0	96
10. Means	JAC	14	244	823	15	104	927	9	0	9	0	54
1996		13	152	507	7	45	552	2	1	3	0	18
1995 w/SD		10	186	730	7	46	776	5	0	5	0	30
3 Yr - TOTALS		37	582	2,060	29	195	2,255	16	1	17	0	102
11. Stewart	JAC	16	136	555	41	336	891	8	1	9	0	54
1996		13	190	723	30	177	900	8	2	10	0	60
1995		14	137	525	21	190	715	2	1	3	0	18
3 Yr - TOTALS		43	463	1,803	92	703	2,506	18	4	22	0	132
12. Bettis	PITT	15	375	1,665	15	110	1,775	7	2	9	0	54
1996		16	320	1,431	22	122	1,553	11	0	11	0	66
1995 w/STL		15	183	637	18	106	743	3	0	3	0	18
3 Yr - TOTALS		46	878	3,733	55	338	4,071	21	2	23	0	138
13. Kirby *	SF	16	125	418	23	279	697	6	1	8	4	52
1996		13	134	559	52	439	998	3	1	4	0	27
1995 w/MIA		16	108	414	66	618	1,032	4	3	7	0	42
3 Yr - TOTALS		45	367	1,391	141	1,336	2,727	13	5	19	4	121
14. A. Smith +	BUF	16	194	840	28	177	1,017	8	0	8	0	48
1996		–	–	–	–	–	–	–	–	–	–	–
1995		–	–	–	–	–	–	–	–	–	–	–
3 Yr - TOTALS		16	194	840	28	177	1,017	8	0	8	0	48
15. Faulk	IND	16	264	1,054	47	471	1,525	7	1	8	0	48
1996		13	198	587	56	428	1,015	7	0	7	0	42
1995		16	289	1,078	56	475	1,553	11	3	14	0	84
3 Yr - TOTALS		45	751	2,719	159	1,374	4,093	25	4	29	0	174

1997 STATISTICAL RESULTS
(RUNNING BACKS — BASIC SCORING METHOD)

NAME	TEAM	GP	RSH	YARDS	REC	YARDS	TOTAL YARDS	RSH TDs	REC TDs	TOTAL TDs	CONV PTS	FAN-TASY PTS
16. Phillips **	**MIA**	**12**	**201**	**677**	**11**	**39**	**675**	**8**	**0**	**8**	**0**	**48**
1996 w/STL		15	193	632	8	28	660	4	1	5	0	30
1995		–	–	–	–	–	–	–	–	–	–	–
3 Yr - TOTALS		27	394	1,309	19	67	1,335	12	1	13	0	78
17. Kaufman	**OAK**	**16**	**272**	**1,294**	**40**	**403**	**1,697**	**6**	**2**	**8**	**0**	**48**
1996		16	150	874	22	143	1,017	1	1	2	0	12
1995		15	108	490	9	62	552	1	0	2	0	12
3 Yr - TOTALS		47	530	2,658	71	608	3,266	8	3	12	0	72
18. George	**TENN**	**16**	**357**	**1,399**	**7**	**44**	**1,443**	**6**	**1**	**7**	**2**	**44**
1996		16	335	1,368	23	182	1,550	8	0	8	0	48
1995		–	–	–	–	–	–	–	–	–	–	–
3 Yr - TOTALS		32	692	2,767	30	226	2,993	14	1	15	2	92
19. F. Lane	**CAR**	**12**	**182**	**809**	**8**	**27**	**836**	**7**	**0**	**7**	**0**	**42**
1996		–	–	–	–	–	–	–	–	–	–	–
1995		–	–	–	–	–	–	–	–	–	–	–
3 Yr - TOTALS		12	182	809	8	27	836	7	0	7	0	42
20. K. Carter	**CIN**	**15**	**128**	**464**	**21**	**157**	**621**	**7**	**0**	**7**	**0**	**42**
1996		15	91	264	22	169	433	8	1	9	0	54
1995		–	–	–	–	–	–	–	–	–	–	–
3 Yr - TOTALS		30	219	728	43	326	1,054	15	1	16	0	96
21. R. Smith	**MINN**	**14**	**232**	**1,266**	**37**	**197**	**1,463**	**6**	**1**	**7**	**0**	**42**
1996		8	162	692	7	39	731	3	0	3	0	18
1995		9	139	632	7	35	667	5	0	5	2	32
3 Yr - TOTALS		31	533	2,590	51	271	2,861	14	1	15	2	92
22. Murrell	**NYJ**	**16**	**300**	**1,086**	**27**	**106**	**1,192**	**7**	**0**	**7**	**0**	**42**
1996		16	301	1,249	17	81	1,330	6	1	7	0	42
1995		15	192	795	71	465	1,260	1	2	3	0	18
3 Yr - TOTALS		47	793	3,130	115	652	3,782	14	3	17	0	102
23. Watters	**PHIL**	**16**	**285**	**1,110**	**48**	**440**	**1,550**	**7**	**0**	**7**	**0**	**42**
1996		16	353	1,411	51	444	1,855	13	0	13	0	78
1995		16	337	1,273	62	434	1,707	11	1	12	0	72
3 Yr - TOTALS		48	975	3,794	161	1,318	5,112	31	1	32	0	192
24. Dunn +	**TB**	**16**	**224**	**978**	**39**	**462**	**1,440**	**4**	**3**	**7**	**0**	**42**
1996		–	–	–	–	–	–	–	–	–	–	–
1995		–	–	–	–	–	–	–	–	–	–	–
3 Yr - TOTALS		16	224	978	39	462	1,440	4	3	7	0	42
25. Vardell	**DET**	**15**	**32**	**122**	**16**	**218**	**340**	**6**	**0**	**6**	**0**	**36**
1996 w/SF		8	58	192	28	179	371	2	0	2	0	12
1995 w/CLE		4	4	9	6	18	27	0	0	0	0	0
3 Yr - TOTALS		27	94	323	50	415	738	8	0	8	0	48
26. Hearst	**SF**	**13**	**234**	**1,019**	**21**	**194**	**1,213**	**4**	**2**	**6**	**0**	**36**
1996 w/CIN		16	225	847	12	131	978	0	1	1	2	8
1995 w./ARIZ		16	284	1,070	29	243	1,313	1	1	2	0	12
3 Yr - TOTALS		45	743	2,936	62	568	3,504	5	4	9	2	56
27. Broussard	**SEAT**	**13**	**70**	**418**	**24**	**143**	**561**	**5**	**1**	**6**	**0**	**36**
1996		9	15	106	6	26	132	1	0	1	0	6
1995		15	46	222	10	94	316	1	0	1	0	6
3 Yr - TOTALS		37	131	746	40	263	1,009	7	1	8	0	48
28. Martin	**NE**	**13**	**274**	**1,160**	**41**	**296**	**1,456**	**4**	**1**	**5**	**0**	**30**
1996		16	316	1,152	46	333	1,485	14	3	17	2	104
1995		16	368	1,487	30	261	1,748	14	1	15	2	92
3 Yr - TOTALS		45	958	3,799	117	890	4,689	32	5	37	4	226
29. Way	**NYG**	**16**	**151**	**698**	**37**	**304**	**1,002**	**4**	**1**	**5**	**0**	**30**
1996		15	22	79	32	328	407	1	1	2	0	12
1995		5	2	6	7	76	82	0	1	1	0	6
3 Yr - TOTALS		36	175	783	76	708	1,491	5	3	8	0	48
30. T. Allen	**WASH**	**10**	**210**	**724**	**20**	**172**	**896**	**4**	**1**	**5**	**0**	**30**
1996		16	347	1,353	32	194	1,547	21	0	21	0	126
1995		16	338	1,309	31	232	1,541	10	1	11	0	66
3 Yr - TOTALS		42	895	3,386	83	598	3,984	35	2	37	0	222

1997 STATISTICAL RESULTS
(RUNNING BACKS — BASIC SCORING METHOD)

NAME	TEAM	GP	RSH	YARDS	REC	YARDS	TOTAL YARDS	RSH TDs	REC TDs	TOTAL TDs	CONV PTS	FAN-TASY PTS
31. Bates	NO	11	119	440	5	42	482	4	0	4	0	27
32. E. Smith	DALL	16	261	1,074	40	234	1,308	4	0	4	2	26
33. Barber +	NYG	12	136	511	34	299	810	3	1	4	2	26
34. Morris	BALT	11	204	774	29	176	950	4	0	4	0	24
35. Hoard	MINN	12	80	235	11	84	319	4	0	4	0	24
36. Zellars	NO	16	156	552	31	263	815	4	0	4	0	24
37. Wheatley	NYG	13	152	583	16	140	723	4	0	4	0	24
38. Ln. Johnson + *	NYJ	16	48	158	16	142	300	2	0	4	0	24
39. Brown	SD	15	253	945	21	137	1,082	4	0	4	0	24
40. C. Warren	SEAT	15	200	847	45	257	1,104	4	0	4	0	24
41. Floyd	SF	15	78	231	37	321	552	3	1	4	0	24
42. Mitchell *	WASH	16	23	107	36	438	545	1	1	4	0	24
43. Bowie	WASH	15	28	100	34	388	488	2	2	4	0	24
44. Hanspard + *	ATL	15	53	335	6	53	388	0	1	3	0	18
45. Richardson	KC	4	2	11	3	6	17	0	3	3	0	18
46. Byars	NE	15	11	24	20	189	213	0	3	3	0	18
47. Gash	NE	12	6	10	22	154	164	0	3	3	0	18
48. Garner	PHIL	16	116	547	24	225	772	3	0	3	0	18
49. Turner	PHIL	15	18	96	48	443	539	0	3	3	0	18
50. Lee	STL	16	28	104	61	825	929	0	3	3	0	18
51. J. Moore	STL	8	104	379	8	69	448	3	0	3	0	18
52. Rhett	TB	6	31	96	0	0	96	3	0	3	0	18
53. R. Thomas	TENN	15	67	310	14	111	421	3	0	3	0	18
54. St. Davis	WASH	11	141	567	18	134	701	3	0	3	0	18
55. Meggett	NE	12	20	60	19	203	263	1	1	2	0	15
56. Evans	MINN	16	43	157	21	152	309	2	0	2	2	14
57. L. Smith	SEAT	12	91	392	23	183	575	2	0	2	2	14
58. Centers	ARIZ	15	101	276	54	409	685	1	1	2	0	12
59. McElroy	ARIZ	14	135	424	7	32	456	2	0	2	0	12
60. J. Graham +	BALT	8	81	299	12	51	350	2	0	2	0	12
61. Holmes	BUF	9	22	106	13	106	212	2	0	2	0	12
62. Greene	CAR	16	45	157	40	277	434	1	1	2	0	12
63. Biakabutuka	CAR	8	75	299	0	0	299	2	0	2	0	12
64. Bieniemy *	CIN	15	21	97	31	249	346	1	0	2	0	12
65. Milne	CIN	15	13	32	23	138	170	2	0	2	0	12
66. S. Williams	DALL	15	121	468	21	159	627	2	0	2	0	12
67. Walker	DALL	10	6	20	14	149	169	0	2	2	0	12
68. L. Warren	IND	12	28	80	20	192	272	2	0	2	0	12
69. Anders	KC	15	79	397	59	453	850	0	2	2	0	12
70. McPhail	MIA	14	17	146	34	262	408	1	1	2	0	12
71. Spikes	MIA	10	63	180	7	70	250	2	0	2	0	12
72. Palmer	MINN	12	11	36	26	193	229	1	1	2	0	12
73. Pegram **	NYG	12	28	95	21	90	185	2	0	2	0	12
74. Jones +	PITT	16	72	235	16	96	331	1	1	2	0	12
75. Strong	SEAT	9	4	8	13	91	99	0	2	2	0	12
76. A. Johnson	CAR	16	97	358	21	158	516	0	1	1	2	8
77. Autry +	CHI	12	112	319	9	59	378	1	0	1	2	8
78. R. Moore **	ARIZ	11	81	278	4	34	312	1	0	1	0	6
79. C. Smith	ARIZ	5	4	5	2	20	25	1	0	1	0	6
80. H. Green	ATL	15	36	78	29	360	438	1	0	1	0	6
81. Christian	ATL	14	7	8	22	154	162	0	1	1	0	6
82. Cotton	BALT	2	2	2	0	0	2	1	0	1	0	6
83. T. Thomas	BUF	16	154	643	30	208	851	1	0	1	0	6
84. Johnston	DALL	5	2	3	18	166	169	0	1	1	0	6
85. Hebron	DEN	10	49	222	3	36	258	1	0	1	0	6
86. D. Smith	DEN	4	4	10	4	41	51	0	1	1	0	6
87. Loville	DEN	3	25	124	2	10	134	1	0	1	0	6
88. Rivers	DET	10	29	166	0	0	166	1	0	1	0	6
89. Schlesinger	DET	7	7	11	5	69	80	0	1	1	0	6
90. Henderson	GB	16	31	113	41	367	480	0	1	1	0	6
91. Hayden	GB	6	32	148	2	11	159	1	0	1	0	6
92. Crockett	IND	15	95	300	15	112	412	1	0	1	0	6

NAME	TEAM	GP	RSH	YARDS	REC	YARDS	TOTAL YARDS	RSH TDs	REC TDs	TOTAL TDs	CONV PTS	FAN-TASY PTS
93. Bennett	KC	12	94	369	7	5	374	1	0	1	0	6
94. Parmalee	MIA	13	18	59	28	301	360	0	1	1	0	6
95. M. Williams	MINN	4	22	59	4	14	73	1	0	1	0	6
96. Grier	NE	6	33	75	0	0	75	1	0	1	0	6
97. Cullors *	NE	5	22	101	2	8	109	0	0	1	0	6
98. Hampton	NYG	2	23	81	0	0	81	1	0	1	0	6
99. R. Anderson	NYJ	14	21	70	26	150	220	0	1	1	0	6
100. Neal	NYJ	7	10	28	8	40	68	0	1	1	0	6
101. Levy *	SF	7	16	90	5	68	158	0	0	1	0	6
102. Heyward	STL	15	34	84	8	77	161	1	0	1	0	6
103. Thompson	STL	4	16	30	0	0	30	1	0	1	0	6
104. Byner	BALT	14	84	313	21	128	441	0	0	0	2	2
105. Le. Johnson	ARIZ	5	23	81	3	4	85	0	0	0	0	0
106. Bouie	ARIZ	3	11	26	0	0	26	0	0	0	0	0
107. Tindale	BUF	1	0	0	4	105	105	0	0	0	0	0
108. Oliver	CAR	4	1	0	6	47	47	0	0	0	0	0
109. A. Carter	CHI	11	9	56	24	152	208	0	0	0	0	0
110. Harmon **	CHI	10	10	36	18	197	233	0	0	0	0	0
111. Hughes	CHI	3	1	3	8	68	71	0	0	0	0	0
112. Salaam	CHI	3	31	112	2	20	132	0	0	0	0	0
113. Hicks	CHI	2	4	14	0	0	14	0	0	0	0	0
114. S. Graham	CIN	2	1	-1	1	1	0	0	0	0	0	0
115. Griffith	DEN	10	9	34	11	55	89	0	0	0	0	0
116. Lynn	DEN	1	0	0	1	21	21	0	0	0	0	0
117. Milburn	DET	4	0	0	5	77	77	0	0	0	0	0
118. Groce	IND	3	10	66	0	0	66	0	0	0	0	0
119. Shelton +	JAC	2	6	4	0	0	4	0	0	0	0	0
120. Jordan	JAC	1	1	2	0	0	2	0	0	0	0	0
121. Hill	KC	16	157	550	12	126	676	0	0	0	0	0
122. Pritchett	MIA	6	3	7	5	35	42	0	0	0	0	0
123. Potts **	MIA	3	2	4	3	27	31	0	0	0	0	0
124. Nealy	MIA	1	1	2	0	0	2	0	0	0	0	0
125. R. Green	MINN	2	6	22	1	5	27	0	0	0	0	0
126. Tr. Davis +	NO	15	75	271	13	85	356	0	0	0	0	0
127. McCrary	NO	4	7	13	4	17	30	0	0	0	0	0
128. Bender	NO	3	5	9	0	0	9	0	0	0	0	0
129. E. Lane	NYG	1	5	13	0	0	13	0	0	0	0	0
130. Sowell +	NYJ	1	7	35	1	8	43	0	0	0	0	0
131. Hall	OAK	8	23	120	1	9	129	0	0	0	0	0
132. Fenner	OAK	7	7	24	14	92	116	0	0	0	0	0
133. Aska	OAK	5	13	5	0	0	5	0	0	0	0	0
134. Davison	OAK	3	2	4	2	34	38	0	0	0	0	0
135. Levitt +	OAK	2	2	3	2	24	27	0	0	0	0	0
136. Staley +	PHIL	2	7	29	2	22	51	0	0	0	0	0
137. Lester	PITT	6	2	9	10	51	60	0	0	0	0	0
138. Whitman	PITT	5	5	11	1	3	14	0	0	0	0	0
139. McAfee	PITT	4	13	41	2	44	85	0	0	0	0	0
140. Fletcher	SD	13	51	161	39	292	453	0	0	0	0	0
141. Craver	SD	8	20	71	4	26	97	0	0	0	0	0
142. Bynum +	SD	5	30	97	2	4	101	0	0	0	0	0
143. Gardner	SD	4	7	20	2	10	30	0	0	0	0	0
144. Edwards +	SF	3	5	17	6	48	65	0	0	0	0	0
145. Ellison	TB	3	2	10	1	8	18	0	0	0	0	0
146. Logan	WASH	4	4	5	3	6	11	0	0	0	0	0

Legend on next page.

+	DENOTES COLLEGE DRAFT PICK		
*	Hanspard	(ATL)	Scored TD's on kickoff returns of 93 and 99 yards.
*	Kirby	(SF)	Scored TD on kickoff return of 101 yards.
*	Ln. Johnson	(NYJ)	Scored TD's on kickoff return of 101 yards and punt return of 66 yards.
*	Mitchell	(WASH)	Scored TD's on kickoff return of 97 yards and punt return of 63 yards.
*	Bieniemy	(CIN)	Scored TD on kickoff return of 102 yards.
*	Cullors	(NE)	Scored TD on kickoff return of 86 yards.
*	Levy	(SF)	Scored TD on punt return of 73 yards.
**	Phillips	(MIA)	Played in 10 games with St. Louis.
**	R. Moore	(ARIZ)	Played in 6 games with St. Louis.
**	Pegram	(NYG)	Played in 3 games with San Diego.
**	Harmon	(CHI)	Played in 10 games with Tennessee.
**	Potts	(MIA)	Played in 1 game with Indianapolis.

RATING THE PLAYERS FOR 1998
(Running Backs—Basic Scoring Method)

GRAB ONE IF YOU CAN

☐ **1. Terrell Davis (Denver Broncos)**
After scoring eight touchdowns as a rookie in 1995, Davis scored 15 touchdowns in each of the last two seasons. That kind of consistency makes him a prime fantasy candidate again in 1998, when I believe he'll again approach or top that 15 touchdown mark.

☐ **2. Barry Sanders (Detroit Lions)**
How would Barry Sanders fare under new head coach Bobby Ross in scoring situations? Sanders jumped to 14 touchdowns in 1997, despite backfield mate Tommy Vardell scoring six short-yardage touchdowns. Ross loves having Sanders as a weapon which should help produce another 12-15 touchdowns in 1998.

☐ **3. Dorsey Levens (Green Bay Packers)**
With Edgar Bennett out for the year with a knee injury in 1997, Levens took over the teams main rushing duties which produced 12 scores. With Bennett now off to Chicago, getting to or surpassing the 12 touchdown mark should again be well within reach in 1998.

☐ **4. Corey Dillon (Cincinnati Bengels)**
It took him a short time to win the starting job away from Ki-Jana Carter as a rookie in 1997, but once he did, look out. Dillon scored ten times playing in only 14 games in 1997. I look for 12 plus scores in 1998 if he stays on track.

☐ **5. Jerome Bettis (Pittsburgh Steelers)**
In the two seasons since coming to Pittsburgh, Bettis has scored 11 and 9 touchdowns respectively as the teams main ground weapon. I believe another 10 to 12 scores are in store again in 1998.

BEST OF THE REST

☐ **6. Terry Allen (Washington Redskins)**
After scoring 11 times in 1995, Allen exploded for 21 scores in 1996. In 1997, however, thumb, knee and ankle injuries limited him to only five touchdowns, playing in just ten games. Assuming he's healthy all of 1998, I look for a return to at least the dozen touchdown range in scoring.

☐ **7. Curtis Martin (New York Jets)**
After scoring 15 and 17 touchdowns his first two years in the league, Martin dropped to only five touchdowns in 1997. Missing three games with a shoulder injury contributed but he just didn't find the end zone often. I look for a rebound to the double-digit range for Martin in 1998, as he is reteamed up with former coach Bill Parcells in New York and has become a Jet.

☐ **8. Ricky Watters (Seattle Seahawks)**
Prior to 1997, Watters had scored 12 and 13 touchdowns since coming to Philadelphia. In 1997, Watters scored only seven times. I look for

Watters to again be a double-digit scorer, with renewed enthusiasm going to a new team, heading to Seattle in 1998.

☐ **9. Jamal Anderson (Atlanta Falcons)**
Quickly gaining respect around the league, Anderson jumped his touchdown totals from 6 in 1996 to 10 last year. Look for another year of double digit scores from Anderson again in 1998.

☐ **10. Emmitt Smith (Dallas Cowboys)**
What happened to Emmitt Smith and the Cowboys in 1997? Smith, after recording 22, 25 and 15 touchdowns respectively the last three seasons dropped to only four touchdowns in 1997. I don't think you can keep Smith or the Cowboys that down for long, I look for a rebound to the 10-touchdown mark or better in 1998.

STRONG LONG SHOTS

☐ **11. Karin Abdul-Jabbar (Miami Dolphins)**
Abdul-Jabbar jumped from 11 touchdowns as a rookie to 16 scores last season. I look for another season in the 10-12 range in 1998, as having Lawrence Phillips around scares me a bit.

☐ **12. Natrone Means (San Diego Chargers)**
Missing two games in 1997, Means still scored nine times for the Jaguars in Jacksonville. Returning to San Diego in 1998 via free-agency, I look for Means to near or top the 10-touchdown mark if healthy.

☐ **13. James Stewart (Jacksonville Jaguars)**
Stewart has recorded 10 and 9 touchdowns respectively the last two seasons. With Natrone Means now off to San Diego, topping the 10-touchdown mark or better should come with ease.

☐ **14. Fred Lane (Carolina Panthers)**
The undrafted, unheralded rookie came on to win the starting job mid-season in 1997. Playing in just 12 games, Lane produced seven scores. What will he do over a full 16 games and more experienced in 1998?

☐ **15. Mike Alstott (Tampa Bay Buccaneers)**
Alstott jumped his touchdown mark from six scores as a rookie in 1996 to ten touchdowns last season. Playing on a young, improving team look for Alstott to again near or top the double-digit scoring mark in 1998.

☐ **16. Edgar Bennett (Chicago Bears)**
Bennett, after a year off with a knee injury, takes his services to Chicago. As the Bears main back I expect him to score in the same range as similar to the 10 touchdowns Raymont Harris recorded in a similar role in 1997.

☐ **17. Eddie George (Tennessee Oilers)**
Despite rushing for 1,300 yards in each of his first two seasons, George has produced only 8 and 7 touchdowns respectively. As the again main ground weapon for the Oilers in 1998, hitting the 10-touchdown mark is well within reach.

☐ **18. Garrison Hearst (San Francisco 49ers)**
In his first year with San Francisco in 1997, Hearst scored six times, while missing three games with a shoulder injury. Returning as the team's main ball carrier, Hearst is likely to near or top double-digit scoring for the high-powered 49ers in 1998.

☐ **19. Antowain Smith (Buffalo Bills)**
As a rookie in 1997, Smith split time and production with veteran Thurman Thomas. Smith scored eight times last year but that should climb as his role expands in 1998.

☐ **20. Marshall Faulk (Indianapolis Colts)**
After scoring 14 times in 1995, Faulk fell victim to injuries in 1996 and scored only seven times. In 1997, Faulk stayed healthy all year and pushed his total one better to eight scores. If he stays healthy, nearing or hitting the 10-touchdown mark is well within his range.

HAVE THE POTENTIAL

☐ **21. Napoleon Kaufman (Oakland Raiders)**
Becoming the full-time main back in 1997, Kaufman jumped to eight touchdowns after producing just two in each of the two previous years. Returning to that main back spot in 1998 should again get him 8-10 touchdowns.

☐ **22. Robert Smith (Minnesota Vikings)**
If he could stay healthy an entire season, who knows what he could produce. Smith did only miss two games in 1997 and scored seven times. When he's healthy, he's got excellent fantasy potential.

☐ **23. Errict Rhett (Baltimore Ravens)**
Rhett, a former 1,000 yard rusher was granted his wish and has moved on to Baltimore. Again becoming a featured back, Rhett should rack up pretty good scoring numbers in 1998.

☐ **24. Warrick Dunn (Tampa Bay Buccaneers)**
As a rookie in 1997, Dunn rushed for just under 1,000 yards and scored seven times. He should be again a featured part of the Buc's offense in 1998 but backfield mate, big Mike Alstott, will continue to steal some of his scoring potential.

☐ **25. Adrian Murrell (Arizona Cardinals)**
Murrell, since taking over as the main back for the Jets, had produced seven touchdowns in each of the last two seasons. However, in 1998 the Jets have brought aboard Curtis Martin which made Murrell expendable. In Arizona, Murrell is likely to win the every down duties which will bring scoring success.

SOLID SLEEPERS

☐ **26. Jerald Moore (St. Louis Rams)**
Moore took over as the main rusher for the Rams late in 1997. Maintaining that role in 1998, Moore should get plenty scoring chances.

☐ **27. Charlie Garner (Philadelphia Eagles)**
With Ricky Watters off to Seattle and Garner signing a 4-year, $6.4 million deal in the offseason, look for his scoring numbers to grow quickly in 1998.

☐ **28. Lamar Smith (New Orleans Saints)**
A leg injury slowed him in 1997, Looking to 1998, however, Smith, coming to New Orleans and expected to see plenty of work, should be able to be a solid touchdown producer for the Saints.

☐ **29. Tiki Barber (New York Giants)**
Scored four times as a rookie in 1997, despite being slowed by a knee injury and missing four games. Staying healthy in 1998 will be the key to better results.

☐ **30. Donnell Bennett (Kansas City Chiefs)**
Most likely to step into the main halfback spot and with Marcus Allen gone will be asked to score as well as produce yardage.

KEEP AN EYE ON

☐ **31. Gary Brown (New York Giants)**
Brown, who rushed for just under 1,000 yards and scored four times for San Diego in 1997, joins the Giant's mix.

☐ **32. Ki-Jana Carter (Cincinnati Bengals)**
Beat out of 'main' ground duties in 1997 by Corey Dillon but Carter could remain a solid scoring weapon.

☐ **33. Ray Zellars (New Orleans Saints)**
Scored four times in 1997 and has the potential to fare much better.

☐ **34. Thurman Thomas (Buffalo Bills)**
The new kid on the block Antowain Smith will continue to steal the majority of show and scores.

☐ **35. Tommy Vardell (Detroit Lions)**
Scored six short-yardage touchdowns in 1997, giving Barry Sanders a break.

☐ **36. Mario Bates (Arizona Cardinals)**
Bates scored four times with New Orleans in 1997, being shifted in and out of the lineup. Coming to Arizona, Bates has a chance to battle Adrian Murrell for playing time and scoring dances.

☐ **37. Byron Hanspard (Atlanta Falcons)**
Hanspard seeing time in the backfield and returning kicks as a rookie in 1997, scored three times, two on kickoff returns. He should see more backfield time in 1998 which should help his scoring numbers.

☐ **38. Larry Centers (Arizona Cardinals)**
One of the league's best receiving backs, Centers always has the potential to hit or top the 6-touchdown mark.

☐ **39. Raymont Harris (Chicago Bears)**
Scored ten times in 1997 but arrival of Edgar Bennett and drafting of

Curtis Enis has him in an undetermined role for 1998.

☐ **40. Chris Warren (Dallas Cowboys)**
Out of the picture now that Ricky Watters has shown up in Seattle but could be a good asset for Dallas but of course Warren will be behind Emmitt Smith, unless he again is injured.

PRIME PROSPECTS

☐ **41. Lawrence Phillips (Miami Dolphins)**
Has the potential to do some things but it will depend on how Jimmy Johnson utilizes him.

☐ **42. Duce Staley (Philadelphia Eagles)**
Will see expanded work now that Ricky Watters has departed to Seattle.

☐ **43. Marc Edwards (San Francisco 49ers)**
With William Floyd, Edwards will likely get his chance at fullback.

☐ **44. William Floyd (Carolina Panthers)**
Should help the Panthers running game as a blocker but can also be a decent touchdown producer himself.

☐ **45. Stephen Davis (Washington Redskins)**
Health of Terry Allen will dictate the success and playing time of Davis.

☐ **46. Charles Way (New York Giants)**
As the injuries to Tyrone Wheatley, Rodney Hampton and Tiki Barber mounted in 1997, Charles Way got his chance. Way scored five times seeing limited action a year ago, however, looking to 1998, the Giants addition of Gary Brown raises questions over Way's role.

☐ **47 Kimble Anders (Kansas City Chiefs)**
Marcus Allen's retirement leaves a big hole for touchdown producer or producers.

☐ **48. Sedrick Shaw/Derrick Cullors (New England Patriots)**
Finding a replacement for the departed Curtis Martin will be a tough task and rookie first-round pick Robert Edwards stands in the way.

☐ **49. Rashaan Salaam (Chicago Bears)**
Salaam's future likely will take him elsewhere with Bears acquisition of Edgar Bennett and drafting of Curtis Enis.

☐ **50. Tim Biakabatuka (Carolina Panthers)**
At least for now Biakabatuka takes a backseat to Fred Lane.

DON'T BE SURPRISED

51. Crockett (IND)
52. Kirby (???)
53. Henderson (GB)
54. Hoard (MINN)
55. R. Thomas (TENN)
56. Turner (PHIL)
57. L. Warren (IND)
58. Graham (BALT)
69. Fletcher (SD)
60. Wheatley (NYG)

YOU NEVER KNOW

61. Mitchell (WASH)
62. Broussard (SEAT)
63. A. Johnson (CAR)
64. Johnston (DALL)
65. Ls. Johnson (NYG)
66. T. Davis (NO)
67. Lee (STL)
68. Bowie (WASH)
69. Ln. Johnson (NYJ)
70. McElroy (ARIZ)

WORTH MENTIONING

71. Hampton (???)
72. Sh. Williams (DALL)
73. Pegram (NYG)
74. Hill (KC)
75. Potts (BALT)

76. Meggett (NE)
77. R. Anderson (NYJ)
78. McPhail (MIA)
79. H. Green (ATL)
80. Holmes (BUF)

ROOKIE PROSPECTS

NAME	TEAM	COMMENT
☐ 1. Fred Taylor	JAC	With Means off to San Diego, opportunity is there
☐ 2. Robert Edwards	NE	Curtis Martin is gone, Edwards will battle for spot.
☐ 3. Curtis Enis	CHI	Bears stockpiled at running back.
☐ 4. John Avery	MIA	More likely a third-down contributor
☐ 5. Robert Holcombe	STL	Workman type back that may push Jerald Moore.
☐ 6. Skip Hicks	WASH	Rushed for over 1,100 yards in '97, insurance behind T. Allen.
☐ 7. Rasheen Shehee	KC	Chiefs in need at RB with Allen and likely G. Hill gone.

A LOOK AT THE WIDE RECEIVERS

(A Guide for the Beginner)

Considerations in Choosing a Wide Receiver

If you have played fantasy football and used the Basic Scoring Method, you know that wide receivers were unpredictable scorers until Jerry Rice came along. Rice, in turn, led the way for the likes of Herman Moore and Carl Pickens, who are developing into consistent scorers when they are healthy. It is still a challenge, however, to guess how most receivers will perform in this method. Let's take a look at some positive and negative characteristics to look for when you're drafting wide receivers.

1. First, look at players' previous performances. Injuries, player movement, holdouts, and suspensions should be noted. Players like Carl Pickens, Isaac Bruce, and Miami rookie Yatil Green all had their seasons marred in 1996.

2. Look for receivers from pass-oriented teams like the 49ers or Packers and more recently the Vikings or Lions, who have become pass-happy. Obviously, these players are more likely to have productive years.

3. Look for receivers who are favorites of a particular quarterback. Many quarterbacks single out a receiver whom they go to in clutch touchdown situations, such as Jerry Rice of the 49ers, who is a favorite target of Steve Young. Carl Pickens is a favorite target for Jeff Blake.

4. Look for quarterback changes to have varying effects on wide receivers. When a quarterback and wide receiver have played together for years, the performance of the receiver may drop off if his regular quarterback leaves. On the other hand, a new quarterback may come to a team and open up the offense, giving receivers more opportunities. Warren Moon did this for Cris Carter in 1994, as did Jeff Blake for Carl Pickens in both 1994 and 1995. Ty Detmer's replacing Rodney Peete in 1996 opened up the Eagles' offense and boosted the stats of Irving Fryar. Jeff George's arrival in Oakland in 1997 helped boost James Jett to 12 scores.

5. Keep an eye on rookie wide receivers, especially from teams looking for a starter at that position. Rookies don't usually draw much coverage, because they are unproven receivers. Such was the case with Seattle's Brian Blades in 1988, as he turned in a very productive eight-touchdown season. Also look at Rob Moore of the Jets, along with Eagle rookie receivers Calvin Williams and Fred Barnett, who all fared well in 1990. In 1991 the performances of Lawrence Dawsey of Tampa Bay and Tim Barnett of Kansas City were impressive. In 1995 Chris Sanders surprised many with a nine-touchdown season for Houston. Rookies Keyshawn Johnson (NY Jets) and Marvin Harrison (Indianapolis) both turned in productive rookie campaigns in 1996.

In the 1997 statistics, players are ranked by their fantasy-point totals. Remember that in the Basic Scoring Method, fantasy points are calculated by awarding six points for every touchdown rushed or caught and three points for every touchdown pass thrown.

1997 STATISTICAL RESULTS
(WIDE RECEIVERS — BASIC SCORING METHOD)

NAME	TEAM	GP	RSH	YARDS	REC	YARDS	TOTAL YARDS	RSH TDs	REC TDs	TOTAL TDs	CONV PTS	FAN-TASY PTS
1. Carter	MINN	16	0	0	89	1,069	1,069	0	13	13	6	84
1996		16	0	0	96	1,163	1,163	0	10	10	0	60
1995		16	1	0	122	1,371	1,371	0	17	17	0	102
3 Yr - TOTALS		48	1	0	307	3,603	3,603	0	40	40	6	246
2. R. Smith	DEN	16	5	16	70	1,180	1,196	0	12	12	0	72
1996		8	1	1	16	237	238	0	2	2	0	12
1995		5	0	0	6	152	152	0	1	1	0	6
3 Yr - TOTALS		29	6	17	92	1,569	1,586	0	15	15	0	90
3. Freeman	GB	15	1	14	81	1,243	1,257	0	12	12	0	72
1996		11	0	0	56	933	933	0	9	9	0	54
1995		5	0	0	8	106	106	0	1	1	0	6
3 Yr - TOTALS		31	1	14	145	2,282	2,296	0	22	22	0	132
4. Jett	OAK	15	0	0	46	804	804	0	12	12	0	72
1996		13	0	0	43	601	601	0	4	4	0	24
1995		11	0	0	13	179	179	0	1	1	0	6
3 Yr - TOTALS		39	0	0	102	1,584	1,584	0	17	17	0	102
5. Galloway	SEAT	15	9	72	72	1,049	1,121	0	12	12	0	72
1996		16	15	127	57	989	1,116	0	7	8	0	48
1995		16	11	154	67	1,039	1,193	1	7	9	0	54
3 Yr - TOTALS		47	35	353	196	3,077	3,430	1	26	29	0	174
6. Emanuel	ATL	16	0	0	65	991	991	0	9	9	0	54
1996		13	0	0	76	931	931	0	6	6	0	36
1995		16	1	0	74	1,039	1,039	0	5	5	0	30
3 Yr - TOTALS		45	1	0	215	2,961	2,961	0	20	20	0	120
7. Irvin	DALL	16	0	0	75	1,180	1,180	0	9	9	0	54
1996		11	0	0	64	962	962	0	2	2	2	14
1995		16	0	0	111	1,603	1,603	0	10	10	0	60
3 Yr - TOTALS		43	0	0	250	3,745	3,745	0	21	21	2	128
8. D. Alexander	BALT	15	1	0	65	1,009	1,009	0	9	9	0	54
1996		15	3	0	62	1,099	1,099	0	9	9	2	56
1995		6	1	29	15	216	245	0	0	1	0	6
3 Yr - TOTALS		36	5	29	142	2,324	2,353	0	18	19	2	116
9. R. Moore	ARIZ	16	0	0	97	1,584	1,584	0	8	8	2	50
1996		16	0	0	58	1,016	1,016	0	4	4	2	26
1995		15	0	0	63	907	907	0	5	5	2	32
3 Yr - TOTALS		47	0	0	218	3,507	3,507	0	17	17	6	108
10. H. Moore	DET	16	0	0	104	1,293	1,293	0	8	8	2	50
1996		16	0	0	106	1,296	1,296	0	9	9	2	56
1995		16	0	0	123	1,686	1,686	0	14	14	0	84
3 Yr - TOTALS		48	0	0	333	4,275	4,275	0	31	31	4	190
11. Calloway	NYG	16	1	-1	58	849	848	0	8	8	0	48
1996		16	1	2	53	739	741	0	4	4	0	24
1995		16	2	-9	56	796	787	0	3	3	0	18
3 Yr - TOTALS		48	4	-8	167	2,384	2,376	0	15	15	0	90
12. Owens	SF	16	0	0	60	936	936	0	8	8	0	48
1996		12	0	0	35	520	520	0	4	4	0	24
1995		–	–	–	–	–	–	–	–	–	–	–
3 Yr - TOTALS		28	0	0	95	1,456	1,456	0	12	12	0	72
13. McCaffrey	DEN	14	0	0	45	590	590	0	8	8	0	48
1996		13	0	0	48	553	553	0	7	7	0	42
1995		14	0	0	39	477	477	0	2	2	2	14
3 Yr - TOTALS		41	0	0	132	1,620	1,620	0	17	17	2	104
14. J. Lewis *	BALT	13	3	35	42	648	683	0	6	8	0	48
1996		4	1	-3	6	85	82	0	1	1	0	6
1995		–	–	–	–	–	–	–	–	–	–	–
3 Yr - TOTALS		17	4	32	48	733	765	0	7	9	0	54
15. Thigpen	PITT	15	1	3	79	1,398	1,401	0	7	7	2	44
1996		4	0	0	12	244	244	0	2	2	0	12
1995		16	0	0	85	1,307	1,307	0	5	5	0	30
3 Yr - TOTALS		35	1	3	176	2,949	2,952	0	14	14	2	86

(WIDE RECEIVERS — BASIC SCORING METHOD)

NAME	TEAM	GP	RSH	YARDS	REC	YARDS	TOTAL YARDS	RSH TDs	REC TDs	TOTAL TDs	CONV PTS	FAN-TASY PTS
16. Proehl	CHI	14	0	0	58	753	753	0	7	7	2	44
1996 w/SEAT		9	0	0	23	309	309	0	2	2	0	12
1995 w/SEAT		4	0	0	5	29	29	0	0	0	0	0
3 Yr - TOTALS		27	0	0	86	1,091	1,091	0	9	9	2	56
17. Brooks	GB	15	2	19	60	1,010	1,029	0	7	7	0	42
1996		5	4	2	23	344	346	0	4	4	0	24
1995		16	4	21	102	1,497	1,518	0	13	13	0	78
3 Yr - TOTALS		36	10	42	185	2,851	2,893	0	24	24	0	144
18. Rison	KC	15	1	2	72	1,092	1,094	0	7	7	0	42
1996 w/GB		15	0	0	47	593	593	0	3	3	0	18
1995 w/CLE		15	1	5	47	701	706	0	3	3	0	18
3 Yr - TOTALS		45	2	7	166	2,386	2,393	0	13	13	0	78
19. Harrison	IND	16	2	-7	73	866	859	0	6	6	4	40
1996		16	3	15	64	836	851	0	8	8	0	48
1995		–	–	–	–	–	–	–	–	–	–	–
3 Yr - TOTALS		32	5	8	137	1,702	1,710	0	14	14	4	88
20. Mathis	ATL	16	3	35	62	802	837	0	6	6	0	36
1996		15	0	0	69	771	771	0	7	7	2	44
1995		14	0	0	78	1,039	1,039	0	9	9	6	60
3 Yr - TOTALS		45	3	35	209	2,612	2,647	0	22	22	8	140
21. Morton	DET	16	3	33	80	1,057	1,090	0	6	6	0	36
1996		16	9	35	55	714	749	0	6	6	0	36
1995		13	3	33	44	590	623	0	8	8	0	48
3 Yr - TOTALS		45	15	101	179	2,361	2,462	0	20	20	0	120
22. J. Reed	MINN	16	0	0	68	1,138	1,138	0	6	6	0	36
1996		16	0	0	72	1,320	1,320	0	7	7	0	42
1995		16	0	0	72	1,167	1,167	0	9	9	0	54
3 Yr - TOTALS		48	0	0	212	3,625	3,625	0	22	22	0	132
23. Fryar	PHIL	16	0	0	86	1,316	1,316	0	6	6	0	36
1996		16	1	-4	88	1,195	1,191	0	11	11	0	66
1995 w/MIA		15	0	0	62	910	910	0	8	8	0	48
3 Yr - TOTALS		47	1	-4	236	3,421	3,417	0	25	25	0	150
24. Martin	SD	15	0	0	63	904	904	0	6	6	0	36
1996		16	0	0	85	1,171	1,171	0	14	14	0	84
1995		16	0	0	90	1,224	1,224	0	6	6	0	36
3 Yr - TOTALS		47	0	0	238	3,299	3,299	0	26	26	0	156
25. Tr. Brown	NE	13	1	-18	41	607	589	0	6	6	0	36
1996		8	0	0	21	222	222	0	0	0	0	0
1995		5	0	0	14	159	159	0	0	1	0	6
3 Yr - TOTALS		26	1	-18	76	988	970	0	6	7	0	42
26. McKnight	SEAT	12	0	0	34	637	637	0	6	6	0	36
1996		1	0	0	1	73	73	0	0	0	0	0
1995		5	0	0	6	91	91	0	0	0	0	0
3 Yr - TOTALS		18	0	0	41	801	801	0	6	6	0	36
27. Hastings	NO	16	4	35	48	722	757	0	5	5	2	32
1996 w/PITT		15	4	71	72	739	810	0	6	6	0	36
1995 w/PITT		15	1	14	48	502	516	0	1	2	0	12
3 Yr - TOTALS		46	9	120	168	1,963	2,083	0	12	13	2	80
28. Tm. Brown	OAK	16	5	19	104	1,408	1,427	0	5	5	2	32
1996		16	6	35	90	1,104	1,139	0	9	9	0	54
1995		16	0	0	89	1,342	1,342	0	10	10	0	60
3 Yr - TOTALS		48	11	54	283	3,854	3,908	0	24	24	2	146
29. Scott	CIN	16	1	6	54	797	803	0	5	5	0	30
1996		15	3	4	58	833	837	0	5	5	0	30
1995		16	5	11	52	821	832	0	5	5	0	30
3 Yr - TOTALS		47	9	21	164	2,451	2,472	0	15	15	0	90
30. McCardell	JAC	16	0	0	85	1,164	1,164	0	5	5	0	30
1996		16	0	0	85	1,129	1,129	0	3	3	4	22
1995 w/CLE		14	0	0	56	709	709	0	4	4	0	24
3 Yr - TOTALS		46	0	0	226	3,002	3,002	0	12	12	4	76

NAME	TEAM	GP	RSH	YARDS	REC	YARDS	TOTAL YARDS	RSH TDs	REC TDs	TOTAL TDs	CONV PTS	FAN-TASY PTS
31. K. Johnson	NYJ	16	0	0	70	963	963	0	5	5	0	30
1996		14	0	0	63	844	844	0	8	8	2	50
1995		–	–	–	–	–	–	–	–	–	–	–
3 Yr - TOTALS		30	0	0	133	1,807	1,807	0	13	13	2	80
32. A. Reed	BUF	15	3	11	60	880	891	0	5	5	0	30
1996		15	8	22	66	1,036	1,058	0	6	6	0	36
1995		6	7	48	24	312	360	0	3	3	0	18
3 Yr - TOTALS		36	18	81	150	2,228	2,309	0	14	14	0	84
33. Metcalf *	SD	15	3	-5	40	576	571	0	2	5	0	30
1996 w/ATL		16	3	8	54	599	607	0	6	6	0	36
1995 w/ATL		16	28	133	104	1,189	1,322	1	8	10	0	60
3 Yr - TOTALS		47	34	136	198	2,364	2,500	1	16	21	0	126
34. Early	BUF	14	0	0	60	853	853	0	5	5	0	30
1996		16	3	39	49	798	837	0	4	4	2	26
1995 w/NO		16	0	0	81	1,087	1,087	0	8	8	0	48
3 Yr - TOTALS		46	3	39	190	2,738	2,777	0	17	17	2	104
35. Ka. Williams *	TB	13	1	5	33	486	491	0	4	5	0	30
1996		10	1	-3	22	246	243	0	0	1	0	6
1995		0	0	0	0	0	0	0	0	0	0	0
3 Yr - TOTALS		23	2	2	55	732	734	0	4	6	0	36
36. Pickens	CIN	12	1	-6	52	695	689	0	5	5	0	30
1996		16	2	2	100	1,180	1,182	0	12	12	2	74
1995		16	1	6	99	1,234	1,240	0	17	17	0	102
3 Yr - TOTALS		44	4	2	251	3,109	3,111	0	34	34	2	206
37. Bruce	STL	11	0	0	56	815	815	0	5	5	0	30
1996		16	1	4	84	1,338	1,342	0	7	7	0	42
1995		16	3	17	119	1,781	1,798	0	13	13	2	80
3 Yr - TOTALS		43	4	21	259	3,934	3,955	0	25	25	2	152
38. Shepherd	WASH	10	4	27	29	562	589	0	5	5	0	30
1996		10	6	96	23	344	440	2	3	5	0	30
1995		14	7	63	29	486	549	1	2	3	0	18
3 Yr - TOTALS		34	17	186	81	1,392	1,578	3	10	13	0	78
39. W. Davis	TENN	15	0	0	43	564	564	0	4	4	0	27
40. F. Sanders	ARIZ	16	1	5	75	1,017	1,022	0	4	4	2	26
41. M. Jackson	BALT	16	0	0	69	918	918	0	4	4	2	26
42. J. Smith	JAC	16	0	0	82	1,324	1,324	0	4	4	0	24
43. Miller	DALL	15	1	6	46	645	651	0	4	4	0	24
44. Stokes	SF	15	0	0	58	733	733	0	4	4	0	24
45. Carruth +	CAR	14	6	23	44	545	568	0	4	4	0	24
46. Anthony +	TB	12	5	84	35	448	532	0	4	4	0	24
47. Ellard	WASH	12	0	0	32	485	485	0	4	4	0	24
48. Solomon	PHIL	11	0	0	29	455	455	0	3	3	2	20
49. Hawkins	PITT	15	5	17	45	555	572	0	3	3	0	18
50. Penn	CHI	14	1	-1	47	576	575	0	3	3	0	18
51. Chrebet	NYJ	14	0	0	58	799	799	0	3	3	0	18
52. Jordan	MIA	13	3	12	27	471	483	0	3	3	0	18
53. C. Sanders	TENN	13	1	-8	31	498	490	0	3	3	0	18
54. Bailey	IND	12	3	20	26	329	349	0	3	3	0	18
55. Westbrook	WASH	10	3	-11	34	559	548	0	3	3	0	18
56. Hughes	KC	5	0	0	7	65	65	0	2	3	0	18
57. Engram	CHI	11	0	0	45	399	399	0	2	2	2	14
58. W. Jackson	JAC	11	3	14	17	206	220	0	2	2	2	14
59. Vanover *	KC	8	5	50	7	92	142	0	0	2	2	14
60. McDuffie *	MIA	16	0	0	76	943	943	0	1	2	0	12
61. Jefferson	NE	16	0	0	54	841	841	0	2	2	0	12
62. Pritchard	SEAT	16	1	14	64	843	857	0	2	2	0	12
63. Hill	NO	15	1	11	55	761	772	0	2	2	0	12
64. Dawkins	IND	14	0	0	68	804	804	0	2	2	0	12
65. R. Ismail	CAR	13	4	32	36	419	451	0	2	2	0	12
66. Graham	NYJ	13	0	0	42	542	542	0	2	2	0	12
67. Timpson	PHIL	13	0	0	42	484	484	0	2	2	0	12
68. C. Johnson	PITT	13	0	0	46	568	568	0	2	2	0	12

NAME	TEAM	GP	RSH	YARDS	REC	YARDS	TOTAL YARDS	RSH TDs	REC TDs	TOTAL TDs	CONV PTS	FAN-TASY PTS
69. Brisby	NE	12	0	0	23	276	276	0	2	2	0	12
70. Dunn	CIN	11	0	0	27	414	414	0	2	2	0	12
71. Guliford *	NO	11	1	-2	27	362	360	0	1	2	0	12
72. Toomer *	NYG	11	0	0	16	263	263	0	1	2	0	12
73. Green	DEN	10	0	0	19	240	240	0	2	2	0	12
74. L. Thomas	MIA	10	0	0	28	402	402	0	2	2	0	12
75. Blades	SEAT	10	0	0	30	319	319	0	2	2	0	12
76. Carrier	CAR	9	0	0	33	436	436	0	2	2	0	12
77. Dawson	KC	9	0	0	21	273	273	0	2	2	0	12
78. Glenn	NE	7	0	0	27	431	431	0	2	2	0	12
79. Patten	NYG	7	1	2	13	226	228	0	2	2	0	12
80. Blackwell + *	PITT	7	2	14	12	168	182	0	1	2	0	12
81. Hundon	CIN	6	0	0	16	285	285	0	2	2	0	12
82. Connell +	WASH	4	1	3	9	138	141	0	2	2	0	12
83. Poole +	NO	2	0	0	4	98	98	0	2	2	0	12
84. VanDyke	NYJ	2	0	0	3	53	53	0	2	2	0	12
85. Stablein	IND	12	0	0	25	253	253	0	1	1	2	8
86. C. Jones	SD	15	4	42	32	423	465	0	1	1	0	6
87. St. Williams	DALL	12	0	0	30	308	308	0	1	1	0	6
88. Small	STL	12	0	0	32	488	488	0	1	1	0	6
89. Kv. Williams	ARIZ	11	1	-2	20	273	271	0	1	1	0	6
90. Perriman **	MIA	11	0	0	25	392	392	0	1	1	0	6
91. Copeland	TB	11	0	0	32	421	421	0	1	1	0	6
92. Seay	PHIL	10	0	0	13	187	187	0	1	1	0	6
93. Kinchen	ATL	9	0	0	16	266	266	0	1	1	0	6
94. K. Alexander	NYG	9	0	0	18	276	276	0	1	1	0	6
95. Walsh	MINN	8	0	0	11	114	114	0	1	1	0	6
96. Ward +	NYJ	8	2	25	18	212	237	0	1	1	0	6
97. Haynes	ATL	7	0	0	12	154	154	0	1	1	0	6
98. Conway	CHI	7	3	17	30	476	493	0	1	1	0	6
99. Shedd *	OAK	7	0	0	10	115	115	0	0	1	0	6
100. Hobbs **	SEAT	7	0	0	7	85	85	0	1	1	0	6
101. Russell	TENN	6	0	0	12	141	141	0	1	1	0	6
102. Mills	CAR	5	0	0	11	127	127	0	1	1	0	6
103. Barnett	MIA	5	0	0	17	166	166	0	1	1	0	6
104. Barlow *	JAC	4	0	0	5	74	74	0	0	1	0	6
105. Kent +	TENN	4	0	0	6	55	55	0	1	1	0	6
106. Truitt	OAK	3	0	0	7	91	91	0	1	1	0	6
107. D. Sanders *	DALL	2	1	-11	1	3	-8	0	0	1	0	6
108. Schroeder	GB	2	0	0	2	15	15	0	1	1	0	6
109. Rice	SF	2	1	-10	7	78	68	0	1	1	0	6
110. Mickens	GB	1	0	0	1	2	2	0	1	1	0	6
111. Moulds	BUF	11	4	59	29	294	353	0	0	0	2	2
112. Muhammad	CAR	7	0	0	27	317	317	0	0	0	2	2
113. Kennison	STL	13	3	13	25	404	417	0	0	0	0	0
114. Still	SD	12	0	0	24	324	324	0	0	0	0	0
115. Edwards	ARIZ	11	0	0	20	203	203	0	0	0	0	0
116. Yarborough	BALT	9	0	0	16	183	183	0	0	0	0	0
117. Uwaezuoke	SF	9	0	0	14	165	165	0	0	0	0	0
118. Mayes	GB	7	0	0	18	290	290	0	0	0	0	0
119. R. Thomas	TB	7	0	0	13	129	129	0	0	0	0	0
120. Mason +	TENN	7	1	-7	14	186	179	0	0	0	0	0
121. Boyd	DET	6	0	0	10	142	142	0	0	0	0	0
122. Crawford	STL	6	1	9	11	232	241	0	0	0	0	0
123. C. Thomas	WASH	6	0	0	11	93	93	0	0	0	0	0
124. Bownes	CHI	5	0	0	12	146	146	0	0	0	0	0
125. C. Jones	PHIL	4	0	0	5	73	73	0	0	0	0	0
126. M. Harris	SF	4	0	0	5	53	53	0	0	0	0	0
127. Roe	BALT	3	0	0	7	124	124	0	0	0	0	0
128. B. Davis	DALL	3	0	0	3	33	33	0	0	0	0	0
129. Manning +	MIA	3	0	0	7	85	85	0	0	0	0	0
130. Hatchette +	MINN	3	0	0	3	54	54	0	0	0	0	0

1997 STATISTICAL RESULTS
(WIDE RECEIVERS — BASIC SCORING METHOD)

	NAME	TEAM	GP	RSH	YARDS	REC	YARDS	TOTAL YARDS	RSH TDs	REC TDs	TOTAL TDs	CONV PTS	FAN-TASY PTS
131.	Bech	NO	3	0	0	3	50	50	0	0	0	0	0
132.	T. Lewis	NYG	3	0	0	5	84	84	0	0	0	0	0
133.	Howard	OAK	3	0	0	4	30	30	0	0	0	0	0
134.	R. Harris	SEAT	3	0	0	4	81	81	0	0	0	0	0
135.	Ross	STL	3	0	0	3	37	37	0	0	0	0	0
136.	E. Smith	CHI	2	1	12	2	22	34	0	0	0	0	0
137.	Twyner	CIN	2	0	0	4	45	45	0	0	0	0	0
138.	Jefers	DEN	2	0	0	3	24	24	0	0	0	0	0
139.	McCorvey	DET	2	0	0	2	9	9	0	0	0	0	0
140.	Horn	KC	2	0	0	2	65	65	0	0	0	0	0
141.	Hilliard +	NYG	2	0	0	2	42	42	0	0	0	0	0
142.	Marsh	PITT	2	1	2	2	14	16	0	0	0	0	0
143.	Floyd	STL	2	0	0	4	39	39	0	0	0	0	0
144.	Brock	ARIZ	1	0	0	1	29	29	0	0	0	0	0
145.	Reese	BUF	1	0	0	1	13	13	0	0	0	0	0
146.	Beebe	GB	1	0	0	2	28	28	0	0	0	0	0
147.	Doering	IND	1	0	0	2	12	12	0	0	0	0	0
148.	W. Moore	JAC	1	0	0	1	10	10	0	0	0	0	0
149.	Lockett +	KC	1	0	0	1	35	35	0	0	0	0	0
150.	Jells	NE	1	0	0	1	9	9	0	0	0	0	0
151.	Adams +	PITT	1	0	0	1	39	39	0	0	0	0	0
152.	T. Davis	SEAT	1	0	0	2	48	48	0	0	0	0	0
153.	J. Thomas	STL	1	0	0	2	25	25	0	0	0	0	0
154.	Harper	WASH	1	0	0	2	65	65	0	0	0	0	0
155.	Thrash	WASH	1	0	0	2	24	24	0	0	0	0	0

+		DENOTES COLLEGE DRAFT PICK	
*	J. Lewis	BALT	Scored TD's on punt returns of 89 and 66 yards.
*	Metcalf	SD	Scored TD's on punt returns of 85, 67, and 83 yards.
*	Vanover	KC	Scored TD on punt return of 82 yards and kickoff return of 94 yards.
*	Ka. Williams	TB	Scored TD on punt return of 61 yards.
*	Blackwell	PITT	Scored TD on kickoff return of 97 yards.
*	Guliford	NO	Scored TD on kickoff return of 102 yards.
*	Toomer	NYG	Scored TD on punt return of 53 yards.
*	Barlow	JAC	Scored TD on kickoff return of 92 yards.
*	D. Sanders	DALL	Scored TD on punt return of 83 yards.
*	Shedd	OAK	Scored TD on fumble return of 25 yards.
*	McDuffie	MIA	Scored TD by recovering fumble in end zone.
**	Perriman	MIA	Played in 3 games with Kansas City.
**	Hobbs	SEAT	Played in 2 games with New Orleans.

RATING THE PLAYERS FOR 1998
(Wide Receivers—Basic Scoring Method)

GRAB ONE IF YOU CAN

☐ **1. Antonio Freeman (Green Bay Packers)**
Despite missing five games because of injuries in 1996, Freeman scored nine times. In 1997, Freeman came back healthy and scored 12 times. As a favorite target of Brett Favre, he should post huge touchdown numbers in 1998.

☐ **2. Cris Carter (Minnesota Vikings)**
Carter has averaged more than 13 touchdowns a season for the last three years, scoring 17, 10 and 13 touchdowns, respectively. I look for another 12-plus scores from him in 1998.

☐ **3. Herman Moore (Detroit Lions)**
Moore's touchdown numbers have declined the last three seasons-14, 9 and 8 times, respectively. During that same time, he has tallied 123, 106 and 104 receptions. Anyone with his height who sees the ball that often is a candidate to reach the 10 to 15 touchdown range.

☐ **4. Jerry Rice (San Francisco 49ers)**
As perhaps the league's best all-time receiver, Rice is always a potential 10 to 15 touchdown scorer. He missed most of 1997 because of knee injuries but he's back to light it up again in 1998.

☐ **5. Carl Pickens (Cincinnati Bengals)**
He's another of the league's premier receivers who fell victim to injury in 1997. Pickens dropped to five touchdowns a year ago after scoring 12 and 17 times the two pervious years. Certainly, when he's healthy, he is a top fantasy choice.

BEST OF THE REST

☐ **6. Rod Smith (Denver Broncos)**
Looking for a go-to receiver in 1997, the Broncos found one in Rod Smith. Smith scored 12 times on 70 receptions and should again reach the 10 to 12 touchdown range in 1998.

☐ **7. Joey Galloway (Seattle Seahawks)**
Galloway continues to improve and boosted his touchdown production from eight scores in 1996 to 12 in 1997. As the Seahawks' main go-to receiver, approaching the dozen touchdown mark is well within his reach.

☐ **8. Tim Brown (Oakland Raiders)**
The 1997 season was an odd one for Brown. He increased his reception level to a career-high 104 but his touchdowns dropped to only five as receiving mate James Jett scored 12 times. Because he's usually a double-digit scorer, I look for Brown to return there in 1998.

☐ **9. Irving Fryar (Philadelphia Eagles)**
Despite having almost exactly the same number of receptions in 1996 (88) as 1997 (86), Fryar dropped from 11 touchdowns to 6. Surely a re-

ceiver who sees the ball that often is likely to score in the 10-touchdown range.

☐ **10. Robert Brooks (Green Bay Packers)**
Brooks recovered from his knee injury to score seven times on 60 receptions in 1997. Two years earlier, Brooks had scored 13 times. As he continues to rebuild his confidence, hitting the 10-plus touchdown range will again be possible.

STRONG LONG SHOTS

☐ **11. Isaac Bruce (St. Louis Rams)**
Nursing a hamstring injury cost him the first five games of 1997, and Bruce scored only five times. I look for a healthy Bruce to again be around the double-digit scoring mark in 1998.

☐ **12. Michael Jackson (Baltimore Ravens)**
Jackson scored 14 times in 1996 when Vinny Testaverde had his career year but dropped to only four scores a year ago. Because his receiving mate Derrick Alexander is now with Kansas City, I look for Jackson's touchdown totals to rebound in 1998. Perhaps the 10-touchdown mark is again possible.

☐ **13. Tony Martin (San Diego Chargers)**
As the prime target for veteran Stan Humphries in 1996, Martin scored 14 times. With Humphries banged up in 1997, Martin dropped to only six scores. He's certainly capable of double-digit scoring, but much depends on the success of his young quarterback in 1998.

☐ **14. Michael Irvin (Dallas Cowboys)**
Irvin, as usual, neared the 10-touchdown mark in 1997, scoring nine times. I expect 1998 will be no different with Irvin nearing the 10-touchdown range again.

☐ **15. Curtis Conway (Chicago Bears)**
A collarbone/shoulder injury limited Conway to 30 receptions and one touchdown in just seven games in 1997. In the two previous years, Conway scored 8 and 12 times.

☐ **16. Rob Moore (Arizona Cardinals)**
Moore jumped to 97 receptions and eight touchdowns in 1997 once he got in sync with rookie quarterback Jake Plummer. With Plummer now at the helm, another big year should be in store for Moore.

☐ **17. Derrick Alexander (Kansas City Chiefs)**
Alexander scored nine touchdowns in each of the last two seasons. In Kansas City, he may struggle a bit more to score in the 8 to 10 touchdown range, but it's very possible.

☐ **18. James Jett (Oakland Raiders)**
Jeff George's arrival in Oakland was a huge blessing for Jett, who scored 12 times on only 46 receptions in 1997. A favorite deep-threat for George, Jett should again score often in 1998.

☐ **19. Marvin Harrison (Indianapolis Colts)**
Harrison has scored eight and six touchdowns in his first two seasons in the NFL. His continued improvement will push him to the 8 to 10 touchdown range in 1998.

☐ **20. Johnnie Morton (Detroit Lions)**
With Brett Perriman's departure in 1997, Morton stepped into an expanded role and recorded 80 receptions, up from 55 a year earlier. He scored only six times, after scoring six and eight times the previous two seasons. His expanded role should give him the chance to score 8 to 10 times in 1997.

HAVE THE POTENTIAL

☐ **21. Charles Johnson (Pittsburgh Steelers)**
With leading receiver Yancey Thigpen off to Tennessee, Johnson will get his chance to increase his reception and touchdown levels in 1998.

☐ **22. Terrance Mathis (Atlanta Falcons)**
Mathis has scored nine, seven and six touchdowns in the last three seasons, respectively, giving you an idea of what he can do and now with Bert Emanuel gone his scoring numbers are likely to grow.

☐ **23. Keyshawn Johnson (New York Jets)**
As a rookie in 1996, Johnson scored eight times on 63 receptions. In 1997, he upped his reception level to 70 but scored only five times. This young talent is very capable of 6 to 10 scores in 1998.

☐ **24. Andre Rison (Kansas City Chiefs)**
Rison's new home resurrected his career in 1997. Rison joined Kansas City and grabbed 72 receptions and seven touchdowns. In 1998, he'll share scoring chances with new acquisition Derrick Alexander.

☐ **25. Ed McCaffrey (Denver Broncos)**
The tall McCaffrey makes an excellent red zone target and, as a result, scored seven and eight touchdowns, respectively, the last two seasons. I look for another 7 to 10 scores in 1998.

SOLID SLEEPERS

☐ **26. Jake Reed (Minnesota Vikings)**
A consistent receiver, Reed is always in the 70-reception range. I look for another solid 70 catches and 7 to 10 touchdowns from him in 1998.

☐ **27. O.J. McDuffie (Miami Dolphins)**
McDuffie scored only two times on 76 receptions in 1997. However, if you look at the two previous years, McDuffie scored eight times in each season.

☐ **28. Yancey Thigpen (Tennessee Oilers)**
Thigpen had 79 receptions and seven touchdowns in 1997 with Pittsburgh. Now, with Tennessee in 1998, he may find it tougher to put together big receiving numbers.

☐ **29. Bert Emanuel (Tampa Bay Buccaneers)**
Emanuel takes his services to Tampa Bay in 1998, where he'll have a tough time nearing totals he produced with Atlanta.

☐ **30. Keenan McCardell (Jacksonville Jaguars)**
Despite recording 85 receptions in each of the last two seasons, McCardell has scored only three and five touchdowns, respectively. However, any receiver who sees the ball that often can't be dismissed as a fantasy pick.

KEEP AN EYE ON

☐ **31. Michael Westbrook (Washington Redskins)**
Injuries continue to hurt Westbrook's scoring. The former first-round pick played in just 10 games in 1997 and tallied only three touchdowns. But the potential is there.

☐ **32. Chris Calloway (New York Giants)**
The Giants continue to pick receivers early in the draft (Ike Hilliard, Amani Toomer, Thomas Lewis). Despite that, they also continue to turn to Chris Calloway. Calloway scored eight times in 1997 and should hit the 7 to 10 touchdown range again in 1998.

☐ **33. Jimmy Smith (Jacksonville Jaguars)**
He only scored four times in 1997 but don't overlook his 82 receptions. Seeing the ball that often provides him with plenty of scoring chances.

☐ **34. Jermaine Lewis (Baltimore Ravens)**
Lewis scored eight times in 1997-twice on punt returns. Derrick Alexander's departure will help Lewis's production but Jim Harbaugh's arrival probably won't in 1998.

☐ **35. Terrell Owens (San Francisco 49ers)**
He scored eight times on 60 receptions in 1997 but Jerry Rice is back healthy.

☐ **36. Darnay Scott (Cincinnati Bengals)**
Scott has scored five touchdowns in each of the last three seasons. In 1997, however, four of his five touchdowns came in the last five weeks. That's a performance he hopes to carry into 1998.

☐ **37. Terry Glenn (New England Patriots)**
Glenn scored six times on 90 receptions as a rookie in 1996. In 1997, he missed nine games with injuries and dropped to 27 catches and two touchdowns. I look for a significant rebound in 1998.

☐ **38. Yatil Green (Miami Dolphins)**
A knee injury forced the Dolphins' No.1 draft pick of 1997 to miss his entire rookie season. Healthy in 1998, he should become a nice big-play receiver.

☐ **39. Quinn Early (Buffalo Bills)**
Early's scoring potential in 1998 greatly depends on who will be at quarterback for Buffalo and how successful that player is.

☐ **40. Frank Sanders (Arizona Cardinals)**
Sanders recorded 75 receptions but only four touchdowns in 1997.

PRIME PROSPECTS

☐ **41. Wayne Chrebet (New York Jets)**
With Jeff Graham off to Philadelphia, Chrebet gets a chance to expand his role and numbers.

☐ **42. Jeff Graham (Philadelphia Eagles)**
Graham brings his services to Philapelphia from the Jets, battling Michael Timpson and Chris T. Jones for playing time.

☐ **43. Andre Reed (Buffalo Bills)**
Reed's getting older but he keeps getting it done. He scored six and five touchdowns in the last two seasons.

☐ **44. Mike Pritchard (Seattle Seahawks)**
Pritchard has pushed for a starting role since coming to Seattle. He scored only two touchdowns on 64 receptions in 1997, and those are numbers he can easily improve.

☐ **45. Ricky Proehl (St. Louis Rams)**
Proehl comes to the Rams after producing 58 receptions and seven touchdowns for Chicago in 1997. He'll battle Eddie Kennison for the No.2 receiver spot opposite Isaac Bruce.

☐ **46. Rae Carruth (Carolina Panthers)**
Carruth, the Panthers' first-round pick in 1997, recorded four touchdowns on 44 receptions as a rookie. Those are numbers he and the Panthers hope he'll improve in 1998.

☐ **47. Reidel Anthony (Tampa Bay Buccaneers)**
Anthony is a No.1 draft pick who recorded four touchdowns as a rookie in 1997, and he did it on just 35 receptions. He's another receiver who's capable of improving his touchdown mark to the six-plus range.

☐ **48. Ike Hilliard (New York Giants)**
The Giants' No.1 draft pick of a year ago missed most of his rookie season because of injuries. They'd like to think he could be a significant factor in their 1998 offense.

☐ **49. Eddie Kennison (St. Louis Rams)**
After scoring 11 times as a rookie in 1996, Kennison, remarkably, did not score in 1997. He'll look to rebound in 1998 but he'll have to fight off new acquisition Ricky Proehl.

☐ **50. Chris T. Jones (Philadelphia Eagles)**
Jones recorded 70 receptions on five touchdowns in 1996 but a knee injury dropped him to only five receptions and no scores in 1997. He'll look to rebound to healthy numbers in 1998.

DON'T BE SURPRISED

51. K. Williams (TB)
52. Dawkins (NO)
53. McKnight (SEAT)
54. Engram (CHI)
55. Shepherd (WASH)
56. Timpson (PHIL)
57. Muhammad (CAR)
58. Stokes (SF)
59. C. Jones (SD)
60. Jefferson (NE)

YOU NEVER KNOW

61. Tr. Brown (NE)
62. Davis (DALL)
63. Sander (TENN)
64. St. Williams (DALL)
65. Hastings (NO)
66. Toomer (NYG)
67. Carrier (CAR)
68. K. Alexander (MIA)
69. Penn (CHI)
70. Hawkins (PITT)

DON'T COUNT THEM OUT

71. Small (IND)
72. Blackwell (PITT)
73. Metcalf (ARIZ)
74. T. Lewis (CHI)
75. Mills (DALL)
76. Ellard (WASH)
77. W. Davis (TENN)
78. Copeland (TB)
79. Perriman (MIA)
80. Hill (NO)

WORTH MENTIONING

81. Blades (SEAT)
82. W. Jackson (JAC)
83. Brisby (NE)
84. Jordan (MIA)
85. Ward (NYJ)
86. Dawson (KC)
87. Still (SD)
88. Moulds (BUF)
89. Van Dyke (NYJ)
90. Stablein (NE)

ROOKIE PROSPECTS

NAME	TEAM	COMMENT
☐ 1. Kevin Dyson	TENN	Dyson looking to help improve Oiler passing game.
☐ 2. Randy Moss	MINN	Talented receiver but must overcome off-field problems.
☐ 3. Marcus Nash	DEN	Caught 76 passes and 13 TD's as favorite target of Peyton Manning in '97.
☐ 4. Jerome Pathon	IND	Colts have their QB—now must build around him.
☐ 5. Tony Simmons	NE	Patriots looking for help at wide receiver.
☐ 6. Michael Ricks	SD	Nice size (6'5") target for young Leaf.
☐ 7. Pat Johnson	BALT	Might fit into mix with Michael Jackson and Jermaine Lewis.
☐ 8. Joe Jurevicius	NYG	Giants always looking for receiver help.

A LOOK AT THE TIGHT ENDS
(A Guide for the Beginner)

Considerations in Choosing a Tight End

1. First, look at players' previous performances. Injuries, player movement, holdouts, and the like should be noted. Brent Jones had his 1997 year-end totals hurt by injury.

2. If a team has one or two good wide receivers, opponents are forced to double-cover them, leaving the tight end open more often, especially in close situations. Mark Chmura is certainly fortunate to play between Antonio Freeman and Robert Brooks.

3. Tight ends from pass-oriented offenses like the 49ers or Packers have a better chance for a productive year than those from running teams.

4. Look for tight ends who seem to be favorite receivers of a particular quarterback. Shannon Sharpe, for example, has become a favorite target of John Elway, and Ben Coates has become Drew Bledsoe's choice. Although tight ends are less likely to be receivers than some other players, scoring receptions by tight ends are more common than before, as tight ends have grown more important in many teams' offensive schemes. Ben Coates and Shannon Sharpe have brought all tight ends more attention.

5. Look for quarterback changes to have an adverse effect on a tight end's productivity. When a quarterback and tight end have played together for years, the performance of the tight end may drop off if his regular quarterback leaves.

In the 1997 statistics, players are ranked by their fantasy-point totals. Remember that in the Basic Scoring Method, fantasy points are calculated by awarding six points for every touchdown rushed or caught and three points for every touchdown pass thrown.

	NAME	TEAM	GP	REC	YARDS	RSH TDs	REC TDs	TOTAL TDs	CONV PTS	FANTASY PTS
1.	**Coates**	NE	**16**	**66**	**737**	**0**	**8**	**8**	**0**	**48**
	1996		15	62	682	0	9	9	2	56
	1995		16	84	915	0	6	6	0	36
	3 Yr - TOTALS		47	212	2,334	0	23	23	2	140
2.	**Dudley**	OAK	**16**	**48**	**787**	**0**	**7**	**7**	**0**	**42**
	1996		13	34	386	0	4	4	0	24
	1995		–	–	–	–	–	–	–	–
	3 Yr - TOTALS		29	82	1,173	0	11	11	0	66
3.	**McGee**	CIN	**15**	**34**	**414**	**0**	**6**	**6**	**2**	**38**
	1996		14	38	446	0	4	4	0	24
	1995		15	55	754	0	4	4	0	24
	3 Yr - TOTALS		44	127	1,614	0	14	14	2	86
4.	**Walls**	CAR	**15**	**58**	**746**	**0**	**6**	**6**	**0**	**36**
	1996		16	61	713	0	10	10	0	60
	1995		16	57	694	0	4	4	2	26
	3 Yr - TOTALS		47	176	2,153	0	20	20	2	122
5.	**Chmura**	GB	**15**	**38**	**417**	**0**	**6**	**6**	**0**	**36**
	1996		11	28	370	0	0	0	0	0
	1995		15	54	679	0	7	7	2	44
	3 Yr - TOTALS		41	120	1,466	0	13	13	2	80
6.	**Bruener**	PITT	**9**	**18**	**117**	**0**	**6**	**6**	**0**	**36**
	1996		7	12	141	0	0	0	2	2
	1995		11	26	238	0	3	3	0	18
	3 Yr - TOTALS		27	56	496	0	9	9	2	56
7.	**Williams**	OAK	**10**	**16**	**147**	**3**	**2**	**5**	**2**	**32**
	1996 (as RB)		13	22	143	0	0	0	0	3
	1995 (as RB)		16	54	375	9	0	9	0	54
	3 Yr - TOTALS		39	92	665	12	2	14	2	89
8.	**Green**	BALT	**14**	**65**	**601**	**0**	**5**	**5**	**0**	**30**
	1996		6	15	150	0	1	1	0	6
	1995 w/MIA		14	43	499	0	3	3	2	20
	3 Yr - TOTALS		34	123	1,250	0	9	9	2	56
9.	**Wycheck**	TENN	**16**	**63**	**748**	**0**	**4**	**4**	**2**	**26**
	1996		15	53	511	0	6	6	0	36
	1995		14	40	471	1	1	2	0	12
	3 Yr - TOTALS		45	156	1,730	1	11	12	2	74
10.	**Drayton**	MIA	**15**	**39**	**558**	**0**	**4**	**4**	**0**	**24**
	1996		12	28	331	0	0	0	2	2
	1995 w/STL		16	47	458	0	4	4	0	24
	3 Yr - TOTALS		43	114	1,347	0	8	8	2	50
11.	**Gedney**	ARIZ	**14**	**23**	**261**	**0**	**4**	**4**	**0**	**24**
	1996		–	–	–	–	–	–	–	–
	1995 w/CHI		5	5	52	0	0	0	0	0
	3 Yr - TOTALS		19	28	313	0	4	4	0	24
12.	**P. Mitchell**	JAC	**14**	**35**	**380**	**0**	**4**	**4**	**0**	**24**
	1996		16	52	575	0	1	1	0	6
	1995		14	41	527	0	2	2	0	12
	3 Yr - TOTALS		44	128	1,482	0	7	7	0	42
13.	**Conwell**	STL	**14**	**38**	**404**	**0**	**4**	**4**	**0**	**24**
	1996 w/STL		6	15	164	0	0	0	0	0
	1995		–	–	–	–	–	–	–	–
	3 Yr - TOTALS		20	53	568	0	4	4	0	24
14.	**C. Lewis**	PHIL	**8**	**12**	**94**	**0**	**4**	**4**	**0**	**24**
	1996		–	–	–	–	–	–	–	–
	1995		–	–	–	–	–	–	–	–
	3 Yr - TOTALS		8	12	94	0	4	4	0	24
15.	**Moore**	TB	**8**	**19**	**217**	**0**	**4**	**4**	**0**	**24**
	1996		12	27	237	0	3	3	0	18
	1995		10	13	102	0	0	0	0	0
	3 Yr - TOTALS		30	59	556	0	7	7	0	42

1997 STATISTICAL RESULTS
(TIGHT ENDS — BASIC SCORING METHOD)

	NAME	TEAM	GP	REC	YARDS	RSH TDs	REC TDs	TOTAL TDs	CONV PTS	FANTASY PTS
16.	Sharpe	DEN	16	72	1,107	0	3	3	2	20
	1996		15	80	1,062	0	10	10	0	60
	1995		12	63	756	0	4	4	0	24
	3 Yr - TOTALS		43	215	2,925	0	17	17	2	104
17.	Baxter	NYJ	13	27	276	0	3	3	0	18
	1996		7	7	114	0	0	0	0	0
	1995		6	18	222	0	1	1	0	6
	3 Yr - TOTALS		26	52	612	0	4	4	0	24
18.	Glover	MINN	12	32	378	0	3	3	0	18
	1996 w/OAK		6	9	101	0	1	1	0	6
	1995 w/OAK		14	26	220	0	3	3	0	18
	3 Yr - TOTALS		32	67	699	0	7	7	0	42
19.	Dilger	IND	10	27	380	0	3	3	0	18
	1996		13	42	503	0	4	4	0	24
	1995		15	42	635	0	4	4	0	24
	3 Yr - TOTALS		38	111	1,518	0	11	11	0	66
20.	Purnell	NE	4	5	57	0	3	3	0	18
	1996		–	–	–	–	–	–	–	–
	1995		–	–	–	–	–	–	–	–
	3 Yr - TOTALS		4	5	57	0	3	3	0	18
21.	Jenkins	WASH	4	4	43	0	3	3	0	18
	1996		1	1	7	0	0	0	0	0
	1995		1	1	2	0	0	0	0	0
	3 Yr - TOTALS		6	6	52	0	3	3	0	18
22.	Riemersma	BUF	12	26	208	0	2	2	2	14
23.	Gonzalez +	KC	12	33	368	0	2	2	2	14
24.	L. Johnson	BUF	15	41	340	0	2	2	0	12
25.	Brady	NYJ	14	22	238	0	2	2	0	12
26.	F. Jones +	SD	13	41	505	0	2	2	0	12
27.	Popson	KC	12	35	320	0	2	2	0	12
28.	Cross	NYG	12	21	150	0	2	2	0	12
29.	B. Jones	SF	12	29	383	0	2	2	0	12
30.	Santiago +	ATL	9	17	217	0	2	2	0	12
31.	LaFleur +	DALL	9	18	122	0	2	2	0	12
32.	Dunn	PHIL	7	7	93	0	2	2	0	12
33.	D. Jones +	JAC	3	5	87	0	2	2	0	12
34.	T. Davis	GB	2	2	28	0	1	2	0	12
35.	Asher	WASH	16	49	474	0	1	1	0	6
36.	Wetnight	CHI	15	46	464	0	1	1	0	6
37.	Crumpler	SEAT	14	31	361	0	1	1	0	6
38.	Hallock	JAC	13	18	131	0	1	1	0	6
39.	Hartley	SD	11	19	246	0	1	1	0	6
40.	Battaglia	CIN	9	12	149	0	1	1	0	6
41.	I. Smith	NO	9	17	180	0	1	1	0	6
42.	Harris	TB	9	20	216	0	1	1	0	6
43.	Carswell	DEN	8	12	96	0	1	1	0	6
44.	Kinchen	BALT	7	11	95	0	1	1	0	6
45.	Farquhar	NO	7	17	253	0	1	1	0	6
46.	J. Johnson	PHIL	7	14	177	0	1	1	0	6
47.	Carter	ARIZ	6	7	44	0	1	1	0	6
48.	West	ATL	6	7	63	0	1	1	0	6
49.	Brown	JAC	6	8	84	0	1	1	0	6
50.	Perry +	MIA	6	11	45	0	1	1	0	6
51.	Kozlowski	ATL	5	7	99	0	1	1	0	6
52.	Clark +	SF	5	8	96	0	1	1	0	6
53.	Laing	STL	5	5	31	0	1	1	0	6
54.	Hape +	TB	5	4	22	0	1	1	0	6
55.	Thomason	GB	4	9	115	0	1	1	0	6
56.	Chryplewicz +	DET	2	3	27	0	1	1	0	6
57.	Bjornson	DALL	13	47	442	0	0	0	2	2
58.	Pollard	IND	6	10	116	0	0	0	2	2
59.	Metzelaars	DET	11	17	144	0	0	0	0	0

1997 STATISTICAL RESULTS
(TIGHT ENDS — BASIC SCORING METHOD)

	NAME	TEAM	GP	REC	YARDS	RSH TDs	REC TDs	TOTAL TDs	CONV PTS	FANTASY PTS
60.	Sloan	DET	11	29	264	0	0	0	0	0
61.	Jennings	CHI	10	14	164	0	0	0	0	0
62.	Pierce	NYG	8	10	47	0	0	0	0	0
63.	Allred +	CHI	7	8	70	0	0	0	0	0
64.	Delong	MINN	7	8	75	0	0	0	0	0
65.	Fauria	SEAT	7	10	110	0	0	0	0	0
66.	Roan	TENN	6	12	159	0	0	0	0	0
67.	Walker	KC	5	5	60	0	0	0	0	0
68.	Goodwin	MINN	5	7	61	0	0	0	0	0
69.	McWilliams	ARIZ	4	7	75	0	0	0	0	0
70.	J. Davis	TB	3	3	35	0	0	0	0	0
71.	Galbraith	DALL	2	2	16	0	0	0	0	0
72.	Slutzker	IND	2	3	22	0	0	0	0	0
73.	Lyons	PITT	2	4	29	0	0	0	0	0
74.	May	SEAT	2	2	21	0	0	0	0	0
75.	Fann	SF	2	5	78	0	0	0	0	0
76.	Jacoby	STL	2	2	10	0	0	0	0	0
77.	E. Smith	ATL	1	1	2	0	0	0	0	0
78.	Cline	BUF	1	1	29	0	0	0	0	0
79.	Mangum +	CAR	1	4	56	0	0	0	0	0
80.	Rasby	CAR	1	1	1	0	0	0	0	0
81.	Allen	CHI	1	1	9	0	0	0	0	0
82.	Chamberlain	DEN	1	2	18	0	0	0	0	0
83.	T. Johnson	NO	1	1	13	0	0	0	0	0
84.	Savoie +	NO	1	1	14	0	0	0	0	0
85.	Botkin	PITT	1	1	11	0	0	0	0	0
86.	Sadowski	PITT	1	1	12	0	0	0	0	0
87.	S. Mitchell	SD	1	1	14	0	0	0	0	0
88.	Pupunu	SD	1	1	7	0	0	0	0	0
89.	Jordan	TB	1	1	0	0	0	0	0	0
90.	R. Lewis	TENN	1	1	7	0	0	0	0	0

+ DENOTES COLLEGE DRAFT PICK

RATING THE PLAYERS FOR 1998
(Tight Ends—Basic Scoring Method)

GRAB ONE IF YOU CAN

☐ **1. Ben Coates (New England Patriots)**
Consistency counts and that's what Ben Coates has been, scoring seven, six, nine and eight touchdowns in the last four seasons, respectively. I look for another 7 to 10 from him touchdowns in 1998.

☐ **2. Shannon Sharpe (Denver Broncos)**
After scoring 10 times on 80 receptions in 1996, Sharpe dropped to only three touchdowns on 72 catches a year ago. I believe he's likely to be back in the seven-plus touchdown range in 1998 as one of the league's best tight ends.

☐ **3. Ricky Dudley (Oakland Raiders)**
Jeff George's arrival in 1997 benefited all the Raiders' receivers, including Dudley. Dudley upped his rookie totals from four touchdowns on 34 receptions in 1996 to seven scores on 48 receptions in 1997. He should match or exceed that performance in 1998.

☐ **4. Mark Chmura (Green Bay Packers)**
With Keith Jackson's retirement in 1997, Chmura returned to a much bigger role and scored six times. Two years earlier as the starter, he scored seven times. That's about what I expect him to do in 1998, 6 to 10 touchdowns, as one of Brett Favre's go-to receivers.

☐ **5. Wesley Walls (Carolina Panthers)**
Always hovering in the 50 to 60 reception range, Walls is a likely candidate to score 6 to 10 times a season. Walls has scored 10 and 6 touchdowns, respectively, the last two seasons.

BEST OF THE REST

☐ **6. Eric Green (Baltimore Ravens)**
Green pushed himself through injuries to record five touchdowns on 65 receptions in 1997. He has returned from a knee injury and should be more productive.

☐ **7. Tony McGee (Cincinnati Bengals)**
McGee's scoring is on the rise. He scored four, four and six touchdowns, respectivel,y during the last three seasons. I look for another five to eight scores from him in 1998.

☐ **8. Troy Drayton (Miami Dolphins)**
As Drayton becomes more involved in the Dolphins' offense, he'll push the four-touchdown mark he hit in 1997 to the five-plus range in 1998.

☐ **9. Mark Bruener (Pittsburgh Steelers)**
Very involved in the Steelers' "red zone" offense in 1997, Bruener scored six times on just 18 receptions. He'll work to keep that role in 1998.

☐ **10. Frank Wycheck (Tennessee Oilers)**
Wycheck, a big part of the Oilers' offense, has produced 53 and 63 receptions while scoring six and four touchdowns over the last two seasons. Wycheck will continue to be a major contributor and to get plenty of scoring chances for the Oilers in 1998.

STRONG LONG SHOTS

☐ **11. Dave Moore (Tampa Bay Buccaneers)**
Moore has scored three and four touchdowns in the last two seasons and looks to boost those numbers since Jackie Harris is with Tennessee in 1998.

☐ **12. Pete Mitchell (Jacksonville Jaguars)**
Mitchell has produced 41, 52 and 35 receptions as the Jaguars' starting tight end for the last three seasons. Mitchell's touchdown numbers jumped to four in 1997 on just those 35 catches. He'll remain a nice touchdown outlet for Jacksonville in 1998, especially with running back Natrone Means' departure.

☐ **13. Tony Gonzalez (Kansas City Chiefs)**
Gonzalez scored twice on 33 receptions as a rookie in 1997 and has shown the potential to score a lot more.

☐ **14. Greg Clark (San Francisco 49ers)**
With Brent Jones retiring, Clark will battle new 49er Irv Smith for the starting job in 1998. The winner of the battle is looking at, potentially, a six-touchdown season.

☐ **15. Jamie Asher (Washington Redskins)**
Asher scored only one touchdown in 1997 while recording a solid 49 receptions. A year earlier, however, he recorded four touchdowns on 42 receptions. That's a level I believe he'll return to or surpass in 1998.

☐ **16. Chris Gedney (Arizona Cardinals)**
After coming to Arizona in 1997, Gedney scored four times on just 23 receptions. Three of his four touchdowns came over the last four weeks of the season, which could be an excellent sign for 1998.

HAVE THE POTENTIAL

☐ **17. Eric Bjornson (Dallas Cowboys)**
In taking over most of the duties of retired Jay Novacek in 1997, Bjornson recorded 47 receptions but failed to score a touchdown. I don't believe that will happen again this year. Bjornson is likely to start finding his way into the end zone with some frequency in 1998.

☐ **18. Ken Dilger (Indianapolis Colts)**
Dilger had scored four touchdowns in both 1995 and 1996 but dropped back a notch to three scores in 1997. This was due partially to a hamstring injury that caused him to miss a number of games. If he's healthy in 1998, I look for another four to six scores from him.

☐ **19. Fred Jones (San Diego Chargers)**
The Chargers' second-round pick of a year ago quickly got himself in-volved in the offense and recorded 41 receptions and two touchdowns in 1997. I believe those numbers will only grow in 1998.

☐ **20. O.J. Santiago (Atlanta Falcons)**
Santiago had produced a couple of touchdowns on 17 receptions as a rookie in 1997 but a leg injury forced him to miss the last five games. He has a good future if he stays healthy and good numbers will follow.

KEEP AN EYE ON   YOU NEVER KNOW

21. I. Smith (SF)	31. Jenkins (WASH)
22. Conwell (STL)	32. Baxter (NYJ)
23. Glover (MINN)	33. Crumpler (SEAT)
24. Wetnight (CHI)	34. Cross (NYG)
25. L. Johnson (BUF)	35. Brady (NYJ)
26. Dunn (PHIL)	36. Farguhar (NO)
27. LaFleur (DALL)	37. Jennings (CHI)
28. Popson (KC)	38. H. Williams (OAK)
29. Sloan (DET)	39. J. Johnson (PHIL)
30. Harris (TENN)	40. Fauria (SEAT)

WORTH MENTIONING

41. Pupunu (NYG)
42. C. Lewis (PHIL)
43. Metzelaars (DET)
44. Hartley (SD)
45. Riemersma (BUF)

ROOKIE PROSPECTS

NAME	TEAM	COMMENT
☐ 1. Cameron Cleeland	NO	Irv Smith's departure to S.F. creates opportunity.
☐ 2. Alonzo Mayes	CHI	Nice size and good downfield ability.
☐ 3. Stephen Alexander	WASH	Decent hands and good jumping ability.
☐ 4. Rod Rutledge	NE	Will have trouble pushing Ben Coates for production.

A LOOK AT THE QUARTERBACKS

(A Guide for the Beginner)

Considerations in Choosing a Quarterback

1. First, look at players' previous performances. Injuries, player movement, holdouts, and the like should be noted. Year-end performances by Brad Johnson, Mark Brunell and Gus Frerotte were all affected in 1997 by injury.

2. Quarterbacks who play for passing teams have the edge. Look for a quarterback with a high number of pass attempts, one who will assure you of at least 25 to 30 touchdown passes for the year. Steve Young, Brett Favre and Scott Mitchell are all good prospects.

3. Look for a quarterback who doesn't mind running the ball, especially near the goal line. Because six points are awarded for a touchdown run and only three points for a touchdown pass, quarterbacks who like to rush for touchdowns are a plus. And if your quarterback is like Steve Young of the 49ers, who throws a lot of touchdowns and runs for several more, you've got yourself a great fantasy candidate.

4. Avoid situations in which the starting quarterback may change from week to week. Some teams use one quarterback one week, then switch the following week, depending on the player's performance. It would obviously hurt you if you didn't know whether your quarterback was going to play. That was the situation in Arizona and Cincinatti during 1997.

In the 1997 statistics, players are ranked by their fantasy-point totals. Remember that in the Basic Scoring Method, fantasy points are calculated by awarding six points for every rushing touchdown and three points for every touchdown pass thrown. No yardage statistics are included, because the Basic Scoring Method awards no points for yardage gained. It is not important how a player's team did, or how he ranks in any category except fantasy points. A player may have a poor passing percentage and may not throw for many yards, but if he ranks high in throwing and rushing touchdowns, he will help you win.

1997 STATISTICAL RESULTS
(QUARTERBACKS — BASIC SCORING METHOD)

NAME	TEAM	GP	RUSHES	COMP	ATT	PCT	RSH TDs	TD PASSES	CONV PTS	FANTASY POINTS
1. Stewart	PITT	16	88	236	440	53.6	11	21	1	130
1996		16	39	11	30	36.7	5	0	0	48
1995		–	–	–	–	–	–	–	–	–
3-Yr Totals		32	127	247	470	52.6	16	21	1	178
2. Favre	GB	16	58	304	513	59.3	1	35	1	112
1996		16	49	325	543	59.9	2	39	2	131
1995		16	39	359	570	63.0	3	38	0	132
3-Yr Totals		48	146	988	1,626	60.8	6	112	3	375
3. McNair	TENN	16	101	216	415	52.0	8	14	1	91
1996		9	31	88	143	61.5	2	6	0	30
1995		4	11	41	80	51.3	0	3	0	9
3-Yr Totals		29	143	345	638	54.1	10	23	1	130
4. George	OAK	16	16	290	521	55.7	0	29	2	89
1996 w/ATL		3	5	56	99	56.6	0	3	0	9
1995 w/ATL		16	27	336	557	60.3	0	24	3	75
3-Yr Totals		35	48	682	1,177	57.9	0	56	5	173
5. Elway	DEN	16	50	280	502	55.8	1	27	1	88
1996		15	50	287	466	61.6	4	26	0	102
1995		16	41	316	542	58.3	1	26	3	87
3-Yr Totals		47	141	883	1,510	58.5	6	79	4	277
6. Bledsoe	NE	16	28	314	522	60.2	0	28	0	84
1996		16	24	373	623	59.9	0	27	4	85
1995		15	20	323	636	55.0	0	13	2	41
3-Yr Totals		47	72	1,010	1,781	56.7	0	68	6	210
7. Moon	SEAT	15	17	313	528	59.3	1	25	0	81
1996 w/MINN		8	9	134	247	54.3	0	7	0	21
1995 w/MINN		16	33	377	606	62.2	0	33	0	99
3-Yr Totals		39	59	824	1,381	59.7	1	65	0	201
8. Young	SF	15	50	241	356	67.7	3	19	0	75
1996		12	52	214	316	67.7	4	14	2	68
1995		11	50	299	447	66.9	3	20	0	78
3-Yr Totals		38	152	754	1,119	67.4	10	53	2	221
9. B. Johnson ***	MINN	13	35	275	452	60.8	0	20	6	72
1996		12	34	195	311	62.7	1	17	2	59
1995		5	9	25	36	69.4	0	0	0	0
3-Yr Totals		30	78	495	799	62.0	1	37	8	131
10. Dilfer	TB	16	33	217	386	56.2	1	21	0	69
1996		16	32	267	482	55.4	0	12	1	37
1995		16	23	224	415	54.0	2	4	0	24
3-Yr Totals		48	88	708	1,283	55.2	3	37	1	130
11. Brunell	JAC	14	48	264	435	60.7	2	18	1	67
1996		16	79	353	557	63.4	3	19	7	82
1995		13	67	201	346	58.1	4	15	1	70
3-Yr Totals		43	194	818	1,338	61.1	9	52	9	219
12. Mitchell	DET	16	37	293	509	57.6	1	19	1	64
1996		14	37	253	437	57.9	4	17	0	75
1995		16	36	346	583	59.3	4	32	1	121
3-Yr Totals		46	110	892	1,529	58.3	9	68	2	260
13. Frerotte	WASH	13	24	204	402	50.7	2	17	0	63
1996		16	23	270	470	57.4	0	12	0	36
1995		13	20	199	396	50.3	1	13	0	45
3-Yr Totals		42	67	673	1,268	53.1	3	42	0	144
14. Chandler	ATL	14	43	202	342	59.1	0	20	0	60
1996 w/HOUS		12	28	184	320	57.5	0	16	0	48
1995 w/HOUS		13	28	225	356	63.2	2	17	2	65
3-Yr Totals		39	99	611	1,018	60.0	2	53	2	173
15. Plummer +	ARIZ	10	39	157	296	53.0	2	15	2	59
1996		–	–	–	–	–	–	–	–	–
1995		–	–	–	–	–	–	–	–	–
3-Yr Totals		10	39	157	296	53.0	2	15	2	59

1997 STATISTICAL RESULTS
(QUARTERBACKS — BASIC SCORING METHOD)

	NAME	TEAM	GP	RUSHES	COMP	ATT	PCT	RSH TDs	TD PASSES	CONV PTS	FANTASY POINTS
16.	Aikman	DALL	16	25	292	518	56.4	0	19	2	59
	1996		15	35	296	465	63.7	1	12	2	44
	1995		16	21	280	432	64.8	1	16	1	55
	3-Yr Totals		47	81	868	1,415	61.3	2	47	5	158
17.	O'Donnell	NYJ	15	32	259	460	56.3	1	17	0	57
	1996		6	6	110	188	58.5	0	4	0	12
	1995 w/PITT		12	24	246	416	59.1	0	17	0	51
	3-Yr Totals		33	62	615	1,064	57.8	1	38	0	120
18.	Testaverde	BALT	13	34	271	470	57.7	0	18	2	56
	1996		16	34	325	549	59.2	2	33	5	116
	1995		13	18	241	392	61.5	2	17	0	63
	3-Yr Totals		42	86	837	1,411	59.3	4	68	7	235
19.	Kramer	CHI	15	27	275	477	57.7	2	14	2	56
	1996		4	8	73	150	48.7	0	3	0	9
	1995		16	35	315	522	60.3	1	29	0	93
	3-Yr Totals		35	70	663	1,149	57.7	3	46	2	158
20.	Marino	MIA	16	18	319	548	58.2	0	16	0	48
	1996		13	10	221	373	59.2	0	17	0	51
	1995		14	11	309	482	64.1	0	24	2	74
	3-Yr Totals		43	39	849	1,403	60.5	0	57	2	173
21.	Banks	STL	16	45	252	487	51.7	1	14	0	48
	1996		14	61	192	368	52.2	0	15	2	47
	1995		–	–	–	–	–	–	–	–	–
	3-Yr Totals		30	106	444	855	51.9	1	29	2	95
22.	Blake	CIN	11	44	184	316	58.2	3	8	1	43
	1996		16	73	308	549	56.1	2	24	1	85
	1995		16	53	326	567	57.5	2	28	2	98
	3-Yr Totals		43	170	818	1,432	57.1	7	60	4	226
23.	Grbac	KC	10	30	179	314	57.0	1	11	2	41
	1996 w/SF		10	23	122	197	61.9	2	8	0	36
	1995 w/SF		9	20	127	183	69.4	2	8	1	37
	3-Yr Totals		29	73	428	694	61.7	5	27	3	114
24.	K. Collins	CAR	13	26	200	381	52.5	1	11	1	40
	1996		13	32	204	364	56.0	0	14	2	44
	1995		15	42	214	433	49.4	3	14	2	62
	3-Yr Totals		41	100	618	1,178	52.5	4	39	5	146
25.	Esiason	CIN	7	8	118	186	63.4	0	13	0	39
	1996 w/ARIZ		10	15	190	339	56.0	1	11	2	41
	1995 w/ARIZ		12	19	221	389	56.8	0	16	0	48
	3-Yr Totals		29	42	529	914	57.9	1	40	2	128
26.	T. Collins	BUF	14	29	215	391	55.0	0	12	0	36
27.	Hoying +	PHIL	7	16	128	225	56.9	0	11	1	34
28.	Gannon	KC	9	33	98	175	56.0	2	7	0	33
29.	Kanell	NYG	12	14	156	294	53.1	0	11	0	33
30.	Harbaugh	IND	12	36	189	309	61.2	0	10	1	31
31.	Detmer	PHIL	8	14	134	244	54.9	1	7	0	27
32.	Graham	ARIZ	8	13	130	250	52.0	2	4	2	26
33.	Brown	NYG	7	15	93	180	51.7	1	5	1	22
34.	Zeier	BALT	5	10	67	116	57.8	0	7	0	21
35.	Cunningham	MINN	4	19	44	88	50.0	0	6	1	19
36.	Beuerlein	CAR	7	4	89	153	58.2	0	6	0	18
37.	Hobert **	NO	6	14	78	161	48.4	0	6	0	18
38.	Whelihan	SD	9	13	118	237	49.8	0	6	0	18
39.	Justin	IND	8	6	83	140	59.3	0	5	2	17
40.	Tolliver **	KC	7	9	64	116	55.2	0	5	0	15
41.	Humphries	SD	8	13	121	225	53.8	0	5	0	15
42.	Hostetler	WASH	6	15	79	144	54.9	0	5	0	15
43.	Van Pelt	BUF	6	11	60	124	48.4	1	2	2	14
44.	Shuler	NO	10	22	106	203	52.2	1	2	1	13
45.	R. Johnson	JAC	5	10	22	28	78.6	1	2	0	12
46.	Wuerffel +	NO	6	6	42	91	46.2	0	4	0	12
47.	Peete	PHIL	5	8	68	118	57.6	0	4	0	12
48.	Foley	NYJ	4	3	56	97	57.7	0	3	0	9

1997 STATISTICAL RESULTS
(QUARTERBACKS — BASIC SCORING METHOD)

	NAME	TEAM	GP	RUSHES	COMP	ATT	PCT	RSH TDs	TD PASSES	CONV PTS	FANTASY POINTS
49.	Kitna	SEAT	3	11	31	45	68.9	1	1	0	9
50.	Mirer	CHI	7	20	53	103	51.5	1	0	2	8
51.	Case	ARIZ	2	7	29	55	52.7	1	0	0	6
52.	Zolak	NE	4	3	6	9	66.7	0	2	0	6
53.	Holcomb	IND	4	5	45	73	61.6	0	1	1	4
54.	Druckenmiller +	SF	4	9	21	52	40.4	0	1	1	4
55.	Tomczak	PITT	5	7	16	24	66.7	0	1	0	3
56.	Everett	SD	4	5	36	75	48.0	0	1	0	3
57.	Graziani +	ATL	2	3	7	23	30.4	0	0	0	0
58.	Stenstrom	CHI	3	1	8	14	57.1	0	0	0	0
59.	Wilson	DALL	6	6	12	21	57.1	0	0	0	0
60.	Garrett	DALL	1	0	10	14	71.4	0	0	0	0
61.	Lewis	DEN	3	5	1	2	50.0	0	0	0	0
62.	Brister	DEN	1	4	6	9	66.7	0	0	0	0
63.	Reich	DET	4	4	11	30	36.7	0	0	0	0
64.	Blundin	DET	1	0	0	1	00.0	0	0	0	0
65.	Bono	GB	2	3	5	10	50.0	0	0	0	0
66.	Pederson	GB	1	3	0	0	00.0	0	0	0	0
67.	Matthews	JAC	2	1	26	40	65.0	0	0	0	0
68.	Erickson	MIA	2	4	13	28	46.4	0	0	0	0
69.	Nussmeier	NO	3	7	18	32	56.3	0	0	0	0
70.	Cherry +	NYG	1	1	0	0	00.0	0	0	0	0
71.	Clements +	NYJ	1	2	0	0	00.0	0	0	0	0
72.	Lucas	NYJ	1	3	3	4	75.0	0	0	0	0
73.	Klingler	OAK	1	1	4	7	57.1	0	0	0	0
74.	Quinn	PITT	1	0	1	2	50.0	0	0	0	0
75.	Philcox	SD	2	1	16	27	59.3	0	0	0	0
76.	Friesz	SEAT	2	1	15	36	41.7	0	0	0	0
77.	Brohm	SF	5	4	16	24	66.7	0	0	0	0
78.	Rypien	STL	4	1	19	39	48.7	0	0	0	0
79.	Walsh	TB	5	6	6	17	35.3	0	0	0	0
80.	Krieg	TENN	3	4	1	2	50.0	0	0	0	0
81.	Ritchey	TENN	1	1	2	2	100.0	0	0	0	0
82.	Green	WASH	1	0	0	1	00.0	0	0	0	0

+   DENOTES COLLEGE DRAFT PICK
**   Hobert   NO   Played in 1 game with Buffalo.
**   Tolliver   KC   Played in 6 games with Atlanta.
***   B. Johnson   MINN   Scored TD on a 3 yard reception.

RATING THE PLAYERS FOR 1998
(Quarterbacks—Basic Scoring Method)

GRAB ONE IF YOU CAN

☐ **1. Brett Favre (Green Bay Packers)**
For four straight seasons, Favre has thrown for more than 30 touchdowns. It's impossible to argue with that kind of consistent success. Look for another 30-plus in 1998.

☐ **2. Kordell Stewart (Pittsburgh Steelers)**
In his first year as the team's starting quarterback, Stewart rewarded the Steelers with 21 passing touchdowns and a whopping 11 rushing scores. I look for his continued success even though he has lost Yancey Thigpen to Tennessee and I believe the Steelers will try to cut back on his rushing touchdowns because of the danger of injuries.

☐ **3. Jeff George (Oakland Raiders)**
Many thought Jeff George's arm fit Al Davis and Raider football and it did. George, in his first season with the Raiders, threw for 29 touchdowns. He'll shoot to beat that mark in 1998.

☐ **4. John Elway (Denver Broncos)**
Elway, a very consistent producer of touchdown passes, has thrown for 26, 26 and 27 touchdowns over the last three seasons. I look for another 25 to 30 touchdown passes in 1998, with targets Rod Smith, Ed McCaffrey and Shannon Sharpe to help.

☐ **5. Steve Young (San Francisco 49ers)**
Without the services of all-world receiver Jerry Rice and being banged up a little himself, Young threw for only 19 touchdowns and ran for three more in 1997. With Rice back healthy, if Young can stay healthy himself, I look for a rebound to the 25-plus touchdown range in 1998.

BEST OF THE REST

☐ **6. Drew Bledsoe (New England Patriots)**
It's been back-to-back productive years for Bledsoe, who has thrown for 27 and 28 touchdowns the past two seasons. I believe he'll be in that range again in 1998.

☐ **7. Scott Mitchell (Detroit Lions)**
Just three years ago, Mitchell threw for 32 touchdowns. His numbers have, however, dropped significantly ever since. I look for Mitchell to try to retain his job by cutting a bit into Barry Sanders' ground numbers and re-establishing himself as a 25 or better touchdown thrower in 1998.

☐ **8. Brad Johnson (Minnesota Vikings)**
Johnson, in his first year as the Vikings' starter, was off to a strong start in 1997 until he suffered a herniated disc in his neck that forced him to miss the last three games of the season. Johnson had thrown 20 touchdown passes in the 13 games he played in. As he continues to improve, he'll expand those numbers, playing over the full 16 games in 1998.

☐ **9. Warren Moon (Seattle Seahawks)**
Brought to Seattle as a backup in 1997, Moon quickly was cast in a starting role following a thumb injury to starter John Friesz in the season opener. Moon exploded for 25 touchdown passes and is ready to try to do it again in 1998.

☐ **10. Steve McNair (Tennessee Oilers)**
McNair took over the starting reins in 1997 and threw for only 14 touchdowns but ran for eight more. His ability to run as well as pass, along with his continuing improvement, make him an attractive fantasy pick for 1998.

STRONG LONG SHOTS

☐ **11. Mark Brunell (Jacksonville Jaguars)**
I believe Brunell is a big statistical success waiting to happen. After missing the first two games of 1998 with a knee injury, Brunell finished with only 18 touchdown passes and two rushing scores. Looking to 1998, having Keenan McCardell, Jimmy Smith and Pete Mitchell makes me believe bigger touchdown numbers are in store for Brunell.

☐ **12. Jeff Blake (Cincinnati Bengals)**
In 1997, an ineffective Jeff Blake lost his starting job to veteran Boomer Esiason. The two previous years, however, Blake had recorded 28 and 24 touchdowns. With Esiason retiring, Blake is likely back as the starter. We know what he's capable of, if he gets his confidence back.

☐ **13. Chris Chandler (Atlanta Falcons)**
In his first year as the quarterback in Atlanta, Chandler threw for 20 touchdowns despite missing two games with injuries. If he is healthy for all of 1998, I look for him to approach the 25-touchdown pass mark, though losing Bert Emanuel to Tampa Bay will hurt.

☐ **14. Jake Plummer (Arizona Cardinals)**
As a rookie in 1997, Plummer eventually won the starting job and finished with 15 touchdown passes and two rushing scores while playing in just 10 games. He looks to have a bright future.

☐ **15. Elvis Grbac (Kansas City Chiefs)**
Missing six games with a shoulder injury in his first season with the Chiefs in 1997, Grbac threw for only 11 touchdowns. Adding Derrick Alexander (Ravens) to Andre Rison, Tony Gonzalez and Ted Popson should help him provide good numbers if he's healthy in 1998.

HAVE THE POTENTIAL

☐ **16. Bobby Hoying (Philadelphia Eagles)**
Hoying didn't get into the lineup until late in the year as a rookie in 1997 but threw for 11 touchdowns playing in just seven games . What can he do over a full season?

☐ **17. Tony Banks (St. Louis Rams)**
Banks actually took a step backward in 1997, throwing for only 14

touchdowns after throwing for 15 as a rookie in1996. Playing without injured Isaac Bruce for the first five weeks hurt. With Bruce healthy and with the addition of Ricky Proehl for 1998, Banks' scoring chances should increase.

☐ **18. Erik Kramer (Chicago Bears)**
Just three short seasons ago, Kramer threw for a lofty 29 touchdown passes. He's played through injuries since but never recaptured that sort of success. He'll have trouble nearing that number in 1998 because the Bears face the league's second-toughest schedule.

☐ **19. Dan Marino (Miami Dolphins)**
Marino's numbers continue to go down. He threw for 24, 17 and 16 touchdowns, respectively, in the last three seasons. Looking to 1998, however, Marino could fare better. The Dolphins face the league's second-easiest schedule and have speedster Yatil Green returning healthy.

☐ **20. Gus Frerotte (Washington Redskins)**
With Heath Shuler off to New Orleans, Frerotte knew the starting job was his for keeps in 1997. Frerotte threw for 17 touchdowns over the first 13 weeks before a hip injury ended his season. If he stays healthy for the full 1998 season, topping the 20 touchdown mark is well within his reach.

KEEP AN EYE ON

☐ **21. Trent Dilfer (Tampa Bay Buccaneers)**
Under new head coach Tony Dungy, Dilfer is playing with newfound confidence and threw for 21 touchdowns in 1997.

☐ **22. Glenn Foley/Neil O'Donnell (New York Jets)**
Foley is believed to have edged high-priced O'Donnell out of a job. With Keyshawn Johnson and Co. to throw to, the Jets should realize decent success.

☐ **23. Troy Aikman (Dallas Cowboys)**
Despite the team's success, which is now also in question, Aikman does not throw for many scores. In the last four seasons, he has thrown for 13, 16, 12 and 19 touchdowns.

☐ **24. Jim Harbaugh (Baltimore Ravens)**
Harbaugh comes to Baltimore but he will again struggle to throw for 15 to 20 touchdowns.

☐ **25. Rob Johnson/Doug Flutie/Todd Collins (Buffalo Bills)**
The Bills are struggling to find a successor for Jim Kelly.

☐ **26. Ryan Leaf/Craig Whelihan (San Diego Chargers)**
I look for the Chargers to run more with Natrone Means returning.

☐ **27. Peyton Manning (Indianapolis Colts)**
I don't see much success here immediately.

☐ **28. Danny Kanell (New York Giants)**
The Giants were happy to see Kanell step in and play well in 1997 but he's unlikely to near the 20-touchdown mark.

☐ **29. Kerry Collins (Carolina Panthers)**
Missing the first two games of the 1997 season because of an injured jaw, Collins threw for only 11 touchdowns. Over the last three seasons, he has thrown for only 14, 14 and 11 scores.

☐ **30. Billy Joe Hobert (New Orleans Saints)**
The Saints' quarterbacks don't really excite me.

ROOKIE PROSPECTS

NAME	TEAM	COMMENT
☐ 1. Peyton Manning	IND	Losing ain't so bad, Colts got their future QB by doing so.
☐ 2. Ryan Leaf	SD	Lots of talent, good leader on field.
☐ 3. Charlie Batch	DET	Future potential only.
☐ 4. John Quinn	JAC	Future potential only.
☐ 5. Brian Griese	DEN	Future potential only.

A LOOK AT THE KICKERS

(A Guide for the Beginner)

Considerations in Choosing a Kicker

1. First, look at players' previous performances. Injuries, player movement, holdouts, and the like should be noted.

2. A kicker can't accumulate points without opportunities to score, so one of your main concerns is the team he's playing for. You're in good shape with a kicker from a strong offensive team that will get close enough for a lot of field-goal attempts. Even a good defensive team will provide its kicker with plenty of scoring opportunities. Mike Hollis continues to see his numbers climb as the Jaguars give him more and more scoring chances.

3. Consider a team's coaching philosophy. In Indianapolis, there's a tendency for the offense to move into field-goal range and let their kickers do their thing. Thus, they get more three-point attempts than a lot of other kickers.

4. A kicker who has played for the same team for a few years is a good bet. Kickers are treated as if they were a dime a dozen, so if one has been with a team for a few years, there must be some confidence that he will be consistent year after year.

5. Consider the opposition a kicker will face in 1998. Favor kickers who will face easy schedules, since this should result in more scoring opportunities. (See Section VI, "Rating the 1998 NFL Team Schedules.")

In the 1997 statistics that follow, players are ranked by their fantasy-point totals. Remember that in the Basic Scoring Method, the Performance Point Method, and the Combined Basic/Performance Scoring Method, fantasy points are calculated by awarding three points for each field goal and one point for each extra point.

1997 STATISTICAL RESULTS
(KICKERS — BASIC, & COMBINED
BASIC/PERFORMANCE SCORING METHODS)

	NAME	TEAM	GP	EXTRA POINTS	EXTRA PT ATT	ACC RATE	FG	FG ATT	ACC RATE	FANTASY POINTS
1.	**Hollis**	**JAC**	**16**	**41**	**41**	**1.000**	**31**	**36**	**.861**	**134**
	1996		16	27	27	1.000	30	36	.833	117
	1995		16	27	28	.964	20	27	.741	87
	3 Yr-TOTALS		48	95	96	2.964	81	99	1.222	338
2.	**Cunningham**	**DALL**	**16**	**24**	**24**	**1.000**	**34**	**37**	**.919**	**126**
	1996		–	–	–	–	–	–	–	–
	1995		–	–	–	–	–	–	–	–
	3 Yr-TOTALS		16	24	24	1.000	34	37	1.088	126
3.	**Anderson**	**SF**	**16**	**38**	**38**	**1.000**	**29**	**36**	**.806**	**125**
	1996 w/PHIL		16	40	40	1.000	25	29	.862	115
	1995 w/PHIL		16	32	33	.970	22	30	.733	98
	3 Yr-TOTALS		48	110	111	2.970	76	95	1.250	338
4.	**Elam**	**DEN**	**15**	**46**	**46**	**1.000**	**26**	**36**	**.722**	**124**
	1996		16	46	46	1.000	21	28	.750	109
	1995		16	39	39	1.000	31	38	.816	132
	3 Yr-TOTALS		47	131	131	3.000	78	102	1.308	365
5.	**Longwell**	**GB**	**16**	**48**	**48**	**1.000**	**24**	**30**	**.800**	**120**
	1996		–	–	–	–	–	–	–	–
	1995		–	–	–	–	–	–	–	–
	3 Yr-TOTALS		16	48	48	1.000	24	30	1.250	120
6.	**Hall**	**NYJ**	**16**	**36**	**36**	**1.000**	**28**	**41**	**.683**	**120**
	1996		–	–	–	–	–	–	–	–
	1995		–	–	–	–	–	–	–	–
	3 Yr-TOTALS		16	36	36	1.000	28	41	1.464	120
7.	**Hanson**	**DET**	**16**	**39**	**40**	**.975**	**26**	**29**	**.897**	**117**
	1996		16	36	36	1.000	12	17	.706	72
	1995		16	48	48	1.000	28	34	.824	132
	3 Yr-TOTALS		48	123	124	2.975	66	80	1.212	321
8.	**Blanchard**	**IND**	**16**	**21**	**21**	**1.000**	**32**	**41**	**.780**	**117**
	1996		16	27	27	1.000	36	40	.900	135
	1995		12	25	25	1.000	19	24	.792	82
	3 Yr-TOTALS		44	73	73	3.000	87	105	1.207	334
9.	**Mare**	**MIA**	**16**	**33**	**33**	**1.000**	**28**	**36**	**.778**	**117**
	1996		–	–	–	–	–	–	–	–
	1995		–	–	–	–	–	–	–	–
	3 Yr-TOTALS		16	33	33	1.000	28	36	1.286	117
10.	**Vinatieri**	**NE**	**16**	**40**	**40**	**1.000**	**25**	**2**	**.862**	**115**
	1996		16	39	42	.929	27	35	.771	120
	1995		–	–	–	–	–	–	–	–
	3 Yr-TOTALS		32	79	82	1.929	52	64	1.231	235
11.	**Stoyanovich**	**KC**	**16**	**35**	**36**	**.972**	**26**	**27**	**.963**	**113**
	1996		16	34	34	1.000	17	24	.708	85
	1995 w/MIA		15	37	37	1.000	27	34	.794	118
	3 Yr-TOTALS		47	106	107	2.972	70	85	1.214	316
12.	**Del Greco**	**TENN**	**16**	**32**	**32**	**1.000**	**27**	**35**	**.771**	**113**
	1996		16	35	35	1.000	32	38	.842	131
	1995		16	33	33	1.000	27	31	.871	114
	3 Yr-TOTALS		48	100	100	3.000	86	104	1.209	358
13.	**Stover**	**BALT**	**15**	**32**	**32**	**1.000**	**26**	**34**	**.765**	**110**
	1996		16	34	35	.971	19	25	.760	91
	1995		16	26	26	1.000	29	33	.879	113
	3 Yr-TOTALS		47	92	93	2.971	74	92	1.243	314
14.	**Davis ******	**SD**	**16**	**31**	**32**	**.969**	**26**	**33**	**.788**	**109**
	1996 w/ ARIZ		8	12	12	1.000	9	14	.643	39
	1995 w/ARIZ		16	19	19	1.000	30	39	.769	109
	3 Yr-TOTALS		40	62	63	2.969	65	86	1.323	257
15.	**Wilkins**	**STL**	**16**	**32**	**32**	**1.000**	**25**	**37**	**.676**	**107**
	1996 w/SF		16	40	40	1.000	30	34	.882	130
	1995 w/SF		7	27	29	.931	12	13	.923	63
	3 Yr-TOTALS		39	99	101	2.931	67	84	1.254	300

	NAME	TEAM	GP	EXTRA POINTS	EXTRA PT ATT	ACC RATE	FG	FG ATT	ACC RATE	FANTASY POINTS
16.	Johnson	PITT	16	40	40	1.000	22	25	.880	106
	1996		16	37	37	1.000	23	30	.767	106
	1995		16	39	39	1.000	34	41	.829	141
	3 Yr-TOTALS		48	116	116	3.000	79	96	1.215	353
17.	Andersen	ATL	16	35	35	1.000	23	27	.852	104
	1996		16	31	31	1.000	22	29	.759	97
	1995		16	29	30	.967	31	37	.838	122
	3 Yr-TOTALS		48	95	96	2.967	76	93	1.224	323
18.	Peterson	SEAT	16	37	37	1.000	22	28	.786	103
	1996		16	27	27	1.000	28	34	.824	111
	1995		16	40	40	1.000	23	28	.821	109
	3 Yr-TOTALS		48	104	104	3.000	73	90	1.233	323
19.	Boniol	PHIL	16	33	33	1.000	22	31	.710	99
	1996 w/DALL		16	24	25	.960	32	36	.889	120
	1995 w/DALL		16	46	48	.958	27	28	.964	127
	3 Yr-TOTALS		48	103	106	2.918	81	95	1.173	346
20.	Christie	BUF	16	21	21	1.000	24	30	.800	93
	1996		16	33	33	1.000	24	29	.828	105
	1995		16	33	35	.943	31	40	.775	126
	3 Yr-TOTALS		48	87	89	2.943	79	99	1.253	324
21.	Daluiso	NYG	16	27	29	.931	22	32	.688	93
	1996		14	22	22	1.000	24	27	.889	94
	1995		16	28	28	1.000	20	28	.714	88
	3 Yr-TOTALS		46	77	79	2.931	66	87	1.318	275
22.	Kasay	CAR	14	25	25	1.000	22	26	.846	91
	1996		16	34	35	.971	37	45	.822	145
	1995		16	27	28	.964	26	33	.788	105
	3 Yr-TOTALS		46	86	88	2.935	85	104	1.224	341
23.	Brien	NO	14	22	22	1.000	23	27	.852	91
	1996		16	18	18	1.000	21	25	.840	81
	1995		14	35	35	1.000	19	29	.655	92
	3 Yr-TOTALS		44	75	75	3.000	63	81	1.286	264
24.	Jaeger	CHI	15	20	20	1.000	21	26	.808	83
	1996		13	23	23	1.000	19	23	.826	80
	1995 w/OAK		10	22	22	1.000	13	18	.722	61
	3 Yr-TOTALS		38	65	65	3.000	53	67	1.264	224
25.	Blanton	WASH	15	34	34	1.000	16	24	.667	82
	1996		16	40	40	1.000	26	32	.813	118
	1995		–	–	–	–	–	–	–	–
	3 Yr-TOTALS		31	74	74	2.000	42	56	1.333	200
26.	Pelfrey	CIN	16	41	43	.953	12	16	.750	77
27.	Ford	OAK	16	33	35	.943	13	22	.591	72
28.	Husted	TB	16	32	35	.914	13	17	.765	71
29.	Murray	MINN	12	23	24	.958	12	17	.706	59
30.	Nedney	ARIZ	10	19	19	1.000	11	17	.647	52
31.	Butler	ARIZ	6	9	10	.900	8	12	.667	33
32.	Carney	SD	4	5	5	1.000	7	7	1.000	26
33.	Bentley	ATL	1	4	4	1.000	2	3	.667	10
34.	Jacke	WASH	1	5	5	1.000	0	0	1.000	5

+   DENOTES COLLEGE DRAFT PICK
**   Davis   SD   Played in 4 games with Minnesota.

Cliff Charpentier's
Fantasy Football Newsletter,
Quick Picks Cheatsheet and More . . .

BE TOTALLY PREPARED FOR YOUR 1998 FANTASY DRAFT. ORDER TODAY.

1. **Preseason Edge '98:** Stay on top of fast breaking preseason developments, (five weekly preseason newsletters). During the preseason, the newsletter updates the digest with player movement, injuries, etc., through the first week of the NFL. Includes a copy of the 1998 NFL rosters and checklist. Faxing & Email are available.

2. **1998 Cliff's Quick Picks—Fantasy Draft At A Glance™:** The ultimate Fantasy Football cheatsheet. Last year, thousands again gave Cliff's Quick Picks rave reviews. This eight-panel foldout, (8½ x 11 each panel), opens up a world of information at your fingertips. Cliff's Quick Picks—Fantasy Draft At A Glance gives you:
   - Key offseason moves, (free-agent trades & signings)
   - Latest injury updates
   - Training camp gossip and fact
   - Cliff's top 100 overall picks, including notes and commentary
   - Cliff's top 50 running back picks, top 50 wide receiver picks, top 25 tight end picks, top 25 quarterback picks, and top 25 kicker picks. All picks are analyzed for basic scoring, and combined scoring/yardage.
   - Team by Team check off areas. A depth chart for fantasy-positioned player.
   - Faxing also available

3. **Preseason Edge '98/Fantasy Quick Picks—Draft At A Glance Package™:** To complete your fantasy draft kit. (A $5.00 savings for ordering both.)

   3a. **Preseason Edge '98/Fantasy Quick Picks—Draft At A Glance Package™:** with 2nd and 3rd update releases.

4. **Commissioner League Organizer:** (For non-computer users) keeps your Fantasy League running smoothly. Contains draft agenda, team rosters, weekly box scores, league draft log, transaction log and weekly standings.

5. **Player Franchise Organizer:** Track your success with this exclusive notebook designed to document your fantasy draft round-by-round, your league roster, and your weekly line-up cards. This organizer is praised by both franchise owners and commissioners. Tell your commissioner to order one for each franchise.

   5a. **Discount packages available for your league:** (Call our office for details)

6. **Kommish™ 1998 for Windows:** Manage your Fantasy Football league with your PC! This one does it all . . . right from your desktop: League and team set-up, drafting, transactions, scoring and more! All with windows point-and-click ease. View and print reports. On-line help screens guide you through the software. This is a must for any state-of-the-art Fantasy Football league!

   6a. **Kommish™ 1998** with yearlong download stats service
   6b. **Kommish™ 1998 Update** (for previous subscribers)
   6c. **Kommish™ 1998 Updated Draft List** (available August 7)

DON'T DELAY! ORDER TODAY!
1-800-233-9809
http://www.fantasydraft.com

ORDER NOW

CALL US TOLL-FREE AT:

1-800-233-9809

WITHIN MINNESOTA CALL:
612-774-8955

SEND ORDER AND PAYMENT TO:
FANTASY SPORTS, INC.
674 E. SIXTH STREET
ST. PAUL, MN 55106
www.fantasydraft.com

NEVER TOO LATE TO FAX OR EMAIL!

NAME _____

ADDRESS _____

CITY _____ STATE _____ ZIP _____

FAX NUMBER (MUST BE INCLUDED) _____

E-MAIL ADDRESS _____

I've marked the packages I want and I have enclosed:

Visa _____ Master _____ Discover _____ Check _____ Money Order _____

Credit Card Number _____ Exp. Date _____

☐ 1. PRESEASON EDGE 1998 (Includes 1998 Roster and Checklist) $19.95
　　　☐ *FAX LAST ISSUE ONLY* $9.95
☐ 2. CLIFF'S 1998 QUICK PICKS—FANTASY DRAFT AT A GLANCE™ $9.95
☐ 2a. CLIFF'S 1998 QUICK PICKS—FANTASY DRAFT AT A GLANCE™ with 2 Updates $14.95
☐ 3. PRESEASON EDGE '98/QUICK PICKS—FANTASY DRAFT AT A GLANCE™ Package $24.95
☐ 3a. PRESEASON EDGE '98/QUICK PICKS—FANTASY DRAFT AT A GLANCE™
　　　Package w/2 Updates $29.95
☐ 4. COMMISSIONER'S LEAGUE ORGANIZER $6.95
☐ 5. PLAYER FRANCHISE ORGANIZER $3.95
☐ 6. THE KOMMISH™ *FOR WINDOWS* $49.95
☐ 6a. THE KOMMISH™ *FOR WINDOWS* with yearlong download stats service $94.95
☐ 6b. THE KOMMISH™ *FOR WINDOWS 1998 Update (for previous subscribers)* $24.95
☐ 6c. THE KOMMISH™ *FOR WINDOWS* Updated Draft List (Available August 7) $9.95
☐ 9. FREE BROCHURE ON ALL PRODUCTS .... FREE

TOTAL $ _____

MINNESOTA RESIDENTS ADD 6.5% SALES TAX $ _____

SHIPPING/HANDLING CHARGE: $ _____

UP TO $25.00	= 5.00	45.01 TO 55.00	= 8.00
FROM 25.01 TO 35.00	= 6.00	55.01 TO 65.00	= 8.50
FROM 35.01 TO 45.00	= 7.00	65.01 AND UP	= 9.00

AMOUNT DUE $ _____

PHONE (_____) _____

RATING THE PLAYERS FOR 1998
(Kickers—Basic and Combined Basic/Performance Scoring Methods)

GRAB ONE IF YOU CAN

☐ **1. Ryan Longwell (Green Bay Packers)**
Longwell stepped in as an undrafted rookie to hit a solid 24 of 30 (.800) field goal attempts and 48 extra point tries in 1997. Kicking for the NFL powerhouse Packers in 1998 should continue to provide him with plenty of scoring opportunities.

☐ **2. Jason Elam (Denver Broncos)**
Elam has been given ample scoring chances and has hit 46 of 46 extra point attempts for two straight seasons. In 1997, he hit 26 of 36 (.772) field goal tries. His success in 1998 will continue because of the frequent scoring chances provided by the high-powered Broncos.

☐ **3. Ritchie Cunningham (Dallas Cowboys)**
Cunningham was another undrafted rookie who performed well in 1997. With the Cowboys' "red zone" offense struggling, Cunningham had 37 field goal tries and hit 34 of them for a sterling .919 kicking percentage. That success makes him a high fantasy pick for 1998.

☐ **4. John Becksvort/???? (San Francisco 49ers)**
The 49ers lost Gary Anderson to the Vikings via free agency. This leaves their 1998 kicking job wide open. Whoever gets the call should benefit both from the 49ers being a good football team and the fact that they face the league's fifth-easiest schedule.

☐ **5. Mike Hollis (Jacksonville Jaguars)**
Hollis has had 36 field goal attempts in each of his last two seasons, which shows that he gets plenty of scoring chances. In 1997, Hollis hit 31 of those 36 chances for a solid .861 kicking percentage. He's a good kicker on a young and improving team.

BEST OF THE REST

☐ **6. Gary Anderson (Minnesota Vikings)**
After hitting 29 of 36 (.806) field goal attempts in 1997, Anderson takes his services to Minnesota for 1998. Anderson has been successful wherever he's been and that trend should continue with the Vikings in 1998.

☐ **7. Jason Hanson (Detroit Lions)**
After a very subpar 1996 campaign in which he hit only 12 of 17 (.706) field goals, Hanson rebounded in a big way to hit an impressive 26 of 29 (.897) attempts in 1997. He's back on track and I look for his continued success in 1998.

☐ **8. Norm Johnson (Pittsburgh Steelers)**
Johnson got only 25 field goal attempts in 1997 but was good on 22 (.880) of them. He did hit all 40 extra-point attempts as the Steeler offense improved behind Kordell Stewart. I look for more field goal attempts in 1998 as the Steelers face the league's toughest schedule.

☐ **9. Adam Vinatieri (New England Patriots)**
Vinatieri hit an impressive 25 of 29 (.862) field goal tries in 1997. I believe he'll continue to see plenty of scoring chances.

☐ **10. Al Del Greco (Tennessee Oilers)**
The Oilers seem to always give Del Greco plenty of opportunities. He has had 30 or more field goal chances in each of the last three seasons. In 1997, Del Greco was good on 27 of 35 (.771) chances. That's a bit of a slide in accuracy for him but he's still very capable.

STRONG LONG SHOTS

☐ **11. Cary Blanchard/Mike Vanderjagt (Indianapolis Colts)**
Blanchard seems to benefit from the Colts' lack of "red zone" success. In the last two seasons, he has had 40 and 41 field goal attempts, respectively. In 1997, he was successful on 32 of 41 (.780) chances. I see little change in 1998, working with a new quarterback situation. Blanchard will face the challenge of Mike Vanderjagt, a free agent Indianapolis signed in the offseason.

☐ **12. John Kasay (Carolina Panthers)**
Just a year earlier, Kasay led the league with 145 points, hitting 37 of 45 (.822) field goals. In 1997, however, the Panthers struggled, creating far fewer chances for Kasay which resulted in a 22 of 26 (.846) performance. The Panthers have to regroup and improve for Kasay's fantasy stock to go back up.

☐ **13. Chris Boniol (Philadelphia Eagles)**
Boniol came to Philadelphia in 1997, following a very successful stint in Dallas. With the Eagles, Boniol hit only 22 of 31 (.710) field goal tries, after hitting 32 of 36 (.889) and 27 of 28 (.964) in 1995 and 1996 with Dallas. Boniol needs to regain his confidence.

☐ **14. Pete Stoyanovich (Kansas City Chiefs)**
The 1997 season was a solid campaign for the aging Stoyanovich as he hit 26 of 27 (.963) field goal attempts. The Chiefs just have to get him more scoring opportunities in 1998.

☐ **15. Olindo Mare/Jon Baker (Miami Dolphins)**
Mare was given the Dolphins' kicking job in 1997 and he responded by hitting 28 of 36 (.778) field goal tries and all 36 extra-point tries. The opportunities should keep coming in 1998 when the Dolphins face a rather easy schedule. Meanwhile, Mare will be challenged for the job in 1998 by free agent signee Jon Baker.

HAVE THE POTENTIAL

☐ **16. John Hall (New York Jets)**
After taking over the Jets' kicking chores in 1997, John Hall hit a woeful 28 of 41 (.683) field goal attempts. However, anyone who gets that many scoring chances deserves decent fantasy consideration, if he keeps his job.

☐ **17. Todd Peterson (Seattle Seahawks)**
A fairly consistent kicker, Peterson hit 22 of 28 (.786) field goal tries in 1997 and all 37 extra point attempts. Peterson, too, needs more scoring chances.

☐ **18. Morton Anderson (Atlanta Falcons)**
Last season was another solid season from one of the league's more consistent kickers. Anderson hit 23 of 27 (.852) field goal tries in 1997 and all 35 extra point attempts. He's a consistent kicker who doesn't seem to get enough scoring chances.

☐ **19. John Carney (San Diego Chargers)**
Don't count out John Carney, who topped the .800 kicking percentage mark for three straight seasons before suffering a knee injury and missing most of 1997. Carney made all seven of his field goal attempts before the injury. The only question for 1998 will be how many scoring chances he'll get with the Chargers' quarterback position in question.

☐ **20. Jeff Wilkins (St. Louis Rams)**
Coming off a strong 1996 season when he hit 30 of 34 (.882) field goals for San Francisco, Wilkins struggled with the Rams in 1997. Wilkins hit only 25 of 37 (.676) attempts and must recover his accuracy to be a good fantasy pick.

KEEP AN EYE ON

☐ **21. Scott Blanton/Danny Kight (Washington Redskins)**
Having key offensive players back healthy should help.

☐ **22. Brad Daluiso (New York Giants)**
The Giants seem to be on the right track, which will help Daluiso's numbers get on track.

☐ **23. Matt Stover (Baltimore Ravens)**
Having Jim Harbaugh run the offense doesn't excite me.

☐ **24. Michael Husted (Tampa Bay Buccaneers)**
He's kicking for an improving team but he had only 17 field goal chances in 1997.

☐ **25. Doug Pelfrey/Jay Kirchoff (Cincinnati Bengals)**
The offensive weapons are there but Pelfrey only had 16 field goal chances in 1997. In 1998, Pelfrey will be challenged by free agent Jay Kirchoff, who was signed in the offseason by Cincinnati.

☐ **26. Cole Ford (Oakland Raiders)**
The 1997 season was a horrible one for Ford (13 of 22 (.591) of field goals) and the Raiders may be looking elsewhere in 1998.

☐ **27. Kevin Butler (Arizona Cardinals)**
The Cardinals always seem to struggle with their kickers.

☐ **28. Steve Christie (Buffalo Bills)**
The quarterback situation has me shying away.

☐ **29. Jeff Jaeger (Chicago Bears)**
The Bears and their tough schedule scare me.

☐ **30. Doug Brien (New Orleans Saints)**
I wouldn't touch a Saints' player.

ROOKIE PROSPECTS
NAME   **TEAM**   **COMMENT**

No kickers were chosen in this year's draft. Rookie free-agents will appear in the team by team section and some in these player ratings.

A 1998 QUICK PICKS— MOCK DRAFT

(My Top "30" Overall Picks for the Basic Scoring Method)

	NAME	TEAM	POS	COMMENTS
1.	Davis	DEN	RB	15 TDs in each of last two seasons puts him at the top of my list.
2.	Favre	GB	QB	30-plus TD passes for four straight years.
3.	Sanders	DET	RB	Rebounded to 14 TDs under Bobby Ross in 1997.
4.	Stewart	PITT	QB	20 passing TDs, 10 rushing, possible again.
5.	Levens	GB	RB	Dozen scores very possible for Packer workhorse.
6.	Dillon	CIN	RB	10 TDs in 14 games as a rookie has me excited for his sophomore campaign.
7.	Freeman	GB	WR	Very capable of 12-plus scores as a favorite of Brett Favre.
8.	Bettis	PITT	RB	Will push, plow and plunge for many scores.
9.	Allen	WASH	RB	Injured in 1997 but scored 21 year before.
10.	George	OAK	QB	Lit it up for 29 TD passes in first year as Raider in 1997.
11.	Martin	NYJ	RB	New team, should be healthy, should produce many scores.
12.	Watters	SEAT	RB	New team, new incentive to rebound scoring numbers.
13.	Carter	MINN	WR	Always capable of 10-15 scores.
14.	Moore	DET	WR	Down year in 1997 but don't count him out.
15.	Rice	SF	WR	Injured in 1997, but remains one of the league's all-time best.
16.	Pickens	CIN	WR	Slowed by injury in '97, but will again be "Picken" apart defenses in '98.
17.	Smith	DEN	WR	Elway found a new go-to guy.
18.	Anderson	ATL	RB	Continuing to mature, improve and improve numbers.
19.	Smith	DALL	RB	Fallen but not beaten, but potential still there.
20.	Means	SD	RB	Will now be "Means" to end, back in San Diego.
21.	Elway	DEN	QB	Has been consistent 25-plus TD thrower last 3 years.
22.	Abdul-Jabbar	MIA	RB	Will score often but likely not to reach 16 of 1997.
23.	Galloway	SEAT	WR	Speedy, rising star who scored 12 in 1997.
24.	Stewart	JAC	RB	Means is gone, should be Stewart's show now.
25.	Young	SF	QB	If he and Rice can avoid injuries. . . .
26.	Longwell	GB	K	Kicking for one of league's best offenses has its benefits.
27.	Lane	CAR	RB	Has found the production and scoring "Lane."
28.	Bledsoe	NE	QB	Last 2 years, he's "Bledsoe" many defenses for 28 and 27 TDs.
29.	Brown	OAK	WR	George's arm and Brown's talent could be awesome.
30.	Fryar	PHIL	WR	Dropped off in '97 to 6 TDs but scored 11 in '96.

This Mock Draft is expanded and updated in *Cliff's Quick Picks: Fantasy Football Draft at a Glance*—a huge cheatsheet that examines the top-100 over-all picks for the Basic and Combined Basic/Performance methods. Potential draft picks are also broken down by fantasy position, including the *top-50* running backs and wide receivers, and the *top-25* tight ends, quarterbacks and kickers. *Cliff's Quick Picks* will be available in mid-August, right around your fantasy draft time. Be sure to order! Details and order form, along with a toll-free phone number, appear on the hard insert in the middle of this book.

IX
RATING THE PLAYERS:
COMBINED BASIC/PERFORMANCE
SCORING METHOD

As the game of fantasy football progressed, leagues began incorporating more player statistics into their scoring. A popular way of doing this was to combine the Basic Scoring and Performance Point methods. I decided to add such a combined method to my book. In several sections, I will evaluate and rate players' performances based on a combination of these two scoring methods. This means that a player will be awarded points both for scoring touchdowns and for the yardage he earns.

Combining the two methods may seem simple when you think of running backs like Barry Sanders, Terrell Davis, or Ricky Watters, who score with frequency and also accumulate a lot of yardage. But how about someone like Marcus Allen, who rushed for only 764 yards in 1993 but scored 15 times? Where does a player like this fit in? How about Curtis Duncan? Duncan had 954 receiving yards in 1992, on 82 receptions, but scored only once. Or how about Ki-Jana Carter, who rushed for only 264 yards in 1996 but scored nine times? And Kareem Abdul-Jabbar who rushed for only 892 yards in 1997 but scored 16 times. Combining the two methods really adds a twist to the game.

In the following pages, I'm going to help you plan your basic drafting strategy. Then I'll follow with some things to keep in mind when choosing players from each position. Next, I'll offer a look at the players' 1997 statistical results. And, finally, I'll rate the players for the 1998 season. No rookies are included in my player ratings. It's too early to size up how rookies will fit into each team's scheme, so I rate them separately, in Section V of this chapter. I will, however, incorporate the rookies in my Quick Picks/Fantasy Draft At a Glance Cheatsheet which comes out in mid-August. This is a more appropriate time to assess how rookies are fitting into their NFL offenses.

Combined Basic/Performance Scoring Method
DRAFTING STRATEGY BY ROUNDS
(A Guide for the Beginner)

1. The draft consists of 12 rounds.

2. Of the 12 players, seven are starters and five are reserves.

3. The starting seven comprise:

1 Quarterback		1 Quarterback
2 Running Backs	OR	2 Running Backs
2 Wide Receivers	FLEX OPTION	3 Receivers
1 Tight End		1 Kicker
1 Kicker		

4. The five reserves can be from any position.

5. Any player from any starting position can be drafted in any round.

ROUND 1: This method makes drafting very interesting, especially in the early rounds. In 1992 Steve Young's 3,465 passing yards, 25 passing touchdowns, 540 rushing yards, and four rushing touchdowns led all scorers, totaling 314 points. In 1993 Young easily did it again, this time totaling 327 points. In fact, both Young and John Elway outscored the closest non-quarterback, Jerry Rice. The gap was even bigger in 1994, when three quarterbacks—Steve Young (366 points), Brett Favre (314 points), and Dan Marino (314 points)—outscored the first non-quarterback, Emmitt Smith (303 points). In 1995 it was a bit closer, as quarterback Brett Favre produced 357 points but running back Emmitt Smith was right behind with 351. In 1996 the quarterbacks again were dominant with six signal-callers outscoring Emmitt Smith, the top running back. In 1997 only Kordell Stewart (314 points) and Brett Favre (311 points) outdistanced running back Barry Sanders' 306 points.

ROUND 2: By the end of the second round, especially if your league has 12 or more franchises, you should try to have both a quarterback with high scoring potential and either a good rushing-receiving back or a very good wide receiver.

ROUND 3: If, for some reason, you decide not to choose a quarterback and running back in the first two rounds, it's almost essential to have both by the end of this round. If you already do have one of each, it's probably time to grab the best non-quarterback available. That means running backs or wide receivers who will be in the 1,000-yard range and who have the potential to score 10 or more times.

ROUNDS 4 and 5: These rounds should be used to fill out your backfield. You should have a quarterback, two running backs, and hopefully both wide receivers by now.

ROUNDS 6 through 9: Up to this point in the draft, because of their low point totals, tight ends and kickers have not been a priority. To fill out your starting lineup, you can select these players in the next four rounds.

ROUNDS 10 through 12: Don't think these final rounds aren't important. You need to draft high-quality backups in case your starters get injured. Also, take a stab at a rookie or two. One might turn out to be a big fantasy player.

A LOOK AT THE RUNNING BACKS
(A Guide for the Beginner)

Considerations in Choosing a Running Back

1. First, look at players' previous performances. Don't overlook players who may have missed portions of the previous year because of injuries, holdouts, and the like. The likes of Terry Allen, Curtis Martin and Garrison Hearst all missed significant time in 1997 because of injuries.

2. Find the running backs who consistently gain 1,500 to 2,000 rushing yards in a season, and who have the potential to cross the goal line 15 times. Barry Sanders should top your list, along with Terrell Davis.

3. Since players tend to earn more points from their yardage (performance points) than from their touchdowns (basic points), choose running backs who carry the ball often and accumulate a lot of yards.

4. Running backs who score lots of short-yardage touchdowns but who don't rush for many yards are *not* good early-round picks.

In the 1997 statistics that follow, you'll find the players ranked by their fantasy-point totals. Remember that in the Combined Basic/Performance Scoring Method, fantasy points are calculated by adding up the following: six points for every touchdown scored, three points for every touchdown thrown, one point for every 10 yards rushing, one point for every 10 yards receiving, and one point for every 20 yards passing.

1997 STATISTICAL RESULTS
(RUNNING BACKS — COMBINED BASIC/PERFORMANCE SCORING METHOD)

NAME	TEAM	GP	RSH TDs	REC TDs	TOTAL TDs	BASIC PTS	RSH YARDS	REC YARDS	TOTAL YARDS	PERF PTS	CONV PTS	FAN-TASY PTS
1. Sanders	DET	16	11	3	14	84	2,053	305	2,358	222	0	306
1996		16	11	0	11	66	1,553	147	1,700	157	0	223
1995		16	11	1	12	72	1,500	398	1,898	175	0	247
3 Yr - TOTALS		48	33	4	37	222	5,106	850	5,956	554	0	776
2. Te. Davis	DEN	15	15	0	15	96	1,750	287	2,037	190	6	286
1996		16	13	2	15	90	1,538	310	1,848	173	0	263
1995		14	7	1	8	48	1,117	367	1,484	137	0	185
3 Yr - TOTALS		45	35	3	38	234	4,405	964	5,369	500	6	734
3. Levens	GB	16	7	5	12	74	1,435	370	1,805	171	2	245
1996		16	5	5	10	60	566	226	792	65	0	125
1995		15	3	4	7	42	120	434	554	44	0	86
3 Yr - TOTALS		47	15	14	29	176	2,121	1,030	3,151	280	2	456
4. Bettis	PITT	15	7	2	9	54	1,665	110	1,775	168	0	222
1996		16	11	0	11	66	1,431	122	1,553	145	0	211
1995 w/STL		15	3	0	3	18	637	106	743	66	0	84
3 Yr - TOTALS		46	21	2	23	138	3,733	338	4,071	379	0	517
5. Kaufman	OAK	16	6	2	8	48	1,294	403	1,697	159	0	207
1996		16	1	1	2	12	874	143	1,017	90	0	102
1995		15	1	0	2	12	490	62	552	47	0	59
3 Yr - TOTALS		47	8	3	12	72	2,658	608	3,266	296	0	368
6. Abdul-Jabbar	MIA	16	15	1	16	96	892	261	1,153	102	0	198
1996		16	11	0	11	66	1,116	139	1,255	112	0	178
1995		–	–	–	–	–	–	–	–	–	–	–
3 Yr - TOTALS		32	26	1	27	162	2,008	400	2,408	214	0	376
7. Faulk	IND	16	7	1	8	48	1,054	471	1,525	140	0	188
1996		13	7	0	7	42	587	428	1,015	90	0	132
1995		16	11	3	14	84	1,078	475	1,553	141	0	225
3 Yr - TOTALS		45	25	4	29	174	2,719	1,374	4,093	371	0	545
8. Dillon +	CIN	14	10	0	10	60	1,129	259	1,388	25	0	185
1996		–	–	–	–	–	–	–	–	–	–	–
1995		–	–	–	–	–	–	–	–	–	–	–
3 Yr - TOTALS		14	10	0	10	60	1,129	259	1,388	125	0	185
9. Watters	PHIL	16	7	0	7	42	1,110	440	1,550	141	0	183
1996		16	13	0	13	78	1,411	444	1,855	170	0	248
1995		16	11	1	12	72	1,273	434	1,707	156	0	228
3 Yr - TOTALS		48	31	1	32	192	3,794	1,318	5,112	467	0	659
10. J. Anderson	ATL	16	7	3	10	60	1,002	284	1,286	119	0	179
1996		16	5	1	6	36	1,055	473	1,528	139	0	175
1995		7	1	0	1	6	161	42	203	16	0	22
3 Yr - TOTALS		39	13	4	17	102	2,218	799	3,017	274	0	376
11. George	TENN	16	6	1	7	44	1,399	44	1,443	135	2	179
1996		16	8	0	8	48	1,368	182	1,550	145	0	193
1995		–	–	–	–	–	–	–	–	–	–	–
3 Yr - TOTALS		32	14	1	15	92	2,767	226	2,993	280	2	372
12. R. Smith	MINN	14	6	1	7	42	1,266	197	1,463	135	0	177
1996		8	3	0	3	18	692	39	731	68	0	86
1995		9	5	0	5	32	632	35	667	61	0	93
3 Yr - TOTALS		31	14	1	15	92	2,590	271	2,861	264	2	356
13. Dunn +	TB	16	4	3	7	42	978	462	1,440	128	0	170
1996		–	–	–	–	–	–	–	–	–	–	–
1995		–	–	–	–	–	–	–	–	–	–	–
3 Yr - TOTALS		16	4	3	7	42	978	462	1,440	128	0	170
14. R. Harris	CHI	13	10	0	10	60	1,033	115	1,148	105	0	165
1996		12	4	1	5	30	748	296	1,044	95	0	125
1995		1	0	0	0	0	0	4	4	0	0	0
3 Yr - TOTALS		26	14	1	15	90	1,781	415	2,196	200	0	290
15. Martin	NE	13	4	1	5	30	1,160	296	1,456	132	0	162
1996		16	14	3	17	104	1,152	333	1,485	138	2	242
1995		16	14	1	15	92	1,487	261	1,748	164	2	256
3 Yr - TOTALS		45	32	5	37	226	3,799	890	4,689	434	4	660

	NAME	TEAM	GP	RSH TDs	REC TDs	TOTAL TDs	BASIC PTS	RSH YARDS	REC YARDS	TOTAL YARDS	PERF PTS	CONV PTS	FAN-TASY PTS
16.	Murrell	NYJ	16	7	0	7	42	1,086	106	1,192	106	0	148
	1996		16	6	1	7	42	1,249	81	1,330	121	0	163
	1995		15	1	2	3	18	795	465	1,260	115	0	133
	3 Yr - TOTALS		47	14	3	17	102	3,130	652	3,782	342	0	444
17.	Hearst	SF	13	4	2	6	36	1,019	194	1,213	112	0	148
	1996 w/CIN		16	0	1	1	8	847	131	978	89	2	97
	1995 w/ARIZ		16	1	1	2	12	1,070	243	1,313	120	0	132
	3 Yr - TOTALS		45	5	4	9	56	2,936	568	3,504	321	2	377
18.	E. Smith	DALL	16	4	0	4	26	1,074	234	1,308	119	2	145
	1996		15	12	3	15	90	1,204	249	1,453	135	0	225
	1995		16	25	0	25	150	1,773	375	2,148	201	0	351
	3 Yr - TOTALS		47	41	3	44	266	4,051	858	4,909	455	2	721
19.	Means	JAC	14	9	0	9	54	823	104	927	86	0	140
	1996		13	2	1	3	18	507	45	552	47	0	65
	1995 w/SD		10	5	0	5	30	730	46	776	72	0	102
	3 Yr - TOTALS		37	16	1	17	102	2,060	195	2,255	205	0	307
20.	A. Smith +	BUF	16	8	0	8	48	840	177	1,017	91	0	139
	1996		–	–	–	–	–	–	–	–	–	–	–
	1995		–	–	–	–	–	–	–	–	–	–	–
	3 Yr - TOTALS		16	8	0	8	48	840	177	1,017	91	0	139
21.	Alstott	TB	15	7	3	10	60	665	178	843	73	0	133
	1996		16	3	3	6	36	377	557	934	82	0	118
	1995		–	–	–	–	–	–	–	–	–	–	–
	3 Yr - TOTALS		31	10	6	16	96	1,042	735	1,777	155	0	251
22.	Stewart	JAC	16	8	1	9	54	555	336	891	77	0	131
	1996		13	8	2	10	60	723	177	900	79	0	139
	1995		14	2	1	3	18	525	190	715	61	0	79
	3 Yr - TOTALS		43	18	4	22	132	1,803	703	2,506	217	0	349
23.	C. Warren	SEAT	15	4	0	4	24	847	257	1,104	99	0	123
	1996		14	5	0	5	32	855	273	1,128	101	2	133
	1995		16	15	1	16	96	1,346	247	1,593	147	0	243
	3 Yr - TOTALS		45	24	1	25	152	3,048	777	3,825	347	2	499
24.	M. Allen	KC	16	11	0	11	66	505	86	591	53	0	119
	1996		16	9	0	9	54	830	270	1,100	96	0	150
	1995		16	5	0	5	30	890	210	1,100	98	0	128
	3 Yr - TOTALS		48	25	0	25	150	2,225	566	2,791	247	0	397
25.	G. Brown	SD	15	4	0	4	24	945	137	1,082	95	0	119
	1996		–	–	–	–	–	–	–	–	–	–	–
	1995 w/HOUS		8	0	0	0	0	293	16	309	27	0	27
	3 Yr - TOTALS		23	4	0	4	24	1,238	153	1,391	122	0	146
26.	F. Lane	CAR	12	7	0	7	42	809	27	836	76	0	118
	1996		–	–	–	–	–	–	–	–	–	–	–
	1995		–	–	–	–	–	–	–	–	–	–	–
	3 Yr - TOTALS		12	7	0	7	42	809	27	836	76	0	118
27.	Way	NYG	16	4	1	5	30	698	304	1,002	86	0	116
	1996		15	1	1	2	12	79	328	407	31	0	43
	1995		5	0	1	1	6	6	76	82	6	0	12
	3 Yr - TOTALS		36	5	3	8	48	783	708	1,491	123	0	171
28.	T. Allen	WASH	10	4	1	5	30	724	172	896	84	0	114
	1996		16	21	0	21	126	1,353	194	1,547	142	0	268
	1995		16	10	1	11	66	1,309	232	1,541	144	0	210
	3 Yr - TOTALS		42	35	2	37	222	3,386	598	3,984	370	0	592
29.	Phillips **	MIA	12	8	0	8	48	677	39	716	65	0	113
	1996		15	4	1	5	30	632	28	660	57	0	87
	1995		–	–	–	–	–	–	–	–	–	–	–
	3 Yr - TOTALS		27	12	1	13	78	1,309	67	1376	122	0	200
30.	Kirby *	SF	16	6	1	8	52	418	279	697	58	4	110
	1996		13	3	1	4	27	559	439	998	92	0	119
	1995 w/MIA		16	4	3	7	42	414	618	1,032	88	0	130
	3 Yr - TOTALS		45	13	5	19	121	1,391	1,336	2,727	238	4	359

1997 STATISTICAL RESULTS
(RUNNING BACKS — COMBINED BASIC/PERFORMANCE SCORING METHOD)

NAME	TEAM	GP	RSH TDs	REC TDs	TOTAL TDs	BASIC PTS	RSH YARDS	REC YARDS	TOTAL YARDS	PERF PTS	CONV PTS	FAN-TASY PTS
31. Morris	BALT	11	4	0	4	24	774	176	950	85	0	109
32. Barber +	NYG	12	3	1	4	26	511	299	810	71	2	97
33. Lee	STL	16	0	3	3	18	104	825	929	79	0	97
34. Zellars	NO	16	4	0	4	24	552	263	815	69	0	93
35. K. Carter	CIN	15	7	0	7	42	464	157	621	50	0	92
36. Wheatley	NYG	13	4	0	4	24	583	140	723	62	0	86
37. Anders	KC	15	0	2	2	12	397	453	850	73	0	85
38. Broussard	SEAT	13	5	1	6	36	418	143	561	47	0	83
39. T. Thomas	BUF	16	1	0	1	6	643	208	851	76	0	82
40. Garner	PHIL	16	3	0	3	18	547	225	772	63	0	81
41. St. Davis	WASH	11	3	0	3	18	567	134	701	62	0	80
42. Centers	ARIZ	15	1	1	2	12	276	409	685	57	0	69
43. Bates	NO	11	4	0	4	24	440	42	482	45	0	69
44. Mitchell *	WASH	16	1	1	4	24	107	438	545	44	0	68
45. S. Williams	DALL	15	2	0	2	12	468	159	627	54	0	66
46. Floyd	SF	15	3	1	4	24	231	321	552	40	0	64
47. L. Smith	SEAT	12	2	0	2	14	392	183	575	49	2	63
48. Bowie	WASH	15	2	2	4	24	100	388	488	39	0	63
49. Turner	PHIL	15	0	3	3	18	96	443	539	44	0	62
50. Vardell	DET	15	6	0	6	36	122	218	340	25	0	61
51. J. Moore	STL	8	3	0	3	18	379	69	448	38	0	56
52. Hill	KC	16	0	0	0	0	550	126	676	55	0	55
53. McElroy	ARIZ	14	2	0	2	12	424	32	456	40	0	52
54. R. Thomas	TENN	15	3	0	3	18	310	111	421	33	0	51
55. A. Johnson	CAR	16	0	1	1	8	358	158	516	42	2	50
56. Hanspard + *	ATL	15	0	1	3	18	335	53	388	31	0	49
57. Hoard	MINN	12	4	0	4	24	235	84	319	23	0	47
58. Ln. Johnson + *	NYJ	16	2	0	4	24	158	142	300	23	0	47
59. J. Graham +	BALT	8	2	0	2	12	299	51	350	32	0	44
60. Greene	CAR	16	1	1	2	12	157	277	434	32	0	44
61. Henderson	GB	16	0	1	1	6	113	367	480	38	0	44
62. McPhail	MIA	14	1	1	2	12	146	262	408	29	0	41
63. Byner	BALT	14	0	0	0	2	313	128	441	38	2	40
64. Autry +	CHI	12	1	0	1	8	319	59	378	31	2	39
65. H. Green	ATL	15	1	0	1	6	78	360	438	32	0	38
66. Biakabutuka	CAR	8	2	0	2	12	299	0	299	26	0	38
67. Bieniemy *	CIN	15	1	0	2	12	97	249	346	26	0	38
68. Crockett	IND	15	1	0	1	6	300	112	412	32	0	38
69. Bennett	KC	12	1	0	1	6	369	5	374	32	0	38
70. Jones +	PITT	16	1	1	2	12	235	96	331	25	0	37
71. Evans	MINN	16	2	0	2	14	157	152	309	22	2	36
72. Parmalee	MIA	13	0	1	1	6	59	301	360	29	0	35
73. Meggett	NE	12	1	1	2	12	60	203	263	23	0	35
74. Fletcher	SD	13	0	0	0	0	161	292	453	35	0	35
75. L. Warren	IND	12	2	0	2	12	80	192	272	20	0	32
76. Byars	NE	15	0	3	3	18	24	189	213	14	0	32
77. R. Moore **	ARIZ	11	1	0	1	6	278	34	312	25	0	31
78. Spikes	MIA	10	2	0	2	12	180	70	250	18	0	30
79. Gash	NE	12	0	3	3	18	10	154	164	12	0	30
80. Holmes	BUF	9	2	0	2	12	106	106	212	16	0	28
81. Hebron	DEN	10	1	0	1	6	222	36	258	22	0	28
82. Tr. Davis +	NO	15	0	0	0	0	271	85	356	28	0	28
83. Palmer	MINN	12	1	1	2	12	36	193	229	15	0	27
84. Rhett	TB	6	3	0	3	18	96	0	96	8	0	26
85. Walker	DALL	10	0	2	2	12	20	149	169	12	0	24
86. Pegram **	NYG	12	2	0	2	12	95	90	185	12	0	24
87. Milne	CIN	15	2	0	2	12	32	138	170	9	0	21
88. Johnston	DALL	5	0	1	1	6	3	166	169	15	0	21
89. Hayden	GB	6	1	0	1	6	148	11	159	14	0	20
90. R. Anderson	NYJ	14	0	1	1	6	70	150	220	14	0	20
91. Rivers	DET	10	1	0	1	6	166	0	166	13	0	19

	NAME	TEAM	GP	RSH TDs	REC TDs	TOTAL TDs	BASIC PTS	RSH YARDS	REC YARDS	TOTAL YARDS	PERF PTS	CONV PTS	FAN-TASY PTS
92.	Richardson	KC	4	0	3	3	18	11	6	17	1	0	19
93.	Levy *	SF	7	0	0	1	6	90	68	158	13	0	19
94.	Harmon **	CHI	10	0	0	0	0	36	197	233	18	0	18
95.	Loville	DEN	3	1	0	1	6	124	10	134	12	0	18
96.	Strong	SEAT	9	0	2	2	12	8	91	99	6	0	18
97.	Christian	ATL	14	0	1	1	6	8	154	162	10	0	16
98.	A. Carter	CHI	11	0	0	0	0	56	152	208	14	0	14
99.	Heyward	STL	15	1	0	1	6	84	77	161	8	0	14
100.	Cullors *	NE	5	0	0	1	6	101	8	109	7	0	13
101.	Hampton	NYG	2	1	0	1	6	81	0	81	7	0	13
102.	Salaam	CHI	3	0	0	0	0	112	20	132	12	0	12
103.	Grier	NE	6	1	0	1	6	75	0	75	6	0	12
104.	Schlesinger	DET	7	0	1	1	6	11	69	80	5	0	11
105.	M. Williams	MINN	4	1	0	1	6	59	14	73	5	0	11
106.	Tindale	BUF	1	0	0	0	0	0	105	105	10	0	10
107.	Hall	OAK	8	0	0	0	0	120	9	129	10	0	10
108.	Neal	NYJ	7	0	1	1	6	28	40	68	3	0	9
109.	Bynum +	SD	5	0	0	0	0	97	4	101	9	0	9
110.	C. Smith	ARIZ	5	1	0	1	6	5	20	25	2	0	8
111.	D. Smith	DEN	4	0	1	1	6	10	41	51	2	0	8
112.	Thompson	STL	4	1	0	1	6	30	0	30	2	0	8
113.	Le. Johnson	ARIZ	5	0	0	0	0	81	4	85	7	0	7
114.	Craver	SD	8	0	0	0	0	71	26	97	7	0	7
115.	Cotton	BALT	2	1	0	1	6	2	0	2	0	0	6
116.	Hughes	CHI	3	0	0	0	0	3	68	71	6	0	6
117.	Milburn	DET	4	0	0	0	0	0	77	77	6	0	6
118.	Groce	IND	3	0	0	0	0	66	0	66	6	0	6
119.	Fenner	OAK	7	0	0	0	0	24	92	116	6	0	6
120.	McAfee	PITT	4	0	0	0	0	41	44	85	6	0	6
121.	Griffith	DEN	10	0	0	0	0	34	55	89	5	0	5
122.	Staley +	PHIL	2	0	0	0	0	29	22	51	5	0	5
123.	Oliver	CAR	4	0	0	0	0	0	47	47	4	0	4
124.	Edwards +	SF	3	0	0	0	0	17	48	65	4	0	4
125.	McCrary	NO	4	0	0	0	0	13	17	30	3	0	3
126.	Sowell +	NYJ	1	0	0	0	0	35	8	43	3	0	3
127.	Bouie	ARIZ	3	0	0	0	0	26	0	26	2	0	2
128.	Lynn	DEN	1	0	0	0	0	0	21	21	2	0	2
129.	Pritchett	MIA	6	0	0	0	0	7	35	42	2	0	2
130.	Potts **	MIA	3	0	0	0	0	4	27	31	2	0	2
131.	Davison	OAK	3	0	0	0	0	4	34	38	2	0	2
132.	Levitt +	OAK	2	0	0	0	0	3	24	27	2	0	2
133.	Lester	PITT	6	0	0	0	0	9	51	60	2	0	2
134.	R. Green	MINN	2	0	0	0	0	22	5	27	1	0	1
135.	E. Lane	NYG	1	0	0	0	0	13	0	13	1	0	1
136.	Gardner	SD	4	0	0	0	0	20	10	30	1	0	1
137.	Hicks	CHI	2	0	0	0	0	14	0	14	0	0	0
138.	S. Graham	CIN	2	0	0	0	0	-1	1	0	0	0	0
139.	Shelton +	JAC	2	0	0	0	0	4	0	4	0	0	0
140.	Jordan	JAC	1	0	0	0	0	2	0	2	0	0	0
141.	Nealy	MIA	1	0	0	0	0	2	0	2	0	0	0
142.	Bender	NO	3	0	0	0	0	9	0	9	0	0	0
143.	Aska	OAK	5	0	0	0	0	5	0	5	0	0	0
144.	Whitman	PITT	5	0	0	0	0	11	3	14	0	0	0
145.	Ellison	TB	3	0	0	0	0	10	8	18	0	0	0
146.	Logan	WASH	4	0	0	0	0	5	6	11	0	0	0

+			DENOTES COLLEGE DRAFT PICK
*	Hanspard	ATL	Scored TD's on kickoff returns of 93 and 99 yards.
*	Kirby	SF	Scored TD on kickoff return of 101 yards.
*	Ln. Johnson	NYJ	Scored TD's on kickoff return of 101 yards and punt return of 66 yards.
*	Mitchell	WASH	Scored TD's on kickoff return of 97 yards and punt return of 63 yards.
*	Bieniemy	CIN	Scored TD on kickoff return of 102 yards.
*	Cullors	NE	Scored TD on kickoff return of 86 yards.
*	Levy	SF	Scored TD on punt return of 73 yards.
**	Phillips	MIA	Played in 10 games with St. Louis.
**	R. Moore	ARIZ	Played in 6 games with St. Louis.
**	Pegram	NYG	Played in 3 games with San Diego.
**	Harmon	CHI	Played in 10 games with Tennessee.
**	Potts	MIA	Played in 1 game with Indianapolis.

RATING THE PLAYERS FOR 1998
(Running Backs—Combined Basic/Performance Scoring Method)

GRAB ONE IF YOU CAN

☐ **1. Terrell Davis (Denver Broncos)**
He just keeps getting better. Davis has recorded, 1,484, 1,848 and 2,037 rushing-receiving yards and 8, 15 and 15 touchdowns, respectively, the last three seasons. That kind of performance will keep him a top fantasy prospect again in 1998.

☐ **2. Barry Sanders (Detroit Lions)**
Under new head coach Bobby Ross, Sanders exploded for 2,358 combined rushing-receiving yards and 14 touchdowns in 1997. It looks like Barry finally has a coach who knows how to exploit his talent properly.

☐ **3. Dorsey Levens (Green Bay Packers)**
With Edgar Bennett injured and out for the year in 1997, Levens's numbers jumped to 1,805 rushing-receiving yards and 12 touchdowns. Bennett has since gone to Chicago leaving Levens to again be the featured back for the high-powered Packers.

☐ **4. Ricky Watters (Seattle Seahawks)**
In Philadelphia, Watters's numbers dropped to 1,550 total rushing-receiving yards and only seven touchdowns. With Watters in Seattle in 1998, I look for his numbers to recover to the 1,700 to 1,900 yard range and top the double-digit touchdown mark.

☐ **5. Jerome Bettis (Pittsburgh Steelers)**
In the two seasons since he came to Pittsburgh, Bettis has produced 11 and 9 touchdowns, along with 1,553 and 1,775 combined rushing-receiving yards, respectively. Because he's the main ground component of the improving Steelers, I look continued big production from him in 1998.

BEST OF THE REST

☐ **6. Corey Dillon (Cincinnati Bengals)**
Despite missing a couple of games as a rookie in 1997, Dillon took over the starting running back duties from Ki-Jana Carter and finished with 1,129 rushing yards, 259 receiving yards and 10 touchdowns. What is his potential over a full season?

☐ **7. Curtis Martin (New York Jets)**
Slowed by a shoulder injury that cost him a number of games, Martin still produced 1,456 combined rushing-receiving yards but only five touchdowns in 1997. Looking back to the two years previous to that injury, Martin had scored 17 and 15 touchdowns. I look for a healthy recovery for Martin and for his production numbers in 1998 as he takes his services to the New York Jets, where he'll be their featured back.

☐ **8. Napoleon Kaufman (Oakland Raiders)**
After becoming the Raiders' main back in 1997, Kaufman jumped to 1,697 rushing-receiving yards, along with eight touchdowns. Continuing as the main back makes Kaufman a good fantasy candidate in 1998.

☐ **9. Terry Allen (Washington Redskins)**
Allen had a disappointing year in 1997 after he had produced a league-high 21 touchdowns along with 1,597 combined rushing-receiving yards in 1996. Allen struggled with an assortment of injuries as he scored just five times and produced fewer than 1,000 yards. A healthy Allen in 1998 should return to much healthier numbers.

☐ **10. Robert Smith (Minnesota Vikings)**
Staying healthy has always been a problem for Smith. He did, however, miss just two games to an ankle injury in 1997 and finished with 1,463 rushing-receiving yards and seven touchdowns. If he stays healthy in 1998, big numbers will follow.

STRONG LONGSHOTS

☐ **11. Garrison Hearst (San Francisco 49ers)**
After becoming the 49ers' main back in 1997, Hearst produced 1,213 rushing-receiving yards and six touchdowns despite missing three games with a shoulder injury. I'm looking for a healthy Hearst to produce 1,500-plus yards and double-digit scores in 1998.

☐ **12. Eddie George (Tennessee Oilers)**
George has had two very consistent seasons since coming into the league. He has produced 1,368 and 1,399 rushing-receiving yards, along with eight and seven touchdowns, respectively. That consistency keeps fantasy owners very aware of his 1998 potential.

☐ **13. Emmitt Smith (Dallas Cowboys)**
Smith went from 2,148 rushing-receiving yards and 25 touchdowns in 1995 to a steady and quick decline in 1996 and 1997. I'm looking for a rebound from the Cowboys in 1998, and for Smith to perhaps be in the 1,500-yard, 10-plus touchdown range.

☐ **14. Marshall Faulk (Indianapolis Colts)**
Faulk stayed healthy in 1997 and rebounded to 1,525 rushing-receiving yards and eight touchdowns. In 1998, he's very capable of reaching or topping those marks, especially since the Colts' quarterback situation is so uncertain.

☐ **15. Karim Abdul-Jabbar (Miami Dolphins)**
Although his overall yardage totals dropped from 1,255 in 1996 to 1,153 in 1997, Abdul-Jabbar's scoring numbers jumped to 16 touchdowns from the 11 he had scored as a rookie in 1996. As the Dolphins' main ground focus again in 1998, he will have good numbers.

16. Warrick Dunn (Tampa Bay Buccaneers)

As a rookie in 1997, Dunn produced 1,440 rushing-receiving yards and seven touchdowns, sharing the Bucs' backfield load with Mike Alstott. I look for his continued development and another 1,300 to 1,500 yards along with 6 to 10 touchdowns in 1998.

17. Fred Lane (Carolina Panthers)

With injuries to Anthony Johnson and Tim Biakabatuka in 1997, undrafted Fred Lane got his chance. Lane took advantage, rushing for 719 of his 809 yards over the last eight games. He also finished with seven touchdowns. Maintaining the starting role should produce much larger numbers in 1998.

18. Jamal Anderson (Atlanta Falcons)

Anderson produced 1,528 and 1,286 rushing-receiving yards and 6 and 10 touchdowns the past two seasons, respectively. Becoming a consistent performer has made him a decent fantasy pick again for 1998.

19. James Stewart (Jacksonville Jaguars)

Stewart has neared the 1,000-yard mark and scored 10 and 9 touchdowns, respectively, the last two seasons. With Natrone Means off to San Diego in 1998, Stewart may finally get his chance.

20. Natrone Means (San Diego Chargers)

After two seasons in Jacksonville, Means returns to the Chargers in 1998. As their main ball carrier, the 1,200-yard range and 8 to 10 touchdowns are well within his reach.

HAVE THE POTENTIAL

21. Errict Rhett (Baltimore Ravens)

Rhett, who lost his starting job in Tampa Bay, moves to Baltimore where he gets another chance to prove himself. Look for good numbers from this former 1,000-yard performer.

22. Antowain Smith (Buffalo Bills)

Smith had 1,017 rushing-receiving yards and eight touchdowns as a rookie in 1997. He'll easily improve on those numbers as his role continues to expand in 1998.

23. Edgar Bennett (Chicago Bears)

Bennett, who missed the 1997 season with an Achilles injury, moves on to Chicago to become its main back. In that capacity, I think he will post 1,000 to 1,200 total yards and 8 to 10 touchdowns.

24. Tiki Barber (New York Giants)

Barber had 810 rushing-receiving yards and four touchdowns as a rookie in 1997 despite missing four games with a knee injury. Staying healthy in 1998 would easily boost those numbers.

25. Carwell Garner (Philadelphia Eagles)

Ricky Watters is off to Seattle, via free agency, which will give Garner an excellent chance to expand his playing time and year end numbers.

SOLID SLEEPERS

☐ **26. Jerald Moore (St. Louis Rams)**
Moore, who came on late in 1997 to show some things, gets his chance over a full season now that Lawrence Phillips has moved to Miami.

☐ **27. Adrian Murrell (Arizona Cardinals)**
Murrell has produced 1,260 and 1,300 rushing-receiving yards along with seven touchdowns in each of the last two seasons. However, in 1998, Murrell takes his services to Arizona where he hopes to be the featured man in the Cardinal's backfield.

☐ **28. Lamar Smith (New Orleans Saints)**
Smith, the sometimes starter for the Seahawks, comes to the Saints as the primary rusher. He's very capable of scoring six to eight times and nearing the 1,000-yard mark.

☐ **29. Mike Alstott (Tampa Bay Buccaneers)**
Teaming with Warrick Dunn in 1997, Alstott produced 843 total yards and 10 touchdowns. In 1998, he'll again be counted on as a scoring force for the Bucs and his yardage numbers could approach 1,000.

☐ **30. Gary Brown (New York Giants)**
The Giants still looking for a durable every-down back signed Brown, who rushed for 945 yards and scored four times for the San Diego Chargers in 1997.

KEEP AN EYE ON

☐ **31. Donnell Bennett (Kansas City Chiefs)**
Bennett could very well fall into the role of the Chiefs' starting halfback, which would obviously dictate plenty of statistical possibilities.

☐ **32. Thurman Thomas (Buffalo Bills)**
Antowain Smith will continue to steal the show and the bulk of the statistical success in 1998.

☐ **33. Larry Centers (Arizona Cardinals)**
One of the league's best receiving backs, Centers always has the potential to produce good yardage and scoring numbers.

☐ **34. Ki-Jana Carter (Cincinnati Bengals)**
He lost his starting role to rookie Corey Dillon in 1997, but Carter should still continue to produce, especially in touchdowns situations.

☐ **35. Ray Zellars (New Orleans Saints)**
He produced 815 rushing-receiving yards and four touchdowns in 1997, but Lamar Smith is now in New Orleans.

☐ **36. Mario Bates (Arizona Cardinals)**
The on-and-off starter for the New Orleans Saints gets his chance in Arizona, where the Cardinals have had trouble finding a consistent back. However. Adrian Murrell also acquired in the offseason stands in the way.

☐ **37. Byron Hanspard (Atlanta Falcons)**
The Falcons' second-round pick of a year ago should continue to see

his backfield duties expand.

☐ **38. Charles Way (New York Giants)**
Injuries to Tyrone Wheatley, Rodney Hampton and Tiki Barber opened the door for Way in 1997. He produced 1,002 rushing-receiving yards and five touchdowns in 1997 but Giants addition of Gary Brown raises questions.

☐ **39. Raymont Harris (Chicago Bears)**
Harris produced 1,148 rushing-receiving yards and 10 touchdowns in 1997 but where does he fit in now that Edgar Bennett and rookie Curtis Enis are in Chicago?

☐ **40. Stephen Davis (Washington Redskins)**
Davis's success depends on the health of Terry Allen.

PRIME PROSPECTS

☐ **41. Tim Biakabatuka (Carolina Panthers)**
The Panthers' former first-round pick has lost his starting job to unheralded Fred Lane, for now.

☐ **42. Chris Warren (Dallas Cowboys)**
Ricky Watters's arrival in Seattle put the talented Warren's future in question, until he was signed by the Cowboys to backup Emmitt Smith.

☐ **43. William Floyd (Carolina Panthers)**
A solid producer when healthy, Floyd takes his talents to Carolina for 1998.

☐ **44. Duce Staley (Philadelphia Eagles)**
Staley should share much of the rushing load with Charlie Garner now that Ricky Watters is gone.

☐ **45. Kimball Anders (Kansas City Chiefs)**
A solid pass-receiver out of the backfield, Anders could produce decent numbers.

☐ **46. Marc Edwards (San Francisco 49ers)**
William Floyd's departure leaves a vacancy for the 49ers' second-round pick of a year ago.

☐ **47. Lawrence Phillips (Miami Dolphins)**
There's plenty of talent here but how will Jimmy Johnson and the Dolphins use him?

☐ **48. Derrick Cullors/Sedrick Shaw (New England Patriots)**
The Patriots are looking for a replacement for the departed Curtis Martin, which won't be easy. The Patriots made Robert Edwards out of Georgia their #1 draft pick and he'll get a good look in training camp.

☐ **49. Rashaan Salaam (Chicago Bears)**
Injuries have riddled his past and now Edgar Bennett and rookie Curtis Enis stand in the way of future success. Salaam will likely have to find work elswhere in 1998.

☐ **50. Amp Lee (St. Louis Rams)**
Lee is likely again to find heavy productivity as a receiver out of the backfield.

DON'T BE SURPRISED

51. Turner (PHIL)
52. R. Thomas (TENN)
53. Kirby (???)
54. Bowie (WASH)
55. J. Graham (BALT)
56. Henderson (GB)
57. Fletcher (SD)
58. Crockett (IND)
69. T. Davis (NO)
60. L. Warren (IND)

YOU NEVER KNOW

61. Mitchell (WASH)
62. Vardell (DET)
63. A. Johnson (CAR)
64. Wheatley (NYG)
65. Le Johnson (NYG)
66. Hoard (MINN)
67. Hill (KC)
68. Hampton (???)
69. Ln. Johnson (NYJ)
70. McElroy (ARIZ)

WORTH MENTIONING

71. Sh. Williams (DALL)
72. Broussard (SEAT)
73. Johnston (DALL)
74. Pegram (NYG)
75. Potts (BALT)

76. Meggett (NE)
77. R. Anderson (NYJ)
78. McPhail (MIA)
79. H. Green (ATL)
80. Holmes (BUF)

ROOKIE PROSPECTS

NAME	TEAM	COMMENT
☐ 1. Fred Taylor	JAC	With Means off to San Diego, opportunity is there.
☐ 2. Robert Edwards	NE	Curtis Martin is gone, Edwards will battle for spot.
☐ 3. Curtis Enis	CHI	Bears stockpiled at running back.
☐ 4. John Avery	MIA	More likely a third-down contributor.
☐ 5. Robert Holcombe	STL	Workman type back that may push Jerald Moore.
☐ 6. Skip Hicks	WASH	Rushed for over 1,100 yards in '97, insurance behind T. Allen.
☐ 7. Rasheen Shehee	KC	Chiefs in need at RB with Allen and likely G. Hill gone.

A LOOK AT THE WIDE RECEIVERS
(A Guide for the Beginner)
Considerations in Choosing a Wide Receiver

1. First, look at players' previous performances. Don't overlook players who may have missed portions of the previous year because of injuries, holdouts, and the like. Injuries hurt the year-end numbers of Carl Pickens, Isaac Bruce, and rookie Yatil Green of Miami in 1997.

2. Grab the wideouts who are both consistent yardage gainers and consistent scorers. You want wide receivers who get you around 1,500 receiving yards and 12 to 15 touchdowns. Jerry Rice would naturally top your list when he's healthy. Then look at Herman Moore, Cris Carter, and Carl Pickens as other prime candidates. Rod Smith and Antonio Freeman are also right there.

3. Favor wide receivers who consistently top the 1,000-yard mark, even if their touchdown totals tend to be fairly low. Michael Irvin and Tim Brown are good examples.

4. If you're in search of a wideout in the later rounds, take a yardage man first. Frank Sanders of Arizona scored only four times in 1997 but on the strength of his 1,017 receiving yards, produced 120 fantasy points.

In the 1997 statistics that follow, players are ranked by their fantasy point totals. Remember that the Combined Basic/Performance Scoring Method awards six points for every touchdown scored, three points for every touchdown pass thrown, one point for every 10 yards rushing, one point for every 10 yards receiving, and one point for every 20 yards passing.

1997 STATISTICAL RESULTS
(WIDE RECEIVERS — COMBINED BASIC/PERFORMANCE SCORING METHOD)

NAME	TEAM	GP	RSH TDs	REC TDs	TOTAL TDs	BASIC PTS	RSH YARDS	REC YARDS	TOTAL YARDS	PERF PTS	CONV PTS	FAN-TASY PTS
1. R. Moore	ARIZ	16	0	8	8	50	0	1,584	1,584	150	2	200
1996		16	0	4	4	26	0	1,016	1,016	95	2	121
1995		15	0	5	5	32	0	907	907	83	2	115
3 Yr-TOTALS		47	0	17	17	108	0	3,507	3,507	328	6	436
2. Freeman	GB	15	0	12	12	72	14	1,243	1,257	120	0	192
1996		11	0	9	9	54	0	933	933	89	0	143
1995		5	0	1	1	6	0	106	106	8	0	14
3 Yr-TOTALS		31	0	22	22	132	14	2,282	2,296	217	0	349
3. R. Smith	DEN	16	0	12	12	72	16	1,180	1,196	115	0	187
1996		8	0	2	2	12	1	237	238	21	0	33
1995		5	0	1	0	6	0	152	152	13	0	19
3 Yr-TOTALS		29	0	15	14	90	17	1,569	1,586	149	0	239
4. Carter	MINN	16	0	13	13	84	0	1,069	1,069	98	6	182
1996		16	0	10	10	60	0	1,163	1,163	109	0	169
1995		16	0	17	17	102	0	1,371	1,371	128	0	230
3 Yr-TOTALS		48	0	40	40	246	0	3,603	3,603	335	6	581
5. Thigpen	PITT	15	0	7	7	44	3	1,398	1,401	134	2	178
1996		4	0	2	2	12	0	244	244	22	0	34
1995		16	0	5	5	30	0	1,307	1,307	124	0	154
3 Yr-TOTALS		35	0	14	14	86	3	2,949	2,952	280	2	366
6. Galloway	SEAT	15	0	12	12	72	72	1,049	1,121	104	0	176
1996		16	0	7	8	48	127	989	1,116	100	0	148
1995		16	1	7	9	54	154	1,039	1,193	107	0	161
3 Yr-TOTALS		47	1	26	29	174	353	3,077	3,430	311	0	485
7. H. Moore	DET	16	0	8	8	50	0	1,293	1,293	122	2	172
1996		16	0	9	9	56	0	1,296	1,296	121	2	177
1995		16	0	14	14	84	0	1,686	1,686	161	0	245
3 Yr-TOTALS		48	0	31	31	190	0	4,275	4,275	404	4	594
8. Tm. Brown	OAK	16	0	5	5	32	19	1,408	1,427	134	2	166
1996		16	0	9	9	54	35	1,104	1,139	106	0	160
1995		16	0	10	10	60	0	1,342	1,342	127	0	187
3 Yr-TOTALS		48	0	24	24	146	54	3,854	3,908	367	2	513
9. Irvin	DALL	16	0	9	9	54	0	1,180	1,180	110	0	164
1996		11	0	2	2	14	0	962	962	89	2	103
1995		16	0	10	10	60	0	1,603	1,603	154	0	214
3 Yr-TOTALS		43	0	21	21	128	0	3,745	3,745	353	2	481
10. Fryar	PHIL	16	0	6	6	36	0	1,316	1,316	125	0	161
1996		16	0	11	11	66	-4	1,195	1,191	114	0	180
1995 w/MIA		15	0	8	8	48	0	910	910	85	0	133
3 Yr-TOTALS		47	0	25	25	150	-4	3,421	3,417	324	0	474
11. J. Smith	JAC	16	0	4	4	24	0	1,324	1,324	127	0	151
1996		16	0	7	7	42	0	1,244	1,244	119	0	161
1995		8	0	3	5	30	0	288	288	23	0	53
3 Yr-TOTALS		40	0	14	16	96	0	2,856	2,856	269	0	365
12. Emanuel	ATL	16	0	9	9	54	0	991	991	93	0	147
1996		13	0	6	6	36	0	931	931	87	0	123
1995		16	0	5	5	30	0	1,039	1,039	98	0	128
3 Yr-TOTALS		45	0	20	20	120	0	2,961	2,961	278	0	398
13. D. Alexander	BALT	15	0	9	9	54	0	1,009	1,009	92	0	146
1996		15	0	9	9	56	0	1,099	1,099	103	2	159
1995		6	0	0	1	6	29	216	245	22	0	28
3 Yr-TOTALS		36	0	18	19	116	29	2,324	2,353	217	2	333
14. Rison	KC	15	0	7	7	42	2	1,092	1,094	104	0	146
1996 w/GB		15	0	3	3	18	0	593	593	53	0	71
1995 w/CLE		15	0	3	3	18	5	701	706	63	0	81
3 Yr-TOTALS		45	0	13	13	78	7	2,386	2,393	220	0	298
15. Jett	OAK	15	0	12	12	72	0	804	804	73	0	145
1996		13	0	4	4	24	0	601	601	54	0	78
1995		11	0	1	1	6	0	179	179	1	0	19
3 Yr-TOTALS		39	0	17	17	102	0	1,584	1,584	128	0	242

(WIDE RECEIVERS — COMBINED BASIC/PERFORMANCE SCORING METHOD)

	NAME	TEAM	GP	RSH TDs	REC TDs	TOTAL TDs	BASIC PTS	RSH YARDS	REC YARDS	TOTAL YARDS	PERF PTS	CONV PTS	FAN-TASY PTS
16.	J. Reed	MINN	16	0	6	6	36	0	1,138	1,138	106	0	142
	1996		16	0	7	7	42	0	1,320	1,320	124	0	166
	1995		16	0	9	9	54	0	1,167	1,167	107	0	161
	3 Yr-TOTALS		48	0	22	22	132	0	3,625	3,625	337	0	469
17.	McCardell	JAC	16	0	5	5	30	0	1,164	1,164	110	0	140
	1996		16	0	3	3	22	0	1,129	1,129	105	4	127
	1995 w/CLE		14	0	4	4	24	0	709	709	65	0	89
	3 Yr-TOTALS		46	0	12	12	76	0	3,002	3,002	280	4	356
18.	Brooks	GB	15	0	7	7	42	19	1,010	1,029	96	0	138
	1996		5	0	4	4	24	2	344	346	32	0	56
	1995		16	0	13	13	78	21	1,497	1,518	145	0	223
	3 Yr-TOTALS		36	0	24	24	144	42	2,851	2,893	273	0	417
19.	Morton	DET	16	0	6	6	36	33	1,057	1,090	100	0	136
	1996		16	0	6	6	36	35	714	749	65	0	101
	1995		13	0	8	8	48	33	590	623	55	0	103
	3 Yr-TOTALS		45	0	20	20	120	101	2,361	2,462	220	0	340
20.	Owens	SF	16	0	8	8	48	0	936	936	86	0	134
	1996		12	0	4	4	24	0	520	520	46	0	70
	1995		–	–	–	–	–	–	–	–	–	–	–
	3 Yr-TOTALS		28	0	12	12	72	0	1,456	1,456	132	0	204
21.	Calloway	NYG	16	0	8	8	48	-1	849	848	76	0	124
	1996		16	0	4	4	24	2	739	741	67	0	91
	1995		16	0	3	3	18	-9	796	787	72	0	90
	3 Yr-TOTALS		48	0	15	15	90	-8	2,384	2,376	215	0	305
22.	F. Sanders	ARIZ	16	0	4	4	26	5	1,017	1,022	94	2	120
	1996		16	0	4	4	24	-4	813	809	75	0	99
	1995		15	0	2	2	16	1	883	884	81	4	97
	3 Yr-TOTALS		47	0	10	10	66	2	2,713	2,715	250	6	316
23.	Harrison	IND	16	0	6	6	40	-7	866	859	79	4	119
	1996		16	0	8	8	48	15	836	851	77	0	125
	1995		–	–	–	–	–	–	–	–	–	–	–
	3 Yr-TOTALS		32	0	14	14	88	8	1,702	1,710	156	4	244
24.	K. Johnson	NYJ	16	0	5	5	30	0	963	963	88	0	118
	1996		14	0	8	8	50	0	844	844	79	2	129
	1995		–	–	–	–	–	–	–	–	–	–	–
	3 Yr-TOTALS		30	0	13	13	80	0	1,807	1,807	167	2	247
25.	Martin	SD	15	0	6	6	36	0	904	904	82	0	118
	1996		16	0	14	14	84	0	1,171	1,171	109	0	193
	1995		16	0	6	6	36	0	1,224	1,224	115	0	151
	3 Yr-TOTALS		47	0	26	26	156	0	3,299	3,299	306	0	462
26.	Proehl	CHI	14	0	7	7	44	0	753	753	70	2	114
	1996 w/SEAT		9	0	2	2	12	0	309	309	27	0	39
	1995 w/SEAT		4	0	0	0	0	0	29	29	0	0	0
	3 Yr-TOTALS		27	0	9	9	56	0	1,091	1,091	97	2	153
27.	M. Jackson	BALT	16	0	4	4	26	0	918	918	86	2	112
	1996		15	0	14	14	88	0	1,201	1,201	115	4	203
	1995		13	0	9	9	54	0	714	714	66	0	120
	3 Yr-TOTALS		44	0	27	27	168	0	2,833	2,833	267	6	435
28.	A. Reed	BUF	15	0	5	5	30	11	880	891	82	0	112
	1996		15	0	6	6	36	22	1,036	1,058	99	0	135
	1995		6	0	3	3	18	48	312	360	31	0	49
	3 Yr-TOTALS		36	0	14	14	84	81	2,228	2,309	212	0	296
29.	Mathis	ATL	16	0	6	6	36	35	802	837	74	0	110
	1996		15	0	7	7	44	0	771	771	71	2	115
	1995		14	0	9	9	60	0	1,039	1,039	100	6	160
	3 Yr-TOTALS		45	0	22	22	140	35	2,612	2,647	245	8	385
30.	Early	BUF	14	0	5	5	30	0	853	853	79	0	109
	1996		16	0	4	4	26	39	798	837	75	2	101
	1995 w/ NO		16	0	8	8	48	0	1,087	1,087	102	0	150
	3 Yr-TOTALS		46	0	17	17	104	39	2,738	2,777	256	2	360

1997 STATISTICAL RESULTS
(WIDE RECEIVERS — COMBINED BASIC/PERFORMANCE SCORING METHOD)

	NAME	TEAM	GP	RSH TDs	REC TDs	TOTAL TDs	BASIC PTS	RSH YARDS	REC YARDS	TOTAL YARDS	PERF PTS	CONV PTS	FAN-TASY PTS
31.	J. Lewis *	BALT	13	0	6	8	48	35	648	683	61	0	109
	1996		4	0	1	1	6	-3	85	82	7	0	13
	1995		–	–	–	–	–	–	–	–	–	–	–
	3 Yr-TOTALS		17	0	7	9	54	32	733	765	68	0	122
32.	Bruce	STL	11	0	5	5	30	0	815	815	77	0	107
33.	Scott	CIN	16	0	5	5	30	6	797	803	72	0	102
34.	McCaffrey	DEN	14	0	8	8	48	0	590	590	53	0	101
35.	McDuffie *	MIA	16	0	1	2	12	0	943	943	88	0	100
36.	Hastings	NO	16	0	5	5	32	35	722	757	66	2	98
37.	McKnight	SEAT	12	0	6	6	36	0	637	637	59	0	95
38.	Pickens	CIN	12	0	5	5	30	-6	695	689	64	0	94
39.	Tr. Brown	NE	13	0	6	6	36	-18	607	589	56	0	92
40.	Stokes	SF	15	0	4	4	24	0	733	733	67	0	91
41.	Chrebet	NYJ	14	0	3	3	18	0	799	799	72	0	90
42.	Pritchard	SEAT	16	0	2	2	12	14	843	857	77	0	89
43.	Jefferson	NE	16	0	2	2	12	0	841	841	76	0	88
44.	Dawkins	IND	14	0	2	2	12	0	804	804	74	0	86
45.	Hill	NO	15	0	2	2	12	11	761	772	70	0	82
46.	Shepherd	WASH	10	0	5	5	30	27	562	589	52	0	82
47.	Miller	DALL	15	0	4	4	24	6	645	651	55	0	79
48.	Metcalf *	SD	15	0	2	5	30	-5	576	571	49	0	79
49.	W. Davis	TENN	15	0	4	4	24	0	564	564	53	0	77
50.	Ka. Williams	*TB	13	0	4	5	30	5	486	491	43	0	73
51.	Carruth +	CAR	14	0	4	4	24	23	545	568	48	0	72
52.	Penn	CHI	14	0	3	3	18	-1	576	575	52	0	70
53.	Westbrook	WASH	10	0	3	3	18	-11	559	548	52	0	70
54.	Hawkins	PITT	15	0	3	3	18	17	555	572	50	0	68
55.	Anthony +	TB	12	0	4	4	24	84	448	532	44	0	68
56.	Ellard	WASH	12	0	4	4	24	0	485	485	43	0	67
57.	C. Johnson	PITT	13	0	2	2	12	0	568	568	51	0	63
58.	C. Sanders	TENN	13	0	3	3	18	-8	498	490	45	0	63
59.	Jordan	MIA	13	0	3	3	18	12	471	483	44	0	62
60.	Graham	NYJ	13	0	2	2	12	0	542	542	49	0	61
61.	Solomon	PHIL	11	0	3	3	20	0	455	455	40	2	60
62.	Timpson	PHIL	13	0	2	2	12	0	484	484	41	0	53
63.	Carrier	CAR	9	0	2	2	12	0	436	436	40	0	52
64.	Glenn	NE	7	0	2	2	12	0	431	431	40	0	52
65.	R. Ismail	CAR	13	0	2	2	12	32	419	451	39	0	51
66.	Conway	CHI	7	0	1	1	6	17	476	493	45	0	51
67.	Small	STL	12	0	1	1	6	0	488	488	44	0	50
68.	Engram	CHI	11	0	2	2	14	0	399	399	35	2	49
69.	Bailey	IND	12	0	3	3	18	20	329	349	30	0	48
70.	Dunn	CIN	11	0	2	2	12	0	414	414	36	0	48
71.	L. Thomas	MIA	10	0	2	2	12	0	402	402	36	0	48
72.	Guliford *	NO	11	0	1	2	12	-2	362	360	32	0	44
73.	C. Jones	SD	15	0	1	1	6	42	423	465	37	0	43
74.	Copeland	TB	11	0	1	1	6	0	421	421	37	0	43
75.	Perriman **	MIA	11	0	1	1	6	0	392	392	33	0	39
76.	Blades	SEAT	10	0	2	2	12	0	319	319	27	0	39
77.	Hundon	CIN	6	0	2	2	12	0	285	285	26	0	38
78.	Kennison	STL	13	0	0	0	0	13	404	417	35	0	35
79.	Dawson	KC	9	0	2	2	12	0	273	273	23	0	35
80.	Brisby	NE	12	0	2	2	12	0	276	276	21	0	33
81.	Toomer *	NYG	11	0	1	2	12	0	263	263	21	0	33
82.	St. Williams	DALL	12	0	1	1	6	0	308	308	26	0	32
83.	Moulds	BUF	11	0	0	0	2	59	294	353	29	2	31
84.	W. Jackson	JAC	11	0	2	2	14	14	206	220	17	2	31
85.	Green	DEN	10	0	2	2	12	0	240	240	19	0	31
86.	Muhammad	CAR	7	0	0	0	2	0	317	317	29	2	31
87.	Patten	NYG	7	0	2	2	12	2	226	228	19	0	31
88.	K. Alexander	NYG	9	0	1	1	6	0	276	276	24	0	30

1997 STATISTICAL RESULTS
(WIDE RECEIVERS — COMBINED BASIC/PERFORMANCE SCORING METHOD)

	NAME	TEAM	GP	RSH TDs	REC TDs	TOTAL TDs	BASIC PTS	RSH YARDS	REC YARDS	TOTAL YARDS	PERF PTS	CONV PTS	FAN-TASY PTS
89.	Stablein	IND	12	0	1	1	8	0	253	253	20	2	28
90.	Still	SD	12	0	0	0	0	0	324	324	28	0	28
91.	Kv. Williams	ARIZ	11	0	1	1	6	-2	273	271	22	0	28
92.	Kinchen	ATL	9	0	1	1	6	0	266	266	22	0	28
93.	Mayes	GB	7	0	0	0	0	0	290	290	27	0	27
94.	Blackwell + *	PITT	7	0	1	2	12	14	168	182	15	0	27
95.	Vanover *	KC	8	0	0	2	14	50	92	142	12	2	26
96.	Ward +	NYJ	8	0	1	1	6	25	212	237	19	0	25
97.	Connell +	WASH	4	0	2	2	12	3	138	141	12	0	24
98.	Hughes	KC	5	0	2	3	18	0	65	65	5	0	23
99.	Crawford	STL	6	0	0	0	0	9	232	241	21	0	21
100.	Barnett	MIA	5	0	1	1	6	0	166	166	15	0	21
101.	Poole +	NO	2	0	2	2	12	0	98	98	8	0	20
102.	Seay	PHIL	10	0	1	1	6	0	187	187	13	0	19
103.	Haynes	ATL	7	0	1	1	6	0	154	154	13	0	19
104.	Russell	TENN	6	0	1	1	6	0	141	141	12	0	18
105.	Mills	CAR	5	0	1	1	6	0	127	127	11	0	17
106.	Mason +	TENN	7	0	0	0	0	-7	186	179	16	0	16
107.	VanDyke	NYJ	2	0	2	2	12	0	53	53	4	0	16
108.	Edwards	ARIZ	11	0	0	0	0	0	203	203	14	0	14
109.	Yarborough	BALT	9	0	0	0	0	0	183	183	14	0	14
110.	Shedd *	OAK	7	0	0	1	6	0	115	115	8	0	14
111.	Uwaezuoke	SF	9	0	0	0	0	0	165	165	13	0	13
112.	Walsh	MINN	8	0	1	1	6	0	114	114	-7	0	13
113.	Hobbs **	SEAT	7	0	1	1	6	0	85	85	7	0	13
114.	Bownes	CHI	5	0	0	0	0	0	146	146	13	0	13
115.	Truitt	OAK	3	0	1	1	6	0	91	91	7	0	13
116.	Rice	SF	2	0	1	1	6	-10	78	68	7	0	13
117.	Boyd	DET	6	0	0	0	0	0	142	142	12	0	12
118.	Barlow *	JAC	4	0	0	1	6	0	74	74	5	0	11
119.	Roe	BALT	3	0	0	0	0	0	124	124	11	0	11
120.	Kent +	TENN	4	0	1	1	6	0	55	55	4	0	10
121.	R. Thomas	TB	7	0	0	0	0	0	129	129	9	0	9
122.	Manning +	MIA	3	0	0	0	0	0	85	85	8	0	8
123.	C. Thomas	WASH	6	0	0	0	0	0	93	93	7	0	7
124.	C. Jones	PHIL	4	0	0	0	0	0	73	73	7	0	7
125.	T. Lewis	NYG	3	0	0	0	0	0	84	84	7	0	7
126.	R. Harris	SEAT	3	0	0	0	0	0	81	81	6	0	6
127.	D. Sanders *	DALL	2	0	0	1	6	-11	3	-8	0	0	6
128.	Schroeder	GB	2	0	1	1	6	0	15	15	0	0	6
129.	Mickens	GB	1	0	1	1	6	0	2	2	0	0	6
130.	Harper	WASH	1	0	0	0	0	0	65	65	6	0	6
131.	Horn	KC	2	0	0	0	0	0	65	65	5	0	5
132.	Hatchette +	MINN	3	0	0	0	0	0	54	54	4	0	4
133.	Bech	NO	3	0	0	0	0	0	50	50	4	0	4
134.	Twyner	CIN	2	0	0	0	0	0	45	45	4	0	4
135.	T. Davis	SEAT	1	0	0	0	0	0	48	48	4	0	4
136.	M. Harris	SF	4	0	0	0	0	0	53	53	3	0	3
137.	E. Smith	CHI	2	0	0	0	0	12	22	34	3	0	3
138.	Hilliard +	NYG	2	0	0	0	0	0	42	42	3	0	3
139.	Floyd	STL	2	0	0	0	0	0	39	39	3	0	3
140.	Lockett +	KC	1	0	0	0	0	0	35	35	3	0	3
141.	Adams +	PITT	1	0	0	0	0	0	39	39	3	0	3
142.	B. Davis	DALL	3	0	0	0	0	0	33	33	2	0	2
143.	Ross	STL	3	0	0	0	0	0	37	37	2	0	2
144.	Brock	ARIZ	1	0	0	0	0	0	29	29	2	0	2
145.	Beebe	GB	1	0	0	0	0	0	28	28	2	0	2
146.	J. Thomas	STL	1	0	0	0	0	0	25	25	2	0	2
147.	Thrash	WASH	1	0	0	0	0	0	24	24	2	0	2
148.	Howard	OAK	3	0	0	0	0	0	30	30	1	0	1
149.	Jefers	DEN	2	0	0	0	0	0	24	24	1	0	1

1997 STATISTICAL RESULTS
(WIDE RECEIVERS — COMBINED BASIC/PERFORMANCE
SCORING METHOD)

	NAME	TEAM	GP	RSH TDs	REC TDs	TOTAL TDs	BASIC PTS	RSH YARDS	REC YARDS	TOTAL YARDS	PERF PTS	CONV PTS	FAN-TASY PTS
150.	Reese	BUF	1	0	0	0	0	0	13	13	1	0	1
151.	Doering	IND	1	0	0	0	0	0	12	12	1	0	1
152.	W. Moore	JAC	1	0	0	0	0	0	10	10	1	0	1
153.	McCorvey	DET	2	0	0	0	0	0	9	9	0	0	0
154.	Marsh	PITT	2	0	0	0	0	2	14	16	0	0	0
155.	Jells	NE	1	0	0	0	0	0	9	9	0	0	0

+		DENOTES COLLEGE DRAFT PICK	
*	J. Lewis	BALT	Scored TD's on punt returns of 89 and 66 yards.
*	McDuffie	MIA	Scored TD by recovering fumble in end zone.
*	Metcalf	SD	Scored TD's on punt returns of 85, 67, and 83 yards.
*	Ka. Williams	TB	Scored TD on punt return of 61 yards.
*	Guliford	NO	Scored TD on kickoff return of 102 yards.
*	Toomer	NYG	Scored TD on punt return of 53 yards.
*	Blackwell	PITT	Scored TD on kickoff return of 97 yards.
*	Vanover	KC	Scored TD on punt return of 82 yards and kickoff return of 94 yards.
*	Shedd	OAK	Scored TD on fumble return of 25 yards.
*	Barlow	JAC	Scored TD on kickoff return of 92 yards.
*	D. Sanders	DALL	Scored TD on punt return of 83 yards.
**	Perriman	MIA	Played in 3 games with Kansas City.
**	Hobbs	SEAT	Played in 2 games with New Orleans.

RATING THE PLAYERS FOR 1998
(Wide Receivers—Combined Basic/Performance Scoring Method)

GRAB ONE IF YOU CAN

☐ **1. Antonio Freeman (Green Bay Packers)**
Having Brett Favre as his quarterback has been a huge benefit for Freeman. Freeman jumped to 1,243 receiving yards and 12 touchdowns as Favre's favorite target in 1997. In 1998, Favre and Freeman will again put up big numbers.

☐ **2. Jerry Rice (San Francisco 49ers)**
Rice missed most of 1997 with knee injuries. When healthy, Rice is very capable of producing 1,300 to 1,800 receiving yards and around 12 touchdowns.

☐ **3. Herman Moore (Detroit Lions)**
Moore is always in the 1,300 to 1,700-yard range and nearing or topping the double-digit touchdown mark. He should again find himself in that range, come 1998.

☐ **4. Carl Pickens (Cincinnati Bengals)**
Pickens missed the last four games of 1997 with a groin injury, which contributed to a huge dropoff in his year-end numbers. However, looking back to the two previous years, Pickens recorded 100 and 99 receptions, 1,180 and 1,234 receiving yards and 17 and 12 touchdowns, giving you a better idea of what he's capable of.

☐ **5. Michael Irvin (Dallas Cowboys)**
Always a productive yardage man, Irvin produced 1,180 receiving yards in 1997 and 1,686 two years earlier in 1995. Irvin's nine touchdowns in 1997 also illustrate his increasing ability to get into the endzone with regularity.

BEST OF THE REST

☐ **6. Rod Smith (Denver Broncos)**
The Broncos, looking for a go-to receiver in 1997, found one in Rod Smith. Smith, who hadn't done much before last year, recorded 1,180 receiving yards and 12 touchdowns. Now that he's claimed the main receiving role, he should continue to produce big numbers in 1998.

☐ **7. Cris Carter (Minnesota Vikings)**
Carter has recorded 1,371, 1,163 and 1,069 receiving yards, along with 17, 10 and 13 touchdowns for the last three seasons, respectively. That's a consistent trend that should continue in 1998.

☐ **8. Tim Brown (Oakland Raiders)**
Brown had recorded consistent yardage numbers the last three seasons with 1,342, 1,139 and 1,427 yards, respectively. However, his touchdown numbers dropped to only five in 1997 after he had scored 9 and 10 the two previous years. I look for another 1,100 to 1,500 yards and double-

digit touchdowns from Brown this season.

☐ **9. Rob Moore (Arizona Cardinals)**
With Jake Plummer eventually taking over as the team's starting quarterback in 1997, Rob Moore's numbers took a jump. Moore finished the year with a whopping 1,584 receiving yards and eight touchdowns. He may not match those numbers in 1998, but he could be near them again.

☐ **10. Irving Fryar (Philadelphia Eagles)**
In the two seasons since he came to Philadelphia, Fryar has recorded 1,195 and 1,316 receiving yards along with 11 and 6 touchdowns, respectively. As the Eagles' best wideout, another 1,100 to 1,300 yard and eight-plus touchdown season should be in store for him.

STRONG LONG SHOTS

☐ **11. Joey Galloway (Seattle Seahawks)**
Continuing to rise is Seahawk wideout Joey Galloway. Galloway hit 1,049 receiving yards and scored 12 times in 1997. I look for another double-digit scoring campaign and 1,000-plus yard season again in 1998.

☐ **12. Robert Brooks (Green Bay Packers)**
Quickly returning to form following his knee injury, Brooks returned to record 1,010 receiving yards and seven touchdowns in 1997. I believe his numbers will continue to climb as he regains his confidence.

☐ **13. Isaac Bruce (St. Louis Rams)**
Slowed by a hamstring injury in 1997, Bruce missed five games and recorded only 815 receiving yards and five touchdowns. Looking back to two years earlier when he recorded 1,798 receiving yards and 13 touchdowns, we get a feel of what he's capable of doing.

☐ **14. Curtis Conway (Chicago Bears)**
An injured collarbone cost Conway much of the 1997 season and resulted in him recording only 476 receiving yards and one touchdown. When he's healthy, as he was in 1995 when he produced 1,062 receiving yards and 12 touchdowns, he can be a huge fantasy factor.

☐ **15. Tony Martin (San Diego Chargers)**
Martin suffered a huge dropoff in 1997 when he tallied only 904 receiving yards and six touchdowns. A year earlier, Martin recorded 1,171 receiving yards and 14 scores. Much of his 1998 success will depend on that of his young quarterback.

☐ **16. Jackie Smith (Jacksonville Jaguars)**
Perhaps the touchdown numbers aren't there, since he scored seven and four touchdowns the last two seasons, but the yardage numbers are. He produced 1,244 and 1,324 yards over that same two-year period.

☐ **17. Jake Reed (Minnesota Vikings)**
The second of the Vikings' talented wideouts, Reed is normally in the 1,100 to 1,400 yard and 6 to 10 touchdown range. He's consistently done it and should again in 1998.

□ **18. Michael Jackson (Baltimore Ravens)**
After scoring 14 times and producing 1,201 receiving yards in 1996, Jackson dropped to just four touchdowns and only 918 receiving yards in 1997. With receiving mate Derrick Alexander off to Kansas City in 1998, look for Jackson's numbers to do a bit of a rebound, although Jim Harbough at quarterback doesn't excite me.

□ **19. Keenan McCardell (Jacksonville Jaguars)**
McCardell is the other half of the talented Jaguar duo that doesn't produce many touchdowns but does produce plenty of yardage. McCardell has produced 1,129 and 1,164 yards over the last two seasons but scored only eight touchdowns in the two years combined.

□ **20. Charles Johnson (Pittsburgh Steelers)**
With Yancey Thigpen off to Tennessee, Johnson likely moves into the No.1 receiving role, which will certainly boost his numbers in 1998.

HAVE THE POTENTIAL

□ **21. Derrick Alexander (Kansas City Chiefs)**
With the Baltimore Ravens the last two seasons, Alexander produced 1,099 and 1,009 receiving yards respectively and nine touchdowns in each of the two seasons. However, since he will be Kansas City in 1998, there's some uncertainty as to just how good his numbers will be.

□ **22. Johnny Morton (Detroit Lions)**
With Brett Perriman leaving after 1997, Morton's playing and yardage numbers took a climb. Surpassing the 1,000-yard mark and scoring six-plus times will again be well within his reach in 1998.

□ **23. Keyshawn Johnson (New York Jets)**
Johnson boosted his yardage numbers to 963 yards in 1997 but saw his touchdown production drop from eight scores as a rookie in 1996 to five last year. Certainly the 1,000-yard mark and 6 to 10 touchdown range are very reachable goals in 1998.

□ **24. Andre Rison (Kansas City Chiefs)**
Rison rebounded after a couple of down years to very respectable numbers in 1997 after coming to Kansas City. Rison recorded 1,092 receiving yards and seven touchdowns. However, there's some question as to how he'll do now that Derrick Alexander has arrived.

□ **25. Yancey Thigpen (Tennessee Oilers)**
Thigpen had 1,398 yards and seven touchdowns as the primary receiver for Kordell Stewart and the Steelers in 1997. With Tennessee in 1998, Thigpen will again do well but probably not reach the same yardage numbers.

SOLID SLEEPERS

□ **26. Terrence Mathis (Atlanta Falcons)**
Always hovering in the 800 to 1,000-yard range and scoring six-plus touchdowns, Mathis is a very capable fantasy pick for 1998, especially with Bert Emanuel departing to Tampa Bay.

☐ **27. Chris Calloway (New York Giants)**
With early-round draft picks Ike Hilliard, Thomas Lewis and Amani Toomer continuing to fizzle, Calloway is blossoming. Calloway recorded 849 receiving numbers and eight touchdowns in 1997. He could expand those numbers in 1998.

☐ **28. James Jett (Oakland Raiders)**
With the arrival of quarterback Jeff George in 1997, Jett's yardage and touchdown numbers got a boost. Jett recorded 804 receiving yards and 12 touchdowns. He'll work to improve on the yardage numbers but he'll struggle to match the touchdown numbers.

☐ **29. Marvin Harrison (Indianapolis Colts)**
Harrison has recorded two 800-yard seasons while scoring eight and six times in his first two years in the NFL. It's time for the talented Harrison to near or top the 1,000-yard mark, along with scoring another six to eight times in 1998.

☐ **30. Frank Sanders (Arizona Cardinals)**
Rookie quarterback Jake Plummer sparked the Cardinals' aerial show in 1997 for both Sanders and Rob Moore. Sanders, like Moore, topped the 1,000-yard mark (1,017) but Sanders scored only four times. If Plummer continues to improve, so will Sanders' numbers in 1998.

KEEP AN EYE ON

☐ **31. Bert Emanuel (Tampa Bay Buccaneers)**
Emanuel has fallen just short of 1,000 receiving yards for the last two seasons while scoring six and nine times. In 1998, going to the Tampa Bay Buccaneers he'll likely have a tougher time producing big numbers.

☐ **32. O.J. McDuffie (Miami Dolphins)**
Nearly 1,000 yards (943) but only two touchdowns for McDuffie in 1997. The two previous years, McDuffie scored seven and six times, and those levels are more like what we can expect in 1998.

☐ **33. Quinn Early (Buffalo Bills)**
If the Bills get their quarterback situation straightened out, Early is capable of putting together solid numbers in 1998.

☐ **34. Mike Pritchard (Seattle Seahawks)**
He's pushing for the No.2 receiving spot alongside Joey Galloway, and should post good numbers in 1998.

☐ **35. Darnay Scott (Cincinnati Bengals)**
Scott finished the 1997 season with four touchdowns and 468 receiving yards in the last five games. However, Carl Pickens was not playing then and returns healthy in 1998.

☐ **36. Terrell Owens (San Francisco 49ers)**
With Jerry Rice out for most of 1997, Owens recorded 936 receiving yards and eight touchdowns. With Rice returning healthy in 1998, Owens's numbers will likely drop a bit.

☐ **37. Terry Glenn (New England Patriots)**
He had an outstanding 90-reception rookie season in 1996 but injuries put a damper on his sophomore campaign.

☐ **38. Michael Westbrook (Washington Redskins)**
The Redskins and fantasy fans are still waiting for the former No.1 draft pick to avoid injuries and other distractions and play to what is believed to be his potential.

☐ **39. Andre Reed (Buffalo Bills)**
He's getting older but he keeps getting it done.

☐ **40. Wayne Chrebet (New York Jets)**
With Jeff Graham off to the Eagles, Chrebet may get his chance to expand his role and his numbers.

PRIME PROSPECTS

☐ **41. Jermaine Lewis (Baltimore Ravens)**
Lewis is looking to boost his 648-yard, eight-touchdown performance of a year ago now that Derrick Alexander has departed. Having Kim Harbaugh as his quarterback doesn't excite me, however.

☐ **42. Ed McCaffrey (Denver Broncos)**
He's perhaps not a big yardage man but tall and talented McCaffrey is always capable of 7 to 10 touchdowns.

☐ **43. Yatil Green (Miami Dolphins)**
The Dolphins' No.1 draft pick of a year ago suffered a knee injury to keep him from any regular-season action. Returning healthy, Green will draw plenty fantasy attention in the preseason, when he could easily push his fantasy stock up.

☐ **44. Jeff Graham (Philadelphia Eagles)**
He's pushing to win the No.2 receiving spot from Chris T. Jones and Michael Timpson.

☐ **45. Rae Carruth (Carolina Panthers)**
The Panthers' first-round pick of a year ago recorded only 545 receiving yards and four scores in 1997. He'll easily improve on those numbers as he continues to see playing time.

☐ **46. Karl Williams (Tampa Bay Buccaneers)**
Williams improved as the 1997 season went on. He has the potential to be a significant contributor for the Bucs.

☐ **47. Leslie Shepherd (Washington Redskins)**
Shepherd produced 562 receiving yards and five touchdowns despite missing the last six games of 1997 with a wrist injury.

☐ **48. Reidel Anthony (Tampa Bay Buccaneers)**
The Buccaneers need their No.1 draft pick to expand on his 448 receiving yard, four-touchdown performance of a year ago.

☐ **49. Ricky Proehl (St. Louis Rams)**
Proehl comes to St. Louis, pushing for playing time after recording 58

receptions for 753 yards and scoring seven times with Chicago in 1997.

☐ **50. Eddie Kennison (St. Louis Rams)**
After a standout rookie season in 1997 with 924 receiving yards and 11 touchdowns, he had a disastrous sophomore season. He'll have to rebound quickly to hold off the challenge of new acquisition Ricky Proehl for the Rams' No.2 receiving spot.

DON'T BE SURPRISED

51. Hilliard (NYG)
52. Engram (CHI)
53. St. Williams (DALL)
54. Dawkins (NO)
55. Timpson (PHIL)
56. C.T. Jones (PHIL)
57. McKnight (SEAT)
58. Stokes (SF)
59. C. Jones (SD)
60. Jefferson (NE)

YOU NEVER KNOW

61. Muhammed (CAR)
62. Toomer (NYG)
63. Penn (CHI)
64. Carrier (CAR)
65. C. Sanders (TENN)
66. Hastings (NO)
67. Tr. Brown (NE)
68. Hawkins (PITT)
69. K. Alexander (MIA)
70. Small (IND)

DON'T COUNT THEM OUT

71. Davis (DALL)
72. Metcalf (ARIZ)
73. T. Lewis (CHI)
74. Mills (DALL)
75. Ellard (WASH)

76. Miller (DALL)
77. Copeland (TB)
78. Perriman (???)
79. Hill (NO)
80. Blades (SEAT)

WORTH MENTIONING

81. W. Jackson (JAC)
82. Brisby (NE)
83. Jordan (MIA)
84. Ward (NYJ)

85. Dawson (KC)
86. Still (SD)
87. Moulds (BUF)
88. Van Dyke (NYJ)

ROOKIE PROSPECTS

NAME	TEAM	COMMENT
☐ 1. Kevin Dyson	TENN	Dyson looking to help improve Oiler passing game.
☐ 2. Randy Moss	MINN	Talented receiver but must overcome off-field problems.
☐ 3. Marcus Nash	DEN	Caught 76 passes and 13 TD's as favorite target of Peyton Manning in '97.
☐ 4. Jerome Pathon	IND	Colts have their QB—now must build around him.
☐ 5. Tony Simmons	NE	Patriots looking for help at wide receiver.
☐ 6. Michael Ricks	SD	Nice size (6'5") target for young Leaf.
☐ 7. Pat Johnson	BALT	Might fit into mix with Michael Jackson and Jermaine Lewis.
☐ 8. Joe Jurevicius	NYG	Giants always looking for receiver help.

A LOOK AT THE TIGHT ENDS

(A Guide for the Beginner)

Considerations in Choosing a Tight End

1. First, look at players' previous performances. Don't overlook players who may have missed portions of the previous year because of injuries, holdouts, and the like. In 1997, 49er tight end Brent Jones had his year-end numbers hurt by injury.

2. Look for a tight end who will get 750 or more receiving yards and who has a shot at seven or more touchdowns. Ben Coates has done well in recent years, as has Shannon Sharpe.

3. Find a tight end who is a certain quarterback's favorite receiver, such as Shannon Sharpe, who is a favorite target for John Elway, or Wesley Wells, who has quickly become Kerry Collins's favorite.

4. Pick a tight end from a predominantly passing team, like Mark Chmura of the Packers.

In the 1997 statistics that follow, players are ranked by their fantasy-point totals. Remember that the Combined Basic/Performance Scoring Method awards six points for every touchdown scored, three points for every touchdown pass thrown, one point for every 10 yards rushing, one point for every 10 yards receiving, and one point for every 20 yards passing.

1997 STATISTICAL RESULTS
(TIGHT ENDS — COMBINED BASIC/PERFORMANCE SCORING METHOD)

NAME	TEAM	GP	RSH TDs	REC TDs	TOTAL TDs	BASIC PTS	RSH YARDS	REC YARDS	TOTAL YARDS	PERF PTS	CONV PTS	FAN-TASY PTS
1. Sharpe	DEN	16	0	3	3	20	0	1,107	1,107	104	2	124
1996		15	0	10	10	60	0	1,062	1,062	102	0	162
1995		12	0	4	4	24	0	756	756	72	0	96
3 Yr - TOTALS		43	0	17	17	104	0	2,925	2,925	278	2	382
2. Coates	NE	16	0	8	8	48	0	737	737	66	0	114
1996		15	0	9	9	56	0	682	682	61	2	117
1995		16	0	6	6	36	0	915	915	85	0	121
3 Yr - TOTALS		47	0	23	23	140	0	2,334	2,334	212	2	352
3. Dudley	OAK	16	0	7	7	42	0	787	787	71	0	113
1996		13	0	4	4	24	0	386	386	34	0	58
1995		–	–	–	–	–	–	–	–	–	–	–
3 Yr - TOTALS		29	0	11	11	66	0	1,173	1,173	105	0	171
4. Walls	CAR	15	0	6	6	36	0	746	746	68	0	104
1996		16	0	10	10	60	0	713	713	66	0	126
1995 w/NO		16	0	4	4	26	0	694	694	62	2	88
3 Yr - TOTALS		47	0	20	20	122	0	2,153	2,153	196	2	318
5. Wycheck	TENN	16	0	4	4	26	0	748	748	67	2	93
1996		15	0	6	6	36	3	511	514	43	0	79
1995		14	1	1	2	12	1	471	472	41	0	53
3 Yr - TOTALS		45	1	11	12	74	4	1,730	1,734	151	2	225
6. Green	BALT	14	0	5	5	30	0	601	601	54	0	84
1996		6	0	1	1	6	0	150	150	14	0	20
1995 w/MIA		14	0	3	3	20	0	499	499	43	2	63
3 Yr - TOTALS		34	0	9	9	56	0	1,250	1,250	111	2	167
7. McGee	CIN	15	0	6	6	38	0	414	414	35	2	73
1996		14	0	4	4	24	0	446	446	37	0	61
1995		15	0	4	4	24	0	754	754	67	0	91
3 Yr - TOTALS		44	0	14	14	86	0	1,614	1,614	139	2	225
8. Drayton	MIA	15	0	4	4	24	0	558	558	49	0	73
1996 w/STL		12	0	0	0	2	0	331	331	26	2	28
1995		16	0	4	4	24	0	458	458	39	0	63
3 Yr - TOTALS		43	0	8	8	50	0	1,347	1,347	114	2	164
9. Chmura	GB	15	0	6	6	36	0	417	417	35	0	71
1996		11	0	0	0	0	0	370	370	33	0	33
1995		15	0	7	7	44	0	679	679	62	2	106
3 Yr - TOTALS		41	0	13	13	80	0	1,466	1,466	130	2	210
10. Conwell	STL	14	0	4	4	24	0	404	404	33	0	57
1996		6	0	0	0	0	0	164	164	14	0	14
1995		–	–	–	–	–	–	–	–	–	–	–
3 Yr - TOTALS		20	0	4	4	24	0	568	568	47	0	71
11. P. Mitchell	JAC	14	0	4	4	24	0	380	380	32	0	56
1996		16	0	1	1	6	0	575	575	51	0	57
1995		14	0	2	2	12	0	527	527	45	0	57
3 Yr - TOTALS		44	0	7	7	42	0	1,482	1,482	128	0	170
12. F. Jones +	SD	13	0	2	2	12	0	505	505	44	0	56
1996		–	–	–	–	–	–	–	–	–	–	–
1995		–	–	–	–	–	–	–	–	–	–	–
3 Yr - TOTALS		13	0	2	2	12	0	505	505	44	0	56
13. Dilger	IND	10	0	3	3	18	0	380	380	34	0	52
1996		13	0	4	4	24	0	503	503	44	0	68
1995		15	0	4	4	24	0	635	635	56	0	80
3 Yr - TOTALS		38	0	11	11	66	0	1,518	1,518	134	0	200
14. Glover	MINN	12	0	3	3	18	0	378	378	31	0	49
1996 w/OAK		6	0	1	1	6	0	101	101	7	0	13
1995 w/OAK		14	0	3	3	18	0	220	220	17	0	35
3 Yr - TOTALS		32	0	7	7	42	0	699	699	55	0	97
15. Asher	WASH	16	0	1	1	6	0	474	474	41	0	47
1996		16	0	4	4	24	0	481	481	41	0	65
1995		6	0	0	0	0	0	172	172	15	0	15
3 Yr - TOTALS		38	0	5	5	30	0	1,127	1,127	97	0	127

NAME	TEAM	GP	RSH TDs	REC TDs	TOTAL TDs	BASIC PTS	RSH YARDS	REC YARDS	TOTAL YARDS	PERF PTS	CONV PTS	FAN-TASY PTS
16. Williams	OAK	10	3	2	5	32	70	147	217	15	2	47
1996 (as RB)		13	0	0	0	3	431	143	514	47	0	50
1995 (as RB)		16	9	0	9	54	1,114	375	1,489	133	0	187
3 Yr - TOTALS		39	12	2	14	89	1,615	665	2,220	195	2	284
17. Wetnight	CHI	15	0	1	1	6	0	464	464	40	0	46
1996		7	0	1	1	6	0	223	223	19	0	25
1995		9	0	2	2	12	0	193	193	15	0	27
3 Yr - TOTALS		31	0	4	4	24	0	880	880	74	0	98
18. Gedney	ARIZ	14	0	4	4	24	15	261	276	21	0	45
1996		–	–	–	–	–	–	–	–	–	–	–
1995 w/CHI		5	0	0	0	0	0	52	52	2	0	2
3 Yr - TOTALS		19	0	4	4	24	15	313	328	23	0	47
19. Gonzalez +	KC	12	0	2	2	14	0	368	368	31	2	45
1996		–	–	–	–	–	–	–	–	–	–	–
1995		–	–	–	–	–	–	–	–	–	–	–
3 Yr - TOTALS		12	0	2	2	14	0	368	368	31	2	45
20. B. Jones	SF	12	0	2	2	12	0	383	383	33	0	45
1996		9	0	1	1	6	0	428	428	38	0	44
1995		16	0	3	3	18	0	595	595	51	0	69
3 Yr - TOTALS		37	0	6	6	36	0	1,406	1,406	122	0	158
21. Bruener	PITT	9	0	6	6	36	0	117	117	8	0	44
22. Moore	TB	8	0	4	4	24	0	217	217	18	0	42
23. L. Johnson	BUF	15	0	2	2	12	6	340	346	28	0	40
24. Popson	KC	12	0	2	2	12	0	320	320	28	0	40
25. Bjornson	DALL	13	0	0	0	2	0	442	442	37	2	39
26. Baxter	NYJ	13	0	3	3	18	0	276	276	21	0	39
27. Crumpler	SEAT	14	0	1	1	6	0	361	361	28	0	34
28. Santiago +	ATL	9	0	2	2	12	0	217	217	19	0	31
29. Brady	NYJ	14	0	2	2	12	0	238	238	17	0	29
30. Riemersma	BUF	12	0	2	2	14	0	208	208	15	2	29
31. C. Lewis	PHIL	8	0	4	4	24	0	94	94	5	0	29
32. Farquhar	NO	7	0	1	1	6	0	253	253	23	0	29
33. Hartley	SD	11	0	1	1	6	0	246	246	20	0	26
34. Harris	TB	9	0	1	1	6	0	216	216	19	0	25
35. Cross	NYG	12	0	2	2	12	0	150	150	11	0	23
36. Sloan	DET	11	0	0	0	0	0	264	264	22	0	22
37. Purnell	NE	4	0	3	3	18	0	57	57	4	0	22
38. Jenkins	WASH	4	0	3	3	18	0	43	43	3	0	21
39. LaFleur +	DALL	9	0	2	2	12	0	122	122	8	0	20
40. I. Smith	NO	9	0	1	1	6	0	180	180	14	0	20
41. J. Johnson	PHIL	7	0	1	1	6	0	177	177	14	0	20
42. Dunn	PHIL	7	0	2	2	12	0	93	93	7	0	19
43. D. Jones +	JAC	3	0	2	2	12	0	87	87	7	0	19
44. Battaglia	CIN	9	0	1	1	6	0	149	149	11	0	17
45. Hallock	JAC	13	0	1	1	6	21	131	152	10	0	16
46. Thomason	GB	4	0	1	1	6	0	115	115	10	0	16
47. Roan	TENN	6	0	0	0	0	0	159	159	14	0	14
48. Clark +	SF	5	0	1	1	6	0	96	96	8	0	14
49. T. Davis	GB	2	0	1	2	12	0	28	28	2	0	14
50. Kinchen	BALT	7	0	1	1	6	0	95	95	7	0	13
51. Kozlowski	ATL	5	0	1	1	6	0	99	99	7	0	13
52. Jennings	CHI	10	0	0	0	0	0	164	164	12	0	12
53. Carswell	DEN	8	0	1	1	6	0	96	96	6	0	12
54. Brown	JAC	6	0	1	1	6	0	84	84	6	0	12
55. Pollard	IND	6	0	0	0	2	0	116	116	9	2	11
56. West	ATL	6	0	1	1	6	0	63	63	4	0	10
57. Metzelaars	DET	11	0	0	0	0	0	144	144	9	0	9
58. Carter	ARIZ	6	0	1	1	6	0	44	44	2	0	8
59. Perry +	MIA	6	0	1	1	6	0	45	45	2	0	8
60. Chryplewicz +	DET	2	0	1	1	6	0	27	27	2	0	8
61. Fauria	SEAT	7	0	0	0	0	0	110	110	7	0	7

1997 STATISTICAL RESULTS
(TIGHT ENDS — COMBINED BASIC/PERFORMANCE
SCORING METHOD)

NAME	TEAM	GP	RSH TDs	REC TDs	TOTAL TDs	BASIC PTS	RSH YARDS	REC YARDS	TOTAL YARDS	PERF PTS	CONV PTS	FAN-TASY PTS
62. Laing	STL	5	0	1	1	6	0	31	31	1	0	7
63. Hape +	TB	5	0	1	1	6	1	22	23	1	0	7
64. Fann	SF	2	0	0	0	0	0	78	78	7	0	7
65. McWilliams	ARIZ	4	0	0	0	0	0	75	75	6	0	6
66. Delong	MINN	7	0	0	0	0	0	75	75	5	0	5
67. Mangum +	CAR	1	0	0	0	0	0	56	56	5	0	5
68. Walker	KC	5	0	0	0	0	0	60	60	4	0	4
69. Goodwin	MINN	5	0	0	0	0	0	61	61	4	0	4
70. Allred +	CHI	7	0	0	0	0	0	70	70	3	0	3
71. J. Davis	TB	3	0	0	0	0	0	35	35	2	0	2
72. Lyons	PITT	2	0	0	0	0	0	29	29	2	0	2
73. May	SEAT	2	0	0	0	0	0	21	21	2	0	2
74. Cline	BUF	1	0	0	0	0	0	29	29	2	0	2
75. Pierce	NYG	8	0	0	0	0	0	47	47	1	0	1
76. Galbraith	DALL	2	0	0	0	0	0	16	16	1	0	1
77. Slutzker	IND	2	0	0	0	0	0	22	22	1	0	1
78. Jacoby	STL	2	0	0	0	0	0	10	10	1	0	1
79. Chamberlain	DEN	1	0	0	0	0	0	18	18	1	0	1
80. T. Johnson	NO	1	0	0	0	0	0	13	13	1	0	1
81. Savoie +	NO	1	0	0	0	0	0	14	14	1	0	1
82. Botkin	PITT	1	0	0	0	0	0	11	11	1	0	1
83. Sadowski	PITT	1	0	0	0	0	0	12	12	1	0	1
84. S. Mitchell	SD	1	0	0	0	0	0	14	14	1	0	1
85. E. Smith	ATL	1	0	0	0	0	0	2	2	0	0	0
86. Rasby	CAR	1	0	0	0	0	0	1	1	0	0	0
87. Allen	CHI	1	0	0	0	0	0	9	9	0	0	0
88. Pupunu	SD	1	0	0	0	0	0	7	7	0	0	0
89. Jordan	TB	1	0	0	0	0	0	0	0	0	0	0
90. R. Lewis	TENN	1	0	0	0	0	0	7	7	0	0	0

+ DENOTE COLLEGE DRAFT PICK

RATING THE PLAYERS FOR 1998
(Tight Ends—Combined Basic/Performance Scoring Method)

GRAB ONE IF YOU CAN

☐ **1. Shannon Sharpe (Denver Broncos)**
Sharpe surpassed the 1,000-yard mark for the second straight season in 1997. His touchdown numbers, however, dropped from 10 in 1996 to three last season. Any tight end who sees the ball often enough to top the 1,000-yard mark for two straight seasons has to be a prime fantasy pick.

☐ **2. Ben Coates (New England Patriots)**
Coates has neared the 10-touchdown mark for each of the last two seasons, scoring nine and eight times. During those two years, he produced 682 and 737 receiving yards, respectively. As a prime target for Drew Bledsoe, Coates will continue to put up good numbers.

☐ **3. Wesley Walls (Carolina Panthers)**
In the two years since he came to Carolina, Walls has produced more than 700 yards in each season and scored 10 and 6 touchdowns, respectively. I look for another 700-plus yard, 6 to 10 touchdown season in 1998.

☐ **4. Ricky Dudley (Oakland Raiders)**
After producing only 386 yards and four touchdowns as a rookie in 1996, Dudley climbed to 787 yards and seven touchdowns in 1997, aided by the arrival of quarterback Jeff George. With George in his second season as a Raider in 1998, Dudley should again post good numbers.

☐ **5. Frank Wycheck (Tennessee Oilers)**
Wycheck's yardage numbers continue to climb. He produced 471, 511 and 748 yards, respectively, in the last three seasons. After scoring only twice in 1995, Wycheck has scored six and four touchdowns in the two years since. Certainly he's become a main ingredient in the Oiler offense, which should help him produce good numbers.

BEST OF THE REST

☐ **6. Troy Drayton (Miami Dolphins)**
After becoming more involved with the Dolphins' offense in 1997, Drayton produced 558 receiving yards and four touchdowns. Those numbers could climb in 1998 as he becomes more of a factor for the Dolphins.

☐ **7. Mark Chmura (Green Bay Packers)**
In recapturing his starting role in 1997 after the retirement of Keith Jackson, Chmura recorded 417 receiving yards and six touchdowns. Two years earlier, he had produced 679 receiving yards and seven touchdowns, giving us a further idea of what he's capable of as a prime target for Brett Favre.

☐ **8. Tony McGee (Cincinnati Bengals)**
He's had good yardage and touchdown numbers in recent years. McGee has recorded 754, 464 and 414 receiving yards, along with four,

four and six touchdowns, respectively, in the last three seasons. His numbers will continue to draw fantasy interest in 1998.

☐ **9. Eric Green (Baltimore Ravens)**
Staying healthy for pretty much all of 1997, Green rebounded to 601 receiving yards and five touchdowns. One drawback in 1998, however, may be the arrival of Jim Harbaugh. He's likely to throw less than Vinny Testaverde and Eric Zeier did.

☐ **10. Jamie Asher (Washington Redskins)**
Asher scored four times and tallied 474 receiving yards on 42 receptions in 1996. He scored only once but tallied 481 receiving yards on 49 receptions in 1997. I look for his touchdown numbers to rebound in 1998 as he again tops the 40-reception mark.

STRONG LONG SHOTS

☐ **11. Erric Conwell (St. Louis Rams)**
After becoming more involved in the Ram offense, Conwell scored four times in 1997 on 38 receptions while producing 404 receiving yards. Conwell will again be a force in the Rams' offense in 1998, providing more decent numbers.

☐ **12. Pete Mitchell (Jacksonville Jaguars)**
Mitchell's yardage numbers dropped to 380 in 1997, after he had produced 575 and 527 the previous two seasons. Mitchell did, however, increase his touchdowns to four. I look for a 400-plus yard season and for Mitchell to again reach or top the four-touchdown mark in 1998.

☐ **13. Eric Bjornson (Dallas Cowboys)**
With Jay Novacek retired, Bjornson stepped in to produce 442 receiving yards but no touchdowns in 1997. I look for his continued involvement in the Cowboy passing game in 1997 and for Bjornson to begin finding his way into the end zone.

☐ **14. Ken Dilger (Indianapolis Colts)**
After recording 635 and 503 receiving yards, respectively, in 1995 and 1996 and scoring four times in each of those two seasons, Dilger's numbers took a drop in 1997. A hamstring injury forced Dilger to miss three games, which resulted in only 380 receiving yards and three scores. We do know, however, how he can perform when healthy.

☐ **15. Fred Jones (San Diego Chargers)**
As a rookie in 1997, Jones stepped right in to record 43 receptions for 505 yards and two touchdowns. His only drawback in 1998 may be uncertainty about who his quarterback will be.

HAVE THE POTENTIAL

☐ **16. Tony Gonzalez (Kansas City Chiefs)**
The Chiefs' No.1 draft pick of a year ago is only going to get better. As a rookie in 1997, Gonzalez produced 368 receiving yards on 33 receptions while scoring only twice. I believe he'll easily improve on those numbers in 1998.

☐ **17. Greg Clark (San Francisco 49ers)**
Although he hasn't shown much, the 49ers like Clark and somebody has to step in for the retired Brent Jones. Still, he will have to contend with new acquisition Irv Smith.

☐ **18. Ryan Wetnight (Chicago Bears)**
Wetnight expanded his role and his numbers in 1997, recording 46 receptions for 464 yards but only one score. Those are numbers he'll work to improve in 1998.

☐ **19. O.J. Santiago (Atlanta Falcons)**
The Falcons' third-round pick of a year ago, O.J. Santiago tallied 217 receiving yards and two touchdowns on just 17 receptions. His low numbers were partially due to a leg injury that forced him to miss the last five games on the year. If he's healthy for all of 1998, he should produce significant numbers.

☐ **20. Chris Gedney (Arizona Cardinals)**
After joining to the Cardinals in 1997, Gedney scored four times on just 23 receptions while producing 261 receiving yards. Those numbers could improve in 1998 if young quarterback Jake Plummer does.

KEEP AN EYE ON

21. I. Smith (SF)
22. Moore (TB)
23. Sloan (DET)
24. LaFleur (DALL)
25. Bruener (PITT)
26. Popson (KC)
27. Farguhar (NO)
28. Glover (MINN)
29. Harris (TENN)
30. Williams (OAK)

YOU NEVER KNOW

31. L. Johnson (BUF)
32. Crumpler (SEAT)
33. Brady (NYJ)
34. Cross (NYG)
35. Metzelaars (DET)
36. Baxter (NYJ)
37. Fauria (SEAT)
38. Jennings (CHI)
39. Battaglia (CIN)
40. J. Johnson (PHIL)

WORTH MENTIONING

41. Pupuna (NYG)
42. C. Lewis (PHIL)
43. Metzelaars (DET)
44. Hartley (SD)
45. Riesmersma (BUF)

ROOKIE PROSPECTS

NAME	TEAM	COMMENT
☐ 1. Cameron Cleeland	NO	Irv Smith's departure to S.F. creates opportunity.
☐ 2. Alonzo Mayes	CHI	Nice size and good downfield ability.
☐ 3. Stephen Alexander	WASH	Decent hands and good jumping ability.
☐ 4. Rod Rutledge	NE	Will have trouble pushing Ben Coates for production.

A LOOK AT THE QUARTERBACKS
(A Guide for the Beginner)
Considerations in Choosing a Quarterback

1. First, look at players' previous performances. Don't overlook players who may have missed portions of the previous year because of injuries, holdouts, and the like. Brad Johnson, Mark Brunell, and Gus Frerotte were all affected in 1997 by injuries.

2. Look for quarterbacks who will give you decent rushing yardage on top of significant passing numbers. They'll occasionally provide a valuable rushing touchdown, as well. Steve Young is always a good consideration when talking of a quarterback who can opt to run but so is Kordell Stewart of Pittsburgh.

3. Look for a quarterback who plays for a predominantly passing team— one who has a chance to throw for over 4,000 yards and close to 30 touchdowns. Brett Favre quickly comes to mind.

4. Stay away from quarterbacks who are not guaranteed a starting assignment week after week. Some teams use one quarterback one week and then switch to another the following week, depending on the players' performances. Such was the case in Arizona in 1997. Quarterbacks in that situation are risky draft choices in fantasy football.

5. Stay away from teams that like to grind it out on the ground. These teams' quarterbacks have little chance of putting together big statistical seasons.

In the 1997 statistics that follow, players are ranked by their fantasy-point totals. Remember that the Combined Basic/Performance Scoring Method awards six points for every touchdown scored, three points for every touchdown pass thrown, one point for every 10 yards rushing, one point for every 10 yards receiving, and one point for every 20 yards passing.

1997 STATISTICAL RESULTS
(QUARTERBACKS — COMBINED BASIC/PERFORMANCE SCORING METHOD)

NAME	TEAM	GP	RSH TDs	PASS TDs	BASIC PTS	RSH YARDS	PS YARDS	PERF PTS	CONV PTS	FANTASY POINTS
1. Stewart	PITT	16	11	21	130	476	3,020	184	1	314
1996		16	5	0	48	171	100	43	0	91
1995		-	-	-	-	-	-	-	-	-
3 Yr - TOTALS		32	16	21	178	647	3,120	227	1	405
2. Favre	GB	16	1	35	112	187	3,867	199	1	311
1996		16	2	39	131	136	3,899	197	2	328
1995		16	3	38	132	181	4,413	225	0	357
3 Yr - TOTALS		48	6	112	375	504	12,179	621	3	996
3. Elway	DEN	16	1	27	88	218	3,635	193	1	281
1996		15	4	26	102	249	3,328	181	0	283
1995		16	1	26	87	176	3,970	204	3	291
3 Yr - TOTALS		47	6	79	277	643	10,933	578	4	855
4. McNair	TENN	16	8	14	91	674	2,665	189	1	280
1996		9	2	6	30	169	1,197	69	0	99
1995		4	0	3	9	38	569	30	0	39
3 Yr - TOTALS		29	10	23	130	881	4,431	288	1	418
5. George	OAK	16	0	29	89	45	3,917	190	2	279
1996 w/ATL		3	0	3	9	10	698	33	0	42
1995 w/ATL		16	0	24	75	17	4,143	200	3	275
3 Yr - TOTALS		35	0	56	173	72	8,758	423	5	596
6. Bledsoe	NE	16	0	28	84	55	3,706	181	0	265
1996		16	0	27	85	27	4,086	198	4	283
1995		15	0	13	41	28	3,507	171	2	212
3 Yr - TOTALS		47	0	68	210	110	11,299	550	6	760
7. Moon	SEAT	15	1	25	81	40	3,678	180	0	261
1996 w/MINN		8	0	7	21	6	1,610	76	0	97
1995 w/MINN		16	0	33	99	82	4,228	208	0	307
3 Yr - TOTALS		39	1	65	201	128	9,516	464	0	665
8. Brunell	JAC	14	2	18	67	257	3,281	176	1	243
1996		16	3	19	82	400	4,367	243	7	325
1995		13	4	15	70	480	2,168	144	1	214
3 Yr - TOTALS		43	9	52	219	1,137	9,816	563	9	782
9. Mitchell	DET	16	1	19	64	83	3,484	172	1	236
1996		14	4	17	75	83	2,917	144	0	219
1995		16	4	32	121	104	4,338	215	1	336
3 Yr - TOTALS		46	9	68	260	270	10,739	531	2	791
10. Young	SF	15	3	19	75	199	3,029	160	0	235
1996		12	4	14	68	310	2,410	139	2	207
1995		11	3	20	78	250	3,200	178	0	256
3 Yr - TOTALS		38	10	53	221	759	8,639	477	2	698
11. Marino	MIA	16	0	16	48	-14	3,780	181	0	229
1996		13	0	17	51	-3	2,795	133	0	184
1995		14	0	24	74	14	3,668	177	2	251
3 Yr - TOTALS		43	0	57	173	-3	10,243	491	2	664
12. B. Johnson ***	MINN	13	0	20	72	139	3,036	161	6	227
1996		12	1	17	59	90	2,258	111	2	170
1995		5	0	0	0	-9	272	11	0	11
3 Yr - TOTALS		30	1	37	131	220	5,566	283	8	408
13. Aikman	DALL	16	0	19	59	79	3,283	160	2	219
1996		15	1	12	44	42	3,126	151	2	195
1995		16	1	16	55	32	3,304	160	1	215
3 Yr - TOTALS		47	2	47	158	153	9,713	471	5	629
14. Banks	STL	16	1	14	48	187	3,254	169	0	217
1996		14	0	15	47	212	2,544	138	2	185
1995		-	-	-	-	-	-	-	-	-
3 Yr - TOTALS		30	1	29	95	399	5,798	307	2	402
15. Testaverde	BALT	13	0	18	56	138	2,971	154	2	210
1996		16	2	33	116	188	4,177	214	5	330
1995		13	2	17	63	62	2,883	141	0	204
3 Yr - TOTALS		42	4	68	235	388	10,031	509	7	744

1997 STATISTICAL RESULTS
(QUARTERBACKS — COMBINED BASIC/PERFORMANCE
SCORING METHOD)

	NAME	TEAM	GP	RSH TDs	PASS TDs	BASIC PTS	RSH YARDS	PS YARDS	PERF PTS	CONV PTS	FANTASY POINTS
16.	Kramer	CHI	15	2	14	56	83	3,011	148	2	204
	1996		4	0	3	9	4	781	37	0	46
	1995		16	1	29	93	39	3,838	186	0	279
	3 Yr - TOTALS		35	3	46	158	126	7,630	371	2	529
17.	Chandler	ATL	14	0	20	60	158	2,692	138	0	198
	1996 w/HOUS		12	0	16	48	113	2,099	104	0	152
	1995 w/HOUS		13	2	17	65	57	2,460	120	2	185
	3 Yr - TOTALS		39	2	53	173	328	7,251	362	2	535
18.	Dilfer	TB	16	1	21	69	99	2,555	125	0	194
	1996		16	0	12	37	124	2,859	142	1	179
	1995		16	2	4	24	115	2,774	140	0	164
	3 Yr - TOTALS		48	3	37	130	338	8,188	407	1	537
19.	O'Donnell	NYJ	15	1	17	57	36	2,796	136	0	193
	1996		6	0	4	12	30	1,147	55	0	67
	1995 w/PITT		12	0	17	51	45	2,970	146	0	197
	3 Yr - TOTALS		33	1	38	120	111	6,913	337	0	457
20.	Frerotte	WASH	13	2	17	63	53	2,682	130	0	193
	1996		16	0	12	36	27	3,453	164	0	200
	1995		13	1	13	45	11	2,751	133	0	178
	3 Yr - TOTALS		42	3	42	144	91	8,886	427	0	571
21.	Plummer +	ARIZ	10	2	15	59	216	2,203	120	2	179
	1996		-	-	-	-	-	-	-	-	-
	1995		-	-	-	-	-	-	-	-	-
	3 Yr - TOTALS		10	2	15	59	216	2,203	120	2	179
22.	Blake	CIN	11	3	8	43	235	2,125	119	1	162
	1996		16	2	24	85	313	3,624	198	1	283
	1995		16	2	28	98	309	3,822	207	2	305
	3 Yr - TOTALS		43	7	60	226	857	9,571	524	4	750
23.	T. Collins	BUF	14	0	12	36	77	2,367	115	0	151
	1996		7	0	4	12	43	739	39	0	51
	1995		7	0	0	0	23	112	4	0	4
	3 Yr - TOTALS		28	0	16	48	143	3,218	158	0	206
24.	K. Collins	CAR	13	1	11	40	54	2,124	104	1	144
	1996		13	0	14	44	38	2,454	119	2	163
	1995		15	3	14	62	74	2,717	133	2	195
	3 Yr - TOTALS		41	4	39	146	166	7,295	356	5	502
25.	Grbac	KC	10	1	11	41	168	1,943	103	2	144
	1996 w/SF		10	2	8	36	21	1,236	60	0	96
	1995 w/SF		9	2	8	37	33	1,469	72	1	109
	3 Yr - TOTALS		29	5	27	114	222	4,648	235	3	349
26.	Harbaugh	IND	12	0	10	31	206	2,060	112	1	143
	1996		14	1	13	45	192	2,630	139	0	184
	1995		15	2	17	65	235	2,575	141	2	206
	3 Yr - TOTALS		41	3	40	141	633	7,265	392	3	533
27.	Kanell	NYG	12	0	11	33	10	1,740	82	0	115
	1996		4	0	1	3	6	227	11	0	14
	1995		-	-	-	-	-	-	-	-	-
	3 Yr - TOTALS		16	0	12	36	16	1,967	93	0	129
28.	Hoying +	PHIL	7	0	11	34	78	1,573	81	1	115
	1996		-	-	-	-	-	-	-	-	-
	1995		-	-	-	-	-	-	-	-	-
	3 Yr - TOTALS		7	0	11	34	78	1,573	81	1	115
29.	Esiason	CIN	7	0	13	39	11	1,478	71	0	110
	1996 w/ARIZ		10	1	11	41	52	2,293	114	2	155
	1995 w/NYJ		12	0	16	48	13	2,275	108	0	156
	3 Yr - TOTALS		29	1	40	128	76	6,046	293	2	421
30.	Detmer	PHIL	8	1	7	27	46	1,567	77	0	104
	1996		13	1	15	51	59	2,911	143	0	194
	1995 w/GB		3	0	1	4	3	81	4	1	8
	3 Yr - TOTALS		24	2	23	82	108	4,559	224	1	306

1997 STATISTICAL RESULTS
(QUARTERBACKS — COMBINED BASIC/PERFORMANCE SCORING METHOD)

	NAME	TEAM	GP	RSH TDs	PASS TDs	BASIC PTS	RSH YARDS	PS YARDS	PERF PTS	CONV PTS	FANTASY POINTS
31.	Gannon	KC	9	2	7	33	120	1,144	64	0	97
32.	Graham	ARIZ	8	2	4	26	23	1,408	66	2	92
33.	Humphries	SD	8	0	5	15	24	1,488	71	0	86
34.	Whelihan	SD	9	0	6	18	29	1,357	64	0	82
35.	Shuler	NO	10	1	2	13	38	1,288	61	1	74
36.	Brown	NYG	7	1	5	22	31	1,023	50	1	72
37.	Beuerlein	CAR	7	0	6	18	32	1,032	50	0	68
38.	Hobert **	NO	6	0	6	18	43	1,024	50	0	68
39.	Justin	IND	8	0	5	17	2	1,046	51	2	68
40.	Zeier	BALT	5	0	7	21	15	958	47	0	68
41.	Hostetler	WASH	6	0	5	15	27	899	44	0	59
42.	Peete	PHIL	5	0	4	12	37	869	43	0	55
43.	Cunningham	MINN	4	0	6	19	127	501	34	1	53
44.	Tolliver **	KC	7	0	5	15	7	677	33	0	48
45.	Van Pelt	BUF	6	1	2	14	33	684	32	2	46
46.	Foley	NYJ	4	0	3	9	-5	705	34	0	43
47.	Wuerffel +	NO	6	0	4	12	26	518	24	0	36
48.	R. Johnson	JAC	5	1	2	12	34	344	19	0	31
49.	Mirer	CHI	7	1	0	8	78	420	22	2	30
50.	Kitna	SEAT	3	1	1	9	9	371	19	0	28
51.	Everett	SD	4	0	1	3	6	457	22	0	25
52.	Holcomb	IND	4	0	1	4	5	454	21	1	25
53.	Case	ARIZ	2	1	0	6	8	316	15	0	21
54.	Druckenmiller +	SF	4	0	1	4	-2	239	11	1	15
55.	St. Matthews	JAC	2	0	0	0	10	275	14	0	14
56.	Rypien	STL	4	0	0	0	1	270	12	0	12
57.	Tomczak	PITT	5	0	1	3	13	185	9	0	12
58.	Nussmeier	NO	3	0	0	0	30	182	10	0	10
59.	Erickson	MIA	2	0	0	0	8	165	8	0	8
60.	Zolak	NE	4	0	2	6	-3	67	2	0	8
61.	Brohm	SF	5	0	0	0	11	164	7	0	7
62.	Philcox	SD	2	0	0	0	3	173	7	0	7
63.	Friesz	SEAT	2	0	0	0	0	138	5	0	5
64.	Reich	DET	4	0	0	0	-4	121	5	0	5
65.	Wilson	DALL	6	0	0	0	-2	115	5	0	5
66.	Lucas	NYJ	1	0	0	0	30	28	4	0	4
67.	Brister	DEN	1	0	0	0	2	48	2	0	2
68.	Garrett	DALL	1	0	0	0	0	56	2	0	2
69.	Graziani +	ATL	2	0	0	0	19	41	2	0	2
70.	Stenstrom	CHI	3	0	0	0	6	70	2	0	2
71.	Walsh	TB	5	0	0	0	-9	58	2	0	2
72.	Bono	GB	2	0	0	0	-3	29	1	0	1
73.	Klingler	OAK	1	0	0	0	0	27	1	0	1
74.	Lewis	DEN	3	0	0	0	2	21	1	0	1
75.	Blundin	DET	1	0	0	0	0	0	0	0	0
76.	Cherry +	NYG	1	0	0	0	-2	0	0	0	0
77.	Clements +	NYJ	1	0	0	0	-3	0	0	0	0
78.	Green	WASH	1	0	0	0	0	0	0	0	0
79.	Krieg	TENN	3	0	0	0	-2	2	0	0	0
80.	Pederson	GB	1	0	0	0	-4	10	0	0	0
81.	Quinn	PITT	1	0	0	0	0	10	0	0	0
82.	Ritchey	TENN	1	0	0	0	6	15	0	0	0

+   DENOTES COLLEGE DRAFT PICK
**   Hobert   NO   Played in 1 game with Buffalo.
**   Tolliver   KC   Played in 6 games with Atlanta.
***   B. Johnson   MINN   Scored TD on a 3 yard reception.

RATING THE PLAYERS FOR 1998
(Quarterbacks—Combined Basic/Performance Scoring Method)

GRAB ONE IF YOU CAN

☐ **1. Brett Favre (Green Bay Packers)**
Favre has thrown for more than 30 touchdowns for four straight seasons and 3,882, 4,413, 2,899 and 3,867 yards, respectively, during that span. His consistency is unmatched and keeps him as a prime fantasy pick again in 1998.

☐ **2. Kordell Stewart (Pittsburgh Steelers)**
Combining the ability to run well with the ball as well as throw, Stewart put together solid numbers in his first year as a starter in 1997. Stewart threw for 3,020 yards and 21 touchdowns while rushing for 476 yards and a whopping 11 rushing touchdowns. He'll continue to mature and improve in 1998, but Pittsburgh faces the league's toughest schedule.

☐ **3. Jeff George (Oakland Raiders)**
In his first year with the Raiders, George threw for just under 4,000 yards and just under 30 touchdowns, and I mean just under. George finished with 3,917 passing yards and 29 touchdown passes. Looks like he's found a team and an offense that fits him perfectly.

☐ **4. John Elway (Denver Broncos)**
For the last three seasons, Elway has been a consistent fantasy performer. He has thrown for 26, 26, and 27 touchdowns, respectively, and 3,970, 3,328 and 3,635 yards during that same period. I believe he'll again reach that level in 1998.

☐ **5. Steve Young (San Francisco 49ers)**
Injuries have adversely affected Young's performance in the last three seasons, including in 1997 when he threw for only 3,029 yards and 19 touchdowns. He was also without standout Jerry Rice for virtually the entire year because of Rice's injury. If Young is healthy, along with Rice, the 3,500 to 4,000 yard and 25 to 30 touchdown range are well within reach.

BEST OF THE REST

☐ **6. Drew Bledsoe (New England Patriots)**
Bledsoe had back-to-back productive seasons in 1996 and 1997, producing 4,086 and 3,706 passing yards along with 27 and 28 touchdowns, respectively. I believe he's become one of the league's more consistent quarterbacks, and I look for another 25 to 30 touchdowns and near 4,000-plus yards in 1998.

☐ **7. Scott Mitchell (Detroit Lions)**
In 1995, Mitchell recorded a whopping 4,338 passing yards and 32 touchdown passes. His performance has been on the downswing ever since. With Barry Sanders's huge numbers in 1997, Mitchell recorded a respectable 3,484 passing yards but only 19 touchdowns. As teams try to stop Barry Sanders in 1998, look for Mitchell's numbers to rebound.

☐ **8. Steve McNair (Tennessee Oilers)**
McNair was finally given the starting quarterback spot in 1997. He threw for only 2,665 yards and 14 touchdowns but was also quite a weapon on the ground, rushing for 674 yards and eight touchdowns. It's his ability to run that will again make him an attractive fantasy pick in 1998.

☐ **9. Warren Moon (Seattle Seahawks)**
Moon's plans to stand on the sidelines while backing up John Friesz in 1997 came to a quick end. Friesz injured his thumb in the season opener and in stepped Moon. Moon threw for 3,678 yards and 25 touchdowns. Moon played so well that the Seahawks ignored his age and will go to him again in 1998.

☐ **10. Brad Johnson (Minnesota Vikings)**
Despite missing three games with a herniated disc in his neck to end the season, Johnson finished 1997 with 3,036 passing yards and 20 touchdowns. If he's healthy in 1998, expect Johnson to push the 3,500-yard, 25-touchdown range.

STRONG LONG SHOTS

☐ **11. Mark Brunell (Jacksonville Jaguars)**
In 1997, Brunell missed the first two games of the year with a knee injury and threw for only 3,281 passing yards and 18 touchdowns. A year earlier, Brunell had thrown for 4,367 yards and 19 touchdowns. If he's healthy for all of 1998, I look for the 3,500 to 4,000-yard and 20-touchdown range.

☐ **12. Jake Plummer (Arizona Cardinals)**
Plummer took over the starting chores a short way into the 1997 season and finished with 2,203 passing yards and 15 touchdowns after playing in 10 games. It'll be interesting to see what he can do over a full season as he continues to improve.

☐ **13. Jeff Blake (Cincinnati Bengals)**
Blake lost his starting job in 1997 to Boomer Esiason, but gets it back since Esiason retired in the offseason. It'll be interesting to see if Blake can regain his confidence and get back on track. In 1995 and 1996, Blake played well and recorded 3,822 and 3,624 passing yards along with 28 and 24 touchdowns, respectively.

☐ **14. Chris Chandler (Atlanta Falcons)**
In his first year as the Falcons' starter, Chandler missed two games with chest and head injuries He finished with 2,692 passing yards and 20 touchdowns. If he stays healthy for all of 1998, I expect him to surpass the 3,000-yard mark and near the 25-touchdown range, though losing Bert Emanuel to Tampa Bay will hurt.

☐ **15. Erik Kramer (Chicago Bears)**
Kramer surprised many by returning from back problems to recapture his starting role in 1998. However, he was not nearly as effective as he had been in 1995 when he threw for 3,838 yards and 29 touchdowns. In 1997, he finished with 3,011 passing yards and only 14 touchdowns but remember, he did not have his best receiver, Curtis Conway, who was

hurt for most of the year. Kramer and the Bears hope to regroup in 1998 but they face the league's second-toughest schedule.

HAVE THE POTENTIAL

☐ **16. Bobby Hoying (Philadelphia Eagles)**
Hoying got his chance at the starting job in 1998 and took full advantage, producing 1,573 passing yards and 11 touchdowns in just seven games. This has fantasy fans very curious about how he'll fare over a full 16 games.

☐ **17. Tony Banks (St. Louis Rams)**
After a fairly impressive rookie season in 1996, perhaps more was expected out of Banks in 1997 than should have been. He had to start the year without star receiver Isaac Bruce, who was hurt for the first five weeks. Banks finished with 3,254 passing yards and only 14 touchdown passes. He hopes to improve those numbers in 1998 with a healthy Bruce all year.

☐ **18. Elvis Grbac (Kansas City Chiefs)**
Stepping in as the Chiefs' starter in 1997, Grbac only saw action in 10 games because of a shoulder injury. He finished with only 1,943 passing yards and 11 touchdowns. He'll easily improve on those numbers in 1998, if he's healthy all year, since the Chiefs have added Derrick Alexander to their receiving corps.

☐ **19. Dan Marino (Miami Dolphins)**
Marino's numbers are certainly not as impressive as they were in his younger years. In 1997, Marino's 3,780 passing yards weren't bad but his lowly 16 touchdown passes were. I still look for another 3,500 to 4,000-yard performance in 1998, along with nearing or topping the 20-touchdown mark, since the Dolphins face a fairly easy schedule.

☐ **20. Gus Frerotte (Washington Redskins)**
Despite missing three games with a hip injury in 1997, Frerotte recorded 2,682 passing yards and 17 touchdown passes. If he's healthy in 1998, 3,000 yards and 20 touchdowns are possible.

KEEP AN EYE ON

☐ **21. Troy Aikman (Dallas Cowboys)**
Surprisingly, despite his fame, Troy Aikman is not a great statistical player. He's normally in the 3,000-yard range (3,304, 3,126 and 3,283 yards the last three seasons) and usually far short of 20 touchdowns, though he threw for 19 a year ago.

☐ **22. Trent Dilfer (Tampa Bay Buccaneers)**
Under new head coach Tony Dungy, Dilfer's confidence continues to grow, as evidenced by the rise in his touchdown pass production to 21 in 1997.

☐ **23. Jim Harbaugh (Baltimore Ravens)**
Harbaugh's never really been a big statistical success, but perhaps he can expand his numbers in Baltimore.

- [ ] **24. Glenn Foley/Neil O'Donnell (New York Jets)**
  Regardless of the starter, Bill Parcells likes a conservative offense.

- [ ] **25. Rob Johnson/Doug Flutie/Todd Collins (Buffalo Bills)**
  There's no Jim Kelly in this group.

- [ ] **26. Ryan Leaf/Craig Whelihan (San Diego Chargers)**
  He's a young quarterback with little time to learn.

- [ ] **27. Peyton Manning (Indianapolis Colts)**
  Success is not likely immediately.

- [ ] **28. Danny Kanell (New York Giants)**
  He's won the starting job but I don't see big numbers in store for him in 1998.

- [ ] **29. Kerry Collins (Carolina Panthers)**
  Collins is not an impressive statistical success because the Panthers like to run the football.

- [ ] **30. Billy Joe Hobert (New Orleans Saints)**
  The Saints' quarterback situation scares me.

ROOKIE PROSPECTS

NAME	TEAM	COMMENT
[ ] 1. Peyton Manning	IND	Losing ain't so bad, Colts got their future QB by doing so.
[ ] 2. Ryan Leaf	SD	Lots of talent, good leader on field.
[ ] 3. Charlie Batch	DET	Future potential only.
[ ] 4. John Quinn	JAC	Future potential only.
[ ] 5. Brian Griese	DEN	Future potential only.

A LOOK AT THE KICKERS

(A Guide for the Beginner)

Considerations in Choosing a Kicker

The scoring for kickers is identical in both the Basic Scoring Method and the Combined Basic/Performance Scoring Method. (See the section on Kickers for the Basic Scoring Method.)

A 1998 QUICK PICKS—MOCK DRAFT
(Top "30" Picks for Combined Basic/Performance Scoring Method)

	NAME	TEAM	POS	COMMENTS
1.	Favre	GB	QB	4,000 passing yards, 30-plus TD passes are norm.
2.	Stewart	PITT	QB	His ability to run for yards and scores makes him a solid fantasy choice.
3.	Davis	DEN	RB	Should near 1,800-2,000 yards range and 15 TD marks.
4.	Sanders	DET	RB	2,000 yards and 12-plus TDs very possible.
5.	George	OAK	QB	Just shy of 4,000 yards and 30 TDs in 1st year as a Raider.
6.	Levens	GB	RB	As Packers' main back, yards and scoring are plentiful.
7.	Watters	SEAT	RB	Taking his services to Seattle should re-ignite fire.
8.	Bettis	PITT	RB	Two very productive years in Pittsburgh going on three.
9.	Elway	DEN	QB	Closing his career with excellent statistical success.
10.	Dillon	CIN	RB	Came on as rookie to explode over last half of '97. 1998 potential looks bright.
11.	Martin	NYJ	RB	Should produce well for Jets in '98, if stays healthy.
12.	Freeman	GB	WR	Favre's favorite could see 1,500 yards and 12 TDs.
13.	Kaufman	OAK	RB	Raiders have found an every-down back.
14.	Young	SF	QB	If he and Rice stay healthy, should see big numbers in '98.
15.	Rice	SF	WR	When healthy is consistent performer.
16.	Allen	WASH	RB	Injured much of 1997, 1,500 yards and 21 TDs a year earlier.
17.	Smith	MINN	RB	When healthy, one of league's most explosive backs.
18.	Moore	DET	WR	More from Moore if Mitchell rebounds in 1998.
19.	Pickens	CIN	WR	Needs Blake to be "Picken" apart defenses again.
20.	Bledsoe	NE	QB	Back-to-back solid years for maturing Bledsoe.
21.	Hearst	SF	RB	49ers have finally found themselves an every-down back.
22.	George	TENN	RB	Plenty of yards first-two seasons, needs to score more.
23.	Mitchell	DET	QB	Needs to rebound from very disappointing 1997.
24.	Smith	DALL	RB	Smith and Cowboys continue to fall. Can they regroup? Don't count Smith out!
25.	McNair	TENN	QB	Ability to run and addition of Thigpen are most attractive fantasy traits.
26.	Faulk	IND	RB	Rebounded some in 1997. In 1998 may be asked to run more due to young QB.
27.	Moon	SEAT	QB	Stepped up in 1997 to show plenty zip left in aging arm.
28.	Irvin	DALL	WR	1,500 yards and 10 TD's possible.
29.	Abdul-Jabbar	MIA	RB	Yardage numbers down but scored 16 in 1997.
30.	Dunn	TB	RB	Youngster who will continue to find ways to get it "Dunn."

This Mock Draft is expanded and updated in *Cliff's Quick Picks: Fantasy Football Draft at a Glance*—a huge cheatsheet that examines the top-100 over-all picks for the Basic and Combined Basic/Performance methods. Potential draft picks are also broken down by fantasy position, including the *top-50* running backs and wide receivers, and the *top-25* tight ends, quarterbacks and kickers. *Cliff's Quick Picks* will be available in mid-August, right around your fantasy draft time. Be sure to order! Details and order form, along with a toll-free phone number, appear on the hard insert in the middle of this book.

X
RATING THE PLAYERS:
DISTANCE SCORING METHOD

Let's review how scoring is done using the Distance Scoring Method. As in the Basic Scoring Method, points are awarded for touchdowns scored by players on offense. The difference between this method and the Basic Scoring Method is that in the Distance Scoring Method, the yardage covered on the touchdown play is used to calculate the points awarded—the longer the touchdown, the more points awarded. This scoring method favors exciting touchdowns and rewards players for the yardage they cover on the play.

The Distance Scoring Method presents unique challenges for your draft selection. It's difficult to determine who is going to score the actual touchdowns. In addition, you must predict who is going to score from enough distance to give you the winning edge.

As we did in the preceding methods, we will now look at basic drafting strategies and review the players' 1997 statistics; finally I will rate the players for 1998. No rookies are included in my player ratings. It's too early to size up how they'll fit into each team's scheme. I rate the rookies separately, in Section V of this chapter.

Distance Scoring Method
DRAFTING STRATEGY BY ROUNDS
(A Guide for the Beginner)

1. The draft consists of 12 rounds.

2. Of the 12 players, seven are starters and five are reserves.

3. The starting seven comprise:

1 Quarterback		1 Quarterback
2 Running Backs	OR	2 Running Backs
2 Wide Receivers	FLEX OPTION	3 Receivers
1 Tight End		1 Kicker
1 Kicker		

4. The five reserves can be from any position.

5. Any player from any starting position can be drafted in any round.

ROUND 1: Remember that points are awarded for actual touchdowns scored. Players are awarded two points for every 10 yards on touchdown plays. Our concerns are primarily to get a player who will score often, and secondly to find someone who might score from some distance. In recent years, some prominent wide receivers have begun to score as consistently as the top running backs. These players, along with running backs like Barry Sanders should be your top picks. In 1997 after Sanders (116 points) and Napolean Kaufman's (84 points) the next nine players were wide receivers in this scoring method.

ROUND 2: Now is probably a good time to pick up a back used as a team's primary ball carrier. He will probably be among the league's elite, if they're not all gone. If you've already grabbed a running back in the first round, take the best wide receiver available.

ROUND 3: In this round, try to grab a good quarterback, one who will throw 25 or more touchdown passes during the year. A consistent quarterback will put points on the scoreboard week after week. Steve Young, when he's healthy, and Brett Favre fall into this category. By the end of the third round, you should have a consistently scoring wide receiver or running back and a solid quarterback.

ROUND 4: In this round, I'd grab either a second running back or a wide receiver, whichever is the best available, to provide a more consistent scoring punch.

ROUND 5: Now it's important to pick up a kicker. Look for a consistent scorer who plays on a team good enough to give him plenty of scoring chances.

ROUNDS 6 through 8: Fill in the starting positions you have left open. If you have followed my suggestions, you lack a tight end and a wide receiver. But if you notice that a player you really like is available at a position you have already partially filled, pick him up, even if you haven't filled all your starting positions. You'll feel better about your lineup, and at the very worst, you'll have either a high-powered reserve or some attractive trade bait.

ROUNDS 9 through 12: These rounds are used to fill in your reserves. It's a good time to take a shot at a rookie. In choosing your reserves, be sure to draft backups for the more injury-prone positions—quarterback, running back, and wide receiver. Even though you're into the less important players by this time, keep alert. Many good picks show up in these late rounds.

Let's now take a look at what to consider when choosing players for each position.

A LOOK AT THE RUNNING BACKS
(A Guide for the Beginner)
Considerations in Choosing a Running Back

1. First, review players' previous performances, especially from last season. Injuries, trades, holdouts, suspensions and the like should be noted. Injuries to Terry Allen, Curtis Martin, and Garrison Hearst greatly affected their seasons.

2. The first priority in selecting a running back is choosing one who will not only score consistently but who is also capable of long touchdown runs. Our first choice is a fast back who scores regularly. Curtis Martin, Terrell Davis, and Barry Sanders can score from anywhere, and all fit the mold perfectly.

3. If a quick, consistent scorer is not available on your turn, you should forget about speed and take a reliable, high-scoring big back. Although his touchdown runs may be shorter, he provides you with consistent scoring. In 1992, Rodney Culver of Indianapolis emerged as a short-yardage touchdown specialist. In 1993, Marcus Allen became Kansas City's designated scorer. In 1996, Cincinnati gave that role to Ki-Jana Carter.

4. Your next preference should be the back who will probably not score many touchdowns but is likely to get some big yardage when he does score. These are the scatback runners who excel in the open but usually give way to the bigger backs in bruising goal-line situations. This type of player may work out as a good second back in your offense. James Brooks was a popular pick in the past. Eric Metcalf has recently shown similar ability. Metcalf gives you breakaway speed and a shot at scoring from anywhere on the field. (Metcalf may not be classified as a running back in some leagues.)

5. Next is a top rookie. Every year there seems to be at least one first-year running back who makes it big. Look at Barry Sanders in 1989; Emmitt Smith in 1990; and Leonard Russell in 1991. In 1992, Rodney Culver of the Colts produced nine touchdowns. In 1993, rookies Ronald Moore (nine TDs), Natrone Means (eight TDs), Jerome Bettis (seven TDs), and Terry Kirby (six TDs) all provided scoring punch. In 1994, Marshall Faulk made a huge impact with 12 scores. In 1996, Karim Abdul-Jabber produced 11 scores. In 1997 Antowain Smith scored eight times.

6. In most cases, shy away from old or injury-prone running backs. If they have been in the league for many years, they probably won't last a full season without injury. In addition, their desire to excel may be dwindling.

7. Finally, beware of players who have injury after nagging injury. They may be good backs, but they can't help you if they're out of the lineup.

In the 1997 statistics that follow, you'll find the players ranked by their fantasy-point totals. Remember that in the Distance Scoring Method, fantasy points are calculated by the length of the touchdown scored—the longer the touchdown play, the more points earned.

NAME	TEAM	GP	RSH	RSH TDs	AVG LGTH	REC	REC TDs	AVG LGTH	TOTAL TDs	AVG LGTH	CONV PTS	FAN-TASY PTS
1. Sanders	DET	16	335	11	37.0	33	3	30.0	14	35.5	0	116
1996		16	307	11	17.8	24	0	0.0	11	17.8	0	54
1995		16	314	11	26.0	48	1	9.0	12	24.6	0	72
3 Yr - TOTALS		48	956	33	26.9	105	4	24.8	37	26.7	0	242
2. Kaufman	OAK	16	272	6	44.7	40	2	46.5	8	45.1	0	84
1996		16	150	1	12.0	22	1	10.0	2	11.0	0	8
1995		15	108	1	16.0	9	0	0.0	2	50.0	0	22
3 Yr - TOTALS		47	530	8	37.0	71	3	34.3	12	40.2	0	114
3. Dillon +	CIN	14	233	10	19.2	27	0	0.0	10	19.2	0	54
1996		–	–	–	–	–	–	–	–	–	–	–
1995		–	–	–	–	–	–	–	–	–	–	–
3 Yr - TOTALS		14	233	10	19.2	27	0	0.0	10	19.2	0	54
4. Dunn +	TB	16	224	4	22.5	39	3	47.0	7	33.0	0	54
1996		–	–	–	–	–	–	–	–	–	–	–
1995		–	–	–	–	–	–	–	–	–	–	–
3 Yr - TOTALS		16	224	4	22.5	39	3	47.0	7	33.0	0	54
5. Te. Davis	DEN	15	369	15	8.5	42	0	0.0	15	8.5	6	52
1996		16	345	13	13.5	36	2	8.0	15	12.8	0	60
1995		14	237	7	11.1	49	1	8.0	8	10.8	0	28
3 Yr - TOTALS		45	951	35	10.9	127	3	8.0	38	10.7	6	140
6. Hanspard +*	ATL	15	53	0	0.0	6	1	10.0	3	67.3	0	44
1996		–	–	–	–	–	–	–	–	–	–	–
1995		–	–	–	–	–	–	–	–	–	–	–
3 Yr - TOTALS		15	53	0	0.0	6	1	10.0	3	67.3	0	44
7. R. Harris	CHI	13	275	10	14.3	28	0	0.0	10	14.3	0	42
1996		12	194	4	4.8	32	1	33.0	5	10.4	0	18
1995		1	0	0	0.0	1	0	0.0	0	0.0	0	0
3 Yr - TOTALS		26	469	14	11.6	61	1	33.0	15	13.0	0	60
8. Kirby *	SF	16	125	6	4.7	23	1	16.0	8	17.9	4	42
1996		13	134	3	12.0	52	1	10.0	4	11.5	0	17
1995 w/MIA		16	108	4	4.5	66	3	16.3	7	9.6	0	22
3 Yr - TOTALS		45	367	13	6.3	141	5	15.0	19	13.5	4	81
9. Broussard	SEAT	13	70	5	30.4	24	1	20.0	6	28.7	0	42
1996		9	15	1	26.0	6	0	0.0	1	26.0	0	6
1995		15	46	1	21.0	10	0	0.0	1	21.0	0	6
3 Yr - TOTALS		37	131	7	28.4	40	1	20.0	8	27.4	0	54
10. Abdul-Jabbar	MIA	16	283	15	3.6	29	1	36.0	16	5.6	0	40
1996		16	307	11	4.7	23	0	0.0	11	4.7	0	24
1995		–	–	–	–	–	–	–	–	–	–	–
3 Yr - TOTALS		32	590	26	4.1	52	1	36.0	27	5.2	0	64
11. R. Smith	MINN	14	232	6	24.3	37	1	12.0	7	22.6	0	40
1996		8	162	3	25.7	7	0	0.0	3	25.7	0	18
1995		9	139	5	16.6	7	0	0.0	5	16.6	2	24
3 Yr - TOTALS		31	533	14	21.9	51	1	12.0	15	21.2	2	82
12. A. Smith +	BUF	16	194	8	16.7	28	0	0.0	8	16.7	0	38
1996		–	–	–	–	–	–	–	–	–	–	–
1995		–	–	–	–	–	–	–	–	–	–	–
3 Yr - TOTALS		16	194	8	16.7	28	0	0.0	8	16.7	0	38
13. Ln. Johnson +	NYJ	16	48	2	1.0	16	0	0.0	4	41.8	0	38
1996		–	–	–	–	–	–	–	–	–	–	–
1995		–	–	–	–	–	–	–	–	–	–	–
3 Yr - TOTALS		16	48	2	1.0	16	0	0.0	4	41.8	0	38
14. Mitchell *	WASH	16	23	1	2.0	36	1	6.0	4	42.0	0	38
1996		15	39	0	0.0	32	0	0.0	0	0.0	0	0
1995		16	46	1	36.0	38	1	22.0	3	39.0	0	26
3 Yr - TOTALS		47	108	2	19.0	106	2	14.0	7	40.7	0	64
15. Levens	GB	16	329	7	10.0	53	5	5.0	12	7.9	2	36
1996		16	121	5	4.8	31	5	5.0	10	4.9	0	26
1995		15	36	3	1.3	48	4	5.0	7	3.4	0	14
3 Yr - TOTALS		47	486	15	6.5	132	14	5.0	29	5.8	2	76

1997 STATISTICAL RESULTS
(RUNNING BACKS — DISTANCE SCORING METHOD)

NAME	TEAM	GP	RSH	RSH TDs	AVG LGTH	REC	REC TDs	AVG LGTH	TOTAL TDs	AVG LGTH	CONV PTS	FAN-TASY PTS
16. **J. Anderson**	**ATL**	**16**	**290**	**7**	**1.8**	**29**	**3**	**24.7**	**10**	**8.7**	**0**	**35**
1996		16	232	5	12.8	49	1	2.0	6	11.0	0	20
1995		7	39	1	3.0	4	0	0.0	1	3.0	0	2
3 Yr - TOTALS		39	561	13	6.1	82	4	19.0	17	9.2	0	57
17. **Bates**	**NO**	**11**	**119**	**4**	**31.5**	**5**	**0**	**0.0**	**4**	**31.5**	**0**	**33**
1996		14	164	4	7.0	13	0	0.0	4	7.0	0	12
1995		16	244	7	13.3	18	0	0.0	7	13.3	0	28
3 Yr - TOTALS		41	527	15	16.5	36	0	0.0	15	16.5	0	73
18. **Martin**	**NE**	**13**	**274**	**4**	**24.8**	**41**	**1**	**21.0**	**5**	**24.0**	**0**	**32**
1996		16	316	14	5.0	46	3	8.0	17	5.5	2	44
1995		16	368	14	4.6	30	1	21.0	15	5.7	2	38
3 Yr - TOTALS		45	958	32	7.3	117	5	13.2	37	8.1	4	114
19. **F. Lane**	**CAR**	**12**	**182**	**7**	**16.3**	**8**	**0**	**0.0**	**7**	**16.3**	**0**	**30**
1996		–	–	–	–	–	–	–	–	–	–	–
1995		–	–	–	–	–	–	–	–	–	–	–
3 Yr - TOTALS		12	182	7	16.3	8	0	0.0	7	16.3	0	30
20. **Murrell**	**NYJ**	**16**	**300**	**7**	**15.5**	**27**	**0**	**0.0**	**7**	**15.5**	**0**	**30**
1996		16	301	6	2.3	17	1	14.0	7	4.0	0	16
1995		15	192	1	2.0	71	2	22.0	3	15.3	0	14
3 Yr - TOTALS		47	793	14	8.9	115	3	19.3	17	10.7	0	60
21. **K. Carter**	**CIN**	**15**	**128**	**7**	**13.0**	**21**	**0**	**0.0**	**7**	**13.0**	**0**	**28**
1996		15	91	8	6.2	22	1	12.0	9	6.8	0	26
1995		–	–	–	–	–	–	–	–	–	–	–
3 Yr - TOTALS		30	219	15	9.4	43	1	12.0	16	9.5	0	54
22. **Alstott**	**TB**	**15**	**176**	**7**	**8.7**	**23**	**3**	**1.7**	**10**	**6.6**	**0**	**28**
1996		16	96	3	6.0	65	3	10.3	6	8.2	0	18
1995		–	–	–	–	–	–	–	–	–	–	–
3 Yr - TOTALS		31	272	10	7.9	88	6	6.0	16	7.2	0	46
23. **Bieniemy ***	**CIN**	**15**	**21**	**1**	**20.0**	**31**	**0**	**0.0**	**2**	**59.5**	**0**	**26**
1996		16	56	2	19.0	32	0	0.0	2	19.0	0	10
1995		14	98	3	2.3	43	0	0.0	3	2.3	0	6
3 Yr - TOTALS		45	175	6	10.8	106	0	0.0	7	23.4	0	42
24. **Phillips ****	**MIA**	**12**	**201**	**8**	**10.0**	**11**	**0**	**0.0**	**8**	**10.0**	**0**	**26**
1996 w/STL		15	193	4	2.3	8	1	11.0	5	4.0	0	12
1995		–	–	–	–	–	–	–	–	–	–	–
3 Yr - TOTALS		27	394	12	7.4	19	1	11.0	13	7.7	0	38
25. **M. Allen**	**KC**	**16**	**124**	**11**	**3.1**	**11**	**0**	**0.0**	**11**	**3.1**	**0**	**25**
1996		16	206	9	1.8	27	0	0.0	9	1.8	0	18
1995		16	207	5	1.0	27	0	0.0	5	1.0	0	10
3 Yr - TOTALS		48	537	25	2.2	65	0	0.0	25	2.2	0	53
26. **Bettis**	**PITT**	**15**	**375**	**7**	**4.1**	**15**	**2**	**18.0**	**9**	**7.2**	**0**	**24**
1996		16	320	11	10.5	22	0	0.0	11	10.5	0	40
1995 w/STL		15	183	3	1.3	18	0	0.0	3	1.3	0	6
3 Yr - TOTALS		46	878	21	7.1	55	2	18.0	23	8.0	0	70
27. **George**	**TENN**	**16**	**357**	**6**	**9.5**	**7**	**1**	**11.0**	**7**	**9.7**	**2**	**24**
1996		16	335	8	11.5	23	0	0.0	8	11.5	0	30
1995		–	–	–	–	–	–	–	–	–	–	–
3 Yr - TOTALS		32	692	14	10.6	30	1	11.0	15	10.7	2	54
28. **Faulk**	**IND**	**16**	**264**	**7**	**4.0**	**47**	**1**	**10.0**	**8**	**4.8**	**0**	**20**
1996		13	198	7	3.6	56	0	0.0	7	3.6	0	16
1995		16	289	11	10.6	56	3	13.0	14	11.1	0	48
3 Yr - TOTALS		45	751	25	6.8	159	4	12.3	29	7.6	0	84
29. **Stewart**	**JAC**	**16**	**136**	**8**	**4.2**	**41**	**1**	**7.0**	**9**	**4.5**	**0**	**20**
1996		13	190	8	3.9	30	2	14.5	10	6.0	0	26
1995		14	137	2	6.0	21	1	7.0	3	6.3	0	6
3 Yr - TOTALS		43	463	18	4.3	92	4	10.8	22	5.4	0	52
30. **Means**	**JAC**	**14**	**244**	**9**	**4.6**	**15**	**0**	**0.0**	**9**	**4.6**	**0**	**20**
1996		13	152	2	3.0	7	1	11.0	3	5.7	0	8
1995 w/SD		10	186	5	5.4	7	0	0.0	5	5.4	0	12
3 Yr - TOTALS		37	582	16	4.7	29	1	11.0	17	5.0	0	40

1997 STATISTICAL RESULTS
(RUNNING BACKS — DISTANCE SCORING METHOD)

	NAME	TEAM	GP	RSH	RSH TDs	AVG LGTH	REC	REC TDs	AVG LGTH	TOTAL TDs	AVG LGTH	CONV PTS	FAN-TASY PTS
31.	McPhail	MIA	14	17	1	71.0	34	1	10.0	2	40.5	0	20
	1996		9	6	0	0.0	20	0	0.0	0	0.0	0	0
	1995		–	–	–	–	–	–	–	–	–	–	–
	3 Yr - TOTALS		23	23	1	71.0	54	1	10.0	2	40.5	0	20
32.	Hearst	SF	13	234	4	11.7	21	2	10.0	6	11.2	0	20
	1996 w/CIN		16	225	0	0.0	12	1	15.0	1	15.0	2	6
	1995 w/ARIZ		16	284	1	1.0	29	1	1.0	2	1.0	0	4
	3 Yr - TOTALS		45	743	5	9.6	62	4	9.0	9	9.4	2	30
33.	Walker	DALL	10	6	0	0.0	14	2	37.5	2	37.5	0	18
34.	Cullors *	NE	5	22	0	0.0	2	0	0.0	1	86.0	0	18
35.	Meggett	NE	12	20	1	5.0	19	1	49.0	2	27.0	0	16
36.	Turner	PHIL	15	18	0	0.0	48	3	19.0	3	19.0	0	16
37.	Watters	PHIL	16	285	7	3.6	48	0	0.0	7	3.6	0	16
38.	Floyd	SF	15	78	3	1.0	37	1	44.0	4	11.7	0	16
39.	Levy *	SF	7	16	0	0.0	5	0	0.0	1	73.0	0	16
40.	Lee	STL	16	28	0	0.0	61	3	22.7	3	22.7	0	16
41.	E. Smith	DALL	16	261	4	7.8	40	0	0.0	4	7.8	2	14
42.	Anders	KC	15	79	0	0.0	59	2	30.0	2	30.0	0	14
43.	Byars	NE	15	11	0	0.0	20	3	16.7	3	16.7	0	14
44.	C. Warren	SEAT	15	200	4	11.5	45	0	0.0	4	11.5	0	14
45.	Bowie	WASH	15	28	2	4.0	34	2	21.0	4	12.5	0	14
46.	Vardell	DET	15	32	6	1.0	16	0	0.0	6	1.0	0	12
47.	Barber +	NYG	12	136	3	2.0	34	1	11.0	4	4.3	2	12
48.	Way	NYG	16	151	4	5.0	37	1	1.0	5	4.2	0	12
49.	Biakabutuka	CAR	8	75	2	19.0	0	0	0.0	2	19.0	0	10
50.	Zellars	NO	16	156	4	3.5	31	0	0.0	4	3.5	0	10
51.	R. Thomas	TENN	15	67	3	11.0	14	0	0.0	3	11.0	0	10
52.	T. Allen	WASH	10	210	4	1.8	20	1	5.0	5	2.4	0	10
53.	McElroy	ARIZ	14	135	2	13.5	7	0	0.0	2	13.5	0	8
54.	Morris	BALT	11	204	4	1.8	29	0	0.0	4	1.8	0	8
55.	Hoard	MINN	12	80	4	3.5	11	0	0.0	4	3.5	0	8
56.	Gash	NE	12	6	0	0.0	22	3	5.3	3	5.3	0	8
57.	Wheatley	NYG	13	152	4	3.3	16	0	0.0	4	3.3	0	8
58.	G. Brown	SD	15	253	4	1.0	21	0	0.0	4	1.0	0	8
59.	R. Moore **	ARIZ	11	81	1	27.0	4	0	0.0	1	27.0	0	6
60.	A. Johnson	CAR	16	97	0	0.0	21	1	14.0	1	14.0	2	6
61.	Greene	CAR	16	45	1	10.0	40	1	1.0	2	5.5	0	6
62.	Richardson	KC	4	2	0	0.0	3	3	2.0	3	2.0	0	6
63.	Evans	MINN	16	43	2	2.0	21	0	0.0	2	2.0	2	6
64.	Pegram **	NYG	12	28	2	12.0	21	0	0.0	2	12.0	0	6
65.	Garner	PHIL	16	116	3	4.0	24	0	0.0	3	4.0	0	6
66.	Jones +	PITT	16	72	1	1.0	16	1	11.0	2	6.0	0	6
67.	L. Smith	SEAT	12	91	2	3.5	23	0	0.0	2	3.5	2	6
68.	J. Moore	STL	8	104	3	3.0	8	0	0.0	3	3.0	0	6
69.	Rhett	TB	6	31	3	2.3	0	0	0.0	3	2.3	0	6
70.	St. Davis	WASH	11	141	3	2.3	18	0	0.0	3	2.3	0	6
71.	Centers	ARIZ	15	101	1	1.0	54	1	1.0	2	1.0	0	4
72.	J. Graham +	BALT	8	81	2	3.0	12	0	0.0	2	3.0	0	4
73.	Holmes	BUF	9	22	2	1.0	13	0	0.0	2	1.0	0	4
74.	Autry +	CHI	12	112	1	3.0	9	0	0.0	1	3.0	2	4
75.	Milne	CIN	15	13	2	1.5	23	0	0.0	2	1.5	0	4
76.	Johnston	DALL	5	2	0	0.0	18	1	13.0	1	13.0	0	4
77.	S. Williams	DALL	15	121	2	2.0	21	0	0.0	2	2.0	0	4
78.	D. Smith	DEN	4	4	0	0.0	4	1	17.0	1	17.0	0	4
79.	Rivers	DET	10	29	1	13.0	0	0	0.0	1	13.0	0	4
80.	Henderson	GB	16	31	0	0.0	41	1	10.0	1	10.0	0	4
81.	L. Warren	IND	12	28	2	2.0	20	0	0.0	2	2.0	0	4
82.	Spikes	MIA	10	63	2	5.0	7	0	0.0	2	5.0	0	4
83.	Palmer	MINN	12	11	1	8.0	26	1	7.0	2	7.5	0	4
84.	Strong	SEAT	9	4	0	0.0	13	2	4.5	2	4.5	0	4

— 247 —

1997 STATISTICAL RESULTS
(RUNNING BACKS — DISTANCE SCORING METHOD)

NAME	TEAM	GP	RSH	RSH TDs	AVG LGTH	REC	REC TDs	AVG LGTH	TOTAL TDs	AVG LGTH	CONV PTS	FAN-TASY PTS
85. C. Smith	ARIZ	5	4	1	1.0	2	0	0.0	1	1.0	0	2
86. Christian	ATL	14	7	0	0.0	22	1	3.0	1	3.0	0	2
87. H. Green	ATL	15	36	1	1.0	29	0	0.0	1	1.0	0	2
88. Byner	BALT	14	84	0	0.0	21	0	0.0	0	0.0	2	2
89. Cotton	BALT	2	2	1	1.0	0	0	0.0	1	1.0	0	2
90. T. Thomas	BUF	16	154	1	2.0	30	0	0.0	1	2.0	0	2
91. Hebron	DEN	10	49	1	1.0	3	0	0.0	1	1.0	0	2
92. Loville	DEN	3	25	1	6.0	2	0	0.0	1	6.0	0	2
93. Schlesinger	DET	7	7	0	0.0	5	1	1.0	1	1.0	0	2
94. Hayden	GB	6	32	1	6.0	2	0	0.0	1	6.0	0	2
95. Crockett	IND	15	95	1	2.0	15	0	0.0	1	2.0	0	2
96. Bennett	KC	12	94	1	9.0	7	0	0.0	1	9.0	0	2
97. Parmalee	MIA	13	18	0	0.0	28	1	7.0	1	7.0	0	2
98. M. Williams	MINN	4	22	1	1.0	4	0	0.0	1	1.0	0	2
99. Grier	NE	6	33	1	2.0	0	0	0.0	1	2.0	0	2
100. Hampton	NYG	2	23	1	1.0	0	0	0.0	1	1.0	0	2
101. Neal	NYJ	7	10	0	0.0	8	1	5.0	1	5.0	0	2
102. R. Anderson	NYJ	14	21	0	0.0	26	1	8.0	1	8.0	0	2
103. Heyward	STL	15	34	1	4.0	8	0	0.0	1	4.0	0	2
104. Thompson	STL	4	16	1	7.0	0	0	0.0	1	7.0	0	2
105. Bouie	ARIZ	3	11	0	0.0	0	0	0.0	0	0.0	0	0
106. Le. Johnson	ARIZ	5	23	0	0.0	3	0	0.0	0	0.0	0	0
107. Tindale	BUF	1	0	0	0.0	4	0	0.0	0	0.0	0	0
108. Oliver	CAR	4	1	0	0.0	6	0	0.0	0	0.0	0	0
109. A. Carter	CHI	11	9	0	0.0	24	0	0.0	0	0.0	0	0
110. Harmon **	CHI	10	10	0	0.0	18	0	0.0	0	0.0	0	0
111. Hicks	CHI	2	4	0	0.0	0	0	0.0	0	0.0	0	0
112. Hughes	CHI	3	1	0	0.0	8	0	0.0	0	0.0	0	0
113. Salaam	CHI	3	31	0	0.0	2	0	0.0	0	0.0	0	0
114. S. Graham	CIN	2	1	0	0.0	1	0	0.0	0	0.0	0	0
115. Griffith	DEN	10	9	0	0.0	11	0	0.0	0	0.0	0	0
116. Lynn	DEN	1	0	0	0.0	1	0	0.0	0	0.0	0	0
117. Milburn	DET	4	0	0	0.0	5	0	0.0	0	0.0	0	0
118. Groce	IND	3	10	0	0.0	0	0	0.0	0	0.0	0	0
119. Jordan	JAC	1	1	0	0.0	0	0	0.0	0	0.0	0	0
120. Shelton +	JAC	2	6	0	0.0	0	0	0.0	0	0.0	0	0
121. Hill	KC	16	157	0	0.0	12	0	0.0	0	0.0	0	0
122. Nealy	MIA	1	1	0	0.0	0	0	0.0	0	0.0	0	0
123. Potts **	MIA	3	2	0	0.0	3	0	0.0	0	0.0	0	0
124. Pritchett	MIA	6	3	0	0.0	5	0	0.0	0	0.0	0	0
125. R. Green	MINN	2	6	0	0.0	1	0	0.0	0	0.0	0	0
126. Bender	NO	3	5	0	0.0	0	0	0.0	0	0.0	0	0
128. McCrary	NO	4	7	0	0.0	4	0	0.0	0	0.0	0	0
127. Tr. Davis +	NO	15	75	0	0.0	13	0	0.0	0	0.0	0	0
129. E. Lane	NYG	1	5	0	0.0	0	0	0.0	0	0.0	0	0
130. Sowell +	NYJ	1	7	0	0.0	1	0	0.0	0	0.0	0	0
131. Aska	OAK	5	13	0	0.0	0	0	0.0	0	0.0	0	0
132. Davison	OAK	3	2	0	0.0	2	0	0.0	0	0.0	0	0
133. Fenner	OAK	7	7	0	0.0	14	0	0.0	0	0.0	0	0
134. Hall	OAK	8	23	0	0.0	1	0	0.0	0	0.0	0	0
135. Levitt +	OAK	2	2	0	0.0	2	0	0.0	0	0.0	0	0
136. Staley +	PHIL	2	7	0	0.0	2	0	0.0	0	0.0	0	0
137. Lester	PITT	6	2	0	0.0	10	0	0.0	0	0.0	0	0
138. McAfee	PITT	4	13	0	0.0	2	0	0.0	0	0.0	0	0
139. Whitman	PITT	5	5	0	0.0	1	0	0.0	0	0.0	0	0
140. Bynum +	SD	5	30	0	0.0	2	0	0.0	0	0.0	0	0
141. Craver	SD	8	20	0	0.0	4	0	0.0	0	0.0	0	0
142. Fletcher	SD	13	51	0	0.0	39	0	0.0	0	0.0	0	0
143. Gardner	SD	4	7	0	0.0	2	0	0.0	0	0.0	0	0
144. Edwards +	SF	3	5	0	0.0	6	0	0.0	0	0.0	0	0

1997 STATISTICAL RESULTS
(RUNNING BACKS — DISTANCE SCORING METHOD)

	NAME	TEAM	GP	RSH	RSH TDs	AVG LGTH	REC	REC TDs	AVG LGTH	TOTAL TDs	AVG LGTH	CONV PTS	FAN-TASY PTS
145.	Ellison	TB	3	2	0	0.0	1	0	0.0	0	0.0	0	0
146.	Logan	WASH	4	4	0	0.0	3	0	0.0	0	0.0	0	0

+   DENOTES COLLEGE DRAFT PICK

*	Hanspard	ATL	Scored TD's on kickoff returns of 93 and 99 yards.
*	Kirby	SF	Scored TD on kickoff return of 101 yards.
*	Ln. Johnson	NYJ	Scored TD's on kickoff return of 101 yards and punt return of 66 yards.
*	Mitchell	WASH	Scored TD's on kickoff return of 97 yards and punt return of 63 yards.
*	Bieniemy	CIN	Scored TD on kickoff return of 102 yards.
*	Cullors	NE	Scored TD on kickoff return of 86 yards.
*	Levy	SF	Scored TD on punt return of 73 yards.
**	Phillips	MIA	Played in 10 games with St. Louis.
**	R. Moore	ARIZ	Played in 6 games with St. Louis.
**	Pegram	NYG	Played in 3 games with San Diego.
**	Harmon	CHI	Played in 10 games with Tennessee.
**	Potts	MIA	Played in 1 game with Indianapolis.

RATING THE PLAYERS FOR 1998
(Running Backs—Distance Scoring Method)

GRAB ONE IF YOU CAN

☐ **1. Barry Sanders (Detroit Lions)**
Nobody is better in the open field. Under new head coach Wayne Fontes, Barry Sanders got back on track in 1997, scoring 14 times with a whopping 35.5-yard average. Sanders scored three touchdowns of 80 yards or more. Look for another 12-plus scores in 1998 with some from long range.

☐ **2. Terrell Davis (Denver Broncos)**
For two straight seasons, Davis has scored 15 touchdowns. He may not have the explosiveness to score many long touchdowns but it's his consistency that makes him a prime fantasy pick again in 1998.

☐ **3. Dorsey Levens (Green Bay Packers)**
With Edgar Bennett out with an injury in 1997, Levens boosted his touchdowns from 10 to 12 as the Packers' featured back. He may not be a threat to score on long runs but he's going to score often again in 1998.

☐ **4. Napoleon Kaufman (Oakland Raiders)**
Becoming the Raiders' main ground force in 1997, Kaufman scored eight times, averaging a lofty 45.1 yards on each. I look for the explosive Kaufman to top the 10-touchdown mark in 1998, which will make him a great fantasy asset in this scoring method.

☐ **5. Curtis Martin (New York Jets)**
After scoring 15 and 17 touchdowns in 1995 and 1996, Martin dropped to only five touchdowns last year. A shoulder injury caused him to miss three games, which slowed his production. I look for a healthy Martin to return to healthy touchdown numbers in 1998, especially since he's going to the New York Jets where he'll rejoin former coach Bill Parcells.

BEST OF THE REST

☐ **6. Corey Dillon (Cincinnati Bengals)**
As a rookie in 1997, Dillon unseated Ki-Jana Carter in short order as the Bengals' main back. Dillon exploded for 10 touchdowns over the last 11 weeks. Look out in 1998 if he's the season-long starter.

☐ **7. Karim Abdul-Jabbar (Miami Dolphins)**
Although he's capable of popping a few long ones, Abdul-Jabbar averaged only 5.6 yards on 16 touchdowns in 1997. Continuing as a prime scoring source for the Dolphins in 1998, Abdul-Jabbar will again be a productive fantasy player.

☐ **8. Robert Smith (Minnesota Vikings)**
Smith has a history of injuries but in 1997 he showed what he can do when he's healthy. He scored seven touchdowns, averaging 22.6 yards each, while healthy for 14 games. The explosive Smith can be a great fantasy candidate when healthy.

☐ **9. Terry Allen (Washington Redskins)**
After a year in which he scored a league-high 21 touchdowns, Allen had a number of injuries in 1997 and scored only five times. With his healthy return in 1998, I look for a return to better scoring numbers.

☐ **10. Ricky Watters (Seattle Seahawks)**
Before 1997, when he scored only seven times, Watters had scored 13, 12, 11, 11 and 11 touchdowns, respectively. His move to Seattle in 1998 will, I believe, spark a new fire in Watters who will again top the double-digit touchdown mark.

STRONG LONGSHOTS

☐ **11. Warrick Dunn (Tampa Bay Buccaneers)**
As a rookie in 1997, Dunn showed some real explosiveness, averaging 33.0 yards on seven touchdowns. He's certainly a back who can score from anywhere and he will again fare very well in this scoring method, although running mate Mike Alstott will steal some of his scores.

☐ **12. James Stewart (Jacksonville Jaguars)**
Stewart has scored 10 and 9 touchdowns in the last two seasons. With Natrone Means off to San Diego, Stewart's scoring total should climb.

☐ **13. Fred Lane (Carolina Panthers)**
Undrafted rookie Fred Lane took advantage of injuries to Anthony Johnson and Tim Biakabatuka to steal the starting running back job in 1997. Lane got better as the season went on, scoring five of six touchdowns over the last eight weeks. What will he do over a full season as a starter?

☐ **14. Emmitt Smith (Dallas Cowboys)**
Smith had scored 25 and 15 touchdowns the two years before his huge dropoff in 1997 when he scored only four times. His fantasy stock has certainly taken a big dip but don't dismiss his potential completely.

☐ **15. Jamal Anderson (Atlanta Falcons)**
Anderson jumped from 6 touchdowns in 1996 to 10 in 1997. As his role has expanded, he has become one of the league's better backs, which makes him a prime fantasy candidate again in 1998.

☐ **16. Jerome Bettis (Pittsburgh Steelers)**
Since coming to Pittsburgh, Bettis has revived his career, scoring 9 and 11 touchdowns, respectively, the last two seasons. He won't score many long touchdowns but 10 to 12 scores are well within his reach.

☐ **17. Natrone Means (San Diego Chargers)**
Means, who scored nine times while playing for Jacksonville in 1997 returns to San Diego in 1998. With the Chargers, Means is very capable of double-digit scoring.

☐ **18. Garrison Hearst (San Francisco 49ers)**
Hearst was slowed by injury in 1997, his first season with the 49ers, and scored only six times. I look for a healthy Hearst to boost those totals in 1997 as he continues to become more of a factor for San Francisco.

☐ **19. Errict Rhett (Baltimore Ravens)**
Joining Baltimore puts Rhett back into a starting role, which will give him plenty of incentive. Rhett can produce some lengthy scores. Nearing or surpassing the 10-touchdown mark should be well within his reach.

☐ **20. Marshall Faulk (Indianapolis Colts)**
Faulk stayed healthy in 1997 and scored eight times for the Colts. If he can stay healthy and if his offensive line improves, he could return to his earlier form of double-digit touchdowns.

HAVE THE POTENTIAL

☐ **21. Mike Alstott (Tampa Bay Buccaneers)**
Alstott only averaged 6.6 yards on his 10 touchdowns in 1997 but any one who scores that frequently deserves considerable fantasy attention.

☐ **22. Antowain Smith (Buffalo Bills)**
As a rookie in 1997, Smith pushed Thurman Thomas for more and more playing time, which resulted in Smith scoring eight touchdowns. Look for the push to continue in 1998, resulting in even bigger scoring production.

☐ **23. Eddie George (Tennessee Oilers)**
For whatever reason, despite two back-to-back 1,300-yard seasons, George has produced only eight and seven touchdowns, respectively, his first two seasons in the NFL. I look for George to finally near or top the double-digit scoring mark in 1998.

☐ **24. Edgar Bennett (Chicago Bears)**
Sidelined for all of 1997 with a leg injury, Bennett returns in 1998 to become the primary rusher for the Bears. In Chicago, as the main back, Bennett will certainly be a frequent touchdown producer.

☐ **25. Charlie Garner (Philadelphia Eagles)**
With Ricky Watters off to Seattle, Garner will become the main focus of the Eagles' ground attack, which will lead to frequent scoring.

SOLID SLEEPERS

☐ **26. Adrian Murrell (Arizona Cardinals)**
As the Jets' main ball carrier, Murrell has scored seven times in each of the last two seasons. However, with Curtis Martin joining the Jets in 1998, Murrell escaped to Arizona where he'll likely capture the featured back role which should provide plenty of scoring chances.

☐ **27. Jerald Moore (St. Louis Rams)**
Moore came on after Lawrence Phillips departed in 1997 to become the Rams' main back and score three times in the last eight games. Keeping the starting role over the full season should help him produce good scoring numbers in 1998.

☐ **28. Lamar Smith (New Orleans Saints)**
Smith signed a four-year deal in the offseason and is presumed to be the featured back for New Orleans in 1998. This role should give him a good number of scoring chances.

☐ **29. Tiki Barber (New York Giants)**
Barber scored only four times as a rookie in 1997, missing four games with a knee injury. In 1998, the talented Barber, who can get it done both on the ground and through the air, should be able to build on his scoring numbers, if Gary Brown and Charles Way step in to take from his scoring potential.

☐ **30. Donnell Bennett (Kansas City Chiefs)**
Bennett may be the best bet to step into the starting halfback role, which should provide significant scoring chances, especially with Marcus Allen retired.

KEEP AN EYE ON

☐ **31. Gary Brown (New York Giants)**
Brown, who scored four times and rushed for just under 1,000 yards in 1997, brings his services to New York. The Giants are in need of an every down producer.

☐ **32. Thurman Thomas (Buffalo Bills)**
Thomas is being phased out in favor of young Antowain Smith, and Thomas's fantasy stock continues to decline.

☐ **33. Ray Zellars (New Orleans Saints)**
Despite the arrival of Lamar Smith, Zellars should still see significant playing time and get scoring chances.

☐ **34. Mario Bates (Arizona Cardinals)**
The Cardinals, unable to find a consistent every-down back, are putting some of their money on Bates. Bates, an on-and-off starter for New Orleans, comes to the Cardinals to battle for playing time and scoring chances with another offseason acquisition, Adrian Murrell.

☐ **35. Ki-Jana Carter (Cincinnati Bengals)**
Carter lost his starting role in 1997 to Corey Dillon. However, Carter still very well could be used in scoring situations. He has produced 16 touchdowns over the last two seasons.

☐ **36. Lawrence Phillips (Miami Dolphins)**
It'll be interesting to see how Jimmy Johnson uses the troubled but talented Phillips.

☐ **37. Raymont Harris (Chicago Bears)**
Harris may have scored 10 times in 1997 but with Edgar Bennett and rookie Curtis Enis now on board in Chicago, there are questions about his 1998 contributions.

☐ **38. Byron Hanspard (Atlanta Falcons)**
Hanspard scored only three times as a rookie in 1997 but two came on kickoff returns. If he expands his backfield role in 1998, much better scoring numbers should follow.

☐ **39. William Floyd (Carolina Panthers)**
One of the league's better fullbacks when healthy, Floyd comes to Carolina in 1998 to provide blocking and short-yardage scores.

☐ **40. Tim Biakabatuka (Carolina Panthers)**
He's another No. 1 draft pick with potential but Fred Lane stands in his way.

PRIME PROSPECTS

☐ **41. Charles Way (New York Giants)**
Finished the '97 season as the Giants most consistent ground weapon but Giants have brought Gary Brown aboard.

☐ **42. Larry Centers (Arizona Cardinals)**
One of the league's best receiving backs, Centers always has the potential to score six-plus touchdowns.

☐ **43. Brian Mitchell (Washington Redskins)**
An excellent return man, good receiver and occasional ground weapon, Mitchell gives you plenty of chances to score.

☐ **44. Chris Warren (Dallas Cowboys)**
Ricky Watters's arrival made Warren dispensable in Seattle but he could become a nice weapon in Dallas as Emmitt Smith's backup.

☐ **45. Duce Staley (Philadelphia Eagles)**
With Ricky Watters off to Seattle, Staley should see more playing time and get more scoring opportunities.

☐ **46. Amp Lee (St. Louis Cardinals)**
Lee recorded 61 receptions in 1997, averaging 27.3 yards on three touchdowns. An excellent receiver, Lee could score a number of long pass-play touchdowns.

☐ **47. Sedrick Shaw/Derrick Cullors (New England Patroits)**
Filling the slot vacated by the departure of Curtis Martin to the Jets won't be easy, and rookie first-round pick Robert Edwards also stands in the way.

☐ **48. Rashaam Salaam (Chicago Bears)**
Edgar Bennett and rookie Curtis Enis arrivals has this former No.1 draft pick looking for work elsewhere.

☐ **49. Tommy Vardell (Detroit Lions)**
His six short-yardage touchdowns in 1997 show his ability around the goal line.

☐ **50. Kimble Anders (Kansas City Chiefs)**
Nice receiver out of the backfield and the Chiefs looking to replace loss of scoring from Marcus Allen's retirement.

DON'T BE SURPRISED

51. Edwards (SF)
52. Kirby (???)
53. Wheatley (NYG)
54. Fletcher (SD)
55. Crockett (IND)
56. Henderson (GB)
57. Turner (PHIL)
58. Tr. Davis (NO)
69. St. Davis (WASH)
60. R. Thomas (TENN)

YOU NEVER KNOW

61. Graham (BALT)
62. Mitchell (WASH)
63. Hoard (MINN)
64. Broussard (SEAT)
65. A. Johnson (CAR)
66. Bowie (WASH)
67. Ln Johnson (NYJ)
68. Le Johnson (NYG)
69. L. Warren (IND)
70. McElroy (ARIZ)

WORTH MENTIONING

71. Hampton (NYG)
72. Sh. Williams (DALL)
73. Johnston (DALL)
74. Hill (KC)
75. Potts (BALT)

76. Meggett (NE)
77. R. Anderson (NYJ)
78. McPhail (MIA)
79. H. Green (ATL)
80. Holmes (BUF)

ROOKIE PROSPECTS

NAME	TEAM	COMMENT
☐ 1. Fred Taylor	JAC	With Means off to San Diego, opportunity is there.
☐ 2. Robert Edwards	NE	Curtis Martin is gone, Edwards will battle for spot.
☐ 3. Curtis Enis	CHI	Bears stockpiled at running back.
☐ 4. John Avery	MIA	More likely a third-down contributor.
☐ 5. Robert Holcombe	STL	Workman type back that may push Jerald Moore.
☐ 6. Skip Hicks	WASH	Rushed for over 1,100 yards in '97, insurance behind T. Allen.
☐ 7. Rasheen Shehee	KC	Chiefs in need at RB with Allen and likely G. Hill gone.

A LOOK AT THE WIDE RECEIVERS
(A Guide for the Beginner)

Considerations in Choosing a Wide Receiver

This method is like the Basic Scoring Method in that the player must score a touchdown to be awarded points. The difference is that a deep-threat receiver will be more valuable, since more points are awarded for the long touchdown play.

1. First, look at players' previous performances. Injuries, player moves, holdouts, suspensions and the like should be noted. In 1997 Carl Pickens, Isaac Bruce, and Miami rookie Yatil Green all had their year-end productivity affected by injuries.

2. The first priority is a receiver from a passing team, preferably a speedy, deep-threat receiver. Jerry Rice of San Francisco always comes to mind. Carl Pickens from Cincinnati also rates high.

3. Look for wide receivers who work well with their current quarterbacks. Such is certainly the case for Carl Pickens and Jeff Blake. Tim Brown and James Jett also have sharpened their numbers when Jeff Hostetler joined the Raiders, and Jeff George's arrival shouldn't hurt.

4. Look for rookie receivers who have a chance to start, especially if they're fast. Defenses pay little attention to rookies until they become established receivers. This certainly was the case for Keyshawn Johnson and Marvin Harrison in 1996 when both scored eight times.

5. Opposing defenses try to clamp down on wide receivers who have just had a great year or consecutive good years, though "great" receivers keep making great plays.

6. Be leery of a receiver on a team going through a quarterback change. If a wide receiver has had a few good years, much of the credit belongs to his timing with his quarterback. A new quarterback will require a period of adjustment, and during that time the wide receiver's productivity may fall off. Such was the case for Issac Bruce in 1996. His touchdown totals dropped from 13 to 7. And with Stan Humphries out much of 1997 Tony Martin saw his numbers drop off significantly.

In the 1997 statistics that follow, you'll find the players ranked by their fantasy-point totals. Remember that in the Distance Scoring Method, fantasy points are calculated by the length of the touchdown scored—the longer the touchdown play, the more points earned.

1997 STATISTICAL RESULTS
(WIDE RECEIVERS — DISTANCE SCORING METHOD)

	NAME	TEAM	GP	RSH	RSH TDs	AVG LGTH	REC	REC TDs	AVG LGTH	TOTAL TDs	AVG LGTH	CONV PTS	FAN-TASY PTS
1.	Galloway	SEAT	15	9	0	0.0	72	12	27.3	12	27.3	0	80
	1996		16	15	0	0.0	57	7	30.3	8	37.5	0	68
	1995		16	11	1	86.0	67	7	36.7	9	48.0	0	94
	3 Yr - TOTALS		47	35	1	86.0	196	26	30.6	29	36.5	0	242
2.	R. Smith	DEN	16	5	0	0.0	70	12	26.3	12	26.3	0	76
	1996		8	1	0	0.0	16	2	34.5	2	34.5	0	16
	1995		5	0	0	0.0	6	1	43.0	1	43.0	0	10
	3 Yr - TOTALS		29	6	0	0.0	92	15	26.0	15	28.5	0	102
3.	Jett	OAK	15	0	0	0.0	46	12	25.4	12	25.4	0	72
	1996		13	0	0	0.0	43	4	24.3	4	24.3	0	22
	1995		11	0	0	0.0	13	1	26.0	1	26.0	0	6
	3 Yr - TOTALS		39	0	0	0.0	102	17	25.2	17	25.2	0	100
4.	J. Lewis *	BALT	13	3	0	0.0	42	6	26.0	8	38.9	0	68
	1996		4	1	0	0.0	6	1	6.0	1	6.0	0	2
	1995		–	–	–	–	–	–	–	–	–	–	–
	3 Yr - TOTALS		17	4	0	0.0	48	7	23.1	9	35.2	0	70
5.	Freeman	GB	15	1	0	0.0	81	12	20.0	12	20.0	0	60
	1996		11	0	0	0.0	56	9	26.5	9	26.5	0	58
	1995		5	0	0	0.0	8	1	11.0	1	11.0	0	4
	3 Yr - TOTALS		31	1	0	0.0	145	22	22.3	22	22.3	0	122
6.	Carter	MINN	16	0	0	0.0	89	13	14.6	13	14.6	6	60
	1996		16	0	0	0.0	96	10	17.1	10	17.1	0	48
	1995		16	1	0	0.0	122	17	14.2	17	14.2	0	68
	3 Yr - TOTALS		48	1	0	0.0	307	40	15.1	40	15.1	6	176
7.	Metcalf *	SD	15	3	0	0.0	40	2	12.5	5	52.0	0	58
	1996 w/ATL		16	3	0	0.0	54	6	12.8	6	12.8	0	22
	1995 w/ATL		16	28	1	23.0	104	8	27.1	10	30.6	0	74
	3 Yr - TOTALS		47	34	1	23.0	198	16	19.9	21	30.6	0	154
8.	D. Alexander	BALT	15	1	0	0.0	65	9	24.8	9	24.8	0	56
	1996		15	3	0	0.0	62	9	22.2	9	22.2	2	52
	1995		6	1	0	0.0	15	0	0.0	1	69.0	0	14
	3 Yr - TOTALS		36	5	0	0.0	142	18	23.5	19	25.9	2	122
9.	McKnight	SEAT	12	0	0	0.0	34	6	38.5	6	38.5	0	56
	1996		1	0	0	0.0	1	0	0.0	0	0.0	0	0
	1995		5	0	0	0.0	6	0	0.0	0	0.0	0	0
	3 Yr - TOTALS		18	0	0	0.0	41	6	38.5	6	38.5	0	56
10.	Thigpen	PITT	15	1	0	0.0	79	7	30.0	7	30.0	2	54
	1996		4	0	0	0.0	12	2	20.0	2	20.0	0	10
	1995		16	0	0	0.0	85	5	22.6	5	22.6	0	28
	3 Yr - TOTALS		35	1	0	0.0	176	14	25.9	14	25.9	2	92
11.	Emanuel	ATL	16	0	0	0.0	65	9	24.4	9	24.4	0	52
	1996		13	0	0	0.0	76	6	9.2	6	9.2	0	18
	1995		16	1	0	0.0	74	5	14.4	5	14.4	0	22
	3 Yr - TOTALS		45	1	0	0.0	215	20	17.3	20	17.3	0	92
12.	Irvin	DALL	16	0	0	0.0	75	9	24.0	9	24.0	0	52
	1996		11	0	0	0.0	64	2	26.0	2	26.0	2	16
	1995		16	0	0	0.0	111	10	21.7	10	21.7	0	52
	3 Yr - TOTALS		43	0	0	0.0	250	21	23.1	21	23.1	2	120
13.	Martin	SD	15	0	0	0.0	63	6	36.8	6	36.8	0	52
	1996		16	0	0	0.0	85	14	18.4	14	18.4	0	70
	1995		16	0	0	0.0	90	6	31.3	6	31.3	0	44
	3 Yr - TOTALS		47	0	0	0.0	238	26	25.6	26	25.6	0	166
14.	Proehl	CHI	14	0	0	0.0	58	7	27.7	7	27.7	2	48
	1996		9	0	0	0.0	23	2	16.0	2	16.0	0	10
	1995 w/SEAT		4	0	0	0.0	5	0	0.0	0	0.0	0	0
	3 Yr - TOTALS		27	0	0	0.0	86	9	25.1	9	25.1	2	58
15.	R. Moore	ARIZ	16	0	0	0.0	97	8	20.9	8	20.9	2	46
	1996		16	0	0	0.0	58	4	17.0	4	17.0	2	20
	1995		15	0	0	0.0	63	5	12.8	5	12.8	2	16
	3 Yr - TOTALS		47	0	0	0.0	218	17	17.6	17	17.6	6	82

1997 STATISTICAL RESULTS
(WIDE RECEIVERS — DISTANCE SCORING METHOD)

NAME	TEAM	GP	RSH	RSH TDs	AVG LGTH	REC	REC TDs	AVG LGTH	TOTAL TDs	AVG LGTH	CONV PTS	FAN-TASY PTS
16. Morton	DET	16	3	0	0.0	80	6	32.0	6	32.0	0	46
1996		16	9	0	0.0	55	6	26.3	6	26.3	0	38
1995		13	3	0	0.0	44	8	15.0	8	15.0	0	32
3 Yr - TOTALS		45	15	0	0.0	179	20	23.5	20	23.5	0	116
17. Owens	SF	16	0	0	0.0	60	8	22.5	8	22.5	0	44
1996		12	0	0	0.0	35	4	32.8	4	32.8	0	32
1995		–	–	–	–	–	–	–	–	–	–	–
3 Yr - TOTALS		28	0	0	0.0	95	12	25.9	12	25.9	0	76
18. A. Reed	BUF	15	3	0	0.0	60	5	35.8	5	35.8	0	42
1996		15	8	0	0.0	66	6	38.3	6	38.3	0	54
1995		6	7	0	0.0	24	3	30.0	3	30.0	0	22
3 Yr - TOTALS		36	18	0	0.0	150	14	35.6	14	35.6	0	118
19. Scott	CIN	16	1	0	0.0	54	5	34.4	5	34.4	0	40
1996		15	3	0	0.0	58	5	20.2	5	20.2	0	28
1995		16	5	0	0.0	52	5	45.6	5	45.6	0	50
3 Yr - TOTALS		47	9	0	0.0	164	15	33.4	15	33.4	0	118
20. McCaffrey	DEN	14	0	0	0.0	45	8	18.0	8	18.0	0	40
1996		13	0	0	0.0	48	7	10.7	7	10.7	0	20
1995		14	0	0	0.0	39	2	13.0	2	13.0	2	8
3 Yr - TOTALS		41	0	0	0.0	132	17	14.4	17	14.4	2	68
21. Brooks	GB	15	2	0	0.0	60	7	23.4	7	23.4	0	40
1996		5	4	0	0.0	23	4	19.0	4	19.0	0	20
1995		16	4	0	0.0	102	13	32.5	13	32.5	0	96
3 Yr - TOTALS		36	10	0	0.0	185	24	27.6	24	27.6	0	156
22. Vanover *	KC	8	5	0	0.0	7	0	0.0	2	88.0	2	40
1996		10	4	0	0.0	21	1	11.0	2	54.0	0	24
1995		12	6	0	0.0	11	2	17.5	5	61.8	0	64
3 Yr - TOTALS		30	15	0	0.0	39	3	15.3	9	65.9	2	128
23. H. Moore	DET	16	0	0	0.0	104	8	16.9	8	16.9	0	38
1996		16	0	0	0.0	106	9	16.2	9	16.2	2	42
1995		16	0	0	0.0	123	14	25.4	14	25.4	0	84
3 Yr - TOTALS		48	0	0	0.0	333	31	20.5	31	20.5	4	164
24. Tr. Brown	NE	13	1	0	0.0	41	6	26.3	6	26.3	0	38
1996		8	0	0	0.0	21	0	0.0	0	0.0	0	0
1995		5	0	0	0.0	14	0	0.0	1	95.0	0	20
3 Yr - TOTALS		26	1	0	0.0	76	6	26.3	7	36.1	0	58
25. Tm. Brown	OAK	16	5	0	0.0	104	5	31.0	5	31.0	2	36
1996		16	6	0	0.0	90	9	17.4	9	17.4	0	42
1995		16	0	0	0.0	89	10	35.9	10	35.9	0	84
3 Yr - TOTALS		48	11	0	0.0	283	24	27.9	24	27.9	2	162
26. Calloway	NYG	16	1	0	0.0	58	8	17.0	8	17.0	0	34
1996		16	1	0	0.0	53	4	16.8	4	16.8	0	18
1995		16	2	0	0.0	56	3	34.7	3	34.7	0	24
3 Yr - TOTALS		48	4	0	0.0	167	15	20.5	15	20.5	0	76
27. Fryar	PHIL	16	0	0	0.0	86	6	24.0	6	24.0	0	34
1996		16	1	0	0.0	88	11	19.1	11	19.1	0	54
1995 w/MIA		15	0	0	0.0	62	8	25.9	8	25.9	0	52
3 Yr - TOTALS		47	1	0	0.0	236	25	22.4	25	22.4	0	140
28. Ka. Williams *	TB	13	1	0	0.0	33	4	17.0	5	25.8	0	32
1996		10	1	0	0.0	22	0	0.0	1	88.0	0	18
1995		–	–	–	–	–	–	–	–	–	–	–
3 Yr - TOTALS		23	2	0	0.0	55	4	17.0	6	36.2	0	50
29. Rison	KC	15	1	0	0.0	72	7	16.7	7	16.7	0	30
1996 w/ GB		15	0	0	0.0	47	3	41.3	3	41.3	0	30
1995 w/CLE		15	1	0	0.0	47	3	8.3	3	8.3	0	8
3 Yr - TOTALS		45	2	0	0.0	166	13	20.4	13	20.4	0	68
30. Hastings	NO	16	4	0	0.0	48	5	21.8	5	21.8	2	30
1996 w/ PITT		15	4	0	0.0	72	6	14.0	6	14.0	0	26
1995 w/ PITT		15	1	0	0.0	48	1	15.0	2	43.5	0	20
3 Yr - TOTALS		46	9	0	0.0	168	12	17.3	13	21.5	2	76

NAME	TEAM	GP	RSH	RSH TDs	AVG LGTH	REC	REC TDs	AVG LGTH	TOTAL TDs	AVG LGTH	CONV PTS	FAN-TASY PTS
31. J. Reed	MINN	16	0	0	0.0	68	6	19.3	6	19.3	0	28
32. Blackwell + *	PITT	7	2	0	0.0	12	1	30.0	2	63.5	0	28
33. C. Sanders	TENN	13	1	0	0.0	31	3	41.0	3	41.0	0	28
34. M. Jackson	BALT	16	0	0	0.0	69	4	25.5	4	25.5	2	26
35. K. Johnson	NYJ	16	0	0	0.0	70	5	21.4	5	21.4	0	26
36. F. Sanders	ARIZ	16	1	0	0.0	75	4	21.0	4	21.0	2	24
37. Harrison	IND	16	2	0	0.0	73	6	10.8	6	10.8	4	24
38. McCardell	JAC	16	0	0	0.0	85	5	17.8	5	17.8	0	24
39. Guliford *	NO	11	1	0	0.0	27	1	16.0	2	57.5	0	24
40. Toomer *	NYG	11	0	0	0.0	16	1	56.0	2	54.5	0	24
41. Early	BUF	14	0	0	0.0	60	5	17.4	5	17.4	0	22
42. Pickens	CIN	12	1	0	0.0	52	5	17.0	5	17.0	0	22
43. Hawkins	PITT	15	5	0	0.0	45	3	33.3	3	33.3	0	22
44. Bruce	STL	11	0	0	0.0	56	5	17.0	5	17.0	0	22
45. Shepherd	WASH	10	4	0	0.0	29	5	16.4	5	16.4	0	22
46. Barlow *	JAC	4	0	0	0.0	5	0	0.0	1	92.0	0	20
47. Hill	NO	15	1	0	0.0	55	2	49.0	2	49.0	0	20
48. Ellard	WASH	12	0	0	0.0	32	4	17.5	4	17.5	0	20
49. Mathis	ATL	16	3	0	0.0	62	6	10.2	6	10.2	0	18
50. Carruth +	CAR	14	6	0	0.0	44	4	18.0	4	18.0	0	18
51. D. Sanders *	DALL	2	1	0	0.0	1	0	0.0	1	83.0	0	18
52. J. Smith	JAC	16	0	0	0.0	82	4	16.5	4	16.5	0	18
53. Jordan	MIA	13	3	0	0.0	27	3	27.0	3	27.0	0	18
54. Chrebet	NYJ	14	0	0	0.0	58	3	24.7	3	24.7	0	18
55. Dunn	CIN	11	0	0	0.0	27	2	35.5	2	35.5	0	16
56. Graham	NYJ	13	0	0	0.0	42	2	36.5	2	36.5	0	16
57. Anthony +	TB	12	5	0	0.0	35	4	15.0	4	15.0	0	16
58. W. Davis	TENN	15	0	0	0.0	43	4	8.8	4	8.8	0	15
59. R. Ismail	CAR	13	4	0	0.0	36	2	33.5	2	33.5	0	14
60. Penn	CHI	14	1	0	0.0	47	3	17.0	3	17.0	0	14
61. Stokes	SF	15	0	0	0.0	58	4	10.7	4	10.7	0	14
62. Westbrook	WASH	10	3	0	0.0	34	3	17.3	3	17.3	0	14
63. Kinchen	ATL	9	0	0	0.0	16	1	53.0	1	53.0	0	12
64. Conway	CHI	7	3	0	0.0	30	1	55.0	1	55.0	0	12
65. Hundon	CIN	6	0	0	0.0	16	2	24.5	2	24.5	0	12
66. Miller	DALL	15	1	0	0.0	46	4	8.5	4	8.5	0	12
67. Bailey	IND	12	3	0	0.0	26	3	12.7	3	12.7	0	12
68. Dawkins	IND	14	0	0	0.0	68	2	23.5	2	23.5	0	12
69. Dawson	KC	9	0	0	0.0	21	2	21.0	2	21.0	0	12
70. Poole +	NO	2	0	0	0.0	4	2	23.0	2	23.0	0	12
71. Patten	NYG	7	1	0	0.0	13	2	24.5	2	24.5	0	12
72. Solomon	PHIL	11	0	0	0.0	29	3	11.3	3	11.3	2	12
73. Pritchard	SEAT	16	1	0	0.0	64	2	20.5	2	20.5	0	12
74. Connell +	WASH	4	1	0	0.0	9	2	24.0	2	24.0	0	12
75. Carrier	CAR	9	0	0	0.0	33	2	18.0	2	18.0	0	10
76. Jefferson	NE	16	0	0	0.0	54	2	19.5	2	19.5	0	10
77. C. Jones	SD	15	4	0	0.0	32	1	44.0	1	44.0	0	10
78. Kv. Williams	ARIZ	11	1	0	0.0	20	1	31.0	1	31.0	0	8
79. Engram	CHI	11	0	0	0.0	45	2	9.0	2	9.0	2	8
80. Green	DEN	10	0	0	0.0	19	2	10.0	2	10.0	0	8
81. W. Jackson	JAC	11	3	0	0.0	17	2	10.0	2	10.0	2	8
82. L. Thomas	MIA	10	0	0	0.0	28	2	15.0	2	15.0	0	8
83. Glenn	NE	7	0	0	0.0	27	2	14.0	2	14.0	0	8
84. K. Alexander	NYG	9	0	0	0.0	18	1	32.0	1	32.0	0	8
85. VanDyke	NYJ	2	0	0	0.0	3	2	17.5	2	17.5	0	8
86. Timpson	PHIL	13	0	0	0.0	42	2	13.0	2	13.0	0	8
87. Small	STL	12	0	0	0.0	32	1	30.0	1	30.0	0	8
88. Haynes	ATL	7	0	0	0.0	12	1	24.0	1	24.0	0	6
89. Hughes	KC	5	0	0	0.0	7	2	9.5	3	6.3	0	6
90. Perriman **	MIA	11	0	0	0.0	25	1	23.0	1	23.0	0	6

NAME	TEAM	GP	RSH	RSH TDs	AVG LGTH	REC	REC TDs	AVG LGTH	TOTAL TDs	AVG LGTH	CONV PTS	FAN-TASY PTS
91. Shedd *	OAK	7	0	0	0.0	10	0	0.0	0	0.0	0	6
92. C. Johnson	PITT	13	0	0	0.0	46	2	12.5	2	12.5	0	6
93. Hobbs **	SEAT	7	0	0	0.0	7	1	20.0	1	20.0	0	6
94. Copeland	TB	11	0	0	0.0	32	1	27.0	1	27.0	0	6
95. Stablein	IND	12	0	0	0.0	25	1	5.0	1	5.0	2	4
96. McDuffie *	MIA	16	0	0	0.0	76	1	10.0	2	5.0	0	4
97. Brisby	NE	12	0	0	0.0	23	2	6.5	2	6.5	0	4
98. Ward +	NYJ	8	2	0	0.0	18	1	19.0	1	19.0	0	4
99. Truitt	OAK	3	0	0	0.0	7	1	19.0	1	19.0	0	4
100. Seay	PHIL	10	0	0	0.0	13	1	19.0	1	19.0	0	4
101. Blades	SEAT	10	0	0	0.0	30	2	7.5	2	7.5	0	4
102. Rice	SF	2	1	0	0.0	7	1	14.0	1	14.0	0	4
103. Kent +	TENN	4	0	0	0.0	6	1	11.0	1	11.0	0	4
104. Moulds	BUF	11	4	0	0.0	29	0	0.0	0	0.0	2	2
105. Mills	CAR	5	0	0	0.0	11	1	2.0	1	2.0	0	2
106. Muhammad	CAR	7	0	0	0.0	27	0	0.0	0	0.0	2	2
107. St. Williams	DALL	12	0	0	0.0	30	1	2.0	1	2.0	0	2
108. Mickens	GB	1	0	0	0.0	1	1	2.0	1	2.0	0	2
109. Schroeder	GB	2	0	0	0.0	2	1	7.0	1	7.0	0	2
110. Barnett	MIA	5	0	0	0.0	17	1	1.0	1	1.0	0	2
111. Walsh	MINN	8	0	0	0.0	11	1	9.0	1	9.0	0	2
112. Russell	TENN	6	0	0	0.0	12	1	2.0	1	2.0	0	2
113. Brock	ARIZ	1	0	0	0.0	1	0	0.0	0	0.0	0	0
114. Edwards	ARIZ	11	0	0	0.0	20	0	0.0	0	0.0	0	0
115. Roe	BALT	3	0	0	0.0	7	0	0.0	0	0.0	0	0
116. Yarborough	BALT	9	0	0	0.0	16	0	0.0	0	0.0	0	0
117. Reese	BUF	1	0	0	0.0	1	0	0.0	0	0.0	0	0
118. Bownes	CHI	5	0	0	0.0	12	0	0.0	0	0.0	0	0
119. E. Smith	CHI	2	1	0	0.0	2	0	0.0	0	0.0	0	0
120. Twyner	CIN	2	0	0	0.0	4	0	0.0	0	0.0	0	0
121. B. Davis	DALL	3	0	0	0.0	3	0	0.0	0	0.0	0	0
122. Jefers	DEN	2	0	0	0.0	3	0	0.0	0	0.0	0	0
123. Boyd	DET	6	0	0	0.0	10	0	0.0	0	0.0	0	0
124. McCorvey	DET	2	0	0	0.0	2	0	0.0	0	0.0	0	0
125. Beebe	GB	1	0	0	0.0	2	0	0.0	0	0.0	0	0
126. Mayes	GB	7	0	0	0.0	18	0	0.0	0	0.0	0	0
127. Doering	IND	1	0	0	0.0	2	0	0.0	0	0.0	0	0
128. W. Moore	JAC	1	0	0	0.0	1	0	0.0	0	0.0	0	0
129. Horn	KC	2	0	0	0.0	2	0	0.0	0	0.0	0	0
130. Lockett +	KC	1	0	0	0.0	1	0	0.0	0	0.0	0	0
131. Manning +	MIA	3	0	0	0.0	7	0	0.0	0	0.0	0	0
132. Hatchette +	MINN	3	0	0	0.0	3	0	0.0	0	0.0	0	0
133. Jells	NE	1	0	0	0.0	1	0	0.0	0	0.0	0	0
134. Bech	NO	3	0	0	0.0	3	0	0.0	0	0.0	0	0
135. Hilliard +	NYG	2	0	0	0.0	2	0	0.0	0	0.0	0	0
136. T. Lewis	NYG	3	0	0	0.0	5	0	0.0	0	0.0	0	0
137. Howard	OAK	3	0	0	0.0	4	0	0.0	0	0.0	0	0
138. C. Jones	PHIL	4	0	0	0.0	5	0	0.0	0	0.0	0	0
139. Adams +	PITT	1	0	0	0.0	1	0	0.0	0	0.0	0	0
140. Marsh	PITT	2	1	0	0.0	2	0	0.0	0	0.0	0	0
141. Still	SD	12	0	0	0.0	24	0	0.0	0	0.0	0	0
142. R. Harris	SEAT	3	0	0	0.0	4	0	0.0	0	0.0	0	0
143. T. Davis	SEAT	1	0	0	0.0	2	0	0.0	0	0.0	0	0
144. M. Harris	SF	4	0	0	0.0	5	0	0.0	0	0.0	0	0
145. Uwaezuoke	SF	9	0	0	0.0	14	0	0.0	0	0.0	0	0
146. Crawford	STL	6	1	0	0.0	11	0	0.0	0	0.0	0	0
147. Floyd	STL	2	0	0	0.0	4	0	0.0	0	0.0	0	0
148. J. Thomas	STL	1	0	0	0.0	2	0	0.0	0	0.0	0	0
149. Kennison	STL	13	3	0	0.0	25	0	0.0	0	0.0	0	0
150. Ross	STL	3	0	0	0.0	3	0	0.0	0	0.0	0	0

1997 STATISTICAL RESULTS
(WIDE RECEIVERS — DISTANCE SCORING METHOD)

	NAME	TEAM	GP	RSH	RSH TDs	AVG LGTH	REC	REC TDs	AVG LGTH	TOTAL TDs	AVG LGTH	CONV PTS	FAN-TASY PTS
151.	R. Thomas	TB	7	0	0	0.0	13	0	0.0	0	0.0	0	0
152.	Mason +	TENN	7	1	0	0.0	14	0	0.0	0	0.0	0	0
153.	C. Thomas	WASH	6	0	0	0.0	11	0	0.0	0	0.0	0	0
154.	Harper	WASH	1	0	0	0.0	2	0	0.0	0	0.0	0	0
155.	Thrash	WASH	1	0	0	0.0	2	0	0.0	0	0.0	0	0

+ DENOTES COLLEGE DRAFT PICK

*	J. Lewis	BALT	Scored TD's on punt returns of 89 and 66 yards.
*	Metcalf	SD	Scored TD's on punt returns of 85, 67, and 83 yards.
*	Vanover	KC	Scored TD on punt return of 82 yards and kickoff return of 94 yards.
*	Ka. Williams	TB	Scored TD on punt return of 61 yards.
*	Blackwell	PITT	Scored TD on kickoff return of 97 yards.
*	Guliford	NO	Scored TD on kickoff return of 102 yards.
*	Toomer	NYG	Scored TD on punt return of 53 yards.
*	Barlow	JAC	Scored TD on kickoff return of 92 yards.
*	D. Sanders	DALL	Scored TD on punt return of 83 yards.
*	Shedd	OAK	Scored TD on fumble return of 25 yards.
*	McDuffie	MIA	Scored TD by recovering fumble in end zone.
**	Perriman	MIA	Played in 3 games with Kansas City.
**	Hobbs	SEAT	Played in 2 games with New Orleans.

RATING THE PLAYERS FOR 1998
(Wide Receivers—Distance Scoring Method)

GRAB ONE IF YOU CAN

☐ **1. Joey Galloway (Seattle Seahawks)**
Over the last three seasons, Galloway has scored 7, 7 and, last year, 12 touchdowns. This fleet-footed receiver averaged 27.3 yards on his 12 scores in 1997 and a whopping 48.0 yards on his seven touchdowns in 1995. Always a deep threat and even more of one now, he's an excellent fantasy candidate in 1998.

☐ **2. Antonio Freeman (Green Bay Packers)**
Freeman averaged 26.5 yards on nine touchdowns in 1996 and 20.0 on 12 scores a year ago. As a favorite go-to receiver of Brett Favre, he should have another big year in store in 1998.

☐ **3. Rod Smith (Denver Broncos)**
With the Broncos looking for a go-to receiver in 1997, Smith stepped into the role and averaged 26.3 yards on 12 touchdowns. If John Elway is around again in 1998, the Broncos' new deep-threat will continue to score off frequent long strikes.

☐ **4. Jerry Rice (San Francisco 49ers)**
Rice missed most of the 1997 season with knee injuries but if we look back to two years earlier, he averaged 25.9 yards on 17 touchdowns. That gives us a feel for what he's capable of.

☐ **5. Tim Brown (Oakland Raiders)**
After scoring 10 and 9 times in 1995 and 1996, Brown dropped to only 5 touchdowns in 1997. However, because he'll have strong-armed Jeff George around in 1998, I look for Brown's touchdown totals to rebound. I expect him to close in on his 1995 performance when he averaged 35.9 yards on 10 touchdowns.

BEST OF THE REST

☐ **6. Carl Pickens (Cincinnati Bengals)**
Until he was slowed by a groin injury in 1997, Pickens had recorded 11, 17 and 12 touchdowns in the three previous seasons. That's a range I believe he'll return to if he's healthy again in 1998.

☐ **7. Cris Carter (Minnesota Vikings)**
Carter does not score on many long touchdown plays but it's his frequency and consistency that make him an attractive fantasy pick. Carter has scored 17, 10 and 13 times, respectively, the last three seasons.

☐ **8. Herman Moore (Detroit Lions)**
In 1995, Moore averaged a solid 25.4 yards on 14 touchdowns. He has seen his touchdown numbers drop over the past two seasons. However, he's still one of the game's best receivers in touchdown situations. I wouldn't overlook him.

☐ **9. Michael Irvin (Dallas Cowboys)**
Perhaps as Emmitt Smith's scoring numbers continue to drop, Michael Irvin's will grow. Irvin scored nine times in 1997, averaging 24.0 yards per score. He's likely to near or top the double-digit touchdown mark again in 1998.

☐ **10. James Jett (Oakland Raiders)**
Oh what a difference a quarterback can make. With Jeff George coming to the Raiders, Jett boosted his touchdown total to 12 (25.4 yard average) from four the year before. With the Raiders' down-field philosophy, George's big-time arm and Jett's speed, 1998 should be another successful year.

STRONG LONG SHOTS

☐ **11. Robert Brooks (Green Bay Packers)**
After returning from a knee injury, Brooks scored only seven times in 1997. Looking back to two years earlier when he was fully healthy, Brooks averaged a whopping 32.5 yards on 13 touchdowns. The potential is there!

☐ **12. Isaac Bruce (St. Louis Rams)**
One of the game's very talented receivers, Bruce missed five games because of a hamstring injury in 1997. However, looking back to 1995 when he averaged 21.4 yards on 13 touchdowns, we get a sense of what he can do.

☐ **13. Tony Martin (San Diego Chargers)**
Martin's touchdown totals dropped from 14 in 1996 to only 6 in 1997, although he averaged 36.8 yards on each. He's certainly one of the game's better deep threats. However, much of his 1998 success will be dictated by how successful his young quarterback will be.

☐ **14. Curtis Conway (Chicago Bears)**
An injured collarbone/shoulder limited Conway to action in just seven games and one 55-yard touchdown in 1997. Looking back to two years previous, however, when he averaged 33.2 yards on 12 touchdowns, we get a good feel of what he's capable of.

☐ **15. Michael Jackson (Baltimore Ravens)**
Jackson's numbers took a huge drop in 1997 when he scored only four times. He's down but not forgotten. Just a year earlier, Jackson scored 14 times with a 22.7-yard average. With receiving mate Derrick Alexander now off to Kansas City, look for Jackson's numbers to rebound in 1998.

☐ **16. Irving Fryar (Philadelphia Eagles)**
Fryar scored only six times in 1997 but did average 24.0 yards on each. A year earlier, Fryar scored 11 times, which gives us the idea that 8 to 12 touchdowns could be in store for him again in 1998.

☐ **17. Johnnie Morton (Detroit Lions)**
Always a nice deep threat, Morton took on an expanded role in 1997 following the departure of Brett Perriman. Morton's 32.0-yard average on

six touchdowns should be a stepping stone to another big year in 1998.

☐ **18. Rob Moore (Arizona Cardinals)**
Rookie Jake Plummer put a little surge into the Arizona offense in 1997 and the results for Moore were 97 receptions and eight touchdowns averaging just over 20 yards. As Plummer continues to improve, so should Moore's numbers.

☐ **19. Derrick Alexander (Kansas City Chiefs)**
Alexander has scored nine touchdowns in each of his last two seasons, averaging 22.2 yards in 1996 and 24.8 yards a year ago on his scores. Coming to Kansas City, however, creates some uncertainty about his scoring frequency.

☐ **20. Terrence Mathis (Atlanta Falcons)**
Mathis scored six times on 62 receptions in 1997 and looks to likely score much more often in 1998 with Bert Emanuel departed to Tampa Bay.

HAVE THE POTENTIAL

☐ **21. Keyshawn Johnson (New York Jets)**
After scoring eight times as a rookie in 1996, Johnson fell back to only five scores in 1997. He's one of the league's talented young receivers, and I look for 7 to 10 touchdowns from him in 1998.

☐ **22. Charles Johnson (Pittsburgh Steelers)**
With the Steelers' top receiver, Yancey Thigpen, moving to Tennessee in the offseason, Johnson will likely get cast into the No.1 receiving role, which should mean an expanded scoring role for Johnson in 1998.

☐ **23. Yancey Thigpen (Tennessee Oilers)**
Yes, he averaged a lofty 30.0 yards on seven touchdowns in 1997, but that was in Pittsburgh. We'll see how often the Oilers will get him the football.

☐ **24. Jake Reed (Minnesota Vikings)**
He's always in the 6 to 10 touchdown range and is capable of scoring on a number of long touchdowns. Reed should get decent fantasy consideration in this scoring method.

☐ **25. Marvin Harrison (Indianapolis Colts)**
The Colts need to get a quarterback in place who can get the ball to talented Harrison more often. Hopefully young Peyton Manning will do just that.

SOLID SLEEPERS

☐ **26. Andre Rison (Kansas City Chiefs)**
Rison scored seven times in 1997 but with Derrick Alexander coming aboard in 1998, he may cut into Rison's numbers.

☐ **27. Michael Westbrook (Washington Redskins)**
Westbrook, with more injuries and other problems, scored only three times in 1997. The Redskins continue to wait for their former No.1 pick to step up and play to his potential.

☐ **28. Bert Emanuel (Tampa Bay Buccaneers)**
With Chris Chandler coming to the Falcons in 1997, Emanuel averaged 24.4 yards on nine touchdowns. However, going to the Tampa Bay Buccaneers in the offseason I don't believe will help his numbers.

☐ **29. Keenan McCardell (Jacksonville Jaguars)**
He averaged 17.8 yards on just five touchdowns in 1997 but he caught 85 passes. Anyone who sees the ball that often has to be a good fantasy consideration.

☐ **30. Andre Reed (Buffalo Bills)**
When will he slow down? Reed, surprisingly, remains one of the league's better deep threats, averaging 38.3 yards on six touchdowns in 1995 and 35.8 yards on five touchdowns a year ago.

KEEP AN EYE ON

☐ **31. Jimmy Smith (Jacksonville Jaguars)**
Smith, like receiving mate Keenan McCardell, had plenty of receptions (82) but didn't score often (four touchdowns) in 1997. Just don't overlook any receiver who sees the ball that often.

☐ **32. Quinn Early (Buffalo Bills)**
He had 60 receptions but only five touchdowns in 1997. He has the potential, depending on who the Bills settle on at quarterback.

☐ **33. Chris Calloway (New York Giants)**
Former early-round picks Ike Hilliard, Thomas Lewis and Amani Toomer have had their chances but it's Chris Calloway who has provided some consistency with eight touchdowns a year ago.

☐ **34. O.J. McDuffie (Miami Dolphins)**
He scored only once in 1997, but as the Dolphins' main receiver, he should get the opportunity to improve that in a big way in 1998.

☐ **35. Terrell Owens (San Francisco 49ers)**
Owens scored eight times on 60 receptions in 1997 but a healthy Jerry Rice returns in 1998.

☐ **36. Darnay Scott (Cincinnati Bengals)**
Scott averaged a lofty 34.4 yards on five touchdowns in 1997.

☐ **37. Ed McCaffrey (Denver Broncos)**
He may not score many long touchdowns but his consistency is worth noting. McCaffrey has scored seven and eight touchdowns in the last two seasons.

☐ **38. Terry Glenn (New England Patriots)**
After scoring six times on 90 receptions as a rookie in 1996, Glenn struggled through ankle and hamstring injuries in 1997 and scored only twice. I'm looking for a healthy rebound from him in 1998.

☐ **39. Jermaine Lewis (Baltimore Ravens)**
Lewis averaged 38.9 yards on eight touchdowns in 1997, including two on punt returns. Jim Harbaugh at a quarterback in 1998 doesn't excite me about his chances, however.

☐ **40. Wayne Chrebet (New York Jets)**
Chrebet should take advantage now that Jeff Graham has moved to Philadelphia.

PRIME PROSPECTS

☐ **41. Mike Pritchard (Seattle Seahawks)**
While fighting for the No.2 receiving spot in Seattle, Pritchard should easily expand on his two touchdowns in 1997.

☐ **42. Yatil Green (Miami Dolphins)**
The Dolphins' speedy No.1 draft pick of a year ago didn't play a down in 1997 because of a knee injury. He's back healthy in 1998.

☐ **43. Eddie Kennison (St. Louis Rams)**
The Rams hope the speedy Kennison, who scored 11 times as a rookie in 1996 but failed to score a single touchdown in 1997, can rebound to respectable numbers in 1998.

☐ **44. Eric Metcalf (Arizona Cardinals)**
Metcalf has the potential as a kick returner and a receiver to put up a number of long scores.

☐ **45. Frank Sanders (Arizona Cardinals)**
Sanders scored only four times on 75 receptions a year ago but with quarterback Jake Plummer's continuing improvement, Sander's numbers should improve, too.

☐ **46. Jeff Graham (Philadelphia Eagles)**
Graham takes his services to Philadelphia to battle Chris T. Jones and Michael Timpson for playing time.

☐ **47. Karl Williams (Tampa Bay Buccaneers)**
Williams averaged 25.8 yards on five touchdowns in 1997, which included returning a punt 61 yards.

☐ **48. Chris Sanders (Tennessee Oilers)**
Sanders averaged 41.0 yards on his three touchdowns in 1997. He has the potential to fare much better, especially with Derrick Alexander now in an Oiler uniform and taking off some of the heat.

☐ **49. Rae Carruth (Carolina Panthers)**
The Panthers are hoping their No.1 draft pick of a year ago can do better than the four touchdowns he scored a year ago.

☐ **50. Reidel Anthony (Tampa Bay Buccaneers)**
Anthony is another No.1 1997 draft pick who needs to expand on the four touchdowns he scored as a rookie.

DON'T BE SURPRISED

51. C.T. Jones (PHIL)
52. Dawkins (NO)
53. McKnight (SEAT)
54. Engram (CHI)
55. Hilliard (NYG)
56. Proehl (STL)
57. Stokes (SF)
58. Timpson (PHIL)
59. Muhammad (CAR)
60. Jefferson (NE)

YOU NEVER KNOW

61. Toomer (NYG)
62. Shepherd (WASH)
63. K. Alexander (MIA)
64. St. Williams (DALL)
65. Penn (CHI)
66. Hastings (NO)
67. C. Jones (SD)
68. Carrier (CAR)
69. Tr. Brown (NE)
70. Hawkins (PITT)

DON'T COUNT THEM OUT

71. Small (STL)
72. Blackwell (PITT)
73. Davis (DALL)
74. T. Lewis (CHI)
75. Mills (DALL)

76. Ellard (WASH)
77. Copeland (TB)
78. Miller (DALL)
79. Perriman (MIA)
80. Hill (NO)

WORTH MENTIONING

81. Blades (SEAT)
82 W. Jackson (JAC)
83. Brisby (NE)
84. W. Davis (TENN)
85. Ward (NYJ)

86. Dawson (KC)
87. Still (SD)
88. Moulds (BUF)
89. Van Dyke (NYJ)
90. Stablein (NE)

ROOKIE PROSPECTS

NAME	TEAM	COMMENT
☐ 1. Kevin Dyson	TENN	Dyson looking to help improve Oiler passing game.
☐ 2. Randy Moss	MINN	Talented receiver but must overcome off-field problems.
☐ 3. Marcus Nash	DEN	Caught 76 passes and 13 TD's as favorite target of Peyton Manning in '97.
☐ 4. Jerome Pathon	IND	Colts have their QB—now must build around him.
☐ 5. Tony Simmons	NE	Patriots looking for help at wide receiver.
☐ 6. Michael Ricks	SD	Nice size (6'5") target for young Leaf.
☐ 7. Pat Johnson	BALT	Might fit into mix with Michael Jackson and Jermaine Lewis.
☐ 8. Joe Jurevicius	NYG	Giants always looking for receiver help.

A LOOK AT THE TIGHT ENDS

(A Guide for the Beginner)

Considerations in Choosing a Tight End

1. First, look at players' previous performances. Injuries, player moves, holdouts and suspensions should be noted. The season of Brent Jones was marred by injury in 1997.

2. Consistency is common among tight ends. The rankings of the top tight ends seem to change little, with an occasional new name creeping onto the list. It's the Shannon Sharpes and Ben Coates who generally seem to top the list. Wesley Walls may soon join that group.

3. Your second priority should be to pick up a good tight end from a passing team, like the 49ers, where Brent Jones excels, year to year, when he's healthy.

4. When choosing a tight end, first check who his fellow receivers are. A tight end between two good wide receivers will often be left open while opponents double-cover the wide receivers. Such is the case in San Francisco, where Jones profits from his position alongside Jerry Rice, and in Denver where Shannon Sharpe excels next to Rod Smith.

5. Any tight end who has the speed to sneak behind the defense for a long touchdown play will reward you with a lot of points. Keith Jackson, of the Packers, comes to mind, along with Shannon Sharpe.

6. As with wide receivers, look for a quarterback change to have an adverse effect on a tight end. In a quarterback–tight end combination that has clicked well for many years, the departure of the quarterback is likely to reduce the tight end's productivity.

In the 1997 statistics that follow, you'll find the players ranked by their fantasy-point totals. Remember that in the Distance Scoring Method, fantasy points are calculated by the length of the touchdown scored—the longer the touchdown play, the more points earned.

1997 STATISTICAL RESULTS
(TIGHT ENDS — DISTANCE SCORING METHOD)

NAME	TEAM	GP	TD PS	RSH	RSH TDs	AVG LGTH	PS REC	REC TDs	AVG LGTH	TOTAL TDs	AVG LGTH	CONV PTS	FAN-TASY PTS
1. **Sharpe**	**DEN**	**16**	**0**	**0**	**0**	**0.0**	**72**	**3**	**46.0**	**3**	**46.0**	**2**	**32**
1996		15	0	0	0	0.0	80	10	15.0	10	15.0	0	46
1995		12	0	0	0	0.0	63	4	5.3	4	5.3	0	10
3 Yr - TOTALS		43	0	0	0	0.0	215	17	18.2	17	18.2	2	88
2. **Coates**	**NE**	**16**	**0**	**0**	**0**	**0.0**	**66**	**8**	**13.0**	**8**	**13.0**	**0**	**30**
1996		15	0	0	0	0.0	62	9	19.6	9	19.6	2	48
1995		16	0	0	0	0.0	84	6	7.5	6	7.5	0	14
3 Yr - TOTALS		47	0	0	0	0.0	212	23	14.1	23	14.1	2	92
3. **Dudley**	**OAK**	**16**	**0**	**0**	**0**	**0.0**	**48**	**7**	**14.9**	**7**	**14.9**	**0**	**28**
1996		13	0	0	0	0.0	34	4	23.2	4	23.2	0	24
1995		–	–	–	–	–	–	–	–	–	–	–	–
3 Yr - TOTALS		29	0	0	0	0.0	82	11	17.9	11	17.9	0	52
4. **Wycheck**	**TENN**	**16**	**0**	**0**	**0**	**0.0**	**63**	**4**	**26.7**	**4**	**26.7**	**2**	**28**
1996		15	0	2	0	0.0	53	6	12.2	6	12.2	0	20
1995		14	0	1	1	1.0	40	1	36.0	2	18.5	0	10
3 Yr - TOTALS		45	0	3	1	1.0	156	11	19.6	12	18.1	2	58
5. **Drayton**	**MIA**	**15**	**0**	**0**	**0**	**0.0**	**39**	**4**	**25.5**	**4**	**25.5**	**0**	**26**
1996		12	0	0	0	0.0	28	0	0.0	0	0.0	2	2
1995 w/STL		16	0	0	0	0.0	47	4	11.0	4	11.0	0	14
3 Yr - TOTALS		43	0	0	0	0.0	114	8	18.3	8	18.3	2	42
6. **Green**	**BALT**	**14**	**0**	**0**	**0**	**0.0**	**65**	**5**	**19.2**	**5**	**19.2**	**0**	**24**
1996		6	0	0	0	0.0	15	1	3.0	1	3.0	0	2
1995 w/MIA		14	0	0	0	0.0	43	3	21.0	3	21.0	2	16
3 Yr - TOTALS		34	0	0	0	0.0	123	9	18.0	9	18.0	2	42
7. **Gedney**	**ARIZ**	**14**	**0**	**0**	**0**	**0.0**	**23**	**4**	**20.5**	**4**	**20.5**	**0**	**22**
1996		–	–	–	–	–	–	–	–	–	–	–	–
1995 w/CHI		5	0	0	0	0.0	5	0	0.0	0	0.0	0	0
3 Yr - TOTALS		19	0	0	0	0.0	28	4	20.5	4	20.5	0	22
8. **Walls**	**CAR**	**15**	**0**	**0**	**0**	**0.0**	**58**	**6**	**12.2**	**6**	**12.2**	**0**	**20**
1996		16	0	0	0	0.0	61	10	12.3	10	12.3	0	32
1995 w/NO		16	0	0	0	0.0	57	4	12.5	4	12.5	2	14
3 Yr - TOTALS		47	0	0	0	0.0	176	20	12.3	20	12.3	2	66
9. **Chmura**	**GB**	**15**	**0**	**0**	**0**	**0.0**	**38**	**6**	**9.0**	**6**	**9.0**	**0**	**20**
1996		11	0	0	0	0.0	28	0	0.0	0	0.0	0	0
1995		15	0	0	0	0.0	54	7	6.1	7	6.1	2	18
3 Yr - TOTALS		41	0	0	0	0.0	120	13	7.5	13	7.5	2	38
10. **L. Johnson**	**BUF**	**15**	**0**	**1**	**0**	**0.0**	**41**	**2**	**39.0**	**2**	**39.0**	**0**	**18**
1996		13	0	0	0	0.0	46	0	0.0	0	0.0	0	0
1995		13	0	0	0	0.0	49	1	2.0	1	2.0	0	2
3 Yr - TOTALS		41	0	1	0	0.0	136	3	26.7	3	26.7	0	20
11. **Williams**	**OAK**	**10**	**0**	**18**	**3**	**1.0**	**16**	**2**	**20.0**	**5**	**8.6**	**2**	**18**
1996 (as RB)		13	1	121	0	0.0	22	0	0.0	0	0.0	0	3
1995 (as RB)		16	10	255	19	6.1	54	0	0.0	9	6.1	0	22
3 Yr - TOTALS		39	11	394	22	5.4	92	2	20.0	14	7.0	2	43
12. **McGee**	**CIN**	**15**	**0**	**0**	**0**	**0.0**	**34**	**6**	**7.7**	**6**	**7.7**	**0**	**16**
1996		14	0	0	0	0.0	38	4	6.8	4	6.8	0	10
1995		15	0	0	0	0.0	55	4	9.5	4	9.5	0	14
3 Yr - TOTALS		44	0	0	0	0.0	127	14	8.0	14	8.0	2	40
13. **Conwell**	**STL**	**14**	**0**	**0**	**0**	**0.0**	**38**	**4**	**13.2**	**4**	**13.2**	**0**	**16**
1996		6	0	0	0	0.0	15	0	0.0	0	0.0	0	0
1995		–	–	–	–	–	–	–	–	–	–	–	–
3 Yr - TOTALS		20	0	0	0	0.0	53	4	13.2	4	13.2	0	16
14. **F. Jones +**	**SD**	**13**	**0**	**0**	**0**	**0.0**	**41**	**2**	**32.5**	**2**	**32.5**	**0**	**16**
1996		–	–	–	–	–	–	–	–	–	–	–	–
1995		–	–	–	–	–	–	–	–	–	–	–	–
3 Yr - TOTALS		13	0	0	0	0.0	41	2	32.5	2	32.5	0	16
15. **Dunn**	**PHIL**	**7**	**0**	**0**	**0**	**0.0**	**7**	**2**	**31.0**	**2**	**31.0**	**0**	**16**
1996		11	0	0	0	0.0	15	2	11.5	2	11.5	0	6
1995		–	–	–	–	–	–	–	–	–	–	–	–
3 Yr - TOTALS		18	0	0	0	0.0	22	4	21.3	4	21.3	0	22

	NAME	TEAM	GP	TD PS	RSH	RSH TDs	AVG LGTH	PS REC	REC TDs	AVG LGTH	TOTAL TDs	AVG LGTH	CONV PTS	FAN-TASY PTS
16.	Bruener	PITT	9	0	0	0	0.0	18	6	5.5	6	5.5	0	14
	1996		7	0	0	0	0.0	12	0	0.0	0	0.0	2	2
	1995		11	0	0	0	0.0	26	3	11.3	3	11.3	0	10
	3 Yr - TOTALS		27	0	0	0	0.0	56	9	7.4	9	7.4	2	26
17.	P. Mitchell	JAC	14	0	0	0	0.0	35	4	9.5	4	9.5	0	12
	1996		16	0	0	0	0.0	52	1	11.0	1	11.0	0	4
	1995		14	0	0	0	0.0	41	2	14.0	2	14.0	0	8
	3 Yr - TOTALS		44	0	0	0	0.0	128	7	11.0	7	11.0	0	24
18.	Dilger	IND	10	0	0	0	0.0	27	3	15.3	3	15.3	0	12
	1996		13	0	0	0	0.0	42	4	8.0	4	8.0	0	12
	1995		15	0	0	0	0.0	42	4	11.8	4	11.8	0	14
	3 Yr - TOTALS		38	0	0	0	0.0	111	11	11.4	11	11.4	0	38
19.	Purnell	NE	4	0	0	0	0.0	5	3	12.0	3	12.0	0	12
	1996		–	–	–	–	–	–	–	–	–	–	–	–
	1995		–	–	–	–	–	–	–	–	–	–	–	–
	3 Yr - TOTALS		4	0	0	0	0.0	5	3	12.0	3	12.0	0	12
20.	D. Jones +	JAC	3	0	0	0	0.0	5	2	26.0	2	26.0	0	12
	1996		–	–	–	–	–	–	–	–	–	–	–	–
	1995		–	–	–	–	–	–	–	–	–	–	–	–
	3 Yr - TOTALS		3	0	0	0	0.0	5	2	26.0	2	26.0	0	12
21.	Riemersma +	BUF	12	0	0	0	0.0	26	2	14.5	2	14.5	2	10
	1996		–	–	–	–	–	–	–	–	–	–	–	–
	1995		–	–	–	–	–	–	–	–	–	–	–	–
	3 Yr - TOTALS		12	0	0	0	0.0	26	2	14.5	2	14.5	2	10
22.	Gonzalez +	KC	12	0	0	0	0.0	33	2	11.5	2	11.5	2	10
	1996		–	–	–	–	–	–	–	–	–	–	–	–
	1995		–	–	–	–	–	–	–	–	–	–	–	–
	3 Yr - TOTALS		12	0	0	0	0.0	33	2	11.5	2	11.5	2	10
23.	Glover	MINN	12	0	0	0	0.0	32	3	11.0	3	11.0	0	10
	1996 w/OAK		6	0	0	0	0.0	9	1	1.0	1	1.0	0	2
	1995 w/OAK		14	0	0	0	0.0	26	3	5.3	3	5.3	0	8
	3 Yr - TOTALS		32	0	0	0	0.0	67	7	7.1	7	7.1	0	20
24.	C. Lewis	PHIL	8	0	0	0	0.0	12	4	7.0	4	7.0	0	10
	1996		–	–	–	–	–	–	–	–	–	–	–	–
	1995		–	–	–	–	–	–	–	–	–	–	–	–
	3 Yr - TOTALS		8	0	0	0	0.0	12	4	7.0	4	7.0	0	10
25.	Moore	TB	8	0	0	0	0.0	19	4	6.3	4	6.3	0	10
	1996		12	0	0	0	0.0	27	3	10.3	3	10.3	0	10
	1995		10	0	1	0	0.0	13	0	0.0	0	0.0	0	0
	3 Yr - TOTALS		30	0	1	0	0.0	59	7	8.0	7	8.0	0	20
26.	Wetnight	CHI	15	0	0	0	0.0	46	1	30.0	1	30.0	0	8
27.	LaFleur +	DALL	9	0	0	0	0.0	18	2	12.5	2	12.5	0	8
28.	Baxter	NYJ	13	0	0	0	0.0	27	3	6.0	3	6.0	0	8
29.	Jenkins	WASH	4	0	0	0	0.0	4	3	7.7	3	7.7	0	8
30.	Kinchen	BALT	7	0	0	0	0.0	11	1	24.0	1	24.0	0	6
31.	Carswell	DEN	8	0	0	0	0.0	12	1	24.0	1	24.0	0	6
32.	Brady	NYJ	14	0	0	0	0.0	22	2	9.5	2	9.5	0	6
33.	B. Jones	SF	12	0	0	0	0.0	29	2	9.5	2	9.5	0	6
34.	Santiago +	ATL	9	0	0	0	0.0	17	2	4.0	2	4.0	0	4
35.	Hallock	JAC	13	0	4	0	0.0	18	1	10.0	1	10.0	0	4
36.	Popson	KC	12	0	0	0	0.0	35	2	2.0	2	2.0	0	4
37.	Cross	NYG	12	0	0	0	0.0	21	2	1.5	2	1.5	0	4
38.	J. Johnson	PHIL	7	0	0	0	0.0	14	1	16.0	1	16.0	0	4
39.	Crumpler	SEAT	14	0	0	0	0.0	31	1	12.0	1	12.0	0	4
40.	Clark +	SF	5	0	0	0	0.0	8	1	10.0	1	10.0	0	4
41.	Carter	ARIZ	6	0	0	0	0.0	7	1	1.0	1	1.0	0	2
42.	Kozlowski	ATL	5	0	0	0	0.0	7	1	2.0	1	2.0	0	2
43.	West	ATL	6	0	0	0	0.0	7	1	1.0	1	1.0	0	2
44.	Battaglia	CIN	9	0	0	0	0.0	12	1	8.0	1	8.0	0	2
45.	Bjornson	DALL	13	0	0	0	0.0	47	0	0.0	0	0.0	2	2

NAME	TEAM	GP	TD PS	RSH	RSH TDs	AVG LGTH	PS REC	REC TDs	AVG LGTH	TOTAL TDs	AVG LGTH	CONV PTS	FAN-TASY PTS
46. Chryplewicz +	DET	2	0	0	0	0.0	3	1	4.0	1	4.0	0	2
47. T. Davis	GB	2	0	0	0	0.0	2	1	2.0	2	2.0	0	2
48. Thomason	GB	4	0	0	0	0.0	9	1	1.0	1	1.0	0	2
49. Pollard	IND	6	0	0	0	0.0	10	0	0.0	0	0.0	2	2
50. Brown	JAC	6	0	0	0	0.0	8	1	2.0	1	2.0	0	2
51. Perry +	MIA	6	0	0	0	0.0	11	1	3.0	1	3.0	0	2
52. Farquhar	NO	7	0	0	0	0.0	17	1	8.0	1	8.0	0	2
53. I. Smith	NO	9	0	0	0	0.0	17	1	1.0	1	1.0	0	2
54. Hartley	SD	11	0	0	0	0.0	19	1	2.0	1	2.0	0	2
55. Laing	STL	5	0	0	0	0.0	5	1	3.0	1	3.0	0	2
56. Hape +	TB	5	0	1	0	0.0	4	1	1.0	1	1.0	0	2
57. Harris	TB	9	0	0	0	0.0	20	1	5.0	1	5.0	0	2
58. Asher	WASH	16	0	0	0	0.0	49	1	8.0	1	8.0	0	2
59. McWilliams	ARIZ	4	0	0	0	0.0	7	0	0.0	0	0.0	0	0
60. E. Smith	ATL	1	0	0	0	0.0	1	0	0.0	0	0.0	0	0
61. Cline	BUF	1	0	0	0	0.0	1	0	0.0	0	0.0	0	0
62. Mangum +	CAR	1	0	0	0	0.0	4	0	0.0	0	0.0	0	0
63. Rasby	CAR	1	0	0	0	0.0	1	0	0.0	0	0.0	0	0
64. Allen	CHI	1	0	0	0	0.0	1	0	0.0	0	0.0	0	0
65. Allred +	CHI	7	0	0	0	0.0	8	0	0.0	0	0.0	0	0
66. Jennings	CHI	10	0	0	0	0.0	14	0	0.0	0	0.0	0	0
67. Galbraith	DALL	2	0	0	0	0.0	2	0	0.0	0	0.0	0	0
68. Chamberlain	DEN	1	0	0	0	0.0	2	0	0.0	0	0.0	0	0
69. Metzelaars	DET	11	0	0	0	0.0	17	0	0.0	0	0.0	0	0
70. Sloan	DET	11	0	0	0	0.0	29	0	0.0	0	0.0	0	0
71. Slutzker	IND	2	0	0	0	0.0	3	0	0.0	0	0.0	0	0
72. Walker	KC	5	0	0	0	0.0	5	0	0.0	0	0.0	0	0
73. Delong	MINN	7	0	0	0	0.0	8	0	0.0	0	0.0	0	0
74. Goodwin	MINN	5	0	0	0	0.0	7	0	0.0	0	0.0	0	0
75. Savoie +	NO	1	0	0	0	0.0	1	0	0.0	0	0.0	0	0
76. T. Johnson	NO	1	0	0	0	0.0	1	0	0.0	0	0.0	0	0
77. Pierce	NYG	8	0	0	0	0.0	10	0	0.0	0	0.0	0	0
78. Botkin	PITT	1	0	0	0	0.0	1	0	0.0	0	0.0	0	0
79. Lyons	PITT	2	0	0	0	0.0	4	0	0.0	0	0.0	0	0
80. Sadowski	PITT	1	0	0	0	0.0	1	0	0.0	0	0.0	0	0
81. Pupunu	SD	1	0	0	0	0.0	1	0	0.0	0	0.0	0	0
82. S. Mitchell	SD	1	0	0	0	0.0	1	0	0.0	0	0.0	0	0
83. Fauria	SEAT	7	0	0	0	0.0	10	0	0.0	0	0.0	0	0
84. May	SEAT	2	0	0	0	0.0	2	0	0.0	0	0.0	0	0
85. Fann	SF	2	0	0	0	0.0	5	0	0.0	0	0.0	0	0
86. Jacoby	STL	2	0	0	0	0.0	2	0	0.0	0	0.0	0	0
87. J. Davis	TB	3	0	0	0	0.0	3	0	0.0	0	0.0	0	0
88. Jordan	TB	1	0	0	0	0.0	1	0	0.0	0	0.0	0	0
89. R. Lewis	TENN	1	0	0	0	0.0	1	0	0.0	0	0.0	0	0
90. Roan	TENN	6	0	0	0	0.0	12	0	0.0	0	0.0	0	0

+ DENOTES COLLEGE DRAFT PICK

RATING THE PLAYERS FOR 1998
(Tight Ends—Distance Scoring Method)

GRAB ONE IF YOU CAN

☐ **1. Shannon Sharpe (Denver Broncos)**
Unmatched at tight end for getting downfield in a hurry, Sharpe averaged 46.0 yards on his three touchdowns in 1997 and twice scored on plays of more than 60 yards. He'll have to find the endzone more often in 1998, perhaps the way he did in 1996 when he scored 10 times.

☐ **2. Ricky Dudley (Oakland Raiders)**
With strong-armed Jeff George coming to Oakland, Dudley's touchdowns jumped from four as a rookie in 1996 to seven in 1997. Dudley is another tight end who can get downfield in a hurry, which makes him a nice fantasy pick for this scoring method.

☐ **3. Ben Coates (New England Patriots)**
It's not so much his ability to score on long plays but his consistency that makes Coates an attractive fantasy pick. Coates has recorded 62 and 66 receptions along with scoring nine and eight times, respectively, over the last two seasons.

☐ **4. Wesley Walls (Carolina Panthers)**
Walls is another producer who's not flashy but consistent. Walls has recorded 57, 61 and 58 receptions, respectively, over the last three seasons (two in Carolina) and scored 4, 10 and 6 touchdowns over that same period.

☐ **5. Frank Wycheck (Tennessee Oilers)**
Highly involved in the Oiler offense, Wycheck scored six times in 1996 and showed his ability to get downfield by averaging a lofty 26.4 yards on four touchdowns in 1997.

BEST OF THE REST

☐ **6. Mark Chmura (Green Bay Packers)**
Perhaps he's unlikely to score on many long plays, but as a favorite scoring weapon of quarterback Brett Favre, Chmura could score 6 to 10 touchdowns.

☐ **7. Troy Drayton (Miami Dolphins)**
Quickly becoming more of a factor in the Dolphins' offense, Drayton expanded to 39 receptions in 1997 and averaged a 25.5 yards on his four touchdowns. Look for continued success from the talented Drayton in 1998.

☐ **8. Eric Green (Baltimore Ravens)**
Green returned to prominence in 1997, recording a whopping 65 receptions while averaging 19.2 yards on five touchdowns. He will be a constant scoring threat for the Ravens.

☐ **9. Fred Jones (San Diego Chargers)**
He may have only scored twice in 1997 as a rookie but he averaged 32.5

yards on those two touchdowns. His 41 receptions also show that he gets the ball often, so watch out for him as a more consistent scoring threat in 1998.

☐ **10. Ernie Conwell (St. Louis Rams)**
With Troy Drayton in Miami, Conwell gained more playing time and better numbers in 1997. He finished with 38 receptions and four touchdowns, and those are numbers he could easily improve on in 1998.

STRONG LONG SHOTS

☐ **11. Tony McGee (Cincinnati Bengals)**
McGee's touchdown production continues to grow. After producing four touchdowns in both 1995 and 1996, McGee jumped to six scores in 1997 on just 34 receptions. He'll again be a scoring force for the Bengals in 1998.

☐ **12. Eric Bjornson (Philadelphia Eagles)**
Getting the bulk of the playing time after Jay Novacek's retirement, Bjornson recorded 47 receptions but did not score a touchdown in 1997. I look for his touchdown numbers to grow in 1998 as he continues to emerge in the Cowboy offense.

☐ **13. Jamie Asher (Washington Redskins)**
Asher actually lifted his reception level from 42 in 1996 to 49 in 1997 but his touchdown production dropped to only one after he scored four times in 1996. Still, as a main wheel in the Redskins' offense, Asher's touchdown numbers should rebound in 1998.

☐ **14. Tony Gonzalez (Kansas City Chiefs)**
Gonzalez will continue to push veteran Ted Popson in Kansas City. As a rookie in 1997, Gonzalez scored twice on 33 receptions. I believe he'll easily improve on those numbers in 1998.

☐ **15. Ken Dilger (Indianapolis Colts)**
Dilger had two consistent seasons in 1995 and 1996 when he recorded 42 receptions and four touchdowns in each season. In 1997, Dilger fell back to only three scores, missing a good number of games with a hamstring injury. Look for another four or more scores from him in 1998.

HAVE THE POTENTIAL

☐ **16. Greg Clark (San Francisco 49ers)**
With Brent Jones retiring after the 1997 season, the 49ers are looking for his replacement. Greg Clark has given them reason to give him a shot but he'll be challenged by new acquisition Irv Smith. Whoever wins the job should see reasonable success while playing for the powerful 49ers.

☐ **17. Pete Mitchell (Jacksonville Jaguars)**
A consistent weapon for the Jaguars, Mitchell has recorded 41, 52 and 35 receptions, respectively, the last three seasons. During that same period, he has scored two, one and four touchdowns. He should continue to see plenty scoring opportunities in 1998 since he sees the ball so often.

☐ **18. Mark Bruener (Pittsburgh Steelers)**
Perhaps he won't score on many long touchdowns but Bruener got much more involved in the red zone offense in 1997, scoring six times on just 18 receptions.

☐ **19. Lonnie Johnson (Buffalo Bills)**
Johnson has produced more than 40 receptions in each of the last three seasons but he hasn't scored much. In 1997, he did score twice, averaging a lofty 39.0 yards on each. If he can continue to find his way into the endzone, he'll be a decent fantasy consideration for 1998.

☐ **20. O.J. Santiago (Atlanta Falcons)**
As a rookie in 1997, Santiago found his way into the endzone only twice, but did it on only 17 receptions and despite playing in just nine games because of a leg injury. If he's healthy in 1998, he should be able to build up those numbers.

KEEP AN EYE ON	YOU NEVER KNOW
21. Popson (KC)	31. Farguhar (NO)
22. I. Smith (SF)	32. Cross (NYG)
23. Sloan (DET)	33. Baxter (NYJ)
24. Gedney (ARIZ)	34. Fauria (SEAT)
25. Moore (TB)	35. J. Johnson (PHIL)
26. Wetnight (CHI)	36. H. Williams (OAK)
27. LeFleur (DALL)	37. Brady (NYJ)
28. Crumpler (SEAT)	38. Carter (ARIZ)
29. Glover (MINN)	39. Jennings (CHI)
30. Harris (TENN)	40. Jenkins (WASH)

WORTH MENTIONING

41. Pupunu (NYG)
42. C. Lewis (PHIL)
43. Metzelaars (DET)
44. Hartley (SD)
45. Riesmersma (BUF)

ROOKIE PROSPECTS

NAME	TEAM	COMMENT
☐ 1. Cameron Cleeland	NO	Irv Smith's departure to S.F. creates opportunity.
☐ 2. Alonzo Mayes	CHI	Nice size and good downfield ability.
☐ 3. Stephen Alexander	WASH	Decent hands and good jumping ability.
☐ 4. Rod Rutledge	NE	Will have trouble pushing Ben Coates for production.

A LOOK AT THE QUARTERBACKS
(A Guide for the Beginner)
Considerations in Choosing a Quarterback

1. First, look at players' previous performances. Injuries, trades, holdouts and suspensions should be noted. In 1997, the seasons of Brad Johnson, Mark Brunell, and Gus Frerotte were hurt by their injuries.

2. Consider quarterbacks who aren't afraid to run the ball in for a touchdown. This opens up an area of scoring possibilities not available to the gimpy-legged quarterback who stays in the pocket. Steve Young of San Francisco, Mark Brunell of Jacksonville, and Kordell Stewart come quickly to mind.

3. Next, does the quarterback's team like to put the ball in the air? The more a team throws the ball, the greater the chance that the quarterback will have a high-scoring year. The Packers' Brett Favre is an obvious early pick.

4. Look for a quarterback who likes to throw deep for those long touchdown passes. Remember, the longer the touchdown, the more points awarded. A quarterback who has a proven deep-threat receiver among his targets is an asset to your team.

5. If you start a quarterback who gets yanked after the first quarter or half of a game, your fantasy team will suffer. Stay away from teams that are struggling to find their weekly signal caller.

In the 1997 statistics that follow, you'll find the players ranked by their fantasy-point totals. Remember that in the Distance Scoring Method, fantasy points are calculated by the length of the touchdown scored—the longer the touchdown play, the more points earned.

1997 STATISTICAL RESULTS
(QUARTERBACKS — DISTANCE SCORING METHOD)

	NAME	TEAM	GP	RSH TDs	TD PS	AVG TD LGTH	COMP	YARDS	YDS PER COMP	CONV PTS	FANTASY POINTS
1.	**Stewart**	**PITT**	**16**	**11**	**21**	**19.9**	**236**	**3,020**	**12.8**	**1**	**91**
	1996		16	5	0	0.0	11	100	9.1	0	48
	1995		–	–	–	–	–	–	–	–	–
	3 Yr - TOTALS		32	16	21	19.9	247	3,120	12.6	1	139
2.	**George**	**OAK**	**16**	**0**	**29**	**24.7**	**290**	**3,917**	**13.5**	**2**	**87**
	1996 w/ATL		3	0	3	12.0	56	698	12.5	0	6
	1995 w/ATL		16	0	24	23.6	336	4,143	12.3	3	72
	3 Yr - TOTALS		35	0	56	23.6	682	8,758	12.8	5	165
3.	**Elway**	**DEN**	**16**	**1**	**27**	**24.4**	**280**	**3,635**	**13.0**	**1**	**85**
	1996		15	4	26	16.2	287	3,328	11.6	0	65
	1995		16	1	26	25.7	316	3,970	12.6	3	85
	3 Yr - TOTALS		47	6	79	22.1	883	10,933	12.4	4	235
4.	**Moon**	**SEAT**	**15**	**1**	**25**	**25.9**	**313**	**3,678**	**11.8**	**0**	**84**
	1996 w/MINN		8	0	7	25.1	134	1,610	12.0	0	21
	1995 w/MINN		16	0	33	19.6	377	4,228	11.2	0	84
	3 Yr - TOTALS		39	1	65	22.6	824	9,516	11.5	0	189
5.	**Favre**	**GB**	**16**	**1**	**35**	**14.3**	**304**	**3,867**	**12.7**	**1**	**74**
	1996		16	2	39	19.7	325	3,899	12.0	2	106
	1995		16	3	38	17.9	359	4,413	12.3	0	97
	3 Yr - TOTALS		48	6	##	17.4	988	12,179	12.3	3	277
6.	**Bledsoe**	**NE**	**16**	**0**	**28**	**16.2**	**314**	**3,706**	**11.8**	**0**	**62**
	1996		16	0	27	15.2	373	4,086	11.0	4	59
	1995		15	0	13	16.4	323	3,507	10.9	2	28
	3 Yr - TOTALS		47	0	68	15.8	1010	11,299	11.2	6	149
7.	**McNair**	**TENN**	**16**	**8**	**14**	**19.2**	**216**	**2,665**	**12.3**	**1**	**61**
	1996		9	2	6	38.0	88	1,197	13.6	0	36
	1995		4	0	3	36.7	41	569	13.9	0	12
	3 Yr - TOTALS		29	10	23	26.4	345	4,431	12.8	1	109
8.	**Mitchell**	**DET**	**16**	**1**	**19**	**22.2**	**293**	**3,484**	**11.9**	**1**	**56**
	1996		14	4	17	19.6	253	2,917	11.5	0	51
	1995		16	4	32	23.6	346	4,338	12.5	1	101
	3 Yr - TOTALS		46	9	68	22.2	892	10,739	12.0	2	208
9.	**Testaverde**	**BALT**	**13**	**0**	**18**	**22.9**	**271**	**2,971**	**11.0**	**2**	**53**
	1996		16	2	33	19.7	325	4,177	12.9	5	92
	1995		13	2	17	22.4	241	2,883	12.0	0	51
	3 Yr - TOTALS		42	4	68	21.2	837	10,031	12.0	7	196
10.	**Aikman**	**DALL**	**16**	**0**	**19**	**19.2**	**292**	**3,283**	**11.2**	**2**	**50**
	1996		15	1	12	15.3	296	3,126	10.6	2	29
	1995		16	1	16	19.4	280	3,304	11.8	1	42
	3 Yr - TOTALS		47	2	47	18.3	868	9,713	11.2	5	121
11.	**Plummer +**	**ARIZ**	**10**	**2**	**15**	**20.3**	**157**	**2,203**	**14.0**	**2**	**49**
	1996		–	–	–	–	–	–	–	–	–
	1995		–	–	–	–	–	–	–	–	–
	3 Yr - TOTALS		10	2	15	20.3	157	2,203	14.0	2	49
12.	**Kramer**	**CHI**	**15**	**2**	**14**	**24.8**	**275**	**3,011**	**10.9**	**2**	**49**
	1996		4	0	3	21.3	73	781	10.7	0	8
	1995		16	1	29	21.0	315	3,838	12.2	0	80
	3 Yr - TOTALS		35	3	46	22.2	663	7,630	11.5	2	137
13.	**Young**	**SF**	**15**	**3**	**19**	**16.9**	**241**	**3,029**	**12.6**	**0**	**49**
	1996		12	4	14	20.4	214	2,410	11.3	2	53
	1995		11	3	20	17.2	299	3,200	10.7	0	51
	3 Yr - TOTALS		38	10	53	17.9	754	8,639	11.5	2	153
14.	**B. Johnson *****	**MINN**	**13**	**0**	**20**	**14.6**	**275**	**3,036**	**11.0**	**6**	**47**
	1996		12	1	17	21.0	195	2,258	11.6	2	51
	1995		5	0	0	0.0	25	272	10.9	0	0
	3 Yr - TOTALS		30	1	37	17.5	495	5,566	11.2	8	98
15.	**Dilfer**	**TB**	**16**	**1**	**21**	**15.8**	**217**	**2,555**	**11.8**	**0**	**47**
	1996		16	0	12	15.6	267	2,859	10.7	1	28
	1995		16	2	4	25.3	224	2,774	12.4	0	21
	3 Yr - TOTALS		48	3	37	16.8	708	8,188	11.6	1	96

	NAME	TEAM	GP	RSH TDs	TD PS	AVG TD LGTH	COMP	YARDS	YDS PER COMP	CONV PTS	FANTASY POINTS
16.	Chandler	ATL	14	0	20	17.2	202	2,692	13.3	0	46
	1996 w/HOUS		12	0	16	21.1	184	2,099	11.4	0	43
	1995 w/HOUS		13	2	17	25.5	225	2,460	10.9	2	56
	3 Yr - TOTALS		39	2	53	21.0	611	7,251	11.9	2	145
17.	Brunell	JAC	14	2	18	13.1	264	3,281	12.4	1	41
	1996		16	3	19	23.4	353	4,367	12.4	7	73
	1995		13	4	15	12.0	201	2,168	10.8	1	38
	3 Yr - TOTALS		43	9	52	16.5	818	9,816	12.0	9	152
18.	Marino	MIA	16	0	16	19.0	319	3,780	11.8	0	40
	1996		13	0	17	16.2	221	2,795	12.6	0	40
	1995		14	0	24	17.0	309	3,668	11.9	2	54
	3 Yr - TOTALS		43	0	57	17.3	849	10,243	12.1	2	134
19.	O'Donnell	NYJ	15	1	17	17.6	259	2,796	10.8	0	40
	1996		6	0	4	37.0	110	1,147	10.4	0	17
	1995 w/PITT		12	0	17	22.5	246	2,970	12.1	0	47
	3 Yr - TOTALS		33	1	38	21.8	615	6,913	11.2	0	104
20.	Frerotte	WASH	13	2	17	15.0	204	2,682	13.1	0	39
	1996		16	0	12	16.4	270	3,453	12.8	0	27
	1995		13	1	13	20.0	199	2,751	13.8	0	35
	3 Yr - TOTALS		42	3	42	16.9	673	8,886	13.2	0	101
21.	T. Collins	BUF	14	0	12	26.3	215	2,367	11.0	0	38
	1996		7	0	4	41.3	55	739	13.4	0	19
	1995		7	0	0	0.0	14	112	8.0	0	0
	3 Yr - TOTALS		28	0	16	30.1	284	3,218	11.3	0	57
22.	Banks	STL	16	1	14	17.1	252	3,254	12.9	0	34
	1996		14	0	15	28.0	192	2,544	13.3	2	53
	1995		–	–	–	–	–	–	–	–	–
	3 Yr - TOTALS		30	1	29	22.7	444	5,798	13.1	2	87
23.	Esiason	CIN	7	0	13	20.3	118	1,478	12.5	0	33
	1996		10	1	11	16.4	190	2,293	12.1	2	28
	1995 w/NYJ		12	0	16	14.7	221	2,275	10.3	0	34
	3 Yr - TOTALS		29	1	40	17.0	529	6,046	11.4	2	95
24.	Hoying +	PHIL	7	0	11	20.8	128	1,573	12.3	1	31
	1996		–	–	–	–	–	–	–	–	–
	1995		–	–	–	–	–	–	–	–	–
	3 Yr - TOTALS		7	0	11	20.8	128	1,573	12.3	1	31
25.	Grbac	KC	10	1	11	17.1	179	1,943	10.9	2	30
	1996 w/SF		10	2	8	16.1	122	1,236	10.1	0	21
	1995 w/SF		9	2	8	32.0	127	1,469	11.6	1	34
	3 Yr - TOTALS		29	5	27	21.2	428	4,648	10.9	3	85
26.	Blake	CIN	11	3	8	20.9	184	2,125	11.5	1	29
	1996		16	2	24	15.6	308	3,624	11.8	1	58
	1995		16	2	28	19.8	326	3,822	11.7	2	78
	3 Yr - TOTALS		43	7	60	18.3	818	9,571	11.7	4	165
27.	Kanell	NYG	12	0	11	20.4	156	1,740	11.2	0	29
	1996		4	0	1	24.0	23	227	9.9	0	3
	1995		–	–	–	–	–	–	–	–	–
	3 Yr - TOTALS		16	0	12	20.7	179	1,967	11.0	0	32
28.	K. Collins	CAR	13	1	11	17.3	200	2,124	10.6	1	27
	1996		13	0	14	12.3	204	2,454	12.0	2	27
	1995		15	3	14	27.8	214	2,717	12.7	2	54
	3 Yr - TOTALS		41	4	39	19.3	618	7,295	11.8	5	108
29.	Humphries	SD	8	0	5	38.4	121	1,488	12.3	0	22
	1996		13	0	18	20.5	232	2,670	11.5	0	47
	1995		15	1	17	22.8	282	3,381	12.0	1	50
	3 Yr - TOTALS		36	1	40	23.7	635	7,539	11.9	1	119
30.	Zeier	BALT	5	0	7	27.3	67	958	14.3	0	22
	1996		1	0	1	2.0	10	97	9.7	0	1
	1995		6	0	4	12.8	82	864	10.5	2	7
	3 Yr - TOTALS		12	0	12	20.3	159	1,919	12.1	2	30

	NAME	TEAM	GP	RSH TDs	TD PS	AVG TD LGTH	COMP	YARDS	YDS PER COMP	CONV PTS	FANTASY POINTS
31.	Harbaugh	IND	12	0	10	12.0	189	2,060	10.9	1	19
32.	Whelihan	SD	9	0	6	24.0	118	1,357	11.5	0	19
33.	Detmer	PHIL	8	1	7	15.9	134	1,567	11.7	0	17
34.	Graham	ARIZ	8	2	4	15.5	130	1,408	10.8	2	15
35.	Gannon	KC	9	2	7	9.7	98	1,144	11.7	0	15
36.	Shuler	NO	10	1	2	54.5	106	1,288	12.2	1	15
37.	Justin	IND	8	0	5	17.0	83	1,046	12.6	2	14
38.	Cunningham	MINN	4	0	6	13.0	44	501	11.4	1	13
39.	Hobert **	NO	6	0	6	16.7	78	1,024	13.1	0	13
40.	R. Johnson	JAC	5	1	2	24.0	22	344	15.6	0	12
41.	Brown	NYG	7	1	5	12.8	93	1,023	11.0	1	12
42.	Van Pelt	BUF	6	1	2	29.0	60	684	11.4	2	11
43.	Beuerlein	CAR	7	0	6	12.5	89	1,032	11.6	0	11
44.	Tolliver **	KC	7	0	5	17.4	64	677	10.6	0	11
45.	Hostetler	WASH	6	0	5	16.2	79	899	11.4	0	11
46.	Wuerffel +	NO	6	0	4	17.0	42	518	12.3	0	9
47.	Foley	NYJ	4	0	3	19.3	56	705	12.6	0	7
48.	Peete	PHIL	5	0	4	11.5	68	869	12.8	0	6
49.	Mirer	CHI	7	1	0	0.0	53	420	7.9	2	4
50.	Zolak	NE	4	0	2	13.0	6	67	11.2	0	4
51.	Druckenmiller +	SF	4	0	1	25.0	21	239	11.4	1	4
52.	Tomczak	PITT	5	0	1	28.0	16	185	11.6	0	3
53.	Everett	SD	4	0	1	21.0	36	457	12.7	0	3
54.	Kitna	SEAT	3	1	1	8.0	31	371	12.0	0	3
55.	Case	ARIZ	2	1	0	0.0	29	316	10.9	0	2
56.	Holcomb	IND	4	0	1	6.0	45	454	10.1	1	2
57.	Graziani +	ATL	2	0	0	0.0	7	41	5.9	0	0
58.	Stenstrom	CHI	3	0	0	0.0	8	70	8.8	0	0
59.	Wilson	DALL	6	0	0	0.0	12	115	9.6	0	0
60.	Garrett	DALL	1	0	0	0.0	10	56	5.6	0	0
61.	Lewis	DEN	3	0	0	0.0	1	21	21.0	0	0
62.	Brister	DEN	1	0	0	0.0	6	48	8.0	0	0
63.	Reich	DET	4	0	0	0.0	11	121	11.0	0	0
64.	Blundin	DET	1	0	0	0.0	0	0	0.0	0	0
65.	Bono	GB	2	0	0	0.0	5	29	5.8	0	0
66.	Pederson	GB	1	0	0	0.0	0	0	0.0	0	0
67.	St. Matthews	JAC	2	0	0	0.0	26	275	10.6	0	0
68.	Erickson	MIA	2	0	0	0.0	13	165	12.7	0	0
69.	Nussmeier	NO	3	0	0	0.0	18	182	10.1	0	0
70.	Cherry +	NYG	1	0	0	0.0	0	0	0.0	0	0
71.	Clements +	NYJ	1	0	0	0.0	0	0	0.0	0	0
72.	Lucas	NYJ	1	0	0	0.0	3	28	9.3	0	0
73.	Klingler	OAK	1	0	0	0.0	4	27	6.8	0	0
74.	Quinn	PITT	1	0	0	0.0	1	10	10.0	0	0
75.	Philcox	SD	2	0	0	0.0	16	173	10.8	0	0
76.	Friesz	SEAT	2	0	0	0.0	15	138	9.2	0	0
77.	Brohm	SF	5	0	0	0.0	16	164	10.3	0	0
78.	Rypien	STL	4	0	0	0.0	19	270	14.2	0	0
79.	Walsh	TB	5	0	0	0.0	6	58	9.7	0	0
80.	Krieg	TENN	3	0	0	0.0	1	2	2.0	0	0
81.	Ritchey	TENN	1	0	0	0.0	2	15	7.5	0	0
82.	Green	WASH	1	0	0	0.0	0	0	0.0	0	0

+   DENOTES COLLEGE DRAFT PICK

**	Hobert	NO	Played in 1 game with Buffalo.
**	Tolliver	KC	Played in 6 games with Atlanta.
***	B. Johnson	MINN	Scored TD on a 3 yard reception.

RATING THE PLAYERS FOR 1998
(Quarterbacks—Distance Scoring Method)

GRAB ONE IF YOU CAN

☐ **1. Brett Favre (Green Bay Packers)**
His four-year string of throwing more than 30 touchdowns in a season, plus receivers Antonio Freeman, Robert Brooks and Mark Chmura, makes Favre a solid choice for fantasy players again in 1998.

☐ **2. Kordell Stewart (Pittsburgh Steelers)**
In his first year as a starter, Stewart threw for 21 touchdowns and ran for 11 more in 1997. With his ability to run, Stewart gives you a double threat to score every game. However, losing his best receiver, Yancey Thigpen, to Tennessee in the offseason hurt.

☐ **3. Jeff George (Oakland Raiders)**
The Raiders have always liked to throw downfield and now they've got a quarterback with an arm to do so. Jeff George threw 29 touchdowns in his first year with the Riaders in 1997. With targets such as James Jett, Tim Brown and Ricky Dudley, he should again have big success in this scoring method in 1998.

☐ **4. John Elway (Denver Broncos)**
There have been three consistent touchdown seasons of 26, 26 and 27 touchdown passes for John Elway over the last three years. Adding Rod Smith as a consistent deep threat weapon makes 1998 look bright as well.

☐ **5. Warren Moon (Seattle Seahawks)**
Moon was thrown into a starting role at the outset of 1997 after an injury to John Friesz. Moon responded in glorious fashion, averaging 25.9 yards on 25 touchdown passes. With speedster Joey Galloway to lead the way, Moon should be looking at another big year in 1998.

BEST OF THE REST

☐ **6. Steve Young (San Francisco 49er)**
Don't count him out! Young has been slowed by injuries in recent years and in 1997, his star receiver Jerry Rice was also hurt. With both Young and Rice back healthy, along with the development of Terrell Owens and J.J. Stokes, Young should rebound to better numbers in 1998.

☐ **7. Drew Bledsoe (New England Patriots)**
There was some question about Bledsoe's year-to-year consistency but after he threw 27 and 28 touchdowns, respectively, the last two seasons, those questions may have disappeared. Bledsoe could use more consistency at the wide receiver position, however, so he doesn't have to rely so heavily on tight end Ben Coates.

☐ **8. Scott Mitchell (Detroit Lions)**
Having targets such as Herman Moore and now Johnnie Morton should make each season a success for Mitchell, but Barry Sanders stole the show in 1997. Mitchell threw for only 19 touchdowns. I look

for teams to do more to stop Sanders in 1998, which will force Mitchell to throw more, enhancing his year-end numbers.

☐ **9. Brad Johnson (Minnesota Vikings)**
Johnson, in his first year as the full-time starter, had thrown 20 touchdown passes in the first 13 games in 1997 before a neck injury forced him out for the year. He's returning healthy in 1998, and I look for Johnson to improve as a player and improve on his numbers.

☐ **10. Steve McNair (Tennessee Oilers)**
The Oilers were looking to their future when they gave young Steve McNair the starting role in 1997. McNair responded with just 14 touchdown passes but added 8 on the ground. Looking to 1998, fantasy owners have to like his ability to run for scores plus the fact that the Oilers picked up Derrick Alexander (from the Ravens) as a receiver.

STRONG LONG SHOTS

☐ **11. Jake Plummer (Arizona Cardinals)**
After taking over the starting quarterback back job a short way into the 1997 season, Plummer ignited the Cardinals' offense. Playing in just 10 games, Plummer threw for 15 touchdowns, averaging just over 20 yards on each. With targets like Rob Moore and Frank Sanders and playing over a full 16 games, Plummer should see even more success in 1998.

☐ **12. Mark Brunell (Jacksonville Jaguars)**
Despite his success in throwing for yardage, Brunell has yet to throw for a substantial number of touchdown passes. In 1997, after missing the first two games of the year, Brunell threw for 18 touchdowns. I believe he can easily better that number in 1998, especially with targets Keenan McCardell and Jimmy Smith, who are both likely to top 80 receptions again. Also, remember that Brunell runs well and is capable of running in a number of scores.

☐ **13. Jeff Blake (Cincinnati Bengals)**
Struggling Blake lost his job in 1997 to veteran Boomer Esiason. Esiason, however, has retired, which likely means Blake gets the starting job back. With the starting job in hand, Blake will try to reach the numbers he recorded in 1995 and 1996 when he threw for 28 and 24 touchdowns, respectively. That won't be an easy task, considering that the Bengals face the league's third-toughest schedule.

☐ **14. Bobby Hoying (Philadelphia Eagles)**
After capturing the starting job midway through 1997, Hoying surprised many by throwing for 11 touchdowns in just seven games. Look for his continued success in 1998 as he gains maturity and confidence.

☐ **15. Elvis Grbac (Kansas City Chiefs)**
Playing in just 10 games in 1997 because of a shoulder injury, Grbac threw for 11 touchdowns in his first year as the Chiefs' starter. If he can stay healthy, he will have Derrick Alexander to team with Andre Rison, and that should breed reasonable success.

HAVE THE POTENTIAL

☐ **16. Chris Chandler (Atlanta Falcons)**
Despite missing two games because of injury in 1997, Chandler threw for 20 scores. Being healthy in 1998 and having target Terrance Mathis should help him gain respectable results, though losing Bert Emanuel to Tampa Bay in the offseason will hurt.

☐ **17. Tony Banks (St. Louis Rams)**
Banks really struggled in 1997, throwing for only 14 touchdowns (17.1 yard average) after averaging a much better 28.0 yards on 15 touchdowns the year before. He missed Isaac Bruce for the first five weeks of the year because of an injury. Speedster Eddie Kennison never caught a touchdown. In 1998, look for Banks to rebound with a healthy Isaac Bruce, the addition of Ricky Proehl, and a contribution from Eddie Kennison.

☐ **18. Erik Kramer (Chicago Bears)**
Kramer returned, surprisingly, from a back problem to again become the Bears' starting quarterback in 1997. He threw for only 14 touchdowns, which was a huge disappointment considering that he had thrown for 29 just two years earlier. Kramer did miss Curtis Conway, who was injured for most of the year but should be back healthy to help Kramer's numbers in 1998.

☐ **19. Dan Marino (Miami Dolphins)**
Age has really taken its toll on Dan Marino's numbers in recent years. In 1997, he threw for only 16 touchdowns. I look for something of a rebound in 1998, however, since Miami faces a very easy schedule and will have last year's first-round pick, Yatil Green, back from an injury.

☐ **20. Troy Aikman (Dallas Cowboys)**
Aikman is a household name but he' not really a big fantasy producer. His 19 touchdown passes of a year ago were actually very good, by his standards. I believe Aikman will continue to throw for more touchdown passes if he's healthy because the Cowboys' running game is no longer dominant.

KEEP AN EYE ON

☐ **21. Glenn Foley/Neil O'Donnell (New York Jets)**
Whoever gets the job has nice targets to throw to, including Keyshawn Johnson, Wayne Chrebet....

☐ **22. Gus Frerotte (Washington Redskins)**
Frerotte threw for 17 touchdowns in 1997 despite missing the last three games with a hip injury.

☐ **23. Trent Dilfer (Tampa Bay Buccaneers)**
Dilfer boosted his confidence and his touchdown numbers to 21 in 1997.

☐ **24. Jim Harbaugh (Baltimore Ravens)**
Harbaugh moves to a team with some interesting targets in Michael Jackson, Jermaine Lewis and Eric Green. However, Harbaugh does not have a reputation for big numbers.

☐ **25. Rob Johnson/Doug Flutie/Todd Collins (Buffalo Bills)**
I don't see a Jim Kelly clone here!

☐ **26. Peyton Manning (Indianapolis Colts)**
I'm not too excited about fantasy potential here yet.

☐ **27. Ryan Leaf/Craig Whelihan (San Diego Chargers)**
Success is unlikely to be immediate.

☐ **28. Danny Kanell (New York Giants)**
Kanell showed some things in 1997. He has some real speedy receivers but, how often will the Giants pass?

☐ **29. Kerry Collins (Carolina Panthers)**
Collins doesn't have the potential for many touchdown passes. He has thrown for 14, 14 and 11 touchdowns the last three seasons.

☐ **30. Billy Joe Hobert (New Orleans Saints)**
There's no reason to go after a Saint quarterback in 1998.

ROOKIE PROSPECTS

NAME	TEAM	COMMENT
☐ 1. Peyton Manning	IND	Losing ain't so bad, Colts got their future QB by doing so.
☐ 2. Ryan Leaf	SD	Lots of talent, good leader on field.
☐ 3. Charlie Batch	DET	Future potential only.
☐ 4. John Quinn	JAC	Future potential only.
☐ 5. Brian Griese	DEN	Future potential only.

A LOOK AT THE KICKERS

(A Guide for the Beginner)

Considerations in Choosing a Kicker

1. First, look at players' previous performances. Injuries, player moves, suspensions and holdouts should be noted.

2. A kicker needs scoring opportunities, and one of our main concerns is the team he's playing for. Get a kicker who plays for a team that consistently moves the ball deep into enemy territory, a good offensive or defensive team.

3. Go for a kicker who has played on the same team for a few years. Kickers are treated as if they were a dime a dozen. If they have been with a team a few years, it's a sign of confidence in their consistency.

4. Look at the schedule to gauge the strength of the opposition a kicker will face in 1998. A soft schedule could mean a lot of points. (See Section VI for a ranking of the 1998 schedules.)

5. A consideration that is unique to this method is the length of the field goal. If it comes to choosing between two nearly equal kickers, go with the one who is more consistent from long distances.

In the 1997 statistics that follow, you'll find the players ranked by their fantasy-point totals. Remember that in the Distance Scoring Method for kickers, fantasy points are calculated by the length of the field goal (see the following table), and one point is awarded for each successful extra point.

FIELD GOALS

0– 9 yards...1 point	40–49 yards...5 points
10–19 yards...2 points	50–59 yards...6 points
20–29 yards...3 points	60–69 yards...7 points
30–39 yards...4 points	70 & over....10 points

1997 STATISTICAL RESULTS
(KICKERS — DISTANCE SCORING METHOD)

#	NAME	TEAM	GP	EXTRA PTS	EXTRA PT ATT	ACC RATE	10-19	20-29	30-39	40-49	50-59	60 & OVER	FG	ATT	ACC RATE	FAN-TASY PTS
1.	**Hollis**	**JAC**	**16**	**41**	**41**	**1.000**	**2/2**	**12/14**	**8/9**	**7/9**	**2/2**	**NA**	**31**	**36**	**.861**	**160**
	1996		16	27	27	1.000	2/2	9/9	12/14	5/8	2/3	NA	30	36	.833	143
	1995		16	27	28	.964	NA	7/9	7/8	4/7	2/3	NA	20	27	.741	108
	3-Yr TOTALS		48	95	96	2.964	4/4	28/32	27/31	16/24	6/8	NA	81	99	.818	411
2.	**Anderson**	**SF**	**16**	**38**	**38**	**1.000**	**NA**	**11/11**	**9/12**	**8/10**	**1/3**	**NA**	**29**	**36**	**.806**	**153**
	1996 w/PHIL		16	40	40	1.000	NA	10/11	8/9	7/9	NA	NA	25	29	.862	137
	1995 w/PHIL		16	32	33	.970	NA	5/5	9/10	8/12	0/3	NA	22	30	.733	123
	3-Yr TOTALS		48	110	111	2.970	NA	26/27	26/31	23/31	1/6	0/0	76	95	.800	413
3.	**Blanchard**	**IND**	**16**	**21**	**21**	**1.000**	**NA**	**9/9**	**12/15**	**10/14**	**1/3**	**NA**	**32**	**41**	**.780**	**152**
	1996		16	27	27	1.000	1/1	11/11	8/9	11/14	5/5	NA	36	40	.900	179
	1995		12	25	25	1.000	NA	5/5	6/8	7/10	1/1	NA	19	24	.792	105
	3-Yr TOTALS		44	73	73	3.000	1/1	25/25	26/32	28/38	7/9	0/0	87	105	.829	436
4.	**Cunningham**	**DALL**	**16**	**24**	**24**	**1.000**	**1/1**	**16/16**	**9/9**	**7/10**	**1/1**	**NA**	**34**	**37**	**.919**	**151**
	1996		—	—	—	—	—	—	—	—	—	—	—	—	—	—
	1995		—	—	—	—	—	—	—	—	—	—	—	—	—	—
	3-Yr TOTALS		—	—	—	—	—	—	—	—	—	—	—	—	—	—
5.	**Elam**	**DEN**	**16**	**46**	**46**	**1.000**	**1/1**	**9/10**	**10/12**	**3/8**	**3/5**	**NA**	**26**	**36**	**.722**	**149**
	1996		15	46	46	1.000	NA	10/10	4/5	6/10	1/3	NA	21	28	.750	126
	1995		16	39	39	1.000	2/2	6/8	13/14	5/7	5/6	0/1	31	38	.816	170
	3-Yr TOTALS		47	131	131	3.000	3/3	25/28	27/31	14/25	9/14	0/1	78	102	.765	445
6.	**Stoyanovich**	**KC**	**16**	**35**	**36**	**.972**	**NA**	**9/9**	**3/3**	**12/13**	**2/2**	**NA**	**26**	**27**	**.963**	**146**
	1996		16	34	34	1.000	NA	8/9	5/7	4/7	0/1	NA	17	24	.708	98
	1995 w/MIA		15	37	37	1.000	1/1	7/10	11/11	6/8	2/4	NA	27	34	.794	146
	3-Yr TOTALS		47	106	107	2.972	1/1	24/28	19/21	22/28	4/7	0/0	70	85	.824	390
7.	**Hall**	**NYJ**	**16**	**36**	**36**	**1.000**	**1/1**	**10/11**	**11/17**	**2/6**	**4/5**	**0/1**	**28**	**41**	**.683**	**146**
	1996		—	—	—	—	—	—	—	—	—	—	—	—	—	—
	1995		—	—	—	—	—	—	—	—	—	—	—	—	—	—
	3-Yr TOTALS		—	—	—	—	—	—	—	—	—	—	—	—	—	—
8.	**Hanson**	**DET**	**16**	**36**	**36**	**1.000**	**NA**	**10/10**	**8/9**	**5/5**	**3/5**	**NA**	**26**	**29**	**.897**	**144**
	1996		16	39	40	.975	NA	4/4	4/5	3/5	1/3	NA	12	17	.706	85
	1995		16	48	48	1.000	2/2	4/4	17/18	4/9	1/1	NA	28	34	.824	158
	3-Yr TOTALS		48	123	124	2.975	2/2	18/18	29/32	12/19	5/9	0/0	66	80	.825	387

	NAME	TEAM	GP	EXTRA PTS	EXTRA PT ATT	ACC RATE	10-19	20-29	30-39	40-49	50-59	60 & OVER	FG	ATT	ACC RATE	FAN-TASY PTS
9.	**Del Greco**	**TENN**	**16**	**32**	**32**	**1.000**	**2/2**	**6/6**	**10/11**	**7/14**	**2/2**	**NA**	**27**	**35**	**.771**	**141**
	1996		16	35	35	1.000	NA	7/7	14/16	10/12	1/3	NA	32	38	.842	168
	1995		16	33	33	1.000	3/3	3/3	8/8	10/12	3/5	NA	27	31	.871	148
	3-Yr TOTALS		48	100	100	3.000	5/5	16/16	32/35	27/38	6/10	0/0	86	104	.827	457
10.	**Vinatieri**	**NE**	**16**	**40**	**40**	**1.000**	**NA**	**11/11**	**7/9**	**6/8**	**1/1**	**NA**	**25**	**29**	**.862**	**137**
	1996		16	39	42	.929	1/1	9/10	8/8	8/14	1/2	NA	27	35	.771	146
	1995		—	—	—	—	—	—	—	—	—	—	—	—	—	—
	3-Yr TOTALS		32	79	82	1.929	1/1	20/21	15/17	14/22	2/3	0/0	52	64	.813	283
11.	**Wilkins**	**STL**	**16**	**32**	**32**	**1.000**	**1/1**	**8/9**	**8/12**	**7/14**	**1/1**	**NA**	**25**	**37**	**.676**	**135**
	1996 w/SF		16	40	40	1.000	NA	16/16	7/8	7/10	NA	NA	30	34	.882	151
	1995 w/SF		7	27	29	.931	1/1	5/5	5/5	1/2	NA	NA	12	13	.923	69
	3-Yr TOTALS		39	99	101	2.931	2/2	29/30	20/25	15/26	1/1	0/0	67	84	.798	355
12.	**Stover**	**BALT**	**15**	**32**	**32**	**1.000**	**NA**	**8/9**	**12/12**	**6/11**	**0/2**	**NA**	**26**	**34**	**.765**	**134**
	1996		16	34	35	.971	NA	8/8	5/6	5/10	1/1	NA	19	25	.760	109
	1995		16	26	26	1.000	1/1	12/12	9/10	7/9	0/1	NA	29	33	.879	135
	3-Yr TOTALS		47	92	93	2.971	1/1	28/29	26/28	18/30	1/4	0/0	74	92	.804	378
13.	**Longwell +**	**GB**	**16**	**48**	**48**	**1.000**	**4/4**	**7/8**	**10/13**	**2/4**	**1/1**	**NA**	**24**	**30**	**.800**	**133**
	1996		—	—	—	—	—	—	—	—	—	—	—	—	—	—
	1995		—	—	—	—	—	—	—	—	—	—	—	—	—	—
	3-Yr TOTALS		16	48	48	1.000	4/4	7/8	10/13	2/4	1/1	0/0	24	30	.800	133
14.	**Davis ****	**SD**	**16**	**48**	**48**	**1.000**	**4/4**	**7/8**	**8/9**	**6/11**	**1/1**	**NA**	**26**	**33**	**.788**	**133**
	1996 w/ARIZ		8	31	32	.969	NA	8/10	0/1	1/3	NA	NA	9	14	.643	42
	1995 w/ARIZ		16	12	12	1.000	1/1	13/14	9/10	6/8	1/6	NA	30	39	.769	132
	3-Yr TOTALS		40	91	92	2.969	5/5	28/33	22/24	13/22	2/4	0/0	65	86	.756	307
15.	**Mare**	**MIA**	**16**	**33**	**33**	**1.000**	**2/2**	**14/15**	**8/10**	**3/6**	**1/3**	**NA**	**28**	**36**	**.778**	**132**
	1996		—	—	—	—	—	—	—	—	—	—	—	—	—	—
	1995		—	—	—	—	—	—	—	—	—	—	—	—	—	—
	3-Yr TOTALS		16	33	33	1.000	2/2	14/15	8/10	3/6	1/3	0/0	28	36	.778	132
16.	**Johnson**	**PITT**	**16**	**40**	**40**	**1.000**	**2/2**	**6/6**	**8/10**	**6/8**	**NA**	**NA**	**22**	**25**	**.880**	**128**
	1996		16	37	37	1.000	1/1	10/12	8/8	3/6	1/3	NA	23	30	.767	124
	1995		16	39	39	1.000	NA	10/10	14/16	8/13	2/2	NA	34	41	.829	173
	3-Yr TOTALS		48	116	116	3.000	3/3	26/28	30/34	19/28	2/4	0/0	79	96	.823	425

	NAME	TEAM	GP	EXTRA PTS	EXTRA PT ATT	ACC RATE	10-19	20-29	30-39	40-49	50-59	60 & OVER	FG	ATT	ACC RATE	FAN-TASY PTS
17.	Brien	NO	14	22	22	1.000	1/1	2/2	10/10	6/9	4/5	NA	23	27	.852	124
	1996		16	18	18	1.000	NA	4/4	9/10	5/7	3/4	NA	21	25	.840	109
	1995 w/NO & SF		14	35	35	1.000	NA	8/8	4/7	6/12	1/2	NA	19	29	.655	111
	3-Yr TOTALS		44	75	75	3.000	1/1	14/14	23/27	17/28	8/11	0/0	63	81	.778	344
18.	Peterson	SEAT	16	37	37	1.000	NA	9/9	7/10	5/7	1/2	NA	22	28	.786	123
	1996		16	27	27	1.000	NA	11/13	7/7	8/11	2/3	NA	28	34	.824	140
	1995		16	40	40	1.000	1/1	5/5	9/10	8/10	2/3	NA	23	28	.821	133
	3-Yr TOTALS		48	104	104	3.000	1/1	25/27	23/27	21/28	3/7	0/0	73	90	.811	396
19.	Andersen	ATL	16	35	35	1.000	1/1	10/10	7/7	3/6	2/3	NA	23	27	.852	122
	1996		16	31	31	1.000	NA	5/5	7/7	7/8	1/5	NA	22	29	.759	123
	1995		16	29	30	.967	1/1	8/8	9/11	3/8	8/9	NA	31	37	.838	162
	3-Yr TOTALS		48	95	96	2.967	2/2	23/23	27/29	13/22	11/17	0/0	76	93	.817	407
20.	Christie	BUF	16	21	21	1.000	2/2	6/6	9/12	8/10	1/1	0/1	24	30	.800	121
	1996		16	33	33	1.000	NA	5/6	12/14	7/8	0/1	NA	24	29	.828	131
	1995		16	33	35	.943	NA	13/14	13/15	3/6	2/5	NA	31	40	.775	151
	3-Yr TOTALS		48	87	89	2.943	0/0	24/26	34/41	18/24	3/7	NA	79	99	.798	403
21.	Boniol	PHIL	16	33	33	1.000	NA	7/7	11/12	4/11	0/1	NA	22	31	.710	118
	1996 w/DALL		16	24	25	.960	1/1	13/13	12/13	5/7	1/2	NA	32	36	.889	144
	1995 w/DALL		16	46	48	.958	NA	11/12	13/13	3/3	NA	NA	27	28	.964	146
	3-Yr TOTALS		48	103	106	2.918	1/1	31/32	36/38	12/21	1/3	0/0	81	95	.853	408
22.	Daluiso	NYG	16	27	29	.931	1/1	6/6	6/7	8/14	1/4	NA	22	32	.688	117
	1996		14	22	22	1.000	2/2	10/10	9/9	3/6	NA	NA	24	27	.889	107
	1995		16	28	28	1.000	NA	7/7	9/10	2/9	2/2	NA	20	28	.714	107
	3-Yr TOTALS		46	77	79	2.931	3/3	23/23	24/26	13/29	3/6	0/0	66	87	.759	331
23.	Kasay	CAR	14	25	25	1.000	1/1	6/7	8/8	4/4	3/6	NA	22	26	.846	115
	1996		16	34	35	.971	2/2	14/14	11/12	7/10	3/7	NA	37	45	.822	177
	1995		16	27	28	.964	NA	5/5	11/15	9/12	1/1	NA	26	33	.788	137
	3-Yr TOTALS		46	86	88	2.935	3/3	25/26	30/35	20/26	7/14	0/0	85	104	.817	429
24.	Jaeger	CHI	15	20	20	1.000	NA	8/9	8/10	4/6	1/1	NA	21	26	.808	102
	1996		13	23	23	1.000	NA	4/4	3/4	12/15	NA	NA	19	23	.826	107
	1995 w/OAK		10	22	22	1.000	NA	4/5	6/7	3/5	0/1	NA	13	18	.722	73
	3-Yr TOTALS		38	65	65	3.000	0/0	16/18	17/21	19/26	1/2	0/0	53	67	.791	282

1997 STATISTICAL RESULTS
(KICKERS — DISTANCE SCORING METHOD)

	NAME	TEAM	GP	EXTRA PTS	EXTRA PT ATT	ACC RATE	10-19	20-29	30-39	40-49	50-59	60 & OVER	FG	ATT	ACC RATE	FAN-TASY PTS
25.	Blanton	WASH	15	34	34	1.000	2/2	4/4	5/6	4/8	1/4	NA	16	24	.667	96
	1996		16	40	40	1.000	2/2	13/13	7/7	2/7	2/3	NA	26	32	.813	133
	1995		–	–	–	–	–	–	–	–	–	–	–	–	–	–
	3-Yr TOTALS		31	74	74	2.000	4/4	17/17	12/13	6/15	3/7	0/0	42	56	.750	229
26.	Pelfrey	CIN	16	41	43	.953	NA	4/4	3/3	5/7	0/2	NA	12	16	.750	90
27.	Ford	OAK	16	33	35	.943	NA	3/5	4/6	5/10	1/1	NA	13	22	.591	89
28.	Husted	TB	16	32	35	.914	NA	5/5	2/3	5/6	1/3	NA	13	17	.765	86
29.	Murray	MINN	12	23	24	.958	NA	7/7	1/3	4/6	0/1	NA	12	17	.706	68
30.	Nedney	ARIZ	10	19	19	1.000	1/1	3/3	4/4	3/7	0/2	NA	11	17	.647	61
31.	Butler	ARIZ	6	9	10	.900	NA	4/4	2/4	2/4	NA	NA	8	12	.667	39
32.	Carney	SD	4	5	5	1.000	NA	3/3	2/2	2/2	NA	NA	7	7	1.000	32
33.	Bentley	ATL	1	4	4	1.000	NA	1/1	1/1	0/1	NA	NA	2	3	.667	11
34.	Jacke	WASH	1	5	5	1.000	NA	NA	NA	NA	NA	NA	0	0	.000	5

+   DENOTES COLLEGE DRAFT PICK

** Davis   (SD)   Played in 4 games with Minnesota.

RATING THE PLAYERS FOR 1998
(Kickers—Distance Scoring Method)

GRAB ONE IF YOU CAN

☐ **1. Ritchie Cunningham (Dallas Cowboys)**
Cunningham stepped in to take over the Cowboys' kicking duties in 1997 and did so in fine fashion. He hit an impressive 34 of 37 (.919) field goal attempts, including 7 of 10 from farther than 40 yards and his only attempt beyond 50. If the Cowboys continue to struggle in the red zone in 1998, look for big success from Cunningham as he gets more field goal attempts.

☐ **2. Jason Elam (Denver Broncos)**
The Broncos got their Super Bowl win in 1997 and look to do more damage in 1998. Jason Elam will again be a good offensive weapon for them, although he'd like to improve on his 26 of 36 (.722) field goal showing of 1997. Elam did make good on three of his five 50-plus yard attempts in 1997.

☐ **3. Mike Hollis (Jacksonville Jaguars)**
Hollis has hit six of eight field goal attempts in the last three seasons, including two of two last year. Kicking for the improving Jaguars should again get him plenty of scoring chances in 1998. Hollis was 31 of 36 (.861) on field goal attempts in 1997.

☐ **4. Jason Hanson (Detroit Lions)**
Hanson rebounded in 1997 after a brutal 12 of 17 (.706) field goal performance in 1996. The Lions got him many more chances and he was 26 of 29 (.897) on field goal tries, including three of five from outside 50 yards. It looks as if he's back on track.

☐ **5. Ryan Longwell (Green Bay Packers)**
Longwell stepped into an envious spot, kicking for the powerful Green Bay Packers. He hit 24 of 30 (.800) field goal attempts in 1997. He did, however, attempt only five field goals from farther than 40 yards, hitting on three of them. Despite not having much of a track record from long distances, kicking for the Packers is enough to make him a huge fantasy consideration for 1998.

BEST OF THE REST

☐ **6. Gary Anderson (Minnesota Vikings)**
Recognized as one of the league's more consistent kickers, Anderson takes his services to Minnesota in 1998. Anderson comes off a year where he hit 29 of 36 (.806) field goal attempts with San Francisco in 1997, including only one of three from beyond 50 yards. I believe he'll find more consistency and accuracy in the friendly, windless Metrodome in 1998.

☐ **7. John Becksvort/???? (San Francisco 49ers)**
With Gary Anderson in Minnesota, the 49ers are looking for a replacement. To me, no matter who that is, he'll be a top fantasy candi-

date because he kicks for the high-powered 49ers, who face a fairly easy schedule in 1998.

☐ **8. Cary Blanchard/Mike Vanderjagt (Indianapolis Colts)**
One of the league's better long-distance kickers, Blanchard was five of five from beyond 50 yards in 1996 but only one of five a year ago. The Colts, especially with their uncertainty situation at quarterback, will continue to get Blanchard in range and take the "3" in 1998. The Colts have also brought in Mike Vanderjagt to push Blanchard for the job.

☐ **9. Adam Vinatieri (New England Patriots)**
Vinatieri improved his accuracy in 1997, hitting on 25 of 29 (.862) field goals. He also showed some leg in hitting six of eight tries from 40 to 49 yards and his lone attempt from beyond 50. The Patriots will continue to get him chances in 1998 and Vinatieri will continue to capitalize.

☐ **10. Pete Stoyanovich (Kansas City Chiefs)**
You'd think that with age, you'd lose leg strength but Stoyanovich proved he could still get it done in 1997, hitting 26 of 27 (.963) field goal tries. This included 12 of 13 attempts from beyond 40 yards and two of two from beyond 50. He's still got it and the Chiefs continue to provide him with chances.

STRONG LONG SHOTS

☐ **11. Al Del Greco (Tennessee Oilers)**
The aging Del Greco keeps getting it done for the Oilers. Del Greco hit 27 of 35 (.771) field goals in 1997. He was only 7 of 14 from 40 to 49 yards but he did hit his two attempts from beyond 50 yards. He's had 30-plus field goal chances in each of the last three years.

☐ **12. Norm Johnson (Pittsburgh Steelers)**
Johnson had only 25 field goal chances in 1997 but he was good on 22 of them. With the Steelers playing the league's toughest schedule in 1998, I look for a few more stalled drives and more field goal chances for Johnson, who'll likely improve his fantasy numbers.

☐ **13. John Kasay (Carolina Panthers)**
Kasay had a huge dropoff in 1997s, just as the Panthers did. After hitting 37 of 45 (.822) field goal attempts in 1996, he hit only 22 of 26 (.846) attempts in 1997. He's still one of the league's better kickers. The Panthers just have to get him more chances.

☐ **14. Morten Anderson (Atlanta Falcons)**
Anderson had only 27 field goal tries in 1997 but he hit 23 of them for a .852 kicking percentage. One of the league's better long-range kickers, Anderson hit two of his three attempts from beyond 50 yards. Because he'll be kicking for an improving Falcon team, I look for Anderson's numbers to improve in 1998.

☐ **15. Todd Peterson (Seattle Seahawks)**
A steady kicker, Peterson's field goal percentage fell below the .800 mark for the first time in three years in 1997, as he hit 22 of 28 (.786) attempts. Look for the Seahawks to provide plenty of scoring chances

in 1998, aided by the addition of Ricky Watters in the offseason.

HAVE THE POTENTIAL

☐ **16. John Carney (San Diego Chargers)**
A knee injury sidelined Carney for most of the 1997 season but if he's healthy in 1998, I wouldn't shy away from him. He hit all seven field goal attempts in 1997 before the injury and he remains one of the league's better kickers. However, the Chargers' quarterback situation scares me.

☐ **17. Jeff Wilkins (St. Louis Rams)**
Wilkins gave two solid performances with the 49ers in 1995 and 1996 but he struggled in his first year with the Rams in 1997. Wilkins hit only 25 of 37 (.676) field goal tries a year ago but he's definitely better than that.

☐ **18. Brad Daluiso (New York Giants)**
With Danny Kanell at quarterback, the Giants look as if they're on a track to improve, which should create scoring opportunities. Now Daluiso just needs to improve on his accuracy, which left him a woeful 22 of 32 (.688) on field goals in 1997.

☐ **19. John Hall (New York Jets)**
Hall had 41 field goal attempts in 1997 but hit only 28 of them for a very poor .683 kicking percentage. In 1998, Hall will have to battle to keep his job but whoever kicks for the Jets should have reasonable success.

☐ **20. Olindo Mare/Jon Baker (Miami Dolphins)**
After stepping in to grab the Dolphins' kicking duties in 1997, Mare hit a respectable 28 of 36 (.778) field goals. I look for more reasonable success in 1998 because the Dolphins face a fairly easy schedule. The Dolphins have signed free agent Jon Baker to push Mare for the job in 1998.

KEEP AN EYE ON

☐ **21. Chris Boniol (Philadelphia Eagles)**
Boniol saw his performance drop well off in 1997 after two productive years in Dallas. Boniol and the Eagles need to get headed back in the right direction.

☐ **22. Cole Ford (Oakland Raiders)**
With Jeff George in town for a second season, Ford's scoring chances may go up but his poor performance in 1997 may have put his job on the line.

☐ **23. Matt Stover (Baltimore Ravens)**
Jim Harbaugh at quarterback doesn't excite me about Stover's scoring chances.

☐ **24. Doug Pelfrey/Jay Kirchoff (Cincinnati Bengals)**
Pelfrey had only 16 field goal attempts in 1997. Jeff Blake at quarterback creates questions. And Pelfrey faces the challenge of free agent Jay Kirchoff, who signed in the offseason.

☐ **25. Michael Husted (Tampa Bay Buccaneers)**
Tampa Bay is a young, improving team that isn't explosive but wins.

☐ **26. Scott Blanton/Danny Kight (Washington Redskins)**
Blanton and the Redskins struggled in 1997. Can they recover and get back on track? Blanton will have competition to push him in or push him out of a job.

☐ **27. Kevin Butler (Arizona Cardinals)**
For some reason, the Cardinals' kickers always seem to struggle.

☐ **28. Steve Christie/Carlos Huerta (Buffalo Bills)**
He's kicking for a young team that's still looking for an identity without Jim Kelly.

☐ **29. Jeff Jaeger (Chicago Bears)**
It's a tough schedule and likely another tough season for Chicago.

☐ **30. Doug Brien (New Orleans Saints)**
This isn't a heavenly team he's kicking for.

ROOKIE PROSPECTS
NAME   TEAM   COMMENT

No kickers were chosen in this year's draft. Rookie free-agents will appear in the team by team section and some in these player ratings.

A 1998 QUICK PICKS— MOCK DRAFT

(My Top "30" Overall Picks for the Distance Scoring Method)

NAME	TEAM	POS	COMMENTS
1. Favre	GB	QB	Targets like Freeman & Brooks help. In addition, Favre has thrown 30-plus TDs 4 straight years.
2. Stewart	PITT	QB	Athleticism will again allow him to throw for 20-plus, and run for a half dozen more.
3. Sanders	DET	RB	Rebounded to 14 TDs in 1997 under Bobby Ross.
4. Davis	DEN	RB	15 TDs in each of last two seasons can't be ignored.
5. George	OAK	QB	Fits Raiders' downfield style, threw for 29 TDs in 1997.
6. Galloway	SEAT	WR	Scored 12 times with 27.3 yard average a year ago.
7. Freeman	GB	WR	Nice deep threat with great QB.
8. Smith	DEN	WR	Broncos' new go-to guy óscored 12 in 1997.
9. Rice	SF	WR	Injured most of 1997 but he's back.
10. Levens	GB	RB	Packer workhorse will again do plenty of scoring.
11. Kaufman	OAK	RB	Raiders' explosive back can get it done from anywhere.
12. Martin	NYJ	RB	New home for Martin to rebound from injuries of 1997.
13. Dillon	CIN	RB	10 TDs as a rookie in 1997 playing in just 14 games.
14. Elway	DEN	QB	25-plus TD passes each of last 3 seasons.
15. Moon	SEAT	QB	Aging, but still has strong arm and fleet-footed Galloway as target.
16. Abdul-Jabbar	MIA	RB	16 TDs as sophomore in 1997.
17. Smith	MINN	RB	If stays healthy, will explode for many scores.
18. Young	SF	QB	Rice back healthy in 1998 should help.
19. Brown	OAK	WR	Very capable of 100 receptions and 12 TDs, by George.
20. Cunningham	DALL	K	Cowboys will continue providing scoring chances.
21. Pickens	CIN	WR	Healthy and will again be "Picken" apart defenses.
22. Carter	MINN	WR	One of the league's consistent go-to WRs.
23. Allen	WASH	RB	Injured much of 1997 but scored 21 year earlier.
24. Bledsoe	NE	QB	Looking for another 25-30 TD passes in 1998.
25. Mitchell	DET	QB	Needs to get the ball more to Moore and Morton.
26. Watters	SEAT	RB	Hopes to again run like "Watters" in Seattle.
27. Dunn	TB	RB	Showed he could get it "Dunn" as rookie in 1997.
28. Moore	DET	WR	"Moore" and hopefully not less than 10 TDs.
29. Irvin	DALL	WR	Big part of Cowboys' offense who must come up big.
30. Jett	OAK	WR	Has the "Jetts" but don't expect another dozen scores in 1998.

This Mock Draft is expanded and updated in *Cliff's Quick Picks: Fantasy Football Draft at a Glance*—a huge cheatsheet that examines the top-100 overall picks for the Basic and Combined Basic/Performance methods. Potential draft picks are also broken down by fantasy position, including the *top-50* running backs and wide receivers, and the *top-25* tight ends, quarterbacks and kickers. *Cliff's Quick Picks* will be available in mid-August, right around your fantasy draft time. Be sure to order! Details and order form, along with a toll-free phone number, appear on the hard insert in the middle of this book.

XI
RATING OPPOSING NFL DEFENSES
HELPING YOU CHOOSE WHICH PLAYERS
TO START FROM WEEK TO WEEK

Now that you've selected your fantasy team, how do you choose whom to start from week to week? Defensive statistics for the teams your players are up against will prove useful in determining which players to start for a given game. (There are now a good number of fantasy leagues that also draft team defenses. The following section, "Drafting a Team Defense," deals specifically with this, although the present section can also be of help, depending on what defensive statistics your league uses.)

You may be fortunate enough to have three good running backs, but you can only play two. Each week you're faced with a tough decision: Which two should you start? This decision can be made easier by examining the defenses the players are up against. If one of the three will face a defense that's very tough against the run, the choice is simple: Bench him and play the other two. The same holds true for selecting a quarterback. Look for the defense that is weaker against the pass or that has allowed more passing touchdowns.

From year to year, especially since the recent explosion of free-agent movement, team defensive statistics have changed quite a bit. As players move, the defensive performances of their teams are affected, obviously, and this makes predicting how a team defense will play during the upcoming year a little more difficult than it used to be. Still, most defenses manage to stay mostly intact, and many teams simply have a history of playing tough defense, despite gains and losses in personnel.

So keep an eye on the last few years' statistics for a base of comparison; but then follow team defensive performances as the 1998 season progresses to get a better feel for how some of these newly thrown together squads will fare. This is just one of the precautions a good fantasy owner takes to ensure success during the season. Every once in a while you're going to pick up a few extra points this way—choosing one player over another, based on the defenses they're facing that week—and those little advantages often make the difference between consistent winning and consistent mediocrity.

As I've said, the statistics in this section are based on how teams did defensively last season, so you may find them useful for only the first few games of 1998. A defense that performed well last year will not necessarily continue to excel this year. To help account for the possibility of a one-year irregularity, however, I have included each team's defensive statistics from both last year and the previous year. This should help you determine whether a defense is improving or on a downward slide; and it should give you an idea of a team defense's consistency against the run or pass.

To evaluate current NFL defenses during the season, you will need to know how they're doing from week to week. I suggest reading a publication that documents current defensive standings. This should definitely help in selecting your weekly fantasy lineup.

In the following charts, I list the defensive rankings according to touchdowns allowed via the pass or rush, and according to yardage allowed via the pass or rush. The defensive touchdown statistics will show fantasy owners who use the Basic, Distance, or Combined Basic/Performance Scoring Methods which teams are toughest to score against via the pass or run. The defensive yardage statistics will help fantasy teams using the Performance Point or Combined Basic/Performance Scoring Method to judge which teams are harder to move the ball against via passing or rushing. The better defenses—the teams tough to score on or pick up yardage against—are at the top of the chart, and the weaker defenses are toward the bottom. Obviously, the higher a defense rates, the less eager you will be to start a player against it.

These statistics show us which defenses were hardest to score on in both 1997 and 1996. Therefore, if your league uses the Basic, Distance or Combined Basic/Performance Scoring Method and you have to choose between playing two quarterbacks, one playing the Cincinnati Bengals or one playing the New York Giants, you would surely choose the one facing the Bengals. The Bengals had the league-high in touchdowns allowed in 1997 (30 touchdowns) while the Giants were tied with Green Bay with the league's best, allowing only 10 touchdowns passes in 1997 and only 15 the year before.

How about making a choice between two running backs, one playing the Oakland Raiders and one playing the San Francisco 49ers? The choice should be simple. The 49ers allowed only five rushing touchdowns in 1997 and only four the year before. The Raiders, on the other hand, allowed 20 rushing scores last year. You would start the running back who is scheduled to face the porous Raider defense.

If your league uses the Performance Point or Combined Basic/Performance Scoring Method, your decision-making process should be the same. Choosing between a quarterback facing the Dallas Cowboys or one facing the New York Giants should again be easy. The Giants were 29th in the league in passing yardage allowed last year. They gave up a whopping 247.3 yards per game on average, while Dallas gave up only 189.1 yards per game, as the league's best pass defense. Obviously, you'd prefer to start a quarterback who faced the Giants.

What if you had to decide between two running backs, one facing the Pittsburgh Steelers and one facing the Washington Redskins? The Steelers' run defense was number one against the run in 1997, allowing only 82.3 yards per game on the ground. A year earlier, the Steelers ranked fourth, allowing 88.4 yards per game. The Redskins, on the other hand, were horrible against the run in both 1996 and 1997. In 1996, the Redskins allowed an average of 141.3 yards per game on the ground, placing dead last in the league. In 1997, the Redskins allowed 138.3 yards per game, finishing 28th in the league against the run. Use the running back facing the much more porous Redskin run defense.

Although these stats can be useful as guidelines, choosing a starting lineup is rarely a cut-and-dried situation. If you have a "franchise" player, like Terrell Davis or Brett Favre, you will probably want to start him no matter which team he's up against. Or if one of your players is especially hot, you may want to continue to start him until he cools off. This all requires a feel for the game, and with time and experience, you'll acquire it.

1997 NFL DEFENSES
RUSHING TOUCHDOWNS ALLOWED

(For Leagues Using the Basic, Distance, or Combined
Basic/Performance Scoring Method)

TEAM	1997 RSH TDs	1996 RSH TDs	1996 LEAGUE RANK
1. Pittsburgh	5	7	5th (Tie)
2. San Francisco	5	4	1st
3. Kansas City	8	11	12th (Tie)
4. Miami	9	10	10th (Tie)
5. N.Y. Jets	9	19	28th
6. Denver	10	6	3rd (Tie)
7. St. Louis	10	22	30th
8. Seattle	10	15	21st (Tie)
9. Tampa Bay	10	13	18th
10. Buffalo	11	12	15th (Tie)
11. New Orleans	11	11	12th (Tie)
12. Carolina	12	6	3rd (Tie)
13. Dallas	12	10	10th (Tie)
14. Jacksonville	12	9	8th (Tie)
15. San Diego	12	9	8th (Tie)
16. Tennessee	12	5	2nd
17. Arizona	13	18	25th (Tie)
18. Minnesota	13	15	21st (Tie)
19. Cincinnati	15	15	21st (Tie)
20. Detroit	15	12	15th (Tie)
21. Philadelphia	15	12	15th (Tie)
22. Washington	15	20	29th
23. Green Bay	16	7	5th (Tie)
24. New England	16	14	19th (Tie)
25. Baltimore	17	18	25th (Tie)
26. N.Y. Giants	17	14	19th (Tie)
27. Atlanta	18	18	25th (Tie)
28. Chicago	18	15	21st (Tie)
29. Indianapolis	18	11	12th (Tie)
30. Oakland	20	7	5th (Tie)

1997 NFL DEFENSES
PASSING TOUCHDOWNS ALLOWED
(For Leagues Using the Basic, Distance, or Combined
Basic/Performance Scoring Method)

TEAM	1997 PS TDs	1996 PS TDs	1996 LEAGUE RANK
1. Green Bay	10	12	3rd (Tie)
2. N.Y. Giants	10	15	5th
3. Tampa Bay	13	17	6th (Tie)
4. New England	14	17	6th (Tie)
5. Washington	14	12	3rd (Tie)
6. Detroit	15	28	27th (Tie)
7. Kansas City	15	19	12th
8. Buffalo	17	11	2nd
9. Carolina	17	17	6th (Tie)
10. Philadelphia	19	18	10th (Tie)
11. Seattle	19	25	23rd (Tie)
12. Dallas	20	10	1st
13. Denver	20	22	16th (Tie)
14. Baltimore	21	27	26th
15. New Orleans	21	22	16th (Tie)
16. Oakland	21	22	16th (Tie)
17. Tennessee	21	24	21st (Tie)
18. Arizona	23	21	13th (Tie)
19. Jacksonville	23	24	21st (Tie)
20. Miami	23	29	29th
21. N.Y. Jets	23	33	30th
22. San Francisco	23	21	13th (Tie)
23. Atlanta	24	26	25th
24. Pittsburgh	24	17	6th (Tie)
25. Chicago	25	22	16th (Tie)
26. Indianapolis	25	25	23rd (Tie)
27. St. Louis	26	23	20th
28. Minnesota	28	18	10th (Tie)
29. San Diego	29	28	27th (Tie)
30. Cincinnati	30	21	13th (Tie)

1997 NFL DEFENSES
RUSHING YARDAGE ALLOWED
(For Leagues Using the Performance Point or Combined
Basic/Performance Scoring Method)

	TEAM	1997 RSH YDs	AVG YDs PER GAME	1996 RSH YDs	AVG YDs PER GAME	1996 RANK
1.	Pittsburgh	1,316	82.3	1,415	88.4	4th
2.	San Francisco	1,372	85.8	1,483	92.7	5th
3.	N.Y. Giants	1,450	90.6	1,755	109.7	16th
4.	Tennessee	1,563	97.7	1,385	86.6	2nd
5.	New England	1,611	100.7	1,506	94.1	6th
6.	Tampa Bay	1,617	101.1	1,892	118.3	22nd
7.	Kansas City	1,621	101.3	1,674	104.6	14th
8.	St. Louis	1,659	103.7	1,853	115.8	20th
9.	Atlanta	1,670	104.4	2,044	127.8	26th
10.	Baltimore	1,690	105.6	1,927	120.4	23rd
11.	San Diego	1,697	106.1	1,756	109.8	17th
12.	Seattle	1,728	108.0	2,086	130.4	28th
13.	Jacksonville	1,745	109.1	1,781	111.3	19th
14.	Chicago	1,772	110.8	1,611	100.7	11th
15.	Buffalo	1,792	112.0	1,665	104.1	13th
16.	Denver	1,803	112.7	1,331	83.2	1st
17.	Miami	1,814	113.4	1,534	95.9	7th
18.	Detroit	1,833	114.6	2,007	125.4	25th
19.	New Orleans	1,864	116.5	2,076	129.8	27th
20.	Green Bay	1,876	117.3	1,412	88.3	3rd
21.	N.Y. Jets	1,890	118.1	2,212	138.3	29th
22.	Minnesota	1,983	123.9	1,976	123.5	24th
23.	Dallas	2,002	125.1	1,568	98.0	9th
24.	Philadelphia	2,011	125.7	1,570	98.1	10th
25.	Indianapolis	2,034	127.1	1,757	109.8	18th
26.	Carolina	2,138	133.6	1,562	97.6	8th
27.	Arizona	2,170	135.6	1,857	116.1	21st
28.	Washington	2,212	138.3	2,260	141.3	30th
29.	Cincinnati	2,227	139.2	1,643	102.7	12th
30.	Oakland	2,246	140.4	1,741	108.8	15th

1997 NFL DEFENSES
PASSING YARDAGE ALLOWED

(For Leagues Using the Performance Point or Combined
Basic/Performance Scoring Method)

	TEAM	1997 PS YDs	1997 AVG YDs PER GAME	1996 PS YDs	1996 AVG YDs PER GAME	1996 RANK
1.	Green Bay	2,946	184.1	3,927	245.4	21st
2.	Dallas	3,025	189.1	3,491	218.2	5th
3.	New Orleans	3,117	194.8	3,967	247.9	22nd
1.	Dallas	2,717	169.8	3,025	189.1	2nd
2.	San Francisco	2,930	183.1	3,461	216.3	12th
3.	Indianapolis	2,967	185.4	3,825	239.1	23rd
4.	Washington	3,098	193.6	3,634	227.1	20th
5.	Denver	3,166	197.9	3,413	213.3	11th
6.	Chicago	3,197	199.8	3,476	217.3	13th
7.	Green Bay	3,225	201.6	2,946	184.1	1st
8.	Tampa Bay	3,342	208.9	3,132	195.8	4th
9.	Carolina	3,345	209.1	3,585	224.1	18th
10.	Seattle	3,355	209.7	3,624	226.5	19th
11.	New Orleans	3,389	211.8	3,117	194.8	3rd
12.	Detroit	3,401	212.6	3,574	223.4`	17th
13.	Buffalo	3,406	212.9	3,409	213.1	10th
14.	Arizona	3,457	216.1	3,639	227.4	21st
15.	Kansas City	3,608	225.5	3,727	232.9	22nd
16.	Pittsburgh	3,611	225.7	3,316	207.3	7th
17.	San Diego	3,632	227.0	3,861	241.3	25th
18.	N.Y. Jets	3,653	228.3	3,542	221.4	16th
19.	Cincinnati	3,668	229.3	4,028	251.8	28th
20.	St. Louis	3,675	229.7	3,856	241.0	24th
21.	Miami	3,682	230.1	3,891	243.2	26th
22.	New England	3,772	235.8	4,055	253.4	29th
23.	Atlanta	3,794	237.1	3,953	247.1	27th
24.	Jacksonville	3,838	239.9	3,541	221.3	15th
25.	Tennessee	3,898	243.6	3,365	210.3	8th
26.	Oakland	3,909	244.3	3,273	204.6	6th
27.	Baltimore	3,956	247.3	4,115	257.2	30th
28.	Minnesota	3,957	247.3	3,384	211.5	9th
29.	N.Y. Giants	3,957	247.3	3,477	217.3	14th
30.	Philadelphia	4,201	262.6	3,243	202.7	5th

XII
DRAFTING A TEAM DEFENSE

A variation of Fantasy Football that has become very popular is drafting a team defense. This variation uses an entire NFL team's defense as an eighth scorer. Points are awarded for every touchdown scored by interception (six points) or fumble recovery (six points), and for every safety (two points). When selecting a defense, look for opportunistic teams that score by taking advantage of their opponents' mistakes. To aid you in selecting a team defense, I'll do two things. First, I'll list last year's defensive fantasy-point totals. Then, because many fantasy leagues also award points for interceptions, fumble recoveries, and sacks, I will lay out how last year's defenses did in those respective categories. Also, to assist you a bit further, I will include each team's totals from the previous year (1996) in these particular categories. The 1997 totals appear in bold face, and the 1996 results appear beside them in parentheses. This comparison may help you determine whether certain defenses have stayed consistent from year to year.

TEAM DEFENSIVE SCORING FOR 1997

TEAM	INTS FOR TDs (1996)	1997	FUMBLES RETURNED FOR TDs (1996)	1997	SAFETIES (1996)	1997	FANTASY POINTS (1996)	1997
1. Denver	(1)	4	(0)	2	(0)	0	(6)	36
2. Green Bay	(3)	3	(2)	3	(2)	0	(32)	36
3. San Diego	(1)	3	(0)	3	(0)	0	(6)	36
4. Seattle	(1)	2	(0)	3	(0)	1	(6)	32
5. Kansas City	(0)	4	(1)	0	(1)	3	(8)	30
6. Detroit	(2)	2	(1)	2	(0)	1	(18)	26
7. Indianapolis	(4)	2	(0)	2	(1)	1	(26)	26
8. New England	(2)	4	(2)	0	(1)	1	(26)	26
9. N. Y. Giants	(3)	4	(1)	0	(2)	1	(28)	26
10. N. Y. Jets	(2)	4	(1)	0	(0)	0	(18)	24
11. Tennessee	(1)	2	(0)	2	(2)	0	(10)	24
12. Washington	(1)	3	(1)	1	(0)	0	(12)	18
13. Dallas	(0)	1	(1)	2	(0)	0	(6)	18
14. San Francisco	(1)	1	(1)	2	(4)	0	(20)	18
15. St. Louis	(4)	1	(1)	2	(1)	0	(26)	14
16. Oakland	(2)	0	(1)	2	(2)	1	(22)	12
17. Arizona	(1)	2	(1)	0	(0)	0	(12)	12
18. Miami	(3)	0	(1)	2	(1)	0	(26)	12
19. Minnesota	(1)	0	(0)	2	(0)	0	(6)	12
20. Philadelphia	(2)	1	(2)	1	(1)	0	(26)	12
21. Pittsburgh	(3)	0	(2)	2	(0)	0	(30)	12
22. Baltimore	(1)	1	(0)	0	(0)	1	(6)	8
23. Cincinnati	(2)	0	(1)	1	(0)	0	(18)	6
24. Jacksonville	(0)	0	(0)	1	(0)	0	(0)	6
25. New Orleans	(0)	0	(0)	1	(0)	0	(0)	6
26. Tampa Bay	(0)	1	(0)	0	(0)	0	(0)	6
27. Buffalo	(0)	0	(2)	0	(0)	1	(12)	2
28. Carolina	(0)	0	(3)	0	(2)	1	(22)	2
29. Chicago	(1)	0	(2)	0	(1)	1	(20)	2
30. Atlanta	(0)	0	(0)	0	(0)	0	(0)	0

TEAM DEFENSIVE STATISTICS FOR 1997
(Interceptions)

TEAM	INTERCEPTIONS (1996)	1997	TEAM	INTERCEPTIONS (1996)	1997
1. N.Y. Giants	(22)	27	16. Buffalo	(14)	15
2. St. Louis	(26)	25	17. San Diego	(23)	15
3. San Francisco	(20)	24	18. Tennessee	(10)	14
4. Green Bay	(26)	21	19. Philadelphia	(20)	14
5. Kansas City	(17)	21	20. Chicago	(17)	13
6. New England	(23)	19	21. Cincinnati	(34)	13
7. N.Y. Jets	(11)	19	22. Jacksonville	(15)	13
8. Pittsburgh	(23)	19	23. Seattle	(14)	13
9. Atlanta	(6)	18	24. Tampa Bay	(16)	13
0. Denver	(24)	18	25. Indianapolis	(13)	12
1. Baltimore	(15)	17	26. Minnesota	(22)	12
2. Detroit	(11)	17	27. Carolina	(22)	11
3. New Orleans	(12)	17	28. Miami	(20)	10
4. Washington	(21)	16	29. Oakland	(17)	10
5. Arizona	(11)	15	30. Dallas	(19)	7

TEAM DEFENSIVE STATISTICS FOR 1997
(Fumble Recoveries)

TEAM	FUMBLE RECOVERIES (1996)	1997	TEAM	FUMBLE RECOVERIES (1996)	1997
1. Miami	(17)	17	16. Pittsburgh	(17)	13
2. N.Y. Giants	(13)	17	17. Tampa Bay	(12)	13
3. San Francisco	(14)	17	18. Dallas	(14)	12
4. Tennessee	(14)	17	19. Oakland	(9)	12
5. Chicago	(10)	16	20. Philadelphia	(12)	12
6. Jacksonville	(14)	15	21. Baltimore	(7)	11
7. Minnesota	(12)	15	22. Carolina	(16)	11
8. New Orleans	(9)	15	23. Green Bay	(14)	11
9. Seattle	(18)	15	24. San Diego	(13)	11
10. Indianapolis	(10)	14	25. Atlanta	(17)	10
11. St. Louis	(13)	14	26. Cincinnati	(10)	10
12. Washington	(9)	14	27. Detroit	(8)	8
13. Denver	(9)	13	28. Buffalo	(15)	7
14. Kansas City	(11)	13	29. N.Y. Jets	(15)	7
15. New England	(11)	13	30. Arizona	(15)	5

TEAM DEFENSIVE STATISTICS FOR 1997
(Sacks)

TEAM	SACKS (1996)	1997	TEAM	SACKS (1996)	1997
1. New Orleans	(41)	58	16. Indianapolis	(28)	42
2. Atlanta	(38)	57	17. Seattle	(46)	42
3. San Francisco	(45)	56	18. Green Bay	(37)	41
4. Kansas City	(32)	54	19. Dallas	(37)	39
5. N.Y. Giants	(30)	53	20. St. Louis	(32)	39
6. Jacksonville	(37)	49	21. Chicago	(29)	38
7. Pittsburgh	(51)	48	22. Washington	(34)	37
8. Buffalo	(47)	46	23. Carolina	(60)	36
9. New England	(33)	46	24. Cincinnati	(32)	36
10. Denver	(40)	44	25. Tennessee	(35)	36
11. Minnesota	(43)	44	26. Arizona	(27)	34
12. Philadelphia	(39)	44	27. Miami	(33)	31
13. Tampa Bay	(34)	43	28. Oakland	(34)	30
14. Baltimore	(33)	42	29. N.Y. Jets	(31)	29
15. Detroit	(32)	42	30. San Diego	(32)	27

FANTASY FOOTBALL BASICS

FORMING A LEAGUE

OPTIONS TO TACKLE THE NFL'S
17-WEEK SEASON (WITH BYE WEEKS)

LEAGUE SCHEDULING FOR 4 TO 16 FRANCHISES

PLAYING THE GAME

RULE CHANGES
OR ADDITIONS FOR 1998

THE FUNDAMENTAL CONCEPT

- From 4 to 16 football fans get together to form a fantasy league. Each member of the group is awarded a franchise for the team he or she will put together.

- The newly founded league selects a commissioner and decides on an amount for a franchise entry fee.

- A predetermined schedule is set up or selected so the teams can meet in head-to-head competition.

- The commissioner organizes a fantasy draft where each franchise owner selects scoring players: quarterbacks, running backs, wide receivers, tight ends, and placekickers. These player selections are made from actual NFL player rosters.

- Trading and picking up players is allowed after the draft; all such transactions are subject to the trade guidelines and deadlines of the league.

- Each franchise submits its weekly starting lineup before the franchises meet in head-to-head competition.

- Following the scoring method selected by the league, the weekly results of scores and standings are determined and posted or mailed out to each franchise by the commissioner.

- The season culminates with playoffs and a Fantasy Bowl, using a predetermined playoff structure as a guideline.

I
FORMING A FANTASY LEAGUE

1. NUMBER OF FRANCHISES:
   Any number of franchises from 4 to 16 can be used in forming a fantasy league. Staying with an even number of franchises, however, makes scheduling for your league easier.

2. ENTRY FEES:
   Another item to consider when forming your league is whether to have an entry fee. It is totally up to the league franchises whether to set up some kind of wager system. There are many leagues that do have some sort of payoff system for the season's winners; there also are many leagues, especially those involving young members, that play the game just for fun.

II
THE LEAGUE COMMISSIONER

1. RESPONSIBILITIES:
   A. Coordinating draft day
   B. Keeping league standings and statistics
   C. Logging trade transactions
   D. Logging weekly team lineups
   E. Serving as league treasurer

2. TERM OF OFFICE:
   The length of time served by the commissioner should be determined by a vote of all the franchise owners, with the majority ruling. NOTE: In many leagues the commissioner serves until he or she no longer wants the job.

3. FEES:
   As an added incentive for taking and keeping the job, the commissioner is usually paid a fee by the league. NOTE: One good form of compensation for a commissioner's services is for that person to be exempt from paying the initial franchise fees.

4. OPTIONS:
   If the opportunity presents itself, the ideal situation would be to have someone who is not a franchise owner serve as your commissioner. Finding someone to agree to this won't be easy, but it would prevent many hassles.

III
LEAGUE SCHEDULING

1. NUMBER OF TEAMS IN YOUR LEAGUE:

   Obviously, your league scheduling will depend upon the number of franchises (teams) you wish to have in your league. There are a few things to consider in selecting the number of teams you will allow in your league. The first thing is how much time your commissioner wishes to spend on league involvement. Don't overload that person so badly that he or she personally won't enjoy the game. I have 16 teams in the league for which I serve as commissioner, and I often wish I could cut back to 12 or even 10. In the leagues I'm familiar with, the most common number of teams is either 8 or 10.

   Another consideration is the availability of quarterbacks. Each team usually drafts two NFL starting quarterbacks, one as the starter and the other as a reserve in case of injury. There are only 30 NFL teams, so if you have more than 14 Fantasy Football league franchises, some of your franchises may be without an NFL starting quarterback as a reserve.

   Finally, I would like to emphasize that it would be much better to go with an even number of teams. This provides far easier scheduling and no byes. Most Fantasy Football players are too addicted to the game to survive a bye.

2. SCHEDULING FOR LEAGUES OF VARIOUS SIZES:

   Your first consideration in devising a schedule is that there are 16 games in the regular NFL season. If you decide to have playoffs in your league, you will have to shorten your regular season to, let's say, 12 or 14 games and then use the remaining weeks for your playoffs. You will be drafting players from all 30 NFL teams. Once the 16-game NFL regular season is complete, only members of the NFL playoff teams will continue playing. This means that if you want all the players from your NFL teams to participate in your playoffs, these playoffs must take place before the end of the 16-game NFL regular season. Again, your playoffs will occur sometime during the last four weeks, depending on how many of your teams are involved in them.

   In the event you decide not to have playoffs and a yearly Fantasy Bowl, you can just play the full 16-game schedule and declare that the winner is the Fantasy Franchise with the best record.

   Another major consideration is the NFL schedule, which is played over 17 weeks. See the next section for options on tackling the NFL's 17-week season with bye weeks.

   The following pages demonstrate various scheduling options for leagues with various numbers of teams, along with options for the 17-week NFL season with bye weeks.

OPTIONS TO TACKLE
THE NFL'S 17-WEEK SEASON
WITH BYE WEEKS

The NFL continues to play its 16-game season over 17 weeks. This gives each NFL team one bye week during the season and will again result in some confusion for Fantasy Football leagues. In several sections of this chapter, I provide suggestions for overcoming problems caused by this schedule. As always, I welcome your ideas and suggestions for dealing with the new NFL schedule.

Tackling the 17-Week NFL Schedule

PLAYING OPTION #1 (for leagues of 10 or fewer teams)

With smaller leagues, you have more options because you have more NFL players to choose from.

1. ROSTER
Expand your original roster from 15 to 20 players.

2. WEEKLY LINEUP SIZE
Maintain the seven-player starting lineup.

3. WEEKLY GAMES
Fantasy teams are allowed to field NFL players only from teams that are playing that week (which is why I don't like this method). For instance, in week #4 you would field from your 15-member fantasy roster a 7-member team of players who are playing that week. If you have Jerry Rice, and the San Francisco 49ers are not playing that week, Rice can't be used. You have to choose from your roster another wide receiver who does play that week.

Leagues using this method should be limited to 10 or fewer teams, because each team has to have at least two starting quarterbacks and two placekickers. Each franchise should be sure not to draft both of its quarterbacks or both of its kickers from the same division. Because the NFL has scheduled its byes somewhat divisionally, a fantasy team that concentrates its players in a single division might not be able to field a certain position if both of its players are off at the same time.

Option #1's Good Points:
This option maintains the immediacy that we fantasy participants have become accustomed to.

Option #1's Drawbacks:
The prime reason I don't care for this option is that there will be one or two weeks when you won't be able to field your top player(s). Worse yet, depending on the NFL schedule, you may be without a quarterback or another player because it just happens that none of your players from that position play that week.

PLAYING OPTION #2 (for leagues of any size)

This option provides both immediate results and much of the playing tradition that our fantasy leagues are used to. It is the option my league will use because it's the least confusing and easiest to use. After using this method for five entire seasons, I am pleased with its results and recommend it for larger leagues.

1. ROSTER
No changes are necessary.

2. WEEKLY LINEUP SIZE
Maintain the seven-player weekly lineup.

3. WEEKLY GAMES
For your fantasy games, weekly scores are tabulated as usual, but if a fantasy player doesn't play on a given week he can be put in the lineup before the previous week's game—with that previous week's performance counting for both weeks. For instance, after all 30 NFL teams have played a couple of weeks into a season, teams begin to get byes. If one of your prime players is scheduled for a bye on week #5 because his team is off that week, you can insert him for week #5 before the start of that player's game in the previous week (which is week #4). His week #4 performance is used for both week #4 and week #5. For this player, week #5 becomes a carryover week—a week in which he does not play but rather carries his performance stats over from the previous week. How many fantasy points does this player score for you during the carryover week? Exactly as many as he scored for you during the previous week. Please note that commissioners should be prepared in week #4 to begin taking lineups for both week #4 and week #5.

This requires you to think ahead and adjust your roster for byes. Any fantasy team not calling in a lineup on a given week is forced to carry the same positions for its players in the lineup as used the previous week. This means it has forfeited its opportunity to make adjustments for the bye week. If a player is injured and a team forgot to call in and replace him in the lineup, his performance—or non-performance—would be locked in for two weeks if that player was involved in a bye week. The benefit for fantasy leagues is immediate weekly results. All fantasy games end on the same weekend. (For further clarification, please see Section VII, point 4b of this chapter, titled "Riding the Same Lineup During Carryover Weeks.")

4. SUDDEN-DEATH TIEBREAKERS
Commissioners, please note: For players not playing in a given week, the previous week's performances are used when you must dip into the list of reserve players to break a tie. (For the basics of tiebreakers, see Section IX.) This means that all players on NFL teams that bye in a given week **MUST** be inserted the previous week. This ensures that all players are given a spot on the following week's lineup card. Commis-sioners should insist on getting a positive comment from every Fantasy Franchise as to where in the following week's lineup—on the active list, in the reserves, on the bench—it wants to put players who have byes the following week.

Any team not heard from will have its bye-week players listed exactly as they were listed in the previous week.

5. LINEUP CHANGES

Lineup changes in this option are twofold. First, concerning the week at hand, only one lineup change is allowed after the weekly lineup is submitted. Second, regarding carryover players—who are submitted one week early to account for a bye the next week—one further lineup change is also allowed. This means that two lineup changes can be allowed per week, but only one change may be used for the current week's lineup. The other may be used only to move players for a forthcoming carryover week. Remember, this change must be made before the carryover player's previous-week game has started.

EXAMPLE: A player is submitted to a starting fantasy lineup for both the current week (week #4) and the following week (week #5) because of an upcoming bye. If he is removed from the starting lineup for the current week (week #4), this is considered the team's lineup change. If you decide to gamble by using his current week's (week #4's) results for only the current fantasy week (week #4) and to remove him from the following week's (week #5) starting lineup, this does not count as week #5's lineup change. If you remove this player from both the current (week #4) and the bye (week #5) starting lineups, it is considered the team's lineup change for the current week but not for the bye week. NOTE: Any player removed from a bye week's starting lineup is automatically placed at the bottom of the bye week's reserve list.

To further clarify:
If a fantasy team elects to change a bye player for the carryover week and does so prior to game time of the current week, this **DOES NOT** count as the current week's lineup change.

6. TRADE NIGHT (Watch Out for Carryover-Player Confusion)

A weekly trade night is allowed, but with one extra guideline for dealing with carryover players. (A carryover player, again, is one whom you keep active, even though his NFL team has a bye, by carrying over his performance from the previous week.)

Your fantasy team can trade or release a carryover player, but the trade or release does not take effect until all of the players involved in this transaction have shed their carryover status. Because a carryover player has already been submitted for your fantasy team's lineup, he will remain officially part of your fantasy team until the carryover week's game—with him in your lineup—has ended. The player you picked up for him may not be used until both the player you traded away and the player you picked up are clear of carryover status.

7. SCHEDULING

See the appropriate scheduling formats in Section III of this chapter.

8. PLAYOFFS

See the appropriate playoff formats in Section III of this chapter.

Option #2's Good Points:
This procedure provides both immediate weekly results and much of the playing tradition that our fantasy leagues are used to.

Option #2's Drawbacks:
This option's only drawback is that a player's performance may count for two games, even if he plays poorly.

NOTE

I highly recommend that commissioners review the consequences of the bye week scheduling format. Address all of your rules issues, including lineups, lineup changes, weekly games, roster transactions, scheduling, and playoff format. And again, please feel free to send me your suggestions. I will certainly look them over for ideas to share with other Fantasy Football participants.

FOUR-TEAM LEAGUE

REGULAR SEASON:
   Play a 15-game regular season. Teams play each other five times. (Two teams have seven home games, and the other two have eight.)

PLAYOFFS:
   The top two teams after 15 games advance to the Fantasy Bowl. This may be played on either week #16 or week #17. If you're undecided about whether to play your Fantasy Bowl on week #16 or #17, you might want to consider this: Many NFL teams, if they have already secured a playoff spot, may elect to sit their star players on week #17 in order to keep those players healthy for the postseason. Because of this, your league might want to hold its Fantasy Bowl on week #16, so that no star players are eliminated from helping their fantasy teams in the big game.

Key: 1. Read down for week #.
   2. Read across top for team # and then down for opponents.
   3. The asterisk (*) indicates a home game for the team heading the column.

FOUR-TEAM LEAGUE

Team #	1	2	3	4
Week #				
1	2	1*	4*	3
2	3*	4	1	2*
3	4*	3	2*	1
4	2	1*	4	3*
5	3	4*	1*	2
6	4	3*	2	1*
7	2*	1	4	3*
8	3*	4*	1	2
9	4*	3	2*	1
10	2	1*	4*	3
11	3	4	1*	2*
12	4	3*	2	1*
13	2*	1	4	3*
14	3*	4*	1	2
15	4	3	2*	1*
16		Bye or Fantasy Bowl		
17		Fantasy Bowl		

SIX-TEAM LEAGUE

REGULAR SEASON:
Play a 15-game regular season. Teams play each other three times each. (Three teams have seven home games, and the other three have eight.)

PLAYOFFS: OPTION #1
The top two teams after 15 games advance to the Fantasy Bowl. This may be played on either week #16 or week #17. If you're undecided about whether to play your Fantasy Bowl on week #16 or #17, you might want to consider this: Many NFL teams, if they have already secured a playoff spot, may elect to sit their star players on week #17 in order to keep those players healthy for the postseason. Because of this, your league might want to hold its Fantasy Bowl on week #16, so that no star players are eliminated from helping their fantasy teams in the big game. (For determining who should advance based on record, see Section IV, Playoffs.)

PLAYOFFS: OPTION #2
The top four teams after 15 games advance to the playoffs. On week #16, the four playoff teams are seeded 1 through 4 based on record, with seed #1 playing seed #4 and seed #2 playing seed #3. The winners then advance to the Fantasy Bowl on week #17.

Key: 1. Read down for week #.
2. Read across top for team # and then down for opponents.
3. The asterisk (*) indicates a home game for the team heading the column.

SIX-TEAM LEAGUE

Team #	1	2	3	4	5	6
Week #						
1	2*	1	4*	3	6*	5
2	3*	6*	1	5*	4	2
3	4	5	6	1*	2*	3*
4	5	3*	2	6	1*	4*
5	6*	4	5*	2*	3	1
6	2	1*	4	3*	6	5*
7	3	6	1*	5	4*	2*
8	4*	5*	6*	1	2	3
9	5*	3	2*	6*	1	4
10	6	4*	5	2	3*	1*
11	2*	1	4*	3	6*	5
12	3*	6*	1	5*	4	2
13	4	5	6	1*	2*	3*
14	5	3*	2	6	1*	4*
15	6*	4	5*	2*	3	1
	(Playoffs: Option #1)			(Playoffs: Option #2)		
16	Bye or Fantasy Bowl			Playoffs		
17	Fantasy Bowl			Fantasy Bowl		

EIGHT-TEAM LEAGUE
(OPTION #1)

REGULAR SEASON:
   Play a 14-game regular season. Teams play each other twice. (Each team has seven home games.)

PLAYOFFS:
   At the end of the 14-game regular season, the top four teams are seeded 1 through 4, as determined by their records. The first round of the playoffs begins on week #15. In the first round, seed #1 plays seed #4 and seed #2 plays seed #3. The winners of round one advance to the Fantasy Bowl during week #16 or week #17. If you're undecided about whether to play your Fantasy Bowl on week #16 or #17, you might want to consider this: Many NFL teams, if they have already secured a playoff spot, may elect to sit their star players on week #17 in order to keep those players healthy for the postseason. Because of this, your league might want to hold its Fantasy Bowl on week #16, so that no star players are eliminated from helping their fantasy teams in the big game. (For determining who should advance based on record, see Section IV, Playoffs.)

Key: 1. Read down for week #.
   2. Read across top for team # and then down for opponents.
   3. The asterisk (*) indicates a home game for the team heading the column.

EIGHT-TEAM LEAGUE
(OPTION #1)

Team #	1	2	3	4	5	6	7	8
Week #								
1	2*	1	4*	3	6*	5	8*	7
2	3*	4*	1	2	8	7*	6	5*
3	4	8*	6*	1*	7	3	5*	2
4	5	6	8	7*	1*	2*	4	3*
5	6*	5*	7*	8	2	1	3	4*
6	7	3	2*	5	4*	8*	1*	6
7	8*	7	5	6*	3*	4	2*	1
8	2	1*	4	3*	6	5*	8	7*
9	3	4	1*	2*	8*	7	6*	5
10	4*	8	6	1	7*	3*	5	2*
11	5*	6*	8*	7	1	2	4*	3
12	6	5	7	8*	2*	1*	3*	4
13	7*	3*	2	5*	4	8	1	6*
14	8	7*	5*	6	3	4*	2	1*
15	Playoffs							
16	Bye or Fantasy Bowl							
17	Fantasy Bowl							

EIGHT-TEAM LEAGUE
(OPTION #2)

DIVISIONS:
Split league into two divisions of four teams each.

REGULAR SEASON:
Play a 17-game regular season. Each team plays each of the other three teams within its division three times, for nine games. Then each team plays each of the teams in the other division twice, for eight more games. This adds up to a total of 17 regular-season games. (Four teams will have nine home games and four teams will have eight.)

PLAYOFFS:
There aren't any! The team with the best regular-season record becomes the league champion.

Key: 1. Read down for week #.
2. Read across top for team # and then down for opponents.
3. The asterisk (*) indicates a home game for the team heading the column.

EIGHT-TEAM LEAGUE
(OPTION #2)

Team#	SPADE DIVISION				CLUB DIVISION			
	1	2	3	4	5	6	7	8
Week #								
1	2*	1	4*	3	6*	5	8*	7
2	3	4*	1*	2	7	8*	5*	6
3	4	3*	2	1*	8	7*	6	5*
4	5*	6	7*	8	1*	2	3*	4
5	6*	7	8	5*	4	1	2*	3*
6	7*	8*	5	6	3*	4*	1	2
7	8	5*	6*	7*	2	3	4	1*
8	2	1*	4	3*	6	5*	8	7*
9	3*	4	1	2*	7*	8	5	6*
10	4*	3	2*	1	8*	7	6*	5
11	5	6*	7	8*	1	2*	3	4*
12	6	7*	8*	5	4*	1*	2	3
13	7	8	5*	6*	3	4	1*	2*
14	8*	5	6	7	2*	3*	4*	1
15	2*	1	4*	3	6*	5	8*	7
16	3	4*	1*	2	7	8*	5*	6
17	4	3*	2	1*	8	7*	6	5*

TEN-TEAM LEAGUE
(Can be used with either Playing Option #1 or #2)

DIVISIONS:
Split league into two divisions of five teams each.

REGULAR SEASON:
Play a 13-game regular season. Each team plays each of the four other teams within the division twice, for eight games. (During the two meetings of any two teams, each should be the home team once.) Then each team plays each of the teams in the other division once, for five more games. (Five teams will have six home games, and the other five will have seven.)

PLAYOFFS:
The top three of the five teams in each division advance to the playoffs. In the first round, the first-place team in each division is awarded a bye. The second- and third-place teams play each other. This takes place on week #14. Winners from week #14 then advance to play the first-place team in their division on week #15. Winners advance to the Fantasy Bowl, to be held either on week #16 or #17. If you're undecided about whether to play your Fantasy Bowl on week #16 or #17, you might want to consider this: Many NFL teams, if they have already secured a playoff spot, may elect to sit their star players on week #17 in order to keep those players healthy for the post-season. Because of this, your league might want to hold its Fantasy Bowl on week #16, so that no star players are eliminated from helping their fantasy teams in the big game. (For determining who should advance based on record, see Section IV, Playoffs.)

Key: 1. Read down for week #.
2. Read across top for team # and then down for opponents.
3. The asterisk (*) indicates a home game for the team heading the column.

TEN-TEAM LEAGUE

	SPADE DIVISION						CLUB DIVISION			
Team #	1	2	3	4	5		6	7	8	9	10
Week #										
1	2*	1	4*	3	6*		5	8*	7	10*	9
2	3*	5*	1	7*	2		10*	4	9*	8	6
3	4	8*	5*	1*	3		9	10	2	6*	7*
4	5	4	9	2*	1*		7	6*	10*	3*	8
5	10	3	2*	5	4*		8*	9*	6	7	1*
6	2	1*	5	6*	3*		4	10*	9	8*	7
7	3	5	1*	9	2*		7*	6	10	4*	8*
8	5*	7*	4	3*	1		8	2	6*	10	9*
9	4*	3*	2	1	10*		9*	8	7*	6	5
10	8	9	7	5*	4		10	3*	1*	2*	6*
11	6	4*	10*	2	8		1*	9	5*	7*	3
12	9*	10	6*	8*	7		3	5*	4	1	2*
13	7*	6	8	10	9		2*	1	3*	5	4*
14					Playoffs						
15					Playoffs						
16					Bye or Fantasy Bowl						
17					Fantasy Bowl						

TWELVE-TEAM LEAGUE
(OPTION #1)

DIVISIONS:
Split league into three divisions of four teams each.

REGULAR SEASON:
Play a 14-game regular season. Each of the four teams in a division plays the other three twice, for a total of six games. Each team also plays all the other eight teams once, for a total of eight games. This makes up the 14-game, regular-season schedule.

PLAYOFFS: OPTION #1 (Four-Team Playoff)
The top team in each division advances to the playoffs, along with one wild-card team (whichever second-place team has the best record). The four teams are seeded 1 through 4. Seed #1 plays seed #4 and seed #2 plays seed #3. The first-round game is played on week #15 with the winners advancing to the Fantasy Bowl on week #16 or #17. If you're undecided about whether to play your Fantasy Bowl on week #16 or #17, you might want to consider this: Many NFL teams, if they have already secured a playoff spot, may elect to sit their star players on week #17 in order to keep those players healthy for the postseason. Because of this, your league might want to hold its Fantasy Bowl on week #16, so that no star players are eliminated from helping their fantasy teams in the big game. (For determining who should advance based on record, see Section IV, Playoffs.)

PLAYOFFS: OPTION #2 (Eight-Team Playoff)
(The benefit of this option is that it keeps more teams in the playoff hunt longer.) The top team in each division advances to the playoffs, along with five wild-card teams. The wild-card teams are the five best teams based on record, not including divisional champions. The eight teams are seeded 1 through 8 based on record. In the first round, seed #1 plays seed #8, seed #2 plays seed #7, seed #3 plays seed #6, and seed #4 plays seed #5. These first-round games take place on week #15. The winners of the first round are then reseeded for the semifinal round played on week #16. Of the remaining four teams seed #1 (based on record) plays seed #4 and seed #2 plays seed #3. The winners then advance to play in the Fantasy Bowl on week #17.

Key: 1. Read down for week #.
  2. Read across top for team # and then down for opponents.
  3. The asterisk (*) indicates a home game for the team heading the column.

TWELVE-TEAM LEAGUE
(OPTION #1)

Team #	Spade Division				Club Division				Heart Division			
	1	2	3	4	5	6	7	8	9	10	11	12
Week #												
1	2*	1	4*	3	6	5*	8	7*	10	9*	12	11*
2	3*	4*	1	2	7*	8*	5	6	11*	12*	9	10
3	4	3	2*	1*	8	7	6*	5*	12	11	10*	9*
4	5	6*	11	12*	1*	2	9*	10	7	8*	3*	4
5	6	7*	9	10*	11*	1*	2	12*	3*	4	5	8
6	12*	11	8*	6	9	4*	10*	3	5*	7	2*	1
7	11*	10	6*	5	4*	3	12	9*	8	2*	1	7*
8	7	8*	12	9*	10	11	1*	2	4	5*	6*	3*
9	8*	9	7*	11*	12*	10*	3	1	2*	6	4	5
10	10*	12	5*	7	3	9*	4*	11*	6	1	8	2*
11	9	5*	10	8	2	12	11	4*	1*	3*	7*	6*
12	2	1*	4	3*	6*	5	8*	7	10*	9	12*	11
13	3	4	1*	2*	7	8	5*	6*	11	12	9*	10*
14	4*	3*	2	1	8*	7*	6	5	12*	11*	10	9
	(Playoffs: Option #1)								(Playoffs: Option #2)			
15	Playoffs								Playoffs			
16	Bye or Fantasy Bowl								Playoffs			
17	Fantasy Bowl								Fantasy Bowl			

— 315 —

TWELVE-TEAM LEAGUE
(OPTION #2)

DIVISIONS:
Split league into two divisions of six teams each.

REGULAR SEASON:
Play a 16-game regular season. Each of the six teams in a division plays each of the other five teams twice, for a total of 10 games. Each team also plays all the teams from the other division once each, for another six games. This makes a total of 16 games. (Each team has eight home games and eight away games.)

PLAYOFFS:
The top team from each division advances to the Fantasy Bowl on week #17.

Key: 1. Read down for week #.
2. Read across top for team # and then down for opponents.
3. The asterisk (*) indicates a home game for the team heading the column.

TWELVE-TEAM LEAGUE
(OPTION #2)

Team #	SPADE DIVISION						CLUB DIVISION					
	1	2	3	4	5	6	7	8	9	10	11	12
Week#												
1	2*	1	4*	3	6*	5	8*	7	10*	9	12*	11
2	3*	6*	1	5*	4	2	9	12*	7*	11*	10	8
3	4	5*	6	1*	2	3*	10*	11	12	7	8*	9*
4	5	3	2*	6	1*	4*	11	9*	8	12*	7*	10
5	6*	4*	5	2	3*	1	12	10*	11*	8	9	7*
6	7	8*	9*	10*	11	12*	1*	2	3	4	5*	6
7	8*	9	10	11	12*	7	6*	1	2*	3*	4*	5
8	9*	10*	11*	12	7*	8	5	6*	1	2	3	4*
9	10	11	12	7*	8	9*	4	5*	6	1*	2*	3*
10	11*	12*	7*	8*	9	10	3	4	5*	6*	1	2
11	12	7	8	9	10*	11*	2*	3*	4*	5	6	1*
12	2	1*	4	3*	6	5*	8	7*	10	9*	12	11*
13	3	6	1*	5	4*	2*	9*	12	7	11	10*	8*
14	4*	5	6*	1	2*	3	10	11*	12*	7*	8	9
15	5*	3*	2	6*	1	4	11*	9	8*	12	7	10*
16	6	4	5*	2*	3	1*	12*	10	11	8*	9*	7
17					Fantasy Bowl							

FOURTEEN-TEAM LEAGUE

DIVISIONS:
Split league into two divisions of seven teams each.

REGULAR SEASON:
Play a 14-game regular season. Each of the seven teams within a division plays every other team twice, for a total of 12 games. Each team also plays two teams at random from the other division, thus making up the 14-game schedule.

PLAYOFFS: OPTION #1 (Four-Team Playoff)
At the end of the regular season, the top two teams in each division are awarded playoff spots. The four playoff teams are then seeded 1 through 4, as determined by record. Seed #1 plays seed #4 and seed #2 plays seed #3. The first-round game is played on week #15 with the winners advancing to the Fantasy Bowl on week #16 or #17. If you're undecided about whether to play your Fantasy Bowl on week #16 or #17, you might want to consider this: Many NFL teams, if they have already secured a playoff spot, may elect to sit their star players on week #17 in order to keep those players healthy for the postseason. Because of this, your league might want to hold its Fantasy Bowl on week #16, so that no star players are eliminated from helping their fantasy teams in the big game. (For determining who should advance based on record, see Section IV, Playoffs.)

PLAYOFFS: OPTION #2 (Six-Team Playoff)
The top team in each division automatically advances to the playoffs. The second- and third-place teams in each division are also awarded playoff spots as wild-card teams. (Another choice within this option would be to take, as wild-card teams, the next four teams in the standings based on record, regardless of division. Either way, you have four wild-card teams.)

In the first round of the playoffs, the divisional winners are awarded byes. The four wild-card teams meet to see who will advance to play the divisional winners. These first-round games will take place on week #15. If you use the second- and third-place teams in each division as wild cards, the winner advances to meet its divisional champ on week #16. On the other hand, if you use the four next-best teams, regardless of division, as your wild-card teams, the winners advance to meet the divisional champs using the following matchups: The divisional champ with the better regular-season record plays the wild-card survivor with the inferior record; and the divisional champ with the inferior record plays the wild-card survivor with the better record.

The winners of these games then meet in the Fantasy Bowl on week #17.

Key: 1. Read down for week #.
2. Read across top for team # and then down for opponents.
3. The asterisk (*) indicates a home game for the team heading the column.

FOURTEEN-TEAM LEAGUE

Team #	SPADE DIVISION							CLUB DIVISION						
	1	2	3	4	5	6	7	8	9	10	11	12	13	14
Week #														
1	2*	1	4*	3	6*	5	14	9	8*	11	10*	13	12*	7*
2	3	7*	1*	5*	4	13	2	10*	14	8	12	11*	6*	9*
3	4*	6	7	1	12	2*	3*	11	13*	14*	8*	5*	9	10
4	5	3*	2*	11	1*	7*	6	12*	10	9*	4*	8	14	13*
5	6*	4	10	2*	7	1	5*	13	11*	3*	9	14*	8*	12
6	7	9	5*	6*	3	4	1*	14*	2*	12	13*	10*	11	8
7	8	5*	6	7	2	3*	4*	1*	12	13*	14	9*	10	11*
8	5*	4*	11*	2	1	7	6*	14	13	12*	3	10	9*	8*
9	2	1*	7*	6	8*	4*	3	5	14*	13	12*	11	10*	9
10	3*	12*	1	7*	6	5*	4	9*	8	14	13	2	11*	10*
11	4	3	2*	1*	7*	9*	5	10	6	8*	14*	13*	12	11
12	13*	7	6*	5	4*	3	2*	11*	10*	9	8	14	1	12*
13	6	5	4	3*	2*	1*	10*	12	11	7	9*	8*	14*	13
14	7*	6*	5	14*	3*	2	1	13*	12*	11*	10	9	8	4
	(Playoffs: Option #1)							(Playoffs: Option #2)						
15	Playoffs							Playoffs						
16	Bye or Fantasy Bowl							Playoffs						
17	Fantasy Bowl							Fantasy Bowl						

— 318 —

SIXTEEN-TEAM LEAGUE
(OPTION #1: 12-game regular season,
with 12 teams in playoffs)

DIVISIONS:

Split league into four divisions of four teams each.

REGULAR SEASON:

Play a 12-game regular season. Each of the four teams within a division plays the other three twice, for a total of six games. Each team also plays two teams from each of the other three divisions once, for a total of 6 more games, to round out the 12-game schedule.

12-TEAM PLAYOFFS: OPTION #1

The top team in each division automatically advances to the playoffs. The second- and third-place teams in each division are also awarded playoff spots. This excludes only the last-place team in each division, leaving 12 playoff teams and keeping a large number of teams in the race as long as possible.

In the first round of the playoffs, the first-place teams are awarded byes. The teams that finished second and third in their divisions meet in the divisional wild-card games on week #13.

The winners advance to meet the divisional champs on week #14. The divisional wild-card winners meet their respective divisional champions to determine who will represent the division in the semifinals.

Week #14's winners advance to the semifinals on week #15. The teams representing the Spade and Club divisions meet, as do the teams representing the Diamond and Heart divisions.

The winners become the Black and Red conference champions, respectively, and meet in the Fantasy Bowl on week #16. (For determining who should advance based on record, see Section IV, Playoffs.)

12-TEAM PLAYOFFS: OPTION #2

The top team in each division automatically advances to the playoffs. Then the eight best remaining teams—based on record and regardless of division—are awarded wild-card playoff spots.

In the first round of the playoffs, the four divisional winners are awarded byes. The eight wild-card teams are seeded 1 through 8, based on record. Seed #1 plays seed #8, seed #2 plays seed #7, seed #3 plays seed #6, and seed #4 plays seed #5. This takes place on week #13.

The winners advance to meet the division champs on week #14. In this round, the division champs are seeded 1 through 4 and the wild-card winners are seeded 5 through 8. Again it will be seed #1 vs. seed #8, seed #2 vs. seed #7, seed #3 vs. seed #6, and seed #4 vs. seed #5. The winners advance to the semifinals on week #15, this time seeded 1 through 4, again based on record. Seed #1 meets seed #4 and seed #2 meets seed #3, with the winners advancing to the Fantasy Bowl on week #16 or #17. If you're undecided about whether to play your Fantasy Bowl on week #16 or #17, you might want to consider this: Many NFL teams, if they have already secured a playoff spot, may elect to sit their star players on week #17 in order to keep those players healthy for the postseason. Because of this, your league might want to hold its Fantasy Bowl on week #16, so that no star players are eliminated from helping their fantasy teams in the big game. (For determining who should advance based on record, see Section IV, Playoffs.)

Key: 1. Read down for week #.
2. Read across top for team # and then down for opponents.
3. The asterisk (*) indicates a home game for the team heading the column.

SIXTEEN-TEAM LEAGUE
(OPTION #1)

| | BLACK CONFERENCE | | | | | | | RED CONFERENCE | | | | | | | |
| | SPADE | | | CLUB | | | | DIAMOND | | | | HEART | | | |
Team #	1	2	3	4	5	6	7	8	9	10	11	12	13	14	15	16
Week #																
1	2*	1	4*	3	6*	5	8*	7	10*	9	12*	11	14*	13	16*	15
2	3	4*	1*	2	7	8*	5*	6	11	12*	9*	10	15	16*	13*	14
3	4*	3*	2	1	8	7*	6	5*	12	11*	10	9*	16	15*	14	13*
4	5	6*	8	7*	1*	2	4	3*	14*	16	13	15*	11*	9	12	10*
5	9*	10	11*	12	13*	14	15*	16	1	2*	3	4*	5	6*	7	8*
6	13	16*	15	14*	9	10*	11	12*	5*	6	7*	8	1*	4	3*	2
7	8*	7	6*	5	4*	3	2*	1	16*	15	14*	13	12*	11	10*	9
8	10	9*	12	11*	16	15*	14	13*	2	1*	4	3*	8	7*	6	5*
9	16*	14	13*	15	10	9*	12*	11	6	5*	8*	7	3	2*	4*	1
10	2	1*	4	3*	6	5*	8	7*	10	9*	12	11*	14	13*	16	15*
11	3*	4	1	2*	7*	8	5	6*	11*	12	9	10*	15*	16	13	14*
12	4	3	2*	1*	8*	7	6*	5	12*	11	10*	9	16*	15	14*	13
13						(12-Team Playoff)										
14						Playoffs (Round 1)										
15						Playoffs (Round 2)										
16						Playoffs (Semifinals)										
17						Bye or Fantasy Bowl										
						Fantasy Bowl										

SIXTEEN-TEAM LEAGUE
(OPTION #2: 14-game regular season,
8 teams in playoffs)

DIVISIONS:

Split league into four divisions of four teams each.

REGULAR SEASON:

Play a 14-game regular season. Each of the four teams within a division plays the other three twice, for a total of six games. In addition, each team plays two teams from the other conference's two divisions once—for four more games—and also plays each of the teams from the other division of its own conference once each—for a total of four more games. This makes a grand total of 14 regular-season games.

PLAYOFFS:

The top team in each division automatically advances to the playoffs. Of the teams that did not win their divisions, the four teams with the best records are awarded playoff spots as wild-card teams. These four teams advance, regardless of division. (Example: If the second- and third-place teams from the Spade Division both have better records than the second-place team from the Heart Division, both Spade teams advance, not the Heart team with the poorer record.)

For the first round of the playoffs, the division champs are seeded 1 through 4 and the four wild-card teams are seeded 5 through 8. Seed #1 plays seed #8, seed #2 plays seed #7, seed #3 plays seed #6, and seed #4 plays seed #5. This first round takes place during week #15. The winners then advance to the semifinals on week #16. Again the teams are seeded, this time 1 through 4, based on record. Seed #1 plays seed #4 and seed #2 plays seed #3. The winners of these semifinal games advance to the Fantasy Bowl on week #17. (For determining who should advance based on record, see Section IV, Playoffs.)

Key: 1. Read down for week #.
2. Read across top for team # and then down for opponents.
3. The asterisk (*) indicates a home game for the team heading the column.

SIXTEEN-TEAM LEAGUE
(OPTION #2)

| | BLACK CONFERENCE | | | | | | | | RED CONFERENCE | | | | | | | |
| | SPADE | | | | CLUB | | | | DIAMOND | | | | HEART | | | |
Team #	1	2	3	4	5	6	7	8	9	10	11	12	13	14	15	16
Week #																
1	2*	1	4*	3	6*	5	8*	7	10*	9	12*	11	14*	13	16*	15
2	3	4*	1*	2	7	8*	5*	6	11	12*	9*	10	15	16*	13*	14
3	4*	3*	2	1	8	7*	6	5*	12	11*	10	9*	16	15*	14	13*
4	5	6*	8	7*	1*	2	4	3*	14*	16	13	15*	11*	9	12	10*
5	9*	10	11*	12	13*	14	15*	16	1	2*	3	4*	5	6*	7	8*
6	13	16*	15	14*	9	10*	11	12*	5*	6	7*	8	1*	4	3*	2
7	8*	7	6*	5	4*	3	2*	1	16*	15	14*	13	12*	11	10*	9
8	10	9*	12	11*	16	15*	14	13*	2	1*	4	3*	8	7*	6	5*
9	16*	14	13*	15	10	9*	12*	11	6	5*	8*	7	3	2*	4*	1
10	7*	8*	5*	6*	3	4	1*	2	15*	13*	16*	14*	10	12	9	11
11	6	5	7	8	2*	1*	3*	4*	13	14	15	16	9*	10*	11*	12*
12	2	1*	4	3*	6	5*	8	7*	10	9*	12	11*	14	13*	16	15*
13	3*	4	1	2*	7*	8	5	6*	11*	12	9	10*	15*	16	13	14*
14	4	3	2*	1*	8*	7	6*	5	12*	11	10*	9	16*	15	14*	13
15	Playoffs (Round 1)															
16	Playoffs (Semifinals)															
17	Fantasy Bowl															

IV
PLAYOFFS & PAYOFFS

PLAYOFFS

Many fantasy leagues will choose the before mentioned playoff structures or may choose to play out the entire regular season and have their Fantasy playoff teams redraft going into the actual NFL playoffs. For a further explanation of this option—see Chapter IX—option 3 in this guide.

Now for further playoff recommendations, see hte following.

1. PLAYOFFS: WHO SHOULD ADVANCE
   For each of the various preceding schedules, I included a suggested playoff structure. You may choose to follow these regular-season schedules and playoff structures, or you may decide to set up your own. Whether you use the structure I suggest or one you have devised yourself, you are also going to need a tiebreaker system in case some teams have identical win-loss records. Here is the tiebreaker system that I like:

   1. Best win-loss record
   2. Most points scored during the regular season
      (There is a reason for putting most points scored as a tiebreaker before head-to-head competition. I feel any fantasy team could get lucky during the season and have a good game against a good team. The true test of a good fantasy team is how it fares throughout the entire season. This is better reflected by a comparison of the point totals scored during the entire season.)
   3. Head-to-head competition (most points vs. team tied with)
   4. Best conference record
   5. Most points allowed
      (The team that allowed more points wins the tiebreaker. This is an indication of which team played a tougher schedule.)
   6. Coin flip

2. PLAYOFFS: DETERMINING THE HOME TEAM
   In the event your league uses a sudden-death tiebreaker, you will need a system to determine which will be the home team. Since the team with the better record should always be the home team, the same system used for determining who should advance to the playoffs would also apply nicely here. Remember the importance of the home team when using the sudden-death tiebreaker. The team that is determined to be the home team will have the first shot at breaking the tie. Again, the system used to determine the home team in the playoffs is the same one used for determining who should advance as listed above.

3. LEAGUE PAYOFFS:
   Our league has a small entry fee that is paid at the beginning of the year by each franchise. The purse that is collected is divided up by first paying the commissioner. (We let our commissioner play for free, which serves as payment for duties and services. Therefore we don't actually take money out of the purse to pay the commissioner, but the purse is smaller because that person has not contributed.) The remainder of the money is divided up to provide payment for the following:

1. First place—Fantasy Bowl winner
2. Second place—Fantasy Bowl runner-up
3. Third place—winner, third-place playoff
4. Fourth place—loser, third-place playoff
5. Trophies for top four teams
6. Stamps, photocopying, & miscellaneous (used by commissioner for issuing weekly results to franchise owners)

V
THE DRAFT

Draft day may become the sports event of the year for most of you, but it can turn into a real headache for your commissioner if he or she is not properly prepared. The following is a layout of how our draft is set up and run. Everything is set up for a 16-team league, but the process can easily be adapted to the number of teams you have in your league.

1. SETTING UP A DRAFT DAY:
   One of the toughest jobs a commissioner faces is selecting a draft day. It is essential to find a day when all the franchises can be represented. In a small league (8 teams or fewer), it shouldn't be very difficult to find a time convenient for all team owners. In leagues of 10 or more, such as the one I'm involved with, select a date that is within two weeks of the National Football League regular-season opener. Then send out a notice more than a month in advance to inform all the teams of the draft date.

2. TEAM REPRESENTATION:
   With each team having a month's advance notice, there shouldn't be any reason that a team can't have a representative there to draft for the franchise, even if the owner can't be present.

   NOTE: After a year or two of having one of your Fantasy Franchise owners draft for both his team and another team that couldn't make it to the draft, you will begin to get many objections from the other franchise owners. Their beef is legitimate: How can an owner from one team put his heart into drafting for another team? It ruins the whole concept of the draft. So in our league, we follow these rules:

   A. No team is allowed to draft for another.
   B. Any team not represented at the draft must make its selections from the players remaining after the draft. (This has never happened.)

3. DRAFT ASSISTANT:
   If a commissioner owns a franchise himself, he may want to seek an assistant for draft day, someone who can take care of logging picks as they are called off, and so on. This leaves the commissioner free to concentrate on his draft. I have done this for the last four years, and it has worked out tremendously for both me and my assistant. In fact, my assistants have thanked me for such a good time.

4. DETERMINING TEAM NUMBERS AND DIVISIONS:
   Once each team is present, the draft can begin. The process for determining each franchise's team number for the purpose of scheduling and naming divisions is as follows:

   A. From a deck of cards select the Ace, Two, Three, and Four of each of the four suits, giving you 16 cards, one for each franchise.

B. The 16 cards are shuffled and cut; each team takes one card to determine both its team number and the division it will be competing in.

C. The 16 cards are interpreted as follows:

Black Conference			**Red Conference**		
Spade	Ace of Spades	— Team #1	**Diamond**	Ace of Diamonds	— Team # 9
Division	Two of Spades	— Team #2	**Division**	Two of Diamonds	— Team #10
	Three of Spades	— Team #3		Three of Diamonds	— Team #11
	Four of Spades	— Team #4		Four of Diamonds	— Team #12
Club	Ace of Clubs	— Team #5	**Heart**	Ace of Hearts	— Team #13
Division	Two of Clubs	— Team #6	**Division**	Two of Hearts	— Team #14
	Three of Clubs	— Team #7		Three of Hearts	— Team #15
	Four of Clubs	— Team #8		Four of Hearts	— Team #16

5. **12 ROUNDS / 7 STARTERS:**
After determining team number and division, we move on to the actual draft. In our league, we draft players in 12 rounds. In selecting these 12 players, we must remember that 7 of them will be used in our starting lineup, which consists of two running backs, two wide receivers, one tight end, one quarterback, and one kicker. The remaining five picks will be reserves and can be from any of the above-mentioned positions.

6. **DRAFTING ORDER:**
We've found that we can best provide a fair draft and parity throughout the league by flopping the drafting order every other round. When determining the order of the draft, we first draw cards for the first round and then reverse that order for the second round.

This works out well, since the franchise that is lucky enough to get the #1 overall pick in the first round won't pick again until the 16th pick in the second round. Another way to look at this is that if you have the misfortune of picking 16th in the first round, you will automatically be given the #1 pick in the second round—two picks in a row. This process has worked out well and keeps the draft balanced pretty evenly. It also prevents someone who is lucky at picking cards from getting all the early picks in each of the rounds.

To determine the order of the draft, 16 cards are preselected from a whole deck. The cards used are the Ace through the Eight of Spades and the Ace through the Eight of Hearts. The 16 cards are shuffled, cut, and passed out. The order of the draft will be as follows:

Ace of Spades	— 1st Pick	Ace of Hearts	— 9th Pick
Two of Spades	— 2nd Pick	Two of Hearts	— 10th Pick
Three of Spades	— 3rd Pick	Three of Hearts	— 11th Pick
Four of Spades	— 4th Pick	Four of Hearts	— 12th Pick
Five of Spades	— 5th Pick	Five of Hearts	— 13th Pick
Six of Spades	— 6th Pick	Six of Hearts	— 14th Pick
Seven of Spades	— 7th Pick	Seven of Hearts	— 15th Pick
Eight of Spades	— 8th Pick	Eight of Hearts	— 16th Pick

Remember, each even-numbered round is in the reverse order of the previous odd-numbered round. So, if you grabbed the Four of Spades for your first-round pick, you would automatically draft 13th in the second round. This procedure is repeated for rounds 3 and 4 and so on, with a new draw of cards every odd round until the 12 rounds are complete.

7. SPEEDING UP YOUR DRAFT:
When drafting 192 players, as we do in our league, the process can sometimes become too long and drawn out. What we have developed is a quicker process for determining the order for all the rounds. Instead of drawing the cards every two rounds, we take six decks of cards which consist of the 16 predetermined cards (Ace through Eight of Spades and Hearts) and label the decks A through F. That means each group of 16 cards is labeled with a letter.

Each of the six decks of cards is shuffled, cut, and spread out, face down, on the table. Each franchise approaches the table and selects one card from each letter group. The following table shows the determination of drafting order for all of the rounds:

Deck marked with letter		
"A" —— Rounds 1 and 2		
"B" —— Rounds 3 and 4		
"C" —— Rounds 5 and 6		
"D" —— Rounds 7 and 8		
"E" —— Rounds 9 and 10		
"F" —— Rounds 11 and 12		

Samples:
Deck "A"

Ace of Spades	——	Draft 1st, 1st Round	——	16th, 2nd Round
Two of Spades	——	Draft 2nd, 1st Round	——	15th, 2nd Round
Ace of Hearts	——	Draft 9th, 1st Round	——	8th, 2nd Round

Deck "D"

Ace of Spades	——	Draft 1st, 7th Round	——	16th, 8th Round
Two of Spades	——	Draft 2nd, 7th Round	——	15th, 8th Round
Two of Spades	——	Draft 2nd, 7th Round	——	15th, 8th Round
Ace of Hearts	——	Draft 9th, 7th Round	——	8th, 8th Round

This process also allows some time for forming last-minute drafting strategies. After determining the drafting order for all the rounds, we take a 10-minute break to allow the teams to set up their picks, now that they know in what order they will draft.

8. TIME LIMIT:
In many cases, such as in our league's draft of 192 players, the draft can last many, many hours. To prevent the draft from dragging on too long, we have established a limit on the time a team has to make each pick.

In the early rounds, this should be no problem, since most of the better, more well-known players are being drafted. However, in the later rounds, selecting a player becomes more involved and may take longer.

The rules on the time limit for drafting players are as follows:

A. Two minutes are allowed per pick.
B. If the time limit has been exceeded, the next team in line will then be able to pick. Following that choice, go back to the team that was skipped.
C. Four minutes are allowed if a team has two consecutive picks (such as when an owner has the last pick of an odd round and automatically has the first pick of the second round).
D. If a team exceeds the four-minute limit for its consecutive picks, it must wait until after the next two teams are allowed picks before being allowed to make its selection(s).
E. A stopwatch should be used, and a warning should be given to the team that is selecting when there are 30 seconds left.

NOTE: Below is a sample of the boards we use at our draft. They are about 2 feet by 3 feet in actual size, making it easy for everyone in the room to see. The draft assistant logs the draft picks as they are called off, making our draft run smoothly and giving it a more professional appearance.

1998
FANTASY FOOTBALL DRAFT
(ROUND #1)

Fantasy Team #	Player Drafted	Pro Team	Pos
1			
2			
3			
4			
5			
6			
7			
8			
9			
10			
11			
12			
13			
14			
15			
16			

VI
ROSTER CHANGES/TRANSACTIONS

Because the 17-week NFL season may affect some transaction procedures, please refer to the suggestions for handling this schedule, found at the beginning of this chapter under "Trade Night."

After the draft has been completed, you may find that you're not happy with all of the players you chose, or, during the course of the season, one of your players may be sidelined with an injury or for some other reason. In either of these events, you may choose to make a trade or pick up another player.

1. PICKUPS AND TRADES:
   During the course of the season, you may elect to pick up or trade for another player. This can be done, provided that your roster never exceeds 12 players. For every player added to your roster, another must be dropped.

   A. Once a player is dropped by an FFL team, he becomes a free agent and is eligible to be picked up by any other franchise. He is, in effect, put on waivers.
   B. There are two types of roster changes that can be made. The first is actually labeled a *pickup*. This occurs when a team decides to pick up a player from the pool of players left unclaimed following the draft. Remember, for every additional player you pick up, you must also drop a player from your current roster to keep it at 12.
   C. Although there will be a limit of only one or two trades between teams, there is no limit to how many players can be picked up from the unclaimed pool.
   D. The other type of transaction is the *trade*. It's a move by one team in the league to trade a player to another team in the league. A limit of one or two of these exchanges or trades should be allowed per year. This prevents any two franchise owners who are close friends from trading between themselves exclusively in an attempt to build one super team between the two of them. In the event of a two-for-one trade, where one team offers two players in exchange for one better player, each team's roster must still end up with 12. This means that the team receiving the two players must drop an additional player besides the one it traded. The team giving up the two players and receiving only one must pick up another player from the unclaimed pool.
   E. Limit the number of transactions per franchise per trade night to three. For leagues using a phone-in method for transactions, this means that one transaction may be made in the first hour allotted, and two may be made in the second hour.

2. COMMISSIONER RESPONSIBILITIES:
   A. To ease the commissioner's load, I suggest having your trade night the same night as you take lineups. This will then tie up only one night in league transactions.

B. Set a time limit of two hours.

C. Keep good records to avoid the possibility of two teams picking up the same player.

D. I suggest the commissioner charge a small fee for each trade, for his or her time and the paperwork involved.

3. LEAGUE HANDLING OF PICKUPS AND TRADES (COMMISSIONER):
There are a number of ways to handle pickups and trades, based on how your league is handled by its commissioner. The first thing to determine is whether league transactions are going to be handled in person or by telephone. Here are some options:

A. Phone-In Leagues

OPTION #1: The Worst Goes First
This method allows the team with the worst record each week to have first chance at making its transactions. (My league tried this the last couple of years and it worked well. I'm sure we'll continue to use it in the future.)

a. In the weeks preceding the season, when transactions are allowed after the league's fantasy draft, the team with the worst record from the previous season will go first, then the team with the next worst record, and so on.

NOTE: OPTION #1
In the event new teams have been added to the league, cards should be drawn at the draft to determine the order of the new teams' transactions. The transaction slots for new teams should be inserted right into the rest of the league's transaction order.

NOTE: OPTION #2
If your league has brought in a number of new teams, you may choose to use the reverse order of the first round of your draft for the weeks prior to the season.

b. On a given transaction night the commissioner calls each franchise, starting with the one with the worst record. For teams with identical records, the following tiebreakers will be used:
1. Worst record
2. Fewest points scored
3. Most points allowed (tougher schedule)
4. Coin flip

c. Each franchise is responsible for giving the commissioner a telephone number where someone can be reached for transactions during the season. If no one will be at the number on a given night, the franchise is responsible for informing the commissioner prior to the transaction day and time, and for leaving a new number where someone can be reached.

d. When a commissioner cannot reach a fantasy team:
1. If a commissioner receives no answer at the given franchise number, he or she will assume that the franchise desires no transactions that evening and, after allowing 10 rings, the

commissioner may go on to the next team. If the team involved calls later in the hour to make transactions, this team will go to the end of the list.

2. If a commissioner gets a busy signal, he or she must continue to call that team for three minutes. If the commissioner still cannot get through on the line, he or she goes on to the next team. If the skipped team calls in and wants to make transactions, it must go to the end of the list for first-hour transactions.

3. If a commissioner reaches a telephone recorder, he or she should leave a message noting the time of the call. If the team calls back and wants to make transactions, it must go to the end of the list.

NOTE: Some owners have called the commissioner back several times a night, in order to stay at the end of the list. The point of this is to find out which players have been dropped by other teams. This is a big nuisance. To prevent this from going on all night, we follow this rule: No team can pick up a player dropped after its original position within that hour. For example, if a franchise owner who is fourth on the list for picking up a player bypasses his moves and wants to drop to the bottom of the list, he may not pick up any player dropped in the fifth position or later. He must wait for his second hour's transaction position to try to obtain one of those dropped players. And a team would have no advantage in moving to the end of the list in the second hour, because it cannot pick up any player dropped after its original transaction position until the following week.

NOTE: If an owner leaves a message on the commissioner's recorder detailing whom the owner wants to pick up, this message should be disregarded by the commissioner. Only transactions made person-to-person over the phone should be considered. The commissioner who receives such a message should ignore it and attempt to contact the owner according to the rules detailed above.

e. Three transactions per night:
(One the first hour, up to two the second hour, for a total of three.)
NOTE: A 2-for-1 trade is considered only one transaction for either team.

If any team was bypassed in the first hour's transactions because of no answer or a busy signal and also failed to contact the commissioner, that team forfeits one of its allowed transactions for the evening. With a maximum of three transactions per transaction night, the first hour's selection would be forfeited. The reason for allowing only one transaction the first hour is to provide each team a shot at obtaining at least one significant player. If the commissioner allowed two transactions in the first hour, very few desirable players would be left by the time the owners choosing later got their chance.

f. Second-hour transactions:

1. The only teams that will be called back by the commissioner are those that expressed an interest in making second-hour transactions when called during the first hour. They should be called back in the same sequence as during the first hour.

2. If any team did not talk to the commissioner during the first hour but wants to make a trade during the second hour, that team goes to the end of the list—behind those that did express, during the first hour, an interest in making second-hour transactions. If more than one team calls in, they will be called back in the sequence they called in.

g. Transaction-position trading:

Two teams may desire to trade their weekly transaction-position numbers. This may come as part of a trade condition. The two teams can be allowed to trade their transaction positions on the condition that both teams must make a first-hour transaction. This will hopefully prevent any two teams in cahoots from just passing their favorable positions to each other. So both teams have to make this first-hour transaction. The commissioner must be assured that this condition has been met before the transaction-position trading is allowed. (This position trading should only be allowed prior to the trade deadline and should not be allowed in the roster-expansion draft or the playoff player-additon draft. The team trading a favorable early position has nothing to gain, since another player or draft pick cannot be included. So such a trade is probably not on the up-and-up, and as a commissioner I would not, and did not, allow such a trade.)

OPTION #2: First Come, First Served

Efficient handling of the weekly phone call-in:

Trades should be handled on a first-come, first-served basis. There may be many trade nights when the teams in your league are looking to pick up the same player. To prevent any hassles or showing of favoritism, state a time you will start taking calls. Take the phone off the hook five minutes before your declared starting time. Then at precisely, say, 6:00 P.M., put the phone back on the hook and begin taking calls.

a. Each franchise may have only one caller trying to place the transaction order. (Some teams have only one owner while others have many.) If more than one owner from a franchise calls within the same hour, the franchise goes to the bottom of the callback list, unless the transactions by the penalized team have already been accepted by the commissioner.

b. Set a limit of one transaction in the first hour and two in the second hour, for a total of three. This will keep you from being on the phone for a long time. This will also give the other teams a chance at the more highly desired players.

c. Offer no advice to teams calling in as to whom you think they should pick up. If a team calls in looking for a player to fill a particular position, let the caller suggest whom he or she wants and offer no help.

d. In the event that you, as commissioner, are looking for a player and want to be fair to both your league and yourself, you could handle it the way I do: If a player goes unclaimed for 10 minutes after the trading hour has started, the commissioner is allowed to pick up the player. Again, the commissioner, like the rest of the owners, can pick up no more than two players at a time. He or she cannot pick up a second or third player until after 10 minutes into the second hour. In the event your league meets on transaction night, the commissioner will draw a card like anyone else to determine the order of pickups.

B. Weekly Get-Together Leagues

OPTION #1: The Worst Goes First
For those leagues that meet weekly, an easy and fair way to handle transactions is the worst-goes-first option, as defined in Option #1 for phone-in leagues. The team with the worst record gets to make its selections first, and so on. If two teams have identical records, the following tiebreakers will be used:
1. Worst record
2. Least points scored
3. Most points allowed (tougher schedule)
4. Coin flip

OPTION #2: Cut the Cards
Use a deck of cards to determine who goes first, and then second, and so on.

OPTION #3: Player Bidding
Another option used in many fantasy leagues for player transactions is *player bidding*. Fantasy teams pick up players from the unclaimed-player pool by bidding for them.

a. Fantasy teams use the trade night to bid on players. If only one team bids on a player, then obviously it acquires the player. If more than one team bids on a player, then the player goes to the team with the highest bid.
Example: Let's say a player goes undrafted but gets hot, so a number of fantasy teams in the league are interested in him. Team A bids $3.00. Team B bids $2.00. Team C bids $5.00. Team C, the highest bidder, gets the player.

b. In the event of two or more teams making the same highest bid, the commissioner will advise each team of this at the end of the evening and let each make another bid, with the highest bidder in this new round of bids getting the player. Or, the league may choose to allow the team with the poorer record at the time to get the player that both teams made identical bids on. (NOTE: If three teams bid on a player but only two have identical high bids, only the two high bidders are allowed to re-bid at the end of the evening.)

c. Because it is not known until the end of the evening which teams get which players, the Fantasy Franchise acquiring the player may not use him as part of its team that week. However, that franchise must announce which player from its team is being released, so the rest of the league is notified of who is going back in the player pool.

d. Do not allow the commissioner, if he or she is also a franchise owner, the advantage of knowing what the other teams are bidding. The commissioner must give his or her bid to another league member at the outset of the evening. In the event the commissioner wants to bid on a player also wanted by the franchise owner whom he normally calls with his bid, he would just place his bid with a different owner that week.

OPTION #4: No-Trade Leagues
For leagues in which the commissioner elects not to get involved in handling trades, you may decide to increase the number of rounds for your league draft. Instead of drafting 12 rounds, you could increase your draft to 15 rounds. This would give each team a chance to stock enough players at each position to survive the year, thus eliminating the need for trades.

NOTE: If a no-trade league is your choice, I'd advise you to hold an "Expansion Draft" midway through the season. By that time, a number of franchises in your league are likely to have multiple injuries and may not be able to field players at various positions.

4. TRANSACTION DEADLINE:
A transaction deadline day that will fall during the season should be established before the season starts. One suggestion would be to have the deadline one week after the halfway point of the season. From that day on, the 12 players who make up a franchise roster must finish the season with that team.

There are a number of ways to help a fantasy team that suffers player injuries after the trade deadline and therefore cannot field a full team. Your league has two options. One deals with a player on injured reserve, and the other simply allows every franchise to obtain more players after the trade deadline, to avoid not having each position covered in the event of an injury. (I prefer the second option. Your league may also elect to use both options, which would allow your franchises to expand rosters after the trade deadline and replace a player who is out for a minimum of four weeks.)

OPTION #1: Injured-Reserve and Cut-Player Options:
a. Injured-Reserve Option:
1. The only exception to the transaction deadline would be the case of a player being injured after this date. In many instances, this would leave a team without a player at a particular position.
2. Any FFL team that suffers an injury after the transaction deadline has an option. If the injured player goes on the NFL injured-reserve list (which puts him out for the season), that franchise may replace him with another player from the unclaimed-player pool. The new player must play the same position as the player released. The injured player, once released from his permanent team after the deadline, is out for the year.

He may not be picked up by any other team. Proof that a player is on injured reserve should be obtained from a current, reliable source of sports information, such as *USA Today, The Sporting News, Pro Football Weekly,* or your local newspaper.

3. Another option would be to replace a player who has missed more than four consecutive weeks and whose NFL team elected not to put him on injured reserve. This player would have to miss four consecutive weeks following the trade deadline. However, this may be difficult to prove in some situations, such as those involving receivers, who may appear in a game without actually catching a pass. This is why this rule should be closely examined and voted on prior to the season by the fantasy league.

NOTE: Unless your league specifically votes otherwise, this rule applies only to players who go on injured reserve. Fantasy players lost because of trades, waivers, or cuts do not fall under this rule. Example: If a fantasy player is cut by an NFL team, his fantasy team is still stuck with him unless your league adopts the cut-player option described later in this section.

NOTE: If you have a good player and you elect to replace him using injured-reserve option #3 above, he is lost to you for the season. However, this may be a necessary loss. You really don't have the luxury of an injured reserve in your fantasy league. You can take an injured player out of the *starting* lineup, but even then he takes up bench space that could be occupied by a healthy player. You just have to decide for yourself whether your good-but-injured player is so valuable that you can afford to have him sit, useless, on your bench, while you wait to find out whether he'll be back or not.

NOTE: Commissioners should require that any FFL team using this rule to pick up a player on injured reserve send in a copy of some statement verifying that this player is out. This is proof in case any questions or protests from other teams arise later.

4. A final option should be considered. The NFL's injured-reserve clause now requires a player on injured reserve to remain there for the rest of the season, as opposed to the previous four-week rule. Because of this, NFL teams may refrain from putting injured players on injured reserve, since that would mean losing the players for the entire season. So some players may be sidelined for weeks without ever being placed on injured reserve. Under previous Fantasy Football rules, this could cause a fantasy team some problems, since the owner of such a player could do nothing with him until he was placed on injured reserve, or until he had missed four consecutive weeks. This is a long time to be without a player, so here is a suggestion for how to deal with this rule:

   a. A fantasy team can now replace an injured player who has not been placed on injured reserve, if that player's prognosis indicates he'll be out for four weeks or longer.

b. The fantasy team wishing to take advantage of this option must present verification of the player's prognosis to the commissioner. This is done via an authoritative publication (*USA Today, TSN, Pro Football Weekly,* local newspaper) agreed upon by the league prior to the beginning of the season.

c. The injured player can only be replaced by another player at the same position.

d. The released player cannot be picked up by any other team. He is unavailable for the remainder of the season in your fantasy league.

b. Cut-Player Option:
Because some franchise owners have been frustrated by being stuck with players cut from NFL teams after the trade deadline, I have included the following option, on which your league can vote.

If a fantasy team possesses a player who has been cut, waived, or released after your league's trade deadline, that player may be replaced under the following provisions:

1. The player being released by the fantasy team must be replaced by a player from the same position.

2. The player being released by the fantasy team, like a player released because he is on injured reserve, cannot be picked up by any other team and is released from the player pool.

3. The fantasy team releasing the player must do so the same week as the player is released from his NFL team. Here are some rules for this release:

   a. If your trade night is Thursday night and the NFL player has been released during the seven days including or preceding your trade day, he must be transacted that night. However, the player's release by his NFL team and the date of that release must be proved on trade night. A clipping from a reliable daily publication is sufficient proof.

   b. If the NFL transaction cannot be proved on trade night—if someone has heard that it occurred earlier that day, for example, but cannot yet offer proof—the fantasy team holding that player must conduct its transaction on the next trade night, the following week.

   c. If the transaction by the fantasy team isn't done in the proper week, that fantasy team is stuck with the player.

4. This rule does *not* apply to NFL players *traded* to another NFL team after your trade deadline. However, it does apply to players cut, waived, or released by an NFL team even if they are picked up by another NFL team that same week.

OPTION #2: Roster-Expansion Draft:
Another alternative for your league is to allow roster expansion after the trade deadline. You could do this instead of, or in addition to, Option #1. Because players suffer minor injuries that don't necessitate their going on injured reserve, many fantasy teams find themselves short a player or two in any given week. To help eliminate this problem, the 12-player limit should be expanded to 14 following the trade

deadline, allowing each franchise two more spots on its roster. This will keep all positions filled despite weekly injuries that may occur. The rules for expanding to 14 players after the trade deadline are as follows:

a. Player Eligibility:
   1. Players drafted for the roster-expansion draft may come only from the unclaimed-player pool.
   2. Any player dropped by a franchise after the trade deadline does not go into the unclaimed-player pool for another team to pick up and may not be used in the playoff player-addition draft. (This may only happen if your league uses both the roster-expansion draft and the Injured-Reserve/Cut-Player Options.)

b. Transaction Procedures:
   1. *Leagues that meet, in person, to make roster-expansion selections:* In leagues where all the franchise owners are able to get together for the roster expansion, the selecting should start with the team with the worst record and work its way through to the team with the best record. The team with the worst record selects one player, and the rest of the teams continue until each franchise has selected its 13th player. Then, starting over again, the team with the worst record selects its 14th player and so on until each franchise has 14 members. The 14-player roster is now permanent. (If two teams have identical records, then the team that has scored the fewest points is designated the "worst" and should select first. If two teams have identical records and identical points, then a coin toss should determine their draft order.)

   NOTE: If a team does not have a representative at the roster expansion draft, it must select its two additional players after all of the other teams are done.

   2. *Leagues that use the phone for expansion selections:* I suggest using a method similar to that used during the year by your league. The drafting should be done in two one-hour periods. The first hour should be to select player #13 on the roster (designated as the first round of the Player Addition Draft), and the second hour should be for player #14 (second round).

NOTE:
   1. If a fantasy team chooses, when called, not to pick up a player but calls back within the first hour of the roster-expansion draft, it may pick up a first-round player but must go to the bottom of the list.
   2. If a fantasy team is not reached by the commissioner and fails to call in at all to take a player during the first round of the roster-expansion draft, that team forfeits its right for the remainder of the year to one of the two players it could have chosen during the roster-expansion draft. That team may, however, select one player during any of the remaining regular-season weeks to add to its roster.
   3. A fantasy team electing to draft one player during the first round of the expansion draft and electing not to pick a second

player during the draft's second round is also eligible to pick up a second selection during any of the remaining regular-season weeks. A fantasy team that does not participate in the first hour of the expansion draft forfeits its right to expand its roster by two players. Such a team may expand by only one and would end up with a maximum of 13 players rather than 14.

4. The order of selecting roster-expansion players following the roster-expansion draft date will follow the transaction procedures used by your league during the season.

OPTION #3: Playoff Player-Addition Draft:
To further ensure Fantasy Franchises against finding themselves short a player at playoff time, I suggest incorporating a playoff player-addition draft. This would expand each playoff team's roster by one player, giving it a possible total of 15.

a. The player can be from any position.

b. The player must be selected from the unclaimed-player pool as it stood prior to the player-transaction deadline. No player dropped by one Fantasy Franchise after the player-transaction deadline may be selected in this draft.

c. The playoff player-addition draft will take place on the trade night prior to the fantasy playoffs.

d. A team not participating in the player-addition draft on that evening forfeits, for the remainder of the playoffs, its right to add a player to its roster.

e. Selections in the playoff player-addition draft will follow the transaction procedures used by your league during the season.

NOTE: Transactions made in the roster-expansion draft and the playoff player-addition draft should carry the normal transaction fees to be paid to the commissioner.

OPTION #4: Injured-Reserve or Cut-Player Option Combined With the Roster-Expansion Draft and the Playoff Player-Addition Draft:
The roster-expansion draft and the playoff player-addition draft were incorporated to try to protect fantasy teams from having to field an incomplete team following the trade deadline. Though these two draft expansions help, they are not fail-safe methods. Injuries to NFL players have become so common in recent years that allowing the injured-reserve and the cut-player options in addition to these drafts may be desirable in many leagues. If a league uses this option, the following rules should be applied.

a. A fantasy team using the injured-reserve or cut-player option to pick up a player must do it in the same transaction order as previously described. So a fantasy team that has an injured-reserve option because one of its players has gone on injured reserve will elect to use either this or the player-addition option when its turn comes that week. If that fantasy team uses its injured-reserve option the first time through transactions on a given night, and wants to make a second move using a player-addition option, the owner must advise the commissioner following the first transaction. That team will then be called back the second time through for the second move.

b. A fantasy team owner who wants to take advantage of the injured-reserve rule must contact the commissioner prior to the transaction night so that the commissioner can insert him in the transaction order.

c. A fantasy team using the injured-reserve option must do so within the transaction week the player is placed on injured reserve. This is enforced so that a fantasy team cannot ride a player's injury until a move will be most advantageous. (If one of your players is placed on injured reserve on Friday, for instance, and your league's transaction night is Thursday, you would have to make your move the following Thursday. If you do not make the move within that transaction week, the player is stuck on your team.)

d. A player picked up using the injured-reserve rule must play the same position as the player released.

OPTION #5: Drafting Team Quarterbacks and/or Team Kickers: Many leagues have opted to draft a team quarterback or kicker, rather than to draft specific quarterbacks or kickers. This is largely due to the high injury rate among quarterbacks and the high turnover at the kicking position. Drafting the Chicago Bears' quarterbacks rather than specifically naming Erik Kramer or Rick Mirer will prevent many transactions and questions. (My league has never used this option and has made the drafting of backup quarterbacks quite a strategy. So it makes it interesting either way.)

VII
LINEUPS

Because the 17-week NFL season may affect some of the handling procedures for transactions, please refer to the suggestions at the beginning of this chapter to see how to handle this change.

The commissioner should set up a night and a period of time (for example, 6:00 to 8:00 p.m.) when he or she is free and can take everyone's lineup. To make it easier on the commissioner, lineup submissions can be scheduled for the same night as trades are taken. The commissioner would then be involved only one night. The following can be used as a commissoner's guide for taking lineups:

1. COMMISSIONER FAVORITISM:

Commissioners, make sure to have your franchise owners prepared when they call you. Each one should be able to call you, read off the lineup, and get off the phone. Don't let them call you and ask your opinion on whom they should start or which NFL teams play which. I've run into this on plenty of occasions and it's really frustrating, especially if it's a good friend doing it to me. Besides taking up a lot of my time, it puts me in an awkward position. I don't feel it is ethical for a league commissioner to show any favoritism and guide a team's choice of whom to start. The easiest way to remedy this kind of problem is to make sure, at the draft, that each team understands: No lineup will be logged in the books unless the team calling it in is ready to give the full lineup without guidance from the commissioner.

2. LINEUP NIGHT:

The day selected for taking lineups should be later in the week, allowing every team in the league a chance to check on its players, via the newspaper or television, for injuries or other late-breaking news that would change its strategy for the game.

NOTE: On the *first* lineup night, there could be a problem if a team forgets to call in its lineup. Since there is no previous week's lineup to carry over, I would suggest handling it this way: Simply insert the team's starting lineup according to the draft order in which the players were taken. In other words, the first players drafted from each starting position are inserted as that team's starters. The first two running backs drafted are the team's starting running backs, the first two wide receivers drafted are the starting wideouts, and so on. Once the starters have been determined, the reserves are listed, also in the order they were drafted, regardless of position. The first player drafted who did not fit into a starting position is the first reserve, the second non-starter drafted is the second reserve, and so on.

3. FANTASY WEEKS THAT START EARLY:

If you elect to take lineups on Thursday nights, for instance, and there is a National Football League game scheduled for that day, your lineup and trade night should automatically be changed to Wednesday. This prevents anybody's calling in his lineup after the Thursday game has started. It's important that all lineups be given prior to the first game played that week.

Even your FFL teams that don't have any players participating in these games still must have their lineups in on the same night as the teams that do have players involved. This gives every team the same amount of time to check the media for injury or other pertinent news. Once the kickoff from the first NFL game of the week occurs, all FFL games for that week have officially begun.

4a. RIDING THE SAME LINEUP:

If a team fails to call the commissioner and submit a lineup, its previous week's lineup will automatically be used. This means that in leagues using carryover-player scores for bye weeks, teams will also be locking in their bye-week players for both weeks if they fail to call in to the commissioner.

4b. RIDING THE SAME LINEUP DURING CARRYOVER WEEKS:

Because of the bye-week player lock-ins from the previous week, your league may run into another problem. The problem comes up when a fantasy team puts in a weekly lineup and changes the position of a carryover player from starter one week to reserve the next. In other words, the team elects to start a carryover player in the current week's game but decides not to use him as a starter the next week. If, the following week, the fantasy team fails to call in its lineup, it is forced to ride the previous week's lineup. But that becomes a problem for the carryover player who was scheduled to move from a starting position the previous week to a reserve position in the carryover week. In this event, the commissioner will automatically use the first player of the same position from the fantasy team's reserve list and insert that player as a starter to fill the carryover player's vacancy.

All the reserves move up a notch until all reserve positions are filled in. There is also a reverse of this. A fantasy team may have a carryover player it elects to use as a reserve the current week and as a starter for the following week's carryover game. If the fantasy team fails to call in its weekly lineup the following week, this again presents a problem. Let's say this player is a running back, for instance. Now you have one starting running back (the carryover player) and two other running backs riding from the previous week's lineup. Which ones are inserted? I recommend, for the sake of consistency, that the first running back listed from the previous week be the other starter alongside the carryover player. The second running back listed should go on the reserves in the spot that the carryover player occupied. Commissioners, take a close look at this, and recommend to your franchises that they carefully choose the order of the players in the lineups they give you. Or suggest that they call in every week to assure themselves they have their lineups just as they desire them. (This situation will come up!)

5. OPTIONS:

A. One Lineup Change: Here is an option I use in our league. After its original starting lineup is called in, each FFL team is allowed one lineup change. This must be done prior to the first National Football League game that week. If your original lineup is called in on Thursday and the first National Football League game for that week is played on Sunday, your commissioner can set up a period of time (between 11:00 a.m. and 12 noon on Sunday, for example) when each team has a chance to call in its one lineup change. This allows every team a chance to check Sunday morning's paper for any late-breaking news. By Sunday morning, a player's playing status should be pretty well determined. The opponent should then be notified of the lineup change prior to the game. The following restrictions apply to any such lineup changes:

1. The lineup change is legitimate if the commissioner is contacted in person prior to the start of the first NFL game.
2. If, for some reason, an owner cannot reach the commissioner to confirm a lineup change, that owner should contact two other franchise owners, notifying them of the intended change.
3. Leaving a lineup change on an answering machine is unacceptable, because the time of the call usually cannot be confirmed. (Recording a message can be acceptable if the answering system automatically records the time of the call, as many now do. This should be voted on by the league prior to the season.)
4. Contacting just your opponent to confirm a lineup change is not acceptable, unless your opponent is also the commissioner. If you cannot reach the commissioner, your opponent can—and should—be one of the two teams you contact (see rule #2 above), but a second team must be notified as well.
5. Both the commissioner and the opposing team should be notified as soon as possible after the decision has been made.

In the event that you replace one of your starters by using this one lineup change, the replaced player then automatically takes the spot of the reserve in your lineup.

NOTE: Because of the new carryover setup, lineup changes involving the following week's carryover players will be handled differently. For rules on trading or releasing a carryover player, consult the section titled "Trade Night," under Playing Option #2 (part of Options to Tackle the 17-Week Season). Also refer to the page preceding this one for rules relating to carryover player lock-ins, when an owner does not call in a lineup.

B. Sudden-Death Tiebreaker: Commissioners, don't forget to write in every team's reserve players for use in the sudden-death tiebreaker. (See Section IX, "Variations on Fantasy Football: Sudden-Death Tiebreaker," for details.)

VIII
SELECTING A SCORING METHOD

After finding the right person to head your league as commissioner, your next step is to establish which method of scoring your league will use. In the following pages, I describe the four methods of scoring that are most commonly used. I have also included a few variations used by different leagues. You may want to expand on the rules a little yourself. After reading through the following rules for the different methods, select the one you feel will give your league the most enjoyment. Before we consider the four methods individually, let's look at the general rules that apply to all of them.

NOTE: Before your regular season begins, you should establish which particular sports-reporting source you are going to use for your game results. This should be done because of possible discrepancies in scoring or possible missing stats. Among your options, of course, are your local newspaper, *USA Today, The Sporting News* (which will be received a week later), and *Pro Football Weekly*. Select one for your league's official results, but in case of a discrepancy, have two backups for help in deciding the correct scoring.

NUMBER OF PLAYERS:
A. At the fantasy draft, each franchise will draft 12 players.
B. Of the 12 NFL players selected on draft day, seven will be used in your starting lineup and the other five will be reserves.
C. Of the starting seven players, the following positions will make up the starting lineup:

*STANDARD OPTION (used by most leagues):
1 Quarterback   2 Wide Receivers   1 Kicker
2 Running Backs   1 Tight End

*FLEX OPTION: Because of the many varieties of formations being used today, like the two-tight-end offense or the H-back (see below), many leagues use the Flex Option in an attempt to simplify the decision of whether a player is qualified as a wide receiver, tight end, or H-back. We suggest that leagues go to three receivers, with no limitations on how many are wide receivers, tight ends, or H-backs.

Here is the FLEX OPTION:
1 Quarterback   3 Receivers   1 Kicker
2 Running Backs

(The position of H-back, a recent phenomenon in the NFL, is used to designate what most would consider a blocking tight end. Usually this player lines up in the backfield and goes in motion either to block or run a pass pattern. If you do not use this Flex Option, H-backs would most likely fall into the tight-end category.)

D. On some occasions, you may find players who are able to play a few positions or who change positions during the course of the year. You may need to set up some sort of rule to clarify at what position that player must be used. An example is Jim Jensen, who played for the

Miami Dolphins in the 1980s. Jensen could have been listed at a variety of positions, including quarterback, wide receiver, and tight end. A number of years ago, the San Diego Chargers converted Rod Bernstine from tight end to running back in the preseason. At our draft, our league elected to vote him in as a running back for the season. Many other leagues left him as a tight end because of preseason publications showing him at that position. It should be determined prior to the season at which position your league will accept these players.

The rule we have established for clarification of position is as follows:

1. Choose one respected sports magazine to use as your league's book. The position listed in this book is the position the player must be drafted for.

2. Your league may choose, in certain instances, to take a vote right at the league's draft to designate a player's position. Such was the case for the Chargers' Rod Bernstine in 1990. We voted Bernstine to be designated a running back based on how our league felt he would most often be used during the season. And last year, Eric Metcalf, used as a running back part of his career and as a wide receiver at other times, was voted to be a wide receiver after being dealt to San Diego.

3. If during the course of the year the player switches positions, a team may change his position with the following provisions:

   a. The fantasy owner must provide evidence to the commissioner that his player has been playing that position for at least two consecutive weeks. The fantasy owner cannot sit on the move. In other words, he or she must make the move when the player is currently playing that new position for his NFL team (with proof that he has been at that position for at least the previous two weeks). The owner may not wait until a player has switched back to his original position, and then choose which of the two positions he or she would prefer that player to play. For example, if Eric Metcalf, who now plays for Arizona, starts the year as a wide receiver in your fantasy league, he will remain a wide receiver unless the Cardinals switch him to running back for at least two weeks. At that point, the fantasy franchise that owns Metcalf can decide to switch him to running back. But if Metcalf is switched back to wide receiver by the Cardinals before the fantasy owner elects to move him to running back, then that owner must play him as a wide receiver. He or she no longer has the option of using Metcalf as a running back, unless the Cardinals switch him again later in the season and the process is repeated.

   b. If that fantasy team owner is the commissioner, two other team owners of the league must approve the switch.

   c. One publication you could use for this rule is *Pro Football Weekly,* which lists the players by position each week.

4. If a team has a protest against an opponent with a player in this situation, the protest must be lodged prior to the start of their game. Once the game has started, no protest may be made. All commissioner decisions should be fair and are final.

THE BASIC SCORING METHOD

The Basic Scoring Method is the most commonly used scoring method. It is the tabulation of actual scoring done in NFL games by various NFL players. Let's take a look at how this is done.

1. SCORING TABULATION BY POSITION:
   The following are the seven starting positions, broken down by the number of points tallied for each score.

   A. Quarterbacks
      1. Three points are awarded for each touchdown pass thrown.
      2. Six points are awarded for each touchdown scored rushing.
      3. Six points are awarded for each touchdown scored receiving a pass (in the event that a quarterback becomes a pass receiver in a play).

   B. Running Backs, Wide Receivers, Tight Ends
      1. Six points are awarded for each touchdown scored, either by running or catching a pass.
      2. Three points are awarded for each touchdown pass thrown (such as in a halfback option).

   C. Kickers
      1. Three points are awarded for each field goal.
      2. One point is awarded for each extra point.

   D. All Fantasy-Positioned Players (Two-point conversions)
      1. If a player (quarterback, running back, wide receiver, tight end) runs in the two-point conversion, he is awarded the two points.
      2. If the two-point conversion involves a pass, the player who catches the pass is awarded two points, and the player who throws the pass is awarded one point. (This is similar to a touchdown pass, where the receiver is awarded six points and the quarterback is awarded three points.)

2. ADDITIONAL SCORING POSSIBILITIES:
   A. If a running back or wide receiver doubles as a punt or kickoff returner and scores a touchdown on a runback, the six points awarded for a touchdown apply.
   B. If any player recovers a fumble in the end zone for a touchdown, the six points for a touchdown are awarded.

3. SAMPLE SCORING FOR A FANTASY FOOTBALL GAME:
   To better explain the scoring process of the Basic Scoring Method, let's look at two fictitious fantasy teams. You will be team #1 and I will be team #2.

   First, let's put together a scorecard listing our starting lineups. (See Detail A.)

Detail A

	TEAM # 1			TEAM # 2
QB	Favre (GB)		QB	Aikman (DALL)
RB	J. Anderson (ATL)		RB	J. Moore (St L)
RB	A. Smith (BUF)		RB	Johnston (DALL)
WR	Fryar (PHIL)		WR	Conway (CHI)
WR	R. Brooks (GB)		WR	Irvin (DALL)
TE	Conwell (St L)		TE	Jennings (CHI)
K	Andersen (ATL)		K	Cunningham (DALL)

As commissioner of a league, I have found the easiest way to tally scores is to use the following key:

A. Quarterbacks, Running Backs, Wide Receivers, and Tight Ends

    1. For each rushing or pass-receiving touchdown, a T is marked to the right of the player's team initials on the scorecard. (Remember, six points are tallied for each.)

    2. For each touchdown pass thrown, a P is marked in the same area. (Remember, three points are tallied for each.)

B. Kickers

    1. For each field goal, an F is marked, again next to a player's team initials. (Remember, three points are tallied for each.)

    2. For each extra point, an X is marked in the same area. (Remember, one point is awarded for each.)

Taking some sample box scores, let's fill in our scorecard.

Looking first at your team (team #1), we will start with your quarterback, Brett Favre of the Green Bay Packers. Using the following box score from the Packers-Bears game (see Detail B), we find that Favre threw two touchdown passes, one to Brooks and one to Chmura. The box score shows him rushing for one touchdown. In our scorecard we would put one T for the rushing touchdown and two Ps for the two touchdown passes.

Detail B

BEARS 23, PACKERS 21

Green Bay	7	7	0	7	—	21
Chicago	7	0	7	9	—	23

Chi-Conway 35 pass from
Kramer (Jaeger kick)
 GB-Favre 1 run (Longwell kick)
 GB-Brooks 31 pass from Favre
(Longwell kick)
 Chi-Engram 22 pass from
Kramer (Jaeger kick)
 Chi-Kramer 6 run (kick failed)
 GB-Chmura 5 pass from Favre
(Longwell kick)
 Chi-FG Jaeger 22
 A-35,908

His score would then add up to 12 points—6 points for the one rushing touchdown and 6 points for the two touchdown passes thrown (3 points each). Now our scorecard would look like this. (See Detail C.)

Detail C

	TEAM # 1			TEAM # 2	
QB	Favre (GB) TPP	12	QB	Aikman (DALL)	
RB	J. Anderson (ATL)		RB	J. Moore (St L)	
RB	A. Smith (BUF)		RB	Johnston (DALL)	
WR	Fryar (PHIL)		WR	Conway (CHI)	
WR	R. Brooks (GB)		WR	Irvin (DALL)	
TE	Conwell (St L)		TE	Jennings (CHI)	
K	Andersen (ATL)		K	Cunningham (DALL)	

Using the following box scores, (Detail D), let's fill in the rest of our scorecard to determine a winner.

Detail D

CARDINALS 31, EAGLES 7

| Philadelphia | 0 0 0 7 — 7 |
| Arizona | 7 7 10 7 — 31 |

Ariz-Centers 12 run (Nedney kick)
Ariz-Rb Moore 10 pass from
Plummer (Nedney kick)
Ariz-FG Nedney
Ariz-McElroy 1 run (Nedney kick)
Ariz-P. Carter 29 pass from
Plummer (Nedney kick)
Phil-C.T. Jones 20 pass from
Detmer (Boniol kick)

RAMS 24, COWBOYS 17

| St. Louis | 7 0 7 10 — 24 |
| Dallas | 0 7 3 7 — 17 |

St L-Conwell 13 pass from
Banks (Wilkins kick), 3:26
Dal-Miller 14 pass from Aikman
(Cunningham kick), 14:43
Dal-FG Cunningham 41, 3:00
St L-Bruce 16 pass from Banks
(Wilkins kick), 7:37
St L-Kennison 8 pass from Banks
(Wilkins kick), 1:06
St L-FG Wilkins 20, 8:00
Dal-Bjornson 2 pass from Aikman
(Cunningham kick), 12:57

FALCONS 31, BILLS 14

| Buffalo | 0 7 0 7 — 14 |
| Atlanta | 3 14 7 7 — 31 |

Atl-FG Andersen 40
Atl-Mathis 7 pass from Chandler
(Andersen kick)
Atl-J. Anderson 10 run (Andersen kick)
Buf-Reed 13 pass from T. Collins
(Christie kick)
Atl-J. Anderson 1 run (Andersen kick)
Atl-J. Anderson 6 pass from
Chandler (Andersen kick)
Buf-Early 28 pass from T. Collins
(Christie kick)

BEARS 23, PACKERS 21

| Green Bay | 7 7 0 7 — 21 |
| Chicago | 7 0 7 9 — 23 |

Chi-Conway 35 pass from
Kramer (Jaeger kick)
GB-Favre 1 run (Longwell kick)
GB-R. Brooks 31 pass from Favre
(Longwell kick)
Chi-Engram 22 pass from
Kramer (Jaeger kick)
Chi-Kramer 6 run (kick failed)
GB-Chmura 5 pass from Favre
(Longwell kick)
Chi-FG Jaeger 22

Continuing with team #1, next we evaluate Jamal Anderson of the Atlanta Falcons. Looking at the Atlanta–Buffalo game, we find that Anderson ran for two touchdowns and caught a touchdown pass. In his slot on the scorecard, we would mark three Ts and give him 18 points.

Next is the other running back, Antowain Smith of the Buffalo Bills. Again, we look at the Atlanta–Buffalo box score, and this time we find that Smith failed to score. So this one is easy; just a put a big zero in his results column.

Move on now to your first wide receiver, Irving Fryar of the Philadelphia Eagles. Looking at the Philadelphia–Phoenix game, we find that Fryar also failed to score, so again we mark a zero in the results column.

Your other wide receiver is Robert Brooks of the Green Bay Packers. This time your luck prevails, as we see Brooks scored on a touchdown pass from your quarterback, Brett Favre. Mark a T and give him six points.

Now check out Ernie Conwell, the tight end of the St. Louis Rams. Conwell scored on a touchdown pass from Tony Banks, so give him a T and six points.

Last would be Morton Andersen, kicker for the Atlanta Falcons. Andersen was successful on one field-goal attempt and four extra-point tries. Give him one F and four Xs, resulting in seven points.

Now let's take a look at my team, team #2, starting with my quarterback, Troy Aikman of the Dallas Cowboys. Looking at the Rams–Cowboys game, we can see that Aikman threw one touchdown to Anthony Miller and one to Eric Bjornson. Give him two Ps and six points.

Next is Jerald Moore of the St. Louis Rams. Looking again at the Rams–Cowboys game, we find Moore did not score. Mark a zero in his slot.

In the Dallas–Los Angeles box score, we find that my other running back, Daryl Johnston, also failed to score, so mark zero in his slot.

Curtis Conway of the Chicago Bears scored once on a touchdown reception against Green Bay. Give him a T and six points.

Michael Irvin of the Dallas Cowboys failed to score in their game with the Rams. Give Irvin a big zero in his slot.

Tight end, Keith Jennings of the Chicago Bears was another one of my players who failed to score. Mark a zero in his space in the scorecard.

Lastly, my kicker, Ritchie Cunningham of the Cowboys, booted one field goal and had two extra points. Give him one F for the field goal and two Xs for the two extra points, totaling five points.

Now our final scorecard should look something like this. (See Detail E.)

Detail E

	TEAM # 1				TEAM # 2	
QB	Favre (GB) TPP	12		QB	Aikman (DALL) PP	6
RB	J. Anderson (ATL) TTT	18		RB	J. Moore (St L)	0
RB	A. Smith (BUF)	0		RB	Johnston (DALL)	0
WR	Fryar (PHIL)	0		WR	Conway (CHI) T	6
WR	R. Brooks (GB) T	6		WR	Irvin (DALL)	0
TE	Conwell (St L) T	6		TE	Jennings (CHI)	0
K	Andersen (ATL) FXXXX	7		K	Cunningham (DALL) FXX	5
		49				17

Congratulations on your first Fantasy Football victory!

What follows are samples of how one league's weekly score sheets may look after the conclusion of its fantasy games.

Basic Scoring Method Samples

FFL Box Scores

	Tm# 3 The Overachievers		VS.		Tm# 1 The Crashdummies	
		Pts				**Pts**
	(Ariz.)	PP			(Seat.)	PP
QB	Plummer	6		QB	Friesz	6
	(G.B.)	T			(Buf.)	T
RB	Bennett	6		RB	Thomas	6
	(Ind.)				(N.Y.J.)	
RB	Faulk	0		RB	Murrell	0
	(Dall.)				(S.F.)	TT
WR	Miller	0		WR	Rice	12
	(Buf.)				(Seat.)	T
WR	Early	0		WR	Blades	6
	(Mia.)				(Tenn.)	
TE	Drayton	0		TE	Wycheck	0
	(N.E.)	FXX			(S.F.)	FFXX
K	Vinatieri	5		K	Anderson	8
	Reserves				**Reserves**	
	(Balt.)				(G.B.)	
1	Mi. Jackson			1	Levens	
	(Den.)				(N.O.)	
2	McCaffrey			2	Hastings	
	(Ariz.)				(N.E.)	
3	Rb. Moore			3	Glenn	
	(K.C.)				(Car.)	
4	Gonzalez			4	Carruth	
	(Ariz.)				(Jac.)	
5	F. Sanders			5	McCardell	
		17				**38**

	Tm# 2 Lodi's Big Daddys		VS.		Tm# 4 East Side Gladiators	
		Pts				**Pts**
	(Balt.)	P			(K.C.)	
QB	Testaverde	3		QB	Grbac	0
	(Phil.)	TT			(Mia.)	
RB	Watters	12		RB	Abdul-Jabbar	0
	(Den.)	T			(Jac.)	T
RB	Davis	6		RB	Means	6
	(Oak.)	T			(S.D.)	
WR	T. Brown	6		WR	Martin	0
	(N.Y.G.)				(Minn.)	
WR	Toomer	0		WR	C. Carter	0
	(T.B.)				(Seat.)	
TE	Harris	0		TE	Fauria	0
	(Det.)	XX			(Atl.)	FXX
K	Hanson	2		K	Andersen	5
	Reserves				**Reserves**	
	(Det.)				(T.B.)	
1	Sanders			1	Alstott	
	(N.Y.J.)				(Det.)	
2	K. Johnson			2	Perriman	
	(Balt.)				(Seat.)	
3	Morris			3	Galloway	
	(Car.)				(Dall.)	
4	Biakabatuka			4	Bjornson	
	(K.C.)				(S.D.)	
5	Rison			5	Humphries	
		29				**11**

	Tm# 7 Mediterranean Meatballs		VS.		Tm# 5 Treanor's Electric Co	
		Pts				**Pts**
	(Oak.)	P			(N.O.)	P
QB	George	3		QB	Shuler	3
	(Wash.)				(Atl.)	TT
RB	T. Allen	0		RB	J. Anderson	12
	(Minn.)				(S.F.)	
RB	R. Smith	0		RB	Hearst	0
	(G.B.)				(Phil.)	
WR	R. Brooks	0		WR	Fryar	0
	(Tenn.)				(Jac.)	T
WR	C. Sanders	0		WR	Smith	6
	(Minn.)	T			(N.Y.G.)	T
TE	Jordan	6		TE	Cross	6
	(Balt.)	XXXX			(S.D.)	XX
K	Stover	4		K	Carney	2
	Reserves				**Reserves**	
	(Car.)				(Phil.)	
1	K. Collins			1	Peete	
	(Det.)				(T.B.)	
2	Morton			2	Anthony	
	(Buf.)				(N.O.)	
3	Reed			3	Davis	
	(Jac.)				(S.F.)	
4	Stewart			4	Floyd	
	(Dall.)				(Atl.)	
5	Johnston			5	Mathis	
		13				**29**

	Tm# 6 F-Troop		VS.		Tm# 8 J.M.D. Warriors	
		Pts				**Pts**
	(S.F.)	PP			(N.Y.G.)	PP
QB	Young	6		QB	Kanell	6
	(T.B.)				(N.Y.G.)	
RB	Dunn	0		RB	Hampton	0
	(Dall.)				(Oak.)	
RB	E. Smith	0		RB	Kaufman	0
	(Ind.)				(N.Y.J.)	
WR	Harrison	0		WR	Graham	0
	(Oak.)	T			(Chi.)	T
WR	Jett	6		WR	Engram	6
	(Balt.)				(G.B.)	T
TE	Kinchen	0		TE	Chmura	6
	(Minn.)	FXX			(St.L.)	FFXXXXX
K	Murray	5		K	Wilkins	11
	Reserves				**Reserves**	
	(Den.)				(G.B.)	
1	Elway			1	Freeman	
	(Car.)				(S.F.)	
2	Carrier			2	Stokes	
	(N.Y.J.)				(N.E.)	
3	O'Donnell			3	Meggett	
	(Ariz.)				(Phil.)	
4	Centers			4	Dunn	
	(N.Y.J.)				(Pitt.)	
5	Chrebet			5	J.L. Williams	
		17				**29**

FFL STANDINGS

(Black Conference)

Spade Division	Team #	Won	Lost	Tie	Points	Points Agst
The Crashdummies	1	7	4	0	314	234
Lodi's Big Daddys	2	6	5	0	241	227
The Overachievers	3	5	6	0	237	283
East Side Gladiators	4	2	9	0	205	317

Club Division	Team #	Won	Lost	Tie	Points	Points Agst
Mediterranean Meatballs	7	8	3	0	283	244
Treanor's Elec. Co.	5	7	4	0	274	247
Armchair Sleepers	6	5	6	0	231	245
J.M.D.Warriors	8	3	8	0	248	287

(Red Conference)

Diamond Division	Team #	Won	Lost	Tie	Points	Points Agst
Costra Nostra	10	8	3	0	220	187
D.C. Express	11	7	4	0	285	236
F-Troop	12	5	6	0	186	224
Boyer's Spoilers	9	4	7	0	197	294

Heart Division	Team #	Won	Lost	Tie	Points	Points Agst
French Connection	13	10	1	0	329	164
The Medics	16	4	7	0	237	242
The Bogarts	14	4	7	0	204	250
The Jayhawks	15	3	8	0	286	296

THIS WEEK'S SCORES

Team # 3 (17)	Team # 2 (29)
Team # 1 (38)	Team # 4 (11)
Team # 5 (29)	Team # 8 (23)
Team # 7 (13)	Team # 6 (17)
Team # 11 (30)	Team # 10 (18)
Team # 9 (9)	Team # 12 (5)
Team # 13 (28)	Team # 14 (16)
Team # 15 (14)	Team # 16 (8)

THIS WEEK'S TRANSACTIONS

Tm#		Dropped/Tm-Pos	Acquired/Tm-Pos
1	5	Dunn TB RB	Bettis Pitt RB
2	7	Reed Minn WR	Reed Buf WR
3	16	Morton Det WR	McCaffrey Den WR
4	12	Drayton Mia TE	Sharpe Den TE
5	13	Fryar Phil WR	R. Brooks GB WR
6	___	_____	_____
7	___	_____	_____
8	___	_____	_____
9	___	_____	_____
10	___	_____	_____

THE PERFORMANCE POINT METHOD

The Performance Point Method is a tabulation of scoring based on a player's yardage performance, not his touchdowns. It differs from the Basic Scoring Method in that less luck is involved. In the Basic Scoring Method, a player may rush for 120 yards in a game, but never score a touchdown, leaving his fantasy franchise unrewarded for his performance. The Performance Point Method, however, looks only at a player's yardage performance and, although the final scores are not typical football scores as in the Basic Method, it is an interesting way to play the game. Let's take a look at this method of scoring.

1. SCORING TABULATION BY POSITION:
   The following is the scoring breakdown by each position:

   A. Quarterbacks, Running Backs, Wide Receivers, Tight Ends
      1. These players are awarded one point for every 20 yards passing.
      2. They are awarded one point for every 10 yards rushing.
      3. They are awarded one point for every 10 yards pass receiving.
      4. No players will have points deducted for having negative yardage in a game. That is, if a player has two rushes that account for minus 12 yards, he is not penalized one point.
      5. You must tabulate the passing, rushing, and pass-receiving scores separately. For instance, if a quarterback passes for 300 yards and rushes for 29 yards, you cannot add the yardage together. You would just award him 15 points for his passing yardage and then 2 more points for his rushing yardage, giving him 17 total points. This also applies to the rushing and pass-receiving yardage of a running back or wide receiver. If, for example, a running back rushes for 97 yards and catches passes for 24 yards, you can't add the yardages together. Again, you just take his 97 rushing yards and award him nine points and then take his 24 pass-receiving yards and award him two more points. This would give him a total of 11 points.

Passing Yardage	Rushing Yardage	Pass-Receiving Yardage
0 — 19 yds: 0 pts	0 — 9 yds: 0 pts	0 — 9 yds: 0 pts
20 — 39 yds: 1 pt	10 — 19 yds: 1 pt	10 — 19 yds: 1 pt
40 — 59 yds: 2 pts	20 — 29 yds: 2 pts	20 — 29 yds: 2 pts
60 — 79 yds: 3 pts	30 — 39 yds: 3 pts	30 — 39 yds: 3 pts
80 — 99 yds: 4 pts	40 — 49 yds: 4 pts	40 — 49 yds: 4 pts
100 — 119 yds: 5 pts	50 — 59 yds: 5 pts	50 — 59 yds: 5 pts
120 — 139 yds: 6 pts	60 — 69 yds: 6 pts	60 — 69 yds: 6 pts
140 — 159 yds: 7 pts	70 — 79 yds: 7 pts	70 — 79 yds: 7 pts
160 — 179 yds: 8 pts	80 — 89 yds: 8 pts	80 — 89 yds: 8 pts
180 — 199 yds: 9 pts	90 — 99 yds: 9 pts	90 — 99 yds: 9 pts
200 — 219 yds: 10 pts	100 — 109 yds: 10 pts	100 — 109 yds: 10 pts
And so on	And so on	And so on

B. Kickers
   Points awarded are the same as in the Basic Scoring Method, except when a kicker for some reason would carry the ball and pick up yardage.
   1. Three points are awarded for each field goal.
   2. One point is awarded for each extra point.
   3. If a kicker rushes for yardage on a blocked kick, for example, he is awarded rushing points for the amount of yardage gained. Or if he completes a pass, he again is awarded the passing points for the yardage gained.

2. SAMPLE SCORING FOR A FANTASY FOOTBALL GAME:
   The following key will help you in logging each player's scoring results:
   A. Quarterbacks, Running Backs, Wide Receivers, Tight Ends
      1. For passing yardage, mark a P followed by a comma and then the number of points associated with that player's passing results. Then put parentheses around that group. For example, (P,14) would show that a player threw for between 280 and 299 yards. He receives 1 point for every 20 yards, giving him 14 passing points.
      2. For rushing yardage, mark an R, again followed by a comma and then the number of points associated with that player's rushing results. Then put parentheses around that group. For example, (R,9) would show that the player rushed for between 90 and 99 yards. He receives one point for every 10 yards, giving him nine rushing points.
      3. For pass-receiving yardage, mark a P with a small r, followed by a comma and the number of points associated with that player's pass-receiving results. Then put parentheses around that group. The notation (Pr,6) would show that the player caught passes resulting in between 60 and 69 yards. He receives one point for every 10 yards, giving him six pass-receiving points.
      4. Also, quarterbacks, running backs, wide receivers, and tight ends may be involved in a two-point conversion. If a player, regardless of his position, successfully passes for a two-point conversion, he is awarded one point. If a player, again regardless of his position, rushes or receives for a two-point conversion, he is awarded two points.
   B. Kickers
      1. For each field goal, mark an F (three points for each).
      2. For each extra point, mark an X (one point for each).
      3. If a kicker is involved in any play where he may have passed for more than 20 yards or rushed or caught a pass amounting to more than 20 yards, the appropriate number of points previously explained applies.

   To explain better and demonstrate the scoring process of the Performance Point Method, we will again set up two fictitious fantasy teams. Use the following lineups in Detail F and the box scores shown in Detail G to figure out the score between team #5 and team #6.

Detail F

TEAM # 5		TEAM # 6	
QB	George (OAK)	QB	Friesz (SEAT)
RB	Sanders (DET)	RB	Brown (SD)
RB	Bettis (PITT)	RB	Kaufman (OAK)
WR	T. Brown (OAK)	WR	Glenn (NE)
WR	Galloway (SEAT)	WR	H. Moore (DET)
TE	Coates (NE)	TE	Green (BALT)
K	Ford (OAK)	K	Hanson (DET)

Detail G

LIONS 23, BUCS 20

Tampa Bay   7 6 0 7 — 20
Detroit   8 10 3 10 — 23
    TB-Harris 4 pass from
Dilfer (Hustad kick)
    Det-Sanders 3 run (Hanson kick)
    Det-FG Hanson 34
    TB-Anthony 29 pass from
Dilfer (kick failed)
    Det-FG Hanson 36
    Det-FG Hanson 38
    Det-H. Moore 6 pass from
Mitchell (Hanson kick)
    TB-K. Williams 29 pass from
Dilfer (Hustad kick)
    A-54,133
    INDIVIDUAL STATISTICS
    RUSHING—Tampa Bay,
Dunn 23-44, Alstott 11-63.
Detroit, Sanders 15-56,
Mitchell 2-20.
    PASSING—Tampa Bay,
Dilfer 28-42-1-373.
Detroit, Mitchell 19-25-0-180.
    RECEIVING—Tampa Bay,
Anthony 8-136, Copeland 8-67,
K. Williams 5-82, Harris 3-49, Alstott
4-39. Detroit, Sanders 5-81,
Morton 2-21, H. Moore 4-46.
    MISSED FIELD GOALS—
Tampa Bay, Hustad 29.
Detroit, Hanson 55.

RAIDERS 30, CHARGERS 14

San Diego   7 0 7 0 — 14
Oakland   7 6 3 14 — 30
    SD-Martin 40 pass from
Whelihan (Carney kick)
    OAK-Kaufman 8 run (Ford kick)
    OAK-FG Ford 21
    OAK-FG Ford 32
    OAK-FG Ford 28
    SD-Brown 2 run (Carney kick)
    OAK-T. Brown 4 pass from
George (Ford kick)
    OAK-Kaufman 5 run (Ford kick)
    A-57,325
    INDIVIDUAL STATISTICS
    RUSHING—San Diego, Brown
18-78, Fletcher 3-5.
    Oakland, Kaufman 16-72,
    PASSING—San Diego, Whelihan
20-36-1-236.
    Oakland, George 21-30-1-332.
    RECEIVING—San Diego,
Brown 5-43, Fletcher 5-40, Jones
3-41, T. Martin 7-112.
    Oakland, Jett 8-134,
T. Brown 6-93, Kaufman 5-49,
Dudley 3-54.
    MISSED FIELD GOALS—None.

RAVENS 30, STEELERS 17

Pittsburgh	3	7	0	7 —	17
Baltimore	9	14	7	0 —	30

Pit-FG Jacke 34
Balt-Mi. Jackson 64 pass from Testaverde (kick failed)
Balt-FG Stover 30
Balt-Alexander 3 pass from Testaverde (Stover kick)
Pit-Stewart 3 run (Jacke kick)
Balt-Green 4 pass from Testaverde (Stover kick)
Balt-Alexander 1 pass from Testaverde (Stover kick)
Pit-Bettis 2 pass from Stewart (Jacke kick)
A-72,313
INDIVIDUAL STATISTICS
RUSHING—Pittsburgh, Bettis 6-40, Stewart 4-29.
Baltimore, Morris 12-66, Graham 15-43, Testaverde 2-(minus 2).
PASSING—Pittsburgh, Stewart 14-33-2-202.
Baltimore, Testaverde 14-22-0-199.
RECEIVING—Pittsburgh, Thigpen 5-66, Bettis 1-9, Bruener 4-96.
Baltimore, Green 4-30, Morris 3-45, Mi. Jackson 1-64, Alexander 2-4, Graham 1-33, Byner 2-16.

SEAHAWKS 24, PATRIOTS 6

New England	0	6	0	0 —	6
Seattle	3	7	7	7 —	24

Sea-FG Peterson 29
Sea-Galloway 46 pass from Friesz (Peterson kick)
NE-Coates 33 pass from Bledsoe (kick failed)
Sea-Broussard 16 pass from Friesz (Peterson kick)
Sea-Friesz 2 run (Peterson kick)
A-59,688
INDIVIDUAL STATISTICS
RUSHING—New England, C. Martin 12-48, Bledsoe 2-4.
Seattle, Warren 26-116, Friesz 2-11.
PASSING—New England, Bledsoe 10-22-1-104,
Seattle, Friesz 13-21-0-230.
RECEIVING—New England, Glenn 4-37, Brisby 4-36, Coates 3-52, C. Martin 2-14.
Seattle, Galloway 7-133, Blades 2-62, Warren 3-26.
MISSED FIELD GOALS—Seattle, Peterson 25.

Starting with team #5, let's take a look at quarterback Jeff George of the Oakland Raiders. First, in looking at his passing stats, we find he completed 21 of 30 passes for 332 yards. In our scorecard, we would mark a P followed by a comma and then a 16, representing one point for every 20 yards he gained passing. Then we would look at both the rushing and pass-receiving stats to see if he had any additional points. As we can see, he didn't. Let's take a look at our scorecard with George's stats logged in. (See Detail H.)

Detail H

TEAM # 5		TEAM # 6	
QB	George (OAK) (P,16)	QB	Friesz (SEAT)
RB	Sanders (DET)	RB	Brown (SD)
RB	Bettis (PITT)	RB	Kaufman (OAK)
WR	T. Brown (OAK)	WR	Glenn (NE)
WR	Galloway (SEAT)	WR	H. Moore (DET)
TE	Coates (NE)	TE	Green (BALT)
K	Ford (OAK)	K	Hanson (DET)

Continuing with team #5, we look at Barry Sanders, running back of the Detroit Lions. Of course, with a running back, we first look at the rushing and pass-receiving stats for his point total, but don't forget to look at the passing stats in the event he may have thrown an option pass. We find Sanders had 15 carries for 56 yards and five receptions for 81 yards. In his slot on the scorecard we would mark (R,5) for his rushing stats and (Pr,8) for his pass-receiving stats, totaling 13 points.

Then move on to Jerome Bettis of the Pittsburgh Steelers. We find Bettis rushing six times for 40 yards and catching one pass for nine yards. In his slot we would mark only (R,4), representing his rushing yardage, because his nine yards of pass-receiving yardage is not enough to qualify him for any pass-receiving points. His total points, therefore, would be only four.

Tim Brown of the Oakland Raiders is next. Looking at the pass-receiving stats first, we find he caught six passes for 93 yards, shown as (Pr,9), but he also carried the ball once for 20 yards, shown as (R,2). This would give him 11 points for his performance.

Now let's look at Joey Galloway of the Seattle Seahawks. Galloway appears only in the pass-receiving stats, where we see he caught seven passes for 133 yards, shown as (Pr,13), totaling 13 points.

On to Ben Coates, tight end of the New England Patriots. Again, Coates appears only in the pass-receiving stats, where we find he caught three passes for 52 yards, shown as (Pr,5), totaling five points.

Team #5's kicker is Cole Ford of the Oakland Raiders. Just to make sure, we check the passing, rushing, and pass-receiving stats and find he gained no yardage. Now, looking at the scoring stats, we find he kicked three field goals and three extra points, shown as FFFXXX, totaling 12 points.

Now let's go on to team #6. First we will look at the quarterback, John Friesz of the Seattle Seahawks. Looking first at his passing stats, we find he was 13 of 21 for 230 yards, shown as (P,11). We also find under the rushing stats that he had two rushes for 11 yards, shown as (R,1). Combining the two, we would give him 12 total points.

Move on to Gary Brown of the San Diego Chargers. In the rushing stats, we find he had 18 rushes for 78 yards, shown as (R,7). In the pass-receiving stats, we find he had five catches for 43 yards, shown as (Pr,4). Again, combining the two, we would total 11 points.

Next comes Napolean Kaufman of the Oakland Raiders. Looking at the rushing stats, we find he rushed 16 times for 72 yards, shown as (R,7), and under the receiving stats, we find he caught five passes for 49 yards, shown as (Pr,4), giving him a total of 11 points.

On to Terry Glenn wide receiver for the New England Patriots. Glenn has only pass-receiving yardage—four catches for 37 yards, shown as (Pr,3), totaling three points.

Herman Moore of the Detroit Lions is next. Moore also has only pass-receiving yardage, with four receptions for 46 yards, shown as (Pr,4), totaling four points.

Now we will look at the tight end, Eric Green of the Baltimore Ravens. Again, we find Green has only pass-receiving yardage, with four catches for 30 yards, shown as (Pr,3), totaling three points.

Lastly, the kicker is Jason Hanson of the Detroit Lions. Hanson has no yardage stats, so we just have to tally his three field goals and two extra points, shown as FFFXX, totaling 11 points.

Let's check to see how our final scorecard will look. (See Detail I.)

Detail I

TEAM # 5				TEAM # 6		
QB	George (OAK) (P,16)	16		QB	Friesz (SEAT) (P,11) (R,1)	12
RB	Sanders (DET) (R,5) (Pr,8)	13		RB	Brown (SD) (R,7) (Pr,4)	11
RB	Bettis (PITT) (R,5)	4		RB	Kaufman (OAK) (R,7) (Pr,4)	11
WR	T. Brown (OAK) (Pr,9) (R,2)	11		WR	Glenn (NE) (Pr,3)	3
WR	Galloway (SEAT) (Pr,13)	13		WR	H. Moore (DET) (Pr,4)	4
TE	Coates (NE) (Pr,5)	5		TE	Green (BALT) (Pr,3)	3
K	Ford (OAK) FFFXXX	12		K	Hanson (DET) FFFXX	11
		74				55

We can see by this final score that typical football scores are rare, but the Performance Point Method can be a very interesting way to play the game.

What follows are samples of how one league's weekly score sheets may look after the completion of its fantasy games.

Performance Point Scoring Method Samples

FFL Box Scores

	Tm# 3			Tm# 1	
	The Overachievers	VS.		The Crashdummies	
		Pts			Pts
QB	(Ariz.) P,19 Plummer	19	QB	(Seat.) P,7 Friesz	7
RB	(G.B.) R,9 Bennett	9	RB	(Buf.) T Thomas	0
RB	(Ind.) R,1 Faulk	1	RB	(N.Y.J.) Murrell	0
WR	(Dall.) Pr,3 Miller	3	WR	(S.F.) Pr,10 Rice	10
WR	(Buf.) Pr,1 Early	1	WR	(Seat.) Pr,6 Blades	6
TE	(Mia.) Drayton	0	TE	(Tenn.) Pr,5 Wycheck	5
K	(N.E.) FXX Vinatieri	5	K	(S.F.) FFXX Anderson	8
	Reserves			**Reserves**	
1	(Balt.) Mi. Jackson		1	(G.B.) Levens	
2	(Den.) McCaffrey		2	(N.O.) Hastings	
3	(Ariz.) Rb. Moore		3	(N.E.) Glenn	
4	(K.C.) Gonzalez		4	(Car.) Carruth	
5	(Ariz.) F. Sanders		5	(Jac.) McCardell	
		38			36

	Tm# 2			Tm# 4	
	Lodi's Big Daddys	VS.		East Side Gladiators	
		Pts			Pts
QB	(Balt.) P,11 Testaverde	11	QB	(K.C.) Grbac	0
RB	(Phil.) R,4 Watters Pr,4	8	RB	(Mia.) Abdul-Jabbar	0
RB	(Den.) R,3 Davis Pr,1	4	RB	(Jac.) Pr,2 Means R,2	4
WR	(Oak.) Pr,11 T. Brown	11	WR	(S.D.) Martin	0
WR	(N.Y.G.) Pr,5 Toomer	5	WR	(Minn.) Pr,4 C. Carter	4
TE	(T.B.) Pr,3 Harris	3	TE	(Seat.) Pr,2 Fauria	2
K	(Det.) XX Hanson	2	K	(Atl.) FXX Andersen	5
	Reserves			**Reserves**	
1	(T.B.) Sanders		1	(T.B.) Alstott	
2	(N.Y.J.) K. Johnson		2	(Det.) Perriman	
3	(Balt.) Morris		3	(Seat.) Galloway	
4	(Car.) Biakabatuka		4	(Dall.) Bjornson	
5	(K.C.) Rison		5	(S.D.) Humphries	
		44			15

	Tm# 7			Tm# 5	
	Mediterranean Meatballs	VS.		Treanor's Electric Co	
		Pts			Pts
QB	(Oak.) P,8 George	8	QB	(N.O.) P,8 Shuler	8
RB	(Wash.) T. Allen	0	RB	(Atl.) R,14 J. Anderson	14
RB	(Minn.) R. Smith	0	RB	(S.F.) Hearst	0
WR	(G.B.) Pr,1 R. Brooks	1	WR	(Phil.) Pr,2 Fryar	2
WR	(Tenn.) Pr,2 C. Sanders	2	WR	(Jac.) Pr,2 Smith	2
TE	(Minn.) Pr,1 Jordan	1	TE	(N.Y.G.) Pr,4 Cross	4
K	(Balt.) XXXX Stover	4	K	(S.D.) XX Carney	2
	Reserves			**Reserves**	
1	(Car.) K. Collins		1	(Phil.) Peete	
2	(Det.) Morton		2	(T.B.) Anthony	
3	(Buf.) Reed		3	(N.O.) Davis	
4	(Jac.) Stewart		4	(S.F.) Floyd	
5	(Dall.) Johnston		5	(Atl.) Mathis	
		16			32

	Tm# 6			Tm# 8	
	F-Troop	VS.		J.M.D. Warriors	
		Pts			Pts
QB	(S.F.) P,13 Young	13	QB	(N.Y.G.) P,9 Kanell	9
RB	(T.B.) Dunn	0	RB	(N.Y.G.) R,4 Hampton	4
RB	(Dall.) R,14 E. Smith	14	RB	(Oak.) R,6 Kaufman	6
WR	(Ind.) Pr,1 Harrison	1	WR	(N.Y.J.) Pr,3 Graham	3
WR	(Oak.) Pr,7 Jett	7	WR	(Chi.) Pr,1 Engram	1
TE	(Balt.) Pr,5 Kinchen	5	TE	(G.B.) Pr,4 Chmura	4
K	(Minn.) FXX Murray	5	K	(St.L.) FFXXXXX Wilkins	11
	Reserves			**Reserves**	
1	(Den.) Elway		1	(G.B.) Freeman	
2	(Car.) Carrier		2	(S.F.) Stokes	
3	(N.Y.J.) O'Donnell		3	(N.E.) Meggett	
4	(Ariz.) Centers		4	(Phil.) Dunn	
5	(N.Y.J.) Chrebet		5	(Pitt.) J.L. Williams	
		45			38

FFL STANDINGS

(Black Conference)

Spade Division	Team #	Won	Lost	Tie	Points	Points Agst
The Crashdummies	1	7	4	0	432	381
Lodi's Big Daddys	2	6	5	0	421	394
The Overachievers	3	5	6	0	373	391
East Side Gladiators	4	2	9	0	307	455

Club Division	Team #	Won	Lost	Tie	Points	Points Agst
Mediterranean Meatballs	7	8	3	0	402	356
Treanor's Elec. Co.	5	7	4	0	388	344
Armchair Sleepers	6	5	6	0	351	365
J.M.D.Warriors	8	3	8	0	310	372

(Red Conference)

Diamond Division	Team #	Won	Lost	Tie	Points	Points Agst
Costra Nostra	10	8	3	0	397	336
D.C. Express	11	7	4	0	346	302
F-Troop	12	5	6	0	323	316
Boyer's Spoilers	9	4	7	0	297	345

Heart Division	Team #	Won	Lost	Tie	Points	Points Agst
French Connection	13	10	1	0	469	317
The Medics	16	4	7	0	398	403
The Bogarts	14	4	7	0	367	367
The Jayhawks	15	3	8	0	343	377

THIS WEEK'S SCORES

Team #	3 (38)	Team #	2 (44)
Team #	1 (36)	Team #	4 (15)
Team #	7 (16)	Team #	6 (45)
Team #	5 (32)	Team #	8 (38)
Team #	11 (45)	Team #	10 (37)
Team #	9 (44)	Team #	12 (30)
Team #	15 (48)	Team #	14 (42)
Team #	13 (52)	Team #	16 (29)

THIS WEEK'S TRANSACTIONS

Tm#		Dropped/Tm-Pos	Acquired/Tm-Pos
1	5	Dunn TB RB	Bettis Pitt RB
2	7	Reed Minn WR	Reed Buf WR
3	16	Morton Det WR	McCaffrey Den WR
4	12	Drayton Mia TE	Sharpe Den TE
5	13	Fryar Phil WR	R. Brooks GB WR
6			
7			
8			
9			
10			

THE COMBINED BASIC/PERFORMANCE SCORING METHOD

Many leagues have decided to add interest to their fantasy games by using a combination of both the Basic Scoring Method and the Performance Point Method. This provides the best of both worlds, since a player is rewarded for the big yardage numbers he earns as well as for the times he crosses the goal line. Using this method, a fantasy team won't be so frustrated when a player rushes or receives for 150 yards but doesn't score any Basic Scoring Method points. On the other hand, if a player rushes three times for six yards but scores twice, he is rewarded more by this method than by the Performance Point Method alone. This Combined Scoring Method is becoming quite popular, especially among established leagues.

Because this Combined Basic/Performance Scoring Method is simply the combination of the previously described Basic Scoring and Performance Point Methods, there is no need for a separate new rules section. A player's total points are tabulated by adding his fantasy points from the Basic Scoring Method (touchdowns and touchdown passes) to his points from the Performance Point Method (yardage). Guidelines for both of these scoring methods are laid out in the previous two sections.

*There is a section in Chapter I (Section X) that concentrates on this new scoring method, giving last year's statistics and giving player ratings for the upcoming 1994 season.

THE DISTANCE SCORING METHOD

The Distance Scoring Method is a tabulation of scoring that uses the yardage covered in a touchdown-scoring play to determine the number of points awarded to the player who scored. This method rewards the "big play" players, those who score on long, exciting plays, as compared to the big fullback who scores on one-yard plunges. Let's take a look at our fourth method of scoring.

1. SCORING TABULATION BY POSITION
   A. Quarterbacks, Running Backs, Wide Receivers, Tight Ends
      1. The following points are awarded for touchdowns scored by either rushing or passing receiving:
      2. The following points are awarded for touchdown passes thrown:

Distance of TD scored	Points Awarded	TD Pass Thrown	Awarded
1 — 9 yards	2 points	1 — 9 yards	1 point
10 — 19 yards	4 points	1 — 19 yards	2 points
20 — 29 yards	6 points	20 — 29 yards	3 points
30 — 39 yards	8 points	30 — 39 yards	4 points
40 — 49 yards	10 points	40 — 49 yards	5 points
50 — 59 yards	12 points	50 — 59 yards	6 points
60 — 69 yards	14 points	60 — 69 yards	7 points
70 — 79 yards	16 points	70 — 79 yards	8 points
80 — 89 yards	18 points	80 — 89 yards	9 points
90 — 99 yards	20 points	90 — 99 yards	10 points

   B. Kickers
      1. The following points are awarded for each field goal:

Distance of Field Goal	Points Awarded
1 — 9 yards	1 point
10 — 19 yards	2 points
20 — 29 yards	3 points
30 — 39 yards	4 points
40 — 49 yards	5 points
50 — 59 yards	6 points
60 — 69 yards	7 points
70 yards & over	10 points

      2. A kicker is awarded one point for each extra point.

TWO-POINT CONVERSIONS

Two-point conversions are scored just like touchdowns. If a player runs in a two-point conversion, he is awarded two points. If the conversion involves a pass, the receiver is awarded two points and the passer is awarded one.

2. SAMPLE SCORING FOR A FANTASY FOOTBALL GAME

The following key will help in logging each player's scoring results. In the area on the scorecard following the player's team name, use the following guidelines:

A. Include with All Players

1. For a touchdown scored by means of rushing or pass receiving, mark a T followed by a comma, then the associated number of points for the distance of the touchdown scored, and lastly surround the group with parentheses. For example, (T,8) would indicate a touchdown scored from between 30 and 39 yards out.

2. For a touchdown pass thrown, mark a P followed by a comma, then the appropriate number of points for the distance of the touchdown pass thrown, and lastly surround the group with parentheses. For example, (P,5) would indicate a touchdown pass thrown from between 40 and 49 yards out.

B. Kickers

1. For field goals, mark an F followed by a comma, then the associated number of points for the distance of the field goal, and lastly surround the group with parentheses. For example, (F,4) would indicate a field goal from between 30 and 39 yards out.

2. For each successful extra point, mark an X (one point for each).

As we did with both the Basic Scoring Method and the Performance Point Method, we will again set up two fictitious fantasy teams to demonstrate further the Distance Scoring Method. We will use the lineups shown in Detail J and the box scores shown in Detail K.

Detail J

TEAM # 7		TEAM # 8	
QB	Young (SF)	QB	Kramer (CHI)
RB	Floyd (SF)	RB	Centers (ARIZ)
RB	Watters (PHIL)	RB	Salaam (CHI)
WR	Miller (DALL)	WR	Anthony (TB)
WR	R. Brooks (GB)	WR	F. Sanders (ARIZ)
TE	P. Carter (ARIZ)	TE	Jones (SF)
K	Anderson (SF)	K	Boniol (PHIL)

Detail K

BEARS 23, PACKERS 21

Green Bay	7	7	0	7 —	21
Chicago	7	0	7	9 —	23

Chi-Conway 35 pass from Kramer (Jaeger kick)
GB-Favre 1 run (Longwell kick)
GB-R. Brooks 31 pass from Favre (Longwell kick)
Chi-Engram 22 pass from Kramer (Jaeger kick)
Chi-Kramer 6 run (kick failed)
GB-Chmura 5 pass from Favre (Longwell kick)
Chi-FG Jaeger 22
A-35,908

CARDINALS 31, EAGLES 7

Philadelphia	0	0	0	7 —	7
Arizona	7	7	10	7 —	31

Ariz-Centers 12 run (Nedney kick)
Ariz-F. Sanders 10 pass from Plummer (Nedney kick)
Ariz-FG Nedney
Ariz-L. Johnson 1 run (Nedney kick)
Ariz-Carter 29 pass from Plummer (Nedney kick)
Phil-C.T.Jones 20 pass from Hoying (Boniol kick)
A-21,902

LIONS 23, BUCS 20

Tampa Bay	7	6	0	7 —	20
Detroit	8	10	3	10 —	23

TB-Harris 4 pass from Dilfer (Hustad kick)
Det-Sanders 3 run (Hanson kick)
Det-FG Hanson 34
TB-K. Williams 29 pass from Dilfer (kick failed)
Det-FG Hanson 36
Det-FG Hanson 38
Det-H. Moore 6 pass from Mitchell (Hanson kick)
TB-Anthony 29 pass from Dilfer (Hustad kick)
A-54,133

RAIDERS 30, CHARGERS 14

San Diego	7	0	7	0 —	14
Oakland	7	6	3	14 —	30

SD-Martin 40 pass from Humphries (Carney kick)
OAK-Kaufman 8 run (Ford kick)
OAK-FG Ford 21
OAK-FG Ford 32
OAK-FG Ford 28
SD-Brown 2 run (Carney kick)
OAK-T. Brown 4 pass from George (Ford kick)
OAK-Kaufman 5 run (Ford kick)
A-57,325

49ERS 42, COWBOYS 17

Dallas	3	7	0	7 —	17
San Francisco	21	0	7	14 —	42

SF-Floyd 6 pass from Young (Anderson kick)
SF-Levy, 56 punt return (Anderson kick)
Dal-FG Cunningham 47
SF-Rice 77 pass from Young (Anderson kick)
Dal-Aikman 1 run (Cunningham kick)
SF-Jones 18 pass from Young (Anderson kick)
Dal-Miller 13 pass from Aikman (Cunningham kick)
SF-Hanks 48 interception return (Anderson kick)
SF-Floyd 16 pass from Young (Anderson kick)
A-59,002

Beginning with team #7, we will start with the quarterback, Steve Young of the San Francisco 49ers. Looking at the box scores from Detail K, we find that in the 49ers–Cowboys game, Young threw four touchdown passes. The first, from six yards, is shown as (P,1). The next, from 77 yards, is shown as (P,8). The third, from 18 yards, is shown as (P,2). The last, from 16 yards, is shown as (P,2). Combining all four gives him 13 total points. Let's check how this would look in our scorecard. (See Detail L.)

Detail L

TEAM # 7			TEAM # 8	
QB	Young (SF) (P,1)	13	QB	Kramer (CHI)
	(P,8) (P,2) (P,2)		RB	Centers (ARIZ)
RB	Floyd (SF)		RB	Salaam (CHI)
RB	Watters (PHIL)		WR	Anthony (TB)
WR	Miller (DALL)		WR	F. Sanders (ARIZ)
WR	R. Brooks (GB)		TE	Jones (SF)
TE	P. Carter (ARIZ)		K	Boniol (PHIL)
K	Anderson (SF)			

Now let's fill in the rest of the scorecard, following the previously mentioned key.

Next for team #7 is William Floyd, running back for the San Francisco 49ers. Looking at the box scores, we find Floyd caught two touchdown passes; the first, from six yards, is shown as (T,2), and the other, from 16 yards, is shown as (T,4). This totals six points.

Let's move on to Ricky Watters of the Philadelphia Eagles. Taking a good look at the Philadelphia–Arizona game, we find that Watters failed to score, giving him zero points.

Okay, how about Anthony Miller of the Dallas Cowboys? Miller did catch a Troy Aikman touchdown pass from 13 yards out, shown as (T,4), totaling four points.

Robert Brooks of the Green Bay Packers is the other wide receiver. Looking at the Green Bay–Chicago game, we find that Brooks failed to score, so mark his slot with a big zero.

The tight end is Pat Carter of the Arizona Cardinals. In the Arizona–Philadelphia box score, we can see Carter scored on a 29-yard pass reception, shown as (T,6), totaling six points.

Team #7's kicker is Gary Anderson of the San Francisco 49ers. In the 49ers–Cowboys box score, we find Anderson was successful on all six extra-point attempts, shown as XXXXXX, totaling six points.

Now let's look at team #8, starting with the quarterback, Erik Kramer of the Chicago Bears. In the Chicago–Green Bay box score, we find Kramer first threw a touchdown pass to Curtis Conway from 35 yards out, shown as (P,4), then threw another touchdown pass to Bobby Engram from 22 yards out, shown as (P,3), and finally ran in a touchdown from six yards out, shown as (T,2). These all combine to make a total of nine points.

Next is Larry Centers of the Arizona Cardinals. Glancing at the Arizona–Philadelphia box score, we find Centers running in a 12-yard touchdown run, shown as (T,4), totaling four points.

The other running back for team #8 is Rashaan Salaam of the Chicago Bears. Salaam failed to score in the Chicago–Green Bay game and thus ends up with a zero in his point-results column.

Let's move on to Reidel Anthony of the Tampa Bay Buccaneers. Anthony a wide receiver, scored on a 29-yard touchdown pass, shown as (T,6), to total six points.

Checking the other wide receiver, Frank Sanders of the Arizona Cardinals, we find Sanders caught a 10-yard touchdown pass in the Philadelphia–Arizona game, shown as (T,4), giving him four points.

Team #8's tight end is Brent Jones of the San Francisco 49ers. In studying the 49ers–Cowboys game, we find Jones was the recipient of one of the four touchdown passes thrown by Joe Montana. The 18-yard touchdown reception by Jones is shown as (T,4), giving him four points.

Last we evaluate the kicker, Chris Boniol of the Philadelphia Eagles. Looking at the Philadelphia–Arizona game, we find Boniol was only able to account for one extra point and had no field goals. This is shown as an X, totaling one point.

Let's take a look at how our final scorecard would appear. (See Detail M.)

Detail M

TEAM # 7		
QB	Young (SF) (P,1) (P,8) (P,2) (P,2)	13
RB	Floyd (SF) (T,2) (T,4)	6
RB	Watters (PHIL)	0
WR	Miller (DALL) (T,4)	4
WR	R. Brooks (GB)	0
TE	P. Carter (ARIZ) (T,6)	6
K	Anderson (SF) XXXXXX	6
		35

TEAM # 8		
QB	Kramer (CHI) (P,4) (P,3) (T,2)	9
RB	Centers (ARIZ) (T,4)	4
RB	Salaam (CHI)	0
WR	Anthony (TB) (T,6)	6
WR	F. Sanders (ARIZ) (T,4)	4
TE	Jones (SF) (T,4)	4
K	Boniol (PHIL) X	1
		28

What follows are samples of how one league's weekly score sheets may look after the completion of its fantasy games.

Distance Scoring Method Samples

FFL Box Scores

Tm# 3 — The Overachievers VS. Tm# 1 — The Crashdummies

	The Overachievers		Pts		The Crashdummies		Pts
	(Ariz.)	P,1			(Seat.)	P,1	
QB	Plummer	P,2	3	QB	Friesz	P,3	4
	(G.B.)	T,2			(Buf.)	T,2	
RB	Bennett		2	RB	Thomas		2
	(Ind.)				(N.Y.J.)		
RB	Faulk		0	RB	Murrell		0
	(Dall.)				(S.F.)	T,14	
WR	Miller		0	WR	Rice	T,2	16
	(Buf.)				(Seat.)	T,6	
WR	Early		0	WR	Blades		6
	(Mia.)				(Tenn.)		
TE	Drayton		0	TE	Wycheck		0
	(N.E.)	FXX,5			(S.F.)	XXF,3	
K	Vinatieri		7	K	Anderson	F,3	8
	Reserves				**Reserves**		
	(Balt.)				(G.B.)		
1	Mi. Jackson			1	Levens		
	(Den.)				(N.O.)		
2	McCaffrey			2	Hastings		
	(Ariz.)				(N.E.)		
3	Rb. Moore			3	Glenn		
	(K.C.)				(Car.)		
4	Gonzalez			4	Carruth		
	(Ariz.)				(Jac.)		
5	F. Sanders			5	McCardell		
			12				**36**

Tm# 2 — Lodi's Big Daddys VS. Tm# 4 — East Side Gladiators

	Lodi's Big Daddys		Pts		East Side Gladiators		Pts
	(Balt.)	P,2			(K.C.)		
QB	Testaverde		2	QB	Grbac		0
	(Phil.)				(Mia.)		
RB	Watters		0	RB	Abdul-Jabbar		0
	(Den.)	T,2			(Jac.)	T,6	
RB	Davis		2	RB	Means		6
	(Oak.)	T,14			(S.D.)		
WR	T. Brown		14	WR	Martin		0
	(N.Y.G.)				(Minn.)		
WR	Toomer		0	WR	C. Carter		0
	(T.B.)				(Seat.)		
TE	Harris		0	TE	Fauria		0
	(Det.)	XX			(Atl.)	XXF,3	
K	Hanson		2	K	Andersen		5
	Reserves				**Reserves**		
	(Det.)				(T.B.)		
1	Sanders			1	Alstott		
	(N.Y.J.)				(Det.)		
2	K. Johnson			2	Perriman		
	(Balt.)				(Seat.)		
3	Morris			3	Galloway		
	(Car.)				(Dall.)		
4	Biakabatuka			4	Bjornson		
	(K.C.)				(S.D.)		
5	Rison			5	Humphries		
			20				**11**

Tm# 7 — Mediterranean Meatballs VS. Tm# 5 — Treanor's Electric Co

	Mediterranean Meatballs		Pts		Treanor's Electric Co		Pts
	(Oak.)	P,8			(N.O.)	P,7	
QB	George		1	QB	Shuler		7
	(Wash.)				(Atl.)		
RB	T. Allen		0	RB	J. Anderson		4
	(Minn.)				(S.F.)		
RB	R. Smith		0	RB	Hearst		0
	(G.B.)				(Phil.)		
WR	R. Brooks		0	WR	Fryar		0
	(Tenn.)				(Jac.)	T,4	
WR	C. Sanders		0	WR	Smith		4
	(Minn.)	T,4			(N.Y.G.)	T,6	
TE	Jordan		4	TE	Cross		6
	(Balt.)	XXXX			(S.D.)	XX	
K	Stover		4	K	Carney		2
	Reserves				**Reserves**		
	(Car.)				(Phil.)		
1	K. Collins			1	Peete		
	(Det.)				(T.B.)		
2	Morton			2	Anthony		
	(Buf.)				(N.O.)		
3	Reed			3	Davis		
	(Jac.)				(S.F.)		
4	Stewart			4	Floyd		
	(Dall.)				(Atl.)		
5	Johnston			5	Mathis		
			9				**23**

Tm# 6 — F-Troop VS. Tm# 8 — J.M.D. Warriors

	F-Troop		Pts		J.M.D. Warriors		Pts
	(S.F.)	P,1			(N.Y.G.)	P,3	
QB	Young	P,7	8	QB	Kanell	P,2	5
	(T.B.)				(N.Y.G.)		
RB	Dunn		0	RB	Hampton		0
	(Dall.)				(Oak.)		
RB	E. Smith		0	RB	Kaufman		0
	(Ind.)				(N.Y.J.)		
WR	Harrison		0	WR	Graham		0
	(Oak.)	T,2			(Chi.)		
WR	Jett		2	WR	Engram		0
	(Balt.)				(G.B.)	T,2	
TE	Kinchen		0	TE	Chmura		2
	(Minn.)	XXF,4			(St.L.)	XXXXF,3	
K	Murray		6	K	Wilkins	F,4	13
	Reserves				**Reserves**		
	(Den.)				(G.B.)		
1	Elway			1	Freeman		
	(Car.)				(S.F.)		
2	Carrier			2	Stokes		
	(N.Y.J.)				(N.E.)		
3	O'Donnell			3	Meggett		
	(Ariz.)				(Phil.)		
4	Centers			4	Dunn		
	(N.Y.J.)				(Pitt.)		
5	Chrebet			5	J.L. Williams		
			16				**20**

FFL STANDINGS

(Black Conference) Spade Division	Team #	Won	Lost	Tie	Points	Points Agst
The Crashdummies	1	7	4	0	444	357
Lodi's Big Daddys	2	6	5	0	404	398
The Overachievers	3	5	6	0	377	374
East Side Gladiators	4	2	9	0	302	419

Club Division	Team #	Won	Lost	Tie	Points	Points Agst
Mediterranean Meatballs	7	8	3	0	396	342
Treanor's Elec. Co.	5	7	4	0	382	322
Armchair Sleepers	6	5	6	0	368	358
J.M.D.Warriors	8	3	8	0	333	372

(Red Conference) Diamond Division	Team #	Won	Lost	Tie	Points	Points Agst
Costra Nostra	10	8	3	0	387	309
D.C. Express	11	7	4	0	316	287
F-Troop	12	5	6	0	366	322
Boyer's Spoilers	9	4	7	0	342	353

Heart Division	Team #	Won	Lost	Tie	Points	Points Agst
French Connection	13	10	1	0	453	329
The Medics	16	4	7	0	427	404
The Bogarts	14	4	7	0	339	345
The Jayhawks	15	3	8	0	326	356

THIS WEEK'S SCORES

Team # 3 (12)　　Team # 2 (20)
Team # 1 (36)　　Team # 4 (11)

Team # 7 (9)　　Team # 8 (20)
Team # 5 (23)　　Team # 6 (16)

Team # 11 (40)　　Team # 10 (12)
Team # 9 (12)　　Team # 12 (7)

Team # 15 (22)　　Team # 14 (16)
Team # 13 (23　　Team # 16 (8)

THIS WEEK'S TRANSACTIONS

Tm#		Dropped/Tm-Pos	Acquired/Tm-Pos
1	5	Dunn TB RB	Bettis Pitt RB
2	7	Reed Minn WR	Reed Buf WR
3	16	Morton Det WR	McCaffrey Den WR
4	12	Drayton Mia TE	Sharpe Den TE
5	13	Fryar Phil WR	R. Brooks GB WR
6	___	_____	_____
7	___	_____	_____
8	___	_____	_____
9	___	_____	_____
10	___	_____	_____

IX
VARIATIONS ON FANTASY FOOTBALL

Up to this point, I have explained the scoring for the three most commonly used methods. Now I want to show you a few variations that some leagues use.

1. DRAFT AN NFL DEFENSE OR SPECIALTY TEAM

In another league, team defense is used an an eighth player. That is, every franchise in the fantasy league would draft a team defense. If any member of the defensive team scores a touchdown, either by way of interception or fumble recovery, six points are awarded. If a team scores by means of a safety, two points are awarded.

Let's say you drafted the San Francisco 49ers to be your team defense. Looking at the box score in Detail O for the 49ers-Cowboys game, we find that Merton Hanks of the 49ers intercepted a pass for a touchdown. This would give your team six additional points.

You will notice that Eric Davis ran back a punt for a touchdown. Although he is a member of the defensive team, the touchdown would not count because it was scored while he was playing on a specialty team. Only a defensive touchdown scored by a member of a defensive team by means of an interception or fumble recovery will be counted.

Detail O

49ERS 42, COWBOYS 17

Dallas   3 7 0 7 — 17
San Francisco   21 0 7 14 — 42
    SF-Floyd 6 pass from Young
(Anderson kick), 2:30
    SF-Davis, 56 punt return (Anderson
kick), 6:37
    Dal-FG Cunningham 47, 10:58
    SF-Rice 77 pass from Young
(Anderson kick), 11:23
    Dal-Aikman 1 run (Cunningham
kick), 6:49
    SF-Jones 18 pass from Young
(Anderson kick), 4:40
    Dal-Miller 13 pass from Aikman
(Cunningham kick), :17
    SF-Hanks 48 interception
return (Anderson kick), 4:32
    SF-Floyd 16 pass from Young
(Anderson kick), 8:31
    A-59,002

Again, let's take a look at our scorecard. (See Detail P.)

Detail P

	TEAM # 1	
QB	Favre (GB) TPP	12
RB	J. Andersen (ATL) TTT	18
RB	A. Smith (BUF)	0
WR	Fryar (PHIL)	0
WR	R. Brooks (GB) T	6
TE	Conwell (St L) T	6
K	Andersen (ATL) FXXX	6
TD	49ers T	6
		54

2. TIEBREAKERS
Because the 17-week NFL season may affect some handling procedures for transactions, please refer to the suggestions in the beginning of this chapter to see how to handle this change.

OPTION #1: Sudden-Death Tiebreaker (for leagues using the Basic Scoring Method or the Distance Scoring Method)
Here is where your reserves come in. In our league we have seven starters and five reserves. When it is time to call in lineups, not only do we list our seven starters, but we also list our five reserves. This listing of our reserves is used in the event of a tie after regulation play. If there is a tie, we go through the reserves to break the tie. The first team scoring any additional points is the winner.

The home team (as predetermined on the league schedule) is granted the first opportunity to break the tie. If the home team's first reserve scores, the game is over; whatever number of points he scored determines the final score. If he failed to score, we go to the vistors first reserve to see if he scored. If he did, his team wins the game. If both of the teams first reserves failed to score, we continue on to the second overtime period. Again, we go to the home team's player first. If he scores, the game is over. If not, we go to the visitors second player. This continues until the tie is finally broken or until all the reserves are used. If none of the reserves from either team can break the deadlock, then the game is declared a tie.

To show how this tiebreaker works, let's take a look at a game between team #3 and team #4 (see Detail Q). First we are going to assume that the score, after tallying each of the teams starters, ended up knotted at 17-17. To break the tie, we would first go to team #3, which was the predetermined home team, to see if its first reserve scored. Team #3's first reserve player is Chris T. Jones of the Philadelphia Eagles. Looking at the box score for the Arizona-Philadelphia game (see Detail R), we find that Jones failed to score.

Next we jump to team #4's first reserve, who is Jake Plummer of the Arizona Cardinals. In checking the game box score, we find that Plummer threw two touchdown passes. Plummer is credited with three points, for throwing a touchdown to break the tie. The second touchdown pass is not needed or used in the tabulation for the final score. Only his first score can be tabulated into the final fantasy game score. (See below, point #1 under "Additional Rules for Tie Breakers.") Now the final score would read team #4, 20, and team #3, 17. There is no need to continue with the rest of the reserves once the tie is broken. Let's take a look at our final scorecard. (See Detail Q.)

Detail Q

TEAM # 5		TEAM # 6	
QB	6	QB	3
RB	0	RB	6
RB	0	RB	0
WR	6	WR	0
WR	0	WR	6
TE	0	TE	0
K	5	K	2
	17		**17**

	Reserves				Reserves	
1	Jones (PHIL)	0		1	Plummer (ARIZ) P	3
2	T. Allen (WASH)			2	Fryar (PHIL)	
3	K. Johnson (NYJ)			3	T. Brown (LARd)	
4	Centers (ARIZ)			4	J. Anderson (ATL)	
5	Stokes (SF)			5	Salaam (CHI)	
		17				**20**

Detail R

CARDINALS 31, EAGLES 7

Philadelphia	0 0 0 7 — 7
Arizona	7 7 10 7 — 31

Ariz-Centers 12 run (Nedney kick)
Ariz-F. Sanders 10 pass from Plummer (Nedney kick)
Ariz-FG Nedney
Ariz-McElroy 1 run (Nedney kick)
Ariz-P. Carter 29 pass from Plummer (Nedney kick)
Phil-Fryar 20 pass from Hoying (Boniol kick)
A-21,902

Formerly, a tie could be broken by any player scoring at least one point. So most fantasy teams carried an additional kicker; this made it very easy to score, because most kickers score at least one extra point. Since a kicker in the NFL cannot kick an extra point to break a tie, why should it be allowed in Fantasy Football? Now a tie can be broken by any scoring player—except a kicker, unless he kicks a field goal. If he kicks seven extra points and no field goals, the tie is not broken. So a tie can be broken in sudden death by:

1) Any player scoring a touchdown
2) Any player (usually a quarterback) throwing a touchdown pass
3) A kicker kicking a field goal (extra points cannot break a tie)
4) A team defense scoring a safety or a touchdown

ADDITIONAL RULES FOR TIEBREAKERS:

1) Only the first score will be used. If a quarterback throws three touchdowns only one will be shown in the final fantasy game score. If a kicker hits three field goals, again only one will be tabulated into the game's final score.
2) In the event that a player who is used as a reserve tie breaker both runs and passes for a score, the score of more value will count. In this case, the touchdown run will be counted for the tie breaker and six points will be awarded in the final score.
3) The points scored to break a tie will be used in the final score and will be used in league standings.

OPTION #2: Reserves Tiebreaker (for leagues using the Performance Point Scoring Method)

Because in the Performance Point Scoring Method almost every player is assured of scoring some points, a tie-breaking method other than sudden death should be used. An effective and fair method for breaking a tie in this case is the Reserves Tie-Breaking Method. Here the team whose reserves score the most total points wins. This keeps any home team with a kicker as first reserve from getting an automatic win. If the score remains tied after adding all the reserve players' points from each team, then revert to sudden death to break the tie, making the home team's first reserve first, and so on. If the score still remains tied, the game is declared a tie. Because so many points are usually added up using this method, the total points from this tie breaker do not count for either team in the Points Scored column of the league standings. (See Detail S.)

Detail S

TEAM # 3			TEAM # 4		
QB	_____	6	QB	_____	3
RB	_____	0	RB	_____	6
RB	_____	0	RB	_____	0
WR	_____	6	WR	_____	0
WR	_____	0	WR	_____	6
TE	_____	0	TE	_____	0
K	_____	5	K	_____	2
		17			**17**

	Reserves			Reserves	
1	Jones (PHIL)	0	1	Plummer (ARIZ)	6
2	T. Allen (WASH)	6	2	Fryar (PHIL)	6
3	K. Johnson (NYJ)	0	3	T. Brown (LARd)	0
4	Centers (ARIZ)	12	4	J. Anderson (ATL)	6
5	Stokes (SF)	6	5	Salaam (CHI)	0
		24			**18**

Because team #3's reserves accounted for 24 points, compared to 18 points for team #4, team #3 is the victor. The final score remains 17-17, and team #3 gets the win. Each team receives 17 points in the standings. Remember, the additional points accumulated by the reserves are not added to the game's final score or the teams yearly point totals. Reserves can accumulate a lot of points, and final scores can wind up in the 70s or 80s as a tie breaker. It would be unfair to use those large totals in the league standings. This is especially true if your league's #1 tie breaker in the win-loss column is most points scored.

3. PLAYOFF REDRAFT

Another twist used by some people is to redraft for their league's play-offs. The teams that make the fantasy league's playoffs will draft from the NFL playoff teams the week immediately following the end of the NFL regular season. (Four fantasy teams is a good number to have for playoff teams, keeping in mind that only 10 NFL teams advance to the playoffs, which greatly decreases the number of players from which to choose.) This twist obviously carries with it many strategies. First, the four teams that advance do not meet in head-to-head competition; rather, the winner is determined by the most points accumulated by the fantasy team through the entire round of the NFL playoffs. With this variation, not only do you want the better players, but you also must keep in mind that valuable players are those from teams you feel will make it beyond the first round, so that they will play in more games and have more chances to score points for you.

Here is a more detailed description of how this is done:

A. Redraft:	16 Players
	2 quarterbacks
	4 running backs
	4 wide receivers
	2 tight ends
	2 kickers
	2 team defenses

B. Player Protection: Any fantasy team can protect up to three of its regular-season players for the playoffs.

C. Drafting order: After the protected players are determined by each fantasyteam,a group of four player cards can be used to determine drafting order, with every round being in the reverse order of the previous round.

D. Scoring:

Quarterbacks:	3 points (TD pass thrown)
	6 points (TD rushing)
Running Backs, Wide Receivers, & Tight Ends:	3 points (TD pass thrown on a halfback option)
	6 points (TD rushing or receiving)
Kickers:	3 points (field goal)
	1 point (extra point)
Team Defense:	6 points (interception or fumble-recovery score)
	2 points (safety)
	1 point (interception)
	1 point (fumble recovery)
Any Player:	2 points (conversion, rushing or throwing)
	1 point (conversion thrown)

All NFL players' performances are counted until their teams are eliminated from the playoffs. The fantasy team amassing the most points through the NFL playoffs, including the Super Bowl, is declared the league's winner.

4. LIFE-LONG FRANCHISES
We have found many fantasy leagues in which the teams from the previous season draft only incoming rookies. This method of playing has many positive and negative sides. On the positive side, it provides ownership like the real thing; you must build on your team each year. If you have a good young team, you may enjoy success for a number of years.

On the other hand, if you have a poor team you may not enjoy waiting for years until your rookies pan out and your franchise finally realizes success. Also, being a little biased, I don't think your fantasy draft would be as enjoyable. In our league the draft is the social event of the year. Being able to start fresh and have a shot at picking a Fantasy Bowl team is truly exciting.

5. PLAYER AUCTIONING

Another option that is used is to hold a player "auction" rather than a player draft. This is done by each franchise's buying into the league for a set number of dollars. These dollars are then used to buy or payroll teams.

Let's take this by steps:

A. An order for choosing which player is to be auctioned is determined. This can be done by a draw of cards or by letting the team with the worst record from the previous year select the first player, and so on.

B. Once a player is up for auction, the bidding begins and goes around the room. For the sake of discussion, we'll establish that this league's entry fee is $100.00 per franchise. The bidding for the player on the auction block begins at $1.00. The bidding goes around the room in clockwise order, with each team having a chance to increase the bid or pass completely.

C. There is no ceiling on the player bids.

D. The bidding for players continues until each team has acquired 12 players.

E. The total cost of the 12 players must not exceed $100.00, or whatever the entry fee is.

SAMPLE OF AUCTION DRAFTING:

ROUND #1

	Player Auctioned			Team#	Price
1	Davis	DEN	RB	6	$27
2	Rice	SF	WR	1	$31
3	Sanders	DET	RB	14	$24
4	Favre	GB	QB	2	$22
5	Watters	PHIL	RB	11	$20
6	Abdul-Jabbar	MIA	RB	13	$21
7	Young	SF	QB	5	$22
8	Carter	MINN	WR	7	$24
9	Murrell	NYJ	RB	3	$22
10	R. Brooks	GB	WR	16	$25
11	E. Smith	DALL	RB	4	$26
12	H. Moore	DET	WR	9	$21
13	Hearst	SF	RB	8	$22
14	Martin	NE	RB	10	$18
15	George	OAK	QB	15	$19
16	Irvin	DALL	WR	12	$22

ROUND #2

Player Auctioned			Team#	Price
1 Bettis	PITT	RB	10	$17
2 Levens	GB	RB	8	$14
3 Kaufman	OAK	RB	7	$18
4 Harris	CHI	RB	2	$15
5 Tm. Brown	OAK	WR	15	$18
6 Pickens	CIN	WR	4	$20
7 Johnson	MINN	QB	12	$17
8 R. Smith	MINN	RB	4	$14
9 Mitchell	DET	QB	3	$16
10 Conway	CHI	WR	13	$12
11 Galloway	SEAT	WR	16	$13
12 Means	JAC	RB	1	$14
13 Brown	SD	RB	6	$13
14 Coates	NE	TE	11	$15
15 Freeman	GB	WR	9	$18
16 Faulk	IND	RB	5	$19

6. DRAFT AN NFL COACH

Some leagues draft an NFL coach who serves as an eighth man in their lineup. If the coach of the NFL team wins his game, the fantasy team is awarded three points. Let's say you had drafted Steve Mariucci of the San Francisco 49ers and the 49ers beat the Cowboys. Three points would have been awarded and your scorecard would have looked like this, with a W marked after Mariucci's team initials to signify the win. (See Detail N.)

Detail N

TEAM # 1	
QB Favre (GB) TPP	12
RB J. Andersen (ATL) TTT	18
RB A. Smith (BUF)	0
WR Fryar (PHIL)	0
WR R. Brooks (GB) T	6
TE Conwell (St L) T	6
K Andersen (ATL) FXXX	7
C Mariucci (SF) W	3
	51

7. WEEKLY OFFICE POOLS

Some week your office may find it fun to throw in a couple of bucks and draft a fantasy team. My research found this to be very popular. Get 4 or even 10 or more football followers each to draft a team for a given weekend's slate of games. To keep it simple and fun, we suggest the following as a guide:

A. Each team selects 7 players
    1 Quarterback
    2 Running Backs
    3 Receivers (can be wide receivers or tight ends)
    1 Kicker

B. Use our Basic Scoring Method for scoring points awarded:

Quarterbacks:	3 points (TD pass thrown)
	6 points (TD rushing)
Running Backs and Receivers:	3 points (TD pass thrown on a halfback option)
	6 points (TD rushing or receiving)
Kickers:	3 points (field goal)
	1 point (extra point)

C. Payoffs
    Up to 6 teams
      1st Place - 75% of pot
      2nd Place - 25% of pot
    6 teams and up
      1st Place - 50% of pot
      2nd Place - 25% of pot
      3rd Place - 15% of pot
      Commissioner - 10% of pot

Winners are determined by the total number of points amassed by the seven players selected by the fantasy team.

1998 NFL SCHEDULE
(ALL TIMES ARE CENTRAL STANDARD TIME)

WEEK #1
(Sunday, September 6)
Atlanta at Carolina 12 PM
Detroit at Green Bay 12 PM
Jacksonville at Chicago 12 PM
New Orleans at St. Louis 12 PM
Pittsburgh at Baltimore 12 PM
Seattle at Philadelphia 12 PM
Tampa Bay at Minnesota 12 PM
Tennessee at Cincinnati 12 PM
Washington at New York Giants 12 PM
Arizona at Dallas 3 PM
Buffalo at San Diego 3:15 PM
Miami at Indianapolis 3:15 PM
New York Jets at San Francisco 3:15 PM
Oakland at Kansas City 7:20 PM

(Monday, September 7)
New England at Denver 7:20 PM

WEEK #2
(Sunday, September 13)
Baltimore at New York Jets 12 PM
Buffalo Bills at Miami 12 PM
Carolina at New Orleans 12 PM
Chicago at Pittsburgh 12 PM
Cincinnati at Detroit 12 PM
Kansas City at Jacksonville 12 PM
Minnesota at St. Louis 12 PM
Philadelphia at Atlanta 12 PM
San Diego at Tennessee 12 PM
Tampa Bay at Green Bay 12 PM
Arizona at Seattle 3:15 PM
Dallas at Denver 3:15 PM
New York Giants at Oakland 3:15 PM
Indianapolis at New England 7:20 PM

(Monday, September 14)
San Francisco at Washington 7:30 PM

WEEK #3
(Sunday, September 20)
Detroit at Minnesota 12 PM
Green Bay at Cincinnati 12 PM
Indianapolis at New York Jets 12 PM
Pittsburgh at Miami 12 PM
St. Louis at Buffalo 12 PM
San Diego at Kansas City 12 PM
Tennessee at New England 12 PM
Chicago at Tampa Bay 3 PM
Washington at Seattle 3PM
Baltimore at Jacksonville 3:15 PM
Denver at Oakland 3:15 PM
Philadelphia at Arizona 7:20 PM

(Monday, September 21)
Dallas at New York Giants 7:20 PM
(Bye Teams: Atlanta, Carolina, New
Orleans, San Francisco)

WEEK #4
(Sunday, September 27)
Arizona at St. Louis 12 PM
Denver at Washington 12 PM
Green Bay at Carolina 12 PM
Jacksonville at Tennessee 12 PM
Kansas City at Philadelphia 12 PM
New Orleans at Indianapolis 12 PM
Oakland at Dallas 12 PM
Seattle at Pittsburgh 3 PM
Atlanta at San Francisco 3:15 PM
Minnesota at Chicago 3:15 PM
New York Giants at San Diego 3:15 PM
Cincinnati at Baltimore 7:20 PM

(Monday, September 28)
Tampa Bay at Detroit 7:20 PM
(Bye teams: Buffalo, Miami, New
England, New York Jets)

WEEK #5
(Sunday, October 4)
Carolina at Atlanta 12 PM
Dallas at Washington 12 PM
Detroit at Chicago 12 PM
Miami at New York Jets 12 PM
New England at New Orleans 12 PM
San Diego at Indianapolis 12 PM
San Francisco at Buffalo 12 PM
Oakland at Arizona 3 PM
New York Giants at Tampa Bay 3:15 PM
Philadelphia at Denver 3:15 PM
Seattle at Kansas City 7:20 PM

(Monday, October 5)
Minnesota at Green Bay 7:20 PM
(Bye Teams, Baltimore, Cincinnati,
Jacksonville, Pittsburgh, St. Louis,
Tennessee)

WEEK #6
(Sunday, October 11)
Buffalo at Indianapolis 12 PM
Carolina at Dallas 12 PM
Kansas City at New England 12 PM
Pittsburgh at Cincinnati 12 PM
San Francisco at New Orleans 12 PM
Tennessee at Baltimore 12 PM
Washington at Philadelphia 12 PM
Chicago at Arizona 3 PM
Denver at Seattle 3:15 PM
New York Jets at St. Louis 3:15 PM
San Diego at Oakland 3:15 PM
Atlanta at New York Giants 7:20 PM

(Monday, October 12)
Miami at Jacksonville 7:20 PM
(Bye teams: Detroit, Green Bay,
Minnesota, Tampa Bay

WEEK #7
(Thursday, October 15)
Green Bay at Detroit 7:20 PM

(Sunday, October 18)
Arizona at New York Giants 12 PM
Baltimore at Pittsburgh 12 PM
Carolina at Tampa Bay 12 PM
Cincinnati at Tennessee 12 PM
Jacksonville at Buffalo 12 PM
New Orleans at Atlanta 12 PM
Washington at Minnesota 12 PM
Indianapolis at San Francisco 3 PM
Dallas at Chicago 3:15 PM
Philadelphia at San Diego 3:15 PM
St. Louis at Miami 3:15 PM

(Monday, October 19)
New York Jets at New England 7:20 PM
(Bye teams: Denver, Kansas City,
Oakland, Seattle)

WEEK #8
(Sunday, October 25)
Atlanta at New York Jets 12 PM
Baltimore at Green Bay 12 PM
Minnesota at Detroit 12 PM
New England at Miami 12 PM
San Francisco at St. Louis 12 PM
Tampa Bay at New Orleans 12 PM
Chicago at Tennessee 3 PM
Cincinnati at Oakland 3:15 PM
Jacksonville at Denver 3:15 PM
Seattle at San Diego 3:15 PM
Buffalo at Carolina 7:20 PM

(Monday, October 26)
Pittsburgh at Kansas City 7:20 PM
(Bye teams: Arizona, Dallas, Indianapolis,
New York Giants, Philadelphia,
Washington)

WEEK #9
(Sunday, November 1)
Arizona at Detroit 12 PM
Denver at Cincinnati 12 PM
Jacksonville at Baltimore 12 PM
Miami at Buffalo 12 PM
Minnesota at Tampa Bay 12 PM
New England at Indianapolis 12 PM
New Orleans at Carolina 12 PM
New York Giants at Washington 12 PM
St. Louis at Atlanta 12 PM
Tennessee at Pittsburgh 12 PM
New York Jets at Kansas City 3 PM
San Francisco at Green Bay 3:15 PM
Oakland at Seattle 7:20 PM

(Monday, November 2)
Dallas at Philadelphia 7:20 PM
(Bye teams: Chicago, San Diego)

WEEK #10
(Sunday, November 8)
Atlanta at New England 12 PM
Cincinnati at Jacksonville 12 PM
Detroit at Philadelphia 12 PM
Indianapolis at Miami 12 PM
New Orleans at Minnesota 12 PM
New York Giants at Dallas 12 PM
Oakland at Baltimore 12 PM
St. Louis at Chicago 12 PM
Carolina at San Francisco 3 PM
Washington at Arizona 3 PM
Buffalo at New York Jets 3:15 PM
Kansas City at Seattle 3:15 PM
San Diego at Denver 3:15 PM
Tennessee at Tampa Bay 7:20 PM

(Monday, November 9)
Green Bay at Pittsburgh 7:20 PM

WEEK #11
(Sunday November 15)
Cincinnati at Minnesota 12 PM
Miami at Carolina 12 PM
New England at Buffalo 12 PM
New York Jets at Indianapolis 12 PM
Philadelphia at Washington 12 PM
Pittsburgh at Tennessee 12 PM
St. Louis at New Orleans 12 PM
San Francisco at Atlanta 12 PM
Seattle at Oakland 3 PM
Baltimore at San Diego 3 PM
Dallas at Arizona 3:15 PM
Green Bay at New York Giants 3:15 PM
Tampa Bay at Jacksonville 3:15 PM
Chicago at Detroit 7:20 PM

(Monday, November 16)
Denver at Kansas City 7:20 PM

WEEK #12
(Sunday, November 22)
Arizona at Washington 12 PM
Chicago at Atlanta 12 PM
Detroit at Tampa Bay 12 PM
Green Bay at Minnesota 12 PM
Indianapolis at Buffalo 12 PM
Jacksonville at Pittsburgh 12 PM
Philadelphia at New York Giants 12 PM
Seattle at Dallas 12 PM
Carolina at St. Louis 3 PM
Baltimore at Cincinnati 3:15 PM
Kansas City at San Diego 3:15 PM
New York Jets at Tennessee 3:15 PM
Oakland at Denver 3:15 PM
New Orleans at San Francisco 7:20 PM

(Monday, November 23)
Miami at New England 7:20 PM

WEEK #13

(Thursday, November 26)
Pittsburgh at Detroit 11:35 AM
Minnesota at Dallas 3 PM

(Sunday, November 29)
Arizona at Kansas City 12 PM
Atlanta at St. Louis 12 PM
Carolina at New York Jets 12 PM
Indianapolis at Baltimore 12 PM
Jacksonville at Cincinnati 12 PM
New Orleans at Miami 12 PM
Tampa Bay at Chicago 12 PM
Buffalo at New England 3 PM
Tennessee at Seattle 3 PM
Philadelphia at Green Bay 3:15 PM
Washington at Oakland 3:15 PM
Denver at San Diego 7:20 PM

(Monday, November 30)
New York Giants at San Francisco
7:20 PM

WEEK #14

(Thursday, December 3)
St. Louis at Philadelphia 7:20 PM

(Sunday, December 6)
Buffalo at Cincinnati 12 PM
Dallas at New Orleans 12 PM
Detroit at Jacksonville 12 PM
Indianapolis at Atlanta 12 PM
New England at Pittsburgh 12 PM
San Diego at Washington 12 PM
San Francisco at Carolina 12 PM
Seattle at New York Jets 12 PM
New York Giants at Arizona 3 PM
Baltimore at Tennessee 3:15 PM
Kansas City at Denver 3:15 PM
Miami at Oakland 3:15 PM
Chicago at Minnesota 7:20 PM

(Monday, December 7)
Green Bay at Tampa Bay 7:20 PM

WEEK #15

(Sunday, December 13)
Arizona at Philadelphia 12 PM
Atlanta at New Orleans 12 PM
Chicago at Green Bay 12 PM
Cincinnati at Indianapolis 12 PM
Denver at New York Giants 12 PM
New England at St. Louis 12 PM
Oakland at Buffalo 12 PM
Pittsburgh at Tampa Bay 12PM
Tennessee at Jacksonville 12 PM
Washington at Carolina 12 PM
San Diego at Seattle 3 PM
Dallas at Kansas City 3:15 PM
Minnesota at Baltimore 3:15 PM
New York Jets at Miami 7:20 PM

(Monday, December 14)
Detroit at San Francisco 7:20 PM

(Saturday, December 19
New York Jets at Buffalo 11:35 AM
Tampa Bay at Washington 3 PM

WEEK #16

(Sunday, December 20)
Atlanta at Detroit 12 PM
Baltimore at Chicago 12 PM
Cincinnati at Pittsburgh 12 PM
Kansas City at New York Giants 12 PM
St. Louis at Carolina 12 PM
San Francisco at New England 12 PM
Tennessee at Green Bay 12 PM
Indianapolis at Seattle 3 PM
Oakland at San Diego 3 PM
New Orleans at Arizona 3:15 PM
Philadelphia at Dallas 3:15 PM
Jacksonville at Minnesota 7:20 PM

(Monday, December 21)
Denver at Miami 7:20 PM

WEEK #17

(Saturday, December 26
Minnesota at Tennessee 11:35 AM
Kansas City at Oakland 3 PM

(Sunday, December 27)
Buffalo at New Orleans 12 PM
Carolina at Indianapolis 12 PM
Detroit at Baltimore 12 PM
Green Bay at Chicago 12 PM
Miami at Atlanta 12 PM
New England at New York Jets 12 PM
Tampa Bay at Cincinnati 12 PM
New York Giants at Philadelphia 3 PM
St. Louis at San Francisco 3 PM
San Diego at Arizona 3:15 PM
Seattle at Denver 3:15 PM
Washington at Dallas 7:20 PM

(Monday, December 28)
Pittsburgh at Jacksonville 7:20 PM

POST SEASON GAMES

(Saturday, January 2)
AFC and NFC Wild Card Games

(Sunday, January 3)
AFC and NFC Wild Card Games

(Saturday, January 9)
AFC and NFC Divisional Playoffs

(Sunday, January 10)
AFC and NFC Divisional Playoff

(Sunday, January 17)
AFC and NFC Championships

(Sunday, January 31)
Super Bowl XXXIII (in Miami)

(Sunday, February 7)
Pro Bowl (in Honolulu)

TO THE AUTHOR

Again I would like to thank those of you who wrote to us in 1996. Your suggestions, rule ideas, and comments help us keep up to date on what you want to see in a Fantasy Football publication. Although I can't answer every letter that is sent to me, I assure you that I do read every one of them. Your input is very valuable in broadening my appreciation of Fantasy Football. In response to your comments, we have done a few things differently in this year's digest and will also change a number of things in the newsletter.

Gentlemen,

Just wanted to drop you a line and tell you that you're doing a great job. Last year was my first as a commissioner of a league, and I don't think I could've pulled it off without your help.

I called several times for your assistance with loading the "Kommish" into my computer. I had just bought it and was I clueless. Your patience was heaven-sent and knowledge golden. Everyone was jealous as to how prepared I was for the draft!

I recommended your fantasy football magazine as the "bible" for our league! Here's to a great 1998 for you and me!

Gratefully,
James R. Caver

Cliff,

Our league in Red Wing is in its 11th year without missing "a beat." It's been a lot of fun but...

This past week, Curtis Martin, RB (NE) was listed as "probable," yet there he was in street clothes on the sidelines for the entire game against Jacksonville. How could something as bizarre as that happen? Needless to say, Martin is on my team so I ended up playing with a six-player lineup. At next year's draft, I think we need to address this problem as I don't think this should happen to any team.

I would appreciate any thoughts or suggestions on some kind of policy that our league might adopt and that would protect any team in our league from having this situation come up again. A suggestion from you might carry more "clout" than any that I might have.

Anxiously awaiting a response, at your conveniece.

Yours in football!
Rick Meier

Rick,

Thanks for taking the time to write. I apologize for such a delay in my response but your letter got lost in the shuffle somewhere along the way.

In regards to your question, having a player who is listed as "probable" wind up sitting on the sidelines and watching the game in street clothes is frustrating. Sometimes there's virtually nothing you can do about it. However, I can tell you that in my league, though we do enforce having our franchise owners submit their starting lineups on Thursday night, we are allowed to make one lineup change up to kickoff time on Sunday. This allows us to track injuries through the week and right up to kickoff and enables us to replace our injured player with a healthy one. It's worked pretty well for us and hopefully your league will look into its benefits.

Thanks again for taking the time to write. Good luck in 1998.

Cliff Charpentier

You can write to us at:
To The Author
Fantasy Sports, Inc.
674 E. Sixth Street
St. Paul, MN 55106
E-Mail: fantasy@skypoint.com

CLIFF CHARPENTIER'S
1997 ALL-FANTASY TEAM

FANTASY PLAYER OF THE YEAR
Running Back: BARRY SANDERS (Detroit Lions)
- 11 rushing touchdowns
- 3 receiving touchdowns
- 2,053 total rushing-receiving yards

Running Back: TERRELL DAVIS (Denver Broncos
- 15 rushing touchdowns
- 0 receiving touchdowns
- 1,170 total rushing-receiving yards

Wide Receiver: ROD SMITH (Denver Broncos)
- 12 touchdowns
- 70 receptions
- 1,180 receiving yards

Wide Receiver: ANTONIO FREEMAN (Green Bay Packers
- 12 touchdowns
- 81 receptions
- 1,243 receiving yards

Tight End: BEN COATES (New England Patriots)
- 8 touchdowns
- 66 receptions
- 737 receiving yards

Quarterback: KORDELL STEWART (Pittsburgh Steelers)
- 21 passing touchdowns
- 11 rushing touchdowns
- 3,020 passing yards
- 476 rushing yards

Kicker: MIKE HOLLIS (Jacksonville Jaguars)
- 31 of 36 (.861) field goal attempts
- 41 of 41 (1.000) extra-point attempts
- 134 total points

1997 FANTASY ROOKIE OF THE YEAR
Running Back: Corey Dillon (Cincinnati Bengals)
- 10 touchdowns
- 1,129 rushing yards
- 259 receiving yards